KARL MARX
FREDERICK ENGELS
COLLECTED WORKS
VOLUME
38

KARL MARX
FREDERICK ENGELS

COLLECTED
WORKS

LAWRENCE & WISHART

LONDON

KARL MARX
FREDERICK ENGELS

Volume
38

MARX AND ENGELS: 1844-51

1982
LAWRENCE & WISHART
LONDON

This volume has been prepared jointly by Lawrence & Wishart Ltd., London, International Publishers Co. Inc., New York, and Progress Publishers, Moscow, in collaboration with the Institute of Marxism-Leninism, Moscow.

Editorial commissions:
GREAT BRITAIN: Jack Cohen, Maurice Cornforth, E. J. Hobsbawm, Nicholas Jacobs, Martin Milligan, Ernst Wangermann.
USA: James S. Allen, Louis Diskin, Philip S. Foner, Dirk J. Struik, William W. Weinstone.
USSR: for Progress Publishers—N. P. Karmanova, V. I. Neznanov, V. N. Sedikh, M. K. Shcheglova; for the Institute of Marxism-Leninism— P. N. Fedoseyev, L. I. Golman, A. I. Malysh, M. P. Mchedlov, A. G. Yegorov.

ISBN 0 85315 459 7

Printed in the Union of Soviet Socialist Republics

Contents

KARL MARX AND FREDERICK ENGELS

LETTERS

October 1844-December 1851

1844

1845

1846

1847

Contents   XIII

Translated by

PETER and BETTY ROSS

Preface

The letters of Karl Marx and Frederick Engels will be published in volumes 38-50 of this edition. These volumes will contain their letters to each other and to their collaborators, friends, relatives, and others. The Appendices will include letters written by others at the request of Marx and Engels, as well as letters addressed to them, and documents giving some idea of the contents of undiscovered letters written by them and providing additional biographical information.

This special group of volumes begins with Engels' earliest surviving letter to Marx, from early October 1844. Their letters, to other people, prior to their historic meeting in Paris in August 1844, before which there was no direct connection between their intellectual development and work, are included in volumes 1-3 of the present edition, together with their separately published works of those years. From the autumn of 1844, the works of Marx and Engels increasingly arise from their close cooperation. Their letters reflect the elaboration of their ideas and their influence on the working class's struggle for emancipation.

Not included in these volumes are letters, appeals and statements addressed to various organisations, editors of newspapers and journals, public employees, etc. These are published in volumes 4-28 of this edition.

The letters of Marx and Engels are extremely rich in ideas and human interest. In them Marx and Engels wrote of their creative plans, of the immense research they undertook in different fields of knowledge, and touched upon a wide range of philosophical, economic, sociological and other problems. They compared the results of their work, shared their impressions of the books they read, discussed the various doctrines and theories of contemporary thinkers, and commented upon the achievements of other scholars—for instance, the progress made in the natural sciences and in engineering—as well as on events and phenomena they witnessed or read about.

The letters show the constant attention Marx and Engels paid to economic and social phenomena, to politics in general, and to the development of the revolutionary movement in particular. Their analysis of current events, class conflicts, diplomatic battles and warfare, political parties and trends, statesmen and politicians, is an important contribution to the Marxist interpretation of the period's history; though it should be borne in mind that very often their judgment of events and people was stated much more sharply, as well as impulsively and emotionally, in their letters than in their works written for publication.

The proletarian class struggle is one of the principal and constant subjects of their correspondence. As the theoreticians of the working class, as well as direct participants in and leaders of proletarian organisations, they were interested most of all in the workers' movement, the conditions and stages of its development, the aims of its programme, its tactics and its organisation. The letters are eloquent testimony of their struggle for the creation of a revolutionary party of the working class, and for the elaboration of a programme and a strategy for the international proletarian movement, giving due consideration both to the general laws of development of the proletarian class struggle and its specific features at different periods of history and in different countries. Many letters contain sharp criticism of the ideological and political antagonists of the working class, and of the various manifestations of opportunism, reformism, sectarianism and dogmatism in the workers' movement. A profoundly scientific, materialist approach to the problems of the proletariat's struggle, a principled defence of revolutionary positions, consistent internationalism, ardent support for those fighting for the oppressed and the exploited, and an irreconcilability towards their enemies, run through the entire correspondence of Marx and Engels.

'If one were to attempt to define in a single word the focus, so to speak, of the whole correspondence,' wrote Lenin, 'the central point at which the whole body of ideas expressed and discussed converges—that word would be *dialectics*. The application of materialist dialectics to the reshaping of all political economy from its foundations up, its application to history, natural science, philosophy and to the policy and tactics of the working class—that was what interested Marx and Engels most of all, that was where they contributed what was most essential and new, and that was what constituted the masterly advance they made in the history of revolutionary thought' (*Collected Works,* Vol. 19, p. 554).

This correspondence is a vital source for the study of both the theoretical and practical activity of Marx and Engels, demonstrating how naturally they combined these two aspects of their revolutionary work. Their letters reflect the development of the three component parts of Marxism—dialectical and historical materialism, political economy and the theory of scientific communism—as well as their study of a whole series of allied disciplines, in particular of world history, law, linguistics, the history of literature, aesthetics, the natural sciences, and military science. In addition, our knowledge of the programme and tactical documents of the Communist League, of the First International and other proletarian organisations founded by Marx and Engels, is augmented by the rich material contained in their letters which illustrate their role as the organisers and leaders of the working-class revolutionary struggle.

Their letters also add in essential ways to many of their published works, drafts and manuscripts of unfinished works, for very often they give original full versions of important theoretical and tactical propositions, showing how one or another idea was conceived, and how it was first presented and subsequently developed. Some of the letters are regular treatises, and some are especially valuable in containing ideas never set down in Marx's and Engels' published works. Many of the letters reveal scientific and literary plans which for one reason or another were never realised, while some are the only evidence that has come down to us that such literary plans existed at all, and from them we can form a general idea of what Marx and Engels intended to write about in such works.

The letters are especially important for the study of those periods in the lives of Marx and Engels when they were unable to write regularly for the press, in which case their correspondence often provides the best or the only source for studying their life and activity. Unfortunately, for some of these years, relatively few letters have been preserved, and they can naturally only supply additional information on the views and activities of Marx and Engels to that which can be derived from their published works.

There can be no better source than their letters from which to study the biographies of Marx and Engels. Readers can follow not just the story of how their works were written and published, or the stages of their theoretical and socio-political activity, but can observe them among their families and friends. They can gain an idea of the circumstances of their life, their everyday occupations, their personal feelings, and so forth. Their letters also show clearly the grim trials which confronted the proletarian revolutionaries in their struggle against the existing state system: police persecutions, legal proceedings, deportation, enforced emigration, publishers refusing to print their works, abuse and slander spread by their enemies, family and personal bereavement. And on top of all that—in the case of Marx—his poverty, leading to the tragic losses in his family, and his own frequent ill health.

And yet, their letters are full of optimism. The staunchness with which they bore up under all their troubles is amazing. They drew this strength from their unswerving loyalty to their revolutionary calling, to the noble idea of serving the cause of the working people's emancipation. It is significant that Marx, who had already experienced several tragic deaths in his family, wrote to Sigfrid Meyer on 30 April 1867: 'I laugh at the so-called "practical" men with their wisdom. If one chose to be an ox, one could of course turn one's back on the sufferings of mankind and look after one's own skin.'

No vicissitudes of life could break their will or spirit, weaken their dedication to the cause of the working class, undermine their faith in the ultimate triumph of the ideas of communism, or shake their historical optimism, their courage and naturally cheerful disposition. Shortly after Marx's death a German bourgeois journalist called him a 'poor wretch' and it is in this connection that Engels wrote indignantly in June 1883: 'If these jackasses ever happened to read my correspondence with the Moor, they would simply gape. Heine's poetry is child's play compared with our bold, jolly prose. The Moor could be furious, but mope—*jamais!* [never]'

The letters testify to the unity of Marx's and Engels' theoretical views and their extraordinary ideological and human closeness. For all the uniqueness of their personalities, there was always complete unanimity between them on the main issues, thanks to the remarkable similarity of their philosophical and political views. Very often we can observe how they arrived at a common point of view through discussion, and then how both expressed that viewpoint in print or in letters to other persons. There are many examples of such creative cooperation.

Their great friendship meant that they kept in constant touch with each other; it is therefore not surprising that they wrote almost daily when they happened to be separated, as they were in the 1850s and the 1860s for example. Their letters speak of their profound mutual respect and affection, and their complete and sincere confidence in one another.

* * *

Volume 38 contains Marx's and Engels' letters from October 1844 to December 1851, covering three stages in the development of Marxism. The first group of letters deals with the formative period and the development of Marxism as the scientific world outlook of the working class, and also shows the first practical steps taken by Marx and Engels to combine the theory of communism with the workers' movement and organise a proletarian party. Their efforts were crowned in 1847 by the establishment of the international communist organisation of the proletariat—the Communist League—and the publication of its programme—the *Manifesto of the Communist Party* (February 1848). Their subsequent letters relate to the period of the bourgeois-democratic revolutions in Europe in 1848-49, which were the first historical test of Marxism, of its theoretical and tactical principles. The third group includes letters written from the end of 1849 to 1851 when priority had to be given to the work of theoretically generalising the experience of the revolutions, of further developing the strategy and tactics of the proletarian revolutionaries, of uniting them in conditions of increasing reaction, and of reorganising the Communist League.

Marx's and Engels' surviving letters from October 1844 to February 1848 show that their efforts were primarily focused on elaborating the theoretical tools that would provide a scientific basis for the workers' movement. Their awareness of the urgency of this task is evident from the very first letters written by Engels from Barmen where he returned in the autumn of 1844 after his meeting with Marx in Paris. Reporting to his friend about the rapid spread of communist and socialist propaganda in Germany, Engels said: 'Failing a few publications in which the principles are logically and historically developed out of past ways of thinking and past history, and as their necessary continuation, the whole thing will remain rather hazy and most people will be groping in the dark' (this volume, p. 3).

At the time, the workers' movement was largely influenced by utopian socialism. Its ideological confusion was aggravated by the circulation of muddled and immature doctrines, in particular those of the Young Hegelians who in 1843-45 preached ideas of subjective idealism and anarchic individualism. That is why in his letters Engels repeatedly urged Marx to hurry up and finish *The Holy Family,* aimed against Bruno Bauer and the other Young Hegelians, and also the book he was planning to write on political economy. In January 1845, Engels wrote: 'Minds are ripe and we must strike while the iron is hot.... We German theoreticians ... cannot yet so much as develop our theory, not even having been able as yet to publish the critique of the nonsense. But now it is high time' (pp. 17-18).

The letters published in this volume enable us to follow the writing of such important works as *The Holy Family, The Condition of the Working-Class in England* (present edition, Vol. 4) and *The German Ideology* (Vol. 5), and provide information about projects never materialised, among them Marx's intention to write a 'Critique of Politics and Political Economy' in two volumes, Marx's and Engels' plans to publish a criticism of the views of the German bourgeois economist Friedrich List, and their plan to start a 'Library of the Best Foreign Socialist Writers' (in German) supplied with critical comments (see this volume, pp. 10-11, 13-14, 15-18, 25-28). The letters also throw light on the journalistic work done by Marx and Engels, their contributions to various papers, the reasons that prompted them to do journalistic work, and the character of a number of the articles written by them.

A whole series of circumstances, relevant not just to the writing but also to the attempt to publish *The German Ideology,* are clarified in the correspondence between Marx and Engels and their letters to other persons, one being the letter written by Marx on 14-16 May 1846 to Joseph Weydemeyer, published for the first time in 1968 (pp. 41-44). In *The German Ideology* Marx and Engels counterposed their materialist understanding of history as an integral conception to the idealist views of Max Stirner and other Young Hegelians, and to the inconsistent materialism of Ludwig Feuerbach. It is apparent from their letters that Marx and Engels originally intended to publish this work in a collection of articles, together with those written by their associates and to criticise the various bourgeois and petty-bourgeois ideological trends. What they wanted was to start a regular quarterly journal for these publications (pp. 41, 533), but these plans failed, as did their other attempts to have these manuscripts printed. However, Marx and Engels were not discouraged for they had achieved their 'main purpose—self-clarification', as Marx wrote in 1859 in the Preface to *A Contribution to the Critique of Political Economy.*

As they developed their dialectical-materialist outlook and intensified their efforts to rally the advanced workers and intellectuals on the basis of the new revolutionary teaching, Marx and Engels felt more and more acutely the necessity to overcome the influence of sectarian utopian teachings, among them the egalitarian communism of Weitling and the petty-bourgeois sentimental 'true socialism', which hindered the formation of working-class consciousness. Of especial danger to the workers' movement was the spread of the reformist views of Proudhon who sowed in the workers' minds the illusion that it was possible to transform capitalism to serve the ideals of petty artisans and peasants.

A number of letters, particularly from Engels in Paris in 1846 to the Brussels Communist Correspondence Committee, show the struggle he had to fight against the influential Weitlingians among the German artisans and workmen living in Paris, and also against the supporters of Proudhon's reformist projects, and Karl Grün who interpreted these projects in the spirit of 'true socialism'. In his letter of 23 October 1846, Engels described the lengthy discussion he had at a workers' meeting in the course of which he succeeded in changing the minds of most of those present, convincing them of the unsoundness of Proudhon's and Grün's views, and clearly defining the aims of the communists as follows: '1. to ensure that the interests of the proletariat prevail, as opposed to those of the bourgeoisie; 2. to do so by abolishing private property and replacing same with community of goods; 3. to recognise no means of attaining these aims other than democratic revolution by force' (p. 82).

The struggle against Proudhon's ideas had a direct bearing on the writing of one of the first works of mature Marxism—*The Poverty of Philosophy*—in which Marx set out the historico-materialist conception earlier developed in *The German Ideology*. This was the first work he published as an economist. His letter of 28 December 1846 to the Russian liberal writer P. V. Annenkov can be regarded as a condensed draft of the book in which the main theses are briefly set out. Marx showed the invalidity of Proudhon's philosophical and sociological views, the utopianism of his reformist projects, his inability to analyse the nature of capitalist relations and social processes as a whole, or to understand the significance of the class struggle of the proletariat. In Proudhon's ideas Marx clearly saw a reflection of the sentiments and world outlook of that class of small private producers who were being ruined by the development of capitalism, and who wanted to eliminate its 'bad sides' while keeping the fundamentals intact. 'Mr. Proudhon is, from top to toe, a philosopher, an economist of the petty bourgeoisie,' Marx wrote (this volume, p. 105).

Proudhon idealistically regarded history as a result of the actions of outstanding men capable of filching 'from God his inmost thoughts' (p. 103), and to counterbalance this view Marx recapitulated the basic principles of historical materialism on the general laws of social development. He pointed to the determining role played in this development by the productive forces, to the dialectical interaction between them and the relations of production (characteristically, here they are called not 'forms of intercourse' as in *The German Ideology* but more precisely 'economic relations', 'social relations'), and to the ultimate dependence of all the other social institutions and superstructural phenomena, including the sphere of ideas, on the mode of production. The discrepancy between the developing productive forces and the outdated relations of production makes it an objective necessity to revolutionise, that is, to change the old mode of production for a new and more progressive one, which would also bring about a change in the entire social superstructure. Marx showed how obsolescent relations of production do not merely hinder the progress of society but are actually capable of pushing it back and denying it the 'fruits of civilisation' (p. 97). The true makers of history—the masses who produce the material wealth—influence its course primarily by participating in the development of the productive forces, Marx pointed out. But they cannot do so arbitrarily since they are not free to choose their productive forces, thus 'every succeeding generation finds productive forces acquired by the preceding generation' (p. 96).

By stressing the need to regard the various forms of production in a given epoch as historical and transitory, Marx established the principle of the historical character of science. He showed that this principle is essential in the study of social phenomena from a truly scientific, dialectical-materialist angle.

The letters of 1846-47 illustrate the efforts of Marx and Engels to organise a proletarian party, to establish and consolidate ties with the representatives of the workers' and socialist movements in different countries, and to set up communist correspondence committees in Belgium, Germany, England and France. The tasks of these committees, formulated in a series of documents (see present edition, Vol. 6, pp. 54-56, 58-60), were also stated in a letter (5 May 1846) to Proudhon, whom Marx still hoped to draw into the work of revolutionary propaganda, '...The chief aim of our correspondence ... will be to put the German socialists in touch with the French and English socialists; to keep foreigners constantly informed of the socialist movements that occur in Germany and to inform the Germans in Germany of the progress of socialism in France and England. In this way differences of opinion can be brought to light and an exchange of ideas and impartial criticism can take place. It will be a step made by the social movement in its *literary* manifestation to rid itself of the barriers of *nationality*' (p. 39).

As Marx and Engels planned it, the communist correspondence committees were to elicit differences of opinion, criticise immature, utopian and sectarian views, work out an ideological and theoretical platform acceptable to the genuinely revolutionary part of the movement, and thus prepare the ground for the organisation of an international proletarian party.

The centre of the network Marx and Engels were organising was to be the Brussels Communist Correspondence Committee, headed by them. Its work is fully described in Engels' letters from Paris to Marx dated 19 August (p. 53) and about 23 October 1846 (pp. 86-88), and in Harney's letter to Engels of 30 March 1846 (published in the Appendices).

The activities of Marx and Engels as theoreticians, journalists and organisers of propaganda helped to develop the views of the members of the League of the Just, a secret organisation of German workers and artisans which emerged in the middle of the 1830s and was also joined by workers of other nationalities. Marx and Engels had established contact with the London leaders of the League—Karl Schapper, Joseph Moll and Heinrich Bauer—already in 1843-45, and in the years that followed they maintained this contact although they criticised the theoretical immaturity and instability of the stand taken by the leaders, and the sectarian, conspiratorial character of the League's organisational structure (pp. 69, 91-92, 83). It was only when they were certain that the London leadership had begun to assimilate the ideas of scientific communism, and showed its readiness to act in this spirit, that Marx and Engels, in January 1847, agreed to join the League, take part in its reorganisation, and draw up a new programme on the basis of the principles they had proclaimed.

From their letters written in 1847 we see how Marx and Engels directed the work of the Communist League, founded by them, trying to strengthen its influence among the masses and encouraging its members to engage in systematic propaganda and organisational work among the proletariat. They themselves did this kind of work in the Brussels German Workers' Society, founded by them in August 1847, which we know from Engels' letter to Marx dated 28-30 September 1847 (p. 130); moreover, they looked upon the Communist League as the nucleus of the future mass proletarian party which was to unite all the militant forces of the working class.

Marx and Engels, being emphatically against sectarian isolation from the general revolutionary movement, guided the Communist League towards the establishment of an alliance with the democrats both on the national and the international scale for joint struggle against the anti-popular regimes. The independence of the ideological and political stand taken by the international proletarian organisation and its right openly to criticise the mistakes and inconsistency of its allies was to be strictly maintained. It took Engels in particular no little effort to secure the cooperation of the French democrats and socialists who grouped round the newspaper *La Réforme*. Engels reported in detail to Marx on his negotiations with the editors Ferdinand Flocon and Louis Blanc in his letters of 25-26 October, 14-15 November 1847, and 14 and 21 January 1848. While commenting most critically on the reformist tendencies in the works of Louis Blanc and the arrogant attitude of 'this little literary lord', Engels considered it imperative to subject his views to public criticism (pp. 155-57).

An international Democratic Association was founded in Brussels in the autumn of 1847 with the active participation of Marx and Engels. Together with several other members of the Communist League they played a leading role in it (see Engels' letter to Marx, 28-30 September, and Marx's letter to Georg Herwegh, 26 October 1847). Marx and Engels maintained regular contact with the leaders of the Left wing of the Chartists, George Julian Harney and Ernest Jones, as well as with the Fraternal Democrats, the international democratic society founded in London (see Engels' letter to Marx dated 14-15 November 1847, and others).

For the wide dissemination of communist ideas the League needed its own newspaper, a point which was repeatedly raised in their letters (pp. 80, 91-92, 120, etc.). In 1846-47 Marx made several attempts to start a theoretical journal as a joint-stock company. In a recently discovered letter to Werner von Veltheim dated 29 September 1847, he said that one of the main tasks of the proposed journal was regularly to criticise the 'political, religious and social parties and aspirations' from materialist positions, consequently that 'political economy would play a leading role' (p. 131) in such a journal. The project, however, did not materialise.

Marx and Engels also wanted to use the emigrant newspaper, the *Deutsche-Brüsseler-Zeitung*, for communist propaganda (see Marx's letter to Herwegh of 8 August 1847, and others), and by assuming control of the editorial affairs they did succeed in turning the paper into an unofficial organ of the Communist League, a herald of the programme and tactical principles of scientific communism.

Of great interest are Engels' letters written at the end of 1847 dealing with his work on the draft programme of the Communist League which was to be confirmed by its second congress. On

23-24 November he wrote to Marx that he was not satisfied with the form of a catechism, or a confession of faith, traditional for many workers' organisations at the time, in which the document was originally written, and proposed calling it a Communist Manifesto (p. 149). Lenin said that this letter, giving in general outline the plan of the future programme document, 'clearly proves that Marx and Engels are justly named side by side as the founders of modern socialism' (Lenin, *Collected Works,* Vol. 19, p. 558).

Written as a programme of the Communist League, the *Manifesto of the Communist Party,* in which the principles of the Marxist revolutionary teaching were systematised for the first time, crowned the theoretical and practical activities of Marx and Engels prior to the revolution of 1848-49. Its publication in February 1848 marked the beginning of a new stage in the development of the international workers' movement.

* * *

Those letters written by Marx and Engels in 1848-49 which have come down to us augment our knowledge of them as revolutionary tribunes and journalists, ideologists and leaders of the proletarian wing of the general democratic revolutionary movement, and as the strategists and tacticians of the revolution.

At the outbreak of the revolution, the Belgian authorities, frightened by the reaction to the February events in Paris, ordered Marx to leave the country at once, and then, on the night of 3 March, arrested both him and his wife. They were released only when the twenty-four hours within which they had to leave the country had passed. The Marxes with their three children had to leave Brussels quickly. In his letters to Marx dated 8-9 and 18 March 1848, Engels told him of the indignation aroused by this act of violence among the democratic public of Belgium, of the protests which appeared in the press and the inquiries made in parliament.

This was not the first time that official authorities had so rudely interfered in Marx's life. Having chosen the road of political struggle, both he and Engels had already suffered the persecutions of reactionary governments, the arbitrariness of censors, and the stratagems of police agents and spies. On the insistence of the Prussian Embassy, the Guizot Government had deported Marx from Paris in February 1845, compelling him to seek asylum in Belgium. 'But I fear that in the end you'll be molested in Belgium too,' Engels wrote him (p. 22), and, true enough, his fears were confirmed three years later by the actions of the Belgian police. Engels himself, living in Paris in 1846-47 where he was engaged in revolutionary propaganda work among the German workers, also expected to be arrested and deported at any time, as we see from his letters, and this indeed occurred at the end of January 1848. There were more persecutions in store for the two friends: summons to the public prosecutor's office, court proceedings, threats of arrest, deportations, and so forth.

The developing events were keenly watched by Marx in Paris, where he arrived on 4 March 1848, and by Engels in Brussels. It was obvious to them that the revolution which had already begun would acutely aggravate the contradictions between the proletariat and the bourgeoisie. Marx wrote to Engels from Paris on 16 March 1848: 'The bourgeoisie here are again becoming atrociously uppish and reactionary, *mais elle verra* [but they'll see]' (p. 162). And Engels, after moving to Paris, wrote to Emil Blank on 28 March 1848 that here 'the big bourgeoisie and the workers are in direct confrontation with each other' (p. 167).

As they observed the beginning of the bourgeois-democratic revolution in Germany and planned how the proletarian revolutionaries were to act in it, they resolutely opposed any attempts to speed up events artificially or to export revolution to Germany. In this connection they strongly criticised Georg Herwegh and Adalbert von Bornstedt for their adventurist scheme of having an armed corps made up of German emigrants invade the territory of Germany and proclaim a republic there, in preference to the plan of having the progressive German workers—mainly those who belonged to the Communist League—return home singly in order to take part in the revolutionary battles. The uncompromising attitude taken by Marx and Engels to the plans of the petty-bourgeois democrats is clearly expressed in Marx's letter to Engels of 16 March and Engels' letter to Marx of 18 March 1848, and elsewhere (pp. 162, 165, 166).

The letters they exchanged upon their return to Germany in April 1848 deal with the situation there, the alignment of class forces, and the state of the local organisations of the Communist League. The revolution had stirred up the political activity of the German workers, but the spontaneous and immature character of their movement was in evidence everywhere. The policy of compromise adopted by the liberal bourgeoisie and the waverings of the petty-bourgeois democrats served the purpose of the feudal-monarchist counter-revolution which, having recovered from the defeats it had suffered, was re-emerging more and more openly. Defining the position of the liberal leaders of Prussia's bourgeoisie who stood at the head of the government, Engels wrote at the end of May 1848: 'In Berlin Camphausen is taking it easy, while reaction, the rule of officials and aristocrats grows daily more insolent, irritates the people, the people revolt and Camphausen's spinelessness and cowardice lead us straight towards fresh revolutions. That is Germany as it now is!' (p. 176).

In this situation, Marx and Engels clearly saw that their main and immediate task was to direct the actions of the German working class into the mainstream of the general democratic movement, guarding it at the same time against ideological subordination to the petty-bourgeois democrats, and fighting for its pursuance of a consistent revolutionary course. The organ of the Left proletarian wing of the democrats became the daily *Neue Rheinische Zeitung* published in Cologne by Marx, Engels and their comrades from the Communist League.

The few surviving letters of that period reflect the enormous work done by Marx and Engels to secure the publication of the paper, to organise the network of correspondents, and ensure its circulation. The editors had their share of cares and troubles: there was the bourgeois shareholders' disapproval of the paper's revolutionary policy, the obstacles put in its way by the Prussian authorities, and money difficulties. In order to keep the paper going, Marx used up his private means, telling Engels in a letter he wrote in November 1848: 'But whatever the circumstances, this *fort* had to be held and the political position not surrendered' (p. 179).

Marx's letters to Engels written in October-November 1848 when the latter, threatened with arrest, was compelled to emigrate temporarily to Switzerland, his letter to Eduard von Müller-Tellering of 5 December, and to Wilhelm Stieber written on or about 29 December 1848, show the grim conditions of police hounding and legal prosecutions in which he and his collaborators had to defend their 'fort'. The paper, however, did not once go back on its principles. It waged a consistent struggle against the advancing counter-revolution, rallied the proletarian circles and all the democratic forces of the country, and determined the tactics of the proletarian revolutionaries in the changing situation. The staunchness and militant spirit of the paper made it widely popular in Germany and in other countries (see Marx's letter to Engels of 29 November 1848, also Engels' letter to Marx of 7-8 January 1849, and others).

Engels' letters to Marx from Berne dated 28 December 1848

and 7-8 January 1849, during his enforced stay in Switzerland, are full of energy, fighting spirit, loyalty to his friends and a wonderful sense of humour.

At the beginning of May 1849, the rearguard battles of the German revolution were fought in Saxony, Rhenish Prussia, Baden and the Palatinate. After the defeat of the insurrections in the Rhine Province, the Prussian authorities did what they had long been preparing to do: they deported Marx from Prussia and took action against the other editors of the *Neue Rheinische Zeitung*. Its farewell issue, printed in red ink, came out on 19 May. After a brief stay in South-Western Germany, Marx left for Paris in anticipation of new revolutionary events in France. From his letter to Engels dated 7 June 1849, it is evident that he was trying to establish contact with the French revolutionary circles (p. 199). Engels, who was in Kaiserslautern at the time, joined Willich's volunteer corps, which formed a part of the Palatinate-Baden insurgent army. From the correspondence of Marx and Engels in July and August 1849, and also from Engels' letters to Jenny Marx, Joseph Weydemeyer and Jakob Schabelitz, it can be seen what an active part Engels took in the fighting against the advancing Prussian and other counter-revolutionary troops. He wrote to Jenny Marx on 25 July 1849: 'I was in four engagements, two of them fairly important, particularly the one at Rastatt' (p. 203).

From the first it was obvious to both Marx and Engels that the petty-bourgeois leaders of the Baden-Palatinate movement were not capable of directing the revolutionary struggle, and it was therefore doomed to failure. But, being in the thick of events, Engels 'had the opportunity of seeing a great deal and learning a great deal', and was later able to expose the 'illusions of the run-of-the mill, vociferous republicans' and the 'despondency lurking beneath the bravado of the leaders' (p. 215). With Willich's detachment, which covered the retreat of the insurgent army, Engels crossed the German-Swiss border and settled temporarily in Switzerland, for if he returned home he was liable to be shot for taking part in the insurrection. In a letter at the end of July 1849 Marx advised him 'to write a history of or a pamphlet on the Baden-Palatinate revolution' (p. 207), a suggestion which coincided with Engels' own intention to publish his 'reminiscences of the farcical Palatinate-Baden revolution' (p. 215). He made his intention good in 1850 by publishing a series of essays under the general title *The Campaign for the German Imperial Constitution* (present edition, Vol. 10).

After the unsuccessful action of the democratic Montagne party on 13 July 1849, the French authorities subjected the proletarian and democratic activists, including foreigners, to even harsher persecution. A new threat hung over Marx. In July, the commissioner of police signed the order for his deportation to Morbihan, a swampy and unhealthy place in Brittany, and the order was carried out on 23 August. Qualifying this act as a 'veiled attempt' on his life, Marx decided to leave France altogether. On 26 August 1849 he arrived in London—a new and, as it turned out, the last place of his exile. After spending a few months in Switzerland, Engels also came to England at the end of 1849. A new phase in their life and work began for both of them.

* * *

Their letters (autumn 1849 till the end of 1851), forming a considerable part of this volume, cover the period which came after the ebbing of the revolutionary tide. By that time, reaction had already triumphed or else reactionary regimes were about to be established in countries recently swept by the revolution. During this period, Marx and Engels set themselves the task of theoretically generalising the experience of the 1848-49 revolution, of further developing the revolutionary theory of the proletariat, and of preserving and training the cadres of the proletarian revolution.

Already at the end of July 1849 Marx wrote to Engels that he 'embarked on negotiations with a view to starting a politico-economic (monthly) periodical in Berlin which would have to be largely written by us two' (p. 207). From the letters that followed we can see how hard he tried to realise his project and how great an importance he attributed to this journal which would allow them successfully to continue with their theoretical and propaganda work, help them to rally the members of the Communist League whom the defeat of the revolution had scattered, and enable them to reorganise and revive the League's activity. This journal which Marx and Engels finally succeeded in starting was the *Neue Rheinische Zeitung. Polilisch-ökonomische Revue,* appearing from January to November 1850. In its columns were published important works of Marxism like Marx's *The Class Struggles in France,* and Engels' *The Campaign for the German Imperial Constitution* and *The Peasant War in Germany,* as well as a series of jointly written international reviews, articles dealing with various questions of theory and tactics of the revolutionary party in the new conditions, and criticisms of anti-proletarian ideological trends (see Vol. 10 of this edition).

The increasing police arbitrariness in Germany, where the journal was printed (in Hamburg) and mainly circulated, and an acute shortage of funds, thwarted plans to make it a bi-weekly, and then a weekly issue (see Marx's letter to Freiligrath of 11 January 1850), and in fact forced Marx and Engels to discontinue publication after the 5th-6th double issue.

From the letters of late 1850 and 1851, we learn of the enormous work done by Marx from his first days in England, and then also by Engels, to re-establish the international connections they had lost and to rally the revolutionary proletarian elements around the Communist League re-organised by them. This work was partly done with the assistance of the Social-Democratic Committee of Support for German Political Refugees, headed by Marx and Engels. They organised the collection of funds for the refugees and their families, helped them to find employment, and did everything within their power to support the people who had fought in the revolutionary battles and now found themselves in exile. We learn this from Marx's and Engels' letters to Joseph Weydemeyer of 9 and 25 April 1850 respectively; from Engels' letter to Theodor Schuster of 13 May, Marx's to Karl Blind of 17 July 1850, and a number of others. In these hard times, in spite of their own difficulties, Marx and Engels were always ready to come to the aid of their comrades. At the same time, these letters also show how firm and uncompromising they were in matters of principle when they had to put up a fight against a divergence from the revolutionary line, or to give a rebuff to any attempt to force immature doctrines and sectarian tactics on the proletarian organisation.

It was this firmness of character that they demonstrated most impressively in the course of the acute ideological struggle between their supporters and the unstable sectarian elements in the Communist League grouped around August Willich and Karl Schapper. Marx's and Engels' theoretical differences with this group had long been coming to a head. From Peter Röser's later and approximate rendering of Marx's letters to members of the Communist League in Cologne (pp. 551-52), an idea can be formed of the disputes which Marx had with Willich in the winter of 1849-50 in the London German Workers' Educational Society. Marx sharply criticised Willich's belief that a communist system could be set up at one go. As for the system itself, Willich pictured it as a barrack-like organisation of society. Marx wrote to his Cologne correspondents that Willich, convinced that communism 'would be introduced in the next revolution, if only by the might of the guillotine', intended to realise it on his 'own and against the will of everyone in Germany' (p. 551). Marx explained, to prove the utter unsoundness of these voluntarist views, that a revolutionary communist transformation of society was a relatively lengthy process, proceeding in several stages. In his argument with Willich he developed some of the important tenets of scientific communism, stressing that the transition to communism had to be made gradually—through a bourgeois-democratic revolution to a proletarian, socialist revolution, and then, after the conquest of power by the working class, through a transitory stage to the new society which, in its development, must also pass through at least two stages. The definite types of society's political organisation, designated in Peter Röser's rendering as 'social', 'socio-communist', and a 'purely communist republic' (p. 554), correspond to this transition period and the two stages of the new society's development. Here, Marx gave his first, rough outline of his teaching on socialism and communism as two phases of communist society, developed in 1875 in his *Critique of the Gotha Programme*.

In the autumn of 1850, the disputes with Willich and his supporters developed into a sharp conflict on questions of tactics. By this time, Marx and Engels had come to the conclusion that in view of the economic rise and the consolidation of the reactionary regimes there could be no revolution in the immediate future. Therefore, the tactical orientation of the Communist League had to be urgently reconsidered. The situation dictated that pro-letarian revolutionaries should be assembled and trained for future battles—a task that took patience and perseverance. The faction, however, ignoring the objective historical conditions and insisting upon immediate revolutionary action, furiously attacked the line taken by Marx and Engels. The meeting of the Central Authority of the Communist League on 15 September 1850 ended in a split. The battle with the separatists, headed by Willich and Schapper, continued in the months that followed.

Marx's and Engels' letters demonstrate their implacable hostility to Willich's and Schapper's dogmatism and sectarianism masked by 'leftist' ultra-revolutionary phrases, and to the separatists' desire to push the workers' movement down the disastrous road of political adventurism and putsches. They poured caustic ridicule on Willich's wild projects to make use of the mobilisation of the *Landwehr* in the Rhine Province, arising from the conflict between Prussia and Austria in the autumn of 1850, for an immediate revolutionary offensive in Western Germany (pp. 284, 287, 560-61). The actions of the Willich-Schapper separatist organisation brought it close to the petty-bourgeois emigrants who nursed similar pseudo-revolutionary schemes and whose appendage it was rapidly becoming. In their

XXXIV   Preface

letters, Marx and Engels showed that factionalism and sectarianism
inevitably led to a decline into an anti-proletarian position and an
ideological subordination to the bourgeoisie and the petty
bourgeoisie (see Marx's letter to Hermann Becker of 28 February
1851, and others).

What worried Marx and Engels especially was the fact that the
adventurist actions of the Willich-Schapper faction and of the
other emigrant groups made it all the easier for the police to
stage all sorts of provocations, incite rumours of imaginary
'communist conspiracies', and under this pretext to prosecute
people prominent in the workers' movement (see Marx's letter to
Engels of 28 May 1851). The arrests of members of the
Communist League which began in Germany in May 1851, and
the intention of the German authorities to stage a public
anti-communist trial, compelled Marx and Engels to make a
statement in the press in defence of the detainees (see Marx's
letter to Engels of 1 December 1851).

The relations between the proletarian revolutionaries headed by
Marx and Engels on the one hand, and the representatives of
various emigrant trends of the petty-bourgeois democrats operating in England and the USA on the other, were all the more
strained the more evident it became to Marx and Engels that the
clamorous campaigns for setting up all kinds of 'revolutionary
committees' and provisional governments, for 'revolutionary loans'
and so forth, would do more harm than good to the democratic
and especially the workers' movement. The rhetorical and
ostentatiously revolutionary campaigning of the petty-bourgeois
emigrants distracted the workers from their own problems and
misled some of them into following the petty-bourgeois leadership.
What is more, insinuations and slander against the proletarian
revolutionaries were spread from these emigrant circles. There is
good reason, therefore, why in their 1851 correspondence Marx and
Engels always spoke with such harsh criticism of the empty
phrase-mongering, petty intrigues and squabbles indulged in by the
leaders of the different German emigrant groups—Arnold Ruge,
Gottfried Kinkel, Karl Heinzen, Gustav Struve, and others.

In his two letters (August and December 1851) to the Frankfurt
journalist Hermann Ebner, Marx draws strikingly satirical portraits of the leaders of the German petty-bourgeois emigrant
groups (pp. 426-33, 499-503). Later, he used these character
sketches when, with Engels, he wrote *The Great Men of the Exile* in
1852 (present edition, Vol. 11, pp. 258, 281-84, 290-93, etc.).

Marx and Engels strongly criticised all manifestations of class and nationalistic narrow-mindedness, an erroneous understanding of revolutionary tasks, and also the miscalculations and mistakes of the emigrant circles, among them the French, the Hungarian and the Italian. Thus, in his letters to Weydemeyer of 11 September and to Engels of 13 September 1851, Marx criticised Mazzini, the Italian bourgeois democrat, for ignoring the interests of the exploited Italian peasantry in his plans for the national unification of Italy and its liberation from Austrian domination, and for failing to see in the peasantry one of the principal motive forces of the national liberation movement. Marx emphasised that only the participation of all the working people in this movement could give it real scope and strength, and guarantee its victory. In the above-mentioned letter to Weydemeyer, Marx said that 'the first step towards gaining Italy's independence was the complete emancipation of the peasants and the transformation of their métayage system into bourgeois freeholdings' (p. 455).

Marx and Engels tried to make the best use of the lull that followed the revolution for enriching their revolutionary teaching, and they urged their closest associates and pupils to concentrate on theoretical knowledge. In this period Marx devoted himself mainly to political economy and again pondered on the plan he had conceived in the 1840s of writing a major work on economics. As he worked on this plan it took on a more and more concrete shape and acquired depth and scope; with great meticulousness Marx selected and prepared the necessary material for a critical review of his predecessors' and contemporary scholars' concepts in the field of political economy. In his letter to Engels of 7 January 1851, he criticised for the first time Ricardo's theory of land rent, voiced certain theses of his own theory of rent, and on 3 February set forth his ideas on the theory of money circulation (pp. 258-63, 273-78).

Taking an all-embracing approach to the examination of economic problems, Marx began to study a number of other sciences, among them, technology and agricultural chemistry, the history of economics, and the economies of different countries, particularly of England, then the classical country of capitalism. Both he and Engels concluded from their analysis of the current economic situation that the post-revolutionary industrial upswing was a temporary phenomena, and that a new economic crisis was inevitable (see Engels' letters to Marx of 1 and 23 September and 15 October 1851, and Marx's letter to Engels of 13 October 1851).

It was Marx's intention, arising from his economic studies, to publish a criticism of Proudhon's new book *Idée générale de la*

2*

Révolution au XIXᵉ siècle, and he gave Engels his opinion of it in his letters of 8 and 14 August 1851, assessing it as a work aimed directly against the revolutionary proletarian world outlook. He said that the book as a whole was in the first place 'a polemic against communism' (p. 423), and asked Engels to write him his opinion of it. Marx thought highly of the thorough critical analysis (published in Vol. 11 of the present edition) which Engels sent him about two months later, and wrote to his friend on 24 November 1851: 'I have been through your critique again here. It's a pity *qu'il n'y a pas moyen* [that there's no means] of getting it printed. If my own twaddle were added to it, we could bring it out under both our names...' (p. 492).

At this time, Engels had undertaken a study of the military sciences, realising that in the coming class battles the military aspect was bound to play a major role. On 19 June 1851 he wrote to Weydemeyer: 'Since arriving in Manchester I have been swotting up military affairs... I was prompted to do this by the immense importance which must attach to the *partie militaire* [military aspect] in the next movement, combined with a long-standing inclination on my part, my articles on the Hungarian campaign in the days of the newspaper and finally my glorious exploits in Baden...' (p. 370).

Marx encouraged his friend's studies in every way, and supplied him with materials and information. In his letter of 23 September 1851, for instance, he gave a detailed rendering of the article 'Umrisse des kommenden Krieges' by Gustav Techow, a petty-bourgeois democrat, which had been published in the American press. Analysing in his reply the probable relation of armed revolutionary and counter-revolutionary forces in Europe in the event of new revolutionary developments, Engels came up with an important idea about the specific formation of revolutionary armies and their behaviour in battle (pp. 469-71).

Engels' work on his *Revolution and Counter-Revolution in Germany* (included in Vol. 11) can be followed from his correspondence with Marx during this period, providing another example of their creative cooperation. At the beginning of August 1851 Marx received an offer from the editor of the *New-York Daily Tribune,* Charles Dana, to become a correspondent of that paper, but as he was fully occupied with political economy at the time, he asked Engels to write a series of articles about the German revolution of 1848-49 (p. 425). His friend agreed at once, and had three articles ready before the end of the year (the rest were written in 1852). In the course of this work Engels kept in constant touch with Marx who also read the articles before mailing them to the USA.

In his turn, Marx unquestionably conceived the idea for *The Eighteenth Brumaire of Louis Bonaparte* as a result of Engels' letter of 3 December 1851. In it Engels gave his opinion of the Bonapartist coup d'état of 2 December 1851, calling it a sorry parody of the coup d'état of 9 November 1799 (the 18th Brumaire according to the republican calender) accomplished by Napoleon Bonaparte; he compared the Second Republic and its leaders to France during the French Revolution and the leaders of the Jacobins, remembering what Hegel said about the recurrence of historical phenomena. The comparisons made by Engels were so apt that Marx decided to use them in his book (see this volume, p. 505, and present edition, Vol. 11, p. 103).

The materials of this volume show how much their friendship meant to both of them in their theoretical work, party struggle, and private life. It helped Marx to bear up under the incredible hardships which confronted him in London, where he found himself without anything like a regular income and at times with no means of subsistence at all. These constant money worries undermined his health, took up all his strength and much of his time, and distracted him from his important theoretical work. The difficult conditions in which the family had to live are eloquently described in his wife's letters to Joseph Weydemeyer of 20 May and 20 June 1850 (pp. 555-60). It was then, at this most critical moment for Marx, that Engels, proving a true friend capable of self-sacrifice, went back to work in the firm of Ermen & Engels, his money orders from Manchester more than once rescuing the Marx family from catastrophe.

Marx's and Engels' letters to Joseph Weydemeyer, Wilhelm Wolff, Roland Daniels, Ernst Dronke, Adolph Cluss and other members of the Communist League, participants in the revolutionary struggle, show how much both treasured their ties of friendship and mutual assistance, and how concerned they were to further the theoretical and political education of their comrades.

Of great historical interest are the letters written by Marx to Heinrich Heine, Ferdinand Freiligrath, Georg Herwegh (until his break with the latter because of his adventurist schemes at the beginning of 1848). These letters speak of the friendly relations which the founders of Marxism had with outstanding German authors, and of the prestige they enjoyed in the circles of progressive German writers.

* * *

This is the first full publication in English of Marx's and Engels' letters. It includes not only letters previously published in editions brought out in Russian, German, and other languages, but also those discovered after the corresponding volumes of these editions had appeared. The letters are printed in chronological order. The form of existing editions has been followed: the date and place of writing are given at the beginning of the letter, irrespective of how they were in the original; when missing in the original, they are given in square editorial brackets. Obvious slips in the text are corrected without comment. The authors' contractions of personal names, geographical names and single words are given in full, except in cases where the contractions were made for the sake of conspiracy or cannot be deciphered. Defects in the manuscripts, where the text is missing or illegible, are indicated by three dots put in square brackets. If the context allows a presumable reconstruction to be made of the missing or illegible words, these words are also in square brackets. Anything crossed out by the authors is reproduced in the footnotes only where the disparity in meaning is considerable. If a letter is a rough copy, a postscript to someone else's letter, or an extract quoted in another document, this is marked either in the text itself or in the Notes.

Foreign words and expressions in the letters are given in italics. If they were underlined by the authors they are given in spaced italics. Words written in English in the original are given in small caps. Longer passages written in English in the original are placed in asterisks.

Information about undiscovered letters mentioned in the text will be found in the Notes. If a fact or event is referred to in several letters, the same note number is used every time.

Volume 38 contains 239 letters written by Marx and Engels. Of these, 172 are given in English translation for the first time; 67 letters have been published in English before, 37 of them only partially. The earlier English publications are mentioned in the Notes. Of the 17 documents included in the Appendices, only two have been published in English before—George Julian Harney's letter to Engels of 30 March 1846 and Jenny Marx's letter to Joseph Weydemeyer of 17 March 1848.

The results of the scientific work done when preparing for print the first volumes of Section III of Marx/Engels *Gesamtausgabe* (*MEGA*$_2$), a new complete edition of the *Works* of Marx and Engels in the original languages, containing their correspondence during the given years, were used in the work on the text and reference material of this volume. The dates of some of the letters were ascertained on the basis of the materials contained in these volumes and also the results of additional research.

The volume was compiled, the text prepared and the preface and notes written by Vladimir Sazonov and edited by Lev Golman (Institute of Marxism-Leninism of the CC CPSU). The name index and the index of periodicals were prepared by Valentina Pekina, the index of quoted and mentioned literature by Yuri Vasin, and the subject index by Marlen Arzumanov (Institute of Marxism-Leninism of the CC CPSU).

The translations were made by Peter and Betty Ross and edited by E. J. Hobsbawm, Nicholas Jacobs (Lawrence & Wishart), Richard Dixon, Natalia Karmanova and Margarita Lopukhina (Progress Publishers), and Larisa Miskievich, scientific editor (Institute of Marxism-Leninism of the CC CPSU).

The volume was prepared for the press by the editors Margarita Lopukhina, Mzia Pitskhelauri and Anna Vladimirova.

KARL MARX
and
FREDERICK ENGELS

LETTERS

October 1844-December 1851

1844

1

ENGELS TO MARX [1]

IN PARIS

[Barmen, beginning of October 1844]

Dear Marx,

No doubt you are surprised, and justifiably so, not to have heard from me sooner; however I still cannot tell you even now anything about my return. I've been stuck here in Barmen for the past three weeks, amusing myself as best I can with few friends and many relations amongst whom, fortunately, there are half a dozen amiable women. Work is out of the question here, more especially since my sister [a] has become engaged to the London communist, Emil Blank, an acquaintance of Ewerbeck's and, of course, the house is now in a hellish state of turmoil. Moreover, it's clear to me that considerable obstacles will continue to be placed in the way of my return to Paris, and that I may well have to spend six months or a whole year hanging about in Germany; I shall, of course, do everything I can to avoid this, but you have no idea what petty considerations and superstitious fears I have to contend with.

I spent three days in Cologne and marvelled at the tremendous propaganda we had put out there. Our people are very active, but the lack of adequate backing is greatly felt. Failing a few publications in which the principles are logically and historically developed out of past ways of thinking and past history, and as their necessary continuation, the whole thing will remain rather hazy and most people will be groping in the dark. Later I was in Düsseldorf, where we also have some able fellows. The ones I like best, by the way, are my Elberfelders, in whom a humane way of

---

[a] Marie

thinking has truly become second nature; these fellows have really begun to revolutionise their family lives and lecture their elders whenever these try to come the aristocrat over the servants or workmen—and that's saying a great deal in patriarchal Elberfeld. But besides this particular group there's another in Elberfeld which is also very good, though somewhat more muddled. In Barmen the police inspector is a communist. The day before yesterday I was called on by a former schoolfellow, a grammar school teacher,[a] who's been thoroughly bitten although he's had no contact whatever with communists. If we could bring direct influence to bear on the people, we'd soon get the upper hand, but such a thing is virtually impossible, especially since we writers have to keep quiet if we're not to be nabbed. Otherwise it's safe enough here, no one bothers much about us so long as we keep quiet, and it seems to me that Hess' fears are little more than phantoms. I've not been molested at all here so far, although the public prosecutor once insistently questioned one of our people about me, but up till now I haven't had wind of anything else.

According to the paper here, Bernays has been charged by the government here and taken to court in Paris.[2] Let me know whether this is true, and also how the pamphlet[b] is getting on; presumably it's finished by now. Nothing has been heard of the Bauers here, nobody knows anything about them. On the other hand, every one is still scrambling to get hold of the *Jahrbücher*.[c] My article on Carlyle[d] has, absurdly enough, earned me a tremendous reputation among the 'mass', whereas only very few have read the one on Economy.[e] That's natural enough.

In Elberfeld, too, the clerical gentry have been preaching against us, at least Krummacher has; for the present they confine themselves to the atheism of the young, but I hope this will soon be followed by a philippic against communism. Last summer the whole of Elberfeld talked of nothing but these godless fellows. By and large, the movement here is remarkable. Since I was here last,[3] the Wupper valley has made greater progress in every respect than in the preceding fifty years. Social manners have become more civilised, participation in politics, in the opposition is widespread, industry has made enormous progress,

---

a Gustav Wurm - b K. Marx and F. Engels, *The Holy Family, or Critique of Critical Criticism*. - c *Deutsch-Französische Jahrbücher* - d F. Engels, 'The Condition of England. *Past and Present* by Thomas Carlyle'. - e F. Engels, 'Outlines of a Critique of Political Economy'.

new districts have been added to the towns, entire woods have been grubbed up, and the level of civilisation throughout the region is indeed above rather than below that in Germany as a whole, whereas only four years ago it was far lower. In other words this promises to be first-rate soil for our principle, and if only we can get our wild, hot-blooded dyers and bleachers on the move, the Wupper valley will surprise you yet. As it is, the workers had already reached the final stage of the old civilisation a few years ago, and the rapid increase in crime, robbery and murder is their way of protesting against the old social organisation. At night the streets are very unsafe, the bourgeoisie is beaten, stabbed and robbed; and, if the proletarians here develop according to the same laws as in England, they will soon realise that this way of protesting as *individuals* and with violence against the social order is useless, and they will protest, through communism, in their general capacity as *human beings.* If only one could show these fellows the way! But that's impossible.

My brother [a] is at present a soldier in Cologne and, so long as he remains above suspicion, will provide a good address to which letters for Hess, etc., may be sent. At the moment I myself am not sure of his exact address and cannot therefore let you have it.

Since writing the above I have been in Elberfeld, where I once again came across several communists I had never heard of before. Turn where you will, go where you may, you'll stumble on a communist. A very impassioned communist, a cartoonist and aspiring historical painter by the name of Seel will be going to Paris in two months' time. I'll direct him to you; the fellow's enthusiasm and his painting and love of music will appeal to you, and he may very well come in useful as a cartoonist. It's possible, but not very probable, that I may be there myself by then.

A few copies of *Vorwärts*[4] arrive here and I have seen to it that others place orders as well; ask the dispatch department to send specimen copies to the following in Elberfeld: Richard Roth, Captain Wilhelm Blank *junior,* F. W. Strücker, Meyer, a Bavarian publican in the Funkenstrasse (a communist beerhouse), all to be sent through Bädeker, the communist bookseller, and under sealed cover. Once the fellows see that copies are coming in, they, too, will place orders. Also to W. Müller, M.D., in

---

[a] Hermann

Düsseldorf; and, if you like, to d'Ester, M.D., Löllchen,[a] the publican, your brother-in-law,[b] etc., in Cologne. All of them, of course, through the booksellers and under sealed cover.

See to it that the material you've collected is soon launched into the world.[5] It's high time, heaven knows! I too shall settle down to work and make a start this very day. The Teutons are all still very muddled about the practicability of communism; to dispose of this absurdity I intend to write a short pamphlet showing that communism has already been put into practice and describing in popular terms how this is at present being done in England and America.[c] The thing will take me three days or so, and should prove very enlightening for these fellows. I've already observed this when talking to people here.

Down to work, then, and quickly into print! Convey my greetings to Ewerbeck, Bakunin, Guerrier and the rest, not forgetting your wife, and write very soon to tell me all the news. If this letter reaches you safely and unopened, send your reply under sealed cover to F. W. Strücker and Co., Elberfeld, with the address written in as commercial a hand as possible; otherwise, to any of the other addresses I gave Ewerbeck. I shall be curious to know whether the postal sleuth-hounds are deceived by the ladylike appearance of this letter.

Goodbye for the present, dear Karl, and write very soon. I have not been able to recapture the mood of cheerfulness and goodwill I experienced during the ten days I spent with you. I have not as yet had any real opportunity of doing anything about the establishment we are to establish.[d]

First published abridged in *Der Briefwech-sel zwischen F. Engels und K. Marx*, Bd. 1, Stuttgart, 1913 and in full in *MEGA*, Abt. III, Bd. 1, Berlin, 1929

Printed according to the original

---

a J. A. Löllgen - b Edgar von Westphalen - c F. Engels, 'Description of Recently Founded Communist Colonies Still in Existence' was published in the *Deutsches Bürgerbuch für 1845* and not in pamphlet form. - d This seems to refer to some literary plan.

2

MARX TO JULIUS CAMPE

IN HAMBURG

Paris, 7 October 1844
rue Vanneau 38

Messrs Hoffmann and Campe, Booksellers, in Hamburg
Julius Campe, Esq.

Dear Sir,

Engels and I have written a pamphlet of some ten sheets against Bruno Bauer and his supporters.[a]

It deals with themes from philosophy, history and idealism, contains a critique of the *Mystères de Paris*,[b] etc., and will not be without interest for Germany. Nor, by and large, will it be objectionable to the censors.

Should you wish to undertake its publication, I would request you to reply forthwith, since the pamphlet cannot but lose in interest if printing is delayed.[6] If Heine is still in Hamburg, would you be so kind as to convey to him my best thanks for the poems he sent. I have not yet advertised them, as I wish to advertise the first part, the ballads, at the same time.[7]

Yours faithfully
Dr Marx

First published in part in *Das Goldene Tor*, Jg. 2, H. 11/12, 1947, S. 1073 and in full in *Hundertundzehn Jahre Verlag Rütten und Loening. Berlin 1844 bis 1954*, [Berlin, 1954,] S. 28

Printed according to the *Hundertundzehn Jahre Verlag Rütten und Loening* text

Published in English for the first time

---

[a] K. Marx and F. Engels, *The Holy Family*. - [b] Novel by Eugène Sue

3

MARX TO HEINRICH BÖRNSTEIN

IN PARIS

[Paris, not later than November 1844]

Dear Sir,

Return the Feuerbach sheets[a] to me as soon as you have printed them.[8]

Yours faithfully
Marx

First published as a facsimile in the book: 石浜 知行： 闘争の跡を訪ねて [Ishihama Tomoyuki, *In the Trace of Battles*], Tokyo, 1926

Printed according to the original

Published in English for the first time

4

MARX TO HEINRICH BÖRNSTEIN

IN PARIS

[Paris, autumn 1844]

Dear Sir,

You would greatly oblige me if you would ascertain by Tuesday at the latest whether or not Frank is willing to undertake *publication* of the pamphlet against Bauer.[b]

It is of complete *indifference* to me which way he decides. I can find a foreign publisher any day. Only, in the case of this particular pamphlet, in which *every* word counts, it would be pleasant to have it printed under my own supervision and to be able to correct it personally.

At any rate I beg you to reply speedily.

Ready to reciprocate,
Yours faithfully
Dr Marx

---

[a] L. Feuerbach, *Das Wesen des Glaubens im Sinne Luther's.* - [b] K. Marx and F. Engels, *The Holy Family.*

P.S. Since the pamphlet is directed *against Bauer* and on the whole contains little to which the censor could object, I should hardly suppose that distribution in Germany would present any great difficulty.

First published in *Der Kampf*, Jg. XXI, H. 10, Wien, 1928

Printed according to the original

Published in English for the first time

5

ENGELS TO MARX [9]

IN PARIS

No. 2

Barmen, 19 November 1844

Dear M.,

About a fortnight ago I received a few lines from you and Bürgers dated 8 October and postmarked Brussels, 27 October.[10] At about the same time you wrote your note, I sent off a letter to you, addressed to your wife,[a] and trust that you received it. In order to make sure in future that our letters are not tampered with, I suggest we number them; thus my present one is No. 2 and, when you write, let me know up to what number you have received and whether one is missing from the series.

A couple of days ago I was in Cologne and Bonn. All goes well in Cologne. Grün will have told you about our people's activities. Hess is thinking of joining you in Paris, too, in a fortnight or three weeks' time, provided he can get hold of sufficient money. You now have Bürgers there as well, and hence enough for a council. You will have all the less need of me and there is all the more need for me here. Obviously I can't come now since it would mean falling out with my entire family. Besides, I have a love affair to clear up first. And after all, one of us ought to be here because all our people need prodding if they are to maintain a sufficient degree of activity and not fall into all manner of shuffling and shifting. Jung, for instance, as well as many others,

---

[a] See this volume, pp. 3-6.

cannot be convinced that the difference between us and Ruge is one of principle,[11] and still persists in believing that it is merely a personal squabble. When told that Ruge is no communist, they don't quite believe it and assert that in any case it would be a pity if such a 'literary authority' as Ruge were to be thoughtlessly discarded. What is one to say to that? One must wait until Ruge once again delivers himself of some monumental stupidity, so that the fact can be demonstrated *ad oculos*[a] to these people. I don't know, but there's something not quite right about Jung; the fellow hasn't enough determination.

We are at present holding public meetings all over the place to set up societies for the advancement of the workers [12]; this causes a fine stir among the Teutons and draws the philistines' attention to social problems. These meetings are arranged on the spur of the moment and without asking the police. We have seen to it that half the rules-drafting committee in Cologne consists of our own people; in Elberfeld, at least one of them was on it and, with the help of the rationalists,[13] we succeeded at two meetings in thoroughly trouncing the pious; by a huge majority, everything Christian was banned from the rules.[14] It amused me to see what a ridiculous figure these rationalists cut with their theoretical Christianity and practical atheism. In principle they entirely agreed with the Christian opposition, although in practice, Christianity, which according to their own assertions forms the basis of the society, must nowhere be mentioned in the rules. The rules were to cover everything save the vital principle of the society! So rigidly did the fellows cling to this absurd position that, even without my putting in a single word, we acquired a set of rules which, as things are now, leaves nothing to be desired. There is to be another meeting next Sunday, but I shan't be able to attend because I am leaving for Westphalia tomorrow.

I am up to my eyebrows in English newspapers and books upon which I am drawing for my book on the condition of the English proletarians.[b] I expect to finish it by the middle or the end of January, having got through the arrangement of the material, the most arduous part of the work, about a week or a fortnight ago. I shall be presenting the English with a fine bill of indictment; I accuse the English bourgeoisie before the entire world of murder, robbery and other crimes on a massive scale, and I am writing an English preface[c] which I shall have printed separately and sent to

---

[a] visibly - [b] F. Engels, *The Condition of the Working-Class in England.* - [c] F. Engels,'To the Working-Classes of Great Britain'.

English party leaders, men of letters and members of Parliament. That'll give those fellows something to remember me by. It need hardly be said that my blows, though aimed at the panniers, are meant for the donkey, namely the German bourgeoisie, to whom I make it plain enough that they are as bad as their English counterparts, except that their sweat-shop methods are not as bold, thorough and ingenious. As soon as I've finished this, I shall make a start on the history of the social development of the English,[15] which will be still less laborious, since I already have the material for it and have sorted it out in my head, and also because I'm perfectly clear about the matter. Meanwhile I shall probably write a few pamphlets, notably against *List*,[16] as soon as I have the time.

You will have heard of Stirner's book, *Der Einzige und sein Eigenthum*,[a] if it hasn't reached you yet. Wigand sent me the specimen sheets, which I took with me to Cologne and left with Hess. The noble Stirner—you'll recall Schmidt of Berlin, who wrote about the *Mystères* in Buhl's magazine[b]—takes for his principle Bentham's egoism, except that in one respect it is carried through more logically and in the other less so. More logically in the sense that Stirner as an atheist sets the ego above God, or rather depicts him as the be-all and end-all, whereas Bentham still allows God to remain remote and nebulous above him; that Stirner, in short, is riding on German idealism, an idealist who has turned to materialism and empiricism, whereas Bentham is simply an empiricist. Stirner is less logical in the sense that he would like to avoid the reconstruction effected by Bentham of a society reduced to atoms, but cannot do so. This egoism is simply the essence of present society and present man brought to consciousness, the ultimate that can be said against us by present society, the culmination of all the theory intrinsic to the prevailing stupidity. But that's precisely what makes the thing important, more important than Hess, for one, holds it to be. We must not simply cast it aside, but rather use it as the perfect expression of present-day folly and, *while inverting it,* continue to build on it. This egoism is taken to such a pitch, it is so absurd and at the same time so self-aware, that it cannot maintain itself even for an instant in its one-sidedness, but must immediately change into communism. In the first place it's a simple matter to prove to

---

[a] The book came out at the end of October 1844, though imprinted as 1845. - [b] Review of *Les Mystères de Paris* by Eugène Sue published in *Berliner Monatsschrift*.

Stirner that his egoistic man is bound to become communist out of
sheer egoism. That's the way to answer the fellow. In the second
place he must be told that in its egoism the human heart is of
itself, from the very outset, unselfish and self-sacrificing, so that
he finally ends up with what he is combatting. These few
platitudes will suffice to refute the *one-sidedness*. But we must also
adopt such truth as there is in the principle. And it is certainly
true that we must first make a cause our own, egoistic cause,
before we can do anything to further it—and hence that in this
sense, irrespective of any eventual material aspirations, we are
communists out of egoism also, and it is out of egoism that we
wish to be *human beings,* not mere individuals. Or to put it another
way: Stirner is right in rejecting Feuerbach's 'man', or at least the
'man' of *Das Wesen des Christentums.*[a] Feuerbach deduces his 'man'
from God, it is from God that he arrives at 'man', and hence 'man'
is crowned with a theological halo of abstraction. The true way to
arrive at 'man' is the other way about. We must take our
departure from the Ego, the empirical, flesh-and-blood individual,
if we are not, like Stirner, to remain stuck at this point but rather
proceed to raise ourselves to 'man'. 'Man' will always remain a
wraith so long as his basis is not empirical man. In short we must
take our departure from empiricism and materialism if our
concepts, and notably our 'man', are to be something real; we
must deduce the general from the particular, not from itself or, *à
la* Hegel, from thin air. All these are platitudes needing no
explanation; they have already been spelled out by Feuerbach and
I wouldn't have reiterated them had not Hess—presumably
because of his earlier idealistic leanings—so dreadfully traduced
empiricism, more especially Feuerbach and now Stirner. Much of
what Hess says about Feuerbach is right; on the other hand he still
seems to suffer from a number of idealistic aberrations—
whenever he begins to talk about theoretical matters he always
proceeds by categories and therefore cannot write in a popular
fashion because he is much too abstract. Hence he also hates any
and every kind of egoism, and preaches the love of humanity, etc.,
which again boils down to Christian self-sacrifice. If, however, the
flesh-and-blood individual is the true basis, the true point of
departure, for our 'man', it follows that egoism—not of course
Stirner's intellectual egoism *alone,* but also the *egoism of the
heart*—is the point of departure for our love of humanity, which
otherwise is left hanging in the air. Since Hess will soon be with

---

[a] *The Essence of Christianity*

you, you'll be able to discuss this with him yourself. Incidentally, I find all this theoretical twaddle daily more tedious and am irritated by every word that has to be expended on the subject of 'man', by every line that has to be read or written against theology and abstraction no less than against crude materialism. But it's quite another matter when, instead of concerning oneself with all these phantasms—for such even unrealised man remains until the moment of his realisation—one turns to real, live things, to historical developments and consequences. That, at least, is the best we can hope for so long as we're confined exclusively to wielding a pen and cannot realise our thoughts directly with our hands or, if need be, with our fists.

But Stirner's book demonstrates yet again how deeply abstraction is rooted in the Berliners' nature. Clearly Stirner is the most talented, independent and hard-working of the 'Free',[17] but for all that he tumbles out of idealistic into materialistic abstraction and ends up in limbo. From all over Germany comes news of the progress made by socialism, but from Berlin not a whisper. When property has been abolished throughout Germany these clever-clever Berliners will set up a *démocratie pacifique*[a] on the Hasenheide—but the fellows will certainly get no further. Watch out! A new Messiah will presently arise in the Uckermark, a Messiah who will tailor Fourier to accord with Hegel; erect a phalanstery upon the eternal categories and lay it down as an eternal law of the self-developing idea that capital, talent and labour all have a definite share in the product. This will be the New Testament of Hegelianism, old Hegel will be the Old Testament, the 'state', the law, will be a 'taskmaster over Christ',[b] and the phalanstery, in which the privies are located in accordance with logical necessity, will be the 'new Heaven' and the 'new Earth', the new Jerusalem descending from heaven decked out like a bride,[c] all of which the reader will be able to find expounded at greater length in the new Revelation. And when all this has been completed, Critical Criticism will supervene, declare that it is all in all, that it combines in its head capital, talent and labour, that everything that is produced is produced by *it,* and not by the powerless masses—and sequestrate everything for itself. That will be the end of Berlin's Hegelian [peace]ful democracy.

If *Critical Criticism*[d] is finished, send me a few copies under

---

[a] An ironical allusion to the Fourierist newspaper *La Démocratie pacifique* known for its sectarian and dogmatic leanings. - [b] Cf. Galatians 3:24 - [c] Cf. Revelation 21:1 and 2. - [d] K. Marx and F. Engels, *The Holy Family.*

sealed cover through the booksellers—they might be confiscated. In case you [didn't re]ceive my last letter, I repeat that you can write to me either [...] F. E. *junior, Barmen,* or under sealed cover to F. W. Strücker and Co., Elberfeld. This letter is being sent to you by a roundabout route.

Write soon—it's more than two months since I last heard from you—how goes it with *Vorwärts?* My greetings to all.

Your[a]

[Address on envelope]

À Monsieur Charles Marx
Rue Vanneau N 38
Faubg. St. Germain, Paris

First published in *Der Briefwechsel zwischen F. Engels und K. Marx,* Bd. 1, Stuttgart, 1913

Printed according to the original

6

MARX TO HEINRICH BÖRNSTEIN

IN PARIS

[Copy]

[Paris, end of December 1844-
beginning of January 1845]

Dear Sir,

It is impossible for me to let you have the review of Stirner before next week. Therefore deliver the specimen copy without my contribution; Bürgers will let you have an article in its stead. You shall have my article next week.[18]

Yours faithfully
Marx

First published in *Katalog 211 des Antiquariats Leo Liepmanssohn,* Berlin, 1924

Printed according to the *Katalog* text

Published in English for the first time

---

[a] The signature is illegible.

1845

7

MARX TO ARNOLD RUGE

IN PARIS

[Paris, 15 January] 1845

To Dr Ruge

I have learned from a reliable source that the Préfecture de Police are now in possession of orders against you, myself and several others, whereby we are to leave Paris within 24 hours and France within the shortest possible time.[19] Börnstein can give you further details. In case you were not yet aware of this news, I deemed it proper to inform you of it.

K. Marx

First published in *Periodikum für wissenschaftlichen Sozialismus*, No. 3, January, Munich, 1959

Printed according to the original

Published in English for the first time

8

ENGELS TO MARX[20]

IN PARIS

[Barmen, about 20 January 1845]

Dear Marx,

If I haven't answered your letter before, it's mainly because I was waiting for the *Vorwärts* you promised me. But as the thing has still not arrived, I've given up waiting, either for that or for the *Critical Criticism*[a] of which I have no further news whatever. As regards Stirner, I entirely agree with you. When I wrote to you, I was still too much under the immediate impression made upon me by the book.[b] Since I laid it aside and had time to think it over, I feel the same as you. Hess, who is still here and whom I spoke to in Bonn a fortnight ago, has, after several changes of mind, come to the same conclusion as yourself. He read me an article, which he is shortly to publish, about the book[c]; in it he says the same as you, although he hadn't read your letter. I left your letter with him,[21] because he still wished to use some things out of it, and so I have to reply from memory. As regards my removal to Paris, there is no doubt that in some two years' time I shall be there; and I've made up my mind too that at any cost I shall spend 4 to 6 weeks there next autumn. If the police make life difficult for me here, I'll come anyway, and as things are now, it may occur to these scum any day to molest us. Püttmann's *Bürgerbuch*[d] will show us just how far one can go without being locked up or thrown out.

My love affair came to a fearful end.[e] I'll spare you the boring details, nothing more can be done about it, and I've already been through enough over it as it is. I'm glad that I can at least get down to work again, and if I were to tell you the whole sorry tale, I'd be incapable of anything this evening.

The latest news is that from 1 April Hess and I will be publishing at Thieme & Butz's in Hagen the *Gesellschaftsspiegel,* a monthly in which we shall depict social *misère* and the bourgeois regime. Prospectus, etc., shortly.[22] In the meantime it would be a good idea if the poetical *Ein Handwerker*[23] would oblige by sending us material on *misère* in *Paris.* Particularly individual cases, exactly what's needed to prepare the philistine for communism. Not much effort will be involved in editing the thing; contributors enough can be found to supply sufficient material for 4 sheets a month—we shan't have much work to do with it, and might exert a lot of influence. Moreover, Leske has commissioned Püttmann to put out a quarterly, the *Rheinische Jahrbücher,* bulky enough to evade censorship,[24] which is to be communism unalloyed. You too will doubtless be able to have a hand in it. In any case it will do no harm if we have part of our work printed twice—first in a periodical and then on its own and in context; after all, banned

---

[a] K. Marx and F. Engels, *The Holy Family.* - [b] M. Stirner, *Der Einzige und sein Eigenthum.* - [c] M. Hess, *Die letzten Philosophen* (published in pamphlet form in June 1845). - [d] *Deutsches Bürgerbuch für 1845* - [e] A reference to the German saying (coined in 1809 by Major Ferdinand von Schill).

books circulate less freely and in this way we'll have twice as much chance of exerting an influence. So you see we here in Germany have our work cut out if we're to keep all these undertakings supplied with material and at the same time elaborate greater things—but we shall have to put our backs into it if we're to achieve anything, and that's all to the good when you're itching to do something. My book on the English workers[a] will be finished in two or three weeks, after which I shall set aside four weeks for lesser things and then go on to the historical development of England and English socialism.[25]

What specially pleases me is the general recognition, now a *fait accompli*, which communist literature has found in Germany. A year ago it began to gain recognition, indeed, first saw the light of day, outside Germany, in Paris, and now it's already worrying the German man-in-the-street. Newspapers, weeklies, monthlies and quarterlies, and reserves of heavy artillery coming up—everything's in the best of order. It's certainly happened devilish fast! Nor has the underground propaganda been unfruitful. Every time I visit Cologne, every time I enter a pub here, I find fresh progress, fresh proselytes. The Cologne meeting[b] has worked wonders. One gradually discovers individual communist groups which have quietly evolved without any direct cooperation on our part.

The *Gemeinnütziges Wochenblatt* which was formerly published together with the *Rheinische Zeitung,* is now also in our hands. It has been taken over by d'Ester who will see what can be done. But what we need above all just now are a few larger works to provide an adequate handhold for the many who would like to improve their imperfect knowledge, but are unable to do so unassisted. Do try and finish your political economy book[c], even if there's much in it that you yourself are still dissatisfied with, it doesn't really matter; minds are ripe and we must strike while the iron is hot. Presumably my English things cannot fail to have some effect either, the facts are too convincing, but all the same I wish I had less on my hands so that I could do some things which would be more cogent and effective in regard both to the present moment and to the German bourgeoisie. We German theoreticians—it may be ludicrous, but it's a sign of the times and of the dissolution of the German national filth—cannot yet so much as develop our theory, not even having been able as yet to publish the critique of

---

[a] F. Engels, *The Condition of the Working-Class in England.* - [b] See this volume, p. 10. - [c] ibid., p. 6.

the nonsense. But now it is high time. So try and finish *before* April, do as I do, set yourself a date by which you will *definitely have finished,* and make sure it gets into print quickly. If you can't get it printed in Paris, have it done in Mannheim, Darmstadt or elsewhere. But it must come out soon.

The fact that you enlarged the *Critical Criticism* to twenty sheets surprised me not a little. But it is all to the good, for it means that much can now be disseminated which would otherwise have lain for heaven knows how long in your escritoire. But if you have retained my name on the title page it will look rather odd since I wrote barely $1^1/_2$ sheets. As I told you, I have as yet heard nothing from Löwenberg,[a] nor anything about the publication of the book, which I most eagerly await.

Yesterday I received *Vorwärts,* which I haven't seen since my departure. I was greatly amused by some of Bernays' jokes; the fellow can make one laugh so heartily, which I seldom do when reading. For the rest, it is definitely bad and neither interesting nor instructive enough to induce many Germans to take it for any length of time. How does it stand now, and is it true, as I hear in Cologne, that it is to be turned into a monthly[18]? We're so terribly overburdened with work here that you can expect no more than an occasional contribution from us. You over there will also have to bestir yourselves. You should write an article every 4 or 6 weeks for it and not allow yourself to be 'governed' by your moods. Why doesn't Bakunin write anything, and why can't Ewerbeck be induced to write at least something humdrum? Poor Bernays is, I suppose, by now in jug.[b] Give him my regards and tell him not to take this dirty business too much to heart. Two months is not an eternity, although it's dreadful enough. What are the lads doing generally? You tell me nothing about it in your letters. Has Guerrier returned, and is Bakunin writing French? What's become of the lot who used to frequent the Quai Voltaire every evening in August? And what are you doing yourself? How goes it with your situation there? Is the *Fouine*[c] still living under your feet? Not long ago, the *Fouine* again let fly in the *Telegraph.*[d] On the subject of patriotism, needless to say. Splendid how he rides it to death, how he doesn't care a rap, provided he succeeds in demolishing patriotism. Probably that was the substance[e] of

---

[a] Löwenberg (lion's mountain) is a pun on Löwenthal (lion's valley), the Frankfort publisher's name. - [b] See this volume, p. 4. - [c] Marten, Arnold Ruge's nickname. - [d] A. Ruge. 'An einen Patrioten', *Telegraph für Deutschland,* Nos. 203 and 204, December 1844. - [e] The original has 'Des Pudels Kern'—Goethe, *Faust,* Erster Teil, 'Studierzimmer'.

what he refused to give Fröbel. German newspapers recently alleged that the *Fouine* intends to return to Germany. If it's true I congratulate him, but it can't be true, else he'd have to provide himself for the second time with an omnibus with privy, and that's out of the question.

Not long ago I spoke to someone who'd come from Berlin. The dissolution of the *caput mortuum*[a] of The Free [17] would appear to be complete. Besides the Bauers, Stirner also seems no longer to have anything to do with them. The few who remain, Meyen, Rutenberg and Co., carry on serenely, foregathering at Stehely's every afternoon at 2 o'clock, as they have done for six years past,[26] and amusing themselves at the expense of the newspapers. But now they have actually got as far as the 'organisation of labour',[b] and they will get no farther. It would seem that even Mr Nauwerck has ventured to take this step, for he participates with zeal in popular meetings. I told you all these people would become *démocrates pacifiques*.[c] At the same time they have much 'acclaimed' the lucidity, etc., of our articles in the *Jahrbücher*.[d] When next the devil drives I shall begin corresponding with little Meyen; one can, perhaps, derive some entertainment *from* the fellows even if one doesn't find *them* entertaining. As it is, there's never any opportunity here for an occasional outburst of high spirits, the life I lead being all that the most splendiferous philistine could desire, a quiet, uneventful existence, replete with godliness and respectability; I sit in my room and work, hardly ever go out, am as staid as a German. If things go on like this, I fear that the Almighty may overlook my writings and admit me to heaven. I assure you that I'm beginning to acquire a good reputation here in Barmen. But I'm sick of it all and intend to get away at Easter, probably to Bonn. I have allowed myself to be persuaded by the arguments of my brother-in-law[e] and the doleful expression on both my parents'[f] faces to give huckstering another trial and for [...] days have been working in the office. Another motive was the course my love affair was taking. But I was sick of it all even before I

---

a Literally: dead head; the term is borrowed from the alchemists and figuratively means 'the remnants'. - b Probably an allusion to Louis Blanc's *Organisation du travail*. - c See this volume, p. 13. - d The reference is to the articles published in the *Deutsch-Französische Jahrbücher*: K. Marx, 'On the Jewish Question' and 'Contribution to the Critique of Hegel's Philosophy of Law. Introduction' and F. Engels, 'Outlines of a Critique of Political Economy' and 'The Condition of England, *Past and Present* by Thomas Carlyle'. - e Emil Blank - f Friedrich and Franziska Engels.

began work; huckstering is too beastly, Barmen is too beastly, the waste of time is too beastly and most beastly of all is the fact of being, not only a bourgeois, but actually a manufacturer, a bourgeois who actively takes sides against the proletariat. A few days in my old man's factory have sufficed to bring me face to face with this beastliness, which I had rather overlooked. I had, of course, planned to stay in the huckstering business only as long as it suited me and then to write something the police wouldn't like so that I could with good grace make off across the border, but I can't hold out even till then. Had I not been compelled to record daily in my book the most horrifying tales about English society, I would have become fed up with it, but that at least has kept my rage on the simmer. And though as a communist one can, no doubt, provided one *doesn't write,* maintain the outward appearance of a bourgeois and a brutish huckster, it is impossible to carry on communist propaganda on a large scale and at the same time engage in huckstering and industry. Enough of that—at Easter I shall be leaving this place. In addition there is the enervating existence in this dyed-in-the-wool Christian-Prussian family—it's intolerable; I might end up by becoming a German philistine and importing philistinism into communism.

Well, don't leave me so long without a letter as I have left you this time. My greetings to your wife, as yet a stranger, and to anyone else deserving of them.

For the time being write to me here. If I have already left, your letters will be forwarded.

Your
F. E.

[Address on envelope]

À Madame Marx. Rue Vanneau N 38
Paris

First published abridged in *Die Neue Zeit,* Bd. 2, No. 44, Stuttgart, 1900-01 and in full in *Der Briefwechsel zwischen F. Engels und K. Marx,* Bd. 1, Stuttgart, 1913

Printed according to the original

9

MARX TO HEINRICH HEINE [27]

IN PARIS

[Paris, end of January-1 February 1845]

Dear Friend,

I hope to have time to see you tomorrow. I am due to leave on Monday.[a]

The publisher Leske has just been to see me. He is bringing out a quarterly[b] in Darmstadt which is not subject to censorship. Engels, Hess, Herwegh, Jung and I, etc., are collaborating with him. He has asked me to solicit your cooperation—poetry or prose. Since we must make use of every opportunity to establish ourselves in Germany, you will surely not decline.

Of all the people I am leaving behind here, those I leave with most regret are the Heines. I would gladly include you in my luggage! Best regards to your wife[c] from mine and myself.

Yours

K. Marx

First published abridged in *Aus dem literarischen Nachlass von Karl Marx, Friedrich Engels und Ferdinand Lassalle*, Bd. 2, Stuttgart, 1902 and in full in *Archiv für die Geschichte des Sozialismus und der Arbeiterbewegung*, Jg. 9, Leipzig, 1921

Printed according to the original

10

ENGELS TO MARX [28]

IN BRUSSELS

Barmen, 22 February-7 March 1845[d]

Dear Marx,

After much writing here and there I have at last received your address from Cologne and at once sit down to write to you. The moment I heard of your expulsion[29] I thought it necessary to

---

[a] 3 February - [b] *Rheinische Jahrbücher* - [c] Mathilde - [d] In the original the first date is written at the beginning of the letter and the second at the end of it.

open a subscription list, so that the extra expense you have incurred thereby should be shared out communist-fashion between us all. The thing has made good progress and three weeks ago I sent fifty odd talers to Jung; I also approached the Düsseldorfers, who have collected the same amount, and in Westphalia, too, I have instigated through Hess the agitation necessary to that end. Meanwhile the subscription list here has not yet been closed. Köttgen, the painter, has been dragging his feet and thus I am not yet in possession of all the money we can expect. However, I hope everything will have come in within a few days, and then I will send you a bill on Brussels. Since I don't, by the way, know whether this will be enough to enable you to set up house in Brussels, I shall, needless to say, have the greatest pleasure in placing at your disposal my fee for my first English piece,[a] some of which at least I hope will soon be paid me, and which I can dispense with for the time being as my old man[b] is obliged to keep me primed. At least the curs shan't have the satisfaction of seeing their infamy cause you pecuniary embarrassment. The fact that you should have been compelled to pay your rent in advance is the height of turpitude. But I fear that in the end you'll be molested in Belgium too,[30] so that you'll be left with no alternative but England.

However, not a word more of the vile business. Kriege will already be with you by the time this arrives. The fellow's a capital agitator. He will tell you a great deal about Feuerbach. The day after he left here I received a letter from Feuerbach—we had, after all, written to the fellow.[31] Feuerbach maintains that until he has thoroughly demolished the religious piffle, he cannot concern himself with communism to the extent of supporting it in print, and also that, in Bavaria, he is too much cut off from the mainstream of life to be able to do so. However, he says he's a communist and that his only problem is how to practise communism. There's a possibility of his visiting the Rhineland this summer, in which case he must come to Brussels and we'll soon show him how.

Here in Elberfeld wondrous things are afoot. Yesterday we held our third communist meeting in the town's largest hall and leading inn.[32] The first meeting was forty strong, the second 130 and the third at least 200. All Elberfeld and Barmen, from the financial aristocracy to *épicerie*,[c] was represented, only the proletariat being

---

[a] F. Engels, *The Condition of the Working-Class in England.* - [b] Friedrich Engels senior, Engels' father - [c] grocers

excluded. Hess gave a lecture. Poems by Müller and Püttmann and excerpts from Shelley were read, also an article from the *Bürgerbuch* on existing communist colonies.[a] The ensuing discussion lasted until one o'clock. The subject is a tremendous draw. All the talk is of communism and every day brings us new supporters. The Wuppertal communism is *une vérité*,[b] indeed, already almost a force. You have no idea how favourable the soil is here. The most stupid, indolent, philistine people, hitherto without any interest in anything in the world, are beginning almost to rave about communism. How long it will still be tolerated I do not know, but the police at any rate are completely at a loss, themselves not knowing where they stand, and just at a time when the chief swine, the District President, is in Berlin. But should they impose a ban, we'll find some way round it and if we can't, we'll at least have stirred things up so mightily that every publication representing our interest will be voraciously read here. As I shall be leaving at Easter, it is all to the good that Hess should settle here and at the same time publish a monthly[c] at Bädeker's in Elberfeld; Kriege, I believe, has a prospectus of this.[22] In any case, as I have probably told you already, I shall be going to Bonn.[d] My projected journey to Paris has now fallen through, there no longer being any reason for me to go there, but anyhow I shall be coming to Brussels instead, the more so since my mother and two sisters[e] will be visiting Ostend in the summer. I must also pay another visit to Bielefeld and the communists there[33] and, if Feuerbach doesn't come, I shall go to him and then, provided I have the time and the money, visit England once again. As you see, I have a good deal ahead of me. Bergenroth told me that he, too, would probably be going to Brussels in a few weeks or so. Together with some Düsseldorfers, he attended our second meeting, at which he spoke. Incidentally, standing up in front of real, live people and holding forth to them directly and straightforwardly, so that they see and hear you is something quite different from engaging in this devilishly abstract quillpushing with an abstract audience in one's 'mind's eye'.

I am to request you once more on Hess' behalf—and do so on my own as well—to send Püttmann something for his quarterly.[f] It's essential that we all appear in the very first issue, so that the

---

[a] F. Engels, 'Description of Recently Founded Communist Colonies Still in Existence'. - [b] a reality - [c] This refers to the *Gesellschaftsspiegel*. - [d] See this volume, p. 19. - [e] Apparently, Elise and Hedwig. - [f] *Rheinische Jahrbücher*

thing acquires some character. In any case, without us it will never so much as materialise.

25 February

Yesterday evening we got news that our next meeting was to be broken up by gendarmes and the speakers arrested.

26 February

Yesterday morning the chief burgomaster [a] forbade Mrs Ober-meyer to permit such meetings on her premises, and I received a tip to the effect that if the meeting was held notwithstanding, arrest and prosecution would follow. We have now of course given it up and can only wait and see whether we shall be prosecuted, though this seems hardly likely as we were wily enough not to provide a pretext, and the whole dirty business could only lead to the government's being made a terrible fool of. In any case the public prosecutors and the entire district court were present and the chief prosecutor himself took part in the discussion.

7 March

Since writing the above I have spent a week in Bonn and Cologne. The people in Cologne are now permitted to hold their meeting in connection with the Association.[34] As regards matters here,[32] a rescript has come in from the Düsseldorf government whereby further meetings are forbidden. Hess and Köttgen have protested. Won't do any good, of course, but these people will see from the tone of the protest that they can't get the better of us. Hess is once more tremendously sanguine because in all other respects everything is going so famously and we have made really tremendous progress. The good fellow is always full of dreams.

Our *Gesellschaftsspiegel* will be splendid, the first sheet has already been censored and everything passed. A mass of contributions. Hess is living in *Barmen,* in the *Stadt London.* It seems unlikely that Bergenroth will come to Brussels in the immediate future, though someone else will, whose name I won't mention as this letter will probably be opened. If it can somehow be managed, I too shall come to see you again in April. At the moment my chief problem is money, since the meeting caused

---

[a] Johann Adolph Carnap

38 rue Vanneau, Paris, where Marx lived
from October 1843 to January 1845

Rue de l'alliance, hors de la porte de Louvain No. 5, Brussels,
where Marx lived

some family ructions, after which my old man made up his mind
to support me only as regards my '*studia*' but not as regards
communist aims of any description.

There's a whole lot more I should tell you if I knew of a safe
address in Brussels, which in any case you must send me. Much of
what has happened here could be harmful to a great many people
if perused in a *cabinet noir*.[35] I shall stay here, then, another four
weeks and leave for Bonn at the beginning of April. Anyhow,
write to me again before then, so that I know how things are with
you. Most of the money has been collected, though I don't yet
know what it amounts to; it will be sent off directly. My
manuscript[a] will be leaving any day now.

The *Critical Criticism* has *still not arrived!*[36] Its new title, *The
Holy Family,* will probably get me into hot water with my pious and
already highly incensed parent, though you, of course, could not
have known that. I see from the announcement that you have put
my name first. Why? I contributed practically nothing to it and
anyone can identify your[b] style.

Let me know by return whether you are still in need of money.
Wigand is due to send me some in about a fortnight's time and
then all you have to do is dispose of it. I fear that the outstanding
subscriptions will not amount to more than 120 or 150 francs.

Apropos, we here are planning to translate Fourier and, if at
all possible, to produce a 'library of the best foreign socialist
writers'.[37] Fourier would seem to be the best to start off with.
We've found people to do the translation. Hess has just told me
about a Fourier glossary brought out in France by some Fourierist
or other. You will know of it. Could you send me particulars at
once and, if possible, post me a copy. At the same time
recommend what French writings you think suitable for translation for our 'library'. But look sharp; the matter is urgent, as we
are already negotiating with a publisher.[c] How far have you got
with your book? I must now get down to my manuscript,[38] so
goodbye for the present and write directly about the points I have
mentioned.

Your
F. E.

Greetings to Kriege and Bürgers.
Is Bernays there?

---

[a] F. Engels, *The Condition of the Working-Class in England.* - [b] The manuscript is
damaged here, but the text is decipherable. - [c] Julius Theodor Bädeker

[On the fourth page of the letter]

À Madame Marx. Bois Sauvage, Plainc Ste Gudule,
Chez Monsieur J. B. Lannoy, Bruxelles

First published abridged in *Die Neue Zeit*,
Bd. 2, No. 44, Stuttgart, 1900-01 and in
full in *Der Briefwechsel zwischen F. Engels
und K. Marx*, Bd. 1, Stuttgart, 1913

Printed according to the original

11

ENGELS TO MARX[28]

IN BRUSSELS

Barmen, 17 March 1845

Dear Marx,

Hess gave me your letter yesterday.[39] As regards the translations, the whole thing is not yet at all organised. I wanted
Fourier—omitting, of course, the cosmogonic nonsense[40]—
translated in Bonn by people there under my own eyes and my
own direction and, the publisher being willing, to issue it as the
first instalment of the proposed 'library'. I talked this over
occasionally with Bädeker, the publisher of the *Gesellschaftsspiegel*,
and he seemed not disinclined, although he lacks the necessary
finances for a *larger* 'library'. But if we produce it in this form, we
would doubtless be better advised to give it to Leske or somebody
else equally able to spend something on it. As for translating the
things *myself*, I simply won't have the time this summer as I have
to finish the English things. The first of them[a] went off to Wigand
this week and since I stipulated that he pay me 100 talers on
receipt of the manuscript, I expect to receive money in a week or
a fortnight, and be able to send it to you. Meanwhile, there are
fr. 122.22 c. on Brussels due 26 March.[b]

Herewith the remainder of the subscriptions; if the business
hadn't been so dreadfully held up by the Elberfelders, who could
have got at least twenty more talers out of their *amis-bourgeois*,[c] the
amount would have been larger and have reached you sooner.

---

[a] F. Engels, *The Condition of the Working-Class in England.* - [b] The words 'fr.
122.22 c. on Brussels due 26 March' were probably added dy Stephan Adolph
Naut. - [c] bourgeois friends

To return to the library, I don't know whether it would be best to produce the things in *historical* sequence. Since Frenchmen and Englishmen would necessarily have to take turn and turn about, the continuity of the development would be constantly interrupted. In any case I believe that it would be better here to sacrifice *theoretical* interest to practical effectiveness, and to start off with the things which have most to offer the Germans and are closest to our principles; the best, that is, of Fourier, Owen, the Saint-Simonists, etc.

Morelly might also appear fairly early on. The historical development could be briefly outlined in the introduction to the series. In this way, even with the arrangement as proposed, people could easily find their bearings. We could do the introduction together—you taking France and I England; this might actually be possible when I come to see you, as I intend to do in three weeks' time. At least we could discuss the matter. But at all events it seems to me essential to start off with things that make a practical, effective impact upon the Germans and save us from repeating what others have said before us. If we were to seek to give a collection of sources on the history of socialism or rather, its history as revealed in and through the sources, a considerable time would, I fear, elapse before we finished it and, moreover, the thing would become boring. Hence I propose that we only use material whose positive content—at least the major part of it—is still of use today. Since you will be providing a *complete* critique of politics,[5] Godwin's *Political Justice* as a critique of politics from the political standpoint and the standpoint of the citizen and society, would, despite the many excellent passages in which Godwin touches on communism, be excluded. And this more especially since, at the *end* of his work, Godwin comes to the conclusion that man must emancipate himself as much as possible from society and use it simply as a luxury article (*Political Justice,* II, Vol. 8, Appendix to Chapter 8), and is altogether distinctly anti-*social* in his conclusions. However, it was a very long time ago that I made excerpts from the book, when many things were still not clear to me, and I must in any case look through it again, for it may well be that there's more to the thing than I found at the time. But if we include Godwin, we cannot leave out his auxiliary, Bentham, although the fellow's so tedious and theoretical.

Write to me about this and then we can consider further what is to be done. Since the idea occurred to both of us, it must be put into effect—the 'library', I mean. Hess will certainly be delighted to have a hand in it, and so will I, once I have the time—as Hess now has, having nothing to do at present save edit the *Gesellschaftsspiegel*.

If we're agreed on the principles, we can thrash out the details and at once get down to work during my visit, which I shall promote even more zealously with this in mind.

The *Critical Criticism*[a]—I think I've already told you it had arrived—is quite outstanding. Your expositions of the Jewish question, the history of materialism and the *Mystères*[b] are splendid and will make an excellent impact. But for all that the thing's too long. The supreme contempt we two evince towards the *Literatur-Zeitung*[c] is in glaring contrast to the twenty-two sheets we devote to it. In addition most of the criticism of speculation and of abstract being in general will be incomprehensible to the public at large, nor will it be of general interest. Otherwise the book is splendidly written and enough to make you split your sides. The Bauers won't be able to say a word. By the way, if Bürgers reviews it in Püttmann's first volume,[d] he might mention the reason— namely my short ten days' stay in Paris—why I covered so little ground, restricting myself to what could be written without delving more deeply into the matter. Anyway, it looks odd, my having but $1^1/_2$ sheets in the thing while you have over 20. You'd have done better to have omitted the piece on the 'conditions of prostitution'. It's too slight and altogether unimportant.

It's curious that another of my plans besides the library should have coincided with yours. I too intended to write a critique of List[e] for Püttmann.[41] Fortunately I learned of your intention in good time through Püttmann. As I wished to discuss List *practically*, to develop the *practical* consequences of his system, I shall enlarge somewhat on one of my Elberfeld speeches (the transactions are to appear in Püttmann's publication) in which I dealt briefly with this among other things.[32] In any case I assume from Bürgers' letter to Hess and from my knowledge of your personality that you will deal with his *premises* rather than with his conclusions.

Just now I'm leading a real dog's life. The business of the meetings[f] and the 'dissolute conduct' of several of our local communists, with whom I, of course, consort, have again aroused all my old man's religious fanaticism, which has been further exacerbated by my declared intention of giving up the huckstering

---

[a] K. Marx and F. Engels, *The Holy Family*. - [b] E. Sue, *Les Mystères de Paris*. - [c] *Allgemeine Literatur-Zeitung* - [d] *Rheinische Jahrbücher* (the review of *The Holy Family* did not appear in the journal). - [e] See this volume, p. 11. - [f] ibid., pp. 22-24.

business for good and all—while my public appearance as a communist has also fostered in him bourgeois fanaticism of truly splendid proportions. Now put yourself in my place. Since I am going away in a fortnight or so, I don't want to cause ructions; I never take umbrage and, not being used to that, they are waxing bold. If I get a letter it's sniffed all over before it reaches me. As they're all known to be communist letters they evoke such piously doleful expressions every time that it's enough to drive one out of one's mind. If I go out—the same expression. If I sit in my room and work—communism, of course, as they know—the same expression. I can't eat, drink, sleep, let out a fart, without being confronted by this same accursed lamb-of-God expression. Whether I go out or stay at home, remain silent or speak, read or write, whether I laugh or whether I don't—do what I will, my old man immediately assumes this lamentable grimace. Moreover my old man's so stupid that he lumps together communism and liberalism as 'revolutionary', and, whatever I may say to the contrary, is constantly blaming me, e.g. for the infamies perpetrated by the English *bourgeoisie* in Parliament. In any case it is now the season of piety in this house. A week ago today a brother and sister of mine[a] were confirmed, today the whole tribe went toddling off to Communion—the body of the Lord did its work; this morning the doleful expressions surpassed themselves. *Pour comble de malheur*[b] I spent yesterday evening with Hess in Elberfeld, where we held forth about communism until two in the morning. Today, of course, long faces over my late return, hints that I might have been in jug. Finally they plucked up enough courage to ask where I had been.—With Hess.—'With Hess! Great heavens!'—Pause, intensified Christian dismay in their faces.— 'What company you keep!'—Sighs, etc. It's enough to drive one mad. You have no idea of the malice of this Christian persecution of my 'soul'. Now all my old man has to do is to discover the existence of the *Critical Criticism* and he will be quite capable of flinging me out of the house. And on top of it all there's the constant irritation of seeing that nothing can be done with these people, that they positively *want* to flay and torture themselves with their infernal fantasies, and that one can't even teach them the most platitudinous principles of justice. Were it not for my mother, who has a rare fund of humanity—only towards my father does she show no independence whatever—and whom I really love, it would not occur to me for a moment to make even

---

[a] Rudolf and Hedwig - [b] To make matters worse

the most paltry concession to my bigoted and despotic old man. But as it is, my mother is making herself ill with her constant fretting, and every time she gets particularly upset about me, she is afflicted with headaches for a week. It's more than I can bear, I must get away, and hardly know how I shall be able to stand the few remaining weeks here.[42] But they'll pass somehow.

Otherwise there's nothing new here. The bourgeoisie talk politics and go to church; what the proletariat does we know not and indeed could hardly know. The address to which you sent your last letter is still safe for the time being. This evening I hope to obtain the money, and Köttgen has just assured me that, as soon as he has more time—in a few days—he will be able to scrape up some more. But I don't altogether credit this; Köttgen is ready and willing if he has a chance to shine, but otherwise is good for nothing and does nothing. *Adios.*

Your
E.

First published in extracts in *Aus dem literarischen Nachlass von Karl Marx, Friedrich Engels und Ferdinand Lassalle*, Bd. 2, Stuttgart, 1902 and in full in *MEGA*, Abt. III, Bd. 1, 1929

Printed according to the original

12

MARX TO HEINRICH HEINE[43]

IN PARIS

Brussels, [24 March 1845]
rue Pachecho vis-à-vis
de l'hôpital St. Jean, No. 35

Dear Heine,

If I write you no more than a few lines today, you must excuse me on the grounds of the multifarious vexations I have had with the Customs.

Püttmann in Cologne has requested me to ask you if you couldn't possibly send a few poems (perhaps also your German fleet?)[a] for the *Jahrbuch*[b] in Darmstadt, a periodical *not subject to censorship.* You can address the material to me. The latest date—but you'll probably have something immediately to hand—is 3 weeks hence. My wife sends her cordial regards to yourself and your wife.[c] The day before yesterday[d] I went to the local Administration de la sûreté publique,[e] where I had to state in writing that here in Belgium I would publish nothing about current politics.

Renouard and Börnstein have had your *Wintermärchen* printed in Paris, New York being given as the place of publication, and have offered it for sale here in Brussels. This pirated edition is said, in addition, to be teeming with printer's errors. More another time.

Yours
Marx

First published in *Archiv für die Geschichte des Sozialismus und der Arbeiterbewegung,* Jg. 9, Leipzig, 1921   Printed according to the original

13

MARX TO ZACHARIUS LÖWENTHAL

IN FRANKFURT AM MAIN

Brussels, 9 May [1845]
rue de l'Alliance, hors de la porte
de Louvain, No. 5
c/o: M. Reinhard

Dear Sir,

I would request you to send *forthwith,* in my name and at my expense—you may again draw a bill on me, including therein the postage on this letter—3 copies of the *Holy Family* to Paris, to Mr *Herwegh,* rue Barbet-Jouy, Faub. St. Germain, Mr *Heine,* rue du Faub. Poissonniére No. 46, and to Mr *Bernays,* 12, rue de Navarin. I have had letters from various quarters complaining that no copies are to be had in *Paris.*

Yours faithfully
Dr Marx

---

[a] H. Heine, 'Unsere Marine'. - [b] *Rheinische Jahrbücher* - [c] Mathilde - [d] 22 March 1845 - [e] police headquarters

You may draw the bill on me forthwith, but I would request you once again to send off the copies in question *immediately*.

[In Engels' handwriting]

Mr Herwegh, rue Barbet-Jouy, Faubg. St. Germain,
Mr H. Heine, rue du Faubourg Poissonniére 46, both in Paris; similarly Mr Bernays, 12, rue de Navarin, Paris.

First published in: Marx and Engels, *Works,* First Russian Edition, Vol. XXV, Moscow, 1934

Printed according to the original

Published in English for the first time

14

ENGELS TO MARIE ENGELS [28]

IN BARMEN

Brussels, Saturday, 31 May 1845

Dear Marie,

To my regret I must today inform you that I shall be unable to be present at your wedding,[a] the reason being the difficulties I have encountered over a passport. Last Wednesday I went to the Administration de la sûreté publique[b] and demanded a passport for Prussia. After some waiting and a lengthy discussion about my emigration and the fact that I could not obtain a passport from the Prussian envoy, I was finally informed that since I had only just arrived, I could not get a passport from him. If I had lived here a little longer, he — Mr Hody, the Directeur of the sûreté publique — would have been empowered to give me passports, but in the circumstances he could not. In any case, foreigners who settled here usually arrived with passports still valid for a year or six months, and hence his instructions were to give visas to newly arrived foreigners, but not to issue them with passports. Incidentally, if I had one or two connections, I would undoubtedly obtain a passport at the Foreign Affairs Ministry. I do indeed have such connections, namely in the person of a German doctor who had actually promised to obtain a passport for me should I run into difficulties. But this doctor was himself married only a fortnight ago and went to the Wallonian watering-places for his honeymoon.

---

[a] with Emil Blank on 3 June 1845 - [b] police headquarters

He returned on Thursday and it was not till yesterday evening that I succeeded in seeing him; he was very willing to help, but he immediately told me that, since he was unable to go to the ministry before this morning, I couldn't possibly get my passport until the day after tomorrow—Monday—and hence must put off my trip until Monday evening or Tuesday morning. I told him that I couldn't wait as long as that, but he again declared that it wouldn't be possible to help me obtain it any sooner; anyhow, he said, he was willing to try again. Well, this morning he sent me a note saying he had indeed made inquiries in person and would be unable to obtain a passport for me before Monday, maybe not until Monday evening. I replied at once, telling him to spare himself further exertion, as in that case I should have to abandon my trip altogether.

As you and the others will readily understand, I would only expose myself to unpleasantness, my other circumstances being what they are, were I to attempt to cross the border without a passport—which, indeed, Mr Hody advised me against, my exit permit being valid *pour sortir de la Prusse, mais pas pour y rentrer,*[a] so it would seem that I must remain here and celebrate your wedding on my own and in my thoughts—sorry though I am for it. Anyhow you may be sure that I shall spend the whole day thinking of you and Emil,[b] and that my best wishes will accompany you in marriage and on your honeymoon, although I shall not have the pleasure of expressing them orally. What I wish you above all is that the love which has brought you together and has made your relationship as beautiful, humane and decent as any I have encountered, will accompany you throughout your lives, help you to surmount all adversity with ease and be the making of your happiness. I rejoice wholeheartedly over your marriage because I know that you cannot be anything but happy in your life together and that—after you have been joined together—neither of you will be disappointed in the other. You may be sure that, of the many good wishes that will be proffered you, none is more sincerely meant, none is more cordial nor warmer than mine! As you know, of all my brothers and sisters, I loved you the best and you were the one in whom I always had most confidence—so you will believe what I say, without any need for solemn asseverations and unnecessary verbiage. Once again, I wish that your love may always remain constant, and there is much else I wish you besides—what, you will be able to guess. Be happy!

---

[a] for leaving Prussia, but not for returning there - [b] Emil Blank

Well, I hope I shall soon receive a letter from Mrs Blank, for I expect Mrs Blank to take just as much interest in me as did Miss Engels. At all events I hope that, after a happy wedding and a happy honeymoon, I shall see you both this summer at Ostend or in England, and till then, once again farewell!

Warmest regards to everyone

Your devoted

Friedrich

First published in *Deutsche Revue*, Jg. 45, Bd. 4, Stuttgart und Leipzig, 1920   Printed according to the original

15

ENGELS TO JULIUS CAMPE [28]

IN HAMBURG

Brussels, 14 October 1845
7, rue de l'Alliance

Dear Sir,

From your esteemed letter [44] I perceive that there is some misapprehension on your part as regards the line we would take in the work we proposed to you for publication.[45] We have no intention of defending protective tariffs any more than free trade, but rather of criticising both systems from our own standpoint. Ours is the communist standpoint, which we have advocated in the *Deutsch-Französische Jahrbücher,* the *Holy Family,* the *Rheinische Jahrbücher,* etc.,[a] and from which, too, my book *The Condition of the Working-Class in England* is written. As you will appreciate, this altogether precludes the submission of our work to the censor, and hence we cannot agree to the same. Should you, however, desist from this and be otherwise inclined to accept the work, we would beg you to be so good as to let us know before we enter into other commitments.

Yours very truly

F. Engels

First published in: Marx and Engels, *Works,* First Russian Edition, Vol. XXV, Moscow, 1934   Printed according to the typescript

---

[a] The journals mentioned carried Marx's 'On the Jewish Question' and 'Contribution to the Critique of Hegel's Philosophy of Law. Introduction' and Engels' 'Outlines of a Critique of Political Economy' and 'The Condition of England. *Past and Present* by Thomas Carlyle'.

1846

16

ENGELS TO MARIE BLANK

IN LONDON

Brussels, 7 March 1846
7, rue de l'Alliance, Saint-Josse-ten-Noode

Dear Marie,

Great was my joy on hearing the news that you had been blessed with a strong, sturdy boy[a] who bears a close resemblance to your beloved spouse. I should have long since sent you my congratulations, having had Mother's notification in my pocket for almost six days now. But so ordinary a letter of congratulation is so ordinary and ceremonious a thing that I should have been truly ashamed to send off promptly by return a polite, conventional communication of this kind to you, my most dearly beloved sister. On the contrary, I have waited six days in order that you may see that I speak from the heart. Anyone can send congratulations by return, but to wait six days is only possible for someone who is particularly affectionate; to send congratulations by return proves absolutely nothing and when done for purely formal reasons is in any case hypocrisy. To wait six days is to show proof of a deep emotion which cannot find expression in words. For that same reason I shall desist from sending the customary good wishes to the young comrade and for a long string of little brothers and sisters to follow him. This last would be superfluous, especially as you are in London where Queen Victoria sets so excellent an example,[46] and besides enough space will probably be left at the end of this letter to enable you to copy out for yourself a sufficiency of choice felicitations, benisons, etc., etc., from whichever letter writer's vade-mecum you may happen to light upon. True, I am sorry that, through your agency, I should already have become an uncle at the age of 26, being in any case too young for that and wanting in the necessary decorum. But the fact that little Elise has already become an aunt at the age of

---

[a] Friedrich

twelve, which is much worse, is some consolation and I can but assure you that I shall be as diligent as possible in the performance of my duties (of which I am totally ignorant) as uncle, provided you think it worth your while to explain them to me in detail beforehand. As I have seven more fellow-sufferers, co-aunts and co-uncles,[a] the one-eighth of the duties devolving upon myself will not in any case prove so very onerous and that is a further consolation. I am happy you are well and that I am too, and hope to see you in Ostend this summer at the latest. I am truly curious to observe you as a mama and to see what effect the earnestness of life, to which as 'wife and mother' you are now obliged to pay heed, has had on you. Lest that effect should become too great, I have written in as jovial a manner as possible. But I would ask you for a reply, a reply, what's more, that gives some hint of the earnestness of life, of the wife and mother, of the painstaking materfamilias or, as the Dutch would say, *welgeliefde Echtgenoot.*[b] So now it is your turn to write when you have the opportunity.

Love to Mother, Emil and Hermann.

Your
Friedrich

First published in: *Friedrich Engels, 1820-1895. Leben und Werk. Eine Ausstellung der Stadt Wuppertal bearbeitet von Dieter Dowe,* Bonn-Bad-Godesberg, 1970

Printed according to the original

Published in English for the first time

17

ENGELS TO EMIL BLANK

IN LONDON

Brussels, 3 April 1846
7, rue de l'Alliance, St. Josse-ten-Noode

Dear Emil,

Be so kind as to send me £6—or approx. 150 fr.—by *return of post.* I shall let you have it back in a week or two. My old man isn't sending the money I was expecting on 1 April; apparently he

---

[a] There were eight children in the Engels family—Frederick, Hermann, Emil, Rudolf, Anna, Hedwig, Elise and Marie. - [b] dearly beloved spouse

intends to bring it with him when he comes for your child's^a christening. But I've now got 150 fr. worth of things in pawn which I must redeem before my people arrive and therefore must have that amount at once. The whole mess is due to the fact that throughout this winter I have hardly earned a farthing from my writing and hence my wife^b and I have had to live almost exclusively on the money I was receiving from home, and that wasn't so very much.[47] Since I now have a fair number of manuscripts either half or completely finished, this isn't very likely to happen to me again. So send me the money and, as soon as I've had my remittance from home, I'll return it.

Your brother Fritz was here these few days and went home yesterday morning. In conclusion I would again enjoin discretion *sur le contenu de cette lettre.*^c

With regards,
Your
F.

First published in: Marx and Engels, *Works,* First Russian Edition, Vol. XXV, Moscow, 1934

Printed according to the original

Published in English for the first time

18

MARX TO HEINRICH HEINE[48]

IN PARIS

Brussels, [beginning of April 1846]
rue de l'Alliance, 5,
hors de la porte de Louvain

My dear Heine,

I am taking advantage of the passage through here of Mr Annenkov, a most engaging and cultured Russian and the bearer of this note, to convey my kindest regards to you.

---

^a Friedrich - ^b Mary Burns - ^c concerning the contents of this letter

A few days ago a short lampoon against you happened to fall into my hands—posthumous letters of Börne's.[a] I should never have held him to be so dull, petty and inept as he here reads in black and white. And what miserable rubbish, too, the addendum by Gutzkow, etc. I shall be writing a detailed review of your book on Börne[b] for a German periodical. A more clumsy treatment than that suffered by this book at the hands of these Christian-Teutonic jackasses would be hard to find in any period of literature, and yet there's no lack of clumsiness in Germany of whatever period.

If perchance you should have anything 'special' to tell me about your piece, do so quickly.

Yours

K. Marx

First published in *Archiv für die Geschichte des Sozialismus und der Arbeiterbewegung*, Jg. 9, Leipzig, 1921

Printed according to the original

19

MARX TO PIERRE-JOSEPH PROUDHON [49]

IN PARIS

Brussels, 5 May 1846

My dear Proudhon,

I have frequently had it in mind to write to you since my departure from Paris, but circumstances beyond my control have hitherto prevented me from doing so. Please believe me when I say that my silence was attributable solely to a great deal of work, the troubles attendant upon a change of domicile,[50] etc.

And now let us proceed *in medias res*[c]—jointly with two friends of mine, Frederick Engels and Philippe Gigot (both of whom are in Brussels), I have made arrangements with the German communists and socialists for a constant interchange of letters which will be devoted to discussing scientific questions, and to keeping an eye on popular writings, and the socialist propaganda

---

[a] L. Börne, *Urtheil über H. Heine. Ungedruckte Stellen aus den Pariser Briefen* (the book contained passages from Börne's letters to Jeannette Wohl with attacks on Heine). - [b] *Heinrich Heine über Ludwig Börne*. Hamburg, 1840 (Marx's review has not been found). - [c] to the matter in hand

that can be carried on in Germany by this means.[51] The chief aim of our correspondence, however, will be to put the German socialists in touch with the French and English socialists; to keep foreigners constantly informed of the socialist movements that occur in Germany and to inform the Germans in Germany of the progress of socialism in France and England. In this way differences of opinion can be brought to light and an exchange of ideas and impartial criticism can take place. It will be a step made by the social movement in its *literary* manifestation to rid itself of the barriers of *nationality*. And when the moment for action comes, it will clearly be much to everyone's advantage to be acquainted with the state of affairs abroad as well as at home.

Our correspondence will embrace not only the communists in Germany, but also the German socialists in Paris and London.[52] Our relations with England have already been established. So far as France is concerned, we all of us believe that we could find no better correspondent than yourself. As you know, the English and Germans have hitherto estimated you more highly than have your own compatriots.

So it is, you see, simply a question of establishing a regular correspondence and ensuring that it has the means to keep abreast of the social movement in the different countries, and to acquire a rich and varied interest, such as could never be achieved by the work of one single person.

Should you be willing to accede to our proposal, the postage on letters sent to you as also on those that you send us will be defrayed here, collections made in Germany being intended to cover the cost of correspondence.

The address you will write to in this country is that of Mr Philippe Gigot, 8 rue de Bodenbroek. It is also he who will sign the letters from Brussels.

I need hardly add that the correspondence as a whole will call for the utmost secrecy on your part; our friends in Germany must act with the greatest circumspection if they are not to compromise themselves.

Let us have an early reply[53] and rest assured of the sincere friendship of

Yours most sincerely

Karl Marx

P.S. I must now denounce to you Mr Grün of Paris. The man is nothing more than a literary swindler, a species of charlatan, who seeks to traffic in modern ideas. He tries to conceal his ignorance with pompous and arrogant phrases but all he does is make himself ridiculous with his *gibberish*. Moreover this man is *dangerous*. He *abuses* the connection he has built up, thanks to his impertinence, with authors of renown in order to create a pedestal for himself and compromise them in the eyes of the German public. In his book on 'French socialists'[a] he has the audacity to describe himself as tutor (*Privatdozent,* a German academic title) to Proudhon, claims to have revealed to him the important axioms of German science and *makes fun* of his writings. Beware of this parasite. Later on I may perhaps have something more to say about this individual.

[From Gigot]

It is with pleasure that I take advantage of the opportunity offered by this letter to assure you how glad I am to enter into relations with a man as distinguished as yourself. Meanwhile, believe me,

Yours most sincerely

Philippe Gigot

[From Engels]

For my part, I can only hope, Mr Proudhon, that you will approve of the scheme we have just put to you and that you will be kind enough not to deny us your cooperation. Assuring you of the deep respect your writings have inspired in me, I remain,

Yours very sincerely

Frederick Engels

First published in *Die Gesellschaft,* Jg. IV, H. 9, Berlin, 1927

Printed according to the original

Translated from the French

Published in English in full for the first time

20

MARX TO KARL LUDWIG BERNAYS

IN SARCELLES

Brussels, 7 May [1846]

Dear Mr Bernays,

The fee due to you for your manuscript—500 fr.—will be paid at the end of the month.[54] In accordance with the contract with

---

[a] K. Grün, *Die soziale Bewegung in Frankreich und Belgien.*

the bookseller-publisher, debts are not payable until after publication of the manuscripts.

I have the honour to be, sir,

Your obedient servant

Dr Charles Marx

First published in *Acta Historica Academiae Scientiarum Hungaricae,* 1977, Budapest, Tomus XXIII, Nr. 3-4

Printed according to *Acta Historica...*

Translated from the French

Published in English for the first time

21

MARX TO JOSEPH WEYDEMEYER

IN SCHILDESCHE NEAR BIELEFELD

Brussels, 14-16 May [1846]

Dear Weiwi,

Herewith a belated letter. All manner of things have intervened. I had already intended to write to you from Liège[55] as arranged. But because of money problems I was averse to doing so. I readily put off such problems from one day to the next. But eventually, of course, one has to take the plunge.

You will shortly be getting an *official* letter from here.[56] The manuscripts will be with you shortly.[a] The second volume is almost ready. As soon as the manuscripts for the first volume arrive (better to send them in *two* consignments) it would be most desirable that printing should begin.[57]

As to your idea about Limburg, it may be all right for pamphlets; books of more than 20 sheets are best printed in Germany proper. I think I've found a way of doing this which 1.

---

[a] K. Marx and F. Engels, *The German Ideology* and other works intended for publication in the planned quarterly.

will *nominally* leave Meyer out of it altogether, 2. will make things very difficult for the governments and 3. strongly commends itself insofar as the dispatch arrangements would be placed in very efficient hands.

Vogler, who resides here and has a commission agent[a] in *Leipzig,* a man chiefly engaged in the dissemination of books liable to confiscation, would, you see, take over the whole bookselling side. The books themselves would be printed in Germany. In each case the *editor* would appear as publisher, i.e. *'Published by the Author'.* Vogler has offered his services on the following terms which I quote word for word from one of his letters to me[b]:

'In return for 10 per cent of the *receipts at the Fair* I undertake responsibility for all charges such as dispatch, carriage, delivery, cash collection, commission and the like, provided the books are delivered to me carriage paid Leipzig.'

Thus Vogler would make out the invoices here, and the books would be sent from the place of publication direct to his commission agent in Leipzig. The place of publication should not, of course, be in *Prussia.* Vogler's account would be settled at each Easter Fair.

It seems to me that for the time being this would be the best course for books of more than 20 sheets. For pamphlets, your suggestion is certainly a good one. As regards a joint-stock bookseller I shall see what I can do. At all events it will create difficulties.

If Meyer agrees to Vogler's proposal we could start at once—it would only be necessary to find some *place of publication outside Prussia.*

I had got thus far when your next letter arrived, the one addressed to Ph. Gigot as well as to me personally. Engels is sitting beside me at this moment to reply to the part concerning us all.[58] I frankly admit that the news it contains has affected me rather disagreeably.

I am, as you know, in a serious financial predicament. In order to make ends meet for the time being here, I recently pawned the last of the gold and silver as well as a large part of the linen. Moreover, so as to economise, I have given up our own establishment for the present and moved to the Bois Sauvage here. Otherwise I should have had to hire a new maid as the youngest child[c] is now being weaned.

---

[a] A. T. Thomas - [b] of 9 May 1846 - [c] Laura, born in September 1845.

I have vainly cast around in Trier (*chez* my mother) and in Cologne *chez* one of her *business acquaintances* with a view to borrowing the 1200 fr. I need to set my affairs in order again. Hence the news about the booksellers is all the more unwelcome since I had hoped to get this money as an advance on the Political Economy.[59]

No doubt there are sundry bourgeois in Cologne who would probably advance me the money for a definite period.[60] But some time ago these people adopted a line that in principle is diametrically opposed to my own, and hence I should not care to be beholden to them in any way.

As to the fee for the publication, only the half for volume 1 is due to me, as you know.

As though one's own misfortunes were not enough, I, as editor of the publication, am also getting a stream of urgent letters, etc., from every quarter. There is, in particular, the unpleasant matter of *Bernays.* As you know, he had already received 104 fr. on account through you. Bernays had given a bill of exchange due 12 May (to his baker), he couldn't pay, so it had to be protested, which gave rise to further expenses, etc., etc. Now the baker wants to have him *locked up.* He wrote to me; I, of course, couldn't help him, but to put the matter off temporarily, took the only possible course:

1. wrote a *fruitless* letter to Herwegh[61] in Paris, asking him to forward the amount to Bernays pending the appearance of his essay[54];

2. wrote a letter in French to Bernays to keep his creditor at bay if need be, in which I informed him that, on publication, he would receive a fee amounting to so and so much.[a] Whereupon the citizen granted him an extension until 2 June. Bernays is liable for the expenses of the protest, etc., *120 fr.* (I can't remember the exact sum).

As you can see, *misère* on all sides! At this moment I'm at a loss what to do.

Some other time I shall write you a more substantial letter. You must excuse my silence on the grounds that all this financial stress has come on top of much work, domestic duties, etc.

Farewell.

Yours

M.

---

[a] See this volume, pp. 40-41.

My wife and I send our warm regards to your betrothed.[a]

Be it noted, and to anticipate any misunderstandings, that *Hess* has *nothing more* due to him from the two volumes I am now editing; on the contrary he still has some to *hand back* to us.[62]

My private address: Au Bois Sauvage. Chez M. Lannoy, Plaine Ste Gudule, N. 19.

When writing to me *privatum* address letters: À Mr Lannoy, Plaine Ste Gudule, Bruxelles, under cover.

First published in *Beiträge zur Geschichte der deutschen Arbeiterbewegung*, Jg. 10, H. 1, 1968

Printed according to the original

Published in English for the first time

22

ENGELS TO MARX

IN BRUSSELS

Ostend, 27 July 1846
11, rue St. Thomas

Dear Marx,

I've been out on several occasions hunting for lodgings for you, but I haven't found anything much. Either too large or too small. Seldom *two* habitable rooms together, the bedrooms for the most part wretchedly cramped. *Enfin*[b] yesterday I discovered 2 lodgings *au choix*[c]: 1. two large rooms, first and second floor respectively; each with bed, for 95 fr. a month, 30 fr. extra for the third bed, breakfast $1/2$ fr. a day per head or stomach. 2. a small house belonging to the same *propriétaire,* one living-room downstairs, upstairs two communicating bedrooms, one of them tolerably large, and a closet, at 150 fr. a month. Breakfast *même prix.*[d] Whoever takes the house will have a maid's services included. The two rooms mentioned above are part of a restaurant, *'au duc de Brabant', rue du lait battu,* so meals could be had there if required. But in this respect you'd be quite independent there. At all events you would do well, if you are considering one of these two lodgings, to put up at the *'duc de Brabant',* it's cheaper than an hotel and, should you not like the rooms, you can ask the woman

---

[a] Louise Lüning - [b] At last - [c] for your choosing - [d] same price

there to show you the house, which is situated in the *rue des sœurs blanches* No. 5, and if that doesn't suit you either, you will no doubt find another. By the way, as compared with last year, there's been a fearsome rise in the cost of lodgings as of everything, or rather, 'and the same for everything'. Fr. 5 will cover the cost of dinner for the whole of your family, beef-steak 1 fr., cutlets *idem*, wine 2-3 fr. Beer bad, cigars bad and expensive, you'd be well advised to bring a few 100 from Brussels, in which case you can assume that the following table of expenses is correct:

	Accommodation	fr.	125-fr. 150	
	Breakfast	"	45- " 45	(if you sometimes
	Dinner	"	150- " 175	eat by the sea)
	Supper, 2-3 beef-steaks	"	60- " 90	(people stuff themselves here)
per month	Afternoon coffee on the beach, very necessary, 2 cups	"	18- " 18	
	Laundering is very dear, at least	"	20- " 30	(In addition bathing ⓐ fr. 1.30-fr. 1.50— Appr. 40 fr.)
		fr.	418-fr. 508	

Besides this it would be desirable to have another 100 fr. for INCIDENTAL EXPENSES, for without it you can be very bored here. You needn't stay here more than a month. Only those with broken backs, or who are complete and utter wrecks both inside and out, stay any longer. But you must so arrange the rent that, should you stay beyond the month, the additional period is paid *à tant par jour*,[a] otherwise they will charge you for a full half month if you stay two days longer.

For the rest, life is very sluggish here. During the first few days a boring philistine from Barmen, *la bête des bêtes*,[b] was, with the exception of my family and imposed upon me by the same, my

---

[a] at so much a day - [b] a monumental ass

one and only companion. Yesterday Blank, whom you know, arrived from London and through him I at last made the acquaintance of a Frenchman *qui a beaucoup d'esprit*[a] and who is an altogether excellent fellow, although he has spent 15 years in Elberfeld and speaks German *par conséquent.*[b]

'Finally I would touch on' the Mrs Hess affair. It's bad, but one cannot possibly let her suffer for the stupidities of the aforementioned Hess; I shall therefore try to smuggle her across the border if, that is, I get enough money from my old man for the journey to Paris, which is still not sure. Send the enclosed scribble to the beloved man of God[c] in Cologne, to cheer him up. So the woman is in Brussels already?

Great men there are none here. They don't arrive till August. No one has yet divulged the identity of the great Germans who are due to arrive. For the time being, therefore, I must content myself with the Prussian Bank project.[63] It's farcical that the gents should imagine they're going to make a lot of money out of it. A few of these big bankers, who want to become 'major stockholders' and conclude their secret agreements with the bureaucrats, e.g. to the effect that their shares are not redeemable, that they are introduced by stealth onto the main board, etc., may perhaps allow themselves to be persuaded. But no one else. Delightful that 'neither the *subscribers* nor the *amounts subscribed* are to be made known'. This means that they're expecting damned little money and are seeking, in true bureaucratic fashion, to cover themselves to some extent in case of failure.

Write soon and let me know whether you're coming and when.[64]

Your
E.

---

[a] who has a very lively mind - [b] as a result - [c] Moses Hess, see this volume, p. 47.

Yesterday these visions were to be seen in the sea by male and female spectators alike.

First published in MEGA, Abt. III, Bd. 1, 1929

Printed according to the original

Published in English for the first time

23

ENGELS AND MARX TO MOSES HESS

IN COLOGNE

Ostend, 27 July 1846
rue St. Thomas, 11

Dear Hess,

As you see, I am no longer writing to you from Brussels. I shall remain here until 10 August and shall probably be leaving Brussels for Paris on the 11th. Marx has sent your letter on to me here. I shall gladly do my utmost to smuggle your wife[a] across the border, but all the same it's unfortunate that she should not have a passport. As I had already left Brussels a few days before her arrival, I know nothing of the whole affair except what you tell me in your letter. As I have said, I will do my utmost.

Your
Engels

[Brussels, about 29 July 1846]

Dear Hess,

In forwarding you these lines from Engels, I would only add that your wife is *quite cheerful.* Seiler is her squire and has introduced her to Vogler and wife, with whom she consorts almost daily. My wife cannot do very much as she is very unwell and mostly has to keep to her bed.

Your
M.

---

[a] Sibylle

I was just about to send this letter off when I read your announcement about Ruge in the *Kölnische Zeitung*.[a] Since the printing of our stuff may be much delayed, I would advise you to get back your article on Ruge.[62] You will be able to use nearly all of it.

I wrote and asked the Westphalians[b] to send the manuscript to Daniels.[65] If he has not yet got it, arrange for the article on Ruge to be sent by them direct to you.

What sort of a book is this of Heinzen's[c]? And what does Dottore Graziano write about you? Write and tell me.

[On the back of the letter in Karl Marx's
and Jenny Marx's handwriting]

Mr. M. Hess in Cologne
Hand to Mr Gottschalk, M. D.

First published in *Rheinische Zeitung*, No. 105, Köln, April 30, 1931

Printed according to the original

Published in English for the first time

24

MARX TO CARL FRIEDRICH JULIUS LESKE[66]

IN DARMSTADT

[Draft]

[Brussels,] 1 August [1846]

Dear Sir,

Your letter in which you expressed your doubts about publication was answered *by return*. As to your query about its 'scientific character', I replied that the book is scientific, but not scientific as understood by the Prussian government, etc. If you would cast your mind back to your first letter, you then wrote in considerable anxiety because you had been cautioned by the Prussians and were then under investigation by the police. I at once wrote to you, saying that I would look around for another publisher.

---

[a] M. Hess, 'Erklärung', *Kölnische Zeitung*, No. 209, 28 July 1846, supplement, announcing Hess' forthcoming article on A. Ruge.- [b] J. Meyer and R. Rempel - [c] A reference to K. Heinzen's collection *Die Opposition* with A. Ruge's articles 'Der teutsche Kommunismus' and 'Der Rabbi Moses und Moritz Hess'.

I *received* yet another letter from you in which, on the one hand, you cancelled publication and, on the other, agreed that the advance be repaid in the form of a draft on the new publisher, whoever it might be.

If you received no further answer to this, it was because I believed I should very shortly be able to give you a *positive* answer, i.e. notification of another publisher. How this came to be delayed, you will presently hear. That I accepted *as a matter of course* your proposal about the repayment of the *advance* will be evident to you from the fact that, at the only place where I took steps to secure publication, I stipulated at the same time that the 1,500 fr. were to be repaid to you on acceptance of the manuscript. The *proof* of this can be produced *at any time. Engels* and *Hess,* by the by, are witnesses.

On the other hand you will recall that in Paris, as in the written contract, *nothing* was agreed about how revolutionary the form of the work was to be, and that, on the contrary, I even believed it necessary at the time to bring out both volumes simultaneously, because the publication of the *first* volume would entail the banning or confiscation of the second. *Heinrich Bürgers* from Cologne was present and can vouch for this. *Legally* speaking you were not therefore *entitled* to lay down new conditions or to refuse to publish as I, for my part, am not bound, from the *legal* viewpoint, either to repay the advance or to accede to your new proposals, or to modify my work. It hardly *needs saying* that I could not for a moment consider adopting a *legal* attitude towards you, more especially since you, for your part, were not contractually obliged to pay me an advance, which I was bound to regard, and did regard, *purely as a friendly gesture.* Though, hitherto, I have often and unhesitatingly released *publishers* (e.g. Wigand and Fröbel in the matter of the *Deutsch-Französische Jahrbücher,* and other publishing houses, as you will presently hear) from their contractual and legally enforceable obligations, despite great financial loss, it has *never* occurred to me to deprive any publisher of a single penny, even when I could *legally* do so. Why I should have made an exception *precisely in the case of yourself,* who had done me a particular favour, I utterly fail to understand.

Now as to the delay in replying:

Several capitalists in Germany[a] had agreed to publish a number of writings by myself, Engels and Hess.[67] In this case there was even a prospect of a really extensive series that would be totally

----

[a] J. Meyer and R. Rempel

immune from the attentions of the police.[68] Moreover, publication of my *Kritik der Ökonomie,* etc., had been virtually assured through a friend of these gentlemen.[a] This same friend remained in Brussels until May so as to convey safely across the border the manuscript of the first volume of the publication brought out under my editorship and with the cooperation of Engels, etc.[b] From Germany he was to write to me, letting me know definitely whether or not the *Nationalökonomie* had been accepted. Such news as I got was indeterminate and a short while ago, after the greater part of the manuscript of the second volume of that publication had been dispatched to Germany, these gentlemen finally wrote informing me that the whole business had come to *nothing,* their capital being employed elsewhere. Hence the delay in giving you a definite reply. When everything had been settled, I arranged with Mr *Pirscher* of Darmstadt, who was staying here, to convey a letter to you from me.

Because publication had been agreed upon with the German capitalists, I had discontinued work on the *Ökonomie.* For it seemed to me very important to *precede* my *positive* development with a polemical piece against German philosophy and *German socialism* up till the present. This is necessary in order to prepare the public for the viewpoint adopted in my Economy, which is diametrically opposed to German scholarship past and present. It is, by the way, the same polemical piece I had already mentioned in one of my letters to you as having to be completed before the publication of the *Ökonomie.*

So much for that.

My answer to your latest letter is as follows:

I. In the event of your not publishing the work, I herewith declare it *to be understood* that you will recover the advance *in the manner you have stipulated.*

But it must be equally understood that, should I receive from another publisher a *fee* less than that agreed on with you, you will share the loss with me, since it was because of you, not me, that recourse had to be had to another publisher.

II. There is a prospect of publication for my book. The day before yesterday I received a letter from Germany[c] in which I was advised of the intention to start a joint-stock company for the publication of communist works, which will be happy to make its début with my book. However, I regard the thing as still so

---

[a] Joseph Weydemeyer - [b] See this volume, p. 41. - [c] A reference to Hess' letter to Marx of 28 July 1846.

ıncertain that I shall, if necessary, address myself to other publishers.

III. Since the all but completed manuscript of the first volume of my book has been lying idle for so long, I shall not have it published without revising it yet again, both as regards matter and style. It goes without saying that a writer who works continuously cannot, at the end of 6 months, publish *word for word* what he wrote 6 months earlier.

There is the further point that the *Physiokraten* in 2 folio volumes did not come out until the *end of July* and will not be arriving here for several days yet, although their publication was announced while I was still in Paris. Full account must now be taken of these.

So much of the book will now be rewritten that it could appear even under *your* imprint. After approval of the manuscript you would, moreover, be at liberty to bring it out under a foreign imprint.

IV. As to dates: because of my very impaired state of health, I am having to take salt-water baths at Ostend during August; moreover I shall be busy editing the 2 volumes of the above-mentioned publication. Hence nothing much can be done during August.

The revised version of the first volume will be ready for publication at the *end of November*. The 2nd volume, of a more historical nature, will be able to follow soon after it.

V. I have already told you in an earlier letter that, partly because of the fresh material collected in England,[69] and partly because of the requirements that have come to light as work proceeded, the manuscript will exceed the agreed number of sheets by more than 20 printed sheets. Since the contract had already been concluded, I had made up my mind, as you will recall from an earlier letter, to be content with the *agreed* fee, although the number of sheets had been increased by about $^1/_3$. It would have spoiled the book had I brought out the fresh material separately. Not for a moment would I object to bearing a commercial loss in the interests of the work. Nor would I wish either to break the *contract* or to *impair* the effect of the book itself.

But since your earlier letter indicated that the resumption of the contract is a matter for me to decide, I feel compelled to include a new condition whereby the printed sheets over and above the agreed number are paid for on the same scale. This request seems to me all the more just as I shall in any case make very little out of the work because of my trip to England and my stay there undertaken solely on its account, and because of the large amount of very expensive literature I had to purchase.

Finally, if it can be done on some kind of reasonable terms, I would like the work to appear under your imprint, since you have always adopted such a liberal and friendly attitude towards me.

If need be, I could produce numerous letters I have received from Germany and France as proof that this work is most eagerly awaited by the public.

Yours faithfully

Dr Marx

I beg you to reply *by return* to the following address: à *Mr Lannoy.* Au Bois Sauvage, Plaine Ste Gudule, N. 19, Bruxelles.

First published in: Marx and Engels, *Works,* First Russian Edition, Vol. XXV, Moscow, 1934

Printed according to the original

25

ENGELS TO MARX

IN BRUSSELS

[Paris,] 19 August 1846
Cercle Valois, Palais Royal

Dear Marx,

Arrived here at last Saturday evening after a fatiguing journey and much tedium.[70] Immediately ran into Ewerbeck. The lad is very cheerful, completely tractable, more receptive than ever; in short I hope that—given a little patience—he and I will come to see pretty well eye to eye in all things. There are no longer any complaints about party strife—for the simple reason that he himself has been compelled to elbow out some of the Weitlingians here. Little has as yet transpired about what actually took place between him and Grün to create a breach between them; all we know is that Grün, by adopting now a fawning, now an arrogant, manner, was able to retain his more or less respectful affection. Ewerbeck has no illusions whatever about Hess, *il n'a pas la moindre sympathie pour cet homme-là.*[a] In any case he has long nourished a private hate against him, going back to the time they lodged together. I duly reprimanded him about the Westphalians.[71] That oaf Weydemeyer had written Bernays a Westphalianly lachrymose letter in which those noble fellows Meyer and Rempel were portrayed as martyrs in a good cause, gladly sacrificing their all, but whom we had rejected with contempt, etc.; and those two gullible Teutons, Ewerbeck and Bernays, sit down together, bemoan our hardness of heart and contentiousness and take the lieutenant at his word. Such superstition can scarcely be credited.

Grün has swindled the workers out of some 300 fr. on the pretext of having a pamphlet of $1\,^1/_2$ sheets printed in Switzerland.[b] Now the money's coming in, but the workers aren't getting a penny of it. Now they're beginning to dun him for it. Ewerbeck realises how foolish it was of him to introduce this fellow Grün among the artisans. He is now afraid to accuse Grün publicly before them because he believes him capable of giving everything away to the police. But what a gullible fellow this Ewerbeck is! The wily Grün had *himself* told Ewerbeck all about his shabby tricks—but presenting them, of course, as undiluted heroic acts *des Dévouements,*[c] and Ewerbeck swallows every word he says. Of the fellow's earlier knaveries he knew only as much as the DELINQUENT himself had thought fit to tell him. Ewerbeck, by the way, has warned Proudhon against Grün. Grün is back here, living away over in Ménilmontant, and scribbling the most dreadful articles for the *Trier'sche.*[d] Mäurer has translated the relevant passages from Grün's book[e] for Cabet; you can imagine Cabet's rage. He has lost all credit even with the *National.*

I went to see Cabet. The old boy was extremely cordial, I listened to all his stuff, told him about God and the devil, etc. I shall go there more often. But we must not bother him with the correspondence.[51] Firstly, he has enough to do and secondly, he's too mistrustful. *Il y verrait un piège*[f] for making improper use of his name.

---

[a] He has not the slightest sympathy for that man. - [b] K. Grün, *Die preussischen Landtags-Abschiede.* - [c] of sacrifice - [d] *Trier'sche Zeitung* - [e] K. Grün, *Die soziale Bewegung in Frankreich und Belgien.* - [f] He would see it as a trap.

I have been leafing quickly through Feuerbach's *Das Wesen der Religion* in *Epigonen*. Apart from a few happy insights, the thing's entirely in the old style. At the beginning, where he confines himself purely to natural religion, he is compelled to remain on rather more empirical ground, but later on it's all at sixes and sevens. Once again full of 'essence', 'Man', etc. I'll read it properly and very soon send you excerpts from the principal passages if they are interesting, so that you'll still be able to use it for the Feuerbach.[72] Meanwhile two passages only.[a] The whole—some 60 pages—opens with the following definition of nature as opposed to the human essence:

'The essence that is different from and independent of the human essence *or God* (!!), whose portrayal is the "Essence of Christianity" (1), the essence *without* human essence (2), human attributes (3), human individuality (4), *is in truth nothing other* than— *nature*' (p. 117).

This is truly a masterpiece of tautology blared forth in tones of thunder. Not only that, but in this proposition he identifies the religious, imaginary *phantom* of nature wholly and entirely with real nature. *Comme toujours.*[b]—Again, a little further on:

'Religion is the acceptance and acknowledgement of that which I am (!) ...To elevate dependence on nature to consciousness, to picture it to oneself, to accept, acknowledge it, means to *elevate oneself to religion*' (p. 118).

Not long ago the minister, Dumon, was caught in his shirt-tails with the wife of a president. The *Corsaire-Satan* relates: 'A lady who had petitioned Guizot said, "It is a pity that so excellent a man as Guizot *est toujours si sévère et boutonné jusqu'au cou.*"[c] Says the wife of an *employé* of *travaux publics,*[d] "*On ne peut pas dire cela de M. Dumon, on trouve généralement qu'il est un peu trop déboutonné pour un ministre*".'[e]

Quelques heures après,[f] during which time I paid a fruitless visit to the Café Cardinal to oblige little Weill—little Weill is somewhat riled because he isn't getting his fees of 1,000 or so francs from the *Démocratie pacifique* which appears to be embroiled in a kind of GREAT CRISIS AND STOPPING OF CASH PAYMENTS, and little Weill is too much

---

[a] *Das Wesen der Religion* is quoted below according to the collection *Die Epigonen,* Bd. 1, Leipzig, 1846. (The end of the second quotation is paraphrased.) - [b] As always. - [c] is always so strict and buttoned up to the neck. (Here and below is a close rendering of items in the *Corsaire-Satan* of 16 and 17 August 1846.) - [d] a public works official - [e] One cannot say as much of Mr Dumon, he is usually thought to be a little too much unbuttoned for a minister. - [f] Some hours later.

of a Jew to allow himself to be fobbed off with banknotes on the first phalanstery of the future. By the way, the Fourierist gents become daily more tedious. The *Phalange* is nothing but nonsense. The information contained in Fourier's posthumous work is confined entirely to the *mouvement aromal*[a] and the mating of the planets which would appear to take place *plus ou moins*[b] from behind. The mating of Saturn and Uranus engenders dung-beetles—which in any case the Fourierists themselves are—but the chief dung-beetle is the Irishman, Mr Hugh Doherty, who in fact isn't even a dung-beetle but only a dung-grub, a dung-larva—the poor creature is floundering about for the tenth time (*10me article*) in the *question religieuse*[c] and still can't discover how he can decently make his EXIT.

I haven't yet seen Bernays. But according to Ewerbeck he isn't getting along too badly and his worst complaint is boredom. The man is said to have grown very robust and healthy, his main activity, gardening, having apparently vanquished care so far as his human frame is concerned. He also, *dit-on*,[d] holds the goats by the horns when his—? wife?—, who can only be thought of between two question marks, is milking them. The poor devil naturally feels ill at ease in these surroundings; save for Ewerbeck who goes there weekly, he doesn't see a soul, potters about dressed in a peasant's blouse, never leaves Sarcelles, which is the most wretched village on this earth and doesn't even have a pub, in short, he's bored to death. We must see if we can get him back to Paris; within a month he would be his old self again. Since Börnstein, in his capacity as informer, must not know of my presence here, we have first written to Bernays[73] suggesting a rendezvous in Montmorency or somewhere else in the neighbourhood; afterwards we shall haul him off to Paris and spend a few francs on thoroughly cheering him up. That will make a different man of him. By the way, don't let him suspect that I've written to you about him in this vein; in his high-flown romantic mood, the good lad might feel it to be a moral injury.

The best of it is that in the house at Sarcelles there are 2 women, 2 men, several children, one of them dubious, and despite all this *on n'y tire pas un coup*.[e] They don't even practise pederasty. *C'est un roman allemand*.[f]

---

[a] aromatic movement - [b] more or less - [c] H. Doherty, 'La question religieuse', *La Phalange*, T. IV, 1846. - [d] it is said - [e] not a thing happens there - [f] It's a German novel.

Madame Hess cherche un mari. Elle se fiche de Hess. S'il se trouverait quelque chose de convenable, s'adresser à Madame Gsell, Faubourg St. Antoine.[a] There's no hurry since the competition isn't keen. Answer soon.

Your
E.

Address: 11, rue de l'arbre sec.

It goes without saying that anything I tell you now or later about Ewerbeck, Bernays and other acquaintances is strictly confidential.

I am not sending this post paid as I am short of money and can't expect any before 1 October. But on that day I shall send a bill of exchange to cover my share of postal expenses.

First published slightly abridged in *Der Briefwechsel zwischen F. Engels und K. Marx*, Bd. 1, Stuttgart, 1913 and in full in *MEGA*, Abt. III, Bd. 1, 1929

Printed according to the original

Published in English for the first time

26

ENGELS TO THE COMMUNIST CORRESPONDENCE COMMITTEE [74]

IN BRUSSELS

Paris, 19 August 1846
11, rue de l'arbre sec

Committee

Carissimi,[b]

Our affair will prosper greatly here. Ewerbeck is quite taken up with it and only asks that a committee should not be officially organised in too great haste, because there's a split in the offing. What remains here of the Weitlingians, a small clique of tailors,[75] is now in process of being thrown out, and Ewerbeck thinks it

---

[a] Mrs Hess is on the look-out for a husband. She doesn't give a fig for Hess. If there should happen to be something suitable, apply to Madame Gsell, Faubourg St. Antoine. - [b] Dear Friends

Chetham's Library in Manchester
where Marx and Engels worked in 1845

The house in Paris where Engels lived
from November 1846 to March 1847

better that this should be accomplished first. However, Ewerbeck doesn't believe that more than four or five of the people here will be available for the correspondence, which number is, indeed, fully adequate. In my next letter I hope to let you know who they are.

These tailors are really astounding chaps. Recently they were discussing quite seriously the question of knives and forks, and whether these had not best be chained.[a] But there are not many of them.

Weitling himself has not replied to the Parisians' last, very rude letter, procured for him by us. He had demanded 300 fr. for practical experiments in connection with his invention,[76] but remarked at the same time that the money had probably been thrown down the drain. You can imagine what sort of answer they gave him.

The cabinet-makers and tanners, on the other hand, are said to be capital fellows. I have not yet seen them. Ewerbeck manages all that with his usual circumspection.

I shall now give you some gleanings from French periodicals, those, of course, which are not to be had in Brussels.

P. Leroux's monthly is almost entirely taken up with articles on St.-Simon and Fourier by P. Leroux himself.[b] In these he exalts St.-Simon to the skies, and does all he can to detract from Fourier and present him as an imitator who has debased and falsified St.-Simon. Thus he is at great pains to prove that the *Quatre Mouvements*[c] are no more than a materialistically conceived plagiarism of *Lettres d'un habitant de Genève*. The fellow's quite mad. Because at one point the latter work maintains that a system which is an encyclopaedic compendium of all the sciences could best be realised by the reduction of all phenomena, etc., to *pesanteur universelle*,[d] it must be from this, we are told, that Fourier derived his whole theory of attraction. Needless to say, none of the evidence, quotations, etc., provide adequate proof that Fourier had even read the *Lettres* when he wrote the *4 Mouvements*. On the other hand the whole Enfantin trend is described as Fourierism surreptitiously introduced into the school. The paper is called *Revue Sociale, ou solution pacifique du problème du prolétariat.*

---

[a] Probably in canteens which the utopian socialists planned to set up by way of experiment. - [b] P. Leroux, 'Saint-Simon et Fourier' (third article from *Lettres sur le fouriérisme*), *Revue Sociale*, No. 11, August 1846. - [c] Ch. Fourier, *Théorie des quatre mouvements et des destinées générales.* - [d] universal gravity

Of the reformist newspaper congress,[77] the *Atelier* relates after the event[a] that, not having attended, it was very surprised to find itself on the list of papers represented there. *Le peuple de la presse*[b] had been kept out until the bases of the reform had been decided upon, and when the doors were then thrown open to the *ouvrier*[c] papers so that they might vote their assent, it had thought it beneath its dignity to go there. The *Atelier* further relates that 150 *ouvriers,* probably Buchezists—which party, the French assure us, is about 1,000 strong—held a banquet, without police permission on 29 July to celebrate the July Days.[d] The police intervened and, because they refused to undertake not to make political speeches or sing any of Béranger's songs, they were dispersed.

Mr Wigand's *Die Epigonen* are here. A dreadful din is heard as Mr Wigand vents his indignation. 'An A. Ruge.' He reproaches the latter with the common misfortunes both have endured during the past four years. Ruge, he says, was unable—in Paris—'to go hand-in-hand with *fanatical communism*'. Communism is a condition

'hatched out in its own, ignorant brain, a *narrow-minded* and *ignorant piece of barbarism* which is to be forcibly imposed on mankind'.

Finally he brags about the great things he will do 'so long as enough lead remains in the world to make type'. The *candidat de la potence,*[e] you see, has not yet given up hope of becoming the *candidat de la lanterne.*[f]

I would draw your attention to the article in today's *National* (*mercredi*[g] 19) on the fall in the number of Parisian voters since 1844 from over 20,000 to 17,000.

Yours
E.

Paris has sunk low. Danton is selling wood in the Boulevard Bourdon. Barbaroux keeps a calico shop in the rue St. Honoré, the *Réforme* no longer has the strength to demand the Rhine, the opposition is searching for talent and cannot find it, the bourgeois gentry go to bed so early that everything has to be closed by 12

---

[a] Reference to the article 'Du manifeste de la presse liberale' in *L'Atelier,* No. 11, August 1846. - [b] The members of the press - [c] workers' - [d] Engels relates the article 'Un Banquet interrompu', *L'Atelier,* No. 11, August 1846. (July Days—revolution of 27-30 July 1830). - [e] candidate for the gallows - [f] candidate for the lamppost. An allusion to the ambiguous position of bourgeois radicals who were threatened with government repressions (gallows) for opposition, and in case of revolution—with reprisals by the people (lamppost) for hostility towards communist aspirations. - [g] Wednesday

o'clock, and *la jeune France*[a] accepts it without turning a hair. The police would certainly not have been able to enforce this had it not been for the early business hours kept by principals, whose motto is: 'Morgenstunde hat usw.'[b]

Mr Grün's pamphlet, printed at the workers' expense, is the one I once saw at Seiler's: *Die preussischen Landtags-Abschiede. Ein Wort zur Zeit* (anonymous); it consists mainly of plagiarisms from Marx's essays (*Deutsch-Französische Jahrbücher*)[c] and monumental nonsense. To him, questions of 'political economy' and of 'socialism' are *identical.* Absolute monarchy developed as follows:

'The Prince created for himself an *abstract domain,* and this intellectual domain was called—the State. The State became the domain of domains; as the ideal of the domain it abolishes the individual domain, just as it lets it subsist, and always abolishes it when it seeks to become absolute, independent, etc.'

This 'intellectual' domain, Prussia, 'almost immediately becomes transformed into a domain in which prayers are said, a *clerical* domain'[d]!! The consequence of all this is: Liberalism in Prussia has already been *overcome* in *theory, hence* the Imperial Estates will no longer concern themselves with bourgeois questions but *directement*[e] with the social question.

'The slaughtering and milling tax is *what really betrays the nature of taxes,* to wit it betrays the fact *that every tax is a poll tax.* But whoever raises a *poll tax is saying:* "Your heads and bodies are my own, you are bound to me *head and body"*.... The slaughtering and milling tax *matches absolutism too well,* etc.'

For two years the jackass has been paying *octroi*[f] without realising it, believing that such a thing exists only in Prussia. Finally, apart from a few plagiarisms and stock phrases, this little pamphlet is *liberal* through and through, and German-liberal to boot.

It is generally held by the workers here that the *Garantien*[g] was *not* written by Weitling *alone.* Besides S. Schmidt, Becker, etc., several Frenchmen are said to have provided him with material and in particular he had manuscripts of one Ahrens, of Riga, a worker in Paris, now in America, who also wrote the main part of *Die Menschheit wie sie ist und sein soll.* The people here once wrote

---

[a] young France - [b] 'Morgenstunde hat Gold im Munde' (early to bed, early to rise makes a man healthy, wealthy and wise) - [c] K. Marx, 'On the Jewish Question' and 'Contribution to the Critique of Hegel's Philosophy of Law. Introduction'. - [d] Engels puns on the words *geistige* (intellectual) and *geistliche* (clerical). - [e] directly - [f] city tolls on imported consumer goods existing since the Middle Ages - [g] W. Weitling, *Garantien der Harmonie und Freiheit.*

to him in London and told him as much, whereat he became exceedingly angry and simply replied that this was slanderous.

[On the back of the letter]

Monsieur Charles Marx, 19, Plaine Ste Gudule, Bruxelles

First published abridged in *Der Briefwech-sel zwischen F. Engels und K. Marx,* Bd. 1, Stuttgart, 1913 and in full in *MEGA,* Abt. III, Bd. 1, 1929

Printed according to the original

Published in English for the first time

27

MARX TO KARL LUDWIG BERNAYS[78]

IN SARCELLES

[Brussels, August 1846]

Only when one previously critically combats these existing (for the sake of brevity let us say 'bad') tendencies, can one write a positive account of one's own with confidence.

First published in *MEGA*$_2$, Abt. III, Bd. 2, Berlin, 1979

Printed according to Bernays' let-ter to Marx of August 1846

Published in English for the first time

28

ENGELS TO THE COMMUNIST CORRESPONDENCE COMMITTEE

IN BRUSSELS

Committee No. 2

[Paris,] Wednesday, 16 September 1846

Dear Friends,

Your news about Belgium, London and Breslau[a] was of great interest to me.[79] I told Ewerbeck and Bernays what was of interest

---

[a] Polish name: Wrocław.

to them. Keep me *au fait*[a] as well with the success of our enterprise and *plus ou moins*[b] the enthusiasm with which the various localities are taking part, so that I can expatiate on that to the workers here in so far as it is politic. What are the Cologne people[c] doing?

There's all manner of news from here.

1. I've had several meetings with the local workers, i.e. with the leaders of the cabinet-makers from the Faubourg St. Antoine. These people are curiously organised. Apart from the business of their league[80] having been thrown into the utmost confusion—as a result of a serious dispute with the Weitlingian tailors—these lads, i.e. 12-20 of them, foregather once a week; they used to hold discussions but, after they ran out of matter, as indeed they were bound to do, Ewerbeck was compelled to give them lectures on German history—starting from scratch—and on an extremely muddled political economy, a popular rendering of the *Deutsch-Französische Jahrbücher*.[d] Meanwhile I appeared. In order to establish contact with them, I twice discussed conditions in Germany since the French Revolution, my point of departure being the economic relations. What they glean from these weekly meetings is thrashed out on Sundays at Barrière meetings[81] attended by Cherethites and Pelethites, wife and children.[e] Here— *abstraction faite de toute espèce de politique*[f]—such things as 'social questions' are discussed. It is a good way of attracting new people, for it's entirely public; a fortnight ago the police arrived and wanted to impose a veto but allowed themselves to be placated and did nothing further. Often more than 200 people foregather.

Things cannot possibly remain as they are now. A degree of lethargy has set in amongst the fellows which comes from their being bored with themselves. For they have nothing to set against the tailors' communism but popularisations *à la* Grün and green-tinted[g] Proudhon,[82] all this having been laboriously dinned into them, partly by no less a person than Mr Grün himself, partly by an old, bombastic master cabinet-maker and minion of Grün's, Papa Eisermann, but partly, too, by *amicus*[h] Ewerbeck. Naturally they soon ran dry, endless repetition ensued and, to prevent them going to *sleep* (literally, this was getting worse and worse at the sessions), Ewerbeck torments them with hair-splitting disquisitions

---

[a] acquainted - [b] more or less - [c] Roland Daniels, Heinrich Bürgers, Karl d'Ester - [d] Reference is probably to Engels' 'Outlines of a Critique of Political Economy'. - [e] 2 Samuel 8:18; 15:18; 20:7, 23 - [f] all politics apart - [g] a play on *Grün* (green) - [h] friend

on 'true value' (this last being somewhat on my conscience) and bores them with the primeval forests of the Teutons, Hermann the Cheruscan, and the most ghastly old German etymology according to—Adelung, all of it quite wrong. By the way, the real leader of these people isn't Ewerbeck but Junge, who was in Brussels[83]; the fellow realises very well what ought to be changed, and might do a great deal since he has them all in his pocket and is ten times more intelligent than the whole clique, but he vacillates too much and always has some new bee in his bonnet. I haven't seen him for nearly 3 weeks—he never turned up and isn't to be found—which is why so little has as yet been achieved. Without him most of them are spineless and irresolute. But one must be patient with the fellows; in the first place we must rid ourselves of Grün, whose enervating influence, both direct and indirect, has been truly dreadful. And then, when we've got these platitudes out of their heads, I hope to be able to achieve something with the fellows, for they all have a strong desire for instruction in economics. This should not take long, as Ewerbeck who, despite his notorious muddle-headedness, now at its fullest flowering, has the best intentions in the world, is completely in my pocket, and Junge, too, is wholly on my side. I have discussed the correspondence[a] with six others; the plan was much acclaimed, specially by Junge, and will be implemented from here. But unless Grün's personal influence is destroyed and his platitudes eradicated, thus reinvigorating the chaps, nothing can be done in view of the considerable material obstacles to be faced (particularly engagements almost every evening). I have offered to confront Grün in their presence and to tax him with his personal rascalities, and Bernays also wishes to be there—Ewerbeck too has a bone to pick with him. This will happen as soon as they have settled their own affairs with Grün, i.e. obtained a guarantee for the money advanced for the printing of Grün's *Landtag* shit.[b] But since Junge didn't turn up and the rest behaved towards Grün±like children, that matter, too, is still not in order, although with a little effort it could have been settled in 5 minutes. The unfortunate thing about it is that most of these fellows are Swabians.

2. Now for something to amuse you. In his new, as yet unprinted book, which Grün is translating,[84] Proudhon has a great scheme for making money out of thin air and bringing the kingdom of heaven closer to all workers. No one knew what it was.

---

[a] See this volume, pp. 38-39, 53, and 56. - [b] [K. Grün,] *Die preussischen Landtags-Abschiede.*

Grün, while keeping it very dark, was always bragging about his philosopher's stone. General suspense. At length, last week, Papa Eisermann was at the cabinet-makers' and so was I; gradually the old coxcomb came out with it, in a naively secretive manner. Mr Grün had confided the whole plan to him. Hearken, now, to the grandeur of this plan for world redemption: *ni plus ni moins*[a] than the already long extant in England, and ten times bankrupt LABOUR-BAZARS or LABOUR-MARKETS, associations of all artisans of all trades, a big warehouse, all work delivered by the *associés* valued strictly in accordance with the cost of the raw product plus labour, and paid for in other association products, similarly valued.[85] Anything delivered in excess of the association's needs is to be sold on the world market, the proceeds being paid out to the producers. In this way the crafty Proudhon calculates that he and his fellow *associés* will circumvent the profit of the middleman. That this would also mean circumventing the profit on *his association's capital,* that this capital and this profit must be *just as great* as the capital and profit of the circumvented middlemen, that he therefore throws away with his right hand what the left has received, has none of it entered his clever head. That his workers can never raise the necessary capital, since otherwise they could just as well set themselves up separately, that any savings in cost resulting from the association would be more than out-weighed by the enormous risk, that the whole thing would amount to spiriting away profit from this world, while leaving the producers of the profit to cool their heals, that it is a truly Straubingerian idyll,[86] excluding from the very outset all large-scale industry, build-ing, agriculture, etc., that they would have to bear only the *losses* of the bourgeoisie without sharing in its gains, all these and a hun-dred other self-evident objections he overlooks, so delighted is he with his plausible illusion. It's all too utterly preposterous. Paterfa-milias Grün, of course, believes in the new redemption and already in his mind's eye sees himself at the head of an association of 20,000 *ouvriers*[b] (they want it *big* from the start), his family, of course, to receive free clothing, board and lodging. But if Proudhon comes out with this, he will be making a fool of himself and all French socialists and communists in the eyes of bourgeois economists. Hence those tears, that polemicising against revolution [87] because he had a peaceable nostrum up his sleeve. Proudhon is just like John Watts. In spite of his disreputable atheism and socialism, the latter regards it as his vocation to acquire respectability in the eyes

---

[a] neither more nor less - [b] workers

of the bourgeoisie; Proudhon, despite his polemic against the economists, does his utmost to gain recognition as a great economist. Such are the sectarians. Besides, it's such an old story![a]

3. Now for another highly curious affair.—The Augsburg *Allgemeine Zeitung* of 21 July, Paris, 16 July. Article on the *Russian Embassy*[b]....

'That is the official Embassy—but quite extraneous to it, or rather *above* it, there is a certain Mr *Tolstoy* who bears no title, is described, however, as *"confidant of the Court"*. Formerly, with the Ministry of Education, he came to Paris charged with a *literary mission;* there he wrote a few memoirs for his Ministry, sent them a few reports on the French daily press, then wrote no more but did all the more. He maintains a splendid establishment, is invited everywhere, receives everyone, busies himself with everything, knows everything and arranges much. He seems to me to be the *actual Russian Ambassador* in Paris.... His intervention works wonders' (—all Poles seeking a pardon addressed themselves to him—) '—at the Embassy *all bow down before him and in Petersburg he is held in great regard.'*

This Tolstoy is none other than our Tolstoy, that noble fellow who told us untruthfully that he wanted to sell his estates in Russia.[88] Besides the apartment to which he took us, the man has a magnificent *hôtel*[c] in the rue Mathurin where he receives the diplomats. This has long been known to the Poles and to *many* of the French, but not to the German radicals amongst whom he thought it better to insinuate himself as a radical. The above article was written by a Pole known to Bernays, and was immediately taken up by the *Corsaire-Satan* and the *National*. On reading the article, all Tolstoy did was laugh heartily and crack jokes about having been found out at last. He is now in London, where he will try his luck, being played out here. It's a pity he is not coming back, otherwise I'd have had a joke or two to try out on him, eventually leaving my card in the rue Mathurin. After this, *c'est clair*[d] that Annenkov, whom he recommended, is also a Russian informer. Even Bakunin, who *must have known* the whole story since the other Russians knew it, is very suspect. I shall, of course, give him no hint of this, but wreak vengeance on the Russians. Even though these spies may not constitute any particular threat to us, we can't let them get away with it. They're good subjects for conspiratorial experiments *in corpore vili*.[e] For that they are not really too bad.

4. Father Hess. After I had happily consigned his spouse,[f] cursing and swearing about same, to oblivion, i.e. to the furthest

---

[a] H. Heine, 'Ein Jüngling liebt ein Mädchen' from *Lyrisches Intermezzo*. - [b] Engels quotes from the article 'Die russische Allianz und die russische Gesandtschaft'. - [c] mansion - [d] it's clear - [e] on the vile body - [f] Sibylle Hess

end of the Faubourg St. Antoine where there is a wailing and gnashing of teeth (Grün and Gsell), I received not long since, through the agency of one Reinhardt, another letter in which the communist papa sought to re-establish relations. It's enough to make one split one's sides. As if nothing had happened of course, altogether *in dulci jubilo*,[a] and moreover altogether the same old Hess. After the remark that he was to some extent reconciled with 'the party' (the 'Yiddish' Circle appears to have become insolvent)—and 'also anxious to resume work' (which event ought to be rung in with a peal of bells), comes the following historical note (dated 19 August):

'A few weeks ago we were *within a hair's breadth* of a *bloody riot* here in Cologne, *large numbers* being already armed' (among them certainly not Moses). 'The affair did not come to a head because the military *did not put in an appearance*' (tremendous triumph for Cologne's pint-sized philistine), etc., etc....

Then he tells of the civic assemblies[89] where 'we', i.e. 'the party' and Mr Moses, '*qua* communists, *won so complete a victory* that we', etc.

'We *drove,* first the moneyed aristocrats ... and then the petty bourgeois, *with glory*' (none of them possessing any talent) '*from the field.* Eventually we *could have* (!) *carried everything* in the assemblies' (e.g. made Moses Chief Burgomaster); 'a programme was adopted to which the assembly pledged its candidates, and which' (hear, hear) '*could not have been more radical even if drawn up by English and French communists*' (!!!) '(and by no one understood more foolishly than by Moses).... '*Keep* an occasional eye' (sic) 'on my [wife]' (both parties would like me to take over the distaff side at my own expense and risk, *j'en ai les preuves*[b]).... 'and pass this onto Ewerbeck as a *heartener.*'

May God bless this 'heartener', this manna from the desert. I, of course, completely ignore the beast—he has now written to Ewerbeck too (and this simply in order that a letter may be conveyed to his distaff side at the former's expense), and is threatening to come here in two months' time. If he visits me, I think I too shall be able to tell him something by way of a 'heartener'.

Now that I'm in full swing, I might as well conclude by telling you that Heine is here again and that the day before yesterday Ewerbeck and I went to see him. The poor devil is dreadfully low. He has grown as thin as a rake. The softening of the brain is spreading, and so is the facial paralysis. Ewerbeck says he might very easily die of pulmonary paralysis or of a sudden cerebral

---

a sweetness and joy - b I have proof of it.

stroke, but could also drag on, sometimes better, sometimes worse, for another three or four years yet. He is, of course, somewhat depressed, melancholy and—most significant of all—extremely benign (and, indeed, seriously so) in his judgments—Mäurer is the only person about whom he constantly cracks jokes. For the rest his intellectual vigour is unimpaired, but his appearance, made stranger still by a greying beard (he can no longer be shaved round the mouth), is enough to plunge anyone who sees him into the depths of depression. The impression made by the sight of so splendid a fellow gradually wasting away is exceedingly painful.

I have also seen the great Mäurer. 'Manikin, manikin, how little you weigh!" The man's really a sight worth seeing, and I was atrociously rude to him, in return for which the jackass evinces a particular affection for me, and tells me I have a kindly face. He resembles Karl Moor six weeks dead. Reply soon.

Yours

E.

Write soon, as I shall in a fortnight's time [...] from here; such a business a letter [...] easily remain lying or be refused at the old place.

At the *Fraternité* there has been a tremendous dispute between materialists [90] and spiritualists.[91] The materialists, outvoted by 23 to 22, walked out. But that has not stopped the *Fraternité* from publishing a very nice article on the various stages of civilisation and their ability to continue developing in the direction of communism.[a]

You'll be amused by the following: *Journal des Économistes,* August of this year, contains, in an article on Biedermann's article on communism,[b] the following: First, all Hess' nonsense, comically Gallicised; next, we read, comes M. Marx.

'M. Marx est un *cordonnier,* comme un autre Communiste allemand, Weitling, est un tailleur. Le premier (Mx) n'a pas une grande estime pour le communisme français (!) qu'il a été assez heureux d'étudier sur les lieux. M. ne sort (du) reste point non plus' (do you not recognise Mr Fix in this Alsatian expression?) 'des formules abstraites et il se garde bien d'aborder aucune question véritablement pratique. Selon lui' (note the nonsense) 'l'émancipation du peuple allemand sera le

---

[a] Engels seems to be writing about a series of articles 'La civilisation' published in the *Fraternité* in 1845 and 1846. The first article was entitled 'La civilisation est l'acheminement de l'esprit humain vers la communauté'. - [b] The reference is to a review of K. Biedermann, 'Unsre Gegenwart und Zukunft' written by Th. Fix and published in the *Journal des Économistes,* Vol. 15, No. 57, August 1846.

signal de l'émancipation du genre humain; la tête de cette émancipation serait la philosophie et son cœur le prolétariat. Lorsque tout sera preparé, le coq gaulois sonnera la résurrection germanique... Marx dit qu'il *faut créer* en Allemagne un prolétariat universel (!!) afin de réaliser la pensée philosophique du Communisme'. [a] Signed T. F. (mort depuis). [b]

That was his last work. The previous issue carried an equally comical review of my book. [c] The September number contains an article on Julius which I have not yet read. [d]

[On the back of the letter]
Monsieur Charles Marx au Bois Sauvage, Plaine Ste Gudule, Bruxelles

First published abridged in *Der Briefwechsel zwischen F. Engels und K. Marx*, Bd. 1, Stuttgart, 1913 and in full in *MEGA*, Abt. III, Bd. 1, 1929

Printed according to the original

Published in English for the first time

29

ENGELS TO MARX [92]

IN BRUSSELS

[Paris,] 18 September 1846
11, rue [de l'arbrc sec]

Dear Marx,

A whole lot of things I wanted to write about privately have found their way into the business letter because that was the one I wrote first. [e] No matter if the others read the rubbish for once.

---

[a] 'Mr. Marx is a *cobbler*, as another German communist, Weitling, is a tailor. The former (M[ar]x) has no great respect for French communism (!) which he has been fortunate enough to study on the spot. For that matter, neither does M. proceed beyond' (do you not recognise Mr Fix in this Alsatian expression?) 'abstract formulas, and he takes the greatest care to avoid broaching any truly practical question. According to him' (note the nonsense) 'the emancipation of the German people will be the signal for the emancipation of the human race; philosophy would be the head of this emancipation, the proletariat its heart. When all has been prepared, the Gallic cock will herald the Teutonic resurrection.... Marx says that a universal proletariat *must be created* in Germany (!!) in order to realise the philosophical concept of communism.' - [b] since deceased - [c] F. Engels, *The Condition of the Working-Class in England* (an anonymous review in the *Journal des Économistes*, Vol. 14, No. 56, July 1846). - [d] The review of G. Julius, 'Bankwesen. Ein neues Gespenst in Deutschland', in the *Journal des Économistes*, Vol. 15, No. 58. September 1846 was also written by Th. Fix which Engels did not know then. - [e] See this volume, pp. 60-67.

Hitherto I have rather dreaded setting to work on the extracts from Feuerbach. Here in Paris the stuff strikes one as utterly insipid. But now that I've got the book[a] at home, I shall apply myself to it at the earliest opportunity. Weydemeyer's sweet nonsense is touching. The fellow first declares that he wants to draft a manifesto in which he pronounces us blackguards and then expresses the hope that this won't give rise to personal differences. Even in Germany such a thing would only be possible on the Hanoverian-Prussian border.

That you should still be in financial straits is abominable. I know of no publisher for our manuscripts[b] other than Leske who, while negotiations are proceeding, must be kept in the dark about our criticism of his firm. Löwenthal will certainly not take it. He has turned down, on all manner of rotten pretexts, a *very good* proposition from Bernays (a life of the old man here[c] in 2 volumes, the first to be printed forthwith and issued the moment the old man dies, the second to follow immediately afterwards). He's also a coward and maintains he might be expelled from Frankfurt. Bernays has a prospect of acceptance by Brockhaus, who believes, of course, that the book is written in a bourgeois spirit.

Have the Westphalians[d] sent the manuscripts to Daniels?

And have you had any further details about the Cologne scheme? Hess wrote about it, you know.[93]

But Lüning's rubbish is the most ludicrous of all. One can almost visualise the fellow as he daringly looses a hypocritical turd into his trousers. If we criticise them for their general baseness,[e] the noble fellow declares this to be '*self*-criticism'.[94] But soon these chaps will experience in their own persons the truth of the saying:

'And if the noble fellow has no bum, on what does he propose to sit?'[f]

And Westphalia seems gradually to be coming to realise that it has no bum or, in Moses'[g] parlance, no 'material basis' for its communism.

Püttmann was not so wrong, where *I* am concerned, when he said that the people in Brussels were collaborating on *Prometheus*. Hear how cunningly this good-for-nothing set about it. Being also

---

[a] L. Feuerbach, *Das Wesen der Religion*. - [b] The reference is to the manuscripts for the quarterly, including that of Marx and Engels' *The German Ideology*. - [c] Louis Philippe - [d] J. Meyer and R. Rempel - [e] K. Marx and F. Engels, 'Circular Against Kriege'. - [f] J. W. Goethe, 'Totalität'. - [g] Moses Hess

in need of money, I wrote to him suggesting that at last he fork out the fee he had owed me for so long.[95] The fellow answered that as to the fee for the first essay which he had printed in the *Bürgerbuch*,[a] he had instructed Leske to pay it to me (naturally not yet to hand), but so far as the one for the second essay in the second of the *Rheinische Jahrbücher*[b] was concerned,—he had already received it from the publisher but, since the German *soi-disant*[c] communists had left him, big P, together with his other big P, *Prometheus,* most shamefully in the lurch—he, P No. 1, had been compelled to use the fees (including those due to Ewerbeck, etc.) for the printing of P No. 2 and would not be able to pay us same for another x weeks. Fine fellows, if you don't give them a manuscript, they keep the money. In such a manner does one become one of the *Prometheus* collaborators and shareholders.

Yesterday evening, when I was with the workers here, I read the 'London Address' already in print.[96] Trash. They address themselves to the 'people', i.e. the presumed proletarians in Schleswig-Holstein which is haunted exclusively by loutish, Low-German peasants and guildish Straubingers.[86] They have learnt from the English this nonsense, this total disregard for actual circumstances, this inability to comprehend an historical development. Instead of answering the question, they want the 'people'—who, in their sense of the word, don't exist at all there—to disregard it and behave peacefully and passively; it doesn't occur to them that the bourgeoisie continues to do as it likes. Except for the denigration of the bourgeoisie, which is somewhat superfluous and entirely at odds with their conclusions (and for which FREE-TRADE catchwords could equally well be substituted), the thing could have been the work of London's FREE-TRADE PRESS, which does not want to see Schleswig-Holstein enter the Customs Union.[97]

That Julius is in the pay of the Prussians and writes for Rother has already been hinted at in the German papers.[98] Bourgeois,[d] who was so delighted with his noble works, according to d'Ester, will be pleased when he hears of it.

A propos Schleswig-Holstein, the day before yesterday the Coachman[e] wrote to Ewerbeck in 3 lines that caution should now be exercised in the matter of letters, since everything is being opened by the Danes. He believes that it could come to armed action.

---

a F. Engels, 'Description of Recently Founded Communist Colonies Still in Existence'. - b F. Engels, 'The Festival of Nations in London'. - c so-called - d Heinrich Burgers - e Georg Weber

Dubito,[a] but it's good that the old Dane[b] should so rudely harry the Schleswig-Holsteiners.[99] By the way, did you read the famous poem 'Schleswig-Holstein, Sea-girt Land', in the *Rheinischer Beobachter*[c]? I can't possibly remember the words, but it goes something like this:

> Schleswig-Holstein, of like stock sprung, Schleswig-Holstein,
> sea-girt land,
> Schleswig-Holstein, German tongue,—Schleswig-Holstein
> German strand,
> Schleswig-Holstein, to action stung, Schleswig-Holstein,
> fiery brand,
> Schleswig-Holstein, hardly wrung, Schleswig-Holstein, make
> a stand,
> Schleswig-Holstein, lustily sung, 'Schleswig-Holstein, may
> Danes be banned.'
> Schleswig-Holstein, loudly rung, 'Schleswig-Holstein',
> throughout th' land!
> Schleswig-Holstein, strong of lung, Schleswig-Holstein,
> weak of hand,
> Schleswig-Holstein, loutish young, Schleswig-Holstein,
> beastly band.

Schleswig-Holstein, of like stock sprung; Keep troth, O Fatherland, is how the drivel ends. It's a ghastly song, worthy of being *sung* by the Dithmarschen,[100] who in turn are worthy of being *besung* by Püttmann.

The Cologne bourgeois are bestirring themselves. They have issued a protest[d] against the gentlemen of the Ministry, which is the most a German citizen can do.[101] The poor Berlin pulpit-drubber[e]! He's at loggerheads with every municipal council in his kingdom; first the Berlin theological controversy,[102] then the Breslau[f] ditto, now the Cologne business. The rascal, by the way, is the spitting image of James I of England, whom he really seems to have taken for his model. No doubt, like the latter, he too will shortly start burning witches.

I did Proudhon a really crying injustice in my business letter. Since there was no room in this last letter, I must make amends here. For I believed he had perpetrated a trifling nonsense, a nonsense within the bounds of sense. Yesterday the matter came up again and was discussed at great length, and it was then I

---

[a] I doubt it. - [b] Christian VIII - [c] M. F. Chemnitz, 'Schleswig-Holsteinische Bundeslied' (music by Bellmann), *Rheinischer Beobachter,* No. 259, 16 September 1846. Below Engels parodies the song. - [d] *Kölnische Zeitung,* No. 253, 10 September 1846. - [e] Frederick William IV - [f] Polish name: Wrocław.

learned that this new nonsense is in truth *wholly unbounded nonsense.* Imagine: Proletarians are to *save* in the form of small shares. This will enable the initial building (needless to say no start can be made with fewer than 10,000-20,000 workers) of one or more workshops devoted to one or more trades, some of the shareholders to be occupied there and the products to be sold, 1) to the shareholders (who thus have no profit to pay for) at the price of the raw material plus labour, and 2) any surplus to be sold on the world market at the current price. As the association's capital is increased by new shareholders joining or by new savings of the old ones, this will be used for building new workshops and factories and so on and so forth, until *all* the proletarians are employed, *all* the country's productive forces have been bought up, thereby depriving the capital still in bourgeois hands of the power to command labour and produce profit! Thus capital is abolished by 'finding an authority under which capital, i.e. the interest system' (Grünification of the erstwhile *droit d'aubaine*,[103] brought somewhat closer to the light of day) 'so to speak disappears.' In this sentence, repeated countless times by Papa Eisermann, hence learned by rote from Grün, you will readily discern a glimmering of the original Proudhonian flourishes. By dint of proletarian savings, and by waiving the profit and interest on their capital, these people intend, for the present, to *buy up* the *whole of France,* no more nor less, and later, perhaps, the rest of the world as well. Was ever more splendid plan devised, and if you want to perform a *tour de force,*[a] what quicker way than to coin five franc pieces out of silver moonshine? And the workers here, fools that they are—the Germans, I mean—*believe* this rubbish, they, who can't keep six sous in their pockets to visit a *marchand de vin*[b] on the evenings of their meetings, propose to buy up *toute la belle France*[c] with their savings. Rothschild and company are mere dabblers compared with these mighty *accapareurs.*[d] It's enough to make anyone throw a fit. Grün has so confused the fellows that the most nonsensical platitude makes more sense to them than the simplest fact adduced for the purpose of economic argument. It is disgraceful that one should still have to pit oneself against such barbaric nonsense. But one must be patient, and I shall not let the fellows go until I have driven Grün from the field and have swept the cobwebs from their brains. The only fellow clear-headed enough to see through the whole nonsense is our Junge who was in Brussels. Ewerbeck, too, has crammed the fellows' heads with

---

[a] feat of strength - [b] wineshop - [c] the whole of beautiful France - [d] buyers-up

the most crackbrained stuff. You've no idea what desperate confusion the fellow is in; at times he verges on madness, being unable to tell you today what he saw with his own eyes, let alone heard, yesterday. To show to what extent he has been under Grün's thumb, it need only be said that when last winter Walthr, of Trier,[104] was complaining to all and sundry about the censors, Grün represented him as a martyr to the censorship, one who was waging the noblest and bravest of battles, etc., and induced Ewerbeck and the workers to draw up and sign a highly pompous address to this jackass, Walthr, thanking him for his heroism in the struggle for freedom of speech!!!! Ewerbeck is hanging his head in shame and is furiously angry with himself; but the stupidity has been done, and now it's a question of knocking out of him and the workers the few *platitudes* he has dinned into his own head with toil and sweat before drumming same into the workers with no less toil and sweat. For he understands nothing until he has learnt it by rote and even then usually misunderstands it. If he were not so tremendously well-intentioned, besides being such an amiable chap—more so now than ever before,—there would be absolutely nothing doing with him. I can't help wondering how I manage to get on with him; sometimes he makes quite apposite remarks, only to relapse at once into some colossal inanity—as, for instance, in his divinely inspired lectures on German history, whose every word is so beset with howlers and follies that it's difficult not to burst out laughing. But, as already mentioned, tremendous zeal and remarkable readiness to join in everything with imperturbable good humour and self-mockery. I like the fellow better than ever, in spite of his silliness.

There is little to be said about Bernays. I have been out there several times and he here once. Coming here probably this winter, only short of money. Westphalians[a] sent him 200 francs by way of a bribe; he accepted the money, but naturally did nothing further about it. Weydemeyer had offered him the money previously; he writes to say he must have *2,000 francs,* otherwise it won't be any use to him. I told him what the Westphalians' answer would be—that they were unable to turn anything into LIQUID cash etc., and so it literally was. In token of his gratitude he is keeping the 200 francs. He is living quite happily, makes no secret to anyone of his whole calamitous story, is on quite happy terms with other people, lives like a peasant, works in the garden, eats well, sleeps, I suspect, with a peasant girl, and has also ceased to parade his

---

[a] Presumably J. Meyer and R. Rempel

sorrows. He is even coming to entertain more lucid and sensible views about party disputes, although, whenever something of the kind occurs, he likes to imagine himself more or less in the role of a Camille Desmoulins, and is generally unsuited to be a party man; there's no arguing with him about his legal opinions because he always tries to break off with the objection that economy, industry, etc., is not his subject and, on the rare occasions we meet, no proper discussion takes place. I think, however, that I have already succeeded in partly breaching his defences and, if he comes here, I shall probably be able to cure him finally of his misapprehensions.

What is everyone doing there?

Your
E.

QUERY: Ought not the people in London[a] to be told the story of the Tolstoy affair,[b] which is *absolutely correct?* If he continues to play the same role among the Germans, they might at some time dreadfully compromise one or two Poles. And supposing the fellow *were to cite you?*

Bernays has written a pamphlet as part of the Rothschild controversy[105]; a German edition[c] is appearing in Switzerland and a French one[d] here in a few days' time.

First published slightly abridged in *Der Briefwechsel zwischen F. Engels und K. Marx*, Bd. 1, Stuttgart, 1913 and in full in *MEGA*, Abt. III, Bd. 1, 1929

Printed according to the original

Published in English in full for the first time

30

ENGELS TO MARX[106]

IN BRUSSELS

[Paris, after 18 September 1846]

...7. they should change the §§ on the sharing of dividends into §§ on the sharing of losses, for, *failing all this,* they would go bankrupt already as a result of the celebrated principle of bearing

---

[a] The London leaders of the League of the Just (K. Schapper, J. Moll and H. Bauer). - [b] See this volume, p. 64. - [c] [K. L. Bernays,] *Rothschild. Ein Ur-theilsspruch vom menschlichen Standpunkte aus.* - [d] [K. L. Bernays,] *Jugement rendu contre J. Rothschild et Georges Dairnvaell, auteur de l'Histoire de Rothschild 1er par le Tribunal de la Seine.*

the whole loss but sharing the profit. They would therefore have to do twice as much business as *any other* publisher in order to keep going—but the fact remains that hitherto all publishers dealing exclusively, or merely for preference, in banned works— Fröbel, Wigand, Leske—have, *in the long run,* been ruined: 1. by confiscation, 2. by being excluded from markets, which ± always happens, 3. by sharp practice on the part of commission agents and retail dealers, 4. by police threats, prosecution, etc., 5. by competition from publishers who only occasionally print something objectionable, who are therefore less subject to police interference and who, moreover, also have a better chance of obtaining manuscripts that will appeal, whereas the above-mentioned stereotypes are left holding the rubbish and books that do not appeal. The book trade's struggle with the police can be waged with profit only if large numbers of publishers take part in it; it is *essentiellement* guerrilla warfare, and one can only make money if one *seldom* takes such a risk. The market is not large enough to make a *spécialité* of the article.

For the rest it makes no difference whether the company is ruined, for ruined it will be no matter what kind of start it makes; but where there's a guarantee, it will be ruined too quickly, a high fever being induced with three crises, of which the third is certainly fatal. In view of the not over-copious supply of manuscripts to be expected, a mild consumption would be more appropriate. It's only regrettable that too big a hole is made in its capital if it does its own printing. It ought to have sufficient to enable it to print for about $1\,^1/_2$ years; for supposing a capital of 3,000 talers expended in the *first year,* the Eastertide settlement would, given profitable trading, produce approx. $^2/_3$, or a minimum of 2,000 talers. Hence for the second year it ought to have at least 1,000 talers over and above those 3,000 talers. Thus $^1/_3$-$^1/_4$ of the capital is permanently tied up in remainders, bad payers, etc. It might be possible to raise this amount by inducing the shareholders to subscribe an additional loan repayable over a period. It is essential, by the way, to consult a publisher first, in order to find out exactly how much of the capital employed remains tied up at the end of the first year, or how much time it takes to turn the total capital over once. I am not sure about it myself, but I have reason to believe that in the above calculations I have underestimated rather than overestimated the capital permanently tied up.

With his 20 per cent of the profits the manager will grow rich. Even if 10 per cent of any losses are passed to the reserve fund, there will be a handsome deficit.

As for the consequences the guarantee would entail for the *authors,* the less said the better. In my opinion it should be *refused* if it is tendered in respect of longer works. Once the company has established itself on that basis, we could no longer offer other publishers anything without their believing that the company had *turned it down.* Quite apart from the fact that the same reasons for which we refused it to the Westphalians[a] obtain here as well. Neither our honour nor our interest would incline us to accept.

To particularise: 7 in the general purposes committee [Tendenz-komitee] is excessive, three, at most 5, is enough Otherwise we shall get jackasses on it, if not intriguers. The general purposes committee must after all be ± resident in Brussels. In which case, with 7 members, how can there be any *choice*? No reason at all to have so many. In any case it's we who will have to do the work, and I am ready to take on my share, so what do we want with all those members? Besides, if it is the same with the opinions of the general purposes committee as with those of the Provincial Diets,[107] what then? All those written opinions will make a devil of a lot of work, but there could be no question of our getting out of it. As I said, I am ready to take on my share.

QUERY: If the bourgeoisie nominates a *truly* socialist supervisory council, which passes *outre*[b] our opinions, what then?

First published in *Der Briefwechsel zwischen F. Engels und K. Marx,* Bd. 1, Stuttgart, 1913

Printed according to the original

Published in English for the first time

31

ENGELS TO MARX[108]

IN BRUSSELS

[Paris, about 18 October 1846]
23, rue de Lille, Faubourg St. Germain

Dear M.,

At last, after much reluctance, I have brought myself to read Feuerbach's twaddle[c] and have discovered that we can't go into it

---

[a] J. Meyer and R. Rempel (see this volume, p. 49). - [b] overrides - [c] L. Feuerbach, *Das Wesen der Religion.*

in our critique.[a] Why, you will see when I have given you the gist of it.

'Das Wesen der Religion', *Epigonen*, Vol. I, pp. 117-78.

'Man's *sense of dependence* is the basis of religion', p. 117.

As man is dependent first of all on Nature, so 'Nature is the first, original object of religion', p. 118.

('Nature is simply a general term to denote beings, things, etc., which man distinguishes *from himself and his products.*')

The first religious manifestations are festivals at which natural processes, changes of season, etc., are symbolised. The particular natural conditions and products in the midst of which a tribe or a people lives, become part of its religion.

In his development man was assisted by other beings which, however, were not beings of a *higher* order, angels, but beings of a lower order, *animals.* Hence animal worship (there follows an apology in which pagans are defended against the attacks of Jews and Christians, trivial).

Nature, even in the case of Christians, always remains concealed behind religion. The attributes upon which the difference between God and Man is founded, are attributes of Nature (primal, basic). Thus omnipotence, eternity, universality, etc. God's true content is no more than Nature; i. e. in so far as God is seen only as the creator of Nature and not as a political and moral law-giver.

Polemic against the creation of Nature by an intelligent being, against creation out of nothing and so on—for the most part vulgar materialism 'humanised', i. e. translated into cosy German, fit to touch the citizen's heart.—Nature in natural religion is not the object as nature, but as

'personal, live, sentient being ... as emotional being, i. e. subjective human being' (p. 138).

Hence men worship it and seek to influence it with human incentives. This is primarily because Nature is fickle.

'The sense of dependence on Nature, combined with the idea of Nature as an arbitrarily active, personal being, is the basis of sacrifice, the most important act in natural religion' (p. 140).

But since the aim of sacrifice is a *selfish* one, it is man who is the *final goal* of religion, the divinity of man its final aim.

---

[a] Reference to Marx and Engels' 'Feuerbach. Opposition of the Materialist and Idealist Outlooks' which preceded other sections of *The German Ideology.*

Next come trivial glosses and solemn disquisitions to the effect that primitive people who still adhere to natural religion, deify things they regard as unpleasant, such as plague, fever, etc.

'As man, from a purely physical being, becomes a *political* being, distinguishing in general between himself and Nature, concentrating upon himself' (!!!), 'so his God also becomes a political being distinct from Nature.' '*Hence* man' arrives at 'the distinction between his being and Nature, and consequently at a God distinct from Nature, initially only by uniting with other men into a *community* in which *powers* distinct from Nature[a] and *existing only in the mind or the imagination*' (!!!), 'the power of the law, of opinion, of honour, of virtue, becomes the object of his sense of dependence....'

(This hideous sentence appears on p. 149.) The power of Nature, the power over life and death, is degraded to an attribute and tool of political and moral power. Intermezzo on p. 151 on oriental conservatives and occidental progressives.

'In the Orient, man does *not* let man *blind him* to Nature.... To him the King himself is not objectified as an earthly, but as a celestial, divine being. But beside a god, man only disappears where the earth is emptied of gods.... Only there do men have space and room for themselves.'

(A nice explanation for the stability of Orientals. It's all those idols and the space they take up.)

'The Oriental is to the Occidental what the countryman is to the townsman, the former is dependent on *Nature,* the latter on men,' etc., etc., 'hence only townsmen make history'

(here, and here alone, we catch a distant, if somewhat evil-smelling, breath of materialism).

'Only he who is able to sacrifice the power of *Nature* to the power of *opinion,* his *life* to his *name,* his existence *in the flesh* to his existence in the mouths and minds of posterity, is capable of historical deeds.'

Voilà.[b] Everything that is not Nature is imagination, opinion, balderdash. Hence, too, 'human "*vanity*" alone is the principle of history'!

P. 152: 'As soon as man becomes conscious of the fact that ... the consequence of vice and folly is unhappiness, etc., that of virtue and wisdom, ... happiness, and hence that intelligence and will are the *powers determining the fate of man* ... he will also see Nature as a being dependent on intelligence and will.'

---

[a] Feuerbach has 'powers of nature' (Naturmächten). - [b] There you are.

(Transition to monotheism—Feuerbach distinguishes the above illusory 'consciousness' from the power of intelligence and will.) With the domination of the world by intelligence and will, supernaturalism makes its appearance, creation from nothing, and monotheism, which is further specifically elucidated in terms of the 'unity of the human consciousness'. Feuerbach deemed it superfluous to point out that without the *One King*, the One God could never have come into being, that the Oneness of the God controlling the multifarious natural phenomena and holding together the conflicting forces of Nature is only the image of the One, the Oriental Despot who apparently or in fact holds together conflicting individuals whose interests clash.

Lengthy drivel against teleology, aping the old materialists. At the same time Feuerbach commits the very howler in regard to the real world which he accuses the theologians of committing in regard to Nature. He makes bad jokes at the expense of the theologians' assumption that without God Nature would dissolve into anarchy (i. e. without belief in God, it would be reduced to tatters), that God's *will, intelligence, opinion* is what binds the world; and he himself believes that it is *opinion,* the fear of public *opinion,* of *laws* and other *ideas,* which now holds the world together.

In the course of an argument against teleology, Feuerbach appears as an out-and-out *laudator temporis praesentis*[a]: The very high death-rate among children in the early years of life is attributable to the fact that

'*Nature* in its opulence sacrifices without compunction thousands of individual members'; ... 'it is the result of natural causes that ... e.g., *one* child in 3-4 dies in the first year of life, and *one* child in 25 in the fifth year, etc.'

With the exception of the few passages here specified, there is nothing worthy of note. Of the historical development of the various religions one learns nothing. At most they provide examples to support the above trivialities. The main bulk of the article consists in polemic against God and the Christians, altogether in his previous manner, except that now that he's run dry, and despite all his repetitions of the old drivel, dependence on the materialists is much more blatantly apparent. If one were to make any comment on the trivialities concerning natural religion, polytheism, and monotheism, one would have to compare

---

[a] Eulogist of the present; paraphrase of 'laudator temporis acti' (Horace, *Ars Poetica*).

them with the true development of these forms of religion, which means they would first have to be studied. But so far as our work is concerned, this is as irrelevant to us as his explanation of Christianity. The article casts no fresh light on Feuerbach's positive philosophical attitude, and the few theses worthy of criticism which I have cited above only confirm what we have already said. If the fellow still holds any interest for you, try and get hold of Vol. I of his *Collected Works*, either directly or indirectly, from Kiessling; he's written a kind of preface to it which might yield something. I have seen passages from it in which Feuerbach speaks of 'ailments of the head' and 'ailments of the stomach', a feeble apology, as it were, for not concerning himself with matters of real import.[109] Exactly what he wrote and told me eighteen months ago.

I have just received your letter[110] which, because of my move, had remained at my old lodgings[a] for a few days. I'll give the Swiss publishers a try. But I hardly imagine that I'll find a taker.[b] None of the fellows have the money to print 50 sheets. In my opinion we shall get nothing printed unless we *split* the things up and try to place the volumes separately, first the philosophical stuff, which is the most urgent, and then the remainder. 50 sheets at once is so dangerously big that many publishers won't accept it simply because they cannot.

Then, of course, there was Kühtmann, or whatever his name is, in Bremen, who was turned against us by Moses[c] and Weitling; the fellow wanted to print bannable books but not pay much; *we could* quite well approach him with this manuscript. What do you say to splitting the stuff up and offering one volume here and the other there? Vogler knows Kühtmann's address in Bremen. I've just about finished List.[111]

I saw the things in the *Volks-Tribun*[d] about three weeks ago.[112] Never before have I come across anything so ludicrously stupid. Brother Weitling reached the peak of infamy in that letter to Kriege. As for the details, incidentally, I can no longer remember enough to make any comment on them. I too am of the opinion

---

[a] See this volume, p. 67. - [b] This refers to attempts to find a publisher for Marx and Engels' *The German Ideology*. - [c] Hess - [d] 'Aus einem Privatbriefe von Wilhelm Weitling' (from W. Weitling's letter to H. Kriege of 16 May 1846), 'Die kommunistischen Literaten in Brüssel und die kommunistische Politik', 'An unsere Freunde' and 'Adresse der deutschen Socialreformer zu Philadelphia an Hermann Kriege und die Socialreformer in New York', *Der Volks-Tribun*, Nos. 25, 26, 27 and 29; 20, 27 June, 4 and 18 July 1846.

that we should reply[113] to both Kriege's and the Straubingers'[86] proclamation, rubbing their noses in the fact that they are denying having said what we reproached them for saying, while at the same time proclaiming in their reply the very stupidities they are denying; and that Kriege in particular, with his high moral pathos and indignation at our mockery, should get the dressing-down he deserves. Since these copies are at the moment going the rounds of the Straubingers here, I shall have to wait 4-5 days before I can get hold of them.

The Straubingers here are baying ferociously at my heels. Notably 3-4 'educated' workers who have been initiated into the secrets of true humanity by Ewerbeck and Grün. But by dint of a little patience and some terrorism I have emerged victorious with the great majority behind me. Grün having abjured communism, these 'educated' ones showed a strong inclination to follow suit. At that I went into action, so intimidating old Eisermann that he no longer turns up, and launched a debate on the pros and cons of *communism* and *non-communism*. This evening a vote will be taken on whether the meeting is communist or, as the 'educated' ones say, 'in favour of the good of mankind'. I am certain of a majority. I stated that, if they were not *communists*, I didn't give a fig for them and would attend no more. This evening Grün's disciples will be definitely overthrown, and then I shall have to start from scratch.

You can't imagine what demands these heducated Straubingers made on me. 'Leniency', 'gentleness', 'warm brotherliness'. But I duly trounced them and every evening managed to silence the whole opposition of 5, 6, 7 fellows (for at the start I had the whole *boutique*[a] against me). More anon about all this business, which shows up Mr Grün in a variety of lights.

Proudhon is expected here in a fortnight. Then the sparks will fly.

There's been some talk of a periodical here.[b] That manikin with the cigar, Mäurer, maintains that he will be able to raise the money for it. But I shan't believe the fellow until the money's actually there. If anything comes of it, we have so arranged matters that the thing will be entirely in *our* hands. I have authorised Mäurer, the ostensible editor, to print his own drivel in it, this being unavoidable. All the rest will pass through my hands, and I have an absolute veto. What I write will, of course, be pseudonymous or anonymous. At all events, should the thing

---

[a] company (literally: shop) - [b] *Die Pariser Horen*

materialise, it will not fall into the hands either of Hess or of Grün, or of any other muddled school. It would have its uses as a *new broom.* But not a word to anyone until it has materialised; it should be decided within the week.[114] Farewell and write soon.

E.

First published in *Der Briefwechsel zwischen F. Engels und K. Marx*, Bd. 1, Stuttgart, 1913

Printed according to the original

Published in English for the first time

32

ENGELS TO THE COMMUNIST CORRESPONDENCE COMMITTEE [115]

IN BRUSSELS

Paris, 23 October 1846

Committee letter (No. 3)

There is little to be said about the Straubinger business [116] here. The main thing is that the various differences I have had to thrash out with the lads hitherto are now settled: Grün's chief follower and disciple, Papa Eisermann, has been chucked out, the rest, so far as their influence over the great majority is concerned, have been completely routed, and I have carried through a unanimous resolution against them.

Briefly this is what happened:

The Proudhonian association scheme was discussed on three evenings. At the beginning I had nearly the whole clique against me and at the end only Eisermann and the three other Grünians. The main thing was to prove the necessity for revolution by force and in general to reject as anti-proletarian, petty-bourgeois, and Straubingerian Grün's true socialism, which had drawn new strength from the Proudhonian panacea. In the end I became infuriated by my opponents' endless repetition of the same arguments and really pitched into the Straubingers, which aroused great indignation among the Grünians but succeeded in eliciting from the worthy Eisermann an *open attack* on communism. Whereupon I lashed him so mercilessly with my tongue that he never showed his face again.

I now made use of the lever—the attack on communism—
provided by Eisermann, the more so since Grün never ceased his
intrigues, going from workshop to workshop, summoning the
people to come to him on Sundays, etc., etc., and, on the Sunday [a]
following the above-mentioned session, was *himself* so abysmally
stupid as to attack communism in the presence of 8-10 Straubingers. I therefore declared that, before I took part in any further
discussion, the question of whether or not we were meeting here
as communists must be put to the vote. If the former were the
case, we must see to it that attacks on communism such as those
made by Eisermann never recur; if the latter, and if they were
simply a random collection of individuals who had met to discuss a
random selection of subjects, I would not give a fig for them, nor
would I ever return. This aroused much horror among the
Grünians who, they said, foregathered here for 'the good of
mankind', for their own enlightenment, men of progress and not
biased system-mongers, etc., etc., the description 'a random
collection' being in no way applicable to such respectable company.
Moreover, they *first wanted to know* what communism really was
(these curs, who for years have called themselves communists and
only deserted out of fear of Grün and Eisermann, these two last
having used communism as a pretext for worming their way in
among them!). Of course I did not allow myself to be caught by
their amiable request to tell them, ignorant as they were, in 2 or 3
words what communism was. I gave them a highly simple
definition which went as far as and no further than the foregoing
points at issue, which, by positing community of goods, *ruled out,*
not only peacefulness, tenderness and consideration for the
bourgeoisie and/or the Straubinger fraternity, but also and finally
the Proudhonian joint-stock society along with its retention of
individual *property* and all that this involves; a definition which,
furthermore, contained nothing that could give rise either to
divagations or to any circumvention of the proposed vote. I
therefore defined the aims of communists as follows: 1. to ensure
that the interests of the proletariat prevail, as opposed to those of
the bourgeoisie; 2. to do so by abolishing private property and
replacing same with community of goods; 3. to recognise no
means of attaining these aims other than democratic revolution by
force.

Two evenings were spent discussing this. During the second, the
best of the 3 Grünians, sensing the mood of the majority, came

---

[a] 18 October 1846

over to me unreservedly. The other two kept contradicting each other without being aware of the fact. Several chaps, who had never spoken before, suddenly opened their traps and declared themselves unequivocally for me. Up till then Junge had been the only one to do so. Some of these *homines novi*,[a] although trembling with fear lest they dry up, spoke quite nicely and all in all seem to have quite a sound intellect. In short, when it was put to the vote, the meeting was declared to be communist in accordance with the above definition by 13 votes to 2, the latter being those of the pair who had remained true to Grün—one of whom subsequently declared himself exceedingly eager to be converted.

Thus a clean sweep has at last been made and we can now begin, so far as is possible, to do something with these fellows. Grün, who was easily able to extricate himself from his financial predicament[b] because the principal creditors were those same Grünians, his principal followers, has gone down a great deal in the opinion of the majority and of some of his followers and, despite all his intrigues and experiments (e. g. attending the Barrière meetings[81] wearing a cap, etc., etc.), has been a resounding failure with his Proudhonian society. Had I not been there, our friend Ewerbeck would have fallen for it. *La tête baissée.*[c]

One could hardly help but admire Grün's stratagem! Doubting his chaps' intelligence, he tells them his stories over and over again until they can rattle them off from memory. After every session—nothing was easier, of course, than to reduce such an opposition to silence—the whole defeated gang went scuttling off to Grün, told him what I had said—naturally all of it distorted—, and had their armoury renewed. When next they opened their traps, one could always tell from the first couple of words exactly what the whole sentence would be. In view of this tale-bearing, I was careful not to provide the fellows with anything general which might assist Mr Grün in further embellishing his true socialism; nevertheless, writing not long ago in the *Kölner*[d] on the occasion of the Geneva Revolution,[117] the cur exploited and variously distorted sundry things I had said to the Straubingers, whereas here in Paris he had drummed the *opposite* into them. He is now engaged in political economy, the worthy man.

---

[a] new men - [b] See this volume, p. 62. - [c] With his eyes shut. - [d] This presumably refers to a report from Paris 'Hr. Guizot beabsichtigt eine Intervention in der Schweiz' published in the *Kölnische Zeitung*, No. 291, 18 October 1846.

You'll have seen Proudhon's book[a] advertised. I shall get hold of it one of these days; it costs 15 fr. so it's too expensive to buy.

The above-mentioned audience, before whom the performance took place, consists of approx. 20 cabinet-makers, who otherwise foregather only at the Barrière and then with all and sundry, having no really closed association of their own, save for a choral club, though some also belong to the rump of the League of the Just.[52] If we could assemble openly we would soon have over 100 chaps from the cabinet-makers alone. I know only a few of the tailors—who also attend the cabinet-makers' meeting. Nowhere in Paris have I been able to find out anything at all about blacksmiths and tanners. Not a soul knows anything about them.

Not long ago Kriege, as one of the Just, laid his report before the 'Halle'[b] (central authority). Of course I read the missive; but since this constituted a breach of the oath, for which the penalty is death by dagger, rope or poison, you must nowhere record same in writing. The letter proves, just as did his riposte to our attack,[c] that he had benefited greatly from the latter and that he was now more concerned with the things of this world. He gave a long account of their difficulties. The first instalment of this American Straubingers' story concerned their misfortunes—evidently Kriege was at the helm and his management of the money side was big-hearted to say the least, the *Tribun*[d] was given away, not sold, the funds consisted in charitable gifts, in short, by trying to re-enact Chapters III-VI of the Acts of the Apostles not even omitting Ananias and Sapphira,[e] they finally found themselves up to their eyes in debt. The second period, in which Kriege became simply the 'registrar', other chaps having apparently taken over the financial side, was that of recovery. Instead of appealing to the fulness of men's hearts, they now appealed to their lightly tripping feet and to their ± uncommunist side generally, discovering to their surprise that all the money they needed could be raised by organising balls, picnics, etc., etc., and that human frailty could be exploited for the benefit of communism. Pecuniarily speaking, they were now thoroughly flush. Among the 'obstacles' they had to overcome, the doughty Tecklenburger[f] also counts the manifold calumnies and aspersions they, amongst others, had had to endure 'and this recently at the hands of the "communist" philosophers in Brussels'. For the rest he indulges in some trivial prattle against the colonies, recommends 'Brother Weitling' to them (i. e. to his

---

[a] P. J. Proudhon, *Système des contradictions économiques, ou Philosophie de la misère.* - [b] The People's Chamber (Volkshalle) - [c] K. Marx and F. Engels, 'Circular Against Kriege'. - [d] *Der Volks-Tribun* - [e] The Acts 5:1 - [f] Hermann Kriege

most inveterate foes), but for the most part remains fairly
down-to-earth, if also somewhat unctuous, and only from time to
time is there a little sighing about brotherliness, etc.

Do you get the *Réforme* there? If you don't read it, let me know
and I will send you accounts of anything special that appears in it.
For the past four days it has been picking on the *National* for
refusing to express unconditional approval of a petition for
electoral reform which is circulating here. This, the *Réforme*
maintains, was entirely due to its partiality for Thiers. Not long
ago it was rumoured here that Bastide and Thomas had resigned
from the *National,* leaving only Marrast, and that the latter had
allied himself with Thiers. This was denied by the *National.*
However, changes have been made in its editorial department, but
I am not aware of the details; for the past year it is known to have
been particularly well-disposed towards Thiers; now the *Réforme* is
pointing out how greatly it has compromised itself by this
partiality.

Moreover, it is only opposition to the *Réforme,* which has of late
led the *National* to commit follies such as denying, purely out of
malice, and until it could do so no longer, etc., the story, first told
by the *Réforme,* of the Portuguese counter-revolution.[118] The
Réforme is now at great pains to carry on a polemic no less brilliant
than that of the *National,* but without success.

Having got to this point in my letter, I once again went to the
Straubingers, where the following transpired: Grün, too impotent
to harm me in any way, is now having me denounced at the
Barrière. Eisermann is attacking communism at the public Barrière meeting at which, owing to the presence of informers, no one,
of course, can answer him back without incurring the risk of being
thrown out; Junge answered him furiously (but yesterday we
warned him against this). Thereupon Eisermann declared Junge
to be the mouthpiece of a third person (myself, of course), who
had suddenly irrupted amongst the people like a bomb, and he
himself well knew how they were primed for the Barrière
discussions, etc., etc. In short, what all his chatter amounted to was
an *out-and-out denunciation* to the police; for four weeks ago the
landlord in whose house the affair happened said: *il y a toujours
des mouchards parmi vous,*[a] and once, at that time, the police
inspector also turned up. He accused Junge in so many words of
being a 'revolutionary'. Mr Grün was present throughout and
prompted Eisermann on what to say. This was the dirtiest trick of

---

[a] There are always informers among you.

all. According to the facts as I know them, I hold Grün fully responsible for everything Eisermann says. There's absolutely nothing to be done about it. That numskull Eisermann cannot be attacked at the Barrière because this would elicit yet another denunciation of the weekly meeting; Grün is too cowardly to do anything *himself* and in his own name. The only thing that can be done is to have it explained to the people at the Barrière that communism wasn't discussed because that might have exposed the whole meeting to danger from the police.

It's high time I heard from you.

Yours
E.

First published in *Der Briefwechsel zwischen F. Engels und K. Marx*, Bd. 1, Stuttgart, 1913

Printed according to the original
Published in English in full for the first time

33

ENGELS TO MARX [119]

IN BRUSSELS

[Paris, about 23 October 1846]

Dear M.,

Have received the thing against Kriege.[120] Not bad. Since you alone signed, Kriege will no doubt put the more peremptory tone of the first document[a] down to my personal account, and eat humble pie in respect of the second, but little do I care. Let him give free rein to his personal malice and paint me as black as may be in the eyes of the American Straubingers,[86] if that gives him any pleasure.

You will see from the Committee letter[b] how successful I was with the Straubingers here. The devil knows, I didn't spare them. I attacked their worst prejudices, and told them they were not proletarians at all. But Grün also played very beautifully into my hands.

---

[a] K. Marx and F. Engels, 'Circular Against Kriege'. - [b] See this volume, pp. 81-86.

For heaven's sake don't stamp your letters to me. If it hadn't been for that damned Leske, who finally sent me a worthless bill of exchange, which I had to return, for the old stuff I had sent to Püttmann[a]—if the cur hadn't left me in the lurch, I'd send you 25 fr. immediately for Committee funds. But meanwhile I shall take upon myself at least the cost of the correspondence with *me*. If I failed to stamp my previous letter, it was because it was too late and I could only get it off by dropping it straight into the letter box. As soon as Leske sends me the money, you'll get a share of it.

None of the Straubingers are to be allowed to see the reply to Kriege. Otherwise it wouldn't be safe from Grün. We must be careful not to let anything disturb the chap until he's finished his work on Proudhon's book, with notes by K. Grün.[b] Then we'll have him. In it he completely retracts a mass of things he has previously said, and delivers himself up body and soul to the Proudhonian system of redemption. Then there'll be no more exploitation, unless he is willing to turn his coat again.

Is Weitling still in Brussels[121]?

I think I shall be able to pull it off with the Straubingers here. True, the fellows are horribly ignorant and, their condition in life being what it is, completely unprepared. There is no competition whatever among them, wages remain constantly at the same wretched level; the struggle with the master, far from turning on the question of wages, is concerned with 'journeymen's pride', etc. The slop-shops are now having a revolutionising effect on the tailors. If only it were not such a rotten trade!

Grün has done a frightful amount of harm. He has turned all that was distinct in these fellows' minds into woolly daydreams, humanitarian aspirations, etc. Under the pretence of attacking Weitlingian and other doctrinaire communism, he has stuffed their heads full of vague literary and petty-bourgeois catch-phrases, maintaining that all else was system-mongering. Even the cabinet-makers, who have *never,* save a few exceptions, been Weitlingians, entertain a superstitious fear of 'bread-and-butter communism' [Löffelkommunismus] and—at least *before* the resolution was passed—would sooner have associated themselves with the woolliest daydreams, peaceable philanthropic schemes, etc., than with this 'bread-and-butter communism'. Here utter confusion reigns.

---

[a] F. Engels, 'Description of Recently Founded Communist Colonies Still in Existence'. - [b] P. J. Proudhon, *Philosophie der Staatsökonomie oder Nothwendigkeit des Elends.* Deutsch bearb. von Karl Grün.

A few days ago I wrote to Harney, gently attacking the pacific nature of the FRATERNAL DEMOCRATS[122] and told him, by the way, that he should continue to correspond with you.

Your

E.

[On the back of the letter]

Monsieur Charles Marx
42 rue d'Orléans
Faubourg de Namur
Affranchi. Bruxelles

First published in *Der Briefwechsel zwischen F. Engels und K. Marx*, Bd. 1, Stuttgart, 1913

Printed according to the original

Published in English in full for the first time

34

ENGELS TO MARX[123]

IN BRUSSELS

[Paris], 2 November [1846]
23, rue de Lille

Where is the long letter you promised so long ago? *Make sure you send Bernays the manuscript,* he only needs what you have[124] since he still has the printed stuff. He has sent nothing to America; whatever may have appeared there was printed without his knowledge or consent.[a] However a lot of copies were printed, and some may have gone as presents from Leske to all points of the compass. We shall investigate the matter. Perhaps through Grün or Börnstein. I have written to Switzerland about the manuscripts,[b] but it would seem that the cur[c] has no intention of replying.[125] Apart from him, there's no one but Jenni; I've played a prank on him and would rather not write, enclose a short note for the fellow in your next. I shall send it on, but it's only for form's sake, the fellow's almost certain to refuse. The first man I

---

[a] [K. L. Bernays,] 'Das entschleierte Geheimniss der Criminal-Justiz. Eine kommunistische Anschauungsweise', *Der Volks-Tribun,* Nos. 26 and 27, 27 June and 4 July 1846. - [b] A reference to K. Marx and F. Engels, *The German Ideology.* - [c] J. M. Schläpter.

wrote to published a short pamphlet by Bernays,[a] but even if he does take the thing, it would appear, *à ce qu'écrit*[b] Püttmann, that he is bankrupt. *Voilà.*[c] I despair of Switzerland. Good advice costs money. Things being what they are, we shall certainly not get rid of 2 volumes together. At most 2 volumes to 2 different publishers. Write about this as well.

Your
E.

I have only just read what the little man[d] has written above about his flight from solitude. It's a good thing we've got him here. He is gradually cheering up again. Greetings to the whole *boutique.*[e]

First published in *Der Briefwechsel zwischen F. Engels und K. Marx,* Bd. 1, Stuttgart, 1913

Printed according to the original

Published in English for the first time

35

ENGELS TO MARX[126]

IN BRUSSELS

[Paris, middle of November-December 1846]

Dear Marx,

The reasons for the brief letter I recently sent Gigot are the following. During the investigation into the disturbances in the Faubourg St. Antoine in October, a multitude of Germans were arrested and questioned, the whole of the second batch consisting of Straubingers.[127] Some of these numskulls, who have now been sent across the border, must have talked a great deal of nonsense about Ewerbeck and myself; IN FACT, in view of their paltriness, nothing else could have been expected of the Straubingers than that they should have been scared to death and have given away all that they knew and more. On top of that, such Straubingers as

---

[a] [K. L. Bernays,] *Rothschild. Ein Urtheilsspruch vom menschlichen Standpunkte aus.* - [b] from what writes - [c] There! - [d] Karl Ludwig Bernays - [e] company (literally: shop)

I was acquainted with, secretive though they were concerning their own miserable affairs, shamefully sounded the alarm about my meetings with them. That's how these lads are.

At the Barrière, as I have already written and told you,[a] the noble Eisermann delivered himself of a further, detailed *avis aux mouchards*[b] in which he attacked me. Junge was also guilty of some gross indiscretions; the fellow is a trifle swollen-headed, he wishes to be sent to Calais and London at the expense of the French government. In short, M. Delessert set one spy after another at the heels of myself and Ewerbeck, who has long been under suspicion and has an expulsion order hanging over his head. These spies succeeded in following us to the *marchand de vins*,[c] where we sometimes foregathered with the Faubourg stalwarts. This was proof enough that we were the leaders of a dangerous clique, and not long afterwards I learned that M. Delessert had requested M. Tanneguy Duchâtel to issue an expulsion order against me and Ewerbeck, and that there was a splendid pile of documents relating to the case in the Prefecture, almost next door to the place where the whores are medically examined. Needless to say, I had no desire to let myself be banished on the Straubingers' account. I had already anticipated something of the kind when I noticed the nonchalance with which the Straubingers were holding forth for all to hear and arguing all over the place about who was right, Grün or I. I was sick and tired of the whole business, there was no putting the lads to rights; even in discussion they wouldn't speak their minds frankly just like the people in London, and I had achieved my main object, the triumph over Grün. It was an excellent opportunity of honourably ridding myself of the Straubingers, vexing as the whole affair was in other respects. I therefore let it be known to them that I could no longer remain their tutor and that, furthermore, they should watch their step. Ewerbeck at once decided to go on a journey and appears, indeed, to have departed forthwith[128]—at any rate, I haven't seen him since. Where he has gone, I do not know. The police had also been looking for the little man (Bernays) who, however, had withdrawn to his old place[d] because of a variety of escapades (it's remarkable what mad scrapes he gets into as soon as he sets foot in the civilised world). When he will return to Paris, I don't know, but in no circumstances will he move into lodgings where he had intended to, hence *the address that was given you is useless.* He

---

[a] See this volume, pp. 85-86. - [b] notification to the informers - [c] wineshop - [d] i. e. Sarcelles

has safely received his manuscript.[a] Meanwhile I can thank the noble police for having reft me from the arms of the Straubingers and reminded me of the pleasures life has to offer. If the suspicious individuals who have been following me for the past fortnight are really informers, as I am convinced some of them are, the Prefecture must of late have given out a great many entrance tickets to the *bals* Montesquieu, Valentino, Prado, etc., etc. I am indebted to Mr Delessert for some delicious encounters with *grisettes* and for a great deal of pleasure, *car j'ai voulu profiter des journées et des nuits qui pouvaient être mes dernières à Paris. Enfin,*[b] since in other respects I've been left in peace up till now, everything would appear to have quietened down. But in future address all letters to Monsieur A. F. Körner, artiste-peintre, 29, rue neuve Bréda, Paris, with an envelope inside bearing my initials, taking care that nothing shows through.

You will understand that, in the circumstances, I have had to leave W. Weitling entirely to his own devices. Having seen none of our people, I have no idea whether he has been or still is here. Nor does it matter. I don't know the Weitlingians at all and, he'd get a fine welcome amongst those I know; because of their eternal clashes with his tailor friends, they feel the most frightful animosity towards him.

The affair with the London people[129] is annoying precisely because of Harney and because they, of all the Straubingers, were the only ones with whom one could attempt to make contact frankly and without *arrière-pensée*. But if the fellows are unwilling, *eh bien,*[c] let them go. In any case one can never know if they won't produce another address as misérable as the one to Mr Ronge or to the Schleswig-Holsteiners.[130] On top of that, there's their perpetual envy of us as 'scholars'. By the way, we have two methods by which we can rid ourselves of them should they rebel: either make a clean break with them, or simply allow the correspondence to lapse. I would be for the latter, if their last letter admits of an answer which, without giving undue offence, is lukewarm enough to rob them of any desire to reply quickly. Then another long delay before answering—and two or three letters will be enough to consign this drowsy correspondence to its last sleep. For how and why should we ridicule these fellows? We have no press organ and even if we had one, they are no writers

---

[a] See this volume, p. 88. - [b] since I wanted to take advantage of the days and nights which might well be my last in Paris. Anyway - [c] well, then

5*

but confine themselves to an occasional proclamation which no one ever sees, still less cares about. If we are to ridicule the Straubingers *at all,* we can always avail ourselves of their fine documents; if the correspondence finally does lapse, well and good; the rupture will be gradual and attract no great attention. In the meantime we shall quietly make the necessary arrangements with Harney, taking care that *they* owe us the final letter (which they will in fact do, once they have been made to wait 6-10 weeks for an answer), and then leave them to clamour. An immediate rupture with the fellows would bring us neither gain nor *gloire.*[a] *Theoretical* disagreements are hardly possible with the fellows since they have no theory and, *sauf*[b] for their possible unspoken misgivings, they wish to learn from us: nor are they able to formulate their misgivings, so that all discussion with them is impossible except, perhaps, face to face. In the case of an open rupture they would bring up against us all that generalised communist thirst-for-learning stuff: we'd have been glad to learn from the learned gentlemen, if they'd had something decent, etc. *Practical* party differences would—since there are only a few of them on the committee and a few of us too—soon degenerate into mere personalities and ill-natured exchanges, at least on the face of it. As a party we can enter the lists against literary men, but not against Straubingers. They are, after all, a couple of 100 strong, vouched for among the English by Harney, proclaimed in Germany by the *Rheinischer Beobachter,* etc., etc., a rabid and by no means impotent communist society; they are, furthermore, the most tolerable of the Straubingers, and can certainly not be bettered so long as there is no change in Germany. We have learnt from this business that, in the absence of a proper movement in Germany, nothing can be done with the Straubingers, even the best of them. It is better after all to let them quietly go their own way, attacking them only as a whole, *en bloc,* than to provoke a dispute which might only serve to sully our reputations. Vis-à-vis ourselves, these lads declare themselves to be 'the people', 'the proletarians', and we can only appeal to a communist proletariat which has yet to take shape in Germany. In addition, the Prussian Constitution is in the offing, and we might then be able to make use of the fellows' signatures, etc., etc.—Anyway, my words of wisdom will doubtless arrive too late and you will already have passed and acted on a resolution in this matter. I would, by the

---

[a] glory - [b] save

way, have written earlier, but I was waiting to see what turn the affair with the police would take.

I have just received a reply from the Swiss publisher.[a] The letter, enclosed herewith, only confirms my belief that the fellow's a scoundrel. No ordinary publisher would accept so amiably after keeping one waiting x weeks. Now we shall have to see what the Bremen man[b] says, and then we can always do as we think fit. Then again there's the fellow at Belle-Vue near Constance; perhaps something might be arranged with him[131]; I could try him again if the Bremen man's not agreeable. Meanwhile I'll make some more enquiries in Herisau—if only we had a decent fellow in Switzerland to whom one could send the manuscript[c] with instructions to hand it over only against payment in cash.[d] But the only one there is that thirsty paterfamilias Püttmann!

During the recent bad spell, one of my innocent, incidental pastimes, besides girls, has been to concern myself to some extent with Denmark and the other northern countries.[132] What an abomination! Rather the smallest German than the biggest Dane! Nowhere else is the *misère* of morality, guilds and estates still carried to such a pitch. The Dane regards Germany as a country which one visits in order to 'keep mistresses and squander one's fortune on them' (*imedens at han reiste i Tydskland, havde han en Maitresse, som fortärede ham den bedste del af hans Midler,*[e] we read in a Danish school book). He calls the German a *tydsk*[f] windbag, and regards himself as the true representative of the Teutonic soul—the Swede in turn despises the Dane as 'Germanised' and degenerate, garrulous and effete—the Norwegian looks down on the Gallicised Swede and his aristocracy and rejoices in the fact that at home in Norge[g] exactly the same stupid, peasant economy is dominant as at the time of the noble Canute, and he, for his part, is treated *en canaille*[h] by the Icelander, who still continues to speak exactly the same language as the unwashed Vikings of anno 900, swills whale oil, lives in a mud hut and goes to pieces in any atmosphere that does not reek of rotten fish. I have several times felt tempted to be proud of the fact that I am at least no Dane, nor yet an Icelander, but merely a German. The editor of the most advanced Swedish newspaper, the *Aftonbladet,* has twice been here in Paris to seek enlightenment on the organisation of labour,

---

[a] Johann Michael Schläpfer - [b] Kühtmann - [c] K. Marx and F. Engels, *The German Ideology.* - [d] Engels here uses the Dutch: *baar Geld.* - [e] while travelling in Germany, he had a mistress who ran through the better part of his fortune - [f] German - [g] Norway - [h] scornfully

has for years taken the *Bon Sens* and the *Démocratie pacifique*; he solemnly conferred with Louis Blanc and Considérant, but found himself out of his depth, and returned home none the wiser. Now as before he loudly advocates free competition or, as the Swedes have it, freedom of *nourishment* or else *själfförsörjningsfrihet*, freedom of self-supply (which sounds even better than freedom to pursue a *trade*). Of course, they're still up to their necks in the guild nonsense and, in the parliaments, it's precisely the bourgeois who are the most rabid conservatives. Throughout the whole country there are only two proper towns, à 80,000 and 40,000 inhabitants respectively, the third, Norrköpping, having only 12,000 and all the rest perhaps 1,000, 2,000, 3,000. At every post station there's one inhabitant. In Denmark things are scarcely better, since they have only one solitary city there, in which the guilds indulge in the most ludicrous proceedings, madder even than in Basle or Bremen, and where you aren't allowed on the promenade without an entrance ticket. The only thing these countries are good for is to show what the Germans would do if they had freedom of the press, viz., what the Danes have actually done, immediately found a 'society for the proper use of the free press', and print almanacs full of Christian good intentions. The Swedish *Aftonbladet* is as tame as the *Kölner Zeitung*, but considers itself 'democratic in the true sense of the word'. On the other hand the Swedes have the novels of Fröken[a] Bremer and the Danes of Councillor of State (Eta traad) Oehlenschläger, Commander of the Order of the Dannebrog.[133] There's also a terrific number of Hegelians there and the language, every third word of which is filched from the German, is admirably suited to speculation.

A report was begun long ago and will follow within the next few days.[134] Write and tell me if you have Proudhon's book.[b]

If you wish to make use of Proudhon's book, which is bad, for your own book,[5] I will send you the very extensive excerpts I have made. It's not worth the 15 francs it costs.

First published slightly abridged in *Der Briefwechsel zwischen F. Engels und K. Marx*, Bd. 1, Stuttgart, 1913 and in full in *MEGA*, Abt. III, Bd. 1, 1929

Printed according to the original

Published in English for the first time

---

[a] Miss - [b] P. J. Proudhon, *Système des contradictions économiques, ou Philosophie de la misère.*

36

MARX TO PAVEL VASILYEVICH ANNENKOV [135]

IN PARIS

Brussels, 28 December [1846] Rue
d'Orléans, 42, Faubourg Namur

My dear Mr Annenkov,

You would long since have had a reply to your letter of
1 November had not my bookseller delayed sending me
Mr Proudhon's book, *Philosophie de la misère*, until last week. I
skimmed through it in two days so as to be able to give you my
opinion straight away. Having read the book very cursorily, I
cannot go into details but can only let you have the general
impression it made on me. Should you so desire, I could go into it
in greater detail in another letter.

To be frank, I must admit that I find the book on the whole
poor, if not very poor. You yourself make fun in your letter of the
'little bit of German philosophy' paraded by Mr Proudhon in this
amorphous and overweening work, but you assume that the
economic argument has remained untainted by the philosophic
poison. Therefore I am by no means inclined to ascribe the faults
of the economic argument to Mr Proudhon's philosophy.
Mr Proudhon does not provide a false critique of political economy
because his philosophy is absurd—he produces an absurd
philosophy because he has not understood present social conditions in their *engrènement*,[a] to use a word which Mr Proudhon
borrows from Fourier, like so much else.

Why does Mr Proudhon speak of God, of universal reason, of
mankind's impersonal reason which is never mistaken, which has
at all times been equal to itself and of which one only has to be
correctly aware in order to arrive at truth? Why does he indulge
in feeble Hegelianism in order to set himself up as an *esprit fort*[b]?

He himself provides the key to this enigma. Mr Proudhon sees
in history a definite series of social developments; he finds
progress realised in history; finally, he finds that men, taken as
individuals, did not know what they were about, were mistaken as
to their own course, i. e. that their social development appears at
first sight to be something distinct, separate and independent of
their individual development. He is unable to explain these facts,

---

[a] intermeshing - [b] Literally: strong intellect

and the hypothesis of universal reason made manifest is ready to hand. Nothing is easier than to invent mystical causes, i.e. phrases in which common sense is lacking.

But in admitting his total incomprehension of the historical development of mankind—and he admits as much in making use of high-flown expressions such as universal reason, God, etc.—does not Mr Proudhon admit, implicitly and of necessity, his inability to understand *economic development*?

What is society, irrespective of its form? The product of man's interaction upon man. Is man free to choose this or that form of society? By no means. If you assume a given state of development of man's productive faculties, you will have a corresponding form of commerce and consumption. If you assume given stages of development in production, commerce or consumption, you will have a corresponding form of social constitution, a corresponding organisation, whether of the family, of the estates or of the classes—in a word, a corresponding civil society. If you assume this or that civil society, you will have this or that political system, which is but the official expression of civil society. This is something Mr Proudhon will never understand, for he imagines he's doing something great when he appeals from the state to civil society, i. e. to official society from the official epitome of society.

Needless to say, man is not free to choose *his productive forces*—upon which his whole history is based—for every productive force is an acquired force, the product of previous activity. Thus the productive forces are the result of man's practical energy, but that energy is in turn circumscribed by the conditions in which man is placed by the productive forces already acquired, by the form of society which exists before him, which he does not create, which is the product of the preceding generation. The simple fact that every succeeding generation finds productive forces acquired by the preceding generation and which serve it as the raw material of further production, engenders a relatedness in the history of man, engenders a history of mankind, which is all the more a history of mankind as man's productive forces, and hence his social relations, have expanded. From this it can only be concluded that the social history of man is never anything else than the history of his individual development, whether he is conscious of this or not. His material relations form the basis of all his relations. These material relations are but the necessary forms in which his material and individual activity is realised.

Mr Proudhon confuses ideas and things. Man never renounces what he has gained, but this does not mean that he never renounces the form of society in which he has acquired certain productive forces. On the contrary. If he is not to be deprived of the results obtained or to forfeit the fruits of civilisation, man is compelled to change all his traditional social forms as soon as the mode of commerce ceases to correspond to the productive forces acquired. Here I use the word *commerce* in its widest sense—as we would say *Verkehr* in German. For instance, privilege, the institution of guilds and corporations, the regulatory system of the Middle Ages, were the only social relations that corresponded to the acquired productive forces and to the pre-existing social conditions from which those institutions had emerged. Protected by the corporative and regulatory system, capital had accumulated, maritime trade had expanded, colonies had been founded—and man would have lost the very fruits of all this had he wished to preserve the forms under whose protection those fruits had ripened. And, indeed, two thunderclaps occurred, the revolutions of 1640 and of 1688. In England, all the earlier economic forms, the social relations corresponding to them, and the political system which was the official expression of the old civil society, were destroyed. Thus, the economic forms in which man produces, consumes and exchanges are *transitory and historical*. With the acquisition of new productive faculties man changes his mode of production and with the mode of production he changes all the economic relations which were but the necessary relations of that particular mode of production.

It is this that Mr Proudhon has failed to understand, let alone demonstrate. Unable to follow the real course of history, Mr Proudhon provides a phantasmagoria which he has the presumption to present as a dialectical phantasmagoria. He no longer feels any need to speak of the seventeenth, eighteenth or nineteenth centuries, for his history takes place in the nebulous realm of the imagination and soars high above time and place. In a word, it is Hegelian trash, it is not history, it is not profane history—history of mankind, but sacred history—history of ideas. As seen by him, man is but the instrument used by the idea or eternal reason in order to unfold itself. The *evolutions* of which Mr Proudhon speaks are presumed to be evolutions such as take place in the mystical bosom of the absolute idea. If the veil of this mystical language be rent, it will be found that what Mr Proudhon gives us is the order in which economic categories are arranged within his mind. It would require no great effort on my part to prove to you that this arrangement is the arrangement of a very disorderly mind.

Mr Proudhon opens his book with a dissertation on *value* which is his hobby-horse. For the time being I shall not embark upon an examination of that dissertation.

The series of eternal reason's economic evolutions begins with the *division of labour*. For Mr Proudhon, the division of labour is something exceedingly simple. But was not the caste system a specific division of labour? And was not the corporative system another division of labour? And is not the division of labour in the manufacturing system, which began in England in the middle of the seventeenth century and ended towards the end of the eighteenth century, likewise entirely distinct from the division of labour in big industry, in modern industry?

Mr Proudhon is so far from the truth that he neglects to do what even profane economists do. In discussing the division of labour, he feels no need to refer to the world *market*. Well! Must not the division of labour in the fourteenth and fifteenth centuries, when there were as yet no colonies, when America was still non-existent for Europe, and when Eastern Asia existed only through the mediation of Constantinople, have been utterly different from the division of labour in the seventeenth century, when colonies were already developed?

And that is not all. Is the whole internal organisation of nations, are their international relations, anything but the expression of a given division of labour? And must they not change as the division of labour changes?

Mr Proudhon has so little understood the question of the division of labour that he does not even mention the separation of town and country which occurred in Germany, for instance, between the ninth and twelfth centuries. Thus, to Mr Proudhon, that separation must be an eternal law because he is unaware either of its origin or of its development. Throughout his book he speaks as though this creation of a given mode of production were to last till the end of time. All that Mr Proudhon says about the division of labour is but a résumé, and a very superficial and very incomplete résumé at that, of what Adam Smith and a thousand others said before him.

The second evolution is *machinery*. With Mr Proudhon, the relation between the division of labour and machinery is a wholly mystical one. Each one of the modes of the division of labour had its specific instruments of production. For instance, between the mid-seventeenth and mid-eighteenth century man did not make everything by hand. He had tools and very intricate ones, such as looms, ships, levers, etc., etc.

Thus nothing could be more absurd than to see machinery as deriving from the division of labour in general.

In passing I should also point out that, not having understood the historical origin of machinery, Mr. Proudhon has still less understood its development. Up till 1825—when the first general crisis occurred—it might be said that the requirements of consumption as a whole were growing more rapidly than production, and that the development of machinery was the necessary consequence of the needs of the market. Since 1825, the invention and use of machinery resulted solely from the war between masters and workmen. But this is true only of England. As for the European nations, they were compelled to use machinery by the competition they were encountering from the English, in their home markets as much as in the world market. Finally, where North America was concerned, the introduction of machinery was brought about both by competition with other nations and by scarcity of labour, i. e. by the disproportion between the population and the industrial requirements of North America. From this you will be able to see what wisdom Mr Proudhon evinces when he conjures up the spectre of competition as the third evolution, as the antithesis of machinery!

Finally, and generally speaking, it is truly absurd to make *machinery* an economic category alongside the division of labour, competition, credit, etc.

Machinery is no more an economic category than the ox who draws the plough. The present *use* of machinery is one of the relations of our present economic system, but the way in which machinery is exploited is quite distinct from the machinery itself. Powder is still powder, whether you use it to wound a man or to dress his wounds.

Mr Proudhon surpasses himself in causing to grow inside his own brain competition, monopoly, taxes or police, balance of trade, credit and property in the order I have given here. Nearly all the credit institutions had been developed in England by the beginning of the eighteenth century, before the invention of machinery. State credit was simply another method of increasing taxes and meeting the new requirements created by the rise to power of the bourgeois class. Finally, *property* constitutes the last category in Mr Proudhon's system. In the really existing world, on the other hand, the division of labour and all Mr Proudhon's other categories are social relations which together go to make up what is now known as *property*; outside these relations bourgeois property is nothing but a metaphysical or juridical illusion. The property of another epoch, feudal property, developed in a wholly different set of social relations. In establishing property as an independent relation, Mr Proudhon is guilty of more than a methodological error: he clearly proves his failure to grasp the bond linking all forms of *bourgeois* production, or to understand the *historical* and *transitory* nature of the forms of production in any one epoch. Failing to see our social institutions as historical products and to understand either their origin or their development, Mr Proudhon can only subject them to a dogmatic critique.

Hence Mr Proudhon is compelled to resort to a *fiction* in order to explain development. He imagines that the division of labour, credit, machinery, etc., were all invented in the service of his *idée fixe*, the idea of equality. His explanation is sublimely naïve. These things were invented for the sake of equality, but unfortunately they have turned against equality. That is the whole of his argument. In other words, he makes a gratuitous assumption and, because actual development contradicts his fiction at every turn, he concludes that there is a contradiction. He conceals the fact that there is a contradiction only between his *idées fixes* and the real movement.

Thus Mr Proudhon, chiefly because he doesn't know history, fails to see that, in developing his productive faculties, i.e. in living, man develops certain inter-relations, and that the nature of these relations necessarily changes with the modification and the growth of the said productive faculties. He fails to see that *economic categories* are but *abstractions* of those real relations, that they are truths only in so far as those relations continue to exist. Thus he falls into the error of bourgeois economists who regard those economic categories as eternal laws and not as historical laws which are laws only for a given historical development, a specific development of the productive forces. Thus, instead of regarding politico-economic categories as abstractions of actual social relations that are transitory and historical, Mr Proudhon, by a mystical inversion, sees in the real relations only the embodiment of those abstractions. Those abstractions are themselves formulas which have been slumbering in the bosom of God the Father since the beginning of the world.

But here our good Mr Proudhon falls prey to severe intellectual convulsions. If all these economic categories are emanations of God's heart, if they are the hidden and eternal life of man, how is it, first, that there is any development and, secondly, that Mr Proudhon is not a conservative? He explains these evident contradictions in terms of a whole system of antagonisms.

In order to explain this system of antagonisms, let us take an example.

Monopoly is good because it is an economic category, hence an emanation of God. Competition is good because it, too, is an economic category. But what is not good is the reality of monopoly and the reality of competition. And what is even worse is that monopoly and competition mutually devour each other. What is to be done about it? Because these two eternal thoughts of God contradict each other, it seems clear to him that, in God's bosom, there is likewise a synthesis of these two thoughts in which the evils of monopoly are balanced by competition and vice versa. The result of the struggle between the two ideas will be that only the good aspects will be thrown into relief. This secret idea need only be wrested from God and put into practice and all will be for the best; the synthetic formula concealed in the night of mankind's impersonal reason must be revealed. Mr Proudhon does not hesitate for a moment to act as revealer.

But take a brief glance at real life. In present-day economic life you will find, not only competition and monopoly, but also their synthesis, which is not a *formula* but a *movement.* Monopoly produces competition, competition produces monopoly. That equation, however, far from alleviating the difficulties of the present situation, as bourgeois economists suppose, gives rise to a situation even more difficult and involved. Thus, by changing the basis upon which the present economic relations rest, by abolishing the present *mode* of production, you abolish not only competition, monopoly and their antagonism, but also their unity, their synthesis, the movement whereby a true balance is maintained between competition and monopoly.

Let me now give you an example of Mr Proudhon's dialectics.

Freedom and *slavery* constitute an antagonism. There is no need for me to speak either of the good or of the bad aspects of freedom. As for slavery, there is no need for me to speak of its bad aspects. The only thing requiring explanation is the good side of slavery. I do not mean indirect slavery, the slavery of proletariat; I mean direct slavery, the slavery of the Blacks in Surinam, in Brazil, in the southern regions of North America.

Direct slavery is as much the pivot upon which our present-day industrialism turns as are machinery, credit, etc. Without slavery there would be no cotton, without cotton there would be no modern industry. It is slavery which has given value to the colonies, it is the colonies which have created world trade, and world trade is the necessary condition for large-scale machine industry. Consequently, prior to the slave trade, the colonies sent very few products to the Old World, and did not noticeably change the face of the world. Slavery is therefore an economic category of paramount importance. Without slavery, North America, the most progressive nation, would be transformed into a patriarchal country. Only wipe North America off the map and you will get anarchy, the complete decay of trade and modern civilisation. But to do away with slavery would be to wipe America off the map. Being an economic category, slavery has existed in all nations since the beginning of the world. All that modern nations have achieved is to disguise slavery at home and import it openly into the New World. After these reflections on slavery, what will the good Mr Proudhon do? He will seek the synthesis of liberty and slavery, the true golden mean, in other words the balance between slavery and liberty.

Mr Proudhon understands perfectly well that men manufacture worsted, linens and silks; and whatever credit is due for understanding such a trifle! What Mr Proudhon does not understand is that, according to their faculties, men also produce the *social relations* in which they produce worsted and linens. Still less does Mr Proudhon understand that those who produce social relations in conformity with their material productivity also produce the *ideas, categories,* i.e. the ideal abstract expressions of those same social relations. Indeed, the categories are no more eternal than the relations they express. They are historical and transitory products. To Mr Proudhon, on the contrary, the prime cause consists in abstractions and categories. According to him it is these and not men which make history. *The abstraction, the category regarded as such,* i.e. as distinct from man and his material activity, is, of course, immortal, immutable, impassive. It is nothing but an entity of pure reason, which is only another way of saying that an abstraction, regarded as such, is abstract. An admirable *tautology!*

Hence, to Mr Proudhon, economic relations, seen in the form of categories, are eternal formulas without origin or progress.

To put it another way: Mr Proudhon does not directly assert that to him *bourgeois life* is an *eternal truth*; he says so indirectly, by deifying the categories which express bourgeois relations in the form of thought. He regards the products of bourgeois society as spontaneous entities, endowed with a life of their own, eternal, the moment these present themselves to him in the shape of categories, of thought. Thus he fails to rise above the bourgeois horizon. Because he operates with bourgeois thoughts and assumes them to be eternally true, he looks for the synthesis of those thoughts, their balance, and fails to see that their present manner of maintaining a balance is the only possible one.

In fact he does what all good bourgeois do. They all maintain that competition, monopoly, etc., are, in principle—i.e. regarded as abstract thoughts—the only basis for existence, but leave a great deal to be desired in practice. What they all want is competition without the pernicious consequences of competition. They all want the impossible, i.e. the conditions of bourgeois existence without the necessary consequences of those conditions. They all fail to understand that the bourgeois form of production is an historical and transitory form, just as was the feudal form. This mistake is due to the fact that, to them, bourgeois man is the only possible basis for any society, and that they cannot envisage a state of society in which man will have ceased to be bourgeois.

Hence Mr Proudhon is necessarily *doctrinaire*. The historical movement by which the present world is convulsed resolves itself, so far as he is concerned, into the problem of discovering the right balance, the synthesis of two bourgeois thoughts. Thus, by subtlety, the clever fellow discovers God's secret thought, the unity of two isolated thoughts which are isolated thoughts only because Mr Proudhon has isolated them from practical life, from present-day production, which is the combination of the realities they express. In place of the great historical movement which is born of the conflict between the productive forces already acquired by man, and his social relations which no longer correspond to those productive forces, in the place of the terrible wars now imminent between the various classes of a nation and between the various nations, in place of practical and violent action on the part of the masses, which is alone capable of resolving those conflicts, in place of that movement—vast, prolonged and complex—Mr Proudhon puts the cacky-dauphin movement [136] of his own mind. Thus it is the savants, the men able to filch from God his inmost thoughts, who make history. All the lesser fry have to do is put their revelations into practice.

Now you will understand why Mr Proudhon is the avowed enemy of all political movements. For him, the solution of present-day problems does not consist in public action but in the dialectical rotations of his brain. Because to him the categories are the motive force, it is not necessary to change practical life in order to change the categories; on the contrary, it is necessary to change the categories, whereupon actual society will change as a result.

In his desire to reconcile contradictions Mr Proudhon does not ask himself whether the very basis of those contradictions ought not to be subverted. He is exactly like the political doctrinaire who wants a king and a chamber of deputies and a chamber of peers as integral parts of social life, as eternal categories. Only he seeks a new formula with which to balance those powers (whose balance consists precisely in the actual movement in which one of those powers is now the conqueror now the slave of the other). In the eighteenth century, for instance, a whole lot of mediocre minds busied themselves with finding the true formula with which to maintain a balance between the social estates, the nobility, the king, the parliaments,[137] etc., and the next day there was neither king, nor parliament, nor nobility. The proper balance between the aforesaid antagonisms consisted in the convulsion of all the social relations which served as a basis for those feudal entities and for the antagonism between those feudal entities.

Because Mr Proudhon posits on the one hand eternal ideas, the categories of pure reason, and, on the other, man and his practical life which, according to him, is the practical application of these categories, you will find in him from the very outset a *dualism* between life and ideas, between soul and body—a dualism which recurs in many forms. So you now see that the said antagonism is nothing other than Mr Proudhon's inability to understand either the origin or the profane history of the categories he has deified.

My letter is already too long for me to mention the absurd case Mr Proudhon is conducting against communism. For the present you will concede that a man who has failed to understand the present state of society must be even less able to understand either the movement which tends to overturn it or the literary expression of that revolutionary movement.

The *only point* upon which I am in complete agreement with Mr Proudhon is the disgust he feels for socialist sentimentalising. I anticipated him in provoking considerable hostility by the ridicule I directed at ovine, sentimental, utopian socialism. But is not Mr Proudhon subject to strange delusions when he opposes his petty-bourgeois sentimentality, by which I mean his homilies about home, conjugal love and suchlike banalities, to socialist sentimentality which—as for instance in Fourier's case—is infinitely more profound than the presumptuous platitudes of our worthy Proudhon? He himself is so well aware of the emptiness of his reasoning, of his complete inability to discuss such things, that he indulges in tantrums, exclamations and *irae hominis probi,*[a] that he

---

[a] the anger of an upright man

fumes, curses, denounces, cries pestilence and infamy, thumps his chest and glorifies himself before God and man as being innocent of socialist infamies! It is not as a critic that he derides socialist sentimentalities, or what he takes to be sentimentalities. It is as a saint, a pope, that he excommunicates the poor sinners and sings the praises of the petty bourgeoisie and of the miserable patriarchal amorous illusions of the domestic hearth. Nor is this in any way fortuitous. Mr Proudhon is, from top to toe, a philosopher, an economist of the petty bourgeoisie. In an advanced society and because of his situation, *a petty bourgeois* becomes a socialist on the one hand, and economist on the other, i.e. he is dazzled by the magnificence of the upper middle classes and feels compassion for the sufferings of the people. He is at one and the same time bourgeois and man of the people. In his heart of hearts he prides himself on his impartiality, on having found the correct balance, allegedly distinct from the happy medium. A petty bourgeois of this kind deifies *contradiction,* for contradiction is the very basis of his being. He is nothing but social contradiction in action. He must justify by means of theory what he is in practice, and Mr Proudhon has the merit of being the scientific exponent of the French petty bourgeoisie, which is a real merit since the petty bourgeoisie will be an integral part of all the impending social revolutions.

With this letter I should have liked to send you my book on political economy,[5] but up till now I have been unable to have printed either this work or the critique of German philosophers and socialists[a] which I mentioned to you in Brussels. You would never believe what difficulties a publication of this kind runs into in Germany, on the one hand from the police, on the other from the booksellers, who are themselves the interested representatives of all those tendencies I attack. And as for our own party, not only is it poor, but there is a large faction in the German communist party which bears me a grudge because I am opposed to its utopias and its declaiming.

Ever yours

Charles Marx

P.S. Perhaps you may wonder why I should be writing in bad French rather than in good German. It is because I am dealing with a French writer.

---

[a] K. Marx and F. Engels, *The German Ideology.*

You would greatly oblige me by not keeping me waiting too long for a reply, as I am anxious to know whether you understand me wrapped up as I am in my barbarous French.

First published in extracts in Russian in *Vestnik Yevropy*, Vol. 15, Book 4, St. Petersburg, 1880 and in full in the French original in *M. M. Stasyulevich i yego sovremenniki v ikh perepiske* [M. M. Stasyulevich and His Contemporaries in Their Correspondence]. Vol. III, 1912

Printed according to the original

Translated from the French

1847

37

ENGELS TO MARX [138]

IN BRUSSELS

[Paris,] Friday, 15 January 1847

Dear Marx,

I would have written to you sooner had Bernays not left me in the lurch. That damned Börnstein, who was one of the people of whom I inquired about your coming here,[139] was never to be found, and I therefore entrusted the matter to Bernays, who said he would come to town on *Monday*[a] at the latest, bringing a letter for you. Instead I received late last night the enclosed scrawl which the lazy fellow had dashed off in Sarcelles the day before yesterday evening, the explanation it contains being hardly of the kind to necessitate 5-6 days' study. But that's the sort of chap he is. I shall, by the way, speak to Börnstein *personally,* for I'm far from satisfied with this explanation and, to be honest, there is no one whose word I trust less than that of Bernays. For six months the man's been drumming into me that you could come here any day, with bag and baggage, and, now that it comes to the point, he makes all this to-do about a passport. As though you needed a passport! No one asks for it at the frontier; Moses[b] came here without anyone asking just as I did and, if you stay with me, I should like to know who is going to ask for it. At most, a Belgian *passeport pour l'intérieur*[c] to establish your identity if necessary, or Mr Leopold's well-known missive: *Cabinet du Roi*[d] — which would suffice for all eventualities. Heine is of exactly the same opinion and, as soon as I can get hold of Börnstein, I'll ask him about it.

Bernays, too, had invented the Tolstoy affair,[e] or rather had been led by Börnstein to believe it, for Börnstein can *make him*

---

[a] 11 January 1847 - [b] Hess - [c] inland passport - [d] King's private secretariat - [e] See this volume, p. 65.

believe anything he choses. All the various items of news contained in
Bernays' earlier letters to us come from the same source and,
having on a number of occasions witnessed the air of infallibility
assumed by Börnstein when spouting his suppositions, his
tittle-tattle and his own fabrications to Bernays, who takes
everything at its face value, I no longer believe *a single word* of all
those important news items 'from the best of sources' which he has
conveyed to us in the past.

I saw with my own eyes how Börnstein, merely by affecting
omniscience, made Bernays believe (and you know with what
enthusiasm Bernays *believes once* he does believe) that the *National*
had been sold lock, stock and barrel, body and soul, to Thiers,
argent± comptant.[a] The little man[b] would have been willing to stake
his life on it. He's as incorrigible in this respect as in his highly
exalted mortally melancholy disposition. *Pendant le cours de la
dernière quinzaine il a été seize fois au bord du désespoir.*[c]

Cela entre nous.[d] I shall ask Börnstein again what he thinks about
your coming here; Heine, as already mentioned, maintains that
you can come in all confidence. Or would you prefer to go to the
French Ambassador[e] and demand a passport on the strength of
your Prussian emigration certificate?

It was very good of you to let me know about Moses' advent.
The worthy man came to see me, didn't find me in, I wrote and
told him to arrange a rendezvous. This took place yesterday. The
man has changed a great deal. His head is adorned with youthful
locks, a dainty little beard lends some grace to his angular jaw, a
virginal blush hovered about his cheeks, but *la grandeur déchue se
peignait dans ses beaux yeux*[f] and a strange modesty had come over
him. Here in Paris I have come to adopt a very insolent manner,
for bluster is all in the day's work, and it works well with the
female sex. But the ravished exterior of that erstwhile world-
shaking high-flyer, Hess, all but disarmed me. However, the
heroic deeds of the true socialists, his disciples (of whom more
anon), and his own, unchanged inner self, restored my courage.[140]
Suffice it to say that my treatment of him was so cold and scornful
that he will have no desire to return. All I did for him was to give
him some good advice about the clap he had brought with him
from Germany. He was also a complete fiasco with a number of
German painters, some of whom he had known before. Only
Gustav Adolf Köttgen has remained faithful to him.

---

a cash more or less down - b K. L. Bernays - c In the course of the past fortnight
he has been sixteen times on the brink of despair. - d This between ourselves. -
e M. H. Rumigny - f fallen greatness was reflected in his fine eyes

The man in Bremen[a] is at any rate preferable to the one in Switzerland.[b] I cannot write to the Swiss, 1. because I have forgotten his address, 2. because I don't want to propose to the fellow a lower fee per sheet than you are proposing to the Bremen man. So [let me know] your proposals for the Bremen man, and at the same time send me the fellow's address. He paid Bernays well for his bad Rothschild pamphlet,[c] but he cheated Püttmann, printing his stuff,[d] but indefinitely postponing payment of the fee on the pretext that his capital was tied up.

Splendid that you should be attacking Proudhon in French. I hope the pamphlet will be finished by the time this reaches you. That you can anticipate as much as you wish of our publication goes without saying *so far as I am concerned.* I too believe that Proudhon's association amounts to the same thing as Bray's plan.[141] I had quite forgotten about the good Bray.

You may have read in the *Trier'sche Zeitung* about the new Leipzig socialist periodical called *Veilchen,*[e] a sheet for *inoffensive* modern criticism!![f] wherein Mr Semmig, as Sarastro, bellows:

"We know no thought of vengeance within these temple walls, where love leads back to duty who'er from duty falls, by frie-ie-ie-iendship's kindly hand held fast, he finds the land of light at last."[g]

But unfortunately, unlike the late Reichel, he hasn't got a bass voice to match. Here Sarastro-Semmig is sacrificing to the 3 deities: 1) Hess—2) Stirner—3) Ruge—all in one breath. The two former have [plumbed] the depths of knowledge. This humble sheet, or humble violet is the craziest thing I have ever read. Such unobtrusive and at the same time insolent insanity is possible only in Saxony.

If only we could rewrite the chapter on 'true socialists' now that they've spread in every direction, now that the Westphalian school, the Saxon school, the Berlin school, etc., etc., have set themselves up separately, alongside the lonely stars of Püttmann, etc.[142] They could be classified according to the celestial constellations. Püttmann the Great Bear, and Semmig the Little Bear, or Püttmann Taurus, and the Pleiades his 8 children. Anyway, he

---

[a] Kühtmann. Reference to a publisher who could possibly print Marx and Engels' *The German Ideology.* - [b] J. M. Schläpfer. - [c] [K. L. Bernays,] *Rothschild. Ein Ur-theilsspruch vom menschlichen Standpunkte aus.* - [d] A reference to Püttmann's *Prometheus.* - [e] Violets - [f] Report from Leipzig of 6 January 1847 in *Trier'sche Zeitung,* No. 12, 12 January 1847. - [g] Mozart's opera *The Magic Flute* (libretto by Emanuel Schikaneder), Act II, aria of Sarastro.

deserves horns if he hasn't already got them. Grün Aquarius and so on.

A propos Grün, I intend to revise the article on Grün's Goethe,[a] reducing it to a $^1/_2$ or $^3/_4$ sheet and adapting it for our publication,[b] *if* you are agreeable; write to me soon about this.[143] The book is too characteristic; Grün extols all Goethe's *philistinisms* as *human*, making out that Goethe, the citizen of Frankfurt and the *official*,[144] is the 'true human being', while passing over if not reviling all that is colossal and of genius. To such an extent that this book provides the most splendid proof of the fact that *human being= German petty bourgeois*. This I had no more than touched on, but I could elaborate it and more or less cut out the remainder of the article, since it isn't suitable for our thing. What do you think?

Your
Engels

[On the back of the letter]

Monsieur Charles Marx, 42, rue d'Orléans, Faubourg de Namur, Bruxelles

First published abridged in *Der Briefwechsel zwischen F. Engels und K. Marx*, Bd. 1, Stuttgart, 1913 and in full in *MEGA*, Abt. III, Bd. 1, 1929

Printed according to the original

Published in English in full for the first time

38

MARX TO ROLAND DANIELS

IN COLOGNE

[Brussels,] 7 March [1847]

Dear Daniels,

You or *one of the others in Cologne* may get a letter from Hess about communist affairs. I would urgently ask that *none* of *you* should answer until I have provided you with documents and

---

[a] K. Grün, *Über Goethe vom menschlichen Standpunkte.* - [b] K. Marx and F. Engels, *The German Ideology.*

letters through W.[a] At all events, I must again *urgently* request you
to *come here.* I have some important things to tell you which cannot
be communicated by post. If *you* can't come, then H. Bürgers must
spend a few days here. You or your representative will stay with
me....[b]

So either you or H. Bürgers come to *Malines* as soon as
possible.

Forward the enclosed letter to *Zulauff,*[145] Grünstrasse, Elberfeld.

Do not come to *Brussels* but to *Malines* and write the day before
to say when you or Bürgers are coming.

You can neglect your bourgeois affairs for a day or two.

Your

Marx

First published in: Marx and Engels,
Works, First Russian Edition, Vol. XXV,
Moscow, 1934

Printed according to the original

Published in English for the first
time

39

ENGELS TO MARX

IN BRUSSELS

[Paris,] Tuesday, 9 March [1847]

Dear Marx,

The wee pamphlet enclosed was delivered to me this morning
by Junge; Ewerbeck had brought it to them a few days ago.
Having looked at the thing, I declared it to be by Moses[c] and
explained this to Junge, point by point. This evening I saw
Ewerbeck, who confessed that he had brought it to them and,
after I had thoroughly demolished the thing, came out with the
information that he himself, Ewerbeck, was the author of the

---

[a] Probably Georg Weerth or Joseph Weydemeyer - [b] The remainder of the letter
is missing, save for the next sentences, which are written in the margin. After the
words 'with me' Marx added 'see above'. - [c] Hess

pretty concoction. He wrote it, he maintains, during the months that followed my arrival here, inspired by the first rapture into which he had been thrown by the novelties I communicated. That's how these lads are. While mocking Hess for decking himself out in borrowed plumes that didn't suit him, and forbidding the Straubingers [146] to convey what I had told them to Grün lest he purloin it, he sits him down and—with the best intentions in the world, as always—conducts himself no whit better. Moses and Grün could not have more thoroughly bungled matters than this homespun clap-doctor. I, of course, first made fun of him a little and ended up by forbidding him ever to give vent to such stuff again. But it's in these people's bones. Last week I sat down and, partly out of foolishness, partly because I absolutely had to have some money, wrote for anonymous publication a letter, pullulating with smutty jokes, in which I expressed gratitude to Lola Montez.[147] On Saturday I read him some bits out of it, and this evening he tells me, with his customary *bonhomie*, that this inspired him to produce something similar and that he did so the very next day on the same subject, handing it in to Mäurer for his anonymous periodical [a] (it really does appear quite sub rosa and only for the benefit of the editors, being censored by Madame Mäurer, who has already blue-pencilled a poem by Heine). He was, he said, telling me about this in good time to save his honour and avoid committing a plagiarism! This fresh masterpiece by this passionately keen author will, of course, simply be my joke translated into a solemnly effusive style. This most recent exercise of the short gut, though of no significance, shows how extremely urgent it is that either your book or our manuscripts [b] should appear as soon as possible. The fellows are all worried by the thought that such splendid ideas should remain so long concealed from the people, and can think up no better way of getting this load off their minds than by voiding as much of it as they think they have *passablement* [c] digested. So don't let the Bremen man [d] slip through your fingers. If he doesn't reply, write again and accept a minimum, if needs must. Each month they lie idle these manuscripts lose 5-10 fr. per sheet in EXCHANGEABLE VALUE. A few months from now, with *la diète prussienne* [148] *en discussion, la querelle bien entamée à Berlin,* [e] Bauer

---

[a] [H. Ewerbeck,] 'Hier Baiern!—Hier Andalusia!', *Die Pariser Horen,* April 1847. - [b] K. Marx, *The Poverty of Philosophy* and Marx and Engels' *The German Ideology.* - [c] tolerably well - [d] Kühtmann - [e] the Prussian Diet in debate, the dispute well under way in Berlin

and Stirner will not fetch more than 10 fr. per sheet. With such a topical work one gradually gets to the stage where the high fee demanded as a writer's *point d'honneur* has to be completely set aside.

I spent about a week with Bernays in Sarcelles. He too does stupid things. Writes for the *Berliner Zeitungs-Halle* and is happy as a sandboy that his *soidisant*[a] communist anti-bourgeois expectorations appear in it. The editors and censors naturally allow anything purely anti-bourgeois to stand, but delete the few references that might also reflect unpleasantly on themselves. Fulminates about juries, 'bourgeois freedom of the press', the representation system, etc. I explain to him that this means literally working *pour le roi de Prusse*,[b] and indirectly, against our party—usual warm-hearted outpourings, impossibility of effecting anything; I point out that the *Zeitungs-Halle* is in the pay of the government, obstinate denials, references to symptoms which, in the eyes of everyone save the sensitive inhabitants of Sarcelles, precisely bear out my contention. Result: Inability of warm heart, ingenuous enthusiasm, to write contrary to its convictions, to comprehend any policy that spares those who hitherto were the objects of its mortal hatred. 'Ain't in me nature!' the inevitable *ultima ratio*.[c] I have read x of these articles dated from Paris; they are *on ne peut plus*[d] in the interests of the government and in the style of true socialism. I feel inclined to give up Bernays and to meddle no more in the high-minded and repellent family woes in which he plays the *heros des dévouements*,[e] of boundless devotion. *Il faut avoir vu cela.*[f] The stench is like five thousand unaired featherbeds, multiplied by the release therein of innumerable farts—the result of Austrian vegetable cookery. And though the fellow should ten times tear himself away from the riff-raff and come to Paris, he will return to them as often. You can imagine the kind of moralising humbug all this puts into his head. The *mode composée*[g] family in which he lives is turning him into a perfect narrow-minded philistine. He'll never get me to come to his *boutique*[h] again, nor is he likely to feel any urgent desire to see so unfeeling an individual as myself.

You will very soon be receiving the pamphlet on the Constitution.[i] I shall write it on separate sheets, so that you can insert and

---

[a] self-styled - [b] for the King of Prussia, i. e. for nothing - [c] last argument - [d] as much as they could be - [e] hero of devotion - [f] It has to be seen. - [g] complex kind of - [h] place (literally: shop) - [i] F. Engels, *The Constitutional Question in Germany.*

discard.[149] If there's any prospect of Vogler paying something, ask him if he will take the Lola Montez joke—approx. $1^1/_2$-2 sheets, but you needn't tell him the thing originated with me. Let me know *by return,* for otherwise I shall try in Belle-Vue. You'll have seen from the *Débats* or the *Constitutionnel* that, as a result of complaints made by Württemberg, the Great Council has made it impossible for the scoundrelly Schläpfer in Herisau to go on publishing revolutionary stuff; he himself has confirmed this in letters to us and has asked that *nothing further* be sent to him. All the more reason, therefore, to maintain contact with the man in Bremen. If nothing at all comes of it with him, there remains only the publishers and booksellers in Belle-Vue near Constance. *Au reste,*[a] should the placing of our manuscripts clash with the placing of your book, then, for heaven's sake, chuck the manuscripts into a corner, for it's far more important that your book should appear. We're neither of us likely to make much out of our work in that quarter.

In yesterday's (Monday's) *Kölner Zeitung* you may have seen a smug article on the scandalous affair of Martin du Nord.[b] That article was by Bernays—from time to time he takes Börnstein's place as correspondent.

The police here are in a very ugly mood just now. It would seem that, by hook or by crook, they are determined to exploit the food shortage to provoke a riot or a mass conspiracy. First they scatter all manner of leaflets about; put up *placats incendiaires,*[c] and now they have even manufactured and strewn around fire-raising devices which, however, *were not set alight,* in order to make plain to the *épicier*[d] the lengths to which diabolical wickedness can go. On top of this they began a fine game with the *communistes matérialistes*[150] arresting a whole mass of fellows, among whom A knows B, B knows C, C knows D, etc., and now, on the strength of these acquaintanceships and a few statements made by witnesses, they transmogrify the whole lot of them, for the most part unknown to each other, into a 'gang'. The trial of this 'gang' is soon to take place, and if the old *complicité morale* be added to this new system, any individual you care to name can be sentenced without more ado. *Cela sent son Hébert.*[e] By this means, nothing could be easier than to pin something even on *père* Cabet.

---

[a] for the rest - [b] Probably a report from Paris 'Affaire Martin du Nord' published in the *Kölnische Zeitung,* No. 67, 8 March 1847. - [c] inflammatory posters - [d] grocer - [e] It stinks of Hébert

If at all possible, do come here some time in April. By 7 April I shall be moving—I don't yet know where to—and about that time I shall also have a little money. So for a time we could enjoy ourselves famously, squandering our all in taverns. However, since the police are being beastly at the moment [151] (besides the Saxon I wrote to you about, my old opponent Eisermann was banished; both have remained here, cf. K. Grün in the *Kölner Zeitung*[a]), it might be as well to follow Börnstein's advice. Try to obtain a passport from the French Ambassador[b] *on the grounds of your emigration*; if that doesn't work, we'll see what can be done at this end—no doubt there is still a conservative deputy who can be persuaded to help. It's absolutely essential that you get out of *ennuyante*[c] Brussels for once and come to Paris, and I for my part have a great desire to go carousing with you. Either *mauvais sujet*[d] or schoolmaster; these are the only alternatives open to one here; a *mauvais sujet* among disreputable good-for-nothings, *et cela vous va fort mal quand vous n'avez pas d'argent,*[e] or schoolmaster to Ewerbeck, Bernays and Co. Or else submit to wise counsel from the leaders of the French radicals which one must later vindicate among the other jackasses lest they unduly flaunt their bloated Germanness. If I had an income of 5,000 fr. I would do nothing but work and amuse myself with women until I went to pieces. If there were no Frenchwomen, life wouldn't be worth living. *Mais tant qu'il y a des grisettes, va! Cela n'empêche pas*[f] one from sometimes wishing to discuss a decent topic or enjoy life with a measure of refinement, neither of which is possible with anyone in the whole band of my acquaintances. You must come here.

Have you seen L. Blanc's *Revolution*[g]? A wild mixture of correct hunches and unbounded craziness. I only read half of the first volume while at Sarcelles *Ça fait un drôle d'effet.*[h] Hardly has he surprised one with some nice observation when he falls head over heels into the most dreadful lunacy. But L. Blanc has a good nose and, despite all the lunacy, the scent he is on is by no means bad. Yet he will get no further than the point he has already reached, being 'rooted to the spot by a spell'—ideology.

---

[a] Reference to [K. Grün,] 'Über die Ausweisung von Eisermann und Anderen', *Kölnische Zeitung*, No. 60, 1 March 1847. - [b] M. H. Rumigny - [c] vexatious - [d] scamp - [e] and that suits you very badly when you have no money - [f] But so long as there are grisettes, well and good! That doesn't prevent - [g] L. Blanc, *Histoire de la révolution française*, t. 1, Paris, 1847. - [h] It makes a curious impression.

Do you know Achille de Vaulabelle's *Chute de l'Empire, Histoire des deux Restaurations?* Came out last year, a republican on the *National,* and in the historiographical manner of the old school— before Thierry, Mignet, etc. Abysmal lack of insight into the most ordinary relations—in this respect even Capefigue in his *Cent jours* does infinitely better—but interesting on account of the Bourbon and allied basenesses, all of which he catalogues, and of a fairly exact representation and criticism of the facts in so far as his national and political interests don't obtrude. On the whole tediously written, however, precisely because of a lack of perspective. The *National* is a bad historian, and Vaulabelle is said to be Marrast's *amicus.*[a]

Moses has vanished completely. He *promises* to give lectures to those *ouvriers*[b] with whom I do *not* 'consort', makes himself out to be Grün's opponent and my intimate friend! God knows and so does Moses that, at our second and last *entrevue*[c] in the Passage Vivienne, the painter Körner and I left him standing agape, in order to lead astray two girls Körner had picked up. Since then I have only met him once, on *mardi gras,*[d] when he was dragging his world-weary self through the most dreadful downpour and the most arid boredom in the direction of the Exchange. We didn't even deign to recognise each other.

I will take care of the letter to Bakunin[152] as soon as I am sure of his address—up to now it is still *chanceux.*[e]

Apropos, do write to Ewerbeck about the wee pamphlet and make fun of him a little; he is most humbly presenting *ambas posaderas*[f] and is anxious to see blows rained down upon them—you know what I mean.

Well then, write soon and see to it that you come here.

Your
F. E.

First published slightly abridged in *Der Briefwechsel zwischen F. Engels und K. Marx,* Bd. 1, Stuttgart, 1913 and in full in *MEGA,* Abt. III, Bd. 1, 1929

Printed according to the original

Published in English for the first time

---

[a] friend - [b] workers - [c] interview - [d] Shrove Tuesday - [e] a matter of chance - [f] both buttocks

40

MARX TO ENGELS

IN PARIS

[Brussels,] 15 May [1847]

Dear Engels,

As you know, Vogler has been under arrest in Aachen since the beginning of May.[a] This has for the time being precluded the possibility of getting the pamphlet[b] you sent here into print. The first $^1/_3$ of it I liked very much. The other 2 will in any case need some alteration. Something more specific on this point in my next.

I enclose the print of your cartoon. I sent it to the Brüsseler-Zeitung.[153]

As for the truly nauseous article by Grün or his associates in the Trier'sche Zeitung,[c] it is of course now too late; it would have been good if at the outset you had published a two-line counter-statement in the same rag.

I cannot go to London, not having sufficient funds. But we hope to send Wolff over. And then it will be enough that the two of you are there.[154]

Voce[d] money:

You will remember that Hess owes me and my brother-in-law Edgar[e] money from the Gesellschaftsspiegel. So I am drawing a bill on him from here, payable 30 days at sight. Bernays likewise has owed me 150 fr. since May of last year. So he too will also be presented with a bill.

I would therefore ask you to do the following:

1. First send me the addresses of both;

2. Inform both of them of the facts and tell the jackasses

3. that if they believe they will be unable to pay the respective sums by 15 June, they are nevertheless to accept the bills. I shall then arrange for cover in Paris. Naturally you will only inform the jackasses of the latter if absolutely unavoidable.

At the moment I'm in such financial straits that I have had to have recourse to drawing bills, and after all I don't intend to make

---

[a] The original is inaccurate: Vogler was arrested at the beginning of April 1847 and returned to Brussels on 17 June. - [b] F. Engels, The Constitutional Question in Germany. - [c] Reference to a report from Paris of 13 April published in the section 'Frankreich' of the Trier'sche Zeitung, No. 107, 17 April 1847. - [d] as regards - [e] Edgar von Westphalen

the two jackasses a present of anything. Should the asses only *feign* acceptance of the bills, I must, of course, know at once.

Since the matter is *very pressing,* I expect you not to let a day go by before setting everything in order and *informing* me.

Here in Brussels I have managed to hunt out an *escompteur.*[a]

I cannot write to you at any greater length. About 12 days ago Breyer let a *vein,* but in my *right* arm instead of the *left.* Since I went on working as though nothing had happened, the wound festered instead of closing. The thing could have been dangerous and cost me my arm. Now it's as good as healed. But the arm's still weak. Mustn't be overtaxed.

Your
Marx

[From Gigot]

My dear Fritzchen,

I am just in the middle of reading your pamphlet—so far it has amused me greatly—and feel really happy that I *ain't no* German. May God or Reason or Race preserve us from the petty bourgeoisie!

Avec laquelle j'ai l'honneur d'être.[b]

YOURS MOST TRULY
Philippe

P.S. Do drop me *un demi mot*[c] sometime.

First published abridged in *Der Briefwechsel zwischen F. Engels und K. Marx,* Bd. 1, Stuttgart, 1913 and in full in *MEGA,* Abt. III, Bd. 1, 1929

Printed according to the original

Published in English for the first time

41

MARX TO GEORG HERWEGH

IN PARIS

Brussels, 27 July [1847]
Faubourg d'Ixelles, rue d'Orléans 42

Dear Herwegh,

Engels has just arrived here for a few weeks from Paris,[155] whence he has brought the following anecdote; I should be glad if you would elucidate it at the earliest opportunity.

---

[a] a bill discounter - [b] With which I have the honour to be - [c] a few words

Bernays told Ewerbeck: Herwegh came to see me and said that Marx had welcomed him in such a friendly manner that he seemed *to want something* of him. Bernays then gave Ewerbeck his unqualified permission to pass on this *bon mot*.

I would not, of course, put pen to paper on account of this piece of gossip had it not achieved a kind of notoriety among my acquaintances in Paris.

I would therefore request you to tell me categorically by return whether or not there is any truth in this.

Your
Marx

First published in: Marx and Engels, *Works,* First Russian Edition, Vol. XXV, Moscow, 1934

Printed according to the original
Published in English for the first time

42

MARX TO GEORG HERWEGH [155a]
IN PARIS

Brussels, 8 August [1847]

Dear Herwegh,

I hasten to acknowledge receipt of your letter. I learn no more from it than I already knew in advance, namely that the whole thing was the most miserable piece of tattle. All I wanted was a few lines from you in order to show Engels in black and white the nature of German petty bourgeois gossip in Paris. I assure you that, since I moved from Paris, and despite all the precautions I have taken to make myself unfindable and inaccessible, these old women have continued to pursue me with trifles of this kind. Only by being excessively rude can one free oneself of these fools.

I am only sorry to have disturbed you with such stuff in your retreat.—It's typical of these old women to want to hush up and sugar over any genuine party struggle while mistaking for revolutionary activity the German habit of gossiping and making trouble. *Les malheureux.*[a] Here in Brussels we don't suffer from that *misère* at least.

---

[a] The wretches.

The Prussian Embassy here has been vigilantly shadowing and observing Bornstedt in order to catch him out in some transgression or other. At last they've succeeded. They *denounced* him and brought down 3 actions on his head: 1) fiscal, for contravening the stamp law, 2) political, for saying in his paper[a] that Louis Philippe ought to be killed, 3) an action for calumniating a Belgian grandee, Mr *Osy*, whom Bornstedt had accused, and rightly so, of profiteering on corn.

None of the 3 actions is of any consequence here, and they will almost certainly result in making the Prussian Embassy, already little esteemed, appear ridiculous. What have Louis Philippe, Osy and the Belgian stamp law to do with them?

The examining magistrate himself[b] declared that all these actions were *pour le roi de Prusse.*[c] The *Brüsseler-Zeitung*, on the other hand, which, despite its many failings, does have some merit and might well have improved,[156] particularly now that Bornstedt has expressed his readiness to help us in every way, is threatened with a sudden pecuniary disaster. How have the noble Teutons behaved in this affair? The booksellers have *cheated* Bornstedt because he couldn't prosecute them. The opposition of all shades, instead of lifting a finger to help, whether in the literary or financial sense, found it more convenient to take exception to the name of Bornstedt. And will such people ever be short of excuses for doing nothing? Now it's the man who's no good, now the wife, now the policy, now the style, now the format—or even the distribution is more or less risky, etc., etc. These gentry want things presented to them on a platter. If there's only *one* opposition paper which is immune from censorship, which is a thorn in the flesh of the government, and whose editor, by the very logic of the enterprise, shows himself complaisant towards all that is progressive, is not this above all an opportunity to be exploited? And, if the paper is inadequate, to make it adequate? But no, our Germans always have 1,000 wise sayings up their sleeve to show why they must let an opportunity slip. An opportunity to do something is to them only a source of embarrassment.

My manuscripts, too, are faring in much the same way as the *Brüsseler-Zeitung*, and on top of that the jackasses keep writing to me day after day, asking why I'm not having anything published, and even reproach me for having written French in preference to

---

[a] *Deutsche-Brüsseler-Zeitung* - [b] Spanoghe - [c] for the King of Prussia, i. e. for nothing.

nothing at all. One will long have to atone for having been born a Teuton.

Farewell. Warm regards to your wife[a] and yourself from my wife and me.

In Paris you'll find an additional list of errata for my French scrawl.[b] Without it some passages are unintelligible.

As soon as you have an hour to spare and nothing better to do, write to your

Marx

[Postscript from Jenny Marx to Emma and Georg Herwegh]

I take advantage of this little space to send you, dear Mrs Herwegh, and your dear husband my hearty greetings. How are you and your two youngsters? They came a little *en retard*[c] compared to my three. We only need a girl to make three couples. My girls[d] are wonderful, but the boy, the boy!![e] *Un petit monstre.*[f] Our best greetings, remember sometimes

Your
Jenny Marx

First published in: *1848. Briefe von und an Georg Herwegh,* Munich, 1896

Printed according to the original

Published in English in full for the first time

43

MARX TO MOSES HESS

IN BRUSSELS

[Brussels,] 2 September [1847]

Dear Hess,

Present yourself today in the *Chaussée d'Etterbeck,* in the Grand Salon, also known as *Palais royal.*

Marx

First published in: Marx and Engels, *Works,* First Russian Edition, Vol. XXV, Moscow, 1934

Printed according to the original

Published in English for the first time

---

[a] Emma - [b] K. Marx. *The Poverty of Philosophy.* - [c] late - [d] Jenny and Laura - [e] Edgar - [f] A little monster.

44

ENGELS TO MARX [157]

IN ZALT-BOMMEL

[Brussels,] 28-30 September 1847

Tuesday, 28 September

Dear Marx,

There has recently been a very curious business here. All those elements among the local Germans who are dissatisfied with us and what we do have formed a coalition for the purpose of overthrowing you, me and the communists in general, and competing with the Workers' Society.[158] *Bornstedt* is exceedingly displeased; the story emanating from Otterberg, passed on and confirmed by Sandkuhl and exploited by Crüger and Moras, to the effect that we were simply exploiting him, Bornstedt, has made him furious with all of us; *Moras* and *Crüger,* who go about complaining of our alleged cavalier treatment of them, have put his back up even further. *Seiler* is annoyed because of the unpardonable neglect he suffered at the founding of the Workers' Society, and because of its good progress, which has given the lie to all his predictions. *Heilberg* is seeking to take spectacular if unbloody revenge for all the slights that have been, and are being, daily meted out to him. Bornstedt, too, is seething because his gifts of books and maps have failed to buy him the status of an influential democrat and honorary membership of, and a place for his bust in, the Society, instead of which his typesetter[a] will, tomorrow evening, put his name to the vote like that of any ordinary mortal. He is also vexed that he, the aristocratic *homme d'esprit,*[b] should find much less opportunity to make fun of the workers than he had hoped. Then Moras is annoyed at having been unable to win over the *Brüsseler-Zeitung* for Heinzen. *Enfin* all these heterogeneous elements agreed upon a coup that was to reduce us one and all to a secondary role vis-à-vis Imbert and the Belgian democrats, and to call into being a society far more grandiose and universal than our uncouth Workers' Society. All these gentlemen were fired by the idea of taking the initiative in something for once, and the cowardly rascals deemed the moment of your absence admirably suited to that end. But they had shamefully miscalculated.

<u>a</u> Karl Wallau - <u>b</u> wit

They therefore decided quite on the sly to arrange a cosmopolitan-democratic supper and there to propose without prior warning
a society *à la* FRATERNAL DEMOCRATS [122] with workers' meetings, etc., etc.
They set up a kind of committee onto which as a matter of form
they co-opted the, to them, completely harmless Imbert. After
hearing all kinds of vague rumours, it was not until Sunday[a]
evening at the Society that I learned anything positive about it
from Bornstedt, and on Monday the meal was to take place. I
could get no details from Bornstedt except that Jottrand, General
Mellinet, Adolf Bartels, Kats, etc., etc., would be there, Poles,
Italians, etc., etc. Although I had no inkling whatever about the
whole coalition (only on Monday morning did I learn that
Bornstedt was somewhat piqued and that Moras and Crüger were
moaning and plotting: about Seiler and Heilberg I knew nothing),
nonetheless I smelled a rat. But it was essential to attend because
of the Belgians and because nothing democratic must be allowed
to take place in little Brussels without our participating. But
something had to be done about forming a group. Wallau and I
accordingly put the matter forward and advocated it vigorously,
upon which some thirty immediately agreed to go. On Monday
morning I was told by Lupus that, besides the *président d'honneur*,
old Mellinet, and the actual chairman, Jottrand, they would have
to have two vice-chairmen, one of whom would be Imbert and the
other a German, preferably a working man. Wallau was, unfortunately, out of the running since he didn't speak French. That's
what he'd been told by Bornstedt. He, Lupus, had replied that in
that case it must be me. I told Lupus that it must be him, but he
refused point-blank. I was also reluctant because I look so awfully
young, but finally I thought that, for all eventualities, it would be
best for me to accept.

We went there in the evening.[159] Bornstedt was all innocence, as
though nothing had as yet been arranged, merely the officials
(*toujours à l'exception de l'Allemand*[b]), and a few registered speakers,
none of whose names, save for Crüger and Moras I was able to
discover; he kept making off to see to the arrangement of the
place, hurried from one person to the next, duping, intriguing,
bootlicking for all he was worth. However I saw no evidence of
any specific intrigue; this didn't transpire till later on. We were at
the Estaminet[c] Liégeois in the Place du Palais de justice. When it
came to electing the officials, Bornstedt, contrary to all that had

---

[a] 26 September - [b] always excepting the German - [c] tavern

6*

been agreed, proposed Wallau. The latter declined through Wolff (Lupus) and had me proposed, this being carried in style. Thus thwarted, the whole plot collapsed. They now ± [a] lost their heads and gave themselves away. After Imbert had proposed the health of the *martyrs de la liberté*, I came out with a toast in French *au souvenir de la révolution de 1792*[b] and, as an afterthought, of the *anniversaire du 1er vendémiaire an I de la république.*[c][160] Crüger followed me with a ludicrous speech during which he dried up and had to resort to his manuscript. Then Moras, who read out an harangue almost entirely devoted to his humble self.[d] Both in German. So confused were their toasts that I have absolutely no recollection of them. Then Pellering in Flemish. The lawyer Spilthoorn of Ghent, speaking French *au peuple anglais*[e] then, to my great astonishment, that hunchbacked spider Heilberg, with a long, school-masterly, vapid speech in French in which he 1) patted himself on the back as editor of the *Atelier Démocratique*; 2) declared that *he*, Maximus Heilberg, had for several months been pursuing— *mais cela doit se dire en français: L'association des ouvriers belges, voilà le but que Je poursuis depuis quelques mois (c. à d. depuis le moment où J'ai daigné prendre connaissance du dernier chapitre de la* Misère de la philosophie).[f] He, then, and not Kats and the other Belgians. '*Nous entrerons dans la carrière quand nos aînés n'y seront plus*',[g] etc., etc. He will achieve what Kats and Jottrand could not do; 3) proposed to found a FRATERNAL DEMOCRACY and to reorganise the meetings; 4) to entrust the elected bureau with the organisation of both.

Well now, what confusion! First lump together the cosmopolitan business and Belgian meetings on Belgian affairs and 2) instead of dropping this proposal because everything's going wrong for you, pass it on to the existing bureau! And if he had my departure in mind, should he not have known that it would be unthinkable to bring anyone else but you into the bureau? But the numskull had already written the whole of his speech and his vanity wouldn't allow him to omit anything by which he could seize the initiative in

---

[a] more or less - [b] in memory of the 1792 revolution - [c] the anniversary of the First Vendémiaire of the first year of the Republic (22 September 1792, the day when the Republic was proclaimed, fell on the First Vendémiaire according to the republican calendar). - [d] [J.] Imbert, [C.] Moras, F. Crüger, [Speeches delivered at the democratic banquet in Brussels on 27 September], *Deutsche-Brüsseler-Zeitung*, Nos. 80 and 83, 7 and 17 October 1847. - [e] to the English people - [f] but that must be said in French: The Association of Belgian Working Men, that is the goal I have been pursuing for several months (i. e. since the moment I deigned to take cognizance of the final chapter of the *Poverty of Philosophy*). - [g] '*We shall enter the lists when our elders are no longer there*' (*Marseillaise* by Rouget de Lisle)

some way. The thing, of course, went through, but in view of the highly *factice*[a] albeit noisy enthusiasm, there could be no question of putting the confused proposal into better order. Next A. Bartels spoke (Jules[b] wasn't there), and then Wallau demanded the floor. But how intense was my astonishment when suddenly Bornstedt thrust himself forward and urgently demanded the floor for Seiler as a speaker whose name was higher up the register. Having got it, Seiler delivered an interminably long, garrulous, silly, absurdly vapid and truly shameful speech (in French) in which he talked the most hair-raising nonsense about *pouvoirs législatif, administratif* et *exécutif,* gave all manner of wise advice to the democrats (as did Heilberg, who invented the most wondrous things about *instruction et question de l'enseignement*[c]), in which Seiler, further posing *en grand homme,*[d] spoke of democratic societies, *auxquelles j'ai participé et que j'ai peut-être même dirigées (littéralement),*[e] and finally, with the *dernières nouvelles arrivées de Paris,*[f] etc., etc., actually dragged in his precious bureau.[161] In short, it was ghastly. Several speakers followed, a Swiss jackass,[g] Pellering, Kats (very good), etc., etc., and at ten o'clock Jottrand (who blushed with shame for the Germans) declared the sitting closed. Suddenly Heilberg called for silence and announced that Weerth's speech at the FREE-TRADE CONGRESS [162] would be appearing next day in a supplement to the *Atelier qui se vendra séparément*[h]*!!!* Then Zalewski also spoke, whining a while *sur l'union de cette malheureuse Pologne et de cette grande, noble et poétique Allemagne—enfin,*[i] all went home quietly enough but very much out of temper.

Thursday, 30 September

Since the above was written a great deal more has happened and various things have been decided. On Tuesday morning, when the whole plot was clear to me, I hurried round to counter it; that same night at 2 o'clock I went to see Lupus at the bureau[j]: could not Bornstedt be balloted out of the Workers' Society? Wednesday called on all and sundry, but everybody was of the opinion that we couldn't do it. On Wednesday evening, when I

---

[a] factitious - [b] Jules Bartels - [c] teaching and questions of education - [d] as a great man - [e] in which I participated and *which I may perhaps even have directed* (literally) - [f] latest news to come from Paris - [g] Marty from Zurich - [h] which would be sold separately - [i] about the union between that unfortunate Poland and that great, noble and poetical Germany—finally - [j] Probably the editorial office of the *Deutsche-Brüsseler-Zeitung.*

arrived at the Society, Bornstedt was already there; his attitude was equivocal; finally Thomis came in with the latest issue; my anti-Heinzen article which I'd brought him as long ago as Monday and, not finding him in (2 o'clock in the afternoon), had taken to the printers, *was not in it*.[a] On my questioning him, he said there had been no space. I reminded him of what you and he had agreed.[163] He denied it; I waited till Wallau arrived and he told me there had been space enough but that on Tuesday Bornstedt had had .the article *fetched* from the printers and had not sent it back again. I went to Bornstedt and very rudely told him as much. He tried to lie his way out. I again reverted to the agreement, which he again denied, save for a few trivial generalities. I passed some insulting remarks— Grüger, Gigot and Imbert, etc., etc., were present—and asked: 'Do you intend to publish the article on Sunday, *oui ou non?*'—'We'll have to discuss it first.'—'I refuse to discuss it with you.'—And thereupon I left him.

The sitting began. Bornstedt, chin cradled in his hands, sat looking at me with a curiously gloating expression. I stared back at him and waited. Up got Mr Thomis, who, as you know, had demanded the floor. He drew a prepared speech out of his pocket and read out a series of the most peculiar aspersions on our sham battle.[164] This went on for some time but, as *cela ne finissait pas*,[b] there was a general muttering, a mass of people demanded the floor, and Wallau called Thomis to order. The latter, Thomis, then read out some half dozen inane phrases on the question and withdrew. Then Hess spoke and defended us pretty well. Then Junge. Then Wolff[c] of Paris who, though he dried up 3 times, was much applauded. Then several more. Wolff had betrayed the fact that our opposition had been purely formal. So I had to take the floor. I spoke—*à la grande déconfiture de*[d] Bornstedt, who had believed that I was too much preoccupied with personal squabbles—I spoke, then, about the revolutionary aspect of the protectionist system, completely ignoring the aforesaid Thomis, of course, and proposed a new question. Agreed.—Pause.— Bornstedt, badly shaken by the vehement way I had addressed him, by Thomis' ratting on him (*il y avait du* Bornstedt *dans son discours*[e]) and by the vehemence of my peroration—Bornstedt came up to me: My dear boy, how terribly impassioned you are,

---

a F. Engels, 'The Communists and Karl Heinzen'. First article (dated 26 September was not printed in No. 78, 29 September; it appeared in the next issue on 3 October 1847). - b it showed no signs of finishing - c Ferdinand Wolff - d to the great discomfiture of - e there were echoes of Bornstedt in his speech

etc., etc. In short, I was to sign the article.—No.—Then at least we should agree on a short editorial introduction.— *Bien, à demain à onze heures au Café Suisse.*[a]

There followed the matter of the admission of Bornstedt, Crüger, Wolff. Hess was the first to get up; he addressed 2 questions to Bornstedt about Monday's meeting. Bornstedt lied his way out, and Hess was weak enough to declare himself *satisfait.* Junge went for Bornstedt personally because of his behaviour at the Society and because he had introduced Sandkuhl under a false name. Fischer came out very energetically against Bornstedt, quite impromptu but very well. Several others likewise. In short, the triumphant Mr von Bornstedt had almost literally to run the gauntlet of the workers. He took a severe drubbing and was so thunderstruck—he, who of course believed he had well and truly bought his way in with his gifts of books—that he could only answer evasively, feebly, concedingly—in spite of the fact that Wallau, fanatically in support of him, was a wretched chairman who permitted him to interrupt the speakers at any and every opportunity. Everything was still hanging in the balance when Wallau directed the candidates to withdraw and called for a vote. *Crüger,* proposed by me as an *exceptionally guileless man, who could in no way harm the Society,* and *purement et simplement* seconded by Wolff, got through. In the case of Bornstedt, Wallau came out with a long, impassioned speech on his behalf. Then I stood up, went into the whole matter of the plot in so far as it concerned the Society, demolished Bornstedt's evasions, each by means of the other, and finally declared: Bornstedt has intrigued against us, has sought to compete with us, but we have won, and hence can now admit him into the Society. During my speech—the best I have ever made—I was constantly interrupted by applause; notably when I said: these gentlemen believed that all had been won because I, their vice-chairman, was going away, but it had not occurred to them that there is, amongst us, one to whom the position belongs by right, one who alone is able to represent the German democrats here in Brussels, and that is Marx— whereupon tremendous applause. In short, no one spoke after me, and thus Bornstedt was not done the honour of being thrown out. He was standing outside the door and listening to it all. I would rather have said my say while he was still in the room, *mais il n'y avait pas moyen,*[b] because I had to spare myself for the final

---

[a] Very well, eleven o'clock tomorrow at the Café Suisse. - [b] but it could not be done

blow, and Wallau broke off the discussion. But, like Wolff and
Crüger, he had heard every word. As opposed to him, Wolff was
admitted almost without a hitch.

In short, at yesterday's sitting Bornstedt, Crüger, etc., etc.,
suffered such an affront that they cannot honourably frequent the
Society again, and they've had enough to last them a long time.
But frequent it they certainly will; the shameless Bornstedt has
been so reduced by our even greater insolence, by the utter failure
of all his calculations, and by our vehemence, that all he can do is
trot around Brussels whining to everyone about his disgrace—*le
dernier degré de l'abaissement.*[a] He came back into the hall raging but
impotent and, when I took my leave of the Society and was
allowed to go with every imaginable mark of respect, he departed
seething. Bürgers, who has been here since the day before
yesterday evening, was present while we discussed Bornstedt.

Throughout, the behaviour of our workers was really *splendid*:
the gifts, 26 books and 27 maps, were never mentioned, they
treated Bornstedt with the utmost frigidity and lack of consideration—and, when I spoke and had reached my peroration, I had it
in my power to have him rejected by a vast majority. Even Wallau
admits as much. But we treated him worse than that by adopting
him with scorn and contumely. The affair has made a capital
impression on the Society; for the first time they have had a role
to play, have dominated a meeting despite all the plotting, and
have put in his place a fellow who was trying to set himself up
against them. Only a few clerks, etc., etc., are dissatisfied, the vast
majority being enthusiastically on our side. They have experienced
what it means to be associated.

This morning I went to the Café Suisse, and who should fail to
turn up but Bornstedt.—Weerth and Seiler, however, were there
to meet me; they had just been talking to Bornstedt, and Seiler
was obsequiousness and ingratiation personified. I, of course, gave
him the cold shoulder. Yesterday's sitting, by the way, was so
dramatic, and evolved so splendidly towards its climax that sheer
aesthetic emotion momentarily turned Wolff of Paris into a party
man. Today I also went to see A. Bartels and explained to him
that the German Society was in no way responsible for what had
happened on Monday, that Crüger, Bornstedt, Moras, Seiler,
Heilberg, etc., etc., were not even members, and that the whole
affair, staged *à l'insu*[b] of the German Society, was in fact a bid to

---

[a] the lowest depths of debasement - [b] without the knowledge

set up a rival faction. A letter in similar vein, signed by all the committee members, is to be sent to Jottrand tomorrow, when I and Lupus will also be going to see Imbert. I have further written the following letter to Jottrand about the place on the organising committee of the Brussels FRATERNAL DEMOCRATS which will become vacant on my departure:

'Monsieur! Obligé de quitter Bruxelles pour quelques mois, je me trouve dans l'impossibilité de remplir les fonctions dont la réunion du 27 de ce mois a bien voulu m'investir.—Je vous prie donc d'appeler un démocrate allemand résidant à Bruxelles à assister aux travaux de la commission chargée d'organiser une société démocratique universelle.— Je me permettrai de vous proposer celui parmi les démocrates allemands de Bruxelles, que la réunion, s'il avait pu y assister, aurait nommé à la charge qu'en son absence on m'a fait l'honneur de me conférer. Je parle de Mr Marx qui dans mon intime conviction a le droit le plus fondé de représenter à la commission la démocratie allemande. Ce ne serait donc pas Mr Marx qui m'y remplacerait, c'était plutôt moi qui à la réunion ai remplacé Mr Marx. Agréez, pp. pp.'[a]

I had in fact already agreed with Jottrand that I would advise him in writing of my departure and propose you for the committee. Jottrand is also away and will be back in a fortnight. If, as I believe, nothing comes of the whole affair, it will be Heilberg's proposal that falls through; if something does come of it, then it will be we who have brought the thing about. Either way we have succeeded in getting you and, after you, myself, recognised as representatives of the German democrats in Brussels, besides the whole plot having been brought to a dreadfully ignominious end.

This evening there was a meeting of the community [165] at which I took the chair. With the exception of Wallau who, by the way, allowed himself to be converted and whose conduct yesterday was,

---

[a] 'Sir, Being obliged to leave Brussels for a few months, I find myself unable to carry out the functions which the meeting of the 27th instant saw fit to entrust to me.—I therefore request you to call on a German democrat resident in Brussels to participate in the work of the committee charged with organising a universal democratic society. I would take the liberty of proposing to you one of the German democrats in Brussels whom the meeting, had he been able to attend it, would have nominated for the office which, in his absence, it honoured me by conferring upon myself. I mean Mr Marx who, I am firmly convinced, has the best claim to represent German democracy on the committee. Hence it would not be Mr Marx who would be replacing me there, but rather I who, at the meeting, replaced Mr Marx. I am, Sir, etc., etc. (cf. pp. 132-33).

indeed, excusable on various grounds for which I made allowance—with this one exception, then, the enthusiasm about the Bornstedt affair was unanimous. The fellows are beginning to feel their own importance. They have at last taken their stand as a society, as a power, vis-à-vis other people, and the fact that everything went with such a splendid swing and that their victory was so complete has made them enormously proud. Junge's in the seventh heaven, Riedel is beside himself with joy, even little Ohnemans goes strutting about like a FIGHTING COCK. Anyway, as I said before, this affair has given, and will continue to give, the Society a tremendous impetus, both internal and external Fellows who otherwise never open their traps have attacked Bornstedt. And even the plot has helped us: firstly Bornstedt went about telling everyone that the German democratic Workers' Society had arranged the meeting and secondly we denied it all and, as a result of both these things, the society has become a general topic of conversation among Belgian democrats and is regarded as a highly significant, *plus ou moins*[a] mysterious power. *La démocratie allemande devient très forte à Bruxelles,*[b] Bartels remarked this morning.

By the way, you too are to be included in the committee's letter to Jottrand. Gigot will sign himself 'Secretary in Marx's absence'.

Settle your financial affairs as quickly as possible and come back here again. I'm itching to get away, but must first wait until these plots have run their course. Just now I can't possibly leave. So the sooner you come the better. But first put your financial affairs in order. At all events I'll remain at my post as long as I possibly can; *si c'est possible,*[c] until you arrive. But for that very reason it's desirable that you come soon.

Your
Engels

First published in *Der Briefwechsel zwischen F. Engels und K. Marx*, Bd. 1, Stuttgart, 1913

Printed according to the original

Published in English for the first time

---

[a] more or less - [b] German democracy is growing very strong in Brussels - [c] if possible

45

MARX TO WERNER von VELTHEIM

IN OSTRAU NEAR HALLE

Zalt-Bommel, 29 September [1847]

Dear Veltheim,

It will surprise you to receive a letter from me, whom you will by now have all but forgotten.

I will explain to you briefly the reason why I am writing.

You know the present state of affairs in Germany respecting the press. The censorship makes virtually every rational undertaking impossible. On the other hand, such a confusion of views prevails that German literature, after having laboriously achieved a certain unity, is threatened with disintegrating again into a host of local literatures—those of Berlin, Saxony, the Rhineland, Baden, etc.[166] Within these fragmented literatures, moreover, we find in turn a welter of the most heterogeneous religious, political and social views.

Friends in Germany have drawn my attention to the fact that precisely now, in this state of anarchy, the needs of the day would be exactly met by a comprehensive and regular review which, while maintaining a critical attitude towards all these parties and views, would not derive its criticism from preconceived principles, but would rather portray the correlation between Germany's political, religious and social parties and aspirations, and also their literature, on the one hand, and German *economic* conditions, on the other—a review in which, therefore, political economy would play a leading role. That a periodical would be out of the question in Germany itself was a point upon which all were agreed.

It was therefore decided in Brussels to bring out, subsequent to an issue of shares, a periodical of this kind, the editorial side of which would be under my supervision. It was also decided to establish our own type-setting and printing shop out of the proceeds of the shares in order to reduce the costs of production.

Since subscriptions for these shares are being collected all over Germany—at 25 talers a share—I should like to ask you whether you and your acquaintances might wish to associate yourselves with this enterprise.

To me it seems beyond dispute that clarity of consciousness can be introduced into the now highly fragmented German movement, as into the modern movement generally, only by elucidating in the first place the relations of production and examining and appraising the other spheres of social existence in connection with them.

An exact statement of income and expenditure would be rendered annually. The number of shares amounts to two hundred.[167]

When you reply kindly do so to the following address: À Mr Charles Marx, Bruxelles, Fbg Namur, Rue d'Orléans 42.

I am only here in Holland for a few days on a family matter and am staying with my uncle.[a]

Yours faithfully
Karl Marx

Have you heard anything of Edgar[b]?

First published in the *Neues Deutschland,* No. 107, 5 May 1976

Printed according to the original

Published in English for the first time

46

ENGELS TO LUCIEN-LÉOPOLD JOTTRAND

IN BRUSSELS

[Brussels, 30 September 1847]

Dear Sir,

Being obliged to leave Brussels for several months, I find myself unable to carry out the functions which the meeting of 27 September saw fit to entrust to me.[159]

I therefore request you to call on a German democrat resident in Brussels to participate in the work of the committee charged with organising a universal democratic society.

I would take the liberty of proposing to you one of the German democrats in Brussels whom the meeting, had he been

---

[a] Leon Philips - [b] Edgar von Westphalen

able to attend it, would have nominated for the office which, in his absence, it honoured me by conferring upon myself. I mean Mr Marx, who, I am firmly convinced, has the best claim to represent German democracy on the committee. Hence it would not be Mr Marx who would be replacing me there, but rather I who, at the meeting, replaced Mr Marx.

Assuring you, Sir, of my profound esteem, I am,

Yours very sincerely
Frederick Engels

Mr Marx, who was absent from Brussels at the time of the meeting, lives at 42, rue d'Orléans, Faubourg de Namur.

First published slightly abridged in *Der Briefwechsel zwischen F. Engels und K. Marx*, Bd. 1, Stuttgart, 1913 and in full in: Marx and Engels, *Works*, First Russian Edition, Vol. XXV, Moscow, 1934

Printed according to the original

Translated from the French

Published in English for the first time

47

ENGELS TO MARX

IN BRUSSELS

Paris, [25-]26 October 1847

Dear Bartholomäus,

Only today am I able to write to you because it was only today that I managed to see little Louis Blanc—after terrible tussles with the *portière*. As a result of my long conversation with him, the little man is prepared to do anything. He was courtesy and friendliness itself, and seems to have no more urgent wish than to associate with us as closely as possible. There is none of the French national patronage about him. I had written to tell him that I was coming with a *mandat formel* to him from the London, Brussels and Rhineland democrats, and also as a CHARTIST AGENT.[168] He asked for details about everything; I described the condition of our party to him in the most glowing terms, spoke about Switzerland, Jacoby, the Badeners as allies[169] etc., etc.

You, I said, were the chief: Vous pouvez regarder M. Marx comme le chef de notre parti (i.e. de la fraction la plus avancée de la démocratie allemande, que je représentais vis-à-vis de lui) et son récent livre contre M. Proudhon [a] comme notre programme.[b] Of this he took most careful note. Then finally he promised to comment on your book in the *Réforme.* He told me a great deal about the *mouvement souterrain,*[c] that is now going on among the workers; he also said that the workers had printed 3,000 copies of his *Organisation du travail* cheaply and that at the end of a fortnight a further edition of 3,000 copies had been needed—he said the workers were more revolutionary than ever, but had learned to bide their time, no riots, only major coups that would be *sure* to succeed, etc., etc. By the way he too would seem to have got out of the habit of patronising the workers.

'Quand je vois des choses comme ce nouveau programme de M. de Lamartine, cela me fait rire! Pour bien juger de l'état actuel de la société française, il faut être dans une position qui vous permet de voir un peu de tout, d'aller le matin chez un ministre, l'après-diner chez un négociant, et le soir chez un ouvrier.'[d]

The coming revolution, he went on, would be quite different from, and much more drastic than, all previous ones, and it would be sheer *bêtise*[e] to keep on thundering only against kings, etc., etc.

By and large, he was very well-behaved and perfectly cordial. You see, the man is ALL RIGHT, *il a les meilleures dispositions du monde.*[f] He spoke of you with great sympathy and said he was sorry that you and he had parted rather *froidement,*[g] ect., etc. He still has a special hankering after a German *and* French review to be published in Paris. Might come in useful later.

As to Ruge, after whom he inquired, I warned him; *il s'est fait le panégyriste de la diète prussienne, et cela même après que la diète s'était*

---

[a] K. Marx, *The Poverty of Philosophy.* - [b] You can regard Mr Marx as the head of our party (i. e. of the most advanced section of German democracy, which I was representing vis-à-vis him) and his recent book against Mr Proudhon as our programme. - [c] underground movement - [d] 'When I see such things as M. de Lamartine's new programme, I can't help laughing! In order to assess the present state of French society properly you have to be in a position which enables you to see a little of everything, to visit a minister in the morning, a merchant in the afternoon, and a working man in the evening.' - [e] stupidity - [f] he has the best intentions in the world - [g] coldly

séparée sans résultat.[170]—*Donc il a fait un pas en arrière*[a]?—Yes, indeed.

With *père* Flocon I am hitting it off well. I first approached him as if I were an Englishman and asked him in Harney's name why he so ignored the *Star*.[b] Well, yes, he said, he was sorry, he'd be only too glad to mention it, only there was no one on the editorial staff who understood English! I offered to write a weekly article for him [171] which he accepted *de grand coeur*.[c] When I told him I was the *Star*'s correspondent, he seemed quite moved.[172] If things go on like this we shall have won over this whole trend in four weeks. Flocon wishes me to write an essay on Chartism for his personal benefit, he hasn't the vaguest idea about it. I shall call on him presently and ensnare him further in our net. I shall tell him that the *Atelier* is making approaches to me (which is true; I am going there this evening), and that, if he behaves decently, I shall turn them down. That will touch his worthy heart.

When I've been here a little longer and have grown more accustomed to writing French, I'll make a start on the *Revue indépendante*.

I quite forgot to ask L. Blanc why he hadn't accepted your Congress article.[173] I shall tax him with it when he next comes to see me. By the way I doubt whether he has, *in fact, received* your book. He was quite unable to remember having done so today. And before I went away he spoke in *very uncertain terms* about it. I shall find out within a day or two. If he hasn't got it, I shall give him my copy.

Just imagine, little Bernays, who trots round here and plays the 'martyr'—one betrayed by everybody, one 'who has helped everybody with money or good advice' (*littéralement*)—this creature has a HORSE AND GIG! It's Börnstein's, of course, but no matter. This same chap who makes himself out to be an oppressed, penniless martyr one day, boasts the next that he is the only one *who knows how to earn money.* He has been plodding away at 21 sheets (!) on the Praslin affair [174] which are coming out in Switzerland.[d] The nub of the matter is this: not *la duchesse* but *le duc* is the martyr! My response to his prating about martyrdom was to remind him that he has long owed me 60 fr. He is becoming every inch the industrialist and brags about it. In any case he's cracked.—Even Ewerbeck is furious with him.

---

[a] he has appointed himself panegyrist of the Prussian Diet, and this even after the Diet had dispersed without a result. So he's taken a step back? (A reference to A. Ruge's 'Adresse an die Opposition des Vereinigten Landtages in Berlin' on 11 June 1847.) - [b] *The Northern Star* - [c] wholeheartedly - [d] K. Bernays, *Die Ermordung der Herzogin von Praslin.*

I have not yet seen Cabet. He is happy, it seems, to be leaving, having noticed that things are showing signs of disintegrating here. Flocon wants to commence the attack, not so L. Blanc, and rightly, although L. Blanc has a finger in all manner of pies and looks forward with glee to seeing the bourgeoisie jolted out of their security by the sudden onset of revolution.

I have been to see *père* Flocon. The good man was cordiality itself, and the honest frankness with which I told him about my affair with the *Atelier* nearly brought tears to his eyes. From the *Atelier* I went on to talk about the *National*: 'Lorsque à Bruxelles nous discutions la question à quelle fraction de la démocratie française on s'adresserait, nous étions unanimement d'accord que dès le premier abord on se mettrait en rapport avec la *Réforme*; car à l'étranger il existe de fortes et de bien fondées préventions contre le *National*. D'abord les préjugés nationaux de cette feuille empêchent tout rapprochement'—'oui, oui, c'est vrai,' said Flocon 'et ceci était même la raison pour laquelle la *Réforme* fut fondée; nous avons déclaré dès le premier jour que nous ne voulons pas des conquêtes'—'et puis,' I went on, 'si je peux en croire mes prédécesseurs, car moi je n'ai jamais été au *National*, ces messieurs se donnent toujours l'air de vouloir protéger les étrangers, ce qui au reste est parfaitement d'accord avec leurs préjugés nationaux; et nous autres, nous n'avons pas besoin de leur protection, nous ne voulons pas de protecteurs, nous voulons des alliés.'—'Ah oui, mais c'est tout à fait différent avec nous, nous n'y pensons pas.'—'C'est vrai, aussi n'ai-je qu'à me louer des procédés des Messieurs de la *Réforme*'.[a]

But how helpful it was that I reminded little Blanc of our affairs. Your Congress speech had, *à ce qu'il paraît*,[b] been mislaid;

---

[a] When in Brussels we were discussing the question of which faction of French democracy to approach, we were unanimously agreed that our very first move should be to make contact with the *Réforme*, there being a strong and well-founded bias against the *National* abroad. In the first place this paper's national prejudices prevent any *rapprochement*—'yes, yes, that's true,' said Flocon, 'and this was precisely why the *Réforme* was founded; we declared from the very outset that we were not out for conquests'—'and then,' I went on, 'if I am to believe my predecessors, for I myself have never been to the *National*, those gentlemen always give the impression of wanting to patronise foreigners, which for that matter is perfectly consistent with their national prejudices; we for our part have no need of their patronage; it is not patrons we want, but allies.'—'Ah, yes, but we're not at all like that; it would never occur to us.'—'True, and I have nothing but praise for the way the gentlemen of the *Réforme* proceed.' - [b] it appears

today he hastened to look for it and send it to Flocon with a very urgent note requesting him to print it forthwith. I explained the thing to Flocon; the man was unable to understand the *cur, quomodo, quando*,[a] because Blanc had sent it to him without any further explanation. Flocon greatly regretted that the thing had become so outdated; while *parfaitement d'accord*[b] with it, he thought it was now too late. Nevertheless he would see whether it could not be included in an article. He would, he said, do his very best.

The article in the *Réforme* on Lamartine's pious intentions was by L. Blanc,[c] as you will have seen. It isn't bad, and in all respects a thousand times better than perpetual Flocon. Undoubtedly he would attack Lamartine very harshly, did he not happen to be his rival just now.

People, you see, are as well-disposed as one could wish. My relations with them are already ten times better than Ewerbeck's ever were. I shall now utterly forbid the latter to write for the *Réforme*. He can relieve himself in the *National* and there compete with Venedey & Co.; he'll do no harm there, and anyway nothing of his will be published.

Afterwards I again visited the *Atelier*. I took with me an amendment to an article in the last issue on English working men [d] which will also be included. The fellows were very well-behaved; I told them *un tas d'anecdotes*[e] about English workers, etc. They requested me most urgently to collaborate, which I shall only do, however, if needs must. Just imagine, the *rédacteur en chef*[f] thought it would be a good idea if the English workers were to dispatch an address to their French counterparts, calling on them to oppose the *libre-échange*[g] movement and champion the cause of *travail national*[h]! *Quel héroïque dévouement!*[i] But in this he failed even where his own people were concerned.

By the way, I was not compelled to make any concessions to these people. I told L. Blanc that nous étions d'accord avec eux sur toutes les questions pratiques et d'actualité, et que dans les questions purement théoriques nous marchions vers le même but; que les principes énoncés dans son premier volume [j] s'accordaient sous beaucoup de rapports avec les nôtres, et que pour le reste il en

---

a why, how and when - b entirely in agreement - c L. Blanc, 'Programme de M. Lamartine', *La Réforme*, 27 October 1847. - d F. Engels, 'The Masters and the Workers in England' written in reply to the article 'Les maîtres et les ouvriers en Angleterre' in *L'Atelier*, No. 1, October 1847. - e a lot of anecdotes - f editor-in-chief - g free trade - h national labour - i What heroic devotion! - j L. Blanc, *Histoire de la révolution française*, t. 1.

trouverait de plus amples développements dans ton livre. Quant à la question religieuse, nous la considérions comme tout-à-fait subordonnée, comme une question qui jamais ne devrait former le prétexte d'une querelle entre les hommes du même parti.[a] For all that, I went on, a friendly discussion of theoretical questions was perfectly feasible and indeed desirable, with which he was *parfaitement d'accord.*

Lupus was perfectly right in assuming that I would very soon meet the management.[175] Barely three days after my arrival here I ran into Seiler in the Boulevard des Italiens. You will long since have heard that he has done a bolt and has no intention of returning. He is going the rounds of the French correspondence bureaux in search of a berth. Since then I have repeatedly failed to find him and don't know how his affairs are going. If he meddles with the *Réforme* we shall have to disown him.

Ask that accursed Bornstedt what he means by not sending me his paper.[b] I cannot forever be chasing after the Straubingers[86] for it. Should he feign ignorance of my address, give it to him, 5, rue Neuve Saint-Martin. I'll send him a few articles as soon as ever I can.

Hellish confusion among the Straubingers. In the days immediately preceding my arrival, the last of the Grünians were thrown out, an entire community of whom, however, half will return. We are now only thirty strong. I at once set up a propaganda community and I rush round speechifying. I was immediately elected to the district[c] and have been entrusted with the correspondence. Some 20-30 candidates have been put up for admission. We shall soon grow stronger again. *Strictly between ourselves,* I've played an infernal trick on Mosi.[d] He had actually put through a delightfully amended confession of faith.[176] Last Friday[e] at the district I dealt with this, point by point, and was not yet half way through when the lads declared themselves *satisfaits. Completely unopposed,* I got them to entrust me with the task of

---

[a] that we were in agreement with them on all practical and current questions and that on purely theoretical questions we were marching towards the same goal; that the principles propounded in his first volume agreed in many respects with our own and that, regarding the rest, he would find it more fully developed in your book. As for the religious question, we regarded this as altogether secondary, as a question which should never be allowed to become a pretext for strife between men of the same party. - [b] *Deutsche-Brüsseler-Zeitung* - [c] Paris District Committee of the Communist League - [d] Moses Hess - [e] 22 October 1847

drafting a new one[a] which will be discussed next Friday by the district and will be sent to London *behind the backs of the communities.* Naturally not a soul must know about this, otherwise we shall all be unseated and there'll be the deuce of a row.

Born will be coming to see you in Brussels; he is going to London.[177] He may arrive before this letter. He will be travelling, somewhat rashly, down the Rhine through Prussia, always provided they don't cop him. Drum something more into him when he arrives; the fellow is the most receptive of all to our ideas and with a little preparation will be able to do good service in London.

Great heavens, I was on the point of forgetting all that avalanche of trash unloosed upon me from the heights of the Alps by the great Heinzen.[b] It is truly fortunate that it should all have been packed into one issue; nobody will plough his way through it. I myself had to break off several times. What a blockhead! Having first maintained that he can't write, I now find myself compelled to add that he can't read either, nor does he seem particularly conversant with the four rules of arithmetic. The ass ought to read F. O'Connor's letter in the last *Star,* addressed to the radical newspapers, which begins with 'YOU RUFFIANS' and ends with 'YOU RUFFIANS',[c] then he would see what a miserable duffer he is in the matter of invective. Well, you will be duly hauling this low, stupid lout over the coals.[d] I'm very glad that you intend to keep your answer quite *brief. I* could never answer such an attack, simply couldn't bring myself to—save perhaps with a box on the ears.

Tuesday

My article[e] has appeared in the *Réforme.* Curiously enough Flocon hasn't altered one syllable, which greatly surprises me.

I have not yet called on *père* Heine. As you can well imagine, with all this business, I've had a devilish lot to do and a fearsome amount of running about and writing.

---

[a] F. Engels, 'Principles of Communism'.- [b] K. Heinzen, 'Ein "Repräsentant" der Kommunisten', *Deutsche-Brüsseler-Zeitung,* No. 84, 21 October 1847 (written in reply to Engels' polemical article 'The Communists and Karl Heinzen'). - [c] F. O'Connor, 'To the Editors of the *Nottingham Mercury,* the *Nonconformist,* the *Dispatch,* the *Globe,* the *Manchester Examiner* and *Lloyds' Trash', The Northern Star,* No. 522, 23 October 1847. - [d] K. Marx, 'Moralising Criticism and Critical Morality'.\- [e] F. Engels, 'The Commercial Crisis in England.—The Chartist Movement.—Ireland'.

I have written to Elberfeld about the FREE TRADE-protective tariff business and am daily expecting a reply.[178] Write again soon. My regards to your wife and children.[a]

Your
Engels

You really should read O'Connor's article in the last *Star* attacking the six radical newspapers; it's a masterpiece of inspired abuse, in many places better than Cobbett and approaching Shakespeare.

Quelle mouche a donc piqué ce pauvre Moses qu'il ne cesse pas d'exposer dans le journal ses fantaisies sur les suites d'une révolution du prolétariat[b]?

First published in *Der Briefwechsel zwischen F. Engels und K. Marx*, Bd. 1, Stuttgart, 1913

Printed according to the original

Published in English for the first time

48

MARX TO GEORG HERWEGH

IN PARIS

Brussels, 26 October [1847] rue d'Orléans, 42, Faubourg Namur

Dear Herwegh,

I wanted to give Engels a letter to bring you, but there was so much pressing business on the day of his departure that this was lost sight of and forgotten.

I had further been asked by Countess Hatzfeldt to write you a few lines of introduction for her. I imagine that by now you will already have made her acquaintance. For a *German woman,* she has developed great vigour sparring with her husband.[179]

Here in Brussels we have founded two public democratic societies.

---

[a] Jenny and Laura - [b] What bug can have bitten poor Moses to make him thus perpetually air in the newspaper his fantasies on the consequences of a revolution by the proletariat? (A reference to M. Hess, 'Die Folgen einer Revolution des Proletariats', *Deutsche-Brüsseler-Zeitung*, Nos. 82, 87, 89 and 90, 14 and 31 October, 7 and 11 November 1847.)

1. A German Workers' Society[158] which already has about 100 members. Besides debates of quite a parliamentary nature, there is also social entertainment with singing, recitation, theatricals and the like.

2. A smaller cosmopolitan-democratic society to which Belgians, French, Poles, Swiss and Germans belong.[159]

If you come up here again you'll find that even in little Belgium more can be done by way of direct propaganda than in big France. Moreover, I believe that, however minor it may be, public activity is infinitely refreshing for everyone.

It is possible, there being now a *liberal* ministry at the helm,[a] that we shall run into some trouble with the police, for liberals always remain liberals.

But we shall be able to deal with them. Here it is not as in Paris, where foreigners confront the government in isolation.

Since it is impossible in present circumstances to make any use of the book trade in Germany, I have agreed with Germans from Germany to produce a review—monthly—supported by subscriptions to shares.[167] In the Rhine Province and Baden a number of shares have already been bought up. We intend to make a start as soon as there's enough money to last 3 months.

If subscriptions in any way permitted, we would establish our own type-setting room here, which could also be used for printing separate works.

Now I should like you to tell me:

1. Whether you, for your part, would also be prepared to drum up a few subscriptions for shares (25 talers per share).

2. Whether you are prepared to collaborate and to figure as a collaborator on the title page.

But I would ask you, since you have in any case long owed me a letter, to overcome for once your aversion to writing and to reply *soon*. I also wanted to request you to ask *Bakunin* by what route, to what address and by what means a letter can be conveyed to *Tolstoy*.

My wife sends her warm regards to you and your wife.

The strange business of the Prussian Embassy in Paris[180] is certainly indicative of our sovereign's[b] mounting and impotent rage.

Farewell.

Your

Marx

---

[a] formed in August 1847 - [b] Frederick William IV of Prussia

[The address written by Jenny Marx on the fourth page of the letter]

Dr Gottschalk, General Practitioner in Cologne.

[Beneath it Karl Marx has written]

Dear Herwegh,

Due to an oversight, the above wrong address nearly appeared on this letter.

First published in: *1848. Briefe von und an Georg Herwegh,* Munich, 1898

Printed according to the original

Published in English for the first time

49

ENGELS TO MARX

IN BRUSSELS

Paris, [14-]15 November 1847

Dear Marx,

Yesterday, having sent friend Reinhardt several times to see Frank about your book,[a] I learned, suddenly and at last, that that cur, Frank, had begun by sending several of the free copies to Frenchmen, in every case demanding 15 sous expenses, and in every case getting the copies back again.[181] Thereupon he *calmly hung on,* not only to those he had got back, but also to such as had not yet been sent out, and *it was not until a few days ago* that he sent them to the addressees without demanding 15 sous. The *conspiration de silence* was thus of Mr Frank's making! I at once hurried along to L. Blanc, whom a few days previously I had again failed to find in because he was *en garde* (*le petit bonhomme en bonnet à poil!*)[b]; this time I did find him in and *the copy had still not arrived*! I have at last got my own copy back, which may be of help in case of need. Today, Sunday, nothing can be done. I have arranged to meet Reinhardt tomorrow, whereupon he will go with me to see Frank, which should have happened earlier but did not happen through negligence on Reinhardt's part. He must intro-

---

[a] K. Marx, *The Poverty of Philosophy.*- [b] on guard (the little mannikin in a busby)

duce me to Frank, since I have no other means of establishing my *bona fides* with the fellow. I shall get him to give me the copy for L. Blanc and take it along with me. But what an ass Flocon is! L. Blanc told me yesterday that Flocon had objected to your *libre-échange*[a] article[173] *qu'il était un peu confus*[b] *!!!!* The muddle-headed creature! I naturally objected, oh, said the little man, *ce n'est pas moi qui ai trouvé cela, tout au contraire, l'article m'a beaucoup plu, et en effet, je ne sais pas ce que M. Flocon ... mais enfin*[c] (with a somewhat equivocal grimace intended for Flocon), *c'est ce qu'il m'a dit.*[d] All in all the editorial board of the *Réforme* is *tout ce qu'il y a de plus*[e] wretchedly constituted. The article on the English crisis and all economic topics *en général* are churned out by a poor, worthy PENNY-A-LINER whose schooling appears to have been confined to the financial articles of a correspondence bureau, and who sees everything through the eyes of a third-rate Parisian clerk in a fourth-rate bank, and judges it with the infallibility peculiar to such an 'EMPIRIC', as the English say. Flocon understands nothing of the matter and seems to me to grow more ignorant day by day. *C'est tout au plus un homme de bonne volonté.*[f] Indeed, L. Blanc also makes no secret of his contempt for him.

                                                                    Monday

I did not find the accursed Reinhardt at home. I shall go there again this evening. Come what may, I must get the whole business cleared up by tomorrow. If I don't write to you again at once, it means that everything's in order.

Yesterday evening the election of delegates took place.[182] After an extremely muddled session I was elected with a $^2/_3$ [majority]. This time I had engaged in no intrigues whatsoever, there had been little opportunity for any. The opposition was merely a fiction; a working man was proposed for appearances' sake, but those who proposed him voted for me.

The money is coming in. Write and tell me whether you and Tedesco are going. If that proves impossible, I can hardly go there and 'congress' on my own, that wouldn't make sense. If neither of you can go, the whole business will fall through and will have to

---

a free-trade - b which was a trifle muddled - c it's not I who thought that, quite the contrary, I liked the article very much, and indeed I don't know what Mr Flocon ... but anyway - d that's what he told me - e quite the most - f At best he's a man of good will.

be postponed for a few months. Should this be the case, write and tell London, so that all can be advised in good time.

Flocon had further told L. Blanc that if your article was to be accepted it would need altering a little, precisely to make it 'clearer'. L. Blanc asked me once again to remind Flocon *de sa part*[a] about the article; but in the circumstances I think it would be far better to let the matter drop. For Flocon to make the article clearer—that would be the last straw! Such block-headed stubbornness is beyond my comprehension and, as I have mentioned, Blanc *plus ou moins*[b] apologised to me for his colleague. But what can be done in such a case? I shall let Flocon do what he wants, have little to do with him and deal mainly with L. Blanc, who is the most reasonable of the lot. There's absolutely nothing one can do with the *National*, it's becoming more narrow-minded every day and is increasingly allying itself with Barrot and Thiers, WITNESS THE LILLE BANQUET.[183]

Seiler will have written to tell you that your book's going very badly here. That's not true. Frank has told Reinhardt that he is pretty well satisfied with the sales. Despite his preposterous behaviour he has, I believe, disposed of some 40 copies. More about this shortly. Seiler—he called on me recently, met with a very cool reception and did not come again—maintains that he has left sufficient in the way of bedding, furniture, paper, etc., etc., to cover Wolff's and Heilberg's needs. See to it, *si cela est*,[c] that Lupus, at least, isn't swindled again, this time by Heilberg. But no doubt it's all so much hot air.

Rothschild has made a profit of 10 million francs on the new loan—4 per cent net.

I shall not be able to pass through Brussels on my way to London, since money is too short. We shall have to arrange to meet in Ostend—on the evening of the 27th (Saturday), and cross over on Sunday so that we can make a start on Monday. On that day, the 29th, the Polish anniversary, there may be something FRATERNALLY democratic going on, in which case we shall have to attend. That would be quite a good thing. You make a French speech in London and then we print it in the *Réforme*.[184] The Germans absolutely must *do* something to hold their own with the French. A single speech would be of more help than ten articles or a hundred visits.

You'll have seen in *The Northern Star*, 2 October, the demand put forward by Harney and the FRATERNALS for a democratic

---

[a] on his behalf - [b] more or less - [c] if that is so

congress.[a] Do lend it your support, as I shall do among the French. We could try and hold it if possible next year in London, perhaps at the same time as our own. Should it come about, it might have a very salutary effect on the French and humble them somewhat. Should it fail to materialise, the fault will lie with the French and they will at least be compelled to declare themselves. It would be even better if Brussels could be the venue [185]; in London Feargus[b] might get up to some kind of foolishness.

Otherwise nothing new. Give the enclosed to Bornstedt[c] and write soon telling me whether you are going to London.

Your
E.

Write to the painter's[d] address if you still have it. It is better. Heine sends his regards. Is extremely weak and somewhat languid. Who actually sent your article to L. Blanc? He says the name at the foot of the letter was quite unknown. That could well be the reason why he allowed the matter to hang fire.

[On the back of the letter]

Monsieur Charles Marx, 42, rue d'Orléans, Faubourg d'Ixelles, Bruxelles

First published in *Der Briefwechsel zwischen F. Engels und K. Marx*, Bd. 1, Stuttgart, 1913

Printed according to the original

Published in English for the first time

---

[a] Manifesto of the Fraternal Democrats. To the Democracy of Europe, from 22 September 1847, *The Northern Star*, No. 519, 2 October 1847. - [b] O'Connor - [c] This seems to refer to Engels' second article in *German Socialism in Verse and Prose;* the first one was published in the *Deutsche-Brüsseller-Zeitung*, 21 November 1847. - [d] A. F. Körner

50

ENGELS TO MARX [186]

IN BRUSSELS

[Paris, 23-24 November 1847]

Dear Marx,

Not until this evening was it decided that I should be coming. Saturday evening,[a] then, in Ostend, Hôtel de la Couronne, just opposite the railway station beside the harbour, AND SUNDAY MORNING ACROSS THE WATER. If you take the train that leaves between 4 and 5, you'll arrive at about the same time as I do.

If, contrary to expectations, there is no packet-boat to Dover on Sundays, write and tell me by return. I. e., since you will receive this letter on Thursday morning, you must make inquiries at once and, should a letter be necessary, it must be posted the same evening—before five o'clock, I think—at the main post office. So if you want to make any changes as regards the meeting place there is still time. If I haven't heard by Friday morning I shall count on meeting you and Tedesco on Saturday evening at the Couronne. We shall then have time enough to talk things over; this congress must be a decisive one, AS THIS TIME WE SHALL HAVE IT ALL OUR OWN WAY.

For a long time now I have been completely at a loss to understand why you have not put a stop to Moses' gossip.[b] It's been giving rise to the most devilish confusion for me here and the most tedious contradictory speeches to the workers. Entire district sittings have been wasted over it, nor is there any possibility of effectively combating this 'vapid' nonsense in the communities; particularly before the elections there could be no question of it.

I expect to see L. Blanc again tomorrow. If not, I shall in any case see him the day after tomorrow. If I have nothing to add at the end of this letter, you will hear the sequel on Saturday.

By the way, Reinhardt talked nonsense to me about the number of copies sold [c]—not 37, but *96* had been sold a week ago today. That same day I myself took your book to L. Blanc. All the copies had been despatched save to Lamartine (not here), L. Blanc and

---

a 27 November 1847 - b Probably a series of articles by Moses Hess. - c K. Marx, *The Poverty of Philosophy.*

A page from Engels' letter to Marx of 23-24 November 1847

Vidal, whose address cannot be found. I have had it taken to the *Presse.*

By the way, Frank's despatch arrangements have been truly appalling.

At least see that Moses doesn't get up to any nonsense during our absence! *Au revoir,* then!

Your
E.

Tuesday evening

Verte[a]

Give a little thought to the Confession of Faith. I think we would do best to abandon the catachetical form and call the thing Communist *Manifesto.*[b] Since a certain amount of history has to be narrated in it, the form hitherto adopted is quite unsuitable. I shall be bringing with me the one from here, which I did[c]; it is in simple narrative form, but wretchedly worded, in a tearing hurry. I start off by asking: What is communism? and then straight on to the proletariat—the history of its origins, how it differs from earlier workers, development of the antithesis between the proletariat and the bourgeoisie, crises, conclusions. In between, all kinds of secondary matter and, finally, the communists' party policy, in so far as it should be made public. The one here has not yet been submitted in its entirety for endorsement but, save for a few quite minor points, I think I can get it through in such a form that at least there is nothing in it which conflicts with our views.

Wednesday morning

Have just received your letter [187] to which the above is an answer. I went to see L. Blanc. I'm remarkably unlucky with him—*il est en voyage, il reviendra p e u t-ê t r e aujourd'hui.*[d] I shall go there again tomorrow and, if necessary, the day after.

I can't be in Ostend by Friday evening because the money won't have been got together until Friday.

This morning your cousin Philips came to see me.

Born should make quite a good speech if you drum something into him. It's good that the Germans are represented by a working man.[188] But Lupus must be purged of all trace of his excessive

---

a PTO - b Cf. K. Marx and F. Engels, *Manifesto of the Communist Party.* - c F. Engels, 'Principles of Communism'. - d he's travelling and will *perhaps* be back today.

modesty. The good fellow is one of those rare people who have to be *thrust* into the foreground. Not Weerth, for heaven's sake, as representative! A man who was always too lazy, until pitchforked by his *succès d'un jour*[a] at the Congress.[189] And who, to boot, wishes to be AN INDEPENDENT MEMBER. *Il faut le retenir dans sa sphère.*[b]

First published in *Der Briefwechsel zwischen F. Engels und K. Marx*, Bd. 1, Stuttgart, 1913

Printed according to the original

Published in English in full for the first time

51

MARX TO PAVEL VASILYEVICH ANNENKOV

IN PARIS

London, 9 December [1847]

Dear Annenkov,

Party considerations, into which I cannot enter here, obliged me to pay a visit to London.[190] I took advantage of this visit both to put the Brussels Democratic Association in touch with the English Chartists and to harangue the latter at a public meeting.[c] You perhaps saw some reports about it in the English and French press.

But when I set out on this trip—and I am compelled to stay here a few days longer—I left my family behind in the most difficult and direst of circumstances. It is not simply that my wife is ill and the children[d] likewise. My economic situation just now is so critical that my wife is being veritably harassed by creditors and is in the most wretched financial straits.

How this crisis came about is easily explained. The German manuscripts are not being published as a whole. Those parts that are being published[e] I am supplying gratis, simply in order to

---

[a] fleeting success - [b] He must be kept to his own sphere. - [c] K. Marx and F. Engels, 'On Poland'. - [d] Jenny, Laura and Edgar - [e] This seems to refer to Marx's critical article on Grün's *Die sociale Bewegung in Frankreich und Belgien* published in *Das Westphälische Dampfboot*, August-September 1847. It is one of the manuscripts of Volume II of Marx and Engels' *The German Ideology*.

launch them on the world. My anti-Proudhon pamphlet[a] has sold very well. However I shall not receive a share of the proceeds until Easter.

By itself, my wife's income is insufficient and I have been negotiating with my own mother for quite some time to extract at least part of my fortune. There would now seem to be an immediate prospect of this. But that is of no help at the present moment.

In this situation, which I am not ashamed frankly to disclose to you, you would in truth save me from the worst if you could arrange to let my wife have a sum of between 100 and 200 francs. I shall, of course, be unable to repay you until my money matters have been settled with my family.

If you are able to agree to my proposal, I would request you to send the money to my old address: M. Charles Marx, Bruxelles, Faubourg Namur, rue d'Orléans, 42. However my wife must not be able to deduce from your letter that I wrote to you from London. I'll tell you the reason later.

Another time, I trust, I shall be able to send you more cheerful news.

Yours

K. Marx

First published in Russian in *Letopisi marksizma*, Book 6, Moscow, 1928

Printed according to the original

Published in English for the first time

---

[a] K. Marx, *The Poverty of Philosophy.*

1848

52

ENGELS TO MARX [191]

IN BRUSSELS

Paris, 14 January 1848

Dear Marx,

If I haven't written to you it was because I have as yet still not been able to get hold of that accursed Louis Blanc. *Décidément il y met de la mauvaise volonté.*[a] But I'm determined to catch him—every day I go to him or lie in wait for him at the café. *Père* Flocon, on the other hand, is proving more amenable. He is delighted at the way the *Brüsseler-Zeitung* and *The Northern Star* defended the *Réforme* against the *National.*[b] Not even the *blâme* against L. Blanc and Ledru-Rollin have succeeded in flustering him, any more than my announcement that we have now decided in London to come out openly as communists. He, of course, made some capital assertions: *vous tendez au despotisme, vous tuerez la révolution en France, nous avons onze millions de petits paysans qui sont en même temps les propriétaires les plus enragés,*[c] etc., etc., although he also abused the peasants,—but *enfin, dit-il, nos principes sont trop rapprochés les uns des autres pour que nous ne devions pas marcher ensemble; quant à nous nous vous appuyerons autant que sera dans notre pouvoir,*[d] etc., etc.

---

[a] Decidedly, he is showing bad will. - [b] Reference to Engels' articles published in *The Northern Star* in November 1847 and January 1848, among them 'Split in the Camp.—The *Réforme* and the *National.*—March of Democracy', 'Reform Movement in France.—Banquet of Dijon', 'The "Satisfied" Majority...' (the last two criticised the nationalist tendencies of Louis Blanc and Ledru-Rollin) and his article 'The *Réforme* and the *National*' in the *Deutsche-Brüsseler-Zeitung*, No. 104, 30 December 1847. - [c] you are tending towards despotism, you will kill the revolution in France, we have eleven million small peasants who at the same time are the most fanatical property owners. - [d] after all, he said, our principles are too similar for us not to march together; as for us, we will give you all the support in our power.

The café 'Au Cygne' in Brussels
where Marx delivered lectures to the Cologne Workers' Association

Amigo prison in Brussels, where Marx was detained
in March 1848

I was enormously tickled by the Mosi[a] business, although annoyed that it should have come to light. Apart from you, no one in Brussels knew of it save Gigot and Lupus—and Born, whom I told about it in Paris once when I was in my cups. *Enfin, c'est égal.*[b] Moses brandishing his pistols, parading his horns before the whole of Brussels, and before Bornstedt into the bargain!!, must have been exquisite. Ferdinand Wolff's inventiveness over the minutes *m'a fait crever de rire*[c]—and Moses believes that! If, by the by, the jackass should persist in his preposterous lie about rape, I can provide him with enough earlier, concurrent, and later details to send him reeling. For only last July here in Paris this Balaam's she-ass[d] made me, *in optima forma*,[e] a declaration of love mingled with resignation, and confided to me the most intimate nocturnal secrets of her ménage! Her rage with me is unrequited love, pure and simple. For that matter, Moses came only second in my thoughts at Valenciennes, my first desire being to revenge myself for all the dirty tricks they had played on Mary.[f]

The *strong wine* proves to be no more than a $^1/_3$ bottle of Bordeaux. It is only to be regretted that the horned Siegfried[g] did not have his unhappy lot publicly minuted by the Workers' Society.[158] He is perfectly at liberty, by the way, to avenge himself on all my present, past and future mistresses, and for that purpose I commend to him 1) the Flemish giantess who lives at my former lodgings, 87 chaussée d'Ixelles *au premier*,[h] and whose name is Mademoiselle Joséphine, and 2) a Frenchwoman, Mademoiselle Félicie[i] who, on Sunday, the 23rd of this month, will be arriving in Brussels by the first train from Cologne on her way to Paris. It would be bad luck if he were to succeed with neither. Kindly pass on this information to him in order that he may appreciate my honourable intentions. I WILL GIVE HIM FAIR PLAY.

It is nearly all up with Heine. I visited him a fortnight ago and he was in bed, having had a nervous fit. Yesterday he was up but extremely ill. He can hardly manage three steps now; supporting himself against the wall, he crawls from armchair to bed and vice versa. On top of that, the noise in his house, cabinet-making, hammering, etc., is driving him mad. Intellectually he is also somewhat spent. Heinzen desired to see him but was not admitted.

---

[a] Moses Hess - [b] Well, no matter. - [c] made me split my sides with laughter - [d] Sibylle Hess - [e] in due form - [f] Mary Burns - [g] An allusion to Hess with a pun on the word *gehörnte*, which, when used to describe Siegfried, the hero of German epic literature, means 'invulnerable', but in other contexts means 'cuckold'. - [h] on the first floor - [i] Félicité André

I was also at Herwegh's yesterday. Along with the rest of his family he has influenza and is much visited by old women. He told me that L. Blanc's 2nd volume[a] has been quite eclipsed by the enormous success of Michelet's 2nd volume.[b] I have not yet read either because shortage of money has prevented me from subscribing to the reading room. By the way, Michelet's success can only be attributed to his suspension[192] and his civic spirit.

Things are going wretchedly with the League[c] here. Never have I encountered such sluggishness and petty jealousy as there is among these fellows. Weitlingianism and Proudhonism are truly the exact expression of these jackasses' way of life and hence nothing can be done. Some are genuine Straubingers,[86] ageing boors, others aspiring petty bourgeois. A class which lives, Irish-fashion, by depressing the wages of the French, is utterly useless. I am now making one last attempt, *si cela ne réussit pas, je me retire de cette espèce de propagande.*[d] I hope that the London papers[e] will arrive soon and help to liven things up somewhat again; then I shall strike while the iron is hot. Not yet having seen any results from the Congress, the fellows are naturally growing completely supine. I am in contact with several new workers introduced to me by Stumpf and Neubeck but as yet there is no knowing what can be made of them.

Tell Bornstedt: 1) In the matter of his subscriptions,[f] his attitude towards the workers here should not be so rigorously commercial, otherwise he'll lose them all; 2) the agent procured for him by Moses is a feeble Jeremiah and very conceited, but the only one who still will and can attend to the thing, so he had better not rub him up the wrong way; the fellow has, moreover, gone to great pains, but he can't put in money—which, for that matter, *he has done already.* Out of the money coming in to him he has to cover the expenses correspondence, etc. involves for him; 3) if he is sending separate issues, he should never send more than 10-15 at most of [...] one issue, and these as *opportunity* offers. The parcels go through Duchâtel's ministry, whence they have to be fetched at considerable expenditure in time and where the ministry exacts a fearsome postal charge in order to ruin this traffic. A parcel of this kind costs 6-8 francs, and what can one do if that's what they ask? Esselens in Liège wanted to appoint a *garde*

---

[a] L. Blanc, *Histoire de la révolution française,* t. 2. - [b] J. Michelet, *Histoire de la révolution française,* t. 2. - [c] the Communist League - [d] if that doesn't succeed, I shall give up this kind of propaganda. - [e] i. e. documents of the Second Congress of the Communist League - [f] to the *Deutsche-Brüsseler-Zeitung*

de convoi[a] to deliver it. Write to Liège and tell them this will be arranged. 4) The issues that were still here have been sent by third party to South Germany. Should occasion offer, Bornstedt should send us a few more issues to be used as propaganda in cafés, etc., etc. 5) Within the next few days Bornstedt will be receiving an article[b] and the thing about the Prussian finances. But you must again cast an eye over the part about the committees of 1843[193] and alter it where necessary, since my memory of the subject was very hazy at the time of writing.

If the Mosi business eventually leads to your attacking him in the *Brüsseler-Zeitung,* I shall be delighted. How the fellow can still remain in Brussels, I fail to understand. *En voilà encore une occasion pour l'exiler à Verviers.*[c] The matter of the *Réforme* will be attended to.[d]

Your
E.

[On the back of the letter]

Monsieur Philipp Gigot
8.-Rue Bodenbroeck, Bruxelles

First published abridged in *Der Briefwechsel zwischen F. Engels und K. Marx,* Bd. 1, Stuttgart, 1913 and in full in *MEGA.* Abt. III, Bd. 1, Berlin, 1929

Printed according to the original

Published in English for the first time

53

ENGELS TO MARX

IN BRUSSELS

Paris, Friday evening, 21 January 1848

Dear Marx,

At last I have run L. Blanc to earth and at the same time found out why I could never get hold of him. *Ecoute plutôt—ce petit grand-seigneur littéraire ne reçoit que les jeudis! et encore l'après-midi*

---

[a] courier - [b] F. Engels, 'The Movements of 1847'. - [c] Here's another opportunity to send him into exile at Verviers. - [d] See this volume, p. 156.

7*

seulement![a] Of this he never informed me, either directly or through his doorkeeper. I found him, of course, surrounded by a crowd of jackasses, amongst whom Ramon de La Sagra, who gave me a pamphlet which I shall send on to you.[b] I have not yet read it. However I was finally able to have a few minutes' talk with him about our affairs. He reluctantly admitted that he had not yet had time to read your book[c] ... *je l'ai feuilleté et j'ai vu que M. Proudhon y est assez vivement attaqué....* Eh bien, I asked, *alors serez vous en mesure de faire l'article pour la 'Réforme' que vous m'aviez promis?—Un article, ah mon Dieu, non, je suis si obsédé par mes éditeurs—mais voilà ce qu'il faut faire: faites l'article vous-même et je le ferai passer à la 'Réforme'.*[d] This was then agreed. *Au fond*[e] you'll lose nothing by it. At least I'll present our views more correctly than he would have done. I shall draw a direct parallel between these and his own—that is the most that can be done: naturally a conclusion *detrimental* to the *Réforme* cannot be drawn in the *Réforme* itself. I shall see to this forthwith.[194]

Why didn't you tell Bornstedt *not* to write to the *Réforme* about your thing? My article was finished when Bornstedt's appeared in the *Réforme* along with the Chartist things[f] whose publication I was awaiting before taking mine in. It was appreciably longer than the brief notice in which, to boot, your name is distorted.[g] I told Flocon he must correct the printer's error; he had not done so yesterday and I haven't seen today's *Réforme*. It is of little moment anyhow. As soon as your speech[h] appears, send me 4-5 copies for the *Réforme*, L. Blanc, de La Sagra (for the *Démocratie pacifique*), etc.; I can now make a longer article of it as the notice was so abominably brief.

---

[a] Just listen—this little literary lord receives visitors only on Thursdays! and then only in the afternoon! - [b] R. de La Sagra, *Organisation du travail*. - [c] K. Marx, *The Poverty of Philosophy*. - [d] I have leafed through it and seen that M. Proudhon is attacked with some acerbity.—Well then, will you be able to write the article for the *Réforme* you promised us?—An article, good gracious no, I'm so hard pressed by my publishers—but I'll tell you what to do: write the article yourself and I'll see that it appears in the *Réforme*. - [e] After all - [f] What is meant is an item about Marx's speech at the meeting of the Brussels Democratic Association on 9 January 1848. It was published in *La Réforme* on 19 January, along with Engels' report 'The Chartist Movement' (his previous report on the subject was published on 10 January). - [g] 'Man' instead of 'Marx' - [h] K. Marx, 'Speech on the Question of Free Trade'.

As for L. Blanc, he deserves to be castigated. Write a review of his *Révolution*[a] for the *Deutsche-Brüsseler-Zeitung* and prove to him in practice how far above him we are; the form amicable, but the content leaving no doubt as to our superiority. *On lui fera parvenir cela.*[b] The petty sultan must be made to quake a little. The theoretical aspect, alas, is for the time being our only strength, but this carries much weight in the eyes of these champions of *science sociale*, of the *loi de la production suffisante*,[c] etc. Comical, these fellows, with their chasing after this unknown *loi*. They wish to find a law by which they will increase production tenfold. Like the waggoner in the fable, they seek a Hercules who will drag the social waggon out of the mire for them. Yet there Hercules is, in their own hands. The *loi de la production suffisante* consists in one's ability to produce *suffisamment*. If they cannot do so, no magic formula will avail. Inventors who take out a *brevet*[d] do more for *production suffisante* than the whole of L. Blanc with his profound, high-flying aspirations to *la science*.

I wrote Bernays a very ironical letter in reply to his last, expressing regret that his impartiality should have robbed me of the ultimate consolation—that of being a beautiful soul misunderstood—*à la* Praslin.[e] Raising his eyebrows reproachfully, he returns me the note,[195] observing that this marks the end of our correspondence. *Sela.*[f]

Otherwise nothing new. Write soon.

Your
E.

[On the back of the letter]

Mr Karl Marx in the German Workers' Society, Brussels

First publshed in *Der Briefwechsel zwischen F. Engels und K. Marx*, Bd. 1, Stuttgart, 1913

Printed according to the original

Published in English for the first time

a L. Blanc, *Histoire de la révolution française*. - b We'll see that it reaches him. - c law of sufficient production - d patent - e An allusion to K. L. Bernays, *Die Ermordung der Herzogin von Praslin*. - f The end.

54

MARX TO ENGELS [196]

IN BRUSSELS

Paris, [between 7 and 12 March 1848]
10, rue neuve Ménilmontant
(Boulevard Beaumarchais)

Dear Engels,

Get Breyer to pay you the *100 francs* which he solemnly promised me to repay within a week, get *30* from Gigot, *10* from Hess. I hope that, as things are now, Breyer will keep his promise.

Maynz will cash the bill for 114 fr. at Cassel's and give you the money. Collect these various sums and use them.

They spoke kindly of you at the *Réforme*. Flocon is ill and I haven't yet seen him. The rumour spread by Seiler is circulating among the Germans generally. Allard has not yet been ousted by the revolution. I advise you to come here.

Central Authority has been constituted here,[197] since Jones, Harney, Schapper, Bauer and Moll are all on the spot. I have been nominated chairman and Schapper secretary. Members are: Wallau, Lupus, Moll, Bauer and Engels.

Jones left for England yesterday; Harney is ill. Salut.

Your
K. M.

First published in *Der Briefwechsel zwischen F. Engels und K. Marx*, Bd. 1, Stuttgart, 1913

Printed according to the original

Published in English in full for the first time

55

ENGELS TO MARX
IN PARIS

Brussels, [8-]9 March [1848]
3, rue Neuve Chaussée de Louvain

Dear Marx,

I hope I shall hear from you tomorrow.

All is quiet here. On Sunday[a] evening Jottrand told the *Association Démocratique* about what had happened to you and

---

a 5 March 1848

your wife.[198] I arrived too late to hear him, and only heard some furious remarks from Pellering in Flemish. Gigot spoke as well, and reverted to the matter. Lubliner published an article about it in the *Émancipation*.[a] The lawyers here are furious. Maynz wants to take the matter up in court and says that you should institute a civil action on the grounds of violation of domicile, etc. Gigot is also to lodge a complaint. It would be capital if this were done, although the government has made it known that the fellow[b] would be dismissed. Yesterday Maynz provided Castiau with the documents he needs to interpellate on this score; I think this will happen tomorrow or the day after.[199] The affair has caused a considerable sensation and has greatly helped to mollify anti-German sentiment.

Lupus was taken to the railway station last Sunday morning at 11 o'clock and packed off to Valenciennes, whence he has written and where he must still be. He did not appear before any tribunal. Nor was he even escorted home to pick up his things! [200]

They've left me unmolested. From various remarks the fellows have let fall, it would seem that they are afraid of expelling me because they previously issued me with a passport, and this might be used against them.

It's a bad business in Cologne. Our three best men are in jug.[201] I have been speaking to someone who took an active part in the business.[c] They wanted to go into the attack, but instead of supplying themselves with weapons, which were easily obtainable, they went to the town hall unarmed and let themselves be surrounded. It is said that most of the troops were on their side. The thing was initiated without rhyme or reason; if the chap's reports are to be believed, they could very well have gone into the attack and in 2 hours all would have been over. But everything was organised with appalling stupidity.

Our *old* friends in Cologne appear to have kept well in the background, although they, too, had decided to go into action. Little d'Ester, Daniels, Bürgers put in a brief appearance but went off again at once, although the little Dr was needed on the city council just then.[202]

Otherwise the news from Germany is splendid. In Nassau a revolution completed, in Munich students, painters and workers in full revolt, in Kassel revolution on the doorstep, in Berlin

---

[a] *L'Émancipation*, No. 67, 7 March 1848. - [b] Darbeck - [c] presumably Peter Nothjung

unbounded fear and indecision, in the whole of western Germany freedom of the press and National Guard proclaimed; enough to be going along with.

If only Frederick William IV digs his heels in! Then all will be won and in a few months' time we'll have the German Revolution. If he only sticks to his feudal forms! But the devil only knows what this capricious and crazy individual will do.

In Cologne the whole of the petty bourgeoisie is for union with the French Republic; at the moment memories of 1797 are uppermost in their minds.[203]

Tedesco's still in jug. I don't know when he'll be appearing in court.

A fulminating article about your affair has gone off to *The Northern Star*.[a]

On Sunday evening remarkable calm at the sitting of the Democratic Association. Resolved to petition the Chambers, demanding their immediate dissolution and new elections in accordance with the new census. The government does not wish to dissolve but will have to. Tomorrow evening the petition will be adopted and signed *séance tenante*.[b]

Jottrand's petition to the Burgomaster[c] and city council met with a very courteous rejection.

You have no idea of the calm that reigns here. Last night, carnival just as usual; the French Republic is scarcely ever mentioned. In the cafés you can get French newspapers with hardly any difficulty or delay. If you didn't know that they *must, tant bien que mal*,[d] you'd think it was all finished here.

On Sunday Jottrand—furious about your persecution—made a really good speech; Rogier's *sévices*[e] have brought him to recognise the class antithesis. He fulminated against the big bourgeoisie and entered into details—perhaps rather trite and illusory but economic nonetheless—to demonstrate to the petty bourgeoisie that a well-paid working class with a high rate of consumption in a republic would provide better custom for them than a Court and a not very numerous aristocracy. Altogether *à la* O'Connor.

It being now too late to catch the post with this letter, I shall finish it tomorrow.

---

[a] F. Engels, 'To the Editor of *The Northern Star*'. - [b] during the session - [c] F. Raucourt - [d] for better or for worse - [e] brutalities

Thursday

Nothing new—I saw your article in the *Réforme*[a]—so there's a rumpus going on in England as well, *tant mieux.*[b]

If you haven't written by the time this arrives, do write at once.

Ironically enough, my baggage has just arrived from Paris—costing me 50 fr.! with customs, etc., etc.

Adieu.

Your
Engels

It would seem that the Deputy Inspector of Police who came to your house has already been dismissed. The affair has aroused great indignation among the petty bourgeois here.

[On the back of the letter]

Monsieur Charles Marx *aux soins de* Madame Gsell, 75, Boulevard Beaumarchais, *Paris.*

First published abridged in *Der Briefwechsel zwischen F. Engels und K. Marx*, Bd. 1, Stuttgart, 1913 and in full in *MEGA*, Abt. III, Bd. 1, 1929

Printed according to the original

Published in English for the first time

56

MARX TO ENGELS[204]

IN BRUSSELS

[Paris,] 16 March 1848

Dear Engels,

I never have a minute these days to write at any length. I confine myself to essentials.

Flocon is very well disposed towards you.

The Straubingers[86] here are all more or less furious with you (set-to with Sch.,[c] etc.).

---

[a] K. Marx, 'To the Editor of *La Reforme*'. - [b] so much the better - [c] apparently reference to Scherzer

As regards my things, take them with you as far as Valenciennes and have them sealed there. Everything will go through exempt. As regards the *silver*, it has already been hallmarked here in Paris. In Valenciennes you must in any case go to the man whose address I enclose.[a] On Vogler's advice my wife sent him the keys to the trunks (which are in Brussels), but without a way-bill. You must fetch these keys from him, otherwise everything will be broken open by the customs here.

As regards the money, tell *Cassel* he must give you the bill if he won't pay it. Then perhaps Baillut will pay it.

Get Gigot to settle accounts and at least give you the balance.

As regards Breyer, you must go to see him again and point out what a *shabby trick* it would be if he made use of my ill-fortune to avoid payment. He must hand over at least part to you. The revolution hasn't cost him a sou.

The bourgeoisie here are again becoming atrociously uppish and reactionary, *mais elle verra*.[b]

Bornstedt and Herwegh are behaving like scoundrels. They have founded a black, red and gold association[205] *contre nous*.[c] The former is to be expelled from the League[d] today.

Your
M.

At the moment I am unable to find the *feuille de route*[e] and this letter must go off.

Dismiss Gigot if he doesn't begin to show signs of activity. Just now the fellow ought to be more energetic.

My warmest regards to Maynz; also to Jottrand. I have received the latest *Débat social*.

My regards to Vogler likewise.

I shall write at length to Maynz and Jottrand.[206]

Farewell.

First published in *Der Briefwechsel zwischen F. Engels und K. Marx*, Bd. 1, Stuttgart, 1913

Printed according to the original

Published in English in full for the first time.

---

[a] probably August Schnee - [b] but they'll see - [c] in opposition to us - [d] the Communist League - [e] way-bill

57

ENGELS TO MARX

IN PARIS

[Brussels,] Saturday [18 March 1848]

Dear Marx,

I shall send off your things.

Write a few lines to M. Victor Faider, *avocat*,[a] either direct or enclosed [in a letter] to Bloss, thanking him for the steps he has taken on behalf of you and your wife, and authorising him to take further steps. Faider, who has suddenly turned out to be a zealous republican, has constituted himself your defence counsel and as such will reply to the *Moniteur belge*,[b] and follow the matter up. He hopes you won't disavow him and, to enable him to take a determined stand, you would do well to send him a note. It is better that a Belgian, rather than Maynz, should pursue the case and, since he has offered his services, he will probably do his job properly.

You really must send the *feuille de route*.[c] The thing is badly needed; Maynz asks after it daily.

Tedesco's been released and left for Liège immediately, without seeing a soul. Esselens was here for a few days, but he didn't see him.

The Bourse, finance, industry and trade here are in the throes of an unprecedented crisis. In the Café Suisse, Commerce is moping about with nothing to do, Messrs Kauwerz, Lauffs and Co. go creeping round with their tails between their legs, the workers have held *rassemblements*[d] and handed in petitions, a general and serious food shortage. Cash is nowhere to be had, and withal an *emprunt forcé*[e] of 60 millions! It'll be the Bourse that will impose the Republic on them here.

Lüning returned here to be confronted with the news that there's a hue and cry after him in Prussia; he is going to send for his wife and come to Paris.

Before he fled, Dronke was accepted into the League[f] by Willich and Co. I subjected him to a fresh examination here,

---

[a] lawyer - [b] Reference to a tendentious item on Marx's expulsion from Belgium in *Le Moniteur belge*, No. 72, 12 March 1848. - [c] way-bill - [d] meetings - [e] a compulsory loan - [f] the Communist League

expounded our views to him and, since he declared himself to be in agreement with them, confirmed his admission. One could hardly have done otherwise, even if there had been an element of doubt. However, the fellow's very modest, very young and seems to all appearances very responsive, so I think that, with a little supervision and some study, he will turn out well. In my presence he retracted all his earlier writings.[a] Unfortunately he lives with Moses[b] who will thus be working on him in between whiles, but, as we know, that is of no consequence. With Lüning, to whom he had become frightfully attached, only a couple of words were needed to unsaddle him.

Moses, by the way, is friendlier than ever—just try to understand the fellow!

I can't do anything with Cassel, since Maynz has the *ordre,*[c] not me. Breyer pleads the financial crisis, the impossibility, just now, of arranging a deferred settlement of his old bills, the refusal of all his patients to pay. He even says that he intends to sell his one and only horse. However I will see what is to be had, for I can hardly manage with the money from Maynz, and Hess' payment, which was the first, has already gone the way of all flesh. Gigot is also in a fix. I shall go and see Breyer again today.

Tomorrow's *Débat social* will contain a detailed refutation, *mot pour mot*[d] of the *Moniteur.*

You must further tell Faider that, if he has to have a special power of attorney, you will send him one.

Also write a few lines to M. Bricourt, *membre de la Chambre des Représentants,* who spoke up admirably on your behalf in the Chamber[199] and, at Maynz's request, put some searching questions to the Minister,[e] and who has instituted an *enquête*[f] into the affair. He is the deputy for Charleroi and, after Castiau, the best of the lot. Castiau has just been to Paris.

Look through the enclosed scrawl[g] and send it to the *Réforme.* The fellows here need to be constantly provoked.

Si c'est possible[h] I shall leave on Monday.[207] But money matters are perpetually thwarting my designs.

I am getting no news at all from England, whether through letters or the *Star.*

---

[a] Reference to E. Dronke's 'Berlin', 'Polizei-Geschichten' and 'Aus dem Volk' published in 1846 and showing influence of 'true socialism'. - [b] Hess - [c] bill - [d] blow by blow; the article 'Encore et toujours l'expulsion de M. Marx' in *Le Débat Social* of 19 March 1848 appears to have been written by V. Faider. - [e] Minister of Justice Fr. Haussy - [f] enquiry - [g] F. Engels, 'The Situation in Belgium' - [h] If possible

In Germany things are going very well indeed, riots everywhere and the Prussians aren't giving way. *Tant mieux.*[a] I hope we shan't have to remain very long in Paris.

How excellent that you are throwing out Bornstedt.[b] The fellow has proved so unreliable that his expulsion from the League is essential. He and Weerth are now allied and Weerth is running round here as a fanatical republican.

Lamartine is becoming daily more depraved. In all his speeches the man addresses himself exclusively to the bourgeoisie and seeks to pacify them. Even the Provisional Government's Electoral Proclamation[c] is directed wholly at the bourgeoisie in order to reassure them. Small wonder that the creatures are becoming uppish.

Adios, au revoir.

F. E.

All letters to be sent here to the address I have given; *en mon absence*[d] Bloss will give them to Gigot.

[On the back of the letter]

M. Marx
Rue neuve Ménilmontant

First published in *Der Briefwechsel zwischen F. Engels und K. Marx*, Bd. 1, Stuttgart, 1913

Printed according to the original

Published in English for the first time

58

ENGELS TO EMIL BLANK

IN LONDON

Paris, 26 March 1848

Dear Emil,

After the glorious February revolution and Belgium's stillborn March revolution, I came back here last week. I wrote to Mother asking for money so that within a few days I could return to

---

a So much the better. - b See this volume, p. 162. - c 'Instruction du Gouvernement provisoire pour l'exécution du décret du 5 mars 1848, relatif aux élections générales', *Le Moniteur universel*, No. 70, 10 March 1848. - d in my absence

Germany [208] where we are starting up the *Rheinische Zeitung* [a] again. Mother is now very anxious to see me back in Germany, partly because she believes that there might again be some shooting here in the course of which I could get hurt, partly because she wants me to return anyway. However she also says in her letter:

'How I can be expected to send you the money, I really don't know, since a few days ago Fould notified Father that he was doing no more business, and since several good bills sent him by Father came back and were protested. Write and tell me, then, how I can be expected to let you have the money.'

The simplest thing would be for you to send me 20 pounds in banknotes, these being highly regarded here, and at once arrange with my old man to reimburse you. In this way I shall get my money quickly and be able to leave, whereas I would otherwise be stuck here for another week before getting money from Barmen, let alone Engelskirchen. I am therefore writing to Barmen this very day for them to repay you the £20, and I would ask you to arrange matters in the way I have just said, since bills are no longer any good.

You can send half of the bisected banknotes to me today, addressed to 19ter rue de la Victoire, Paris, and the remainder next day to Mlle Félicité André, same street and No. This will foil letter thieves.

Here things are going very well, [209] i.e. the bourgeoisie, who were beaten on 24 February and 17 March, [b] are once more raising their heads and railing horribly against the Republic. But the only result of this will be that a thunderstorm quite unlike anything they have known before will very soon break over them. If the fellows persist in their insolence, some of them will very soon be strung up by the people. In the provisional government they have a certain party, namely Lamartine, the soft-soaper, whose life will also soon be forfeit. The workers here, 200,000-300,000 strong, will hear of no one but Ledru-Rollin, and they are right. He is the most resolute and radical of all. Flocon, too, is very good; I've been to see him once or twice and am about to do so again; he's a thoroughly honest fellow.

We have nothing to do with the great crusade which is departing from here to set up the German republic by force of arms. [210]

---

[a] *Neue Rheinische Zeitung* - [b] See this volume, p. 168.

My kindest regards to Marie[a] and the little ones and reply by return.

In haste,
Your
Frederick

First published in: Marx and Engels, *Works,* First Russian Edition, Vol. XXV, Moscow, 1934

Printed according to the original

Published in English for the first time

59

ENGELS TO EMIL BLANK[211]

IN LONDON

Paris, 28 March 1848

Dear Emil,

Today I received the first four halves of the 4 £5 notes and would ask you to send the other halves *immediately,* since I must get away as soon as possible. Many thanks for your willingness to come so promptly to my assistance in this EMERGENCY. Your subscription to the *Rheinische Zeitung*[b] has been registered.

As regards the parties here, there are, properly speaking, three major ones, not counting the minor ones (Legitimists[c] and Bonapartists who simply intrigue, mere sects without influence among the people, in part wealthy, but no hope whatever of victory). These three are, first, those defeated on 24 February, i.e. the big bourgeoisie, speculators on the Bourse, bankers, manufacturers and big merchants, the old conservatives and liberals. Secondly, the petty bourgeoisie, the middle class, the bulk of the National Guard which, on 23 and 24 Febr. sided with the people, the 'reasonable radicals', Lamartine's men and those of the *National.* Thirdly, the people, the Parisian workers, who are now holding Paris by force of arms.

The big bourgeoisie and the workers are in direct confrontation with each other. The petty bourgeois play an intermediary but altogether contemptible role. The latter, however, have a majority in the provisional government (Lamartine, Marrast, Dupont de l'Eure, Marie, Garnier-Pagès and, occasionally, Crémieux as well).

---

[a] Marie Blank, Engels' sister - [b] *Neue Rheinische Zeitung* - [c] supporters of the Bourbon dynasty overthrown in 1830

They, and the provisional government with them, vacillate a great deal. The quieter everything becomes, the more the government and the petty-bourgeois party incline towards the big bourgeoisie; the greater the unrest, the more they join up with the workers again. Recently, for instance, when the bourgeois had again become fearfully uppish and actually dispatched a column of National Guards 8,000 strong to the Town Hall[a] to protest against a decree of the provisional government, and more especially against Ledru-Rollin's vigorous measures,[212] they did in fact succeed in so intimidating the majority of the government, and in particular the weak-kneed Lamartine, that he publicly disavowed Ledru. But on the following day, 17 March, 200,000 workers marched on the Town Hall, proclaimed their implicit confidence in Ledru-Rollin and compelled the majority of the government and Lamartine to recant. For the time being, then, the men of the *Réforme* (Ledru-Rollin, Flocon, L. Blanc, Albert, Arago) again have the upper hand. They, more than anyone else in the government, still represent the workers, and are communists without knowing it. Unfortunately little Louis Blanc is making a great ass of himself with his vanity and his crack-brained schemes.[213] Ere long he will come a terrible cropper. But Ledru-Rollin is behaving very well.

The most unfortunate thing is that the government, on the one hand, has to make promises to the workers and, on the other, is unable to keep any of them because it lacks the courage to secure the necessary funds by revolutionary measures against the bourgeoisie, by severe progressive taxation, succession duties, confiscation of all émigré property, ban on the export of currency, state bank, etc. The men of the *Réforme* are allowed to make promises which they are then prevented from keeping by the most inane conservative decisions.

In addition there is now a new element in the National Assembly: the peasants who make up $5/_7$ of the French nation and support the party of the *National,* of the petty bourgeoisie. It is highly probable that this party will win, that the men of the *Réforme* will fall, and then there'll be another revolution. It's also possible that, once in Paris, the deputies will realise how things stand here, and that only the men of the *Réforme* can stay the course in the long term. This, however, is improbable.

The postponement of the elections for a fortnight is also a victory for the Parisian workers over the bourgeois party.[214]

---

[a] seat of the provisional government

The men of the *National,* Marrast and Co., cut a very poor figure in other respects as well. They live in clover and provide their friends with palaces and good positions. Those from the *Réforme* are quite different. I've been to see old Flocon several times; the fellow lives as before in poor lodgings on the fifth floor, smokes cheap shag in an old clay pipe, and has bought nothing for himself but a new dressing-gown. For the rest his way of life is no less republican than when he was still editor of the *Réforme,* nor is he any less friendly, cordial and open-hearted. He's one of the most decent fellows I know.

Recently I lunched at the Tuileries, in the Prince de Joinville's suite, with old Imbert who was a *réfugié* in Brussels and is now Governor of the Tuileries. In Louis-Philippe's apartments now the wounded lie on the carpets, smoking stubby pipes. In the throne-room the portraits of Soult and Bugeaud have been torn down and ripped and the one of Grouchy cut to shreds.

Going past at this very moment, to the strains of the *Marseillaise,* is the funeral cortège of a working man who died of his wounds. Escorting him are National Guards and armed populace at least 10,000 strong, and young toffs from the Chaussée d'Antin, have to escort the procession as mounted National Guards. The bourgeois are enraged at seeing a working man thus given the last honours.

Your
F. E.

First published in: Marx and Engels, *Works,* First Russian Edition, Vol. XXV, Moscow, 1934

Printed according to the original

60

MARX AND ENGELS TO ÉTIENNE CABET

IN PARIS

Paris, 5 April 1848

Dear Citizen,

During the last two days of our stay in Paris we presented ourselves at your house several times. But we always found your offices[a] so crowded with people that our all too limited time prevented us from taking our turn and waiting. We therefore regret that we have to leave without having had one last interview with you.

Mr Ewerbeck, who will be delivering this, will take it upon himself to inform us of the address we should use when writing to you.[215]

We do not doubt for one instant that we shall shortly be able to give you favourable news of the progress of the communist movement in Germany.

Meanwhile, please accept our respectful greetings.

Yours very sincerely
K. Marx, F. Engels

First published in English in the journal *Science and Society*, Vol. IV, No. 2, 1940

Printed according to Engels' manuscript

Translated from the French

61

ENGELS TO EMIL BLANK

IN LONDON

Barmen, 15 April 1848

Dear Emil,

I am safely back here again.[216] The whole of Barmen is waiting to see what I shall do. They believe I'm going to proclaim the republic forthwith. The philistines are trembling with vague fear—what of, they themselves don't really know. At any rate, it is believed that, now I am here, much will speedily resolve itself. C. and A. Ermen were quaking visibly when I walked into their office today. I, of course, am not meddling in anything but waiting quietly to see what happens.

The panic here is ineffable. The bourgeoisie are calling for confidence but confidence has gone. Most of them are fighting for existence, as they themselves put it. This doesn't fill the workers' bellies, however, and from time to time they rebel a little. General dissolution, ruin, anarchy, despair, fear, rage, constitutional

---

[a] editorial offices of *Le Populaire*

enthusiasm, hatred of the Republic, etc., are rampant, and the fact is, for the time being, the richest people are the most tormented and frightened. And the exaggerations, the lies, the ranting and the railing, are enough to drive one out of one's mind. The most placid of citizens is a real *enragé*.[a]

But they're in for a surprise when once the Chartists make a start. The business of the procession was a mere bagatelle. In a couple of months, my friend, *G. Julian Harney*, to whom pray address the enclosed letter, *9 Queen Street, Brompton,* will be in Palmerston's shoes.[217] I'LL BET YOU TWOPENCE AND IN FACT ANY SUM.

All is well with your mother and mine. They are expecting your brother Hermann; Anna is in Hamm. My regards to Marie[b] and the children. *À bientôt.*

Your
F.

First published in: Marx and Engels, *Works,* First Russian Edition, Vol. XXV, Moscow, 1934

Printed according to the original

Published in English for the first time

62

MARX TO ENGELS

IN BARMEN

Cologne [about 24 April 1848]
Apostelnstrasse Nr. 7

Dear Engels,

A good many have already been subscribed for here, and we shall probably soon be able to make a start.[218] But now you must without fail make demands on your old man and in general declare *definitively* what is to be done in Barmen and Elberfeld.

A prospectus (written by Bürgers),[c] etc., has been sent from here to Hecker in Elberfeld.

---

[a] madman (ironically comparing the German citizens with the men of the most radical trend during the French Revolution) - [b] Anna and Marie are Engels' sisters. - [c] H. Bürgers, 'Prospectus for the Founding of the *Neue Rheinische Zeitung*' (see present edition, Vol. 7, pp. 539-41), later published in *Das Westphälische Dampfboot,* No. 12, 17 May 1848.

Have you no address for Dronke? He must be written to forthwith.

Answer by return. I might come to your part of the world if things don't look too fearsome with you.[219]

Your
M.

First published in *Der Briefwechsel zwischen F. Engels und K. Marx*, Bd. 1, Stuttgart, 1913

Printed according to the original

Published in English for the first time

63

ENGELS TO MARX[220]

IN COLOGNE

B[armen,] 25 April 1848

Dear Marx,

I have just received the prospectus[a] along with your letter. There's damned little prospect for the shares here. Blank,[b] to whom I had already written about it[221] and who is still the best of the lot, has become practically a bourgeois; the others even more so since they became established and came into conflict with the workers. All these folk shun the discussion of social questions like the plague, calling it seditious talk. I have lavished on them the finest rhetoric, and resorted to every imaginable diplomatic ploy, but always hesitant answers. I am now going to make one final effort; if it fails, that will be the end of everything. In 2-3 days you'll have definite news about how things have gone. The fact is, *au fond*,[c] that even these radical bourgeois here see us as their future main enemies and have no intention of putting into our hands weapons which we would very shortly turn against themselves.

---

[a] H. Bürgers, 'Prospectus for the Founding of the *Neue Rheinische Zeitung*.-
[b] Wilhelm Blank - [c] after all

Nothing whatever is to be got out of my old man. To him even the *Kölner Zeitung* is a hotbed of agitation and, sooner than present us with 1,000 talers, he would pepper us with a thousand balls of grape.

The most advanced of the bourgeois here find their party represented pretty much to their satisfaction by the *Köln. Zeitung.* *Que veux-tu qu'on fasse, alors?*[a]

Moses'[b] agent, Schnaake, who was here last week, would seem to have been calumniating us too.[222]

I have no address for Dronke except: Adolf Dominicus, merchant, Coblenz (his uncle). His old man is living in Fulda, a grammar school headmaster, I think. It's a little backwater: Dr E. Dronke junior, Fulda, would probably reach him if he's there. But it's foolish of him not to write, if only to let us know his whereabouts.

I have had a letter from Ewerbeck asking whether we have received a supposedly important letter which he sent to the agreed address in Mainz. If you haven't had it, write and inform Mainz (Philipp Neubeck, teacher candidate, Rentengasse (Heiliger Geist), Mainz).

Ewerbeck is having the *Manifesto*[c] translated into Italian and Spanish in Paris and to that end wants us to send him 60 fr. which he has undertaken to pay. Yet another of those schemes of his. They will be splendid translations.[223]

I am working on the English translation, which presents more difficulties than I thought. However, I'm over half way through, and before long the whole thing will be finished.[224]

If even a single copy of our 17 points[d] were to circulate here, all would be lost for us. The mood of the bourgeoisie is really ugly. The workers are beginning to bestir themselves a little, still in a very crude way, but as a mass. They at once formed coalitions. But to *us* that can only be a hindrance. The Elberfeld political club[225] issues addresses to the Italians, advocates direct election but resolutely eschews any discussion of social questions, although in private these gentlemen admit that such questions are now *coming* to be the order of the day, always with the proviso that we should not take precipitate action!

---

[a] So what do you want us to do? - [b] Hess - [c] K. Marx and F. Engels, *Manifesto of the Communist Party.* - [d] K. Marx and F. Engels, 'Demands of the Communist Party in Germany'.

Adios. Write soon in greater detail. Has the letter been sent to Paris, and did it have any results? [226]

Your

E.

First published in *Der Briefwechsel zwischen F. Engels und K. Marx*, Bd. 1, Stuttgart, 1913

Printed according to the original

Published in English in full for the first time

64

ENGELS TO MARX

IN COLOGNE

[Barmen,] 9 May 1848

Dear Marx,

Herewith:

1. The list of the shares so far subscribed for, 14 in number.
2. A proxy for you. [227]
3. One for d'Ester (Bohnstedt is an acquaintance of his).
4. One for Bürgers.

It was unavoidable that Bohnstedt and Hecker should have given their proxies to personal acquaintances.

Hühnerbein will appear there in person on behalf of himself and two others here.

The list is not yet closed. Although I have called on Laverrière and Blank x times, I haven't found them at home. Zulauff has taken over the former.

Two others, with whom I made no headway, will be worked upon by Hecker.

Today Zulauff is going to Ronsdorf, where he has good prospects.

The two kinds of people who prove the most difficult are, firstly, the young *républicains en gants jaunes,*[a] who fear for their fortunes and smell communism in the air and, secondly, the local panjandrums, who regard us as rivals.

---

[a] republicans in kid gloves (a nickname of the moderate bourgeois republicans in France, followers of Armand Marrast)

Neither Nohl nor Bracht were to be persuaded. Of the jurists, Bohnstedt is the only one with whom anything can be done. All in all we've made fruitless moves enough.

Tomorrow I am going to Engelskirchen for 2 days. Let me know at once the results of the shareholders' meeting.

A beginning has also been made with a community of the League.[a]

Your
Engels

First published in *Der Briefwechsel zwischen F. Engels und K. Marx*, Bd. 1, Stuttgart, 1913

Printed according to the original

Published in English for the first time

65

ENGELS TO EMIL BLANK [228]

IN LONDON

Cologne, 24 May 1848
14, Höhle

Dear Emil,

I arrived here in Cologne last Saturday.[b] The *Rheinische Zeitung*[c] will be appearing on 1 June. But if we are not at once to come up against obstacles, some preliminary arrangements must be made in London, and we are taking the liberty of entrusting these to you since there's nobody else there.

1. Arrange at any NEWSMAN'S for a subscription to *The Telegraph* (DAILY PAPER) and *The Economist*, WEEKLY PAPER, from the time this letter arrives until 1 July. The NEWSMAN, whose address you can give us to save being bothered again later on, should include both papers in one wrapper or paper band—in the way papers are customarily sent—and dispatch them daily, addressed to Mr W. Clouth, St Agatha, 12, Cologne, via Ostend.[229]

2. Please forward the enclosed letters.

3. Pay the cost of the subscription to the two papers, the postage of this letter, etc., etc., and charge them at once to the dispatch

---

[a] the Communist League - [b] 20 May - [c] *Neue Rheinische Zeitung*

department of the *Neue Rheinische Zeitung*, St Agatha, 12, Cologne, stating to whom the sum is to be sent, and it will be done at once.

The necessary capital for the newspaper has been raised. Everything is going well, all that remains is the question of the papers, and then we can start. We are already getting *The Times* and, for the first month, we need no other English papers than the two above-mentioned. Should you ever happen upon something worthy of note in another paper, we should be grateful if you would send it to us. Any expense will, of course, immediately be refunded. Papers containing detailed information on trade, the state of business, etc., etc., are also desirable. Write some time and let me know what papers are now to be had there, so that we know how we stand.

I didn't, of course, see Marie,[a] as I had to leave before she arrived. But I'll be going over there some time soon, when things here are really under way. Barmen, by the way, is more boring than ever and is filled with a general hatred for what little freedom they have. The jackasses believe that the world exists solely to enable them to make tidy profits and, since these are now at a low ebb, they are screeching gruesomely. If they want freedom they must pay for it, as the French and English have had to do; but these people think they ought to have everything for nothing. Here things are looking up a little, if not very much. The Prussians are still the same as ever, the Poles are being branded with lunar caustic and, at the moment of writing, *Mainz is being bombarded by the Prussians* because the Civic Guard arrested a few drunken and rampaging soldiers[230]—the sovereign National Assembly in Frankfurt hears the firing and doesn't seem to take any notice.[231] In Berlin Camphausen is taking it easy, while reaction, the rule of officials and aristocrats grows daily more insolent, irritates the people, the people revolt and Camphausen's spinelessness and cowardice lead us straight towards fresh revolutions. That is Germany as it now is! Adieu.

Your
F. E.

First published in: Marx and Engels, *Works*, First Russian Edition, Vol. XXV, Moscow, 1934

Printed according to the original

Published in English in full for the first time

---

[a] Marie Blank

66

ENGELS TO KARL FRIEDRICH KÖPPEN

IN BERLIN

Cologne, 1 September 1848

My dear Köppen,

I return your article herewith. I should already have sent it before but had lost your address in the turmoil of the removal and the mass of business this involved.[232]

Marx will have told you how often we thought of you during the sleepless night of exile. I can assure you that you were the only one of the Berliners whom we recalled with pleasure. Come to that, the sleepless night of exile was pleasurable *après tout*[a] and I look back on it longingly from out of this tedious philistine farce known as the German revolution! But one must be able to make sacrifices for the dear fatherland, and the greatest sacrifice is to return to that fatherland and write leading articles for this gross and boorish public. Farewell.

Tout à vous[b]

F. Engels

First published in French in *L'Humanité*, No. 6093, 28 November 1920

Printed according to the original

Published in English for the first time

67

MARX TO ENGELS[233]

IN GENEVA

Cologne, [about 29 or 30 October] 1848

Dear Engels,

As your letter only arrived this evening, there is no time left to make enquiries about bills. I haven't even time to go home. I send you the enclosed, which happens to be to hand and, in addition, a

---

[a] after all - [b] Yours ever

draft of 50 talers from Schulz on a citizen of Geneva[a] where you might also obtain help in other ways.

I sent 50 talers to you and Dronke in Paris a long time ago and at the same time sent your passport to Gigot in Brussels.

Since 11 October the paper has been appearing again, *tale quale*.[b] It is not the time now to go into details, as haste is necessary. As soon as you can, write some news items and longer articles. Now that everyone save Weerth is away, Freiligrath having only joined us a few days ago, I am up to my eyes and unable to undertake work of a more detailed kind, and in addition the public prosecutor's office is doing all it can to rob me of my time.

Write by return. Shall I send your underclothing, etc.? Plasmann ready to do so immediately.[234] Your father has paid him, by the way.

By the way, your old man has written to Gigot asking where you are. He wants, so he says, to send you some money. I sent him your address.

Your

K. Marx

[From Louis Schulz]

P. S. Should be obliged if you would open enclosed letter to J. Köhler by the Lake, or rue du Rhône, and deliver same, whereupon he will pay you 250 fr. for my account against sight draft on me. Friendly greetings.

Louis Schulz

First published in *Der Briefwechsel zwischen F. Engels und K. Marx*, Bd. 1, Stuttgart, 1913

Printed according to the original

Published in English for the first time

68

MARX TO ENGELS

IN LAUSANNE

[Cologne, first half of November 1848]

Dear Engels,

I am truly amazed that you should still not have received any money from me. *I* (not the dispatch department) sent you 61

---

[a] J. Köhler - [b] quite unchanged

talers ages ago, 11 in notes, 50 as a bill, to Geneva, enclosed in a letter to the address you gave. So make inquiries and write immediately. I have a postal receipt and can reclaim the money.

I had further sent 20 talers to Gigot and, later, 50 to Dronke for all of you, each time out of my cashbox. A total of some 130 talers.

Tomorrow I shall send you some more. But inquire about the money. The bill included a note recommending you to one of Lausanne's financial philistines.

I am short of money. I returned from my journey with 1,850 talers; I received 1,950 from the Poles. I spent 100 while still on my journey. I advanced 1,000 to the newspaper (and also to yourself and other refugees). This week there are still 500 to be paid for the machine. Balance 350. And withal I haven't received a cent from the paper.[235]

As regards your editorship, I 1) announced in the very first issue that the committee was to remain unchanged,[a] 2) explained to the idiotic reactionary shareholders that they are at liberty to regard any of you as no longer belonging to the editorial staff, but that I am at liberty to *pay as high fees as I wish* and hence that they will be no better off financially.

It would have been, perhaps, more sensible not to advance so large a sum for the newspaper, as I have 3-4 court actions hanging over me,[236] can be locked up any day and then pant for money as doth the hart for cooling streams. But whatever the circumstances, this *fort* had to be held and the political position not surrendered.

The best thing—once you have settled the financial business in Lausanne—is to go to Berne and carry out your proposed plan. Besides, you can write for anything you want. Your letters always arrive in reasonably good time.

To suppose that I could leave you in the lurch for even a moment is sheer fantasy. You will always remain my friend and confidant as I hope to remain yours.

K. Marx

Your old man's a swine and we shall write him a damned rude letter.

First published abridged in *Der Briefwechsel zwischen F. Engels und K. Marx*, Bd. 1, Stuttgart, 1913 and in full in *MEGA*, Abt. III, Bd. 1, 1929

Printed according to the original

Published in English for the first time

---

[a] K. Marx, 'Editorial Statement Concerning the Reappearance of the *Neue Rheinische Zeitung*'.

69

MARX TO FERDINAND LASSALLE

IN DÜSSELDORF

[Cologne, 13 November 1848]

Dear Lassalle,

At your democratic-monarchist club [237] you should resolve the following:

1. *General refusal to pay taxes*—to be advocated specially in rural areas;

2. Dispatch of volunteer corps to Berlin;

3. Cash remittance to the Democratic Central Committee in Berlin. [238]

For the Rhenish Democratic Provincial Committee [239]

K. Marx

(Private)

Dear Lassalle,

If you could send me some money, whether it be the 200 talers or the amount for the loan certificates, you would greatly oblige me. Send it to my wife, Cecilienstrasse 7. I have had a summons [240] today and it is generally believed that I shall be arrested tomorrow.

Your

Marx

First published in *Düsseldorf 1848. Bilder und Dokumente*, Düsseldorf, 1948

Printed according to the original

Published in English for the first time

70

MARX TO ENGELS

IN BERNE

Cologne, 29 November [1848]

Dear Engels,

The papers have been sent to you. If this was not done sooner the fault lies with that jackass Korff who, because I was overworked, a circumstance aggravated by repeated summonses, has so far failed to carry out my orders.

In the meantime remain in Berne. I shall write to you as soon as you can come. Seal your letters better. One of them had been opened, as I indicated in the paper, without, of course, mentioning your name.[a]

Write in detail about *Proudhon* and, since your geography is good, about the dirty business in Hungary (nations swarming like bees).[b] Don't forget me[c] in the piece on Proudhon, since our articles are reprinted by a great many French newspapers.

Write something, too, attacking the Federal Republic, to which end Switzerland provides the best opportunity.[d]

K. Heinzen has published his old trashy piece attacking us.[e]

Our paper continues to stand by the principle of *émeute,*[f] but despite all my summonses in court, it has succeeded in sailing clear of the *Code pénal.*[241] It is now very much *en vogue.* We are also issuing posters daily.[242] *La révolution marche.*[g] Write diligently.

I have devised an infallible plan for extracting money from your old man, as we now have none. Write me a begging letter (as crude as possible), in which you retail your past vicissitudes, but in such a way that I can pass it on to your mother. The old man's beginning to get the wind up.

I hope to see you again soon.

Your

Marx

First published abridged in *Der Briefwechsel zwischen F. Engels und K. Marx,* Bd. 1, Stuttgart, 1913 and in full in *MEGA,* Abt. III, Bd. 1, 1929

Printed according to the original

Published in English for the first time

---

[a] K. Marx ['Letters Opened']. - [b] In compliance with this request Engels wrote the articles '[Proudhon]' and 'The Magyar Struggle'. - [c] Marx means his book *The Poverty of Philosophy.* - [d] F. Engels, 'The National Council'. - [e] K. Heinzen, *Die Helden des teutschen Kommunismus,* Bern, 1848. - [f] uprising - [g] The revolution is on the march.

71

MARX TO EDUARD von MÜLLER-TELLERING

IN VIENNA

[Cologne, 5 December 1848]

My dear Tellering,

You would already have had the missing issues,[a] but most of them are missing. Hence I am still busily trying to get hold of the copies you lack.

As regards your feuilleton, you must excuse me for not having read it through yet, owing to my being overworked. If it is not suitable for our newspaper you shall have it back.

Regarding the *addresses,* all your letters have arrived. As a precaution, write to *Herr Werres, Unter Huthmacher 17.* The address is wholly above suspicion.

Just now our newspaper is *sans sou.*[b] But the subscribers [...][c] The jackasses are at last beginning to feel that our prophecies have invariably been right; unless we're suppressed by the government we shall have surmounted our troubles by the beginning of January, and then I shall do everything in my power to reward you in accordance with your services. Your articles are incontestably the best we receive, completely in line with our own tendency, and since they have been reprinted from our paper by French, Italian and English periodicals, you are contributing a great deal to the enlightenment of the European public.[243]

I cannot describe to you what sacrifices in terms of money and patience I have had to make to keep the newspaper going. The Germans are crack-brained jackasses.

Give my kindest regards to your wife[d] and rest assured of my constant friendship.

Yours
K. Marx

First published in the *Volksstimme,* Frankfurt a. M., No. 247, 22 October 1897

Printed according to the original

Published in Englısh for the first time

---

[a] *Neue Rheinische Zeitung* - [b] penniless - [c] word indecipherable (probably *träumen—* dream) - [d] Amalie

72

ENGELS TO MARX

IN COLOGNE

Berne, 28 December [1848]

Dear Marx,

How are things? Now that Gottschalk and Anneke have been acquitted,[244] shan't I be able to come back soon? The Prussian curs must surely soon tire of meddling with juries. As I have said, if there are sufficient grounds for believing that I shall not be detained for questioning, I shall come at once. After that they may, so far as I'm concerned, place me before 10,000 juries, but when you're arrested for questioning you're not allowed to smoke, and I won't let myself in for that.

In any case the whole September affair[245] is crumbling away to nothing. One after another they're going back. So write.

Apropos, some money would come in very handy towards the middle of January. By then you should receive plenty.

Your
E.

First published in *Der Briefwechsel zwischen F. Engels und K. Marx*, Bd. 1, Stuttgart, 1913

Printed according to the original

Published in English for the first time

73

MARX TO WILHELM STIEBER[246]

IN BERLIN

[Draft]   [Cologne, about 29 December 1848]

The editorial department is in receipt of your letter and accepts the correction dated Frankfurt.[a] As to your threat of a libel action, this only reveals your ignorance of the *Code pénal,* whose paragraph relating to libel does not apply to the report appearing

---

a 'Stieber', *Neue Rheinische Zeitung*, No. 182, 30 December 1848, supplement.

in No. 177.[247] Moreover, to set your mind at rest be it said that this report was sent to us by a Frankfurt Deputy[a] before the *Neue Preussische Zeitung* divulged the same news. Your earlier activities in Silesia did not seem to us to belie the contents of the said report, although we did, on the other hand, think it strange that you should exchange your more remunerative and honourable post in Berlin for one which, albeit *legal,* is precarious and equivocal.

As to your protestations regarding your activities in Silesia,[b] we shall endeavour to place material at your disposal, either publicly or in private, as you wish.

On the grounds of their novelty, we shall excuse the lectures on democracy and democratic organs contained in your letter.

First published in: Marx and Engels, *Works,* First Russian Edition, Vol. XXV, Moscow, 1934

Printed according to the original

Published in English for the first time

---

[a] Probably Friedrich Wilhelm Schlöffel, 'Dr Stieber', *Neue Rheinische Zeitung,* No. 177, 24 December 1848. - [b] *Neue Preussische Zeitung,* No. 148, 20 December 1848.

Gürzenich, a building where the Cologne Workers' Association
held their meetingsin 1848 and 1849

The house in Anderson Street, London,
where Marx lived from 1849 to April 1850

1849

74

ENGELS TO MARX

IN COLOGNE

Berne, 7[-8] January 1849

Dear Marx,

Having recovered, after several weeks of sinful living, from my exertions and adventures,[233] I feel, firstly, a need to get down to work again (striking proof of this being the enclosed Magyar-Slav article[a]), and, secondly, a need for money. The latter is the more urgent and if by the time this arrives, you haven't yet sent me anything, do so forthwith, for I've been *sans le sou*[b] these past few days, and it's impossible to touch anyone in this rotten town.

If only something worth writing about happened in this rotten country. But it's all local rubbish of the rottenest kind. However I'll shortly be sending a few general articles[c] about it. If I have to stay abroad much longer I shall go to Lugano, particularly if something blows up in Italy, as seems likely.

But I keep thinking that I shall soon be able to return. This lazing about in foreign parts, where you can't really do anything and are completely outside the movement, is truly unbearable. I am rapidly coming to the conclusion that detention for questioning in Cologne is better than life in free Switzerland. So do write and tell me if there isn't some chance of my being treated as favourably as Bürgers, Becker,[d] etc., etc.[248]

---

[a] F. Engels, 'The Magyar Struggle'. - [b] penniless - [c] F. Engels, 'Herr Müller.—Radetzky's Chicanery towards Tessin.—The Federal Council.—Lohbauer', 'The Swiss Press', 'Protectionist Agitation.—Recruiting into the Neapolitan Army', 'Müller.—The Freiburg Government.—Ochsenbein'. - [d] Hermann Becker

Raveaux is right: even in grace and favour Prussia[249] one is freer than in free Switzerland. Every little nonentity here is at one and the same time a police spy and an *assommeur*.[a] I saw an example of this on New Year's Eve.

Who the devil was responsible for inserting recently that boring religio-moral article from Heidelberg[b] on the March Association[250]? To my pleasure I have also noticed that Henricus occasionally exhales an article—witness the sighs extending over 2 issues on the subject of the Ladenberg circular.[c]

Our newspaper is now much quoted in Switzerland, the *Berner Zeitung* borrows a lot as does the *National-Zeitung*,[d] and this then goes the rounds of all the other papers. Also much quoted, more so than the *Kölnische,* according to the *National,* etc., etc., in Swiss papers in the French language.

You'll have included the advertisement.[e] Herewith a copy of ours in the *Berner Zeitung.* Greetings to the whole company.

Your
E.

Missed the post yesterday. Today, then, I'll merely add that since 1 January the *Neue Rheinische Zeitung has no longer been arriving here.* Do ascertain whether it's being regularly dispatched. I've looked into the question of a subscription, but it's no good. I'd have to subscribe for a $^1/_2$ year; I shan't be staying as long as that and anyway I haven't any money. As I said, it's important it should arrive here, not simply on my own account, but mainly because the *Berner Zeitung,* which is well disposed towards us and edited by a communist,[f] is doing everything to make it *en vogue* here.

First published in *Der Briefwechsel zwischen F. Engels und K. Marx,* Bd. 1, Stuttgart, 1913

Printed according to the original

Published in English for the first time

---

[a] assassin - [b] 'Ein Aktenstück des Märzvereins', *Neue Rheinische Zeitung,* No. 181, 29 December 1848. - [c] [H. Bürgers,] 'Hr. v. Ladenberg und die Volksschullehrer', *Neue Rheinische Zeitung,* No. 182, 30 December 1848. The planned continuation of this article did not appear in the newspaper. - [d] *Schweizerische National-Zeitung* - [e] This seems to refer to the advertisement about the daily publication of the *Berner Zeitung* as from 1 January 1849 printed in the *Neue Rheinische Zeitung,* Nos. 185, 187 and 189, 3, 5, and 7 January. - [f] Niklaus Niggeler

A cartoon of Frederick William IV and the Prussian bourgeoisie drawn by Engels on the back of E. Voswinkel's letter to Marx (22 January-beginning of February) about the elections to the Prussian Diet (1849)

75

MARX TO EDUARD von MÜLLER-TELLERING

IN RATIBOR

Cologne, 15 January [1849]

Dear Tellering,

You always calculate your posting days wrongly because you imagine that the post from Austria and Berlin arrives here regularly. But it's always 1-2 days late and is exceedingly irregular. I got your first letter from Vienna on the evening of the 10th. On the 11th I promptly sent a post-restante letter to *Oderberg*,[a] enclosing 50 talers in money orders.[251] Hence you'll have to return to Oderberg in any case, so as to pick up the money.

You will receive the newspapers, provided you write and tell me, immediately you get back from Oderberg, whereabouts you intend to live in the interim.

Despite Geiger's malevolence, I hope to see the matter of your passport finally settled within 2-3 days. But you must also tell me where our Berlin friend is to send your passport to.

If you have to keep away from Vienna—which would be an irreparable loss to the paper[b] and would mean your appointing a deputy responsible for day-to-day information—Breslau[c] would seem to me to be the most suitable place to stay. I frequently think sorrowfully of your wife,[d] who deserves a more comfortable lot.

I am enclosing an issue of the 'Neue Rheinische Zeitung', which will, I trust, be of interest to you *on account of the leading article on the Magyars*.[e]

Write to me as soon as you possibly can. In France the fun will begin anew in the spring. The bourgeois republic's infamy has advanced too rapidly towards the 'heyday of its transgressions'.[f]

Yours

K. Marx

First published in: Marx and Engels, *Works,* First Russian Edition, Vol. XXIX, Moscow, 1946

Printed according to the original

Published in English for the first time

---

[a] Polish name: Bohumin - [b] *Neue Rheinische Zeitung* - [c] Polish name: Wrocław - [d] Amalie - [e] F. Engels, 'The Magyar Struggle'. - [f] Shakespeare, *Hamlet,* Act I, Scene 5.

76

MARX TO ERNST DRONKE

IN PARIS

Cologne, 3 February [1849]

Dear Dronke,

Your letter,·passed on to me by Engels, I shall answer briefly as follows:

1. As regards your coming here: When I wrote 'Don't come to Germany until I write to you', *Kratz* had told me that your case was not yet quite settled.[252]

2. Later I wrote to Kapp instead of to you because Kapp was bombarding me with threatening letters. The draft I gave Kapp wasn't honoured by Korff. In the meantime I had declared at the shareholders' meeting that either Korff or I must resign from the paper.[a] Moreover, *during this period Plasman* had again sequestered the postage money, and the paper, as Engels discovered on his arrival, was expecting to announce its insolvency any day.

3. As regards the Meyerbeer business, I know *nothing whatever* about it. You will appreciate that in a situation in which the compositors were daily rebelling over a few talers, I would hardly have spurned 150 talers.

4. As regards my letter about Kapp, I was justified in writing it. During the most ghastly period of all, Kapp was threatening to attack us publicly. If you put yourself in *our* situation at that time, you will understand my vexation. As regards Weerth's comment (which, by the by, referred *not to you*, but to *Imandt*, who was writing to us incessantly), this is the first I have heard of it.

5. As regards the 25 talers remitted on *14 January*, these were dispatched to you in the presence of witnesses via Ewerbeck's address. The Post Office here will provide information about this tomorrow. Nota bene: *Kapp* received 15 talers from me at the same time.

6. As regards my not answering, Lupus will testify that I wrote to·you frequently.

7. If the tone of one of my letters was waspish, this was, a) because I was going through an atrociously bad patch with the

---

[a] *Neue Rheinische Zeitung*

paper and was under attack from all the paper's correspondents and creditors, b) because, in a letter to Freiligrath, *Imandt* depicted you, Kapp, etc., as complaining bitterly about me, while the precious Beust, I think it is *Beust* (I am not quite sure), was sending similar letters here.

Within a few days the paper must either *go under* or else *consolidate* itself, in which case we shall immediately send you more money of which, at the moment, there is a *complete* lack. However the business of the 25 talers must be cleared up.

That I have constantly regarded you as co-editor of the paper is apparent not only from the new announcement in the various papers,[a] but also from the fact that I placed your article about the expulsion of the Frankfurt refugee[b] under 'Cologne'.[c]

Your
Marx

[From Wilhelm Wolff]

In entire agreement with the above

Your
Lupus

First published in: Marx and Engels, *Works*, First Russian Edition, Vol. XXV, Moscow, 1934

Printed according to the original

Published in English for the first time

77

ENGELS TO DANIEL FENNER von FENNEBERG

IN FRANKFURT AM MAIN

Cologne, 1 March 1849

Dear Sir,

I would have replied to you before now had I not first had to consult various other people about your matter. I do not think it advisable for you to make any sort of public appearance here; out

---

a 'Bestellungen auf die *Neue Rheinische Zeitung* für das nächste Quartal, Januar bis März 1849'. - b F. Wiedecker - c [E. Dronke,] 'Allianz der europäischen Polizei', *Neue Rheinische Zeitung*, No. 192, 11 January 1849.

of craving for advancement, the chief of police[a] here is *capable de tout*,[b] as we have experienced only today in the unjustified expulsion of a local Polish refugee. I would further advise you, should your passport not be *absolutely impeccable,* to choose any route to Paris other than via Cologne and Brussels. You would get through Cologne well enough, but you would undoubtedly be arrested at the Belgian border and transported by prison van to the French border, after having, perhaps, spent several days in prison. I myself experienced this 5 months ago,[233] and every day fresh reports reach us of these infamies perpetrated against the refugees by the Belgians. You even run the risk of having all your money taken from you by the scoundrels and not getting a farthing back, as happened to the refugee, von Hochstetter.

If I can be of service to you in any other way, it would be a pleasure.

Yours faithfully

F. Engels

First published in: Marx and Engels, *Works,* Second Russian Edition, Vol. 27, Moscow, 1962

Printed according to the original

Published in English for the first time

78

MARX TO COLONEL ENGELS

IN COLOGNE

[Draft]

Cologne, 3 March [1849]

To Colonel Engels, Deputy Commandant

Sir,

The day before yesterday two non-commissioned officers[c] of the 8th Company, 16th Infantry Regiment, came to my rooms to speak to me privately. I had left for Düsseldorf. They were

---

[a] W. A. Geiger - [b] capable of anything - [c] Dust and Hover

therefore turned away. Yesterday afternoon two of these gentlemen again presented themselves and demanded a private interview.

I had them shown into a room where I joined them almost
immediately. I invited the gentlemen to sit down and asked them
what they wanted. They told me they wanted to know the name of
the writer of the article (No. 233 of the *Neue Rheinische Zeitung* of
28 February) against Captain von Uttenhoven.[253] I replied to these
gentlemen, 1) that the article in question had nothing to do with
me since it had appeared below the line and was therefore an
advertisement; 2) that they were at liberty to insert a refutation
gratis; 3) that they were at liberty to sue the paper. Upon the
gentlemen's remarking that the whole of the 8th Company felt
themselves to be insulted by the advertisement, I returned that
nothing but the signatures of all the members of the 8th Company
would convince me of the accuracy of that statement, which in any
case was irrelevant.

The non-commissioned officers thereupon declared that if I
failed to name, to 'deliver up' the 'man', they would 'no longer be
able to restrain their men', and 'evil would result'.

I told the gentlemen that little or nothing was to be achieved by
trying to threaten or intimidate me. They then withdrew
muttering under their breath.

Relaxation of discipline must have gone very far and all sense of
law and order must have ceased if, like a robber band, a Company
can send delegates to an individual citizen and attempt with
threats to extort this or that confession from him. In particular, I
fail to understand the meaning of the sentence: 'We can no longer
restrain our men'.

Are these 'men', perhaps, to exercise jurisdiction on their own
initiative, do these 'men' have other than legal resources at their
command?

I must beg you, Sir, to institute an inquiry into this incident and
to give me an explanation for this singular presumption. I would
be sorry to be obliged to have recourse to publicity.

First published in: Marx and Engels,
Works, First Russian Edition, Vol. XXV,
Moscow, 1934

Printed according to the original

Published in English for the first
time

79

MARX TO COLONEL ENGELS

IN COLOGNE

[Draft]

[Cologne, before 15 April 1849]

To Colonel Engels, Commandant

Sir,

Being convinced that Royal Prussian non-commissioned officers[a] would not deny words spoken in private, I did not call in *any witnesses* to the conversation in question.[b] As to my alleged remark that *'the courts, as has recently been seen, can do nothing to me'*,[254] even my political opponents will concede that, were I to harbour such a foolish thought, I would not express it before a third party. And do not the non-commissioned officers themselves admit that I explained to them that things *below the line* are no concern of mine and that in any case I am responsible only for the section of the paper signed by me? Hence there was absolutely no reason to speak of *my* position vis-à-vis the courts.

I am all the happier to refrain from pressing for a further inquiry as it was my concern, not that the non-commissioned officers should be punished, but simply that they should be reminded, from the lips of their superiors, of the limits of their duties.

As for the kind remark with which you conclude, the *Neue Rheinische Zeitung* has demonstrated, by its silence over the recent friction among the military themselves, how great is its consideration for the prevailing mood of unrest.

First published in: Marx and Engels, *Works*, First Russian Edition, Vol. XXV, Moscow, 1934

Printed according to the original

Published in English for the first time

---

[a] Dust and Hover - [b] The words 'although a co-editor of the *Neue Rheinische Zeitung* happened to be in my rooms at the time' are deleted in the original.

80

MARX TO ENGELS

IN COLOGNE

[Cologne, before 15 April 1849]

Dear Engels,

Leave out the article on B. Dietz until *the facts have been ascertained*. We shall ourselves write to Brussels on the subject.

By the way, try to find out the name of the printer's apprentice who reported the matter to Dietz without authority.

Your
Marx

[On the back of the letter]

Herr Engels, local

First published in: Marx and Engels, *Works,* First Russian Edition, Vol. XXI, Moscow, 1929 and in *MEGA,* Abt. III, Bd. 1, 1929

Printed according to the original

Published in English for the first time

81

MARX TO ENGELS

IN COLOGNE

Hamburg, 23 April [1849]

Dear Engels,

Your letter didn't reach me till today,[255] as I had already left Bremen on Wednesday[a] morning. Nothing doing in Bremen. Rösing went bankrupt a year ago and is now living solely on the interest from what remains of his wife's capital. Hence nothing doing.

On the other hand I shall certainly be able to make shift here.

As for the signature, cannot *Werres* sign?

---

[a] 18 April 1849

As for interim money arrangements, as long as I'm away the following should be noted: before I left, Plasmann solemnly promised to make whatever advances were necessary. Perhaps St. Naut feels some scruple about resorting to this source. If necessary, do *so yourself*.

All this week the paper[a] has been very skimpy, which assorts ill with my present mission.

Warmest regards to my wife and the others.

Write by return whatever happens, and keep your chin up. *Les choses marcheront.*[b]

Your
K. Marx

[Inside the envelope]

Address: Rohde, Merchant, Bleichenbrücke.

<table>
<tr><td>First published in Der Briefwechsel zwischen F. Engels und K. Marx, Bd. 1, Stuttgart, 1913</td><td>Printed according to the original

Published in English for the first time</td></tr>
</table>

82

MARX TO HERMANN BREHMER

IN BRESLAU

Harburg, 6 May [1849]

To Mr Brehmer in Breslau[c]

I warmly recommend to you the bearer of these lines, Mr Bruhn, whose name you will still recall from the events in Southern Germany last year.[256]

Yours very truly
Karl Marx

<table>
<tr><td>First published in: G. Becker, 'Neue Dokumente von Karl Marx aus dem Jahre 1849', Zeitschrift für Geschichtswissenschaft, 1974, Heft 4</td><td>Printed according to the original

Published in English for the first time</td></tr>
</table>

---

[a] *Neue Rheinische Zeitung* - [b] Things will go all right. - [c] Polish name: Wrocław

83

MARX TO EDUARD von MÜLLER-TELLERING

IN BRESLAU

Harburg, 6 May 1849

Dear Tellering,

I warmly recommend to you the bearer, Mr. Bruhn, who is one of our principal agitators in Germany.

Yours very truly

Dr Karl Marx

First published in: G. Becker, 'Neue Dokumente von Karl Marx aus dem Jahre 1849', *Zeitschrift für Geschichtswissenschaft*, 1974, Heft 4

Printed according to the original

Published in English for the first time

84

MARX TO ANDREAS STIFFT

IN VIENNA

Harburg, 6 May [1849]

To Dr. Stifft in Vienna

Dear Stifft,

Post tot discrimina rerum,[a] I am glad to have an opportunity of reminding you of my existence. Each new number of the Vienna paper[b] gives me the real satisfaction of knowing beyond doubt that you have not been swallowed up by the counter-revolutionary monster.[257] I trust that we shall yet find ourselves seated side by side at a convention.

The bearer, Bruhn, is one of my best friends and a proficient, active revolutionary. I recommend him to you most highly.

Yours

K. Marx

First published in: G. Becker, 'Neue Dokumente von Karl Marx aus dem Jahre 1849', *Zeitschrift für Geschichtswissenschaft*, 1974, Heft 4

Printed according to the original

Published in English for the first time

---

[a] After so many vicissitudes (Virgil, *Aeneid*, I). - [b] *Der Radikale*

85

MARX TO JOSEPH WEYDEMEYER [258]

IN FRANKFURT AM MAIN

[Bingen, 1 June 1849]

Dear Weydemeyer,

I beg you in *my own* and *Freiligrath*'s names to take the printer of Freiligrath's poem[a] to court for piracy and sue him for damages.

My general attorney is *St. A. Naut* in Cologne, and I should be much obliged if you would write to him about this matter.

Vale faveque.[b]

K. Marx

First published in: Marx and Engels, *Works,* First Russian Edition, Vol. XXV. Moscow, 1934

Printed according to the original

Published in English for the first time

86

MARX TO ENGELS [259]

IN KAISERSLAUTERN

Paris, 7 June [1849]
45, rue de Lille

Dear Engels,

I am not writing to you at any great length in this letter. First I want you to tell me in your reply whether it arrives *intact*. I believe that letters are again being opened *con amore.*[c]

---

[a] Reference to F. Freiligrath's 'Abschiedswort der *Neuen Rheinischen Zeitung*' published in the newspaper's last number (No. 301, 19 May 1849) printed in red ink. - [b] Good-bye and farewell. - [c] enthusiastically

Here a royalist reaction is in full swing, more barefaced than under Guizot, and comparable only to that after 1815. Paris is *morne*.[a] On top of that the cholera is raging mightily. For all that, never has a colossal eruption of the revolutionary volcano been more imminent than it is in Paris today. Details to follow. I consort with the whole of the revolutionary party and in a few days' time I shall have *all* the revolutionary journals at my disposal.

As for the Palatinate-Baden envoys here, Blind, alarmed by a real or pretended attack of cholera, has moved into the country some hours away from Paris.

Quant à[b] Schütz, the following should be noted:

1. The Provisional Government has placed him in a false position by failing to keep him informed. The French demand *des faits*[c] and where can he get them from if not a soul writes to him? Dispatches must reach him as often as possible. It is clear that at this moment he can achieve nothing. All that can be done is to throw dust in the eyes of the Prussian Government by enabling him to have frequent meetings with the leaders of the Montagnards.[260]

2. A second, unpardonable mistake on the part of the *Gouvernement provisoire du Palatinat*[d] is their entrusting a crowd of rotten Germans with this or that mission behind the back of the official envoy. This will have to cease once and for all if Schütz is to maintain at least the prestige of his position vis-à-vis the Montagnards and just now—vis-à-vis Prussia—that is the whole point of his mission.

Apart from that, it goes without saying that he doesn't learn very much, since he consorts only with a few *official* Montagnards. I shall, incidentally, keep him always *au courant*.[e]

For my part I must ask you to write to me at least twice a week regularly and immediately every time anything important happens.

The *Kölnische Zeitung* feuilleton on the Palatinate movement, dated Dürkheim an der Haardt, states among other things:

'Some anger has been aroused by Mr Marx, editor of the *Rheinische Zeitung*.[f] He is said to have told the Provisional Government that since his time had not yet come, he intended temporarily to retire.'[g]

---

[a] dreary - [b] As for - [c] facts - [d] provisional government of the Palatinate - [e] informed - [f] *Neue Rheinische Zeitung* - [g] 'Briefe aus Baden und der Pfalz. IV. Dürkheim a. d. Haardt, 1. Juni', *Kölnische Zeitung*, No. 136, 6 June 1849.

How does that fit in? The miserable Germans here, with whom, by the way, I avoid any meeting, will seek to proclaim this throughout the whole of Paris. I therefore think it advisable for you to see that an item appears in the *Karlsruher Zeitung* or the *Mannheimer Abendzeitung* stating expressly that I am in Paris as the representative of the *democratic Central Committee*. Another reason why I think this would be useful is that for the time being, as no immediate results are to be obtained here, the Prussians must be made to believe that the most frightful intrigues are going on here. *Il faut faire peur aux Aristocrates.*[a]

Ruge is a complete nonentity here.

What is Dronke doing?

You must, by the way, see that *you raise money for me somewhere.* You know that I spent the latest sums received *pour faire honneur aux obligations de la 'Nouvelle Gazette Rhénane',*[b] and, in the present *circonstances,*[c] I cannot live a completely retired life, still less get into financial difficulties.

If at all possible let me have an article in French in which you sum up the whole Hungarian affair.[261]

Show this letter to d'Ester, to whom my best regards. If I am to write to a different address, let me have it.

M.

Write to me at the following address: M. Ramboz, 45 rue de Lille

[On the back of the letter]

Herrn *Fr. Engels,* inquire at Dr d'Ester's.

First published abridged in *Der Briefwechsel zwischen F. Engels und K. Marx*, Bd. 1, Stuttgart, 1913 and in full in *MEGA*, Abt. III, Bd. 1, 1929

Printed according to the original

Published in English for the first time

---

[a] We must frighten the aristocrats. - [b] to honour the obligations of the *Neue Rheinische Zeitung*. - [c] circumstances

87

MARX TO JOSEPH WEYDEMEYER

IN FRANKFURT AM MAIN

Paris, 13 July [1849]
45, rue de Lille
Address: M. Ramboz

Dear Weydemeyer,

Dronke will already have written to tell you that you must sell the red newspapers at any price.[262]

I am here with my *famille, sans le sou.*[a][263] And yet an opportunity has come my way of making 3,000-4,000 fr. in a few weeks. For my pamphlet against Proudhon,[b] which he has done everything in his power to suppress, is beginning to sell here, and it is up to me to infiltrate reviews of it into the more important papers, thus necessitating a second edition. But for this to be of any help I would have to buy up the copies still available in Brussels and Paris in order to become sole *propriétaire.*

300-400 talers would enable me to carry out this operation and at the same time maintain myself here during the early days. You might, perhaps, be able to help me in this.

Namely, as follows:

A lady in Rheda—Lüning is also in touch with her—sent 1,000 talers to Carl Post for the *Neue Rheinische Zeitung,* but recovered the money when that paper went under. Might she not, perhaps, be persuaded by your intervention to make me this advance? My claim to such an advance is, I believe, all the greater as I contributed more than 7,000 talers to the *Neue Rheinische Zeitung* which, after all, was a party enterprise.

If at all possible, pursue this matter, but without mentioning it to anybody. I tell you that, unless help is forthcoming from one quarter or another, I shall be *perdu,*[c] since my family is also here and the last piece of my wife's jewellery has already found its way to the pawnbrokers.

I await your reply by return.

Your

K. Marx

First published in: Marx and Engels, *Works,* First Russian Edition, Vol. XXV, Moscow, 1934

Printed according to the original

Published in English for the first time

---

[a] family, penniless - [b] K. Marx, *The Poverty of Philosophy.* - [c] lost

88

MARX TO CAROLINE SCHÖLER[a]

IN COLOGNE

Paris, 14 July 1849
45, rue de Lille

Dear Lina,

Would you be so kind, when you write to my wife, as to enclose a note to the red Orlando furioso[b]? You must help me a little in the act I am putting on.

Yours very sincerely
K. Marx

First published in *MEGA*₂, Abt. III, Bd. 3, Berlin, 1981

Printed according to the original

Published in English for the first time

89

ENGELS TO JENNY MARX[264]

IN PARIS

Vevey, Vaud Canton,
25 July 1849

Dear Mrs Marx,

You as well as Marx will be wondering why you have not heard from me for so long. *En voici les causes.*[c] On the same day as I wrote to Marx (from Kaiserslautern) there came news that the Prussians had occupied Homburg, thereby cutting off communications with Paris. So I couldn't send the letter off and went to join Willich. In Kaiserslautern I had completely disassociated myself from the *soi-disant*[d] revolution; but when the Prussians arrived, I

---

[a] Appended to Jenny Marx's letter to the same addressee (see this volume, pp. 546-48). - [b] Ferdinand Wolff (red Wolff) is compared to the title character of L. Ariosto's poem. - [c] Here are the reasons. - [d] so-called

couldn't resist the urge to take part in the war. Willich being the
only officer who was any good, I joined him and became his
adjutant. I was in four engagements, two of them fairly important,
particularly the one at Rastatt,[265] and discovered that the
much-vaunted bravery under fire is quite the most ordinary
quality one can possess. The whistle of bullets is really quite a
trivial matter and though, throughout the campaign, a great deal
of cowardice was in evidence, I did not see as many as a dozen
men whose conduct was cowardly *in battle*. But all the more 'brave
stupidity'. *Enfin*,[a] I came through the whole thing unscathed, and
au bout du compte,[b] it was as well that one member of the *Neue
Rheinische Zeitung* was present, since the entire pack of democratic
blackguards were in Baden and the Palatinate, and are now
bragging about the heroic deeds they never performed. It would
have been said again that the gentlemen of the *Neue Rheinische
Zeitung* were too cowardly to fight. But of all the democratic
gentry, the only ones to fight were myself and Kinkel. The latter
joined our corps as a musketeer and did pretty well; in the first
engagement in which he took part, his head was grazed by a bullet
and he was taken prisoner.

Having covered the withdrawal of the Baden army, our corps
entered Switzerland 24 hours later than everyone else, and
yesterday we arrived here in Vevey. During the campaign and the
march through Switzerland it was quite impossible for me to write
so much as a line. But now I hasten to send some news, and write
to you with all the more dispatch for having heard—somewhere
in Baden—that Marx had been arrested in Paris. Since we never
received any newspapers, we learnt nothing. Whether or not it is
true, I have never been able to find out. You can imagine the state
of anxiety I am in as a result, and I beg you most urgently to set
my mind at rest and to put an end to my doubts about Marx's
fate. Since I have had no confirmation of this rumour of Marx's
arrest, I still hope it is false. But that Dronke and Schapper are in
jug, I can hardly doubt. Enough—if Marx is still at liberty send
him this letter with the request that he write to me immediately. If
he should not feel safe in Paris, he will be completely safe here
in the Vaud Canton. The government describes itself as red
and *partisane de la révolution permanente*.[c] In Geneva likewise.
Schily from Trier is there; he held a command in the Mainz
corps.

If I get any money from home, I shall probably go to Lausanne

---

[a] In short - [b] as it turns out - [c] supporter of permanent revolution

or Geneva and see what I can do. Our column, which fought well, bores me and there isn't anything to do here. In battle, Willich is brave, cool-headed and adroit, and able to appreciate a situation quickly and accurately, but when not in battle he is a *plus ou moins*[a] tedious ideologist[b] and a true socialist. Most of the people in the corps whom one can talk to have been sent elsewhere.

If only I could be sure that Marx is at liberty! I have often thought that, in the midst of the Prussian bullets, my post was much less dangerous than that of others in Germany and especially Marx's in Paris. So dispel my uncertainty soon.

Tout à vous[c]

Engels

Address: F. Engels, refugié allemand, Vevey, Suisse (If possible under cover as far as Thionville or Metz.)

First published in *Der Briefwechsel zwischen F. Engels und K. Marx*, Bd. 1, Stuttgart, 1913

Printed according to the original

Published in English in full for the first time

90

MARX TO FERDINAND FREILIGRATH

IN COLOGNE

[Paris,] 31 July [1849]

Dear Freiligrath,

I must confess that I am much astonished by Lassalle's behaviour. I had approached him personally and, since I myself had at one time made the countess[d] a loan and was, besides, aware of Lassalle's liking for me, it would never have occurred to me that he would compromise me in this way. On the contrary, I had impressed upon him the need for the utmost discretion. The direst straits are better than public begging. I have written to him on the subject.[266]

---

[a] more or less - [b] meaning: follower of philosophical idealism - [c] Yours ever - [d] Sophie von Hatzfeldt

I find the business unspeakably annoying.

Parlons de politique,[a] since it will distract us from this private unpleasantness. In Switzerland things are becoming ever more complicated and now, as regards Italy, there is Savoy into the bargain. It would seem that, if needs be, Austria proposes to recoup her loss of Hungary at Italy's expense. The incorporation of Savoy by Austria would, however, be the undoing of the present French government if tolerated by the latter. The majority in the French Chamber is clearly falling apart. The Right is splitting up into Philippists pure and simple, Legitimists who vote with the Philippists, and Legitimists pure and simple, who have recently been voting with the Left.[267] What Thiers and company are planning is to make Louis Napoleon Consul for ten years, until the coming-of-age of the Count of Paris[b] who will then replace him. If, as is almost certain, the *assemblée* reimposes the *droits*[c] on drink,[268] it will arouse the antagonism of all the wine-growers. With each reactionary measure it alienates yet another section of the population.

But most important of all just now is England. We must have no illusions about the so-called Peace Party,[269] of which Cobden is the acknowledged leader. Nor should we have any illusions about the 'unselfish enthusiasm' of the English for Hungary, which has resulted in the organisation of meetings throughout the country.

The Peace Party is simply a *cloak* for the FREE-TRADE *Party*. The same content, the same object, the same leaders. Just as, at home, the Free Traders attacked the aristocracy in its material basis with the repeal of the Corn and Navigation Laws,[270] so now in their foreign policy, they are attacking it in its European connections and ramifications—by seeking to break the Holy Alliance.[271] The English Free Traders are radical bourgeois who wish to break radically with the aristocracy in order to rule without let or hindrance. What they overlook is the fact that they are thus, *malgré eux,*[d] bringing the people onto the stage and into power. Exploitation of the peoples, not by means of medieval warfare but solely by means of trade warfare—that's your Peace Party. Cobden's behaviour in the Hungarian affair had an immediately practical nexus. Russia is now seeking to negotiate a loan. Cobden, the representative of the industrial bourgeoisie, forbids

---

[a] Let us talk politics - [b] Louis Philipp Albert - [c] duties, taxes - [d] willy-nilly.

this deal of the financial bourgeoisie's, and in England the Bank is ruled by industry, whereas in France industry is ruled by the Bank.

Cobden's attack on Russia has been more formidable than any of either Dembinski or Görgey.[a] He revealed how pitiable was the condition of her finances. She is, he says, the MOST WRETCHED NATION. Each year the Siberian mines bring the State no more than £700,000: the duty on spirits brings it 10 times as much. True, the gold and silver reserve in the vaults of the Bank of Petersburg amounts to £14,000,000, but it serves as a metallic reserve for a paper circulation of £80,000,000. Hence, if the Tsar[b] dips into the vaults of the Bank, he will depreciate the paper money, and thus bring about a revolution in Russia herself. Consequently, the proud English bourgeois exclaims, the absolutist colossus cannot stir unless we make him a loan, and this we shall not do. Once again we are waging, by purely bourgeois means, the bourgeoisie's war against feudal absolutism. The golden calf is mightier than all the calves on the thrones in the world. Of course the English FREE TRADERS also have a direct interest where Hungary is concerned. Instead of Austrian trade barriers, as hitherto, a trade agreement and some sort of FREE TRADE with Hungary. The money, which they are now without doubt secretly remitting to the Hungarians, they will assuredly get back 'with profit and interest' in *retour*[c] by way of trade.

The English bourgeoisie's attitude to continental despotism is a reversal of the campaign they conducted against the French from 1793 to 1815. The importance of this development cannot be overrated.

Kindest regards to you and your wife[d] from me and my wife.

Your

K. Marx

First published in part in *Die Neue Zeit*, Ergänzungshefte No. 12, 1911-12 and in full in: Marx and Engels, *Works*, First Russian Edition, Vol. XXV, Moscow, 1934

Printed according to the original

Published in English in full for the first time

---

[a] Reference to Cobden's speech at a meeting held on 23 July 1849 in support of Hungary, see *The Times*, No. 20236, 24 July 1849 and *The Northern Star*, No. 614, 28 July 1849.- [b] Nicholas I - [c] return - [d] Ida

91

MARX TO ENGELS[43]

IN VEVEY

[Paris, end of July 1849]

Dear Engels,

I have suffered a great deal of anxiety on your account and was truly delighted when yesterday I received a letter in your own hand.[a] I had got Dronke (who is here) to write to your brother-in-law[b] asking for news of you. He, of course, knew nothing.

My whole family is here[263]; the government wanted to banish me to Morbihan, the Pontine marshes of Brittany.[272] So far I have frustrated their intention. But if I am to write to you in greater detail, both about my own circumstances here and about affairs in general, you must let me have a safer address, for things are really appalling here.

You now have the best opportunity to write a history of or a pamphlet on the Baden-Palatinate revolution.[273] Had you not taken part in the actual fighting, we couldn't have put forward our views about that frolic. It would be a splendid chance for you to define the position of the *Neue Rheinische Zeitung* vis-à-vis the democratic party generally. I am positive that the thing will sell and bring you money.

I have embarked on negotiations with a view to starting a politico-economic (monthly) periodical in Berlin which would have to be largely written by us two.[274]

Lupus[c] is also in Switzerland, I believe in Berne. Weerth was here yesterday; he is setting up an agency in Liverpool. Red Wolff[d] is living here with me. Finances are, of course, in a state of chaos.

Freiligrath is in Cologne now as heretofore. If my wife were not in an *état par trop intéressant*,[e] I would gladly leave Paris as soon as it was financially possible to do so.

---

[a] See this volume, pp. 202-04. - [b] Emil Blank - [c] Wilhelm Wolff - [d] Ferdinand Wolff - [e] all too interesting condition (on the birth of Marx's son, see this volume, p. 220)

Farewell. Convey my kindest regards to Willich and write by return to the address: M. Ramboz, rue de Lille, 45.

Your
K. M.

First published in *Der Briefwechsel zwischen F. Engels und K. Marx*, Bd. 1, Stuttgart, 1913   Printed according to the original

92

MARX TO JOSEPH WEYDEMEYER[275]

IN FRANKFURT AM MAIN

[Paris, end of July 1849]

Dear Weydemeyer,

I have heard from Dronke that it's no go with the Westphalian lady.[a] Well, it can't be helped.

Now I should appreciate your advice as to how best to publish pamphlets.

I should like to start with the pamphlet on *wages* of which only the beginning appeared in the *Neue Rheinische Zeitung*.[b] I would write a short political foreword to it on the present *status quo*. Do you think that, e.g., Leske would be agreeable? But he would have to pay, as soon as he had the manuscript in his hands, and pay well, since I know that this pamphlet will attract and will find a mass of subscribers in advance. My present financial *état*[c] will not permit me to settle my outstanding *compte*[d] with Leske.[276]

Were Leske then to find that the thing is well received, we could continue in this way.

Yesterday I had a letter from Engels[e]; he is in Switzerland and, as Willich's adjutant, has taken part in four encounters.

The sword of Damocles still hangs over my head; my expulsion[f] has neither been rescinded nor, for the moment, is it being enforced.

---

[a] See this volume, p. 201. - [b] K. Marx, *Wage Labour and Capital*. - [c] condition - [d] account - [e] See this volume, pp. 202-04. - [f] ibid., pp. 207, 211, 212.

Awkward though the present state of affairs may be for our personal circumstances, I am nevertheless among the *satisfaits. Les choses marchent très bien*[a] and the Waterloo suffered by official democracy may be regarded as a victory.[277] 'Governments by grace of God' are taking it upon themselves to avenge us on the bourgeoisie, and to chastise them.

One of these days I may perhaps send you a short article for your paper[b] on the state of affairs in England.[278] Just now I find it too boring, having already discussed the matter in a number of private letters.

Write to me *direct* and to *my own* address: 45, rue de Lille, Monsieur Ramboz.

My best regards to your wife[c] and yourself from my wife and me. The former is *très souffrante, conséquence naturelle de son état par trop intéressant.*

Adieu, mon cher,[d] and reply soon.

Your
K. M.

First published in *Die Gesellschaft,* Jg. VII, Bd. 2, Berlin, 1930

Printed according to the original

Published in English in full for the first time

93

MARX TO JOSEPH WEYDEMEYER

IN FRANKFURT AM MAIN

[Paris, mid-August 1849]

Dear Weydemeyer,

I will gladly fall in with Rühl's suggestion[279] if he agrees to take over the whole of the business side, at which I am no good and for which he will be paid a commission.

1) But I have no publisher on hand to make the necessary advances,

---

[a] satisfied. Things are going very well - [b] *Neue Deutsche Zeitung* - [c] Louise - [d] very poorly, the natural consequence of her all too interesting condition. Good-bye, my friend (on the birth of Marx's son, see this volume, p. 220).

2) the subscription lists seem to me superfluous. Announcements in the *Westdeutsche* and other papers in the Rhineland and elsewhere would achieve the same purpose. The thing should be advertised particularly in the Berlin, Hamburg, Leipzig and Breslau[a] papers.

The news about your paper[b] is very bad. I shall at once write and inform Naut, the trusty old business manager of the *Neue Rheinische Zeitung,* and acquaint you with the result.[280]

You would already have had my article[c] but for the fact that the illness of my wife and all the children has meant that I have been a kind of male nurse for the past week.

Best regards to your wife.

Your
K. M.

I hope for a reply as soon as possible.

First published in: Marx and Engels, *Works,* First Russian Edition, Vol. XXV, Moscow, 1934

Printed according to the original

Published in English for the first time

94

MARX TO ENGELS[228]

IN VEVEY

Paris, 17 August [1849]

Dear Engels,

I don't know whether my first letter—in reply to the first one you sent my wife[d]—arrived safely, since your address was very uncertain. I would have already replied to your second[281] had I not been prevented by the fact that the whole of my family here was ill. Let me repeat once again how anxious my wife and I were on your account and what a delightful surprise it was to have definite news of you.

You will see from the date that, as a result of my protest, the Ministry of the Interior has for the time being left me unmolested here in Paris. The Morbihan *département,* to which I had been

---

[a] Wrocław - [b] *Neue Deutsche Zeitung* - [c] See this volume, p. 209. - [d] ibid., pp. 202-04 and 207-08.

directed, is lethal at this time of year—the Pontine marshes of Brittany.[282] It would not be prudent just now to write about the 13 June affair.[260] I don't believe, or at least don't know whether secrecy of the mails is being observed.

The general situation here may be summed up in a couple of words: the majority disintegrating into its original, mutually hostile elements, Bonapartism hopelessly compromised, ill-will among the peasants because of the retention of the 45 centimes, the wine-growers furious at the threatened retention of the tax on drink,[268] the current of public opinion once again anti-reactionary, in the Chamber, now prorogued, and in the Ministry, reaction, growing exclusive and concerned with expelling the Barrot-Dufaure clique from the Cabinet.[283] As soon as this comes about you can look for an early revolutionary resurrection.

I don't know whether in Switzerland you have any chance of following the English movement. The English have taken it up again at exactly the same juncture at which it was broken off by the February revolution. As you are aware, the Peace Party[269] is nothing but the Free-trade party under a new guise. But this time the industrial bourgeoisie is acting in a manner even more revolutionary than during the Anti-Corn League agitation.[270] In two ways: 1) the aristocracy, whose roots have been attacked at home by the repeal of the Corn Laws and the Navigation Acts, is further to be ruined in the sphere of foreign policy, in its European ramifications. Reversal of Pitt's policy. Anti-Russian-Austrian-Prussian, in a word, pro Italy and Hungary. Cobden has formally threatened to proscribe bankers who make loans to Russia, has unleashed a veritable campaign against Russian finances. 2) Agitation for universal suffrage, in order to effect the total political severance of the tenants from the landed aristocracy, to give the towns an absolute majority in Parliament, to nullify the House of Lords. Financial reform, in order to curb the Church and cut off the political revenues of the aristocracy.

Chartists and Free Traders have joined hands in these two propaganda campaigns. Harney and Palmerston apparently friends. At the last meeting held in London, O'Connor and Colonel Thompson both of one mind.[284]

Consequences of this economic campaign against feudalism and Holy Alliance incalculable.

Hungary splendid. But this rotten Prussia? *Qu'en dis-tu?*[a] The pallid canaille[b] are now being fattened in Saxony, Baden, the

---

[a] What do you think of it? - [b] H. Heine, *Deutschland. Ein Wintermärchen,* Kapit VIII.

Palatinate. If they send an army to the aid of the Austrians, it will be so contrived that they themselves remain in Bohemia and wax fat there. But wretched Prussia—I only fear that it's too craven—*perdu*[a] as soon as it participates in the Hungarian affair, which in any case is turning into a *guerre universelle*.[b]

Maintenant, mon cher, que faire de notre part? Il faut nous lancer dans une entreprise littéraire et mercantile, j'attends tes propositions.[c]

Red Lupus[d] is here, in the same house as myself; Dronke in Paris likewise, *mais c'est un tout petit homme de l'école de E. Meyen.*[e] Lupus[f] is in Zurich. Address: Dr. Lüning. You don't need to write separately to M. Ramboz. *C'est mon pseudonyme.*[g]

So the address is simply:

Monsieur Ramboz, 45, rue de Lille.

Salut!

Ch. M.

First published abridged in *Der Briefwechsel zwischen F. Engels und K. Marx*, Bd. 1, Stuttgart, 1913 and in full in *MEGA*, Abt. III, Bd. 1, 1929

Printed according to the original

Published in English in full for the first time

95

MARX TO ENGELS[43]

IN LAUSANNE

[Paris,] 23 August [1849]

Dear Engels,

I am being banished to the Morbihan *département*, the Pontine marshes of Brittany.[272] I need hardly say that I shall not consent to this veiled attempt on my life. So I am leaving France.[285]

They won't give me a passport for Switzerland, hence I must go to London, and that tomorrow. In any case, Switzerland will soon be hermetically sealed and the mice would be trapped all at one go.

---

[a] lost - [b] general war - [c] Now, my dear friend, what should we for our part do? We must launch out into a literary and commercial venture, I await your proposals. - [d] Ferdinand Wolff - [e] but he's an insignificant little chap of the school of E. Meyen. - [f] Wilhelm Wolff - [g] It's my pseudonym.

Besides, in London there is a *positive* prospect of my being able to start a German newspaper.[a] I am *assured* of part of the funds.

So you must leave for London at once. In any case your safety demands it. The Prussians would shoot you twice over: 1) because of Baden, 2) because of Elberfeld.[286] And why stay in a Switzerland where you can do nothing?

You will have no difficulty in coming to London, whether under the name of Engels or under the name of Mayer. As soon as you say you want to go to England, you will receive a one-way passport to London from the French Embassy.

I count on this *absolutely*. You *cannot* stay in Switzerland. In London we shall get down to business.

For the time being my wife will remain here. Continue to write to her at the same address: 45, rue de Lille, M. Ramboz.

But once again, I confidently count on you not to leave me in the lurch.

Your
K. M.

Lupus[b] is at Dr Lüning's, Zurich. Write and tell him also about my plan.

First published abridged in *Der Briefwech-sel zwischen F. Engels und K. Marx*, Bd. 1, Stuttgart, 1913 and in full in *MEGA*, Abt. III, Bd. 1, 1929

Printed according to the original

96

ENGELS TO JOSEPH WEYDEMEYER [287]

IN FRANKFURT AM MAIN

Lausanne, 23 August 1849
8, Place de la Palud

Dear Weydemeyer,

Post tot discrimina rerum[c]—after umpteen arrests in Hesse and the Palatinate,[288] after 3 weeks of sybaritic living in Kaiserslautern, after a glorious 4 weeks' campaign in which, for a change, I buckled on my sword-belt and acted as Willich's adjutant, after 4

---

[a] *Neue Rheinische Zeitung. Politisch-ökonomische Revue* - [b] Wilhelm Wolff - [c] After so many vicissitudes (Virgil, *Aeneid*, I).

weeks of tedious cantoning with the refugee detachment in the Vaud Canton, I am at last finding my feet here in Lausanne. The very first thing I shall do is sit down and compose a merry tale of the whole Palatinate-Baden frolic.[a] But since I no longer have any contact with Germany and do not even know which towns are or are not under martial law, I don't know what publisher to approach. I'm no longer acquainted with such folk. You are on the spot and hence will be better able to say which are the right publishers with whom to negotiate something of this kind; it will, of course, be quite innocuous and will not involve any risk of confiscation or prosecution. There might be such a one in Frankfurt. But he must have money. Please be good enough to write to me about this, if possible by return, so that I can take the necessary steps at once.

I recently saw your red Becker,[b] very jaunty, in Geneva; he was tippling with the popular man, Esselen, and other easy-going *diis minorum gentium*[c] in the country.

Warm regards to your wife and all our acquaintances

from your
Engels

First published in: Marx and Engels. *Works,* First Russian Edition, Vol. XXV. Moscow, 1934

Printed according to the original
Published in English in full for the first time

97

ENGELS TO JAKOB LUKAS SCHABELITZ

IN BASLE

Lausanne, 24 August 1849
8, Place de la Palud

Dear Schabelitz,

I am most obliged to you for promptly forwarding a letter to me. Since I cannot have my letters sent direct and knew of no other address, I was compelled to put you to this trouble. You

---

[a] F. Engels, *The Campaign for the German Imperial Constitution.* - [b] Max Joseph Becker - [c] second-rate luminaries (literally: gods of minor peoples)

may be receiving one or two more for me and would, perhaps, be kind enough to send these on to me also.

I am at present stuck in Lausanne where I am writing my reminiscences of the farcical Palatinate-Baden revolution.[a] You know me too well to credit me with political participation in this affair which was lost before it began. In Karlsruhe and Kaiserslautern I poked quiet fun at the provisional government's blunders and lack of resolution, I refused all posts, and it was not until the Prussians arrived that I joined Willich at Offenbach and took part in the campaign as his adjutant. Now at headquarters, now in the face of the enemy, the whole time in correspondence with the High Command, in constant touch with d'Ester, who, as 'red camarilla', was spurring on the government, in various engagements and, finally, at the battle of Rastatt,[265] I had the opportunity of seeing a great deal and learning a great deal. As you know, I am sufficiently critical not to share the illusions of the run-of-the-mill, vociferous republicans and to detect the despondency lurking beneath the bravado of the leaders.

As befits the *Neue Rheinische Zeitung,* the thing will take a view of the affair different from that of other prospective accounts. It will disclose many a shabby trick and, in particular, will contain much that is new concerning the goings-on in the Palatinate, about which hitherto virtually nothing has been known. It won't be big—about 4-6 sheets.

Up till now I have not had leisure enough to look round for a publisher. I would not care to send the manuscript to Germany, there is a danger of its being intercepted in the post. Since I am largely unfamiliar with the book trade in Switzerland, I thought I would write and ask you whether your old man[b] might be the kind of publisher who would accept such work and—NB—*pay* for it, for I need money, *il faut que l'on vive.*[c] That the thing will be pleasant to read goes without saying, and my name is guarantee enough that it will be bought in Germany (it won't be liable to confiscation, *le sujet n'y prête pas*[d]). If, then, your worthy papa is prepared to do business, I shall rely on you, if not, it can't be helped. In that case you will not, at any rate, refuse to advise me about other possible German publishers, since I am very much in the dark in regard to the German book trade as well.

---

[a] F. Engels, *The Campaign for the German Imperial Constitution.* - [b] Jacob Christian Schabelitz - [c] one has to live - [d] the subject doesn't lend itself thereto

Write and tell me about this if possible by return.
Best regards

from your
F. Engels

First published in: Marx and Engels, *Works,* First Russian Edition, Vol. XXV, Moscow, 1934

Printed according to the original

Published in English for the first time

98

MARX TO FERDINAND FREILIGRATH [43]

IN COLOGNE

London, 5 September [1849]

Dear Freiligrath,
Address: Karl Blind, 18 Roberts Street,
Peterson's Coffeehouse, Grosvenor Square;
therein the letter to me under cover.

I can only write a word or two since I have had a kind of cholerine for the past 4-5 days and feel dreadfully listless.

My wife has written and asked me to acknowledge receipt of your letter enclosing 100 fr. Just imagine what blackguards the Paris police are; they have even been harassing my wife and it was only with difficulty that she succeeded in obtaining permission to remain in Paris until 15 September. We had rented our lodgings there up to that date.

I am now in a really difficult situation. My wife is in an advanced state of pregnancy,[a] she is obliged to leave Paris on the 15th and I don't know how I am to raise the money for her journey and for settling her in here.[289]

On the other hand there are excellent prospects of my being able to start a monthly review[b] here; but I am pressed for time and the first weeks constitute the real difficulty.

Lassalle seems to have been offended by my letter to you and another I wrote to him.[c] This was certainly very far from my

---

[a] See this volume, p. 220. - [b] *Neue Rheinische Zeitung. Politisch-ökonomische Revue* -
[c] See this volume, p. 204.

intention, and I should already have written to him, if my present condition did not make letter-writing a real burden to me.

Once I am more or less on my feet again I shall write to you in greater detail about politics. I look forward to a few lines from you soon. Best regards to your wife,[a] Daniels, etc.

Your

K. Marx

First published in: Fr. Mehring, 'Freilig-rath und Marx in ihrem Briefwechsel', *Die Neue Zeit*, Ergänzungsheft, No. 12, 12 April 1912, Stuttgart

Printed according to the original

99

ENGELS TO GEORGE JULIAN HARNEY[290]

IN LONDON

Genova,[b] 5 October 1849

My dear Harney,

You will have got the few lines I sent you through Colonel Willich.[291] This is to inform you, and by you Marx, that I am this morning arrived here in Genova, and that, wind and weather favourable, I am going under sail for *London* to-morrow morning on board the English schooner *Cornish Diamond,* Capt-n *Stevens.* My journey will be of about 4 or 5 weeks so that by the middle of November I shall be in London.

I am very happy to have found so soon an opportunity of leaving this damned police atmosphere—indeed I never saw it so organised as here in Piedmont.

Ever truly thine

F. Engels

First published in: Marx and Engels, *Works,* First Russian Edition, Vol. XXV, Moscow, 1934

Reproduced from the original

---

[a] Ida - [b] Genoa

100

MARX TO LOUIS BAUER

IN LONDON

[Draft]

London, 30 November [1849]

Sir,

In view of the inimical relations now obtaining between the two societies to which we belong—in view of your direct attacks upon the refugee committee here,[292] at any rate upon my friends and colleagues in the same—we must break off social relations if we are not mutually to expose ourselves to equivocal interpretations. Yesterday evening I thought it unseemly, in the presence of my wife, to express my views on this collision.

While expressing my utmost obligation to you for your medical assistance, I would beg you to send me your account.

Yours truly
Dr K. Marx

First published in: Marx and Engels, *Works*, First Russian Edition, Vol. XXV, Moscow, 1934

Printed according to the original

Published in English for the first time

101

MARX TO JOSEPH WEYDEMEYER[293]

IN FRANKFURT AM MAIN

London, 19 December [1849]
4 Anderson Street, Kings Road, Chelsea

Dear Weydemeyer,

An unconscionable time has elapsed since I last wrote to you. Civil vexations of every kind, all manner of business and, finally, the general difficulty I have in bringing myself to write a letter, will explain to you my long silence. I have at last, *post tot discrimina rerum,*[a] succeeded in giving reality to my *Revue,*[b] that is to say, I have a printer and a distributor in Hamburg.[c] Otherwise we do everything at our own expense. The worst of it is that in Germany so much time is always lost before one can get to the point of publication. I have little doubt that by the time 3, or maybe 2, monthly issues have appeared, a world conflagration will intervene and the opportunity of temporarily finishing with political economy will be gone.[294]

As you live in the heart of Germany and hence are more familiar with the details than we are, you might perhaps find time to describe, for our *Revue,* briefly and concisely in a few main features, the present condition of South Germany and everything connected with it.[295]

I would further request you to insert the following announcement in your paper[d] but *not until* you have seen the announcement in the *Kölnische Zeitung* for which the bookseller in Hamburg will be responsible. Perhaps you could send a copy to *Westphalia.* For you will see from the announcement that, besides our circulation through the book trade, we want to establish another by asking our party comrades to draw up subscription lists and send them to us here. For the time being we shall have to keep the price fairly high and the number of sheets low. Should our resources increase as a result of a wider circulation, this defect will be remedied.

What do you think of the row between Proudhon, Blanc and Pierre Leroux?[296]

Willich sends you his regards, and likewise Engels, red Wolff[e] and Weerth.

Here in England the most important movement is probably taking place at this moment. On the one hand, protectionist agitation supported by the fanaticised rural population—the consequences of the free CORN TRADE are now beginning to be felt in the form I predicted years ago[f]—on the other, the Free Traders who, as FINANCIAL AND PARLIAMENTARY REFORMERS,[284] are extending the wider political and economic logic of their system to home affairs and, as PEACE PARTY,[269] to foreign affairs; finally, the Chartists who, while acting in concert with the

---

[a] after so many vicissitudes (Virgil, *Aeneid,* I) - [b] *Neue Rheinische Zeitung. Politisch-ökonomische Revue* - [c] J. E. M. Köhler and J. Schuberth - [d] K. Marx and F. Engels, 'Announcement of the *Neue Rheinische Zeitung. Politisch-ökonomische Revue'* was published in the *Neue Deutsche Zeitung* (edited by Weydemeyer), Nos. 14, 23 and 31, 16 and 26 January and 5 February 1850. - [e] Ferdinand Wolff - [f] K. Marx, 'Speech on the Question of Free Trade'.

bourgeoisie against the aristocracy, have at the same time resumed with increased vigour their own party activity against the bourgeois.[297] The conflict between these parties will be tremendous and the outward form of agitation will become more tempestuously revolutionary if, as I hope—and not without good reason—the Tories come to power in place of the Whigs. Another *événement*,[a] as yet imperceptible on the Continent, is the mighty industrial, agricultural and commercial crisis now looming up. Were the Continent to postpone its revolution until after the onset of this crisis, England might from the start have to be an ally, albeit an unpopular one, of the revolutionary Continent. An earlier outbreak of revolution—unless directly motivated by Russian intervention—would in my view be a *malheur*[b] since at this particular time, with trade still *en ascendant*,[c] the mass of the workers in France, Germany, etc., as well as the entire strata of tradesmen, etc., though perhaps revolutionary in words, are certainly not so *en réalité*.[d]

You know that my wife has made the world richer by one citizen[e]? She sends her warm regards to you and your wife.[f] My best regards to the latter also.

Write soon.

Your

K. Marx

Apropos, can you find out Citizen *Hentze*'s address for me?

You will have seen friend Heinzen's inane bragging in the newspapers.[g] This fellow, who was done for by the revolution in Germany—before that his things enjoyed a certain vogue *parce que le petit bourgeois et le commis-voyageur s'amusèrent à lire imprimées en pleins caractères les bêtises et les rodomontades qu'ils débitaient eux-mêmes mystérieusement chez le marchand de vin entre le fromage et le biscuit*[h]—is endeavouring to rehabilitate himself by compromising the other refugees in Switzerland and England—those who have really worked—in the eyes of those countries' governments,[298] by

---

[a] event - [b] misfortune - [c] on the up and up - [d] in reality - [e] Heinrich Guido (Fawksy) - [f] Louise - [g] K. Heinzen, 'Lehren der Revolution', *Deutsche Londoner Zeitung*, Nos. 241 and 242, 9 and 16 November 1849. - [h] because the petty bourgeois and the commercial traveller liked to see printed in black and white the idiocies and rodomontades they themselves served mysteriously between the cheese and the biscuits at the wine-shop.

kicking up a row, and earning himself a lucrative martyrdom by threatening shortly to gobble up a hundred THOUSAND OF MILLIONS OF MEN at *déjeuner à la fourchette*.[a]

First published in: Marx and Engels, *Works*, First Russian Edition, Vol. XXV, Moscow, 1934

Printed according to the original

Published in English in full for the first time

102

ENGELS TO JAKOB LUKAS SCHABELITZ

IN BASLE

London, 22 December 1849
6 Macclesfield Street,
Dean Street, Soho

Dear Schabelitz,

I received your letter and, if I failed to answer it from Lausanne, it was for a variety of reasons, but more especially my great circumnavigation of the globe from Genoa to London, which kept me 5 weeks afloat. The reason I didn't let Bamberger have my manuscript[b] was because I wanted to have it published either as a pamphlet of my own or, failing that, in the *Revue* which we already had in mind at the time. This *Revue* has now come into being and in January the first issue will appear in Germany—as you will have already seen from a somewhat premature announcement in the *Berner Zeitung*.[c] We should be very pleased if you or your old man[d] would make yourselves more or less responsible for sales in Switzerland and open an account direct with us. The copies would reach you through our Hamburg commission agent,[e] and you might perhaps be able to take over some kind of general agency for Switzerland, since we prefer in any case to work only with sound houses and I don't know the fellow who put his name to the announcement in Berne.[f] You might tell me some time whether the man's any good. Consider, then, how this might be arranged and let me know on what terms. At all events, these would have to provide for quarterly accounts and payments, at

---

[a] luncheon - [b] *The Campaign for the German Imperial Constitution* - [c] *Berner Zeitung*, No. 361, 27 December 1849 - [d] Jacob Christian Schabelitz - [e] Julius Schuberth - [f] Davoine

least as regards sums received from regular subscribers. We also require this of our Hamburg commission agent.[a]

Kindly have the enclosed announcement inserted in the *National-Zeitung*[b] and, should you from time to time require a fill-in, use this one for preference.

Besides the general introduction (by Marx), the first issue will contain a first article by me on the campaign for an imperial constitution, an article by little Wolff[c] on the last days of the Frankfurt and Stuttgart parliaments, a survey of events by Marx and myself[d] and, if feasible, the first of a series of lectures on economics which Marx is giving at the Workers' Society here.[299] Also miscellanea, perhaps something more by red Wolff.[e] The latter, Marx, Weerth and I, are now here and Lupus will, if at all possible, be joining us shortly.

All in all, things are going quite well here. Struve and Heinzen are intriguing with all and sundry against the Workers' Society and ourselves, but without success. They, together with some wailers of moderate persuasion who have been thrown out of our society, form a select club at which Heinzen airs his grievances about the noxious doctrines of the communists.[300]

Write to me as soon as possible on the business question.

Your
F. Engels

Happy New Year in advance.

Be so kind as to send me *forthwith* a parcel containing *Mieroslawski's 'Rapports sur la campagne en Bade', Daul's 'Tagebuch eines pp.'*, the Becker-Esselen screed,[f] and anything else *of importance* that has appeared on the Baden business, i.e. that contains *facts* and not hot air. You can either draw the amount on me, or charge it to the account of the *Neue Rheinische Zeitung* against future business transactions.

First published in: Marx and Engels, *Works*, First Russian Edition, Vol. XXV, Moscow, 1934

Printed according to the original

Published in English for the first time

---

[a] Theodor Hagen - [b] K. Marx and F. Engels, 'Announcement of the *Neue Rheinische Zeitung. Politisch-ökonomische Revue*' published in the *Schweizerische National-Zeitung*, No. 8, 10 January 1850. - [c] Wilhelm Wolff - [d] K. Marx and F. Engels, 'Review [January-February 1850]'. - [e] Ferdinand Wolff - [f] A. Daul, *Tagebuch eines politischen Flüchtlings während des Freiheitskampfes in der Rheinpfalz und Baden;* J. Ph. Becker and Ch. Esselen, *Geschichte der süddeutschen Mai-Revolution des Jahres 1849.*

1850

103

MARX TO EDUARD von MÜLLER-TELLERING

IN LONDON

[Copy]

[London,] 1 January 1850

Dear Tellering,

Engels, Seiler, Weerth, Willich and I shall not be appearing at the meeting arranged for 3 January,[301] for the following reasons amongst others:

1. The list of political refugees invited has been arbitrarily compiled. Thus, for example, C. Schramm and F. Wolff are not included.

2. Not one of the workers, who for years have been in the vanguard of German democracy in London, has been invited.

Your
K. Marx

First published in: Marx and Engels, *Works,* First Russian Edition, Vol. XXV, Moscow, 1934

Printed according to a copy by Engels

Published in English for the first time

104

MARX TO JOSEPII WEYDEMEYER[a]

IN FRANKFURT AM MAIN

London, 8 January 1850

Dear Weydemeyer,

I [enclose] the pawn-ticket herewith. Would you be so kind as to renew it and to deduct the cost [from the] subscriptions.[b] Kindest regards to your wife[c] from mine, likewise to yourself.

K. Marx

First published in: Marx and Engels, *Works,* Second Russian Edition, Vol. 27, Moscow, 1962

Printed according to the original

Published in English for the first time

105

MARX TO FERDINAND FREILIGRATH

IN COLOGNE

London, 11 January [1850]

Dear Freiligrath,

Today I am writing you just a couple of lines on an urgent matter.

Both for our *Revue* and for its gradual transformation into a fortnightly and weekly and, if circumstances permit, back into a daily newspaper—and also for our other *propagandist* interests—we need money. Money is to be had only in America, where all the semi-revolutionaries—e.g. a certain Anneke who did an ignominious bunk in the Palatinate, thereby proving that he's not even a soldier—are now plucking the golden apples.

---

[a] This is a postscript by Marx to Conrad Schramm's letter to Joseph Weydemeyer of 8 January 1850 (see this volume, p. 548-50). - [b] To the *Neue Rheinische Zeitung. Politisch-ökonomische Revue.* - [c] Louise

We have therefore decided to send *C. Schramm* to America forthwith, as our emissary. For the lengthy journey we have in mind we need at least 150 talers. While requesting you to collect contributions to that end with the utmost possible dispatch, we would at the same time request you to send by return letters of introduction for C. Schramm, manager of the *N.Rh.Z.* (restored to our party as a result of his daring escape from the Wesel fortress).

I have also written to G. Jung about the money matter.[302]

Awaiting an early reply.

Your
K. Marx

The Chartists and French *réfugiés* here are also giving mandates to our emissary.

This is a League[a] matter.

It is essential, my dear Freiligrath, that in your letter of introduction, you leave no doubt about the position of the *N.Rh.Z.* in Germany and its revolutionary significance.

First published in: Marx and Engels, *Works,* First Russian Edition, Vol. XXV, Moscow, 1934

Printed according to the original

Published in English for the first time

106

MARX TO JOSEPH WEYDEMEYER

IN FRANKFURT AM MAIN

London, 4 February 1850

Dear Weydemeyer,

The reason for your getting such a late reply to your letter is that I was seriously ill for a fortnight.

The *Revue* will be appearing next week. Your article will be in it. We are awaiting the continuation.[295]

The publication of the periodical was delayed through my illness. Actually we had arranged it so that two issues should

---

[a] the Communist League

appear simultaneously but the publisher[a] was opposed to this out of commercial considerations which we thought correct. So a further change was necessary and this happened to coincide with my unlucky illness.

You will receive 100 copies from Cologne. Please send two of them to *C. Biringer* in Höchst near Frankfurt. He ordered them from here. You will probably undertake to get payment for them.

I have passed on your message to Tellering. The fellow is quite unsuited to be an English correspondent. In Vienna it was alright for him to bluster. Here you have to study matters. More another time.

Your
K. Marx

Best regards to your wife[b] from my wife and self. In Hamburg about 1,500 copies have already been ordered.

First published in: Marx and Engels, *Works*, First Russian Edition, Vol. XXV, Moscow, 1934

Printed according to the original

Published in English for the first time

107

MARX TO LOUIS BAUER

IN LONDON

[Rough copy]

[London,] 5 February [1850]
20 Queen's Road

I am *only now* answering your letter of 30 January because I am not inclined to let you prescribe 'time limits' for what I do.

In reply to your letter the following:

1. When Schramm wrote that my debt to you was not yet 'due', it only meant that one cannot be sued for a SURGEON's bills until six months have elapsed, certainly not that the debt does not exist.

2. Far from having conceded to Mr Heidemann that your bill was not 'too steep', I told him the contrary, as he himself admitted

---

[a] Julius Schuberth - [b] Louise

on 22 January in the letter to my wife. *Nevertheless* I informed him that I was willing to pay. As I told him, I hoped that by January I should be in possession of the necessary amount although I could not guarantee this. The impertinence of Mr Heidemann in sending a woman a demand for payment under a *black seal,* which she mistook for the announcement of a death, moved me to have him informed in writing that I wished to have no further contact with him.

3. As to your bill, I *now* insist that you *itemize* it. I fail to understand how you could have disbursed £1 on my behalf. You travelled out to me in Chelsea at my express request on only three occasions, once by cab. As to the confinement,[a] accoucheurs over here (except in the case of the bourgeois) charge for *9 days—while you* attended my wife on only 4 days out of the 9, as Willich can testify—one GUINEA. Where, then, do you get £4.10 from? By the way, I am told that, immediately upon receipt of my letter,[b] you held a confabulation with Heidemann and decided 'to fleece' me. So first of all an itemized bill, which I shall then pay.

K. Marx

First published in: Marx and Engels, *Works,* Second Russian Edition, Vol. 50, Moscow, 1981

Printed according to the original

Published in English for the first time

108

ENGELS TO EDUARD von MÜLLER-TELLERING

IN LONDON

[Copy]

[London, 7 February 1850] Thursday morning

Dear Tellering,

Your note[303] arrived so late that, even with the best will in the world, it would have been difficult to get you a ticket for today's ball. Since moreover you have failed, even though accepted by the society as a member, either to take out your card or to attend any

---

[a] for the birth of Heinrich Guido - [b] See this volume, p. 218.

of the meetings, and only the day before yesterday an individual in a similar situation was expelled from the society, I for my part find it entirely impossible to accede to your request.

Tout à vous[a]

Engels

First published in: Tellering, *Vorge-schmack in die künftige deutsche Diktatur von Marx und Engels*, Cologne, 1850

Printed according to a copy by Tellering

Published in English for the first time

109

ENGELS TO JULIUS SCHUBERTH

IN HAMBURG

AND THEODOR HAGEN AND STEPHAN ADOLPH NAUT

IN COLOGNE

[Draft]

[London,] 4 March 1850

1. Schuberth. Letter answered. The 2nd issue[b] must, as promised, not cost more than the first. As regards the 450 copies, no change can now be made for the first quarter. For the 2nd he should put forward proposals. The arrangement for Köhler's payment has nothing to do with this.

What Schuberth says about success contradicts his earlier information and our reports.

In future nothing to be set aside without asking us. For the 3rd issue 'To Die for the Republic'[c] can stand.

50 copies to be sent here. The correspondence from South Germany[d] no longer to be used.[295]

2. Hagen. Same as Schuberth. Should organise proper supervision of the printer[e] and also obtain from the latter a certificate *re*

---

[a] Yours ever - [b] *Neue Rheinische Zeitung. Politisch-ökonomische Revue.* - [c] F. Engels, *The Campaign for the German Imperial Constitution*, IV. - [d] by Joseph Weydemeyer - [e] H. G. Voigt

number of copies.[304] The correspondence from South Germany no longer to be used.

He should vigorously oppose the censor's presumption and place his name on the title page as the responsible editor.[305] Should section IV of *The Campaign for the German Imperial Constitution* create difficulties, this should be reported at once.

3. Naut. Terms for printer—price as in Hamburg; for Eisen: 25 per cent for Cologne, 50 per cent for all other copies, incl. all expenses, excepting, perhaps, postage from London and advertisements ordered by us.

The printer must deliver 5 sheets in 10 days and fix penalty for breach of contract.

First published in: Marx and Engels, *Works*, First Russian Edition, Vol. XXV, Moscow, 1934

Printed according to the original

Published in English for the first time

110

MARX TO EDUARD von MÜLLER-TELLERING[43]

IN LONDON

[Rough copy]

London, 12 March 1850

For the letter you wrote yesterday to the Workers' Society, I would send you a challenge, were you still capable of giving satisfaction after your disgraceful calumnies against Engels and after the well-founded sentence of expulsion pronounced by the Workers' Society executive committee.[306] I await you on a different field to strip you of the hypocritical mask of revolutionary fanaticism behind which you have so far skilfully contrived to hide your petty interests, your envy, your unassuaged vanity and your angry discontent over the world's lack of appreciation for your great genius—a lack of appreciation that began with your failure to pass your examination.

Had you reflected a little, you would have been obliged to assume that if, as a *witness,* I was compelled to report a fact detrimental to yourself, I for my part would do everything in my power to avoid a scandal which must doubly compromise me: in the eyes of the Workers' Society, to which you were recommended *by me,* and in the eyes of the public, for whom you exist only in as much as you were a contributor to *my newspaper.*[a]

Your letters to me, and they are available for publication, prove that you did all you could to foist upon me the role of 'democratic Dalai Lama and incumbent of the future'. What proof have you that I ever accepted that absurd role? The only thing you could reproach me with is that I did not immediately break with you or denounce you to the others after the Klapka affair, on the compromising nature of which I forthwith bluntly expressed my views to you in the presence of witnesses.[307] I admit my weakness. Only Becker's[b] statement that, 4 weeks prior to the appearance of your glib pamphlet attacking the *Westdeutsche Zeitung,*[c] you again offered to collaborate on that paper, a statement supported by the testimony of Freiligrath and Hagen, only your wholly unsubstantiated calumnies against Engels convinced me that what I had regarded as an isolated instance of precipitancy was the connecting link of an entire system. It was, by the way, wise of you not after all to appear yesterday at the final appointment which Willich had yet again arranged for you at your request. You knew what was to be expected from a confrontation with me.

K. Marx

First published in: Marx and Engels, *Works,* First Russian Edition, Vol. XXV, Moscow, 1934

Printed according to the original

111

MARX TO JOSEPH WEYDEMEYER

IN FRANKFURT AM MAIN

London, 9 April [1850]
4 Anderson Street, King's Road, Chelsea

Dear Weydemeyer,

I should be greatly obliged if you would write and tell me *by return* how the sales of the *N.Rh.Z.*[d] are going and whether we

---

[a] *Neue Rheinische Zeitung* - [b] Hermann Becker - [c] E. Tellering, *Westdeutscher Zeitungsjammer* - [d] *Neue Rheinische Zeitung. Politisch-ökonomische Revue*

may not soon receive some money. You people in little Germany have no conception of what things are like here.

The 3rd issue is coming out on the 10th of this month. The chap in Hamburg[a]—why, we don't yet really know—has been frightfully dilatory over the thing. This will now be put a stop to.

I have also been requested by the Refugee Committee to appeal to your committee.[308] We now have 60 refugees on our hands; several hundred, who have been expelled from Switzerland, have already been announced. Hence our refugee fund will soon be down to its last *monaco*,[b] and then the people will be out on the street again.

Warm regards to your wife,

Your
K. Marx

First published in *Die Gesellschaft*, Jg. VII, Bd. 2, Berlin, 1930

Printed according to the original

Published in English for the first time

112

ENGELS TO JULIUS SCHUBERTH

IN HAMBURG

[Draft]

[London, about 11 April 1850]

Attention *Schuberth*

1. Following dispatch of the 3rd issue,[c] we now await *at the earliest possible date* the statement concerning the sales of the 3 issues and *an adjustment of the balance,* and if this cannot be done before 15 April, he is to write and tell us. But at all events, to advise by return how many copies of the 3rd issue have been run off and what proportion of these are against firm orders. Only a few hundred in excess of firm orders are to be run off.

2. Since Schuberth does not consider it necessary for Mr Hagen

---

[a] Julius Schuberth - [b] a small copper coin current in the Principality of Monaco - [c] *Neue Rheinische Zeitung. Politisch-ökonomische Revue*

to act as responsible editor, he is *in no circumstances to alter a single word of the manuscript.* We hereby inform him that, should this none the less occur, we must forthwith sever our connection with him. Hagen is instructed to ensure that nothing is altered.

3. Since, *contrary* to our instructions, Schuberth sent Naut 300 copies instead of 450, Naut is to take such copies as he needs from the 150 which Schuberth sent to Eisen. We further expect that the dispatch of copies to Naut will, in future, always be made *at the same time* as those to Eisen. Should we receive further complaints, we shall have to take other measures. Similarly we expect that in future the 50 copies for London will be dispatched by the first steamer after the issue is ready.

(A letter to be written to Hagen and enclosed with Schuberth's.)

First published in: Marx and Engels, *Works,* First Russian Edition, Vol. XXV, Moscow, 1934

Printed according to the original

Published in English for the first time

113

ENGELS TO JOSEPH WEYDEMEYER

IN FRANKFURT AM MAIN

London, 22 April 1850
6 Macclesfield Street, Soho

Dear Weydemeyer,

Could you insert the statement overleaf[a] in the *Neue Deutsche Zeitung.* The attempts of the 'great men' here to regain a position for themselves at the expense of the refugees, and their attempted manoeuvrings to that end in the press at large, are discouraging people from sending money here.[309] We have now received and distributed some £120-130 for the refugees, and the others have raised *summa summarum*[b] £2.15 s., and now they are trying to make themselves out to be the champions of the 'helpless' refugees. Unless we get some money now, our 50-60 refugees will, within a week, be out on the street and without a penny. This

---

[a] K. Marx and F. Engels, 'Statement. 20 April 1850'. - [b] all in all

evening the bigwigs intend to hold a refugee meeting to see what they can devise. We'll leave them to it. Naturally there will again be big words and vast schemes, but no money for the refugees. Anyway, they're likely to fail, even though none of us will be going.

Marx is waiting anxiously for your reply to his last letter, which went off to you about a fortnight ago.[a]

Best regards to your wife[b] and to Lüning's also from

Your

F. Engels

First published in *Die Gesellschaft*, Jg. VII, Bd. 2, Berlin, 1930

Printed according to the original

Published in English for the first time

114

ENGELS TO JOSEPH WEYDEMEYER [310]

IN FRANKFURT AM MAIN

London, 25 April 1850

Dear Weydemeyer,

Your letter to Marx arrived today, together with £5 for the refugee fund and an enclosure for me. You will meanwhile have received two letters[c] containing the Refugee Committee's statements, its appeal, and its record of accounts.[d] Get these printed as quickly as possible and do whatever you can in the vicinity to collect funds for the refugees. How things are in general, you will see from the enclosed letter to Dronke.[311] Perhaps something could be raised in Franconia, Nuremberg, Bayreuth, etc., etc. The *N.Rh.Ztg.* has a very large circulation there. If you have an address in Munich, write there likewise. You will realise that now, when those jackasses, Struve and Company, are trying, on the eve

---

[a] See this volume, pp. 230-31. - [b] Louise - [c] See this volume, p. 232 (the second letter has not survived). - [d] K. Marx and F. Engels, 'Statement. 20 April 1850'; Accounts of the Social-Democratic Refugee Committee in London. 23 April 1850; and the appeal may be the Appeal for Support for German Political Refugees. 20 September 1849.

of the revolution, to make use of the refugees to get their names into the papers again, it becomes a matter of honour for us to go on supporting at least our own refugees, and not to let the best of the new arrivals fall in their turn into the clutches of those jackasses.

We believed that the two following issues of the *Revue* had been in your hands, the 2nd for 5 weeks, and the 3rd for several days at the least. So that jackass, Naut, never sent them to you! A rude letter has already gone off to him today, telling him to send them to you forthwith.[312] He must have had the 3rd issue for a week. But wait till you've also got the 3rd issue, which brings the first series of articles[a] to a definitive close, before writing a critique of it.

Adieu, your

F. E.

We have just heard that those wretches, Struve, Tellering, Schramm, Bauer[b] (of Stolpe), etc., etc., have put it about in sundry German papers that our committee[c] is itself swallowing up the refugee funds. This infamy is also being spread by letter. You cannot have read of it anywhere, otherwise you would have entered the lists long ago on our behalf. You know that the revolution has cost all of us money and has never brought us in a centime. Not even the *Neue Preussische Zeitung*, etc., have ever dared to reproach us with such things. The rotten democrats, the impotent 'great men' of the petty bourgeoisie, alone were vicious enough to stoop to such baseness. Our committee has now rendered accounts on 3 occasions,[d] on each of which the donors were invited [to appoint] representatives to verify the books and receipts. What other committee has done that much? A receipt is to hand for every centime. *Not one* committee member has ever received a centime from the funds, nor would he ever ask for one, however much he was down on his luck. Not one of our best friends has ever received more than the least of the refugees;

---

[a] F. Engels, *The Campaign for the German Imperial Constitution.* - [b] Rudolf Schramm, Louis Bauer - [c] the Social-Democratic Refugee Committee - [d] Accounts of the Committee of Support for German Refugees in London. 3 December 1849; Accounts of the Social-Democratic Refugee Committee in London. Beginning of March 1850; Accounts of the Social-Democratic Refugee Committee in London. 23 April 1850.

no one who had a source of income received so much as a sou.
If Dronke is no longer there, open his letter, read it, and send it on to him.

First published in *Die Gesellschaft*, Jg. VII,   Printed according to the original
Bd. 2, Berlin, 1930

115

ENGELS AND MARX TO FRANÇOIS PARDIGON

IN LONDON

[Rough copy]

London, 6 May 1850

Dear Pardigon,

We have just this minute heard that it is intended to submit your programme on behalf of your society to the German Society in Greek Street and to ask them whether or not they will give it their support.[313]

After our conversation on Saturday,[a] we don't believe it; but if you or your society were to denounce an individual or a number of different individuals to us as a mere bad lot, we should simply show them the door without asking whether they were willing to adhere to our programme.

We have denounced the ringleaders of this society to you as charlatans and swindlers. Swindlers and charlatans will sign anything. They would probably have signed our manifesto had we been prepared to accept their repeated proposals of union and concord.

It will be clear to you that, were a similar proposal to be adopted by your society, we should be honour bound to sever forthwith all connections with the members of Rathbone Place.

Greeting and Fraternity

F. Engels
K. Marx

First published in: Marx and Engels,   Printed according to the original
Works, First Russian Edition, Vol. XXV,
Moscow, 1934   Translated from the French

Published in English for the first
time

---

[a] 1 May 1850

116

ENGELS TO THEODOR SCHUSTER

IN FRANKFURT AM MAIN

London, 13 May 1850

Mr Th. Schuster in Frankfurt a. M.

Through Mr Weydemeyer of that city we have received for the account of the Refugee Committee there [308] £10.0s.0d. n/c[a] on Mr Stiebel here, of receipt and due entry of which we herewith gratefully advise you.

Should it be possible to send us further donations from there or the vicinity for the refugees here, we should be most grateful to you. The number of refugees grows daily, and the above £10 is barely sufficient to meet the most pressing day-to-day requirements for a week. Funds are beginning to come in less plentifully, while on the other hand the refugees now in need of assistance almost exclusively belong to occupations offering little if any prospect of employment here.

Greeting and Fraternity
The Social-Democratic Refugee Committee
F[oreign] D[epartment]

F. Engels
Secretary

It is requested that all donations be sent through Mr Weydemeyer to Mr Marx or Mr C. Pfänder, 21 King Street, Soho Square, London.

First published in *Die Gesellschaft*, Jg. VII, Bd. 2, Berlin, 1930

Printed according to the original

Published in English for the first time

---

[a] not specified

117

MARX TO JOSEPH WEYDEMEYER

IN FRANKFURT AM MAIN

[London,] 8 June[a] [1850]
64 Dean Street, Soho

Dear Weydemeyer,

How are things with our *Revue*? The money, especially? The question is becoming all the more urgent as the Prussians are making every effort to induce the British Government to expel me from England too.[314] Were I not stuck here *sans le sou*[b] I should already have withdrawn into the heart of England and the Government would have lost sight of me.

How are things with the 'red issue'[c]?[262] We have orders for it from America. How much of it has been sold? How many copies have you left?

Your paper[d] seems to have joined the rest to form a *conspiration du silence* in regard to our *Revue*. However, I realise that, to the readers of the *Neue Deutsche Zeitung*, Raveaux must be more interesting.

Regards to Dronke and to your wife.[e]

Your
K. M.

First published in *Die Gesellschaft*, Jg. VII, Bd. 2, Berlin, 1930

Printed according to the original

Published in English for the first time

118

MARX TO HEINRICH BÜRGERS[315]

IN COLOGNE

[London, 25 June 1850]

[...] the Cologne people, including Daniels, were *as usual* much taken up with *being wise after the event* [...]

---

[a] A slip of the pen in the original: May. - [b] without a penny - [c] *Neue Rheinische Zeitung*, No. 301, 19 May 1849. - [d] *Neue Deutsche Zeitung* - [e] Louise

[...] Like any other place Cologne can, if it so wishes, declare itself a Centre of any kind. Indeed it would conform better than any other place to Spinoza's dictum whereby the periphery coincides with the centre [...][a]

Published for the first time

Printed according to Daniels' letter to Marx of 28 June 1850 and that of the Cologne leading district to the Communist League Central Authority of 10 July 1850

119

MARX TO JOSEPH WEYDEMEYER[316]

IN FRANKFURT AM MAIN

London, 27 June[b] [1850]
64 Dean Street, Soho Square

Dear Weydemeyer,

Send the money to Naut. The fellow's not a bad old jackass. I shall explain the matter to you some other time. Pray do not be offended by my wife's agitated letters.[c] She is nursing her child,[d] and our situation here is so extraordinarily wretched that an outburst of impatience is excusable.

Lüning's critique—I have seen 1 and 2[e]—shows that he doesn't understand what he is trying to criticise. Maybe I shall explain a few things to him in our *Revue*.[317]

This is an important day. There is a possibility that today the Ministry may fall.[318] Then a truly revolutionary movement will get

---

[a] Marx may have had in mind Spinoza's letter to Walter Tschirnhaus of January 1673. - [b] A slip of the pen in the original: July. - [c] See this volume, pp. 555, 559. - [d] Heinrich Guido - [e] O. Lüning's review of the *Neue Rheinische Zeitung. Politisch-ökonomische Revue* in the *Neue Deutsche Zeitung*, Nos. 148 and 149, 22 and 23 June 1850. The end of the review was published in Nos. 150 and 151, 25 and 26 June.

under way here. We ourselves may be the Tories' first victims. Then our long-intended expulsion might actually come about.

Your

K. Marx

First published in: Marx and Engels, *Works,* First Russian Edition, Vol. XXV, Moscow, 1934

Printed according to the original

Published in English in full for the first time

120

MARX TO KARL BLIND

IN PARIS

[Rough copy]

London, 17 July 1850
64 Dean Street, Soho

Dear Blind,

Our long silence was due to a misunderstanding. For we believed that the Central Authority's second circular[a] had been brought you 6 weeks or 2 months ago [by] our emissary, Klein, and we were waiting for your answer. [Now] it transpires that Klein has [brought] back nothing of the kind to Brussels.

Write to me as soon as possible and in a special enclosure to the [Central Authority]. We are thinking of convening a congress here in a few (8) weeks' time.[319] What do you [make] of the Holstein business?[320] We shall shortly be dispatching an emissary [who] worked there for two years and knows [exactly] who is who and what is what.[b]

Concerning my own fortunes and the manifold vicissitudes which I [...] in, some other time.

I am approaching you this time about a private matter [...], that, if at all possible, you will not refuse me your assistance. I had arranged with my family that I would settle my financial affairs with my uncle Philips in Holland [...] weeks, [for which] purpose I was to visit Holland in person. An [...] illness of my wife constantly

---

[a] K. Marx and F. Engels, 'Address of the Central Authority to the League, June 1850'. - [b] This seems to refer to C. Schramm.

rendered my departure impossible. And now I shall not be able to go there for several weeks, because two of my uncle's daughters are being married, one after the other, from his house, so th[at] business matters cannot be settled till several weeks later.

With this affair in mind, I meanwhile drew a bill for £20 (500 fr.) with a [merchant] firm[a] here in London on the strength of this arrangement. The bill matures on Monday or Wednesday.[b] If I were unable to pay it, I would lay myself open to a public [...] which, given the present state of the parties here, and [my] relations with the Prussian Embassy and the English Ministry, [could] have most disagreeable consequences.

Now I hear that *Goegg* in Paris has a considerable amount of capital available just now. Would you write to him *immediately*, explaining the circumstances to him and inquiring whether he could advance me the money on a promissory note or a bill. *Periculum in mora.*[c]

Pending the arrangement in Holland I am, in the literal sense of the word, *dépourvu,*[d] save for my last shilling.

I rely on you to do your utmost.

Your
K. Marx

First published in German in *International Review for Social History,* Vol. IV, Leiden, 1939

Printed according to the original

Published in English for the first time

121

MARX TO JOSEPH WEYDEMEYER[43]

IN FRANKFURT AM MAIN

London, 29 October 1850
64 Dean Street, Soho

Dear Weydemeyer,

I beg you to carry out the following transaction for me:

Borrow from Schuster or somebody else the money necessary to redeem my silver from the Frankfurt pawnbroker's,[321] then *sell* the

---

[a] Probably a firm headed by Simon Bamberger. - [b] i. e. 19 or 21 July - [c] Delay spells danger (Titus Livius, *ab urbe condita libri*). - [d] destitute

silver to a goldsmith or wherever it can be sold in Frankfurt, repay the man who loaned you the money for redeeming the silver, and send the balance to me here.

Neither you nor the other man will be incurring any risk for, should you not be able to sell the stuff at a higher price, all you have to do is take it back to the pawnbroker's.

On the other hand my present circumstances are such that I must at all costs raise some money, even to be able to continue working.

The only items I would ask you to return to the pawnbroker's, since they have no saleable value, are 1) a small silver mug, 2) a silver plate, 3) a small knife and fork in a case—all belonging to little Jenny.[a]

I very much approve of your plan for a popular work on political economy and only hope that you will soon make a start on it.[322] Warm regards to your wife[b] from my wife and self.

Your
K. Marx

First published in: Marx and Engels, *Works*, First Russian Edition, Vol. XXV, Moscow, 1934

Printed according to the original

122

MARX TO ENGELS[323]

IN MANCHESTER

[London,] 19 November 1850

Dear Engels,

Just a line or two to let you know that our little gunpowder-plotter, Fawksy,[324] *died* at ten o'clock this morning. Suddenly, from one of the convulsions he had often had. A few minutes before, he was still laughing and joking. The thing happened quite unexpectedly. You can imagine what it is like here. Your absence at this particular moment makes us feel very lonely.

---

a Marx's eldest daughter - b Louise

In my next letter I shall tell you something about Harney from which you will see what an ominous situation he's in.

Your
K. Marx

If you happen to feel so inclined, drop a few lines to my wife. She is quite distracted.

First published in *Der Briefwechsel zwischen F. Engels und K. Marx*, Bd. 1, Stuttgart, 1913

Printed according to the original

123

MARX TO ENGELS

IN MANCHESTER

London, 23 November 1850

Dear Engels,

Your letter did my wife a great deal of good.[325] She's in a really dangerous state of excitation and exhaustion. She had nursed the child[a] herself and had fought for its existence under the most difficult circumstances and at the greatest sacrifice. And on top of this, the thought that the poor child was a victim of bourgeois *misère,* although it never wanted for any particular care.

Mr Schramm[b] is thoroughly beseilered[c] and is just now at his most loathsome. For two whole days, 19 and 20 November, he never showed his face in our house, then came for a moment and immediately disappeared again after one or two fatuous remarks. He had volunteered to accompany us on the day of the funeral; he arrived a minute or two before the appointed hour, said not a word about the funeral, but told my wife that he had to hurry away so as not to be late for a meal with his brother.[d] With my wife in such an irritable state, you can imagine how offensive was the conduct of this person, to whom so much friendship has been extended in our house.

---

[a] Heinrich Guido - [b] Conrad Schramm - [c] Marx coins a verb from the name Seiler - [d] Rudolf Schramm

Jones has explained Harney's true situation to me. He is *sous le coup de la justice*.[a] The entire contents of his paper[b] are such as to make it liable to stamp duty.[326] The government is merely waiting for its circulation to increase in order to nab him. The proceedings against Dickens have been instituted solely as a precedent in respect of Harney.[327] If he is arrested he may, besides the actual sentence, have to serve 20 years through being unable to produce SECURITIES.

Bauer[c] and Pfänder have won their case.[328] Their counsel was Roberts.

Your
K. M.

First published abridged in *Der Briefwechsel zwischen F. Engels und K. Marx*, Bd. 1, Stuttgart, 1913 and in full in *MEGA*, Abt. III, Bd. 1, 1929

Printed according to the original

Published in English for the first time

124

ENGELS TO MARX

IN LONDON

[Manchester,] 25 November 1850

Dear Marx,

I am writing today just to tell you that I am unfortunately still not in a position to send you the £2 I promised you for today in my last letter.[329] Ermen[d] has gone away for a few days and, since no proxy has been authorised with the bank, we are unable to make any remittances and have to content ourselves with the few small payments that happen to come in. The total amount in the cash box is only about £4 and you will therefore realise that I must wait a while. As soon as Ermen returns I shall at once send you the money. I trust the first remittance arrived safely.

---

a threatened with prosecution - b *The Red Republican* - c Heinrich Bauer - d Peter Ermen

Schramm's[a] behaviour is really despicable.

The Harney business is indeed extremely ominous. If they are actually determined to arrest him, changing the paper's name won't help.[b] Nor can he give it up altogether, and if *this* paper falls into the category liable to stamp duty, I can't see any possibility at all of bringing out an unstamped political weekly. In any case, he'd do better to omit his 'LABOUR RECORD' from page 8, this being NEWS and unquestionably subject to stamp duty. But from what you write it would seem that, in Jones' opinion, the content of his analytical articles is equally liable to be stamped. And that would be the limit.

So the outraged Schramm, to judge by Mr Seiler's begging letter, would seem to be again on the best of terms with his brother[c] and even showing him some *égards*[d]!

I hope your wife is feeling better. Warm regards to her and the rest of your family from your

F. E.

In the course of this week I shall send your wife a parcel of COTTON THREAD which I hope she will find to her liking.

[On the back of the letter]

Charles Marx Esq.
64 Dean Street. Soho Square. London

First published abridged in *Der Briefwechsel zwischen F. Engels und K. Marx*, Bd. 1, Stuttgart, 1913 and in full in *MEGA*, Abt. III, Bd. 1, 1929

Printed according to the original

Published in English for the first time

125

MARX TO ENGELS

IN MANCHESTER

London, 2 December [1850]
64 Dean Street, Soho

Dear Engels,

For several days I have been seriously unwell and hence this letter, together with advice of receipt of the two POST OFFICE ORDERS, will reach you later than I would have wished. I have remitted

---

[a] Conrad Schramm; see this volume, p. 242. - [b] *The Red Republican*, to avoid persecution, in December 1850 changed its name to *The Friend of the People*. - [c] Rudolf Schramm - [d] consideration

7/6d to Seiler. As regards the *Indépendance*[a] we neither of us owe him anything for the time being, as he opportunely got himself thrown out by his landlord, leaving behind in return for the £10 he owed him nothing but unsold copies of the *Indépendance,* personal effects to the value of 18 pence, and 2 or 3 books which he had borrowed from myself and others. Truly, he possesses IN A HIGH DEGREE the ability to liquidate, American-fashion, the excess of his expenditure over his revenue.

The great *Heilberg* has arrived here with a young wife, *soi-disant.*[b] I have not yet had the honour of seeing the legendary Tuck, who has been cast back across the ocean, considerably aggrandised, of course—a dangerous rival for Seiler. He completely monopolises Bamberger, calling him 'little brother', and the old Amschel, 'auntie'.

As yet I have neither seen nor heard anything of our *Revue.*[c] I am negotiating with Cologne about the publication of the quarterly.[d]

Partly because of ill-health, partly on purpose, I never foregather with the others at the Pulteney Stores[330] except on the official days. Since these gentlemen have so extensively debated whether or not this company is *ennuyante,*[e] I, of course, am leaving them to agree amongst themselves upon the solace to be derived from their discourse. I, however, make myself scarce. As we have both of us experienced, one loses these people's esteem to the same extent that one is liberal with them. Moreover, I'm tired of them and wish to employ my time as productively as possible. Friend Schramm,[f] who for several weeks has been playing the malcontent and has finally come to the conviction that no one is in the least inclined to place obstacles in the way of the natural course of his emotional ups and downs, is gradually readapting himself to the type of humour compatible with the MODEL-LODGING-HOUSE.

At the Great Windmill considerable annoyance reigns over the loss of £16 as a result of a court ruling.[331] Lehmann, in particular, is seething. His rage will not abate until Bauer and Pfänder are publicly branded as thieves and miscreants by every newspaper in Europe. Now, of course, little Bauer maintains with suppressed moral fury that the payment of a single penny, whether to the Great Windmill or to a public poor box, would be an unpardona-

---

[a] *L'Indépendance belge* - [b] so-called - [c] *Neue Rheinische Zeitung. Politisch-ökonomische Revue,* No. 5-6. - [d] See this volume, pp. 251-52. - [e] dull - [f] Conrad Schramm

ble affront to the English courts and 'recognition of the bourgeoisie'.

Meanwhile the great men of Great Windmill Street have experienced a triumph, as the following[a] shows:

'*Aux démocrates de toutes les nations!*

Citoyens! Proscrits Refugiés en Angleterre et mieux placés *par cela même pour* juger des mouvements politiques du Continent, nous' (note well! An out-and-out solecism in this *single* phrase which they have daringly tacked on to subject, copula and predicate, and should in any case read: et ainsi mieux placés *que* vous autres *pour*) 'avons pu suivre et surveiller activement toutes les combinaisons des Puissances coalisées se préparant à une nouvelle invasion de la *France*, où' (very naice!) 'les Cosaques du Nord sont attendus par leurs complices, *pour*' (yet again attendus pour) 'éteindre dans son foyer même' (the birthplace of Barthélemy and Pottier) 'le volcan de la Révolution Universelle.—Les Rois et les aristocrates de l'Europe ont compris qu'il était temps d'élever des digues pour arrêter la marée populaire' (should read: le marasme populaire) 'qui menace d'engloutir leurs trônes ébranlés.—Des troupes nombreuses levées en Russie, en Autriche, en Prusse, en Bavière, dans le Hanovre, dans le Würtemberg, en Saxe et enfin dans tous les états de l'Allemagne, sont déjà réunies.' (Des troupes ... sont déjà réunies!) 'En Italie 130 000 hommes menacent la frontière suisse. Le Vorarlberg est occupé par 80 000 hommes. Le Haut Rhin est couvert par 80 000 hommes, Würtembergeois, Bedois et Prussiens. Le Main est gardé par 80 000 Bavarois et Autrichiens. Tandis que 370 000 hommes occupent les points que nous venons d'indiquer, la Prusse a mobilisé 200 000 soldats qu'elle tient disponible' (sic) 'pour être lancé sur les frontières de la Belgique et de la France: la Hollande et la Belgique, contraintes par les coalitions, soutiendront le mouvement d'invasion avec une armée forte de 150 000 hommes. En Bohême 150 000 hommes se tiennent prêts et n'attendent qu'un ordre pour se réunir à l'armée du Main, qui serait alors forte de 230 000 hommes. Autour de Vienne sont concentrés 80 000 hommes. 300 000 Russes campent en Pologne, et 80 000 dans les environs de St. Petersbourg: ces armées réunies composent une force d'un million trois cents trente mille combattants, qui n'attendent que le signal de l'attaque. Derrière ces troupes se tiennent aussi (!) prêts 180 000 Autrichiens, 200 000 Prussiens, 100 000 hommes fournis par les principautés de l'Allemagne, et 220 000 Russes. Ces armées forment ensemble, comme troupes de réserve 700 000 hommes; sans compter les hordes innombrables' (sic) 'de Barbares que l'Attila Moscovite ferait surgir du fond de l'Asie, pour lancer, comme autrefois (!) sur la civilisation Européenne. Des journaux allemands' (here a note is appended with a piffling sentence from the *Neue Deutsche Zeitung* to put Lüning in a good mood) 'et nos *renseignements particuliers* nous *font connaître les secrètes intentions des Puissances* dont les Plénipotentiaires se sont réunis à Varsovie le 25 Octobre dernier.[332] Il a *été décidé*, dans la (!) conférence, qu'une guerre feinte' (My God! what diplomats!) 'entre la Prusse et l'Autriche, servirait de prétexte au mouvement des soldats que la *volonté* du Czar transforme en instruments aveugles et en sicaires féroces contre les défenseurs de la liberté.' (Bravo!) 'En présence de ces faits, il n'est plus possible de douter: on organise en ce moment le massacre, déjà commencé (!!) de tous les Républicains. Les journées de Juin 1848 avec leurs exécutions sanglantes et les proscriptions que les ont suivies—la Hongrie dévastée

---

[a] Published in *Le Constitutionnel*, 18 December 1850.

et asservie par l'Autriche—l'Italie livrée au Pape et aux Jésuites, après l'égorge-
ment de la République Romaine par les soldats du Gouvernement de la France
n'ont point assouvi la rage de nos ennemis: ils rêvent l'asservissement de tous les
peuples qui combattent pour le triomphe de la liberté commune. Si la démocratie
n'y prend garde, la Pologne, la Hongrie, l'Allemagne, l'Italie et la France seront
bientôt encore vouées aux fureurs de la soldatesque sauvage de Nicolas qui, pour
exciter les Barbares au combat leur promet la dévastation et le pillage de l'Europe.
    Devant ce danger qui nous menace, *debout! Debout!*... Républicains Français,
Allemands, Italiens, Polonais, et Hongrois, sortons de cet engourdissement'
(Toping Schapper and Willich!) 'qui énerve nos forces et prépare une victoire facile
à nos oppresseurs. *Debout!*... Aux jours de repos et de honte du présent, faisons
succéder les jours de fatigue et de gloire, que nous prépare la guerre sainte de la
liberté! En examinant ces dangers que nous vous signalons, vous comprendrez,
comme nous, qu'il y aurait folie d'attendre plus longtemps l'attaque de l'ennemi
commun; nous devons tout préparer et aller au devant du péril qui nous
environne.' (Just try au devant d'une chose qui vous *environne!*) 'Citoyens
Démocrates Socialistes, notre salut n'est qu'en nous mêmes: nous ne devons
compter que sur nos propres efforts; et éclairés des exemples du passé, nous
devons nous prémunir contre les trahisons de l'avenir. Évitons, évitons surtout le
piège qui nous est tendu par les serpens (!) de la diplomatie. Les émules des
Metternich et des Talleyrand méditent en ce moment d'éteindre le flambeau de la
Révolution, en suscitant à la France, par l'invasion qu'ils préparent, une guerre
nationale dans laquelle les peuples s'égorgeraient au profit des ennemis de leur
affranchissement. Non, Citoyens! plus de guerre nationale! Les barrières que les
despotes avaient élevées entre les nations qu'ils s'étaient partagées, sont désormais
tombées pour nous, et les *peuples* confondus' (really: *confondus*) 'n'ont plus qu'un
drapeau, sur lequel nous avons écrit avec le sang fécond de nos martyrs: *République
Universelle Démocratique et Sociale.*'
    Pour *Leurs Sociétés:* 'Les membres du comité de la société des proscrits
Démocrates Socialistes Français à Londres: Adam (Cambreur), Barthélemy
(Emmanuel), Caperon (Paulin), Fanon, Gouté, Thierry, Vidil (Jules); les délégués
de la commission permanente de la section de la démocratie polonaise à Londres:
Sawaszkiewicz, Warskiroski; les membres du comité démocrate socialiste des
refugiés allemands et de la société ouvrière allemande: Dietz (Oswald), Gebert (A.),
Mayer (Adolphe), Schärttner (A.), Schapper (Charles), Willich (Auguste). Les
délégués de la société démocratique hongroise à Londres: Molikoy, Simonyi.
Londres le 16. Novembre 1850.' [a] [333]

---

[a] '*To the democrats of all nations!*
    Citizens! Proscribed refugees in England who, *for that very reason,* are in a better
position *to* judge the political movements on the Continent, we' (note well! An
out-and-out solecism in this *single* phrase which they have daringly tacked on to
subject, copula and predicate, and should in any case read: and hence in a better
position *than* the rest of you *to*) 'have been able actively to keep track of and
observe all the combinations of the coalition powers preparing for a fresh invasion
of *France,* where' (very naice!) 'the Cossacks of the North are awaited by their
accomplices *to*' (yet again 'awaited to') 'extinguish at its very centre' (the birthplace
of Barthélemy and Pottier) 'the volcano of the Universal Revolution.— The kings
and aristocrats of Europe have realised that it was time to put up dykes to arrest
the popular tide' (should read: popular stagnation) 'which is threatening to engulf

their tottering thrones.—Large numbers of troops raised in Russia, in Austria, in Prussia, in Bavaria, in Hanover, in Württemberg, in Saxony and, in short, in all the states of Germany, have already mustered' (troops ... have already mustered!). 'In Italy 130,000 men are threatening the Swiss frontier. The Vorarlberg is occupied by 80,000 men. The Upper Rhine is covered by 80,000 men, Württembergers, Badeners and Prussians. The Main is guarded by 80,000 Bavarians and Austrians. While 370,000 men occupy the localities indicated above, Prussia has mobilised 200,000 soldiers which she is holding available' *(sic)* 'for launching against the frontiers of Belgium and France. Holland and Belgium, constrained by the coalitions, will support the invasion move with an army 150,000 strong. In Bohemia 150,000 men are holding themselves ready and only await the order to join up with the army of the Main, which will thus be 230,000 strong. 80,000 men are concentrated round Vienna. 300,000 Russians are encamped in Poland, and 80,000 in the neighbourhood of St. Petersburg: all together these armies make up a force of one million three hundred and thirty thousand combatants who are only awaiting the signal to attack. Behind these troops and also (!) holding themselves ready are 180,000 Austrians, 200,000 Prussians, 100,000 men provided by the German principalities, and 220,000 Russians. Taken together these armies form a reserve of 700,000 men; not counting the innumerable' *(sic)* 'hordes of barbarians which the Muscovite Attila will unleash from the heart of Asia to be launched, as of yore (!), against European civilisation. From German newspapers' (here a note is appended with a piffling sentence from the *Neue Deutsche Zeitung* to put Lüning in a good mood) 'and from our own *sources of information* we *learn the secret intentions of the Powers* whose Plenipotentiaries foregathered in Warsaw on 25 October last. *It was decided,* in the (!) conference, that a feint war' (My God! what diplomats!) 'between Prussia and Austria would serve as a pretext for the movement of troops whom the *will* of the Czar is transforming into blind instruments and ferocious bravoes to combat the defenders of liberty.' (Bravo!) 'In the face of these facts, there can no longer be any possible doubt: at this moment they are organising the massacre, already begun (!!), of all republicans. The days of June 1848, with their bloody executions and the proscriptions that followed them—Hungary devastated and enslaved by Austria—Italy delivered up to the Pope and the Jesuits, after the Roman Republic had been butchered by the soldiers of the French Government, have in no way assuaged the fury of our enemies: they dream of the enslavement of all those people who are fighting for the victory of common liberty. If democracy is not on its guard, Poland, Hungary, Germany, Italy and France will soon again fall victim to the fury of the brutal soldiery of Nicholas who whets the barbarians' appetite for battle with the promise that they may devastate and pillage Europe.

In the face of this danger by which we are threatened, *arise! Arise* ... French, German, Italian, Polish and Hungarian republicans, let us emerge from this torpor' (Toping Schapper and Willich!) 'which debilitates our strength and paves the way for an easy victory for our oppressors. *Arise!*... Let us ensure that the present days of inactivity and shame are succeeded by the days of fatigue and glory which await us with the holy war of liberty! On examining these dangers we have pointed out to you, you will realise, like us that it would be folly to wait any longer for our common enemy to attack; we must make every preparation and go out to face the peril which surrounds us.' (Just try going out to face something which *surrounds* you!) 'Citizens, Socialist Democrats, our salvation lies only with ourselves: we cannot count on anything but our own efforts; and, enlightened by the examples of the past, we must provide against the betrayals of the future. Let us avoid, let us avoid above all, the trap that has been laid for us by the serpents (!)

The house where Engels lived in Manchester

28 Dean Street, Soho, London, where Marx lived
from 1850 to 1857

If that's not champion drivel, then I really don't know what is.[a]
Having read the Rollin, Mazzini, Ruge, etc. manifesto addressed to
the Germans,[b] wherein they are invited to sing the *Bardiet*[c] and
reminded that their forbears were called 'Franks', and wherein the
King of Prussia[d] had already agreed to be whacked by Austria, I
thought I had plumbed the depths of stupidity. *Mais non!* For here is
the Fanon-Caperon-Gouté manifesto, as the *Patrie* calls it,[e] of the *dii
minorum gentium*[f] with, as it rightly remarks, the same content but
devoid of chic, devoid of style, with the most pathetic rhetorical
flourishes such as *serpents* and *sicaires*[g] and *égorgements*.[h] The
Indépendance, quoting a few sentences from this masterpiece, relates
that it was composed by the *soldats les plus obscurs de la
Démocratie*[i] and that these poor devils had sent it to the London
correspondent of that paper, despite the latter's conservatism.
Such was their longing to appear in print. In retribution it names
no names, and similarly the *Patrie* names only the three
mentioned above. To compound the *misère* they gave one of the
Straubingers[86] here (yesterday this same person told Pfänder the
sorry tale) 50 copies to take to France. Just off Boulogne he
hurled 49 of them into the sea; on reaching Boulogne Brother

---

of diplomacy. The emulators of the Metternichs and the Talleyrands are at this
moment contemplating how they may extinguish the torch of the Revolution by
instigating in France, through the invasion they are preparing, a national war in
which the peoples will butcher each other for the benefit of the enemies of their
liberation. Nay, Citizens! No more national war! For us the barriers, set up by
despots between the nations they had shared out among them, are henceforward
fallen, and the *peoples*, confounded,' (really: *confounded*), 'have only one flag
upon which, with the fertile blood of our martyrs, we have written: *Universal
Democratic and Social Republic.*'
    On behalf of *Their Societies:* 'The members of the Committee of the Society
of Exiled French Socialist Democrats in London: Adam (Cambreur), Barthélemy (Emmanuel), Caperon (Paulin), Fanon, Gouté, Thierry, Vidil (Jules); the delegates of the Permanent Commission of the Polish Democracy Section in London: Sawaszkiewicz, Warskiroski; the members of the Socialist Democratic Committee of German Refugees and the German Workers' Society: Dietz (Oswald),
Gebert (A.), Mayer (Adolphe), Schärttner (A.), Schapper (Karl), Willich (August).
The delegates of the Hungarian Democratic Society in London: Molikoy, Simonyi.
London, 16 November 1850.'
[a] Marx adapts here a saying current in the Mark. - [b] 'Le Comité central
démocratique européen, aux Allemands, 13 novembre 1850' published in *La Voix
du Proscrit,* No. 4, 17 November 1850 and other papers. - [c] Teutonic war
song - [d] Frederick William IV - [e] G. de Molinari, 'Un nouveau manifeste rouge', *La
Patrie,* 28 November 1850. - [f] second-rate luminaries (literally: gods of minor
nations) - [g] assassins - [h] butchery - [i] the most obscure soldiers of Democracy
(*L'Indépendance belge,* No. 323, 19 November 1850); the newspaper has: 'soldats ... de
la démagogie'.

Straubinger was sent back to London for lack of a passport, and declares 'that he is now off to Boston'.

Farewell and write by return.

Your
K.Marx

Apropos! Do write sometime to the worthy Dronke telling him to reply about League matters and not to write only in the case of begging letters. The gentlemen in Cologne[a] have sent no news. 'Haude', who is now back, having lost all his worldly goods in Germany,[334] is described by Weydemeyer as an 'otherwise stout lad'.

You must seriously consider what you are going to write about.[335] England won't do, there being 2 articles on the subject already,[b] perhaps 3 with Eccarius.[c] Nor is there a great deal to say about France. Could you not perhaps, in conjunction with Mazzini's latest things, tackle the rotten Italians along with their revolution? (His *Republic and Monarchy* etc., as well as his religion, the Pope, etc.)[d]

[From Jenny Marx]

Dear Mr Engels,

Your kind sympathy over the heavy blow dealt us by fate through the loss of our little darling, my poor little child of sorrow,[e] has been a great comfort to me, the more so as, in the last few sorrowful days, I have found cause for the most bitter complaint in our friend Schramm. My husband and all the rest of us have missed you sorely and have often longed to see you. However, I am very glad that you have left and are well on the way to becoming a great COTTON LORD. See that you entrench yourself firmly between the two warring brothers[f]; their tussle is bound to place you in a position of indispensability vis-à-vis your respected Papa, and in my mind's eye I already see you as Friedrich Engels JUNIOR and partner of the SENIOR. But of course the best thing about it is that, notwithstanding the COTTON TRADE and all the rest, you are still the same old Fritze and, in the words of those three arch-democrats, Frederick William the First,[g] Kinkel and Mazzini,

---

[a] members of the Cologne Central Authority of the Communist League - [b] F. Engels, 'The English Ten Hours' Bill' and K. Marx and F. Engels, 'Review. May to October [1850]'. - [c] J. G. Eccarius, 'Die Schneiderei in London oder der Kampf des grossen und des kleinen Capitals', *Neue Rheinische Zeitung. Politisch-ökonomische Revue*, No. 5-6, 1850. - [d] J. Mazzini, *Republic and Royalty in Italy* published in several issues of *The Red Republican* in June-November 1850; G. Mazzini, *Le Pape au dix-neuvième siècle*. - [e] Heinrich Guido - [f] Gottfried and Peter Ermen - [g] August Willich

you will not become 'estranged from *the sacred cause of freedom*'. Karl has told you something about the mummery here. I might add some *nova*.[a] That obese ruffian, Haude, shed all his fat during his muckraking tour of the German provinces and trips over his own legs whenever he sees anyone. It would seem that a little hippopotamus of dubious origin has joined the dictator hippopotamus,[b] and that the Great Windmill Knight, Hohenzoller Willich, has reinforced his guard of nobles with a few qualified footpads and blackguards. Our own people dawdle along from one day to the next with the help of a few borrowed pence. Rings is now earning something as a claqueur with the Duke of Brunswick, who is once more loudly pontificating before the courts.

The last Polish banquet, at which were foregathered the French, German, Hungarian and Polish *crapauds*[c] (Willich, Fieschi, Adam, etc.),[336] ended up in a free-for-all. Apart from that we've heard nothing of the crew. Last night we attended Ernest Jones' first lecture on the history of the papacy. His lecture was marvellous and, by English standards, advanced, though not quite *à la hauteur*[d] for us Germans who have run the gauntlet of Hegel, Feuerbach, etc. Poor Harney was dangerously ill of an abscess of the windpipe. He is not allowed to speak. An English doctor has made two incisions without finding the affected spot. His *Red [Republican]* has turned into *The Friend of the People*. Well, enough for today. The children chatter a great deal about Uncle Angels and, thanks to your estimable tuition, dear Mr Engels, little Till[e] now gives a splendid rendering of the song about the 'journeyman's pelt and the nimble broom'.

I hope we shall see you at Christmas.

Yours

Jenny Marx

First published abridged in *Der Briefwechsel zwischen F. Engels und K. Marx*, Bd. 1, Stuttgart, 1913 and in full in *MEGA*, Abt. III, Bd. 1, 1929

Printed according to the original

Published in English for the first time

126

MARX TO HERMANN BECKER

IN COLOGNE

London, 2 December [1850]
64 Dean Street, Soho

Dear Becker,

I know that you felt greatly offended by a letter I wrote to Bürgers.[f] However, in this letter, which was written under very trying circumstances, I had no intention of offending you any more

---

[a] news - [b] Karl Schapper - [c] philistines - [d] up to the mark - [e] Edgar Marx - [f] Presumably Marx's letter to Bürgers of 25 June 1850 (see this volume, pp. 237-38).

10*

than my other friends in Cologne. I believe that this explanation will satisfy you and that, without harking back to the past, I can proceed straight to the proposals I have to make to you.

1. You know how wretchedly Mr Schuberth has managed our *Revue*. I believe that in a few days' time he will have brought out the last two issues. I wish to continue the enterprise as a quarterly (from February onwards), 20 sheets every quarter. The increased size would allow the inclusion of more varied material. Can you undertake publication, and on what terms?

2. A friend of mine [a] has translated my anti-Proudhon piece [b] from the French into German and has written his own introduction to it.[337] I would put the same question to you as above.

3. I have devised a scheme by which socialist literature consisting of a series of small pamphlets could be launched on the public in successive publications. A start could not be made until March. Should you be willing to undertake something of this kind, the things would be got ready in the meantime. I believe that, after its recent cheering experience of *haute politique,* the German public will BY AND BY find itself obliged to turn its urgent attention to the real content of present-day struggles. I beg you to reply soon.

Your
K. Marx

First published in: Marx and Engels, *Works,* First Russian Edition, Vol. XXIX, Moscow, 1946

Printed according to the original

Published in English for the first time

127

ENGELS TO EMIL BLANK

IN BARMEN

Manchester, 3 December 1850

Dear Emil,

I have received your parcel and thank you for your prompt dispatch of the cigars, which have found general acclaim. The underpants are also fine.

---

[a] Probably Wilhelm Pieper - [b] K. Marx, *The Poverty of Philosophy.*

Father wrote to me a few days ago. His preference is for Gottfried Ermen, with whom he would prefer to continue in case of a rupture; under no circumstances will he remain with Peter any longer than necessary. I shall collect all the notes available on Ermen Bros' business. That they have done extensive business is certain, the average profit, Gottfried Ermen maintains, being £600 a year, and more in recent years. In this business it is difficult to lose money in an average year; they possess and need little capital, and the article—low quality sewing and knitting yarn—also goes better compared with the fine qualities, which are falling off considerably.

The balance for the year 1849/50 has not yet been struck; debits and credits are still in the most splendid confusion. Father would seem to have been pressing them again, so I hear, and tomorrow they will set about putting this in order.

Accordingly Mr Peter arrived here this morning or yesterday evening! He sent for old Hill—he is living in an hotel two doors away from our office—was very nice, inquired about indifferent matters, but so far, at any rate, has failed to put in an appearance at the office. If his intention is to plague me, he has chosen the wrong man. Father does not wish to intervene in the brothers' squabbles, nor will I do so. But Gottfried is in such a fix that he has to keep in with me; he will tell me everything without my having to ask him about it.

If Peter Ermen takes over the management of the office, which very probably will happen in the end, this will greatly interfere with my examination of the books. Hitherto I have only been able to do this 4 days a week in DINNER-HOURS, when I was on my own, but it's precisely during DINNER-HOURS that he is accustomed to go sniffing about the office. I have abstracted the essentials, however, and little remains save the very involved task of comparing the prices at which Ermen Bros have been selling to us with the current prices on each occasion, and a search through old invoices, etc., etc., so as to see whether one may not perhaps light upon this or that. In a few days' time I shall send Father Ermen Bros' complete accounts for 1849/50, duly classified and set out, as also those of Ermens' bleaching concern, so that he may see how these gentlemen carry on business with his capital.

Debit Father with the cost of the cigars, that would be the simplest.

My love to Marie, Hermann and the children.

Your
Frederick

First published in: Marx and Engels, *Works,* First Russian Edition, Vol. XXV, Moscow, 1934

Printed according to the original

Published in English for the first time

128

ENGELS TO MARX

IN LONDON

Manchester, 17 December 1850

Dear Marx,

I have been exceptionally busy of late and have had other interruptions which have forced me out of my customary routine and prevented me from writing. Hence my belated reply.

The Fanon-Caperon-Gouté manifesto[a] is truly a masterpiece, both in form and content. *Crânerie*[b] has found its ultimate expression, and Monsieur Barthélemy has at last given the world an example of *ce que c'est que de parler carrément.*[c] The military dispositions of the *homme de marbre*[d] are equally funny; the *bonhomme*[e] has counted most of the Austrian army corps twice over, as the most cursory REFERENCE to the newspapers will show. Incidentally, it's really taking effrontery too far after all the fiascos since 1848, and with all the nations, *crapauds*[f] first and foremost, in their present easy-going mood, to speak of a *marée populaire qui menace d'engloutir des trônes.*[g] The collection of names at the bottom is undoubtedly the finest FEATURE of the whole. No such European congress has ever been seen before. Ledru-Rollin, Mazzini and Co. actually acquire a certain importance from this puerile affair. For that matter, I'd like to know in what way that milksop Sawaszkiewicz, who appears at the bottom, differs from Ledru-

---

[a] See this volume, pp. 246-47. - [b] Swagger - [c] what blunt speaking is - [d] man of marble (iron) - [e] chap - [f] philistines - [g] a popular tide which is threatening to engulf thrones

Rollin's Polack Darasz, and to what extent the two Hungarians, who appear at the bottom, are to be preferred to Mazzini. True, Schapper and Ruge are more or less equally matched and, unless the cockroach Dietz tips the scales heavily in favour of the new European committee, these gentry will hardly be able to compete with their prototype.[338]

Recently I went to see John Watts; the fellow seems skilled in sharp practice and now has a much larger SHOP in Deansgate, somewhat further up. He has become a consummate radical mediocrity, is concerned with nothing but the EDUCATIONAL MOVEMENT, raves about MORAL FORCE[339] and has accepted Mr Proudhon as his lord and master. He has translated the *Contradictions économiques*[a] and some other stuff and has lost a great deal of money at it, since English workers have not yet sufficient 'education' to enable them to understand these marvellous things. From a few instances he gave me, it transpired that he knows very well how to boost his tailoring business by parading his bourgeois liberalism. On the EDUCATIONAL COMMITTEES he sits fraternally alongside his once inveterate foes, the dissenting ministers,[340] from time to time accepting their vote of thanks FOR THE VERY ABLE ADDRESS HE DELIVERED ON THAT EVENING. It seemed to me that the fellow has lost all his wits in the metamorphosis and I have not been to see him since. For people hereabouts who are thus transmuted into a state of bourgeois respectability, Proudhon is, of course, heaven sent; though seemingly going further than anyone else, further even than Owen, he is nevertheless FULLY RESPECTABLE.

I have no objection to writing about Mr Mazzini and the Italian business. Only—save for the thing in *The Red* [*Republican*][b]—I haven't got a single one of Mazzini's writings. However I shan't be able to do anything before Christmas since I shall be in London a week hence. I shall then bring back with me what I need. But perhaps by that time something else will have occurred to us.

Very many thanks to your wife for her amiable note.[c] As for the COTTON LORD, it hasn't come to that yet; my old man doesn't seem at all inclined to keep me here any longer than is absolutely necessary. *Cependant nous verrons.*[d] Peter Ermen is going round in circles like a fox that has left its brush in a trap, and is trying to

[a] P. J. Proudhon, *Système des contradictions économiques, ou Philosophie de la misère.* -
[b] J. Mazzini, *Republic and Royalty in Italy.* - [c] See this volume, pp. 250-51. -
[d] However, we shall see.

make things too hot for me here—the stupid devil imagines *he* could annoy me!

Dronke has been written to.[341]

My regards to your wife and children.

Your
F. E.

First published abridged in *Der Briefwechsel zwischen F. Engels und K. Marx,* Bd. 1, Stuttgart, 1913 and in full in *MEGA,* Abt. III, Bd. 1, 1929

Printed according to the original

Published in English for the first time

1851

129

MARX TO ENGELS

[London,] 6 January [1851]

Dear Engels,

You would very much oblige me, *s'il est possible*,[a] by sending me the money by return. My landlady is VERY POOR, this is the second week she has not been paid, and she's dunning me with dreadful determination.

At yesterday's district meeting Wolff[b] appeared, but not Liebknecht or Schramm.[c] Once the new Rules[342] had been adopted, I adjourned the wretched thing indefinitely.

Your
K. M.

Our *Revue* will probably appear afresh in Switzerland. Work out SOMETHING then, so that I have the manuscript READY if needs be.

First published in *Der Briefwechsel zwischen F. Engels und K. Marx,* Bd. 1, Stuttgart, 1913

Printed according to the original

Published in English for the first time

---

[a] if possible - [b] Ferdinand Wolff - [c] Conrad Schramm

130

MARX TO ENGELS [343]

IN MANCHESTER

London, 7 January 1851

Dear Engels,

I am writing to you today, to lay before you a *questiuncula theoretica*,[a] naturally *naturae politico-economicae*.[b]

You know, to begin *ab ovo*,[c] that according to Ricardo's theory, rent is nothing else but the difference between the production costs and the price of agricultural produce, or, as he also expressed it, the difference in the price at which the produce of the poorest land must be sold in order to cover costs (the tenant-farmer's profit and interest being always included in the costs), and that at which the produce of the best land can be sold.

The increase in rent proves, according to his own exposition of his theory, that:

1. Recourse is had to ever poorer types of soil, or that the same amount of capital, successively employed on the same land, does not give the same yield. In a word: the soil deteriorates in like proportion to the increasing demands the population must make upon it. It becomes relatively less fertile. Wherein Malthus discovered the real basis for his theory of population, and wherein his disciples now seek their last sheet-anchor.

2. Rent can only rise when the price of corn rises (at least according to *economic laws*); it must fall when the latter falls.

3. When *a country's overall rental* rises, this can only be explained by the fact that a very large mass of relatively poorer land has been brought under cultivation.

Now these 3 PROPOSITIONS are everywhere refuted by history.

1. There is no doubt that, with the advance of civilisation, ever poorer types of soil are brought under cultivation. But equally, there is no doubt that, as a result of the progress of science and industry, these poorer types of soil are relatively good as against those previously regarded as good.

2. Since 1815 the price of corn has fallen, irregularly but steadily, from 90 to 50 shillings and, before the repeal of the Corn

---

[a] a small question of theory - [b] of a politico-economic nature - [c] at the beginning (literally: from the egg)

A page from Marx's letter to Engels of 7 January 1851

Laws,[270] even lower. Rent has steadily risen. Thus in England. *Mutatis mutandis* everywhere on the Continent.

3. In all countries, as Petty has already observed, we find that, when the price of corn fell, the country's overall rental rose.

The main point of all this is to adjust the law of rent to progress in fertility in agriculture generally, this being the only way, firstly, to explain the historical facts and, secondly, to eliminate the Malthusian theory of the deterioration, not only of the 'hands', but also of the soil.

I believe that the matter can be explained simply, as follows:

Let us assume that, at a given state of agriculture, the price of wheat is 7 shillings a quarter[a] and one acre of the best quality land, subject to a rent of 10 shillings, produces 20 bushels. The return per acre thus=20×7 or=140 shillings. In this case the production costs amount to 130 shillings. Hence 130 shillings is the price of the product of the poorest land under cultivation.

Let us assume that there is a general improvement in agriculture. If this be presupposed, we at the same time assume that science, industry and population are in a state of growth. A general increase in the fertility of the land resulting from improvements presupposes these conditions, as against the fertility fortuitously induced by a favourable season.

Say the price of wheat falls from 7 to 5 shillings a quarter.[a] The best land, No. 1, which formerly yielded 20 bushels now yields 30 bushels. This now returns, instead of 20×7, or 140 shillings, 30×5, or 150 shillings. I. e. a rent of 20 shillings instead of 10 as formerly. The poorest land, which bears no rent, must produce 26 bushels, for, in accordance with our foregoing assumption, the requisite price of these is 130 shillings and 26×5=130. If the improvement, i. e. the general progress of science, which goes hand in hand with the overall progress of society, growth of population, etc., is not so general as to enable the poorest land that must be brought under cultivation to produce 26 bushels, the price of corn cannot fall to 5 shillings a quarter.[a]

As before, the 20 shillings rent is an expression of the difference between production costs and the price of corn on the best land, or between the production costs on the poorest and those on the best land. Relatively speaking, one piece of land is no less infertile by comparison with the other than before. But *fertility in general* has improved.

---

[a] Presumably this should be 'bushel'.

All that is presupposed is that, if the price of corn falls from 7 to 5 shillings, consumption or demand increases correspondingly, or that productivity does not exceed the demand that may be expected when the price is 5 shillings. False though this hypothesis might be if the price had fallen from 7 to 5 as the result of an exceptionally abundant harvest, it is a necessary one where fertility has increased gradually and as a result of measures taken by the producers themselves. In any case, all we are concerned with here is the economic feasibility of this hypothesis.

From this it follows that:

1. Rent may rise although the price of agricultural produce falls, and yet *Ricardo's law still holds good.*

2. The law of rent, as laid down by Ricardo in its simplest form and leaving aside its exposition, does not presuppose the diminishing fertility of the land, but only—and this *despite the general increase in fertility that accompanies the development of society*—the *varying* fertility of fields or the varying results obtained by the capital successively employed on the same land.

3. The more general the improvement in the land, the greater the variety of the fields it will embrace, and the country's overall rental may rise, although there is a general fall in the price of corn. E. g., given the above example, it is simply a question of the number of fields producing over 26 bushels at 5 shillings without actually having to go as high as 30, i.e. of the extent to which the quality of the land varies as between the best and the poorest. This has nothing to do with the RATIO of rent of the best land. In fact it has nothing to do directly with the RATIO of rent at all.

As you know, the real joke where rent is concerned is that it is generated by evening out the price for the resultants of varying production costs, but that this law of market price is nothing other than the law of bourgeois competition. Even after the elimination of bourgeois production, however, there remains the snag that the soil would become relatively more infertile, that, with the same amount of labour, successively less would be achieved, although the best land would no longer, as under bourgeois rule, yield as dear a product as the poorest. The foregoing would do away with this objection.

I should like to have your views on the matter.

Having bored you with this muck, I am sending you by way of comic relief the enclosed bundle of letters from Dr *Magnus Gross* (doubly great Great! Greatest of the Great!) of Cincinnati.[344] You will see that if Monsieur Gross is not *grand,* he is nevertheless *gros.*[a] Tellering II *in nuce.*[b] These Coblenzers are all alike![c] Send the things back to me with, if you have the time and the inclination, a line or two for Dronke.

Your
K. M.

First published in *Der Briefwechsel zwischen F. Engels und K. Marx,* Bd. 1, Stuttgart, 1913

Printed according to the original

Published in English in full for the first time

131

ENGELS TO MARX

IN LONDON

Manchester, 8 January 1851

Dear Marx,

Herewith Post Office Order for £1, particulars as before. My buyer[d]—our clerk—having apparently paid out a great deal of late, seems anxious not to take too much money from the firm all at once. He is rather reluctant—I don't press him overmuch, *cela se conçoit.*[e] I myself have been involved in very heavy outlays as a result of my trip to London,[345] otherwise I would gladly send you the whole amount; as it is, I must for today confine myself to fulfilling the obligation of an ordinary consignee and send you half the amount in part payment. The second half will follow—at the latest—in the early part of February, perhaps sooner; as soon, that is, as the firm sends my old man a letter containing the payments made to me.

Jones was up here and bearded his opponents at a public meeting in their own den.[346] Leach and Donovan opposed him. The debate, however, wasn't quite what I had expected. Petty stratagems on both sides; much *chronique scandaleuse*[f] which partly made up for the absence of some of London's amenities. On

---

a Pun on the French words *grand* (great) and *gros* (big). - b in miniature - c Probably an allusion to the fact that Müller-Tellering came from Coblenz. - d This presumably concerns the *Historischer und geographischer Atlas von Europa* belonging to Marx, who had instructed Engels to sell it. - e as is understandable - f tittle-tattle

Jones' part, superiority of rhetorical talent. Leach, on the other hand, tremendously IMPERTURBABLE but at times abysmally absurd. Donovan, a common, intriguing, local panjandrum. Jones, by the way, because of the *Neue Rheinische Zeitung*[a] and my presence, was compelled to proclaim himself a RED REPUBLICAN and supporter of the NATIONALISATION OF LANDED PROPERTY, while Leach, on the other hand, took his stand as the wholehearted representative of the CO-OPERATIVE SOCIETIES, insofar as they reject political agitation. These societies, incidentally, would now seem to be very numerous in Lancashire, and Jones and his friends are afraid that, if some sort of alliance were formed between them and the Chartists, they would gain control of the CHARTIST MOVEMENT. This circumstance explains many of the concessions Harney thought fit to make them.

The success of Jones' performance here was all that could be expected; he put forward as the point to be decided between himself and the Manchester CHARTIST COUNCIL the question of recognising the Executive in London; the votes were evenly divided, although Leach and Co. had had about 3 hours in which to fetch their people to the meeting and a crowd of them had duly turned up. At the beginning, when the company was simply a random gathering (Leach had counted on Jones' not arriving before 9 o'clock but, much to the former's chagrin, he was there as early as 8), Jones was given an enthusiastic reception.

When in the company of Chartists whom he wishes to win over or attach more closely to his person, Jones is by no means as naive as he is with us. HE IS VERY WIDE AWAKE. Perhaps a little too much so—at least, the likes of us 'notice the design'.[b]

One of Harney's friends here is a boring Scotsman of infinite sensibilities and hence interminable speeches; a second is a small, resolute, aggressive lad, about whose intellectual capacity I have not yet made up my mind; a third, a man whom Harney did not mention to me, one Robertson, seems to me to be far and away the most intelligent. I shall try to start up a small club with these fellows, or organise regular meetings to discuss the *Manifesto*[c] with them. Harney and Jones have a host of friends here, and O'Connor a host of hidden enemies but, until he makes a downright fool of himself in public, it won't be possible to bring about his—official—downfall here. At the meeting, by the way,

---

[a] *Neue Rheinische Zeitung. Politisch-ökonomische Revue* - [b] Goethe, *Torquato Tasso*, 3. Auszug, 1. Austritt. - [c] K. Marx and F. Engels, *Manifesto of the Communist Party*.

Jones referred to him and Reynolds with the scantest possible respect.

Recently my brother-in-law[a] told me some good news concerning myself: my prospective American partner was in London and from a conversation between the two of them it transpired that I was not the man to be of use to his firm. Thus America is put off pretty well indefinitely, since no fresh plan can now be hatched without my consent.

Best regards to your wife and children.

Your
F. E.

First published in *Der Briefwechsel zwischen F. Engels und K. Marx*, Bd. 1, Stuttgart, 1913

Printed according to the original

Published in English for the first time

132

MARX TO ENGELS

IN MANCHESTER

[London,] 22 January 1851

Dear Engels,

You are *taciturne comme la mort*.[b] Enclosed I send you 1) a statement by Oswald Dietz in the Basle *National-Zeitung* against Pfänder and Bauer,[c] 2) a tattling article against us concocted by Mr A. Ruge in company with Struve and Willich.[d] You must return the garbage to me within two days at the latest, telling me what action you think we should take against No. 2. If you would like to draft some sort of statement, send it along as well.

C. Schramm is going to issue his own statement.

What do you think of this *coup de maître*[e] by Atta Troll[f] and, entrenched behind him, that 'outstanding, resolute man, Struve',

---

[a] Emil Blank - [b] silent as the grave - [c] O. Dietz. 'An die deutschen Arbeiter-Verein', *Schweizerische National-Zeitung*, No. 5, 7 January 1851 (on the alleged appropriation of Educational Society funds by Heinrich Bauer and Carl Pfänder see this volume, pp. 245-46). - [d] A. Ruge, 'London, 13 January', *Bremer Tages-Chronik*, No. 474, 17 January 1851. - [e] master stroke - [f] Title character of Heine's satirical poem. Here meaning Arnold Ruge.

not to speak of the 'valiant Willich'. *C'est un peu fort.*[a] I happened to light upon the paper at Bamberger's. Who else would either read or know of the *Bremer Tages-Chronik. Organ der Demokratie?*

Bauer and Pfänder naturally won't answer and silence would, indeed, seem to be the most advisable course for them just now.

I have as yet had no news, either from Schabelitz, who wished to take over our *Revue*[b] or from Becker, who was going to see to the publication of my essays.[347] None of my approaches to Mr Schuberth have so far been of any avail. If Haupt can find a lawyer who will take over the case, he will bring an action against him.[348]

What are Mary and Lizzy[c] doing? And above all you yourself? Harney was here one evening with Pieper, Eccarius, etc., and very gay, until his 'dear spouse'[d]—'half drew she him, half sank he in'[e]—carried him off almost by force.

Your
K. M.

First published abridged in *Der Briefwechsel zwischen F. Engels und K. Marx,* Bd. 1, Stuttgart, 1913 and in full in *MEGA,* Abt. III, Bd. 1, 1929

Printed according to the original

Published in English for the first time

133

ENGELS TO MARX

IN LONDON

[Manchester,] Saturday [25 January 1851]

Dear Marx,

Je te trouve joli en me disant que je suis taciturne comme la mort.[f] However, I'll refrain from making any further riposte.

The perfidy of that Pomeranian blackguard, Ruge, is crude beyond all measure.[g] It would be the simplest if you were to draft

---

[a] It's a bit too much. The words quoted are from Ruge's article. - [b] *Neue Rheinische Zeitung. Politisch-ökonomische Revue* - [c] Sisters Mary and Lizzy Burns - [d] Mary - [e] Goethe, 'Der Fischer'. - [f] You're a fine one to tell me I'm silent as the grave. - [g] See this volume, p. 265.

a statement to be signed by us both.[a] A few personal remarks could, if necessary, be appended in the form of notes and signed separately by each of us. I don't know whether I should add something on my own account, if only to say that, in my commercial employment, I have maintained complete independence and hence do not have to let myself be ordered by my 'principals', as Mr Ruge was by his superior Mazzini, despite all his earlier atheistic boasting,[349] to append my signature to moving appeals to the *bon dieu*[b]; and that I have adopted this LINE so as not to fall into the necessity, congenial enough to other worthy gents held up to us as an example by Mr Ruge, namely, of living on democratic charity—or some such. Tell me if you think this is necessary.

The article, by the way, with its moral indignation and its monumental lies, provides splendid stuff for ridicule. It immediately puts one on the track of Ruge's intrigues. It's very natural that Mr Ruge and Mazzini's European Committee should be as incense in the nostrils of the worthy Reverend Dulon, and that Mazzini's sublime manifestos should find their only fertile soil in Germany among those wailing North German, Lower-Saxon democrats swimming in Bremen-concocted, belletristic, drivel-sauce. These gentlemen's Friendship of Light[350] was bound to find desirable allies in Ronge-Mazzini and in the now once more god-fearing Ruge, while the honour of officially corresponding as the 'German Committee' with the greatest men of respectable European democracy must inevitably have made that malleable parson Dulon receptive to the worst scurrilities levelled against the 'frivolous' and godless folk of the *Neue Rheinische Zeitung*. Ruge, too, has only plucked up courage since coming to believe that the *Revue* is dead. But I think he is mistaken and will shortly bring down a pretty thunderstorm upon his ludicrous cranium.

Would it not be a good idea—since we cannot possibly raise a real shindy about this article or reply to it anywhere save in the *Tages-Chronik*[c]—to have the aforesaid Dulon secretly worked upon by his friend, red Becker[d]? After these scurrilities we can't even be sure that our reply will be accepted.

But it is clear as day that it was only Schramm's[e] fatuous manner and the ill-considered prating which, to judge by this article, he indulged in at his brother's,[f] that inspired these

---

[a] K. Marx and F. Engels, 'Statement. 27 January 1851.' - [b] Good Lord - [c] *Bremer Tages-Chronik* - [d] Hermann Becker - [e] Conrad Schramm - [f] Rudolf Schramm

jackasses with sufficient courage to vent themselves so vulgarly against us, the 'isolated and forsaken by all'. The fellow will now himself realise how base are the machinations whose tool he has become, and he must also realise that his stupidity harms himself more than others. The great Ruge doesn't even pay him the half-hearted court he pays to Tellering. 'C. Schramm, not to be confused!'[a] What's the fellow up to now? *Cette affaire est de peu d'importance.*[b] Trumped-up and misconstrued tittle-tattle, clumsy and incomprehensible insinuations and moral bombast—*nous avons soutenu, Dieu merci, de bien autres charges!*[c] The only unpleasantness is that the thing will upset your wife so much, which, as things are now, is undesirable.[351]

Next week in *The Friend of the People* I shall duly take the European Committee to task and have already notified Harney.[352] I must stop now, as the office is just closing and it's nearly time for the post. More anon.

Your
F. E.

First published in *MEGA*, Abt. III, Bd. 1, 1929

Printed according to the original

Published in English for the first time

134

MARX TO ENGELS

IN MANCHESTER

[London,] 27 January 1851

Dear Engels,

Enclosed you will find the statement for signature.[d] There can be *no question of sending it* to Dulon, for Ruge has made himself *co-proprietor* of the *Bremer Chronik.*[e] It must be sent to the

---

[a] Ruge's article has: 'Conrad Schramm (not to be confused with the Berlin deputy Rudolf Schramm)....' - [b] The affair's of small significance. - [c] We have, God be praised, survived far worse accusations. - [d] K. Marx and F. Engels, 'Statement. 27 January 1851'. - [e] *Bremer Tages-Chronik*

conservative paper, the *Weser-Zeitung* in Bremen.[353] Write to its editors when you send the statement; tell them to send us two copies to London, to my address, 28 Dean Street, at the same time informing us what the announcement will cost and how it is to be paid for. Don't forget, however, to prepay the letter.

Now, as it's nearly time for the post, no more than the following:

1. Did you forward to *Weerth* the letter[354] which my wife sent with a few lines for you[a]?

2. Did you get my letter in which I sent you *Dr Magnus Gross' scrawl,* etc., and to which I wanted to know your answer[b]? If you haven't received it, *I beg you to complain to the Post Office at once.* I sent you this letter the day *after* I had received *yours—about a fortnight ago, that is.*

Write soon and tell me whether you approve of the statement.

Your
K. M.

I think it would be superfluous to add any special notes to the statement.

P.S.

You mustn't forget, either, to tell the Bremen editors, i.e. the editors of the *Weser-Zeitung,* to make sure they observe the right sequence, putting Schramm's[c] statement *after,* and not *before* ours. Apropos! If you have really not received the 2 letters, write to me in *English,* after you yourself have made inquiries in Manchester, telling me how I should write to the Post-Master General. In my letter of a fortnight ago I apprised you of a new viewpoint about land rent[d] on which I must have your opinion.

Your
K. M.

[From Wilhelm Pieper]

Dear Engels, I must inform you in haste that Marx is highly indignant at your complete silence on the subject of his new theory of land rent about which he recently wrote to you. Marx leads a very retired life, his only friends being John

a See this volume, pp. 561-62. - b ibid., pp. 262-63. - c Conrad Schramm - d See this volume, pp. 258-63.

Stuart Mill and Loyd, and whenever one goes to see him one is welcomed with economic categories in lieu of greetings.

On ne peut pas vivre qu'avec toi, après tout,[a] and if one wishes to live uneconomically, as I love doing, I have to indulge my extravagance quietly, there being no longer anyone here for me to consort with. In between times I try to do some copying, and even sometimes do exercises in composition on my own account, but I still very much doubt whether I shall achieve anything worthwhile. I am glad to hear that you are in good spirits and shall before long find the time to write you something rather more coherent.

Cordial greetings,
W. Pieper

First published in *MEGA*, Abt. III, Bd. l, 1929

Printed according to the original

Published in English for the first time

135

ENGELS TO MARX[220]

IN LONDON

[Manchester,] Wednesday evening,
29 January [1851]

Dear Marx,

Your silence and your astonishment at my silence became suddenly explicable to me when today my old witch of a landlady, AFTER SOME SHARP CROSS-EXAMINATION hunted out your letter of 7 inst. from among a pile of books in my room where it had been peacefully slumbering since 8 January.[b] I happened to be out that evening, and this person had simply placed the letter on top of the books; later, when tidying up, she had in her haste put another book on top of it, and as that pile of books has remained untouched all this while, the letter might, without your reminder, have gone on slumbering there till Doomsday. Had I been studying Russian this month instead of physiology, this wouldn't have happened.

Anyhow, your new thing about land rent is absolutely right. The

---

[a] After all, one cannot live with you alone. - [b] See this volume, pp. 258-63.

increasing infertility of the land concomitant with an ever-increasing population in Ricardo has always seemed to me implausible, nor have I ever been able to discover any evidence in support of his ever-rising price of corn, but with my notorious sloth *en fait de théorie*,[a] I have silenced the inward grumbling of my better self and have never gone to the root of the matter. There can be no doubt that you have hit on the right solution, thereby entitling yourself afresh to the title of economist of land rent. If there were still right and justice on this earth, all land rents for at least a year would now be yours, and that would be the least which you could claim.

I have never really been able to accept Ricardo's simple proposition in which he represents land rent as the difference in the productivity of various types of land and, seeking to prove this proposition, 1) acknowledges no other factor than the bringing under cultivation of ever poorer types of soil, 2) completely ignores advances in agriculture and 3) finally abandons almost entirely the bringing under cultivation of poorer types of soil, and instead continually proceeds from the assumption that capital, employed successively on a particular field, contributes less and less to the increase in the yield. Convincing as was the proposition to be proved, the factors adduced in proof of that same proposition were wholly alien to it. You will remember that, in the *Deutsch-Französische Jahrbücher,* I already invoked the progress made by scientific agriculture as against the theory of increasing infertility[b]—of course very CRUDE and not at all closely argued. You have now cleared up the matter, which is yet another reason why you must make haste to finish the Economy and get it published. If we could somehow get an article of yours on land rent into an English periodical, it would create a tremendous stir. Think it over. *Je me charge de la traduction.*[c]

Enclosed I return Mr Great-Gross.[d] In my next I shall include a line or two for the delectable Dronke, but tonight I'm too sleepy to do any more work. A fine band of scallywags, Gross, Wilhelmi, and the progressive pamphleteer from Cincinnati[e]! The fellows must really imagine that we're on our physical, moral and intellectual beam ends to ask such things of us.[344] *C'est amusant, cependant,*[f] and I laughed heartily at these backwoods saviours of society and their proposals, including fee for Dronke. Dr Siegfried

---

[a] in matters of theory - [b] F. Engels, 'Outlines of a Critique of Political Economy'. - [c] I will attend to the translation. - [d] See this volume, pp. 262-63. - [e] L. A. Hine - [f] It's amusing, however

Weiss' 'sharp and spicy'[355] is OUTDONE by the 'red, piquant, sarcastic and versatile' of the 'Adonis of a long-forgotten Beauty'. *Que Dieu le bénisse!*[a]

Tomorrow the statements will go off to Bremen together with the necessary instructions.[b] Mr Schramm[c] might really have rewritten his; it's so wretchedly scrawled that it will probably give rise to misunderstanding.

The O'Connor conference here has turned out to be sheer humbug.[356] Ostensibly representing the whole of English Chartism, it consists of *8* men who represent *4* towns: Manchester, Bradford, Warrington and Sowerby. Of these, Warrington and Bradford belong to the opposition and see eye to eye with the Executive. Mantle, the Warrington representative, who doesn't give a fig for the majority, opened the PROCEEDINGS with the motion that the conference, SEEING THEIR UTTER INSIGNIFICANCE AND CONTEMPTIBILITY, should resolve to go home forthwith, and tomorrow he will extort from them a vote of confidence for the Executive, i.e. for Harney and Jones, from which O'Connor will be unable to abstain. On the question of union with the FINANCIAL REFORMERS[284] 3 voted for and 2 against, 3 abstaining, among them O'Connor, whom Mantle had unfortunately intimidated by his insolent conduct; otherwise the fellow would have voted in favour, thereby making a colossal and irretrievable fool of himself. At the conference O'Connor, Leach, McGrath, Clark and a certain Hurst formed the majority. At a dinner given for O'Connor on Monday, Mr Thomas Clark proposed the following toast: THE QUEEN: HER RIGHTS AND NO MORE; THE PEOPLE: THEIR RIGHTS AND NO LESS. Here again Mantle, a fiery, undiplomatic hothead, stopped O'Connor from getting up and drinking the toast.

The letter to Weerth[d] has gone off and should be in his hands within a few days, provided he isn't buried in the heart of Morocco.

No more for today.

Your
F. E.

First published in *Der Briefwechsel zwischen F. Engels und K. Marx*, Bd. 1, Stuttgart, 1913

Printed according to the original

Published in English in full for the first time

---

[a] May God bless him! - [b] K. Marx and F. Engels, 'Statement. 27 January 1851' (see also this volume, p. 267). - [c] Conrad Schramm - [d] See this volume, p. 269

136

MARX TO HERMANN BECKER[357]

IN COLOGNE

[London, about 1 February 1851]

...You would very greatly oblige me by sending me Willich's letters.[a] Partly because we here by the rivers of Babylon[b] should also be vouchsafed a share of your Homeric laughter. And on the other hand because the man is exploiting the 'alleged' connection in order to brag in front of foreigners and, at the same time, make denunciations. Finally I feel it necessary that you should convey a note to him, either through me or direct, in which you most politely decline further correspondence on the grounds that, while humour may not greatly endanger him in London, for you in Cologne—and not for you alone but, by way of repercussion, for our party comrades in Germany—its effects may be dire. And what could be more ominous and at the same time more absurd than to be nailed to the cross as a result of a trick played through some mere whim of the 'carpenter's'[358]...

First published in *Anklageschrift gegen P. G. Roeser, J. H. G. Bürgers, P. Nothjung, W. J. Reiff, H. H. Becker, R. Daniels, C. W. Otto, A. Jacobi, J. J. Klein, F. Freiligrath*, Cologne, 1852

Printed according to *Anklageschrift*

Published in English for the first time

137

MARX TO ENGELS

IN MANCHESTER

[London,] 3 February 1851

Dear Engels,

Is it on Mary[c] you're studying physiology, or elsewhere? If the first, I can understand that this *n'est pas de l'hébreux*,[d] nor even *Russian*.

---

[a] See this volume, pp. 282, 284. - [b] Psalms 137:1 - [c] Mary Burns - [d] isn't *Hebrew*

Up till now all that my new theory of rent has yielded is the commendable state of mind to which every worthy man necessarily aspires. However, I am at least satisfied that you should be satisfied with it. An inverse relationship of the fertility of the soil to human fertility must needs deeply affect a strong-loined paterfamilias like myself, the more so since *mon mariage est plus productif que mon industrie*.[a]

I shall now submit to you just one illustration of the CURRENCY theory, my study of which might be described by Hegelians as a study of 'otherness', of the 'alien', in short of the 'holy'.

The theory of Mr Loyd and *tutti frutti*,[b] from Ricardo onwards, consists in the following:

Let us assume that we have a purely metallic CURRENCY. If there were too much of it here, prices would rise and hence the export of commodities decrease. Their import from abroad into this country would increase. Thus IMPORTS would rise above EXPORTS. Hence an unfavourable balance of trade. An unfavourable rate of exchange. Hard cash would be exported, the CURRENCY would shrink, the prices of commodities would fall, IMPORTS decrease, EXPORTS increase, money flow back again; in short, the SITUATION would attain its former equilibrium.

In the converse case likewise, *mutatis mutandis*.

The moral of this: since paper money must imitate the movement of METALLIC CURRENCY, and since artificial regulation must here take the place of what, in the other case, is natural law, the Bank of England must increase its paper issues if BULLION flows in (e.g. by the purchase of GOVERNMENT SECURITIES, EXCHEQUER BILLS, etc.) and reduce it by the reduction of discounts, or by the sale of government paper, if BULLION decreases. However I contend that the Bank should take the opposite course and *increase* its discounts if BULLION *decreases* and let them take their normal course if it increases. Upon pain of unnecessarily intensifying the impending commercial crisis. However, more of that *une autre fois*.[c]

What I wish to elucidate here goes to the basic principles of the matter. For my contention is that, *even with a purely metallic CURRENCY, the quantity thereof, its expansion or contraction, has nothing to do with the outflow and inflow of precious metals, with the favourable or*

---

[a] my marriage is more productive than my industry. - [b] all sorts of others - [c] some other time

unfavourable balance of trade, with the favourable or unfavourable rate of exchange, except in the most extreme cases, which practically never occur but are theoretically determinable. The same contention is made by Tooke, but I have found no proof of it in his *History of Prices* for 1843-47.

As you can see, it's an important matter. Firstly, the whole theory of circulation is denied in its very fundamentals. Secondly, it is shown that the progress of crises, even though the *credit system* be a condition of the same, is concerned with CURRENCY only in so far as crackbrained meddling by the authorities in its regulation may aggravate an existing crisis, as in 1847.

Note that in the following illustration it is assumed: The *inflow* of BULLION goes hand in hand with flourishing trade, prices not yet high but rising, a surplus of capital, excess of EXPORTS over IMPORTS. The outflow of gold vice versa, *mutatis mutandis.* Now this is the assumption of those against whom the polemic is directed. They cannot gainsay it. In reality there may be 1,001 cases in which there is an outflow of gold, although the prices of other commodities in the country exporting it are far lower than in those to which the gold is being sent, e.g. as in England in 1809-11 and 1812, etc., etc. Yet the *general assumption* is, firstly, right *in abstracto* and, secondly, accepted by the CURRENCY chaps.[359] Hence not to be debated here for the time being.

Let us assume, then, that *a purely metallic* CURRENCY is in circulation *in England.* But that does not presuppose that the *credit system* has ceased. Rather, the Bank of England would turn itself into both a *deposit* and *lending bank.* Save that its loans would consist simply in cash. If this assumption were to be rejected, what appears here as a DEPOSIT *of the Bank of England* would appear as HOARDS *of private individuals* and the loans of the Bank as loans of private individuals. *Thus, in this context, the term Bank of England* DEPOSITS is simply *an abbreviation, to present the process, not in fragmented form,* but concentrated in a FOCUS.

Case I. *Influx of* BULLION. Here the matter is very simple. A great deal of idle capital, hence increase in deposits. In order to make use of them the Bank would lower its *rate of interest.* Hence, expansion of business in the country. The *circulation* would *only* rise if business increased to the extent that additional CURRENCY was required to conduct it. Otherwise the surplus CURRENCY issued would flow back into the Bank as DEPOSITS., etc., as a result of maturing bills, etc. Thus CURRENCY does not act here as a *cause.* Its increase is ultimately the *consequence* of a greater amount of capital put to use, not vice versa. (Hence, in the case under discussion, the *first* consequence would be *growth of* DEPOSITS, i.e. of idle capital, not of circulation.)

Case II. This is where the matter really begins. EXPORT OF BULLION is assumed. Beginning of a period of PRESSURE. Unfavourable rate of exchange. At the same time a poor harvest, etc. (or else dearer raw materials for industry) necessitate ever larger imports of commodities. Suppose that the accounts of the Bank of England at the beginning of such a period appear as follows:

a) CAPITAL £14,500,000	GOVERNMENT SECURITIES £10,000,000
REST ....£ 3,500,000	BILLS OF EXCHANGE £12,000,000
DEPOSITS £12,000,000	BULLION OR COIN .... £ 8,000,000
£30,000,000	£30,000,000

The Bank is in debt, since *it has been assumed* that no *notes* exist, only the 12 millions of DEPOSITS. According to its principle (in common with the DEPOSIT and circulation banks, only a third of its LIABILITIES have to be IN CASH), its 8 millions of BULLION is too large by half. To make more profit it *lowers the interest rate* and raises its DISCOUNTS, e.g. by 4 millions, which are exported for corn, etc. The Bank's accounts then appear as follows:

b) CAPITAL £14,500,000	GOVERNMENT SECURITIES £10,000,000
REST ....£ 3,500,000	BILLS OF EXCHANGE £16,000,000
DEPOSITS £12,000,000	BULLION OR COIN .... £ 4,000,000
£30,000,000	£30,000,000

From these FIGURES it follows that:

Merchants, as soon as they have to export *gold,* act *first* upon *the Bank's* BULLION RESERVE. The gold thus exported *diminishes* its (the Bank's) reserve without having the slightest effect on the CURRENCY. Whether the 4 millions are in its cellars or aboard a ship bound for Hamburg is *all the same* so far as the CURRENCY is concerned. It finally becomes evident that a significant DRAIN of BULLION, in this case £4 millions sterling, can take place without in any way affecting either the CURRENCY or the business of the country in general. Throughout the whole period, that is, during which the BULLION RESERVE, which was *too large* in relation to LIABILITIES, is being reduced to no more than its DUE PROPORTION to the same.

c) But let us suppose that the circumstances which necessitated the DRAIN of 4 millions continue, shortage of corn, rise in the price of raw cotton, etc. The Bank grows concerned about its security. It *raises the interest rate* and limits its DISCOUNTS. Hence, PRESSURE in the world of commerce. What effect does this PRESSURE have? Withdrawals are made from the Bank's DEPOSITS, its BULLION falls proportionately. Should the DEPOSITS fall to 9 millions, i.e. be reduced by 3 millions, those 3 millions must come from the Bank's BULLION reserve. This would therefore fall (4 millions – 3 millions) to 1 million against DEPOSITS of 9 millions, a proportion which would be dangerous to the Bank. If, then, the Bank wishes to maintain its BULLION RESERVE at one third of the DEPOSITS, it will diminish its DISCOUNTS by 2 millions.

The accounts would then appear as follows:

CAPITAL	£14,500,000	GOVERNMENT SECURITIES	£10,000,000
REST	£ 3,500,000	BILLS UNDER DISCOUNT	£14,000,000
DEPOSITS	£ 9,000,000	BULLION OR COIN	£ 3,000,000
	£27,000,000		£27,000,000

It follows that, as soon as the DRAIN becomes so great that the BULLION RESERVE reaches its DUE PROPORTION in relation to DEPOSITS, the Bank will raise the interest rate and reduce the DISCOUNTS. But then the DEPOSITS begin to be *affected* and, as a result of their decrease, the BULLION RESERVE decreases but so, to an even greater extent, does the DISCOUNT of BILLS. The CURRENCY is not in the least affected. A portion of the BULLION and DEPOSITS withdrawn *fills* the vacuum which the contraction of the Bank's accommodation creates in the circulation at home, while another portion finds its way abroad.

d) Supposing that imports of corn, etc., continue and the DEPOSITS sink to 4,500,000, the Bank, in order to maintain the necessary reserve against its LIABILITIES, would reduce its DISCOUNTS by a further 3 millions, and the accounts would appear as follows:

CAPITAL	£14,500,000	GOVERNMENT SECURITIES	£10,000,000
REST	£ 3,500,000	BILLS UNDER DISCOUNT	£11,000,000
DEPOSITS	£ 4,500,000	BULLION OR COIN	£ 1,500,000
	£22,500,000		£22,500,000

On this assumption the Bank would have reduced its DISCOUNTS from 16 to 11 millions, that is, by 5 millions. The necessary requirements of the circulation replaced by the DEPOSITS withdrawn. But simultaneously shortage of capital, rise in the price of raw materials, decrease of demand, hence of business activity, hence *ultimately* of the circulation, of the necessary CURRENCY. The surplus portion of the same would be sent abroad in the form of BULLION to pay for imports. The CURRENCY is *the last* to be affected, and it would only be *reduced* to less than the necessary quantity should the BULLION RESERVE fall below the minimal proportion to DEPOSITS.

With regard to the above, it should also be noted that:

1. Instead of reducing its DISCOUNTS, the Bank could dispose of its PUBLIC SECURITIES, which, on this assumption, would be unprofitable. However same result. Instead of reducing its own RESERVE and DISCOUNTS, it would reduce those of private persons who put their money in PUBLIC SECURITIES.

2. I have assumed here a DRAIN of 6,500,000 on the Bank. In 1839 there was one of 9-10 millions.

3. The process assumed in the case of a purely METALLIC CURRENCY can lead, as with paper, to a closure of the till, as happened twice in Hamburg in the eighteenth century.

Write soon.

Your
K. M.

First published in *Der Briefwechsel zwischen F. Engels und K. Marx*, Bd. 1, Stuttgart, 1913

Printed according to the original

Published in English for the first time

138

ENGELS TO MARX [220]

IN LONDON

Manchester, 5 February 1851

Dear Marx,

Herewith the remaining £1 for the atlas,[a] which I was unfortunately not able to send you sooner.

Tell Harney when you see him that by the end of this week he will receive at the very least the 1st half of a series of articles on CONTINENTAL DEMOCRACY [352]—the articles so arranged that each one of

---

[a] *Historischer und geographischer Atlas von Europa* (see this volume, pp. 263, 301).

them will not fill more than 2-2 $^1/_2$ columns in his *Friend of the People*. I shall use the above as a pretext for crying down the whole democratic establishment and rendering it suspect to the English proletariat by putting it—Mazzini, Ledru-Rollin, etc. included— on the same footing as the FINANCIAL REFORMERS.[284] The European Committee WILL CATCH IT NICELY. These gentry will be dealt with one by one, Mazzini's writings, Ledru-Rollin's splendid acts of heroism in February-June 1848—not, of course, forgetting Mr Ruge. I shall make it quite plain to the Italians, Poles and Hungarians that they are to keep their traps shut on all current issues. This business of the hoax Harney is perpetrating with Mazzini & Co.'s begging letters is really going too far and, since there's no other way of reforming him, I shall be obliged to expose in his own journal the fatuity and baseness of these fellows and to unveil the mysteries of continental democracy for the benefit of the English Chartists. A detailed polemical article is always more salutary in Harney's case than any amount of debate. Unfortunately I have damned little material here.

What I have at the moment is Sarrans *jeune*,[a] *Lafayette et la révolution de Juillet*. If I could find a few more sources, I could do an article for our *Revue* on the July Revolution and subsequent events up till the February Revolution, at the same time subjecting the *Histoire de dix ans*[b] to a friendly criticism. These '10 ans' have remained largely unchallenged by advanced opinion and, in Germany as in France, constitute a very important formative element in the revolutionary party as a whole. It would do no harm, I think, to reduce the influence of this book to the appropriate limits; hitherto it has been an uncontested authority.

Mr Russell, the craven cur, has made a splendid fool of himself yet again. First he breathes fire and brimstone against PAPAL AGGRESSION,[360] then, realising that the MANCHESTER MEN have absolutely no intention of getting embroiled in the mummery, he is brought to bed of an heroic measure, namely wanting to ban the use of English titles by Catholic bishops. And then the nice hint, dropped at his behest by Mr Peto, that it would indeed have been desirable to extend the franchise during the present session, but since LAW-REFORM came next on the agenda, the franchise would have to be postponed till next year! A prime example of Whig logic. The MPs, by the way, are very captious and unsure of themselves, with

---

[a] the Younger - [b] L. Blanc, *Histoire de dix ans. 1830-1840.*

elections in the offing; they have to make liberal or protectionist FLOURISHES and, but for the fact that the EXHIBITION[a] happens to coincide with the most lively period of the session's *grande politique*,[b] things might go ill with the little manikin.[c] And even so, *qui sait*.[d]

In general the daily political bread is growing ever drier. The happy situation in which *la belle France* now delights is, indeed, edifying. For there is no denying that Messieurs the Burgraves[361] are becoming less and less representative of the bourgeois fraction or rather, that the bourgeoisie is moving further and further away from its erstwhile Legitimist and Orleanist leaders. First, the important minority in favour of Baroche at the session in which he was unseated by the coalition, a minority which also consisted of a great many non-Bonapartists, former Orleanists, etc., etc.; next the unmistakable mood of the conservative bourgeoisie *en masse*, which is far more favourable to Napoleon than hitherto. The mass of these fellows are now resolutely opposed to Orleanist no less than to Legitimist plots for a restoration; *les solutions les embêtent*,[e] and what they want is the daily round of the presidential present. The fellows are neither royalist, nor republican, nor imperialist, but presidential; but the best thing about it is that such delicious indecision is possible only in the mass, and that anyone who wished to make his mark as official representative of this tendency would, within six months, find himself compelled to abandon his neutrality in favour of a definite royalist or imperialist fraction. By the way, the only French papers I have here are the *Débats* and the *Charivari* which, sad to say, *grâce à l'esprit exquis du peuple dans ces parages*,[f] is coming to seem almost witty again.

From a stupid Hungarian refugee whom I recently happened upon, I heard that this noble breed are once again jabbering about murder plots and riots on the occasion of the GREAT EXHIBITION. Amidst the din I seemed almost to detect the heroic voices of those London hotspurs, Willich and Barthélemy. There's really no getting away from the creatures; recently a fellow accosted me in the street and lo, it was a Great Windmill Street refugee[331] now employed in Liverpool. 'If I take the wings of the morning, and dwell in the uttermost parts of the sea',[g] I shall not escape that band.

---

[a] The Great Exhibition held in London in May-October 1851. - [b] high politics - [c] John Russell - [d] who knows - [e] the solutions annoy them - [f] thanks to the exquisite wit of the people hereabouts - [g] Psalms 139:9

Heinrich Heine

P. V. Annenkov

Joseph Weydemeyer

George Julian Harney

The FREE TRADERS here are exploiting the prosperity or semi-prosperity to buy the proletariat, with John Watts for broker. You will be familiar with Cobden's new plan: a NATIONAL FREE SCHOOL ASSOCIATION for the purpose of putting through a BILL by which the TOWNSHIPS would be authorised to impose local taxes for the building of schools. The thing is being splendidly promoted. In addition, Salford already has a FREE LIBRARY and museum—lending library and reading room gratis. In Manchester the Hall of Science was purchased—and here, as the Lord Mayor of Manchester most graciously acknowledged, Watts really was the broker—by a committee out of the proceeds of public collections (some £7,000 in all) and is to be turned into a FREE LIBRARY. The thing is to be opened at the end of July—with 14,000 volumes TO BEGIN WITH. All the meetings and assemblies held for this purpose resound with praise for the workers, and in particular for the good, modest, helpful Watts who is now on the best of terms with the Bishop of Manchester. I am already looking forward to the indignant uproar over the workers' ingratitude which will break out on all sides when the first SHOCK makes itself felt.

Not long ago my worthy pater wrote me a pleasant letter expressing the wish that I remain here indefinitely, that is, for as long as the trouble with the Ermens lasts (and that might mean until 1854). Very agreeable to me, of course, *s'il me paie bien mon ennui*.[a] Of this, naturally, I give no hint, but 'sacrifice' myself for the 'firm' and express my readiness 'to remain here for the time being and see how circumstances develop'. He's coming over next summer, and I shall then try to make myself so indispensable to him that he will have to agree to anything.

Kind regards to your wife and children.

Your

F. E.

PARTICULARS on the POST OFFICE ORDER as before.

First published in *Der Briefwechsel zwischen F. Engels und K. Marx*, Bd. 1, Stuttgart, 1913

Printed according to the original

Published in English in full for the first time

---

[a] provided he pays me well for my boredom

11-1543

139

MARX TO HERMANN BECKER [357]

IN COLOGNE

[London,] 8 February 1851

...apropos! Willich and Schapper in company with Barthélemy, etc., have, by monstrous bragging about their influence in Germany and by monstrous calumnies against ourselves, at long last succeeded in bamboozling Louis Blanc to such an extent that he has combined with this 'scum' to arrange a banquet for February and, in concert with same, has issued a programme of festivities along with a kind of manifesto. The little man walked into the trap out of vanity, so as to show Ledru-Rollin that he, too, could wag a German-French-Polish-Hungarian tail. Now the business is *en pleine déroute*[a] again and the little man suspects that he has compromised himself for nothing and has committed a fruitless piece of perfidy against ourselves who, since 1843, have maintained a kind of lukewarm alliance with him.

But do you know what Willich impresses strangers[b] by most? His *tremendous influence in Cologne.* Hence it is all the more necessary for you to send me the letters,[c] so that a dyke can be thrown up against the 'carpenter's'[358] machinations. Adieu....

First published in *Anklageschrift gegen P. G. Roeser, J. H. G. Bürgers, P. Nothjung, W. J. Reiff, H. H. Becker, R. Daniels, C. W. Otto, A. Jacobi, J. J. Klein, F. Freiligrath,* Cologne, 1852

Printed according to *Anklageschrift*

Published in English for the first time

---

[a] in utter disarray - [b] The indictment has *Freunden* (friends) instead of *Fremden* (strangers). Later Becker himself expressed the opinion that this change had been made arbitrarily by those who drew up the indictment. - [c] See this volume, pp. 273, 284.

140

MARX TO ENGELS

IN MANCHESTER

[London,] 10 February 1851
28 Dean Street, Soho

Dear Engels,

When you wrote saying that it would soon be time to attack Louis Blanc, you were a *clairvoyant,* to say the least.

Now hearken to the following story:

A few days or perhaps a week ago, I ran into Landolphe and, from the embarrassed way in which he greeted me and my wife, noted that there was something 'rotten' in the state[a] of our *ami chevaleresque,*[b] our Bayard of the Montagne.[260] *Eh bien!*[c] *Landolphe and Louis Blanc* have joined up with the *Willich-Schapper* committee, from which Mr Adam has resigned! And only a fortnight previously Landolphe had been raving and ranting about Barthélemy and I had been telling him about the affair of Messrs Willich and Schapper. *Qu'en dis-tu?*[d] Not a word from these worthies to apprise me of it.

The nub of the matter is as follows:

On 24 February Church Street[362] are holding a banquet to which they have invited Blanc and Ledru-Rollin and, among others, Landolphe. Louis Blanc, anxious to show Ledru-Rollin that he too has a cosmopolitan committee behind him, and to punish Church Street for treating him and Ledru as 'of equal importance', rallied his army from Great Windmill Street[331] and from the pub where the feckless Poles foregather.

Encore un coup! Qu'en dis-tu?[e]

A few days ago Church Street received a printed circular (combining a *manifesto*) with an invitation to a monster banquet on 24 February, and signed *primo*[f] Landolphe and, immediately after, Schapper, L. Blanc. Intense indignation in Church Street! Intense delight in Great Windmill Street!

In the circular-manifesto Louis Blanc does not speak in the name of a nation, but in the name and on behalf of the eternal formula: *liberté, égalité, fraternité!* The only fly in the ointment so

---

[a] Cf. 'Something is rotten in the state of Denmark', Shakespeare, *Hamlet,* Act I, Scene 4. - [b] chivalrous friend - [c] Well now! - [d] What do you say to that? - [e] Yet another coup! What do you say to that? - [f] first

11*

far as I'm concerned is that I still owe Landolphe £1.10s. which ought now to be sent him forthwith through Wolff.[a]

You can easily imagine how greatly Willich and Schapper have grown in their own esteem and how they fancy us beaten!

But we'll beat them in a different sense. We are well on the way to driving Corporal and Carpenter Willich[358] *mad, literaliter*[b] mad.

You will recall the letter written to Willich by Schramm on Becker's behalf,[c] in which he offered him military dictatorship, abolished the press, and cast mild aspersions on Schapper's moral character.

Eh bien! Willich, the uneducated, four times cuckolded jackass, fell into the trap. He has been bombarding Becker with letters, already has an envoy awaiting dispatch, treats Schapper *de haut en bas*,[d] ignores, insults and intrigues against that worthy man in every possible manner, has already adopted the overbearing manner of a Cromwell II, has grown irascible, no longer tolerates contradiction, and has entrusted Becker with the task of starting a revolution in Cologne, after which he declares himself ready to assume the supreme leadership.

A short time ago, while in company, he suddenly jumped up shouting that his letters from Paris and Cologne had not yet arrived—it was on the occasion of the last French ministerial crisis—complained that his (stupid head) was in a whirl, whirl, whirl, dashed off to Bond Street and had a bucket of water poured over it. I now have a showerbath prepared for him which should have quite the opposite effect. In a few days' time Becker is going to let me have Willich's letters and then I shall spring the mine.

A fresh swarm of democratic scallywags here, Frenchmen driven out of Brussels, Heise from Cassel, Oppenheim from Brussels, Günther from Frankfurt, etc. Fortunately, however, I have seen none of the latter.

You did receive my last letter, didn't you?

Your

K. M.

First published abridged in *Der Briefwechsel zwischen F. Engels und K. Marx,* Bd. 1, Stuttgart, 1913 and in full in *MEGA,* Abt. III, Bd. 1, 1929

Printed according to the original

Published in English for the first time

---

[a] Ferdinand Wolff - [b] literally - [c] Hermann Becker - [d] superciliously

141

MARX TO ENGELS[43]

IN MANCHESTER

[London,] 11 February 1851

Dear Engels,

Iterum Crispinus![a]

I have just learned that there was a meeting earlier this evening in the Tottenham Court Road in honour of the late *Bem*. On the platform were: *Chairman* Schapper, etc., Louis Blanc and the remaining members of the new League of Peoples Committee. In one of the front rows of the auditorium sat Harney and wife. The bulk of those present were from Great Windmill Street.[331] Applause greeted Schapper's inevitable speech, 'WAR TO THE KNIFE', delivered in English. Louis Blanc spoke no better. *Vive la guerre!*[b] *Tausenau*, also present, spoke about Bem. *Harney* delivered a long and, they say, good harangue in which he finally hailed Blanqui, Barbès and, last of all, Louis Blanc, as the socialist Messiah.

Qu'en dis-tu?[c]

Suppose you attended a meeting presided over by *Th. Clark* Esq., and it was your presence and your speeches alone that *lent* any real weight to the meeting, would friend Harney regard that as loyal?

Not content, then, with boosting Ruge in his *Friend of the People,* he must needs indirectly boost Schapper-Willich as well.

Last Sunday he sent for me. The purpose being to persuade Jones to accept the title, 'Friend of the People'. I didn't go. If that's what he wants, let him turn to L. Blanc, Landolphe, Schapper or Willich. I am *fatigué*[d] of this public incense so tirelessly used by Harney to fill the nostrils of *les petits grands hommes.*[e]

Apart from this accident, namely, that you, too, Brutus (Harney), if you don't take sides against us at least play the neutral, while Engels does his best for you in Manchester, Eccarius[f] writes for your paper[363] and I occasionally work on

---

[a] *Ecce iterum Crispinus* (Behold, this Crispinus again). Juvenal, *Satiraes,* IV, 1 (figuratively: the same again) - [b] Hurrah for war! - [c] What do you say to that? - [d] tired - [e] the petty panjandrums - [f] Johann Georg Eccarius

Jones for you—apart from that, I am greatly pleased by the public, authentic isolation in which we two, you and I, now find ourselves. It is wholly in accord with our attitude and our principles. The system of mutual concessions, half-measures tolerated for decency's sake, and the obligation to bear one's share of public ridicule in the party along with all these jackasses, all this is now over.

Now, I'd appreciate an early answer to this note, too. I hardly see anyone here save Pieper and live in complete retirement. So you'll realise that I miss you all the more and feel the need to talk things over with you.

You'll see from tomorrow's newspapers that the grant was rejected by a majority of 102 votes.[364]

Your
K. M.

First published in *Der Briefwechsel zwischen F. Engels und K. Marx*, Bd. 1, Stuttgart, 1913   Printed according to the original

142

ENGELS TO MARX

IN LONDON

[Manchester,] Wednesday [12 February 1851]

Dear Marx,

I have just found your letter at home and am at once writing by today's post to tell you that by the end of this or the beginning of next week at the latest, I shall somehow arrange to send you the £1.10s. for Landolphe so that this business, which must be protracted no longer, is settled once and for all.[a] *Notre ami*[b] Landolphe has once again shown what an old woman he is, while the fatuous vanity of the hyperclever L. Blanc is taking such a

---

[a] See this volume, p. 284. - [b] Our friend

turn as to brand the sublime dwarf a fool pure and simple. *C'est bien.*[a] One comes to realise more and more that emigration is an institution which inevitably turns a man into a fool, an ass and a base rascal unless he withdraws wholly therefrom, and unless he is content to be an independent writer who doesn't give a tinker's curse for the so-called revolutionary party. It is a real SCHOOL OF SCANDAL AND MEANNESS in which the hindmost donkey becomes the foremost saviour of his country. At any rate the little popularity-monger will atone for it once we have a press organ again. As you know, I have none of my papers with me here, so I'd like you to suggest a few more sources on French affairs between 1830 and 1848 which you may happen to know about, and I shall endeavour to shovel coals of fire, at least in a literary sense, under the worthy pretender's backside. At all events, in my articles in *The Friend of the People,* I shall call on him to publish—provided you have no objection, since it was you to whom he told the story—the information given him by Mr Mazzini concerning the character of the European Central Committee and its attitude towards socialists and communists, and shall make such allusions as are necessary for this to be understood.[352] *Pourquoi nous gênerions-nous?*[b]

Today Harney will be getting 3 articles by way of introduction, pretty lengthy, a gentle hint dropped here and there. The awkward part of it is that it's difficult to attack Ledru & Co., without at least partially identifying oneself with the Willich-Barthélemy clique in the eyes of the English proletariat and Harney's readers. Ultimately the only way out will be to devote a few special articles to that clique. Not, however, in the first 3 articles, which have been written for Harney's benefit, TO PUT HIM IN THE RIGHT TRACK, rather than for any other purpose. But in numbers 4-9 Ledru, Mazzini, Ruge, etc., etc., will be attacked in rapid succession and in as direct and personal a manner as possible.

The Willich affair is *impayable.*[c] *Only do make sure that you get hold of the letters.*[d] I'd like to witness the moral indignation when the bomb goes off. It would seem that for some time past you've again had good spies in Great Windmill Street[331]; *cela ne fait pas de mal*[e] and at least provides some entertainment. I confess I could never have thought the fellow so stupid. He will, incidentally, be well and truly on fire now that the Prussian ministerial press is holding

---

[a] Well and good. - [b] Why should we make any bones about it? - [c] priceless - [d] See this volume, p. 284. - [e] that does no harm

out the prospect of war with Switzerland and the reserve guardsmen—as they were informed on parade—are being kept under arms for that very reason.[365] The governments of the Holy Alliance[271] are playing into the hands of these fantastic idiots in a truly irresponsible way and, were it not for Palmerston, the next 'emancipation of general stupidity' might well see the light of day six months prematurely.

Your latest economic discovery is at present being subjected to my most earnest scrutiny. I have no time today to go into it further, but the thing seems to me to be absolutely right. But figures are not to be trifled with and I am therefore considering the matter in detail.

Quelle bête que ce Louis-Napoléon![a] He sells his doubts about the electoral law to the assembly, and himself to Montalembert, for 1,800,000 fr. which in the end he does not get after all.[366] There's nothing you can do with an adventurer of this stamp. If, for the space of four weeks, he allows himself to be guided by ingenious intriguers, you may be quite sure that, come the fifth, he will in the most fatuous fashion bring to nought all that has been accomplished. *Aut Caesar aut Clichy!*[b]

Not long ago we inaugurated a new CHARTIST LOCALITY here. These English are far less conscientious than we honest, timid Germans in the matter of democratic forms. There were thirteen of us, and it was immediately resolved to elect a COUNCIL of thirteen members, namely those present. Thereupon each man proposed one of those present and, in place of myself, since I, of course, refused, one who was absent and, in less than five minutes, these PRIVATE GENTLEMEN had turned themselves into a COUNCIL, and yet each one of them had been elected, and this comical PROCEEDING PASSED OFF VERY SERIOUSLY AND AS A MATTER OF COURSE. What will come of this business I shall see ere long. For today, *prosit.*[c]

Your
F. E.

First published abridged in *Der Briefwechsel zwischen F. Engels und K. Marx*, Bd. 1, Stuttgart, 1913 and in full in *MEGA*, Abt. III, Bd. 1, 1929

Printed according to the original

Published in English for the first time

---

[a] What an idiot Louis Napoleon is! - [b] Either Caesar or Clichy (Clichy—a debt prison in Paris): paraphrase of 'Aut Caesar aut nihil' (either Caesar or nothing), a motto of the fifteenth-century Italian politician, Cesare Borgia. - [c] your health

143

ENGELS TO MARX

IN LONDON

[Manchester,] Thursday, 13 February 1851

Dear Marx,

I had been more or less expecting this business with Harney.[a] I saw the notice of the Bem meeting in *The Friend of the People*,[b] which stated that the Germans, French, Poles and Hungarians, as well as the FRATERNAL DEMOCRATS[122] would be taking part, and it was quite clear that these could be none other than Great Windmill Street[331] & Co. I forgot to draw your attention to this announcement before. There's no possibility of my pursuing the matter any further today. But tomorrow I shall write a letter to Harney in which I shall tell him not to print the manuscript I sent him, as I shall not be providing a sequel,[367] and in which I shall at the same time explain the whole business to him in detail. If this letter is of no avail, the whole rigmarole will have to be dropped until Mr Harney returns of his own accord, which will happen very soon. I have a very strong suspicion that he will be up here shortly and then I shall duly take him to task. It's about time he realised that we're in earnest with him, too. At any rate, so as to save time and avoid writing twice I shall send the letter to you to be passed on to him as quickly as possible once you've read it.

Personally I find this inanity and want of tact on Harney's part more irritating than anything else. But *au fond*[c] it is of little moment.

At long last we again have the opportunity—the first time in ages—to show that we need neither popularity, nor the SUPPORT of any party in any country, and that our position is completely independent of such ludicrous trifles. From now on we are only answerable for ourselves and, come the time when these gentry need us, we shall be in a position to dictate our own terms. Until then we shall at least have some peace and quiet. A measure of loneliness, too, of course—*mon Dieu*, I've already had a 3 months' spell of that in Manchester and have grown used to it, and this,

---

[a] See this volume, p. 285. - [b] 'Honour to General Bem, the Patriot and Hero', *The Friend of the People*, No. 9, 8 February 1851. - [c] basically

moreover, as a BACHELOR, which here, at any rate, is excessively boring. Besides we have no real grounds for complaint if we are shunned by the *petits grands hommes*[a]; haven't we been acting for years as though Cherethites and Plethites[b] were our party when, in fact, we had no party, and when the people whom we considered as belonging to our party, at least officially, *sous réserve de les appeler des bêtes incorrigibles entre nous,*[c] didn't even understand the rudiments of our stuff? How can people like us, who shun official appointments like the plague, fit into a 'party'? And what have we, who spit on popularity, who don't know what to make of ourselves if we show signs of growing popular, to do with a 'party', i.e. a herd of jackasses who swear by us because they think we're of the same kidney as they? Truly, it is no loss if we are no longer held to be the 'right and adequate expression' of the ignorant curs with whom we have been thrown together over the past few years.

A revolution is a purely natural phenomenon which is subject to physical laws rather than to the rules that determine the development of society in ordinary times. Or rather, in revolution these rules assume a much more physical character, the material force of necessity makes itself more strongly felt. And as soon as one steps forward as the representative of a party, one is dragged into this whirlpool of irresistible natural necessity. By the mere fact of keeping oneself INDEPENDENT, being *in the nature of things* more revolutionary than the others, one is able at least for a time to maintain one's independence from this whirlpool, although one does, of course, end up by being dragged into it.

This is the position we can and must adopt on the next occasion. Not only no official *government* appointments but also, and for as long as possible, no official *party* appointments, no seat on committees, etc., no responsibility for jackasses, merciless criticism of everyone, and, besides, that serenity of which all the conspiracies of blockheads cannot deprive us. And this much we are able to do. We can always, in the nature of things, be more revolutionary than the phrase-mongers because we have learnt our lesson and they have not, because we know what we want and they do not, and BECAUSE, AFTER WHAT WE HAVE SEEN FOR THE LAST THREE YEARS, WE SHALL TAKE IT A GREAT DEAL MORE COOLLY THAN ANY ONE WHO HAS AN INTEREST IN THE BUSINESS.

The main thing at the moment is to find some way of getting

---

[a] petty panjandrums - [b] 2 Samuel 15:18 - [c] with the reservation that between ourselves we called them incorrigible fools

our things published; either in a quarterly in which we make a frontal attack and consolidate our position so far as *persons* are concerned; or in fat books where we do the same without being under the necessity of mentioning any one of these vipers. Either way suits me; in the long run, and with reaction on the increase, it seems to me that the feasibility of the former is decreasing and that the latter will come more and more to be the expedient to which we must apply ourselves. What price all the tittle-tattle the entire émigré crowd can muster against you, when you answer it with your political economy?

Tomorrow, the letter for Harney. *En attendant, salut.*[a]

Your
F. E.

First published in *Der Briefwechsel zwischen F. Engels und K. Marx*, Bd. 1, Stuttgart, 1913

Printed according to the original

Published in English for the first time

144

MARX TO ENGELS[220]

IN MANCHESTER

London, 23 February [1851]

Dear Engels,

For a week you've had no news of me, firstly because I was awaiting the documents from Cologne[b] and wished to tell you about them, secondly because I had to wait for further details about our 'EXFRIEND'. The former have not yet arrived. As to the latter, I am now rather better informed.

Harney received your letter all right.

---

[a] Meanwhile, greetings. - [b] i.e. Willich's letters which were to be sent to Marx by Johann Becker (see this volume, pp. 273, 282, 284).

According to what I am told by Tessier du Mothay, who is now here, the Louis Blanc affair originated as follows:

The association in Church Street[362] gave itself out to be a philanthropic association for assistance to French political *réfugiés*. Ledru-Rollin, L. Blanc, Adam, everyone, in short, made this a pretext for participating in it. Politics were banned by the statutes. Then 24 February[a] hove into view. As you know, when presented with the opportunity of making themselves important, the French prepare for it as long in advance and treat it with as much solemnity as the prospective lying-in of a pregnant woman. Even if the association was merely a philanthropic one, so the argument ran, its members in their capacity as Frenchmen must nevertheless celebrate 24 February. A definite evening was fixed for a debate on this important matter. On that evening both Ledru and Blanc were present. The latter delivered a carefully prepared, spuriously temperate, jesuitical speech, in which he sought to prove that a political banquet contravened the association's statutes, that it would simply make France aware of their dissensions, etc., and, amidst much pious talk of *fraternité,* the Corsican mandrake, vented his chagrin at not having been included in the provisional government[368] by Ledru and Mazzini. He got his answer. Despite his speech, which none admired more sincerely than he did, it was decided to hold the banquet.

And what does *la blanche Louise*[b] do now? She declares that, as a result of this decision, the association has dissolved itself thereby restoring to each his individual freedom, and that he will make use of this restitution of his 'free will' and organise a banquet without any spirit of faction, pure *fraternité* and other delectable tidbits.

His eyes turned naturally to Barthélemy, knowing as he did that the latter, the Germans, Poles, etc., together formed a compact mass. On the other hand Landolphe, *le bel homme,*[c] was entrusted with the mission of winning over our DEAR Harney. L. Blanc was even gracious enough to invite Harney to the dinner, though, during the past six months, he and Landolphe have been consigning him to the devil. What magnanimity!

On the other hand L. Blanc drafted a manifesto which, as our DEAR would say, is OUT AND OUT. You will have read it in *The Friend of the People.* It even repudiates the *'aristocracy of the mind',* thereby on

---

[a] the anniversary of the February 1848 revolution in France - [b] white Louise (Louis Blanc) - [c] the fine figure of a man

the one hand ostensibly providing a motive for condescending to the *dii minorum gentium*[a] and, on the other, holding out to Schapper & Co. the immediate and cheerful prospect of an *'aristocracy of stupidity'.* But this manifesto—feeble platitudes, naturally—is regarded by L. Blanc as the 'wisest possible thing' to which human nature, under the MOST HAPPY CIRCUMSTANCES, could aspire. It was intended not only to astound the whole of Europe but also and more particularly to give Ledru-Rollin a slap in the face, and to lead all the Blanquists in France to believe that, out of sheer intrepidity of principle, the INCORRUPTIBLE LITTLE MAN had disassociated himself from Church Street.

Thus the worthy Harney has made himself the tool of a vulgar intrigue and, what is more, an intrigue directed against Ledru-Rollin to whom, at the same time, he goes running and whose banquet he will also honour with his presence tomorrow. In order further to nettle this, despite his *qualités très aimables* and *respectables,*[b] highly *impressionable plebeian*—impressionable, that is, to famous names, in whose shadow he feels touched and honoured—and in order at the same time to show Ledru-Mazzini that the Napoleon of socialism cannot be thwarted with impunity, the little man goes and solicits the felicitations of the Parisian workers. These 'Parisian workers', whose appearance on the scene was bound to make the blood rise to our DEAR's head, are, of course, none other than the notorious 25 *délégués des Luxembourg,* who have never been delegated by anyone, and who, throughout Paris, are the object, now of the hatred, now of the *risée*[c] of the other workers,—fellows whose importance is no greater than that of the members of the Pre-parliament or the Committee of Fifty in Germany.[369] They feel a need for a *petit bon dieu quelconque,*[d] a fetish, and there is something monstrous about the little man's appearance which all along has made it a suitable object of worship. He for his part assures them that they are the greatest men and the truest socialists on earth. And had he not already nominated them *pairs*[e] of the future Workers' Republic? Hence, whenever he raises a finger, they offer their felicitations and, whenever they offer their felicitations, he publicly expresses his heartfelt thanks. And he raised a finger this time. In these professional felicitators Harney, of course, sees Paris, the whole of Paris.

Before I take leave of the mandrake, two more items which I

---

[a] second-rate luminaries (literally: gods of the minor nations) - [b] most amiable and respectable qualities - [c] ridicule - [d] a little god of some sort - [e] peers

learned from Tessier, both of them highly characteristic of this *fausse pleureuse*.[a]

Louise never speaks extempore. He writes down every word of his speeches and learns them *by heart* in front of the looking-glass. Ledru, on the other hand, always improvises and, on important occasions, confines himself to a few MATTER OF FACT notes. Hence, quite aside from the difference in personal appearance, Louise is completely incapable of making the slightest impression when *alongside* Ledru. He therefore welcomed any pretext that permitted him to avoid comparison with this dangerous rival!

So far as his historical works are concerned, he wrote them in the same way that A. Dumas wrote his feuilletons. He never studies more material than is needed for the next chapter. This is how such books as the *Histoire des dix ans* are produced. In this way it lends a certain freshness to his accounts. For what he's conveying is at least as new to him as it is to the reader; on the other hand the thing as a whole is weak.

So much for L. Blanc. Now for our DEAR.

He was not content with merely attending the fellows' meeting. Indeed not. He has turned their banquet of 24 February which, without him, would have been a complete fiasco, into a *London event*. A thousand tickets have already been sold for the banquet, which is being held in the City. It was Harney who placed *the majority of the tickets,* as Jones informed me the day before yesterday. O'Connor, Reynolds, hundreds of Chartists will be there. Harney has been drumming them up. Again according to Jones, he is *en route*[b] all day, carrying out L. Blanc's orders.

He has even perpetrated a little piece of perfidy with regard to Jones by getting him to translate L. Blanc & Co.'s manifesto and then asking him whether he would have any objection to being named as the translator. That was on Wednesday.[c] So by then he already had your letter, although he gave no hint of this to Jones. Jones saw in his question merely an appeal to his own 'socialist' sentiments—and naturally replied that he had no objection.

Jones told me that, as a result of my arguments, he might stay away from the banquet, though he couldn't say for certain. The reason for his indecision' is perfectly sensible. Were he not to turn up, he would forfeit some of his popularity since, thanks to our DEAR, this banquet has become a Chartist occasion. He is also afraid that Reynolds might intrigue behind his back.

---

[a] crocodile - [b] on the go - [c] 18 February

Jones disapproves of the behaviour of our DEAR, whom I have not 'seen again'. He tried to excuse it on the grounds that, if the Chartists failed to attend either of the banquets, they would be accused of political apathy, or of antipathy towards the foreign revolutionaries. To this I replied that in that case Harney, etc., should have held a Chartist meeting to celebrate the rotten 24 February instead of constituting a pedestal for a dwarf and half a dozen jackasses—a dwarf who never describes Harney as anything but a 'brave garçon',[a] and who, if a movement were to go into action in London tomorrow, or in one year's or 20 years' time, would produce official documents to prove that he had set these *pauvres Anglais dans la route du progrès*,[b] a path which led from 1688 to 24 February 1851, when Louis Blanc heard himself acclaimed by the whole of London, as once before by 50,000 workers in the courtyard of the *Réforme,* which holds barely 50 men. And how many crocodile's tears about this event that never happened will he consign to paper!

Harney has become embroiled in this business, firstly, because of his inordinate admiration for official great men, which we have often derided in the past. Secondly, because he loves theatrical effects. He is truly avid of applause, if not actually *vaniteux.*[c] There is no disputing that he himself is profoundly susceptible to the stock phrase and generates the most copious and impassioned gas. Is more deeply bogged in the democratic mire than he would care to admit. He has a twofold SPIRIT, one inculcated by Frederick Engels, and one that is all his own. The former is for him a kind of straitjacket. The latter is he himself in *puris naturalibus.*[d] But there is in addition a third, a *spiritus familiaris,*[e] and that is his worthy spouse.[f] She has a great predilection for *gants jaunes*[g] *à la* Landolphe and Louis Blanc. She hates me, for one, as a frivolous fellow who might endanger her 'PROPERTY TO BE WATCHED UPON'. I have irrefutable proof that this female has more than one of her long plebeian fingers in this pie. The extent of Harney's thraldom to this *spiritus familiaris,* and of the petty Scottish wiliness with which she conducts her intrigues, will be apparent to you from the following: You will recall how on New Year's Eve she insulted Miss Macfarlane in the presence of my wife. Later she told my wife, with a smile on her lips, that Harney had not seen Miss Macfarlane throughout the evening. Later she told him that she

---

[a] good lad - [b] poor English on the path of progress - [c] vain - [d] in a state of nature - [e] familiar spirit - [f] Mary - [g] dandies

had DECLINED her acquaintanceship because the cleft dragoon had evoked the dismay and ridicule of the whole company and of my wife in particular. And Harney was idiotic and cowardly enough not to give Miss Macfarlane a chance to avenge the insult, thus breaking in the most unworthy manner with the only collaborator on his insignificant little rag[a] who really had any ideas. On his rag, a *rara avis*.[b]

What lends added weight to this meeting is the stir created in London by LITTLE JOHNNY's[c] resignation and the *avènement*[d] of Stanley-d'Israeli.[370]

There's nothing the FRENCHMEN fear more than a general amnesty. It would rob all the local cardboard heroes of their halos.

A. Ruge, in company with Struve, Kinkel, Schramm,[e] Bucher, etc., has been trying to bring into being a *Volksfreund* or, as our Gustav[f] would have it, a *Deutscher Zuschauer*. Came to nought. Some of the others did not want Winkelried's[g] patronage, some, like the 'easy-going' Kinkel, demanded payment in cash, *ce qui ne fait pas le compte de M. Ruge*.[h] His chief aim was, as you will know, to extract money from the reading public. This was frustrated by Julius, since he too wants to bring out a paper here.

K. Heinzen is *redacteur en chef*[i] of the bankrupt New York *Schnellpost* and has entered into a hair-raising polemic with Weitling.

You would do well to write sometime soon to Red Becker[j] in New York and inform him about *l'état actuel des choses*.[k]

Enclosed a letter from Dronke. Send it back to me by return; if you wish to write yourself with it, *tant mieux*.[l]

Your remittance was a great help to me as I couldn't possibly go on owing the *bel homme*[m] a FARTHING any longer.

In my next letter, something about French literature of 1830-48. Write, too, and tell me whether my sums are right.

Your

K. M.

---

[a] *The Friend of the People* - [b] rare bird - [c] John Russell - [d] accession to power - [e] Rudolf Schramm - [f] Gustav Struve - [g] Arnold Ruge (nicknamed Winkelried after a semi-legendary Swiss warrior whose name was Arnold) - [h] which doesn't suit Mr Ruge's book - [i] editor-in-chief - [j] probably Max Joseph Becker - [k] the present state of things - [l] so much the better - [m] that fine figure of a man (Landolphe—see this volume, pp. 284, 286)

Incidentally, in our dealings with our DEAR—for he will seek to come back as soon as he has done with this great historical event [371]—we must assume an air of superiority and make him feel that he has 'lost'.

Apropos! Harney has had himself elected to a Chartist deputation to Church Street, whence, having made his *entrée,* he will repair to the City, where he will make himself at home.

Since, incidentally, there was nothing naive about his action, it follows that he arranged everything with the *'bel' homme behind my back* and was *no* less reticent towards *yourself.*

First published abridged in *Der Briefwechsel zwischen F. Engels und K. Marx,* Bd. 1, Stuttgart, 1913 and in full in *MEGA,* Abt. III, Bd. 1, 1929

Printed according to the original

Published in English in full for the first time

145

MARX TO ENGELS [43]

IN MANCHESTER

[London,] 24 February 1851
28 Dean Street, Soho

Dear Engels,

It is now one o'clock in the morning. About an hour ago Pieper came rushing in, hatless, dishevelled, his clothing in tatters. This is what had happened.

Earlier this evening the meeting or banquet took place in the City. *Willich presided.* Jones, in accordance with his promise, didn't go. Our DEAR [a] was wearing a red armlet. Some 700 men were present, 150 Frenchmen, about 250 Germans, 200 Chartists and the remainder Poles and Hungarians. Blanc read out the addresses received from his brethren in Paris, Willich one from La Chaux-de-Fonds. There was none from Germany. An address from Poles in Paris was also read.

---

[a] Harney

The speeches were, it seems, ludicrous and, despite all the *fraternité*, the sweat of tedium beaded men's brows and lamed their tongues.

Schramm[a] and Pieper had bought tickets in order to watch the fun. They were molested from the very start. Schramm went across to one of the stewards, the worthy, chivalrous Landolphe, and begged him to ensure that, in return for their money, they should at least be left in peace. The worthy fellow replied that this was not the place to embark on explanations.

By AND BY the Great Windmill Streeters[331] began to grow restive. They set up a shout of, 'SPY, SPY', Haynau, Haynau,[372] whereupon Schramm and Pieper were man-handled out of the hall, their hats torn off; in the courtyard outside the hall they were kicked, stamped on, cuffed, nearly rent in pieces, handfuls of hair torn out, etc. Barthélemy came up and said of Schramm: '*C'est un infâme! Il faut l'écraser.*'[b] Schramm replied: '*Vous êtes un forçat libéré!*'[c]

Some 200 individuals took part in the scuffle, Germans, Frenchmen, and, no less 'plucky', the fraternal gentry,[d] against two unarmed men.

Post festum who should arrive but our DEAR; instead of intervening energetically however, as behoved him, he stammered something about knowing these people and would have launched into long explanations. A fine remedy, of course, at such a moment.

The two defended themselves as bravely as lions.

The Windmillers yelled: 'It was him who stole 19 shillings from our cash box!'

So much for today. *Qu'en dis-tu, mon cher?*[e] If revolution breaks out in London tomorrow, Willich-Barthélemy will assuredly come to power.

Your

K. M.

First published in *Der Briefwechsel zwischen F. Engels und K. Marx,* Bd. 1, Stuttgart, 1913   Printed according to the original

---

[a] Conrad Schramm - [b] 'He's infamous! He must be crushed.' - [c] You're an ex-convict! - [d] Fraternal Democrats - [e] What do you say to that, dear friend?

146

ENGELS TO MARX

IN LONDON

[Manchester,] Tuesday, 25 February [1851]

Dear Marx,

A week ago yesterday I sent you a letter for Harney[a] and have had no answer from you since; this might put me in a bit of a quandary if a letter from Harney, which may arrive any day, should require a speedy answer, or if the new Chartist clique here succeeds in negotiating a visit by Harney, and one fine morning I find he has turned up at the pub. I hope that you received everything safely and that it's not ill-health that is preventing you from writing. Perhaps you don't care for the letter or the way I acted off my own bat without further consultation with you. But that was precisely why I sent it to you, and if there had been anything you took exception to, nothing could have been simpler than to let Harney know he wasn't to print my article[b] for the time being, and to return me the letter with marginal comments, WHICH YOU KNOW WOULD HAVE HAD ALL DUE ATTENTION.

In any case, I have long owed you an answer to the CURRENCY business.[c] In my opinion the thing as such is perfectly correct and will go a long way towards reducing the crazy theory of circulation to simple and lucid FUNDAMENTAL FACTS. As regards the exposition in your letter I have only the following remarks to make:

1. Given that, at the beginning of a PERIOD OF PRESSURE the Bank of England accounts show, as you say, £12,000,000 DEPOSITS and £8 million BULLION or COIN. In order to get rid of the surplus £4 million BULLION, you suggest it [the Bank] should lower the discount rate. I don't believe that it needs to do this, and as far as I remember the discount rate has never yet been lowered at the beginning of the PRESSURE. In my view the PRESSURE would immediately affect the DEPOSITS and very soon not only establish an equilibrium between BULLION and DEPOSITS, but also compel the Bank to raise the discount rate so that the BULLION would not fall below $^1/_3$ of the DEPOSITS. To the extent that PRESSURE increases, the circulation of capital, the turnover of goods will stagnate. Once bills have been drawn, however, they mature and have to be honoured. Hence the reserve capital — the DEPOSITS — has to be set in motion — not *qua* CURRENCY, as you will appreciate, but *qua* CAPITAL, and thus the simple

---

a See this volume, p. 289. - b ibid., p. 287. - c ibid., pp. 274-78.

DRAIN OF BULLION, combined with PRESSURE, will of itself suffice to rid the Bank of its surplus BULLION. This takes place without the Bank having to *lower its* rate of interest under circumstances which simultaneously *raise* the general interest rate throughout the country.

2. In a period of growing PRESSURE, it seems to me, the Bank (so as not to get into difficulties) must increase the proportion of BULLION to DEPOSITS to the same extent that PRESSURE increases. The 4 surplus millions would be a boon and a blessing, and the Bank would release them as slowly as possible. With increasing PRESSURE, according to your assumptions, a proportion of BULLION to DEPOSITS of the order of $^2/_5$:1, $^1/_2$:1 and even $^3/_5$:1 would be in no way excessive, and, all the easier to bring about as, with the decrease of DEPOSITS, the BULLION RESERVE would also decrease in absolute terms, though relatively speaking it would increase. In this case a RUN on the Bank is just as possible as with paper money and may be induced by perfectly normal commercial conditions without any ruinous effect on the Bank's credit.

3. 'The CURRENCY is *the last* to be affected', you say. Your own assumptions that it is affected as a result of stagnating commercial activity, and that then, of course, less CURRENCY is required, lead to the conclusion that the CURRENCY contracts simultaneously with commercial activity, and that part of it becomes surplus to the extent that PRESSURE increases. Admittedly it is only at the end, in a condition of high PRESSURE, that it contracts *perceptibly*. But looked at as a whole this process is well under way from the beginning of the PRESSURE, even though this cannot be factually demonstrated in detail. But in so far as this SUPERSEDING of part of the CURRENCY is a *consequence* of the other commercial conditions, of PRESSURE which is independent of the CURRENCY, and all other commodities and commercial conditions are affected *before* the CURRENCY, and also in so far as *in practice* the currency is the last to be sensitive to this decrease, so it will, indeed, be the last to be affected by the crisis.

These comments, as you see, are entirely confined to your *modus illustrandi*[a]; the thing itself is quite unexceptionable.

Your
F. E.

First published in *Der Briefwechsel zwischen F. Engels und K. Marx*, Bd. 1, Stuttgart, 1913

Printed according to the original

Published in English for the first time

---

[a] method of presentation

147

ENGELS TO MARX

IN LONDON

[Manchester,] Wednesday, 26 February [1851]

Dear Marx,

Your letter of the 23rd, postmarked the 25th, arrived this morning. In future you should always write to me 'care of Messrs Ermen & Engels, Manchester'. Your letters will reach me more surely and quickly since my homecomings are often irregular, and in any case the letters addressed to my lodgings are sometimes delivered by the post to the office—where I go at least once a day anyway. If possible send them by the first evening post from London—up till 6 from Charing Cross, or half past five from the smaller offices, and the letters will certainly reach the office by ten the next morning.

You forgot to enclose the letter from Dronke. Send it soon, as I want to write to him, particularly so as to resume my correspondence with Lupus, of whose whereabouts I know nothing, as I receive no reply to any of my letters.[373] If you would rather not bear the cost of postage of overseas letters and of pre-paid replies, send them, or have them addressed, to me, and I shall charge it to the firm.

According to the *Constitutionnel*, d'Ester has been banished from Switzerland and has already left— *en sais-tu quelque chose*[a]?

Your atlas[b] has been saved. In the end I refused to sell it and am keeping it here for the time being as I need it badly; I am now reading the history of the *Consulat* and *Empire* in the works of French and English historians, particularly military. The best I have found so far in this LINE is W. P. Napier (now General), *History of the War in the Peninsula*. Like all Napiers, the fellow has his quirks but also an enormous amount of COMMON SENSE and, what is more, shows a very true eye in evaluating Napoleon's military and administrative genius. A Frenchman would be utterly incapable of writing such a book. So far as historical reliability and even correct judgment are concerned, Thiers[c] is no whit better

---

[a] do you know anything about it? - [b] *Historischer und geographischer Atlas von Europa* - [c] A reference to A. Thiers' *Histoire du Consulat et de l'Empire*.

than that wretched Tory, Southey, late POET LAUREATE, who has also written a history of the Peninsular War replete with invective and rodomontade.[a] Napier, however, gives too much prominence to his commander-in-chief, Wellington, but I haven't yet read enough of his account to be able to give a definite opinion.

I shall take due note of the information on citoyens[b] Blanc and Harney. As yet I have heard nothing from the latter. I rather suspected that his spiritus familiaris[c] had a finger in this pie. She has unbounded admiration for great men, and has become generally increasingly disagreeable. He must, incidentally, be made to feel this when he turns up again. As for that little man Blanc, it could do no harm if we were to go over his oeuvres complètes[d] at the earliest opportunity — you the Organisation du travail and the Histoire de la révolution, I the Dix ans, sauf à critiquer ensemble l'association du travail mise en pratique après février, et les 'Pages d'histoire'.[e] I shall be coming to London at Easter and something might be done then. The things themselves should be obtainable here cheaply in a Belgian reprint. Since my ploy with my old man has proved wholly successful, at least up till now, I can definitely settle down here, and shall in any case be sending for my books from Brussels. If you by chance have anything to be sent for from Cologne, let me know; I shall be writing to Daniels about my things in the next few days, and then it could all be sent in one parcel. NB. Everything, except English books reprinted on the Continent. How matters are developing with my old man, and the new ploy I had to think up, firstly, to prolong my indispensability here and 2, to spare myself undue work in the office, I will tell you when we meet; in any case Easter is only six weeks away and it's an involved story. What is certain is that my old man is going to pay through the nose in cash to compensate me for everything, especially once he's been here and I've got him even further embroiled. The difficulty is this: to be given an official appointment vis-à-vis the Ermens as my old man's representative, and yet to have no official appointment within the firm here, which would involve working for and drawing a salary from the firm. I hope, however, to bring it off; my old man is enchanted with my business letters and he regards my remaining here as a great

---

[a] R. Southéy, History of the Peninsular War. - [b] citizens - [c] familiar spirit (Harney's wife) - [d] complete works - [e] save that we shall jointly criticise the labour association as put into practice after February, and the Pages d'histoire (a reference to L. Blanc's Pages d'histoire de la révolution)

sacrifice on my part. *Ceci me vaut, ou me vaudra sous peu, £5 additionelles par mois, sauf additions futures.*[a]

Your
F. E.

Don't forget to send me the titbits from Cologne with which to solace my loneliness, as soon as you have received and read them.[b]

<table>
<tr>
<td>First published in Der Briefwechsel zwischen F. Engels und K. Marx, Bd. 1, Stuttgart, 1913</td>
<td>Printed according to the original

Published in English for the first time</td>
</tr>
</table>

148

MARX TO ENGELS

IN MANCHESTER

[London, 26 February 1851]

Dear Engels,

I am sending you Pieper's and Schramm's[c] letters so that you may learn the facts from the actual participants. This is the best way for you to form your own opinion. Incomprehensible *lâcheté*[d] on the part of the 200 FRATERNAL[e] MURDERERS who discharged their revolutionary energies upon two individuals, incomprehensible *lâcheté* on the part of our DEAR,[f] of Landolphe, of Louis Blanc, etc., who calmly looked on, memorising their fraternal slogans.

One further point from Schramm's conversation with Harney: Harney emphasised that Schapper was a 'long-standing acquaintance' of his, and had been on the most intimate terms with him while we were in Brussels.

Apropos! Messrs L. Blanc & Co. had *already* sent a *complete report* of the meeting to a Paris paper *the day before.*[374]

---

[a] That's worth, or shortly will be worth, an extra £5 a month, apart from future increments. - [b] See this volume, pp. 282, 284. - [c] Conrad Schramm - [d] cowardice - [e] i.e. Fraternal Democrats - [f] Harney

Legal proceedings would ruin L. Blanc. You can imagine what a feast it would be for *The Times*, more especially as *Barthélemy*, the *galérien*, the *meurtrier*,[a] etc., would appear as the accused and *provocateur à l'assassinat*.[b] For in the middle of the brawl, Barthélemy said pointing to Schramm: '*C'est un infâme, il faut l'écraser*.'[c]

Nothing but ill can come of litigation: Harney's and Jones' projected paper in the soup, Harney and the FRATERNALS in the soup, *The Times* will be jubilant, Pieper will lose his job (he's magnanimous enough not to bother about it), and Schramm, etc., will end up by having to take on all the Chartists at once. *Que faire?*[d] I shall discuss this tomorrow with Jones. Friend Harney, like Schapper, seems to count on the whole affair quietly blowing over. Hence he has thought it not worth his while to take the necessary STEPS with regard to us or to make the necessary concessions. In this way the jackass is aggravating the situation. One can't allow this dirty business to go unavenged.

If Harney writes to you, there's one thing you must guard against. In your letter[e] you dwell too much on Ledru's and Blanc's theoretical criticism. Harney now makes out that we demanded that he should form part of our *queue*.[f] Hence, what above all must be pointed out to him is that:

1. the *one and only* issue is his relationship with Schapper and Willich, in that he has constituted himself the *supporter* of our immediate, personal, rascally foes and, in the eyes of Germany, has thrown what weight he has into the scales for them against us. And did he not together with us break off all connections with Vidil, with Barthélemy and with Willich *in writing*?[375] How, then, could he resume them without us, behind our *backs*, and *against* our wishes! If that is FAIR it's beyond me.

2. He has *disavowed us* in that, *after* the incident with Schramm and Pieper, he failed to make immediate public amends at the meeting and then withdraw forthwith. Instead of which he did everything to make out to his friends that the thing was irrelevant.

Enclosed Dronke's letter. You must write and tell him in detail about the whole mummery, including the most recent affair. I have masses to write to Cologne, Hamburg, etc.

---

[a] convict sentenced to the galleys; murderer - [b] inciter to murder - [c] 'He's infamous, he must be crushed.' - [d] What's to be done? - [e] See this volume, pp. 287, 299. - [f] retinue

If today's letter hasn't been stamped, you must excuse me. It is too late to go out for STAMPS, and it is essential that the letter be posted this evening.

Your

K. Marx

First published in *Der Briefwechsel zwischen F. Engels und K. Marx*, Bd. 1, Stuttgart, 1913

Printed according to the original

Published in English for the first time

149

ENGELS TO MARX

IN LONDON

[Manchester,] Wednesday [26 February 1851]

Dear Marx,

I have just come upon your 2nd letter. I at once wrote another one to Harney: if you approve of it, send it on to him forthwith.[a] This infamous affair is altogether too much, and he's got to be made aware of the fact. If he allies himself with the others, *tant pis pour lui*,[b] I CARE THE DEVIL.

Enclosed a letter which looks very odd to me.[376] What's behind the whole business? I don't know to what extent red Wolff[c] is his own master. Besides, there's so much that's crack-brained about the letter that I can't reply to it without having further information. So let me know at once what kind of a DODGE this is and return the piffle to me. One o'clock in the morning.

Your

F. E.

Having no STAMPS, I shan't be able to put any on this letter as I am now going out to post it.

First published abridged in *Der Briefwechsel zwischen F. Engels und K. Marx*, Bd. 1, Stuttgart, 1913 and in full in *MEGA*, Abt. III, Bd. 1, 1929

Printed according to the original

Published in English for the first time

---

[a] See this volume, pp. 306, 311. - [b] so much the worse for him. - [c] Ferdinand Wolff

150

ENGELS TO MARX

IN LONDON

[Manchester,] Thursday, 27 February 1851

Dear Marx,

When last night at 12 o'clock I arrived home and found your letter with its account of the infamy perpetrated upon Schramm and Pieper,[a] I at once sent off to you a letter for Harney. From that letter, the shaky hand, the passionate indignation, the bumbling, stumbling train of thought and the not exactly harmonious whole, it will have been evident to you that it was written under the influence of a glass or two of strong rum-punch which I had unwontedly imbibed that evening, and you will therefore not have sent it off. IN FACT, I was so enraged that I couldn't have gone to bed without sending it off and hence, more to calm myself than to convey my opinion in all haste to Harney, I dashed off to the post at 1 o'clock. You'll have received the letter around midday today, and since today there's no post until the evening, it has not been possible to send you another letter before this one. I now enclose an amended letter for Harney, which you will kindly convey to him if, as I hope, you haven't yet forwarded the first.[377]

In future address letters to me as follows:

1. All letters which you send from the Charing Cross office before six in the evening, or before half past five from smaller offices, to the office (Ermen and Engels). Then I shall get them at 10 in the morning.

2. All letters posted *after* 6 o'clock in the evening to Great Ducie Street. I shall get them the following evening at 6 o'clock, whereas in the office I wouldn't get them until the following morning.

Hühnerbein wrote to me recently. Mirbach got away safely and is leaving Paris to follow his wife to Athens.

Your

F. E.

First published in *Der Briefwechsel zwischen F. Engels und K. Marx*, Bd. 1, Stuttgart, 1913

Printed according to the original

Published in English for the first time

---

[a] See this volume, pp. 297-98.

151

ENGELS TO MARX

IN LONDON

[Manchester,] Friday [28 February 1851]

Dear Marx,

Your letter of the day before yesterday didn't arrive till this morning. Had I already had all these details yesterday I would have written to our DEAR Harney in quite a different vein. But sooner or later he'll turn up and then I'll let him have a piece of my mind.

It would not, I believe, be a great deal of use to take serious legal proceedings over this business. Apart from Harney and Jones and the Chartists, the business would fizzle out in mutual recriminations and accusations. With the help of any advocate, the others would cause the most impudent questions to be put to Schramm and Pieper, e.g. whether Schramm had not stolen funds from Great Windmill Street,[378] etc., etc., which, however vigorously they were parried, would be enough to ruin the whole effect. The defendants' witnesses would swear that Schramm had said such and such, they would recall certain of Schramm's scenes in Great Windmill Street and inflate them out of all proportion so as to depict Schramm as a DISTURBER OF PUBLIC MEETINGS, etc., and the MAGISTRATE, only too happy to see the demagogues dubbing each other rascals, would allow anything that might throw a compromising light on either party. Schramm, however, should use it as a threat.

Besides, he is taken FOR A CARE-THE-DEVIL, RECKLESS SORT OF CHARACTER, and they'll believe him capable of such excesses. He should give Landolphe a box on the ears and practise shooting; the chap's always getting involved in such affairs[379] and, more than anyone else, he should know how to shoot.

The case would after all end up with nothing more than the rudest of snubs for both parties from the MAGISTRATE — especially as it would be heard up in Islington, where heaven knows what sort of old jackasses the MAGISTRATES are. And if Landolphe, *représentant du peuple*,[a] were to state that Schramm could only have come with

---

[a] representative of the people

the intention of making trouble, etc., don't you think that ultimately this would impress the public more than Schramm's and Pieper's statement? A great scandal could be made of the business, but then Schramm would risk having part of the scandal rebound on him in the form of insinuations.

And again, one sure consequence of such a scandal would be the introduction of a new Aliens Bill[380] to protect the honest reactionaries coming over from the Continent for the Exhibition.

But when given the cold shoulder by Landolphe, why the devil didn't Schramm go straight to Harney *pour le mettre en cause*?[a]

Just time for the post. Adieu.

Your
F. E.

First published abridged in *Der Briefwechsel zwischen F. Engels und K. Marx*, Bd. 1, Stuttgart, 1913 and in full in *MEGA*, Abt. III, Bd. 1, 1929

Printed according to the original

Published in English for the first time

152

MARX TO HERMANN BECKER[357]

IN COLOGNE

[London,] 28 February [1851]

Dear Becker,

I trust you have received the *Rh.Z.*[b] I cannot understand your silence. Had you sent me *Willich's letters* for which I asked you,[c] I would not have had to report the abominations related below. I must again insist on your *sending these letters forthwith*.... The

---

a to call him to account - b *Neue Rheinische Zeitung. Politisch-ökonomische Revue* - c See this volume, pp. 273, 282.

following report is to be read out to all our friends, who must make it known throughout the whole of Germany.

It concerns the banquet held in London on 24 February, at which two of our friends and party comrades[a] were publicly 'haynaued'[372] under the chairmanship of the bold Chevalier de *Willich*. To help you understand what follows, a few preliminary remarks:

The French émigrés, like all the others, had split up into various factions. Thereupon they combined to found an association in Church Street.[362] It was to be of a *philanthropic* nature, for the assistance of refugees. Politics were excluded. Thus all shades of French émigré opinion were provided with a neutral terrain. In this way, then, Ledru-Rollin and Louis Blanc, Montagnards[260] and Cabetists, Blanquists, etc., happened to be here at the same time.

24 February was approaching. As you know, when presented with such a chance of appearing important, the French prepare for it, discuss it, examine its every aspect as long in advance as they would do a woman's impending lying-in. Accordingly, the Church Street association convened a general meeting in order to arrange the celebration of this 'glorious' day. L. Blanc and Ledru-Rollin were present. Little Blanc—NB he cannot improvise but writes his speeches and learns them by heart in front of a looking-glass—rose and made a cleverly couched, elaborate, jesuitical speech in which he sought to prove that this association, being of a philanthropic nature, could not stage a *political* banquet and hence could not celebrate the February Revolution. Ledru-Rollin replied. In the heat of replying, little Blanc blurted out that, since *Ledru and Mazzini had not included him in the European Central Committee*,[338] he would not partake of any banquet with them. He was told that it was not the European Central Committee which was giving the banquet, but the Church Street association, comprising all shades of French émigré opinion.

The following day that association received a letter from L. Blanc in which he notified them that he intended to stage a rival monster banquet....[b]

So L. Blanc secured Harney and with him part of his following, for his banquet. The English foundations had been laid. But the

---

[a] Conrad Schramm and Wilhelm Pieper - [b] In the indictment the following is written over a passage omitted here: 'The following describes how L. Blanc won over his friend Harney with the progressive faction of the Chartists for his banquet.'

continental background, which was also to have all the colours of a European central rainbow, was still missing. To that end Louis Blanc ran a knowledgeable eye over the caricature of Mazzini's committee — the *Willich-Schapper-Barthélemy-Vidil-Peter and Paul committee.*

Just a few words about the origins and nature of this committee and its various hangers-on from the respective associations.

When Willich and Schapper, along with their association, were thrown out of the League,[a] they joined up with Vidil and Barthélemy ... and the dregs of the Polish, Hungarian and Italian émigrés, by which rabble they had themselves dubbed European Central Committee.... Schapper and Willich, who could reasonably hope that, from a distance, this dirty, tasteless and paltry piece of mosaic might be taken for a work of art, also had the particular aim of showing the German communists that it was themselves, not we, who had the European émigrés behind them and that, whether Germany liked it or not, they were determined to take over her government at the earliest opportunity....

In order to conduct his intrigue against Church Street, L. Blanc was not above associating himself with this gang he so despised. They, of course, were delighted. At last they were to attain a *position.* Although these gentlemen wish to exclude all writers, they welcome with open arms any writer of repute who places himself at their disposal. Schapper and Willich saw their day of triumph approaching ... when the German communists would assuredly not be able to resist, and would repentantly return to seek shelter beneath their wings....

The banquet took place in Islington on 24 February. Two of our friends, *Schramm* and *Pieper* attended.... Addresses were read out. L. Blanc read an address from his delegates, Landolphe one from Deputy Greppo (no other was to be had from Paris), a Pole an address from a few fellow thinkers in Paris, and the great Willich, who *presided,* one from La Chaux-de-Fonds. They had been unable to get hold of any from Germany....[b]

Now it is up to you to do everything in your power to brand

---

[a] The Communist League - [b] In the indictment the following is written over a passage omitted here: 'When, following this, the ill-treatment inflicted on these their friends, who both, according to the above, belonged to the League, has been described, the whole ends thus:'

these cowardly, calumnious, infamous assassins before the German proletariat, and wherever else this can be done.

To that end it is essential that you send us Willich's letters forthwith....

First published in *Anklageschrift gegen P. G. Roeser, J. H. G. Bürgers, P. Nothjung, W. J. Reiff, H. H. Becker, R. Daniels, C. W. Otto, A. Jacobi, J. J. Klein, F. Freiligrath*, Cologne, 1852

Printed according to *Anklageschrift*

Published in English for the first time

153

MARX TO ENGELS

IN MANCHESTER

[London,] Saturday, 1 March 1851

Dear Engels,

You must have the most singular post-horses, seeing that all my letters reach you too late.

As you will very well know, if you have given due attention to the letters you have received, everything you advise has already happened, with the exception of the box on the ears for Landolphe, which I do not consider a proper remedy. If anybody is to be done an injury, it must be the little HIPHIPHIPHURRAH Scotsman, George Julian Harney, and no other, and then it is Harney who will have to practise shooting.

With both your letters to Harney in front of me,[a] I sent the *first,* because in my opinion it was better written and more apt than the second, amended, edition.

Both Harney and Landolphe have been sufficiently threatened with legal proceedings. Your fear that Landolphe would testify against Schramm unfounded. Rather, he will swear that he, as a committee member, was approached by Schramm before the scandal and asked to keep order among the gang.

Since, then, the 'threat' of legal proceedings is of no avail, *que faire*[b] except quietly swallow blows, 'spy', and Schapper-Willich triumph!

All your fears concerning scandal justified. But we, too, will

---

[a] See this volume, p. 306. - [b] what can be done

have a SHARP advocate on our side. A little disrepute, whether more or less, can be of no moment to Schramm. But if he lets the matter drop, now that the Church Street[362] Frenchmen have become embroiled in it, he will be *perdu*[a] unless he either obtains public satisfaction from the Chartists or takes the matter to court. One thing or the other.

Jones, as I told you in my letter, wasn't at Monday's meeting. I had arranged a meeting with him at my house, but as early as Tuesday rushed round to see him, didn't find him in, left a note asking him to come without fail on Wednesday. Didn't come. Went there on Thursday. Was turned away. Left a note of invitation. Didn't come. Thursday evening I wrote him a lengthy letter[381] calmly, simply and clearly setting forth the whole dirty business from the beginning, placing, for his benefit, the repulsive consequences in their perspective, demanding public satisfaction, and finally requesting him to call on me and discuss matters. Didn't come, although he was in town, nor yet any written reply from him. So Jones has clearly been worked upon by that little Scottish intriguer, who is afraid of leaving him alone with me. You see, then, no prospect of public satisfaction from the Chartists. There only remains legal proceedings. *Adviendra que pourra.*[b] The only drawback being that Pieper will lose his job as a result and that we may well have *plus ou moins*[c] the whole of the Chartist mob at our heels.

The *introduction of an Aliens Bill*[380] would be the *most fortunate* event so far as we are concerned. Where would those jackasses be without a public demonstration every day?

There's only *one* other way of settling the matter without creating an almighty scandal, and that is for you to *come down, immediately* and without delay.[382] You could stay with me, as I have now rented two additional rooms. There is, I definitely assure you, no other way. Letters confuse, delay and achieve nothing.

Your
K. M.

First published slightly abridged in *Der Briefwechsel zwischen F. Engels und K. Marx*, Bd. l, Stuttgart, 1913 and in full in *MEGA*, Abt. III, Bd. l, 1929

Printed according to the original

Published in English for the first time

---

[a] lost - [b] Come what may. - [c] more or less

154

MARX TO ENGELS

IN MANCHESTER

[London,] 8 March[a] 1851

Dear Engels,

No more than a MATTER OF FACT line or two today.

As you will have seen, *The Times* didn't accept the stuff.[b] *Mais ça ne nous regarde plus.*[c]

Harney had already written to Schramm the day before yesterday morning. That idle jackass went out at 9 in the morning and didn't return home until one o'clock at night. So he did not find the letter till yesterday.

Harney is publishing his statement.[d] Has written a satisfactory introduction to it. Addresses Schramm as 'DEAR Schramm' and reminds him that he too must abide by his obligations and not have recourse to the POLICE COURT—this document is aimed at the French.

Yesterday the *Patrie*[e] (and today the *Constitutionnel*) carried a statement by Messrs Blanc, Barthélemy, Schapper, Willich and all the rest of the committee, in which these gentlemen declare that Blanqui had not sent the toast to any member of the committee. The *Patrie*'s comment is that it had not wished to print the statement without first making inquiries. Whereupon it had been informed by Mr Antoine—Blanqui's brother-in-law—that the toast had been dispatched to Barthélemy, one of the co-signatories, who had acknowledged receipt of same. You can imagine the lamentations in that camp!

Mais ce n'est pas tout.[f]

Yesterday morning, then, Wolff[g] sent Wdloff, in company with a real live Englishman, to see Landolphe. The fellow behaved like a discountenanced *Grec*,[h] first lamenting, declaiming, vapouring, expostulating, arms and legs all over the place, and then relapsing into a state of total and ineffectual pusillanimity. Will be placed on

---

[a] A slip of the pen in the original: February. - [b] F. Engels, 'To the Editor of *The Times*'. - [c] But that no longer concerns us. - [d] C. Schramm, 'To the Editor of *The Friend of the People*', *The Friend of the People*, No. 14, 15 March 1851 (a protest against the insulting attitude to him and Pieper at the meeting on 24 February 1851). - [e] *La Patrie*, No. 66, 7 March 1851. - [f] But that's not all. - [g] Ferdinand Wolff - [h] Greek (here: cheat)

record this evening before the miserable *crapauds*[a] of Church Street.[362]

Finally, bad news from my mater. She has made everything dependent on Bommel.[b] I shall probably have to hazard a *coup de désespoir.*[c]

Your
K. Marx

I have received Willich's letters from Becker.[d] You will get them on Tuesday.

First published in *Der Briefwechsel zwischen F. Engels und K. Marx*, Bd. 1, Stuttgart, 1913

Printed according to the original

Published in English for the first time

155

ENGELS TO MARX

IN LONDON

[Manchester,] Monday, 10 March 1851

D. M.,

This morning I received the enclosed letter from Weerth and am at once sending it on to you. So the business between Schramm[e] and Harney is now settled. If you can inveigle that idle fellow into doing it, get him to send Harney a copy of the translation of Blanqui's toast; *cela fera son effet.*[f] It would be an altogether good idea if, now that he is again on the best of terms with Harney, he was to maintain the connection—after all, Harney has a paper.[g] A copy of the article that was sent to *The Times*[h] might also be sent to Blanqui in Belle-Isle. Schramm

---

a philistines - b probably Marx's uncle Lion Philips of Zalt-Bommel - c desperate act - d Hermann Becker; see this volume, pp. 273, 282, 308. - e Conrad Schramm - f it will have its effect (the reference is to the English translation of L. A. Blanqui's toast 'Avies ou people') - g *The Friend of the People* - h F. Engels, 'To the Editor of *The Times*' (with an English translation of L. A. Blanqui's toast).

shouldn't be too lackadaisical in this matter—for he would thereby secure his rear in various directions. Money tomorrow.

Your
F. E.

Barthélemy has made a prize ass of himself—that's *one* consolation.

Tell Schramm to put the whole story down on paper for Harney. Then we shall have GIVEN NOTICE, and that's always something that may later carry weight.

First published in *Der Briefwechsel zwischen F. Engels und K. Marx*, Bd. 1, Stuttgart, 1913

Printed according to the original

Published in English for the first time

156

ENGELS TO MARX

IN LONDON

[Manchester,] 17 March 1851

Dear Marx,

I have had a very tiresome attack of influenza, which has rendered me incapable of anything, whether sensible or otherwise, hence my silence. All I could do last week was send you a POST OFFICE ORDER—which you'll have received. The 5 shillings are for Lenchen, who happened to be out when I left your house. If at all possible, I will send you the £2 for HIPHIPHURRAH[a] if not this week, then next week at the latest. Schramm can take it to him. Not having heard anything from you up to the present—since sending you Weerth's letter—I, of course, am completely in the dark and am, moreover, still awaiting Willich's precious letters.[b] I have not seen *The Friend of the People* containing Schramm's statement[c]; the thing arrives here at very irregular intervals. Ask Schramm to send me a copy *sous bande*[d]; he should be able to get

---

[a] Harney - [b] See this volume, p. 314. - [c] C. Schramm, 'To the Editor of *The Friend of the People*', *The Friend of the People*, No. 14, 15 March 1851. - [d] in a wrapper

12*

one easily enough if he has none to hand. It is good to hear that Landolphe has in the end turned out to be an arrant coward. I am still waiting for him to send me the famous letter.

I am dreadfully irritated by the stupidity of the arrangements here, which make regular and uninterrupted swotting virtually impossible. I have no access to one of the libraries, and in the other, public one, things of immediate interest to me are only to be found sporadically, and the hours are inconvenient, hence all I have to fall back on is the wretched Athenaeum, where nothing is to be had and whose library is in the most frightful disorder. For instance, I have again been vainly pursuing the Napier,[a] and it always takes 2-3 weeks before one can get hold of the next volume. In despair I have taken out Cicero's *Letters*,[b] which I have been using to study the *règne de* Louis Philippe and the corruption of the Directoire. A very jolly *chronique scandaleuse*. Cicero is really priceless; Professor Krug and Sebastian Seiler rolled into one. Since the world began the ranks of respectability have been able to boast no more infamous canaille than this fellow. I shall duly take excerpts from this charming little volume. No more for today.

Your
F. Engels

First published in *Der Briefwechsel zwischen F. Engels und K. Marx*, Bd. 1, Stuttgart, 1913

Printed according to the original

Published in English for the first time

157

MARX TO ENGELS

IN MANCHESTER

London, 17 March 1851

Dear Engels,

I haven't written for a week. For one thing, I too had influenza, out of elective affinity. For another, was *criblé de petites misères*,[c] all of which came to a head this fateful week.

---

[a] W. F. P. Napier, *History of the War in the Peninsula and in the South of France, from the Year 1807 to the Year 1814*. - [b] Marcus Tullius Cicero, *Epistolae*. - [c] riddled with minor ailments

Enclosed you will find the Chevalier de Willich's hilarious letters.[a]

Heinzen's disgusting rag[b] contains what purports to be a letter from Paris, concocted here in London, in which, I need hardly say, we two are attacked first, and then Rudolf Schramm, the deputy, because 'he did not scruple to fritter away his wife's money', and then the 'half-men Tausenau, Julius and Bucher'; finally, and with much bitterness, the great *Kinkel.* Heinzen will never, ever, forgive him for competing with him in the begging business. Praise is meted out only to the great Ruge and Struve. In this letter from Paris, Ruge lets it be said that he made a one-day excursion from Brighton to London. This scandal-mongering article derived from gossip in a private letter from Ruge and a private letter from Bamberger, i.e. two diametrically opposed accusations, thrown together and edited by Heinzen.

The great banquet, where Ruge performed the part of the 'Infinite Dullard'—Wolff[c] and Liebknecht heard him with their own ears—was not attended by deputies from either Berlin or Frankfurt.[d] They don't want a Ruge-Struve hegemony.[383] The R. Schramm, Count Reichenbach (the Frankfurt Reichenbach, not the party's beard),[e] and Oppenheim, Bucher clique and, finally, Julius off his own bat, have all resumed their intrigues against the deities of dullness. Of course for noble reasons. *Je vous dis, de la merde, la merde tout pure, toute cette canaille-là.*[f]

At the banquet Kinkel, who is publishing the scandalous allegations about us, adopted his best red morocco manner, to speak wistfully of conciliation, 'from the simple champion of the Constitution even unto the red republican.'

All the jackasses, while sighing for a republic, and Kinkel even on occasion for a red republic, paid the most abject homage to the English Constitution, a contradiction to which even the innocent *Morning Chronicle* deigned to draw their attention as being short on logic.

Nothing further about Landolphe. As befits an *homme d'honneur,*[g] he goes his way unruffled by the knowledge of being a *Grec*[h] unmasked.

---

[a] See this volume, p. 314. - [b] *Deutsche Schnellpost* - [c] Ferdinand Wolff - [d] i.e. deputies of the Prussian National Assembly of 1848 and the All-German National Assembly of 1848-49 in Frankfurt am Main - [e] i.e. Oskar Reichenbach, not Eduard Reichenbach - [f] Shits, I tell you, shits pure and simple, all this canaille. - [g] man of honour - [h] Greek (here: cheat)

The Blanqui comedy was not yet over. Vidil, the *ancien capitaine*,[a] sent the *Patrie*[b] a statement in which he declared that his sense of honour and feeling for truth compelled him to make a statement to the effect that, in the original statement, L. Blanc, and all the others including himself, had been lying. The committee had consisted of 13 persons, not 6. All of them had been shown Blanqui's toast and all of them had discussed it. He had been among the 6. A few days later the noble Barthélemy, without having seen this letter, also sent a statement to the *Patrie*[c] saying that *he* had received the toast but had not informed the others; he thus reveals himself to be a threefold liar. Beneath this letter, the *Patrie* appended the remark that it would accept nothing more from these jackasses. Its introductory comment was as follows:

'Nous nous sommes demandés souvent—et la question est difficile à résoudre—qui l'emportait chez les démagogues, de la vantardise ou de la stupidité? Une quatrième lettre de Londres augmente encore notre perplexité à cet égard. Ils sont là nous ne savons combien de pauvres diables, tourmentés à tel point de la rage d'écrire et de voir leurs noms cités dans les journaux *réactionnaires*, qu'ils ne reculent pas même devant la perspective d'une confusion et d'une dépréciation sans borne. Peu leur importe la risée et l'indignation publiques: le 'Journal des Débats', 'l'Assemblée nationale' et la 'Patrie', inséreront leur prose; pour obtenir ce bonheur, rien ne coûte à la Démocratie cosmopolite etc. Nous accueillons donc au nom de la *commisération* littéraire, la lettre suivante du citoyen Barthélemy... C'est une nouvelle, et nous l'espérons bien, une dernière preuve à l'appui du trop célèbre toast Blanqui, qu'ils ont tous nié d'abord, et pour l'affirmation duquel ils se prennent maintenant aux cheveux.'[d]

Is that not SUPERB?
I received your POST OFFICE ORDER. If you pay such rates of

---

[a] former captain - [b] *La Patrie*, No. 69, 10 March 1851. - [c] *La Patrie*, No. 71, 12 March 1851. On the statement of Blanqui and others see this volume, p. 313. - [d] 'We have often asked ourselves, and it is a difficult question to answer, whether the demagogues are notable more for their boastfulness or their stupidity. A fourth letter from London has increased our perplexity. There they are, we do not know how many poor wretches, who are so tormented by the longing to write and to see their names published in the *reactionary* press that they are undeterred even by the prospect of infinite humiliation and mortification. What do they care for the laughter and the indignation of the public—the *Journal des Débats*, the *Assemblée nationale* and the *Patrie* will publish their stylistic exercises; to achieve this no cost to the cause of cosmopolitan democracy can be too high.... In the name of literary *commiseration* we therefore include the following letter from "citizen" Barthélemy—it is a novel, and, we hope, the last proof of the authenticity of Blanqui's famous toast whose existence they first all denied and now fight among themselves for the right to acknowledge.' P. Mayer, [Comments on Barthélemy's letter,] *La Patrie*, No. 71, 12 March 1851.

interest in your business, either your profits or your losses must be vast.

Don't forget to write to Dronke. Galeer is dead. Hence enclosed to be sent to Th. Schuster in Frankfurt.

Your

K. Marx

First published in *Der Briefwechsel zwischen F. Engels und K. Marx*, Bd. 1, Stuttgart, 1913

Printed according to the original

Published in English for the first time

158

ENGELS TO MARX

IN LONDON

[Manchester,] Wednesday, 19 March 1851

Dear Marx,

The business of Blanqui's toast is coming on very nicely indeed. Vidil's statement[a] with regard to Louis Blanc is priceless— the fellow branded a common liar in the eyes of France and England. Barthélemy has got himself wonderfully embroiled.— There's part of your letter I don't understand: Vidil declares: 'The committee had consisted of 13 persons, not 6.... He had been among the 6.' Who are the 6? The signatories of the first statement or, perhaps, the faction which voted in favour of reading out Blanqui's toast?[384]

The tittle-tattle among the Germans also makes agreeable reading. I saw the account of the banquet in the *Daily News*[b]—since the thing was respectable it was an occasion which even Mr Mazzini felt able to attend without embarrassment. 'General Haug IN THE CHAIR!' That fellow shows promise of becoming a caricature of *Général* Dubourg as he was in 1830. To judge by the advertisement in *The Times,* Göhringer's Golden Star TAVERN is now very RESPECTABLE. Since I must collect together all the tittle-tattle, it might not be a bad idea to send out a patrol to

---

[a] *La Patrie*, No. 69, 10 March 1851. - [b] The banquet held on 13 March 1851 to celebrate the anniversary of the revolution in Vienna on 13 March 1848 (*The Daily News*, 14 March 1851).

reconnoitre there— *il s'en trouvera bien un qui voudra mettre son nez dans cette merde-là, même au risque d'être mis à la porte.*[a]

Last—but not least—the Willichiana[b] did a great deal to enliven my breakfast this morning. What a numskull! How he could regard Schramm's[c] letter as an answer to his first one, I really cannot conceive. But the chance of a military dictatorship in the Rhine province, without a press to plague him, *sapristi,*[d] that would be quite enough to turn the dense oaf's head. *Capitaine d'armes*[e] and sergeant, no more nor less! Social revolution by means of providing paupers' victuals for *Landwehr*[385] families; statistics reduced to a register of 'rations, livestock, vehicles, and troops'! This plan for revolution knocks into a cocked hat the earlier one for conquering Germany with 5,000 men. If *that* doesn't make sense to the *Landwehr,* one can only despair of humankind. 'I would take a few men with me and *call upon* others'—and do you know what the fellow's intention was? 'Citizen Karl Marx is called upon to present himself in Cologne within 48 hours and to take charge of public finance and social reforms under the supervision and control of Citizen Gebert. Failure to comply with this order and any contrariness or argument, as also unseemly jokes, will be punishable with death. Citizen Marx will be provided with a guard of one corporal and six men.'—And now, hearken to what this fellow says of Schapper: '*Nous ne voulons plus de jouisseurs!*'[f] So even the spartan pot half and half and the fat pig's unresisting inamorata count for sybaritism with this self-sufficient sergeant who tipples gratis. Indeed, who knows whether, if Cologne were to be besieged, the fat pig would not imitate the conduct of the noble Palafox at Saragossa who, throughout the whole of the second (the real) siege of Saragossa,[386] never put in an appearance because, together with 3-4 dissolute fellows and a crowd of whores, he was busying himself among the wine barrels in the bomb-proof cellar of a convent, and didn't show his nose until the time came to conclude the capitulation.

But to what is Willich replying in the third, jubilant letter which betrays a certainty of victory and a lack of nothing but funds? Had Schramm written him a second one, or had Becker replied to Willich's 2nd letter? *Explique-moi cela*[g] and let me know whether you need the things back yet; I'd like to keep them here for the present so that I can occasionally make what notes I want.

---

[a] there's sure to be someone prepared to nose about in that muck, even at the risk of being thrown out - [b] i.e. Willich's letters to Hermann Becker, see this volume, p. 314. - [c] Conrad Schramm - [d] great heavens - [e] Master-at-arms - [f] We will no longer tolerate sybarites. - [g] Explain that to me

Speculation in railways is again reaching dazzling heights—since 1 January most shares have risen by 40 per cent, and the worst ones more than any. *Ça promet!*[a]

Your
F. Engels

First published in *Der Briefwechsel zwischen F. Engels und K. Marx*, Bd. 1, Stuttgart, 1913

Printed according to the original

Published in English for the first time

159

MARX TO ENGELS[387]

IN MANCHESTER

[London, 22 March 1851]

Dear Engels,

Above you will find the splendid document which I got Pieper to copy out for you. On the pretext of having guaranteed Mazzini's loan, Ruge is calling for money to be converted into 'public opinion'. Among the 'Prussians' here, Bucher, Elsner, Zimmermann, etc., there is great indignation at these 'vigorous provisionals'.

As for the 'six' who have caused you so much TROUBLE,[b] those 6 were Landolphe and Blanc, Willich and Schapper, Barthélemy and Vidil, in a word, the 6 matadors; Hungarians, Poles, etc., the unconsulted mob, did not figure.

In the 3rd letter Willich is replying to nothing but the expression of his own thoughts. *N'a reçu ni lettre ni rien de la part des Becker et des Schramm.*[c] Today will be an agreeable day for the lad. About a fortnight ago Wolff[d] encountered him in a whores' coffee house at 2 o'clock in the morning and loudly exclaimed: 'What? The virtuous Willich here?' Whereupon the virtuous one sloped off.

The actual CONTRIVER of the German central DODGE[e] is the tireless,

---

a That's promising! - b See this volume, p. 319. - c Has received neither letter nor anything else from the Beckers and the Schramms. - d Ferdinand Wolff - e the Committee for German Affairs

leathery Struve, *bunion specialist* and herbivore. All the fellow's up to is the old business of using cranioscopy, morality and suchlike trivialities to draw attention to himself. A quack, and one with a hoarse, laryngitical voice to boot. For the past 25 years the jackass has been writing a 'democratic political encyclopaedia'[a] and a 'democratic universal history',[388] the first being, nothing more than Welcker-Rotteck[b] translated into Struvese, the second, Rotteck[c] democratically paraphrased. And Ruge has sunk so low that only the compassion of the police prevented him from printing this nonsense in Germany.

That dim-witted Kinkel is good at ridding the philistines of their illusions. No better means of unmasking this jackass than for him to fall into the hands of such *highly experienced harlequins* as Struve and Ruge. In that company, at any rate, he'll lose his lion's skin.

Your
K. Marx

A few days ago Jones came to see me and, especially in view of the latest revelations, is congratulating himself on having been saved by me from taking part in the banquet.

First published in *Der Briefwechsel zwischen F. Engels und K. Marx*, Bd. 1, Stuttgart, 1913

Printed according to the original

Published in English for the first time

160

MARX TO ENGELS [43]

IN MANCHESTER

[London,] 31 March 1851
28 Dean Street, Soho

Dear Engels,

While you busy yourself with military history, I am conducting a little campaign in which I am likely to be vanquished BY AND BY,

---

[a] G. Struve, *Grundzüge der Staatswissenschaft*, Bd. 1-4. - [b] K. Rotteck and K. Welcker, *Das Staats-Lexikon*. - [c] K. Rotteck, *Allgemeine Weltgeschichte für alle Stände*.

and from which neither Napoleon nor even Willich—the communist Cromwell—would have been able to extricate themselves.

You should know that I had to pay £31.10 shillings to old Bamberger[a] on 23 March, and £10 to the Jew, Stiebel, on the sixteenth, all on current bills. I first got Jenny to ask my mother-in-law[b] outright. The answer to this was that Mr Edgar[c] had been sent back to Mexico with the remainder of *Jenny's money*, and I couldn't extract a *single* centime.

Then I wrote to my mother, threatening to draw bills on her and, in case of non-payment, to go to Prussia and get myself locked up. I had really intended to take the latter course if such should be the case, but this device ceased to be feasible from the moment the jackasses began to fill the press with their jeremiads about the workers deserting me, my declining popularity and the like. As it was, the thing would have looked like a piece of political histrionics, a more or less deliberate imitation of Jesus Christ-Kinkel. The time-limit I set my mater was 20 March.

On 10 March she wrote and told me they intended to write to our relations; on 18 March she wrote to say the relations had *not* written which was intended to mean the matter was concluded. I at once replied, saying that I stood by my first letter.[389]

On 16 March, with Pieper's help, I paid Stiebel his £10. On 23 March, after I had made a number of fruitless moves, the bill for old Bamberger was inevitably protested. I had a frightful scene with the old man who, moreover, was frightfully abusive about me to the worthy Seiler. Through his BANKER in Trier the idiot had asked for information about me from the banker, Lautz. This fellow, my mater's banker and my personal enemy, naturally wrote and told him the most absurd things about me and, on top of that, thoroughly stirred up my mater against me.

As regards old Bamberger, I had no alternative but to make out two bills for him, one on him in London to run for 4 weeks from 24 March, the other, payable in Trier in 3 weeks, on my mater in order to cover the first. I at once advised my mater of this. Today, at the same time as your letter, one arrived from my mater in which, full of moral indignation, she addresses me in the most *insolent* terms, declaring *positivement* that she will protest any bill I draw on her.

---

[a] Simon Bamberger - [b] Caroline von Westphalen - [c] Edgar von Westphalen

So when 21 April comes round I shall have to expect the very worst from a thoroughly incensed old Simon Bamberger.

At the same time my wife was brought to bed on 28 March.[a] Though the confinement was an easy one, she is now very ill in bed, the causes being domestic rather than physical. And thereby I have *verbalement*[b] not a FARTHING in the house, so that tradesmen's bills—butcher's, baker's AND SO FORTH—keep mounting up.

In 7 or 8 days' time, I shall have a copy of the will from Scotland.[390] If anything's to be made of it, little Bamberger[c] is the one to do so, if only in his own interest. But I can't rely on it.

You will admit that this is a pretty kettle of fish and that I am up to my neck in petty-bourgeois muck. And at the same time one is also said to have exploited the workers! and to aspire to dictatorship! *Quelle horreur!*[d]

Mais ce n'est pas tout.[e] The manufacturer who, in Brussels, loaned me money from Trier, is dunning me for it because his iron-works are doing badly. *Tant pis pour lui.*[f] I can't do as he asks.

But finally, to give the matter a tragi-comic turn, there is in addition a *mystère* which I will now reveal to you *en très peu de mots.*[g] However, I've just been interrupted and must go and help nurse my wife. The rest, then, in which you also figure, in my next.

Your
K. M.

Apropos, how do merchants, manufacturers, etc., account for the portion of their income which they themselves consume? Is this money too fetched from the BANKER or how is it arranged? I'd be glad to have your answer to this.

First published slightly abridged in *Der Briefwechsel zwischen F. Engels und K. Marx*, Bd. 1, Stuttgart, 1913 and in full in *MEGA*, Abt. III, Bd. 1, 1929

Printed according to the original

---

[a] Jenny Marx gave birth to a daughter Franziska on that day. - [b] literally - [c] Louis Bamberger - [d] How terrible! - [e] But that's not all. - [f] So much the worse for him. - [g] in a very few words

161

MARX TO ENGELS [220]

IN MANCHESTER

[London,] 2 April[a] 1851

Dear Engels,

I return herewith the cover of the letter I received from you today. Might it have been opened by Pitt Ermen? You must *éclaircir*[b] this matter.

Your post office order arrived most opportunely. And this time celerity has increased the capital tenfold, like *Signore* Proudhon's railway revenues.[391]

As you can imagine, I'm not being idle. And with the *avances*[c] you are making, I hope to collect what is wanting from various parts of the world.

I'm not writing to you about the *mystère* since, *coûte que coûte,*[d] I shall be coming in any case to see you at the end of April. I must get away from here for a week.[392]

The worst of it is that I now suddenly find myself hampered in my work at the library. I am so far advanced that I will have finished with the whole economic stuff in 5 weeks' time. *Et cela fait,*[e] I shall complete the political economy at home and apply myself to another branch of learning at the Museúm.[f] *Ça commence à m'ennuyer. Au fond,*[g] this science has made no progress since A. Smith and D. Ricardo, however much has been done in the way of individual research, often extremely discerning.

Send me an answer to the question I put to you in my last letter. As you are now devoting yourself to military science, couldn't you embark on a fresh study of the Hungarian campaigns with the help of the *Neue Rheinische Zeitung*, Palmerston's Blue Book,[h] etc.? *Ça serait très utile.*[i] Sooner or later I shall be bringing out 2 volumes of 60 sheets, and that would fit in splendidly.[393] If you wish to find out any details about intrigues, battles, personalities, all you have to do is send me the inquiries in unsealed letters addressed to Baroness von Beck. I have established contact with her. She was a spy for Kossuth. And she's a veritable chronicler of

---

a The original has March. - b clear up - c advance payments - d cost what it may - e And having done that - f British Museum - g It's beginning to bore me. Basically - h 'Correspondence Relative to the Affairs of Hungary 1847-49' - i It would be most useful.

the Hungarian muck. *Il faut l'exploiter.*[a] She's too stupid to be able to conceal the truth. I have done some experiments to find out.

My wife, alas, has been delivered of a girl,[b] and not a *garçon.*[c] And, what is worse, she's very poorly.

Enclosed a letter from Daniels, to whom I wrote at length about his *Physiologie.*[d] What little sense there is in his letter is a reflection of my own to him.[394] At any rate let me have the scrawl back and *tell me what you think of it.*

Your
K. M.

You would, by the way, oblige me if, *dans les circonstances actuelles,*[e] you wrote to me as often as possible. As you know, my acquaintanceship here is confined *plus ou moins*[f] to stupid youngsters.

First published in *Der Briefwechsel zwischen F. Engels und K. Marx,* Bd. 1, Stuttgart, 1913

Printed according to the original

Published in English in full for the first time

162

ENGELS TO MARX

IN LONDON

[Manchester,] 3 April [1851]

Dear Marx,

The business of my opened letter is strange indeed. It could only have been opened by our clerk in the office and I doubt whether he possesses the nerve; besides, he could only have done it in old Hill's absence and I don't believe the latter left the office for as much as a second. None of the Ermens was in town. It is, of course, impossible to get to the bottom of the matter as there would seem to be a strong possibility—*vu*[g] questions in Parliament

---

[a] She must be exploited. - [b] Franziska - [c] boy - [d] R. Daniels' manuscript 'Mikrokosmos. Entwurf einer physiologischen Anthropologie'. - [e] in the present circumstances - [f] more or less - [g] in view of

concerning refugees—that it actually happened at the post office. I had already noticed that the clerk, who is more a servant of Ermen Brothers than of Ermen and Engels, had been regarding me with some suspicion of late, but from there to tampering with letters *il y a loin encore*.[a] In any case I shall know how to forestall that sort of thing in future. Even if the fool actually read the letter, it would be of no great moment; for if the fellow ever tried to make use of the information, e.g. if my old man were to come here, it would so compromise him that he would at once get the sack. Anyhow, as I have said, I doubt whether he possesses the nerve.

As to the question raised in your last letter but one, it is not entirely clear. However, I think the following might suffice.

In commerce the merchant as a firm, as a producer of profits, and the same merchant as a consumer are two entirely different people who confront one another as antagonists. The merchant as a firm means capital account and/or profit and loss account. The merchant as a guzzler, toper, householder and procreator means household expense account. Hence the capital account debits the household expense account with every centime that makes its way from the commercial to the private purse and, since the household expense account shows only a debit but no credit and is thus one of the firm's worst debtors, the total debit standing to the household expense account at the end of the year is pure loss and is written off the profit. In the balance sheet, however, and in calculating the percentage of profit, the sum expended for housekeeping is usually regarded as being still in hand, as part of the profit; e.g. if, on a capital of 100,000 talers, 10,000 talers are earned but 5,000 frittered away, it is calculated that a profit of 10 per cent has been made and, when everything has been correctly entered, the capital account in the following year figures with a debit of 105,000 talers. The actual procedure is rather more complicated than I have described here, in that the capital account and the household expense account seldom come in contact save at the end of the year, and the household expense account generally figures as a debtor to the cash account, which serves as broker; but in the end this is what it amounts to.

Where there are several partners, the matter is very simple. E.g. A has 50,000 talers in the business and B likewise 50,000; they make a profit of 10,000 talers and each spends 2,500 talers. So at

_____
[a] it's still a far cry

the end of the year the accounts appear as follows—in single
entry book-keeping and omitting the imaginary accounts:

A Credit with A & B—capital invested	50,000	talers
A ” ” ” —share of profit	5,000	”
	55,000	talers
Debit with A & B—for cash	2,500	”
A Credit for the following year	52,500	talers

Similarly B. Yet the firm continues to calculate that it has made
10 per cent profit. In a word: the merchants, when calculating the
percentage of profit, ignore the partners' living expenses, whereas
they allow for them in calculating the increase in capital resulting
from the profit.

I'd be happy enough to write about the Hungarian campaign—
or better still, if that were possible, about the campaigns of
1848/50 as a whole—if only all the sources were available. The
Neue Rheinische Zeitung could only serve for comparison with the
Austrian bulletins, and you know how much these leave to be
desired. I should require at least 10-12 works on this campaign
alone, and even then wouldn't have what I needed most—Kossuth's *Közlöny* (*Moniteur*). There's no easier way to make an ass of
oneself than by trying to argue about military history without
having at one's finger-tips all the facts concerning strength,
provisioning, munitions, etc. That may be allright for a newspaper
when all journals are equally ill-informed and reduced to drawing
correct inferences from the few data at their disposal. But I don't
believe that as yet sufficient material on the Hungarian war is
available to the public to enable one to say *post festum* of every
crucial occasion: 'Here such and such ought to have been done,
and here what was done was right, even though the outcome
might seem to belie it.' Who, for instance, will provide me with
data on the establishment of the Austrian and Hungarian armies
and of the various corps on the eve of every battle and of every
important movement? For that Kossuth's and Görgey's memoirs
would have to be published first, and an authentic version of the
battle and campaign plans submitted by Dembinski be available.
However, even with the existing material, much could be
elucidated and perhaps quite an interesting article produced.
What is already clear is that, at the beginning of 1849, it was the
winter alone which saved the Hungarian insurrection, as it did the

Polish in 1830, and the Russian Empire in 1812.[a] Hungary, Poland
and Russia are the only countries in Europe where invasion is
impossible in winter. But it's always fatal when an insurrection is
saved merely by the bottomless mud which surrounds it. If the
business between Austria and Hungary had come to a head in
May instead of in December, a Hungarian army would never have
been organised and the whole mess would have ended up like
Baden, *ni plus ni moins*.[b] The more I mug up on war, the greater
my contempt for heroism—a fatuous expression, heroism, and
never heard on the lips of a proper soldier. When Napoleon was
not haranguing or making proclamations but speaking COOLLY he
never spoke of *glorieux courage indomptable*,[c] etc., but would say at
most, '*il s'est bien battu*'.[d]

Incidentally, should a revolution break out in France next year,
there can be no doubt that the Holy Alliance[271] will advance *at
least* as far as the gates of Paris. And, despite the remarkable
attainments and rare energy of our French revolutionaries, it still
remains highly questionable whether the forts and the enceinte of
Paris are so much as armed and provisioned. But even if 2 forts
are taken, e.g. St Denis and the next one to the east, it will be all
to hell with Paris and the Revolution, *jusqu'à nouvel ordre*.[e] Soon I
shall explain this to you exactly in military terms,[f] together with
the only countermeasure that might at least temper the invasion:
the occupation of the Belgian fortresses by the French, and of
those on the Rhine by means of a highly problematic insurrection-
al *coup de main*.

I think you'll enjoy the following joke about the nature of your
Prussian foot-sloggers which throws light on the later defeat at
Jena,[395] etc. So inspired was Prussian General Bülow, of the same
school as old Fritz,[g] father or uncle to the later Bülow of 1813, by the
apparently reckless but *au fond*[h] exceedingly sure blows struck by
Napoleon at Marengo,[396] that he arrived at the following insight: 1)
To lay down a system of warfare based on the absurd for the purpose
of 'confounding' the enemy with one folly after another and, 2) to
provide the infantry, not with bayonets, but with lances as in the
Thirty Years' War![397] In order to beat Napoleon, one does away with
gun-powder, *qu'en dis-tu?*[i]

I'm delighted that, despite everything, you should be coming

---

[a] i.e., during Napoleon's invasion - [b] no more nor less - [c] glorious and undaunted
courage - [d] he fought well - [e] until further orders - [f] F. Engels, 'Conditions and
Prospects of a War of the Holy Alliance against France in 1852'. - [g] Frederick
II - [h] at bottom - [i] what do you say to that?

here at the end of the month. But you must make use of the opportunity to bring me the complete run of the *Neue Rheinische Zeitung*, from which I shall compile dossiers on all the German democratic jackasses and the French ones likewise—a task that must in any case be done before we again find ourselves precipitated into some kind of mess. It would be good if for this purpose the worthy Liebknecht, *qui est assez bon pour cela*,[a] could go to the Museum[b] and look up details of the voting in the Berlin, Frankfurt and Vienna assemblies, which must be there (in stenographic records), and make extracts for the whole of the Left.

You know, I haven't read Daniels' conclusion.[c] That the fellow should insist on 'concepts' as mediating between human beings, etc., is explicable; nor will you ever persuade one who writes about physiology that it is not. In the final count he can always argue that, every time an actual fact affects men, it provokes concepts in them, and hence that the reaction to this fact, though in the second instance a consequence of the fact, is, in the first instance, a consequence of the concept. Of course there is no objection to this formal logic, and it all really depends on the manner, which I do not know, of its presentation in the manuscript.[d] I think it would be best to write and tell him that, knowing now to what misinterpretations certain sections are open, he should so alter them that his 'true' opinion plainly emerges. That is all you can do, unless you yourself rewrite the more questionable passages of the manuscript, which is not feasible either.

Let me know how your wife is, and give her my warm regards.

I'm glad that you've at long last finished with political economy. The thing has really been dragging on far too long, and so long as you have in front of you an unread book which you believe to be important, you won't be able to settle down to writing.

What are the prospects of finding a publisher for the two volumes of 60 sheets you have in mind? If that turns out ALL RIGHT, we might be able to inveigle the fellow into getting the necessary material for the Hungarian article—I'd let him know about it—the cost to be deducted later, *au besoin*,[e] from the fee. In that case I should also need a *very good* special map of Hungary and Transylvania, if possible battle-plans which, to the best of my knowledge, are not contained in existing works—and the map

---

[a] who is good enough for that - [b] British Museum - [c] See this volume, p. 326. - [d] R. Daniels' manuscript 'Mikrokosmos. Entwurf einer physiologischen Anthropologie'. - [e] if need be

alone could cost some 15-20 talers. I would arrange for Weydemeyer to look for one. Apropos, do you know his address? I'd like to ask him about the military ABC books on organisation and tactics, since I can't get that sort of stuff here. You might also see if you can get any books on Hungary out of the Beck woman, or else through her. I shall also need the Decker, which you still have.[a]

Your
F. E.

First published in *Der Briefwechsel zwischen F. Engels und K. Marx*, Bd. 1, Stuttgart, 1913

Printed according to the original

Published in English for the first time

163

MARX TO HERMANN BECKER [357]

IN COLOGNE

[London,] 9 April 1851

Dear Becker,

Herewith the jolly scribble from the School of Kinkel. 15 shillings have accumulated here for the League.[b] 10 shillings are still outstanding, having been promised but not yet collected. I shall proceed in the manner you indicate. So debit me with £1. For, owing to the reduced circumstances of the member who should pay it, five shillings cannot be collected....

First published in *Anklageschrift gegen P. G. Roeser, J. H. G. Bürgers, P. Nothjung, W. J. Reiff, H. H. Becker, R. Daniels, C. W. Otto, A. Jacobi, J. J. Klein, F. Freiligrath*, Cologne, 1852

Printed according to *Anklageschrift*

Published in English for the first time

---

[a] C. von Decker, *La Petite guerre, ou Traité des opérations secondaires de la guerre* (see this volume, pp. 405-06). - [b] Communist League

164

ENGELS TO MARX

IN LONDON

[Manchester,] 11 April 1851

Dear Marx,

I thought that by today I would at last have been done with my grand strategical treatise.[a] Partly because of interruptions, partly through having to look up details, and partly because the thing is turning out longer than I thought, I shall hardly finish it before the small hours. It is, by the way, wholly UNFIT for publication, is for PRIVATE INFORMATION only, and a kind of exercise for me.

I am gradually gaining a clearer conception of Wellington. A self-willed, tough, obstinate Englishman, with all the *bon sens*,[b] all the resourcefulness of his nation; slow in his deliberations, cautious, never counting on a lucky chance despite his most colossal luck; he would be a genius if COMMON SENSE were not incapable of rising to the heights of genius. All his things are exemplary, not one of them masterly.[c] A general like him is as if created for the English army where every soldier, every second lieutenant, is a miniature Wellington in his own sphere. And he knows his army, its self-willed, DEFENSIVE DOGGEDNESS, which every Englishman brings with him from the boxing ring, and which enables it, after eight hours of strenuous defensive fighting that would bring any other army to its knees, to launch yet another formidable attack in which lack of élan is compensated by uniformity and steadiness. The defensive battle of Waterloo,[277] until the Prussians arrived, would have been too much for any army not having a nucleus of 35,000 Englishmen.

During the Peninsular War, incidentally, Wellington showed greater insight into Napoleon's military art than those nations upon whose backs Napoleon left the imprint of the superiority of his military art. Whereas the Austrians simply became confused, and the Prussians, because their judgment *n'y voyait que du feu*,[d] declared imbecility and genius to be identical, Wellington showed a measure of finesse and avoided the blunders committed by the Austrians and Prussians. He never imitated Napoleon's man-

---

[a] F. Engels, 'Conditions and Prospects of a War of the Holy Alliance against France in 1852'. - [b] common sense - [c] A pun on the words *musterhaft* (exemplary) and *meisterhaft* (masterly). - [d] could not understand it

oeuvres, but made it exceedingly difficult for the French to employ their manoeuvres against himself. He never made a single mistake, unless compelled by political considerations; on the other hand I have never discovered the least evidence of his having ever betrayed so much as a spark of genius. Napier himself[a] says of him that, on occasions when a stroke of genius would have been decisive, no such thing ever entered his mind. So far as I can learn, he never knew how to exploit such an opportunity. He is great in his own way, as great, that is, as it is possible to be without ceasing to be mediocre. He has all the qualities of the soldier, all of them equally developed and in remarkable harmony one with the other; but it is precisely this harmony which prevents any one individual quality from evolving to the point of genius. *Tel soldat, tel politique.*[b] Peel, his political bosom friend, is to some extent his replica. Both represent a Toryism which has enough *bon sens* decently to surrender one position after another and to merge with the bourgeoisie. It is the retreat to Torres Vedras.[398] *Voilà* Wellington.

Your
F. E.

First published in *Der Briefwechsel zwischen F. Engels und K. Marx*, Bd. 1, Stuttgart, 1913

Printed according to the original

Published in English for the first time

165

MARX TO ENGELS

IN MANCHESTER

[London,] 15 April 1851

Dear Engels,

You have not had a letter and are getting no more than these few lines now, because FROM DAY TO DAY I have been awaiting your letter—the one you promised. Enclosed a letter from Lupus. I wrote to him 4 days ago, but didn't answer the questions addressed to you.[399]

---

[a] W. F. P. Napier, *History of the War in the Peninsula...* - [b] As the soldier is, so are his politics.

A letter from a Fischer in America whom I don't know. In the meantime I have asked Liebknecht to write to him.

I shall send you a letter from Rothacker in my next. That jackass, too, is an editor in America. From his letter it transpires that, from the extreme FAR WEST to the east we are being loudly inveighed against, both in speech and in print. In his rag Weitling published an article said to be from Paris but in fact by Willich, attacking me and you.[a] Schnauffer, on the other hand, has attacked the great Willich.

As for *Struve,* no sooner had he made himself answerable for the 10 millions, than he distributed a leaflet in the City begging for money to help him emigrate to America, together with Amalia.[b] In this he was successful. Last Friday he pushed off, still with Amalia.

Willich, with Göhringer for mentor, is said to have become very devoted to the TRICKER. Incidentally, for a fortnight after receiving the latest reply from pseudo-Becker, enclosing the toast, he suffered from a bilious fever. For 2 weeks never left the chapel, i.e. the barracks. And on his return to the Windmill,[331] he brought up for discussion the question of the toast and the introductory comment,[c] presumably so as to equip himself with a *testimonium paupertatis.*[d]

Schapper has framed a constitution for England since, after mature consideration and lengthy discussion in that same Windmill, they decided that England had no written constitution and must therefore be given one. And Schapper-Gebert will provide her with this constitution. It's already written.

Schimmelpfennig has been travelling round Germany and has everywhere been busily engaged in intrigues against us, in the common interest of Willich-Schapper, Ruge-Kinkel, Becker[e]-Sigel. Especially at the seats of Kinkel-mania, and more particularly in Westphalia, Osnabrück, Bielefeld, etc., where they've never been well-disposed towards us, there is no end to the tittle-tattle.

Your

K. M.

First published abridged in *Der Briefwech-sel zwischen F. Engels und K. Marx,* Bd. 1, Stuttgart, 1913 and in full in *MEGA,* Abt. III, Bd. 1, 1929

Printed according to the original

Published in English for the first time

---

[a] 'Paris, 2. Januar 1851', *Die Republik der Arbeiter,* No. 2, February 1851. - [b] Amalie Struve - [c] See K. Marx and F. Engels, 'Introduction to the Leaflet of L. A. Blanqui's Toast Sent to the Refugee Committee'. - [d] certificate of poverty - [e] Johann Philipp Becker

166

ENGELS TO MARX

IN LONDON

Manchester, Tuesday, 15 April [1851]

Dear Marx,

Herewith POST OFFICE ORDER for £5.

If your wife's state of health and your other circumstances permit, come up the day after tomorrow, Thursday.[392] There are three trains for you to choose from: 1. at half past six in the morning, arriving here at 2 o'clock (has 2nd class); 2. the PARLIAMENTARY TRAIN[400] at seven in the morning (2nd and 3rd class), arriving at half past six in the evening; 3. at 12 o'clock midday, arriving at 9 in the evening (2nd class). Then, from Friday to Monday we could make a tour of the neighbourhood.

Anyway, write and tell me by return whether you're coming and by which train; I shall then be at the station. If you can't come up on Thursday, although *sous beaucoup de rapports*[a] that would be preferable, then come up on Friday. At any rate, let me know at once how and when.

All else I'll leave for verbal discussion, since I'd better go and get the POST OFFICE ORDER straight away. My regards to your wife and children.

Your
F. E.

Once again the Post Office was too crowded—enclosed half a five-pound note—the other half by the next post.

First published in: Marx and Engels, *Works,* First Russian Edition, Vol. XXII, Moscow, 1929

Printed according to the original

Published in English for the first time

---

[a] in many respects

167

ENGELS TO MARX

IN LONDON

[Manchester,] 1 May 1851

Dear Marx,

Within a few days, a week at the most, you will receive another £5—I'd have sent it today, had I not just had to pay out £10 in cash.

For the past few days I have been vainly searching for the letters from Lupus[a] and Dronke. You must have taken them both with you.[401] If you find them, send them to me by return and I shall then write at once. Nor have I been able to find Fischer's letter from New Orleans.

Ne nous plaignons pas trop de la mauvaise queue.[b] I happen to have Savary's memoirs[c] at home. Heaven knows, Napoleon was similarly afflicted. Savary himself providing a splendid example. Nothing could be more mediocre than this fellow. Just as some people think they're UP TO THE MARK, yet don't even understand the *Communist Manifesto*,[d] so too Savary imagines that he's got the measure of Napoleon, that he's one of the few elect who can comprehend the full greatness of the fellow, and yet he has failed to comprehend one single campaign- or battle-plan. When he wrote these memoirs, virtually no proper account of these campaigns had been written and, since the thing's an apologia both for Napoleon and for himself, he would certainly not have failed to do his best in this respect; instead, we find nothing but a few general platitudes and a disconnected jumble of detail as seen through the eyes of a subordinate. All the fellow knows about Austerlitz,[402] for instance, is that the enemy was surprised by a flanking march, and was split up into as many fragments as there were French columns—a word-for-word copy of Napoleon's bulletin. But how it happened, he has no idea. For the rest, a vast amount of Empire and Consulate tittle-tattle; a real prize *crapaud,*[e]

---

a Wilhelm Wolff (see this volume, p. 333) - b Let us not complain too much about our poor following. - c A.-J.-M.-R. Savary, *Mémoires du duc de Rovigo...* - d K. Marx and F. Engels, *Manifesto of the Communist Party.* - e philistine boastful, mendacious, servile, positively revelling in the noble activities of the policeman, both as regards the pleasures of spying and the delight in wielding authority when making an arrest; at the same time lending himself to all manner of tomfooleries and intrigues, yet so mediocre, so obsequious and so blinkered that he had always to be kept on a short rein and issued with definite orders. *Enfin,*[a] a far from impressive character, *au fond,*[b] neither better nor worse, neither more reliable nor more shady than certain *amici,*[c] and yet in course of time Napoleon made a passable machine of him, a Duke of Rovigo and a courtier who did him no discredit with the Tsar of Russia.[d] But indeed fellows such as these have to be bought, and that means above all money and power.

Savary's memoirs, which were pretty well known in France, have, by the way, been copied by the worthy Thiers[e] with an effrontery which, in terms of plagiarism, yields nothing to that of the English economists, and this not only where tittle-tattle is concerned. Here and there he also uses Mr Savary as his main source on questions of administration, etc., etc.

To go by *The Times,* things must be pretty terrible in London now that the Tatars, French, Russians and other barbarians have taken complete possession of it. And, withal, the prospect of brigades of informers arriving from all parts of the world, and even Prussian gendarmes, not to speak of German democratic friends *à la* Otterberg, who'll be turning up in June to see the Great Exhibition[f] and the great men. A fine how-d'ye-do. If you're not careful, you'll have foisted upon you people, with or without letters of introduction, who will demand to be shown Ledru, Mazzini, L. Blanc and Caussidière and who, once back in Germany, will grumble furiously because you failed to procure them an invitation to dinner with Feargus O'Connor. There'll be people coming to you and saying: 'Mr Marx?—Delighted—You'll have heard of me, I'm Neuhaus, leader of the Thuringian movement!'

You probably read about the fracas in the Cologne City Council over Deputy Burgomaster Schenk's address to the Prince of Prussia,[g] and also about the latter's insolent speech.[403] 'The press is bad, the press in Cologne has got to improve!'[h] *Ce pauvre*[i] Brüggemann—he, of course, is seizing on the occasion to write a

---

a In brief - b at bottom - c friends - d Alexander I - e A. Thiers, *Histoire du Consulat et de l'Empire.* - f in London in 1851 - g Wilhelm I - h 'Köln, 24. April', *Kölnische Zeitung,* No. 99, second edition, 25 April 1851. - i poor

lot of twaddle such as, in all modesty and with the best intentions, one used to take the immense liberty of writing under the censorship. But now 'our Stupp' is burgomaster into the bargain, and the greatest man in Cologne, while your brother-in-law[a] is confiscating books with praiseworthy zeal. My only fear is that *en Brutus prusso-bureaucrate*[b] he will soon be laying violent hands on your stuff, and that might put an unwelcome stop to the payment of fees. This noble fellow's other brother-in-law, what-you-may-call-him Florencourt, has, as announced in the German papers, betaken himself *tambour battant et mèche allumée*[c] to the bosom of the Catholic Church. Your family is at least interesting, whereas in mine it's I alone who have to cut the capers.

Apropos, you'd do me a very great favour if you would arrange for Daniels, or anyone else you think suitable in Cologne, to send me a letter (direct here and so with a Cologne postmark) as soon as possible, in which he acknowledges receipt of two five-pound notes, as well as one sent previously, that is, £15 in all, adding that he paid this money to specific individuals in accordance with my instructions, and that my accounts with various people in Cologne are settled in full. He could throw in a few casual remarks, greetings, etc., so that the letter doesn't look contrived. For I foresee a discussion about the monies that have been raised, and hence must have a document which will help me if necessary to prove that I have paid debts in Cologne. The sooner I have the letter the better. How you broach the matter I leave entirely to you, and I would rather it was you who procured the document for me, since the business we two transact between us concerns nobody else. For all I care, you can write and say that it was women who got me into debt, or that, for League purposes, I once stood security for this sum and have now been compelled to pay up, or anything else you choose—*n'importe.*[d] The letter will, by the way, be returned promptly in June to the writer. The main thing is the Cologne postmark, date-stamped sometime in the first half of May.

How goes it with your household? My regards to your wife and children, and write soon.

Your
F. E.

---

[a] Ferdinand von Westphalen - [b] like a Prusso-bureaucratic Brutus - [c] with drums beating and flags flying - [d] no matter

I have just found the letters from Lupus and Fischer—but I can't find the one from Dronke. I shall write to Lupus today.[a] When you write to Cologne, it would be a good idea to press them for Lupus' fare—you know what these Cologne people[b] are!

First published slightly abridged in *Der Briefwechsel zwischen F. Engels und K. Marx*, Bd. 1, Stuttgart, 1913 and in full in *MEGA*, Abt. III, Bd. 1, 1929

Printed according to the original

Published in English for the first time

168

ENGELS TO WILHELM WOLFF

IN ZURICH

[Manchester, 1 May 1851]

Dear Lupus,

From the date on your letter which Marx brought me when he visited me here in Manchester a few days ago, I am horrified to see that it is nearly a month old. However Marx tells me that he wrote to you at once.[c]

As to your American plans,[404] dismiss them from your mind. They are superfluous and you'll find something in London straight away, since you know English and there is a demand for people as well-grounded as yourself in ancient languages, especially if you have your testimonials with you. After all, quite insignificant persons have been given the most excellent positions. The American journal[d] affair is nothing but humbug; do you imagine that if there were anything in it, the fellow[e] would write to Europe for an editor and wait so long? Who knows what is really the case and what has happened in the meantime? You might have to wait till doomsday before being advanced the money for your trip. Moreover at best the thing isn't such as to warrant your going to Chicago on the strength of it; 4 dol-

---

a See this volume, pp. 339-41. - b i.e. members of the Central Authority of the Communist League in Cologne - c See this volume, p. 333. - d *Illinois Staats-Zeitung* - e Bernhard Höffgen

lars a week is less than the lowliest wood-cutter's daily wage, and, on top of that, one week's notice, which is very general there!

[...] I hope that you'll have it by now and, as soon as it is in your possession, pack your bags, obtain a passport to London and up anchor. I see that newspapers on the Continent are implying that the British Government are not admitting any more refugees. Stuff! Don't let anything put you off, not even, say, a directive from the police that you must have a visa from the British Ambassador in Berne. You need nothing of the kind. All you need is a visa enabling you to cross France, i.e. from the French Embassy, which the Swiss will procure for you. You simply pass through the country and cross over here. Even should the French—and they're quite capable of this—direct you to Le Havre and thence to America, all you have to do at Le Havre is board the steamer for Southampton or London. You know that no one is ever stopped at a port of entry here, and despite all the empty chatter in the reactionary press, I hope to see you in London for the Exhibition.[a] As I have told you, don't let anything put you off but, whatever happens, insist on going to London. Should you experience difficulties over transit with the French Government, and if funds permit, it might even be preferable to take the route I took[405] [...] write Lorenzo Chiozza [...] very nice letter saying you have been given his address by a compatriot of his, and would be much obliged if he would advise you whether any vessels and which, bound for England, are lying there (sailing vessels, there are also steamers) and approximately when they are due to sail. Ask him, too, for the names of the captains. Then you can either communicate with these captains by letter (addressed to them aboard their vessels), or go to them direct. My passage, including food, cost me six pounds (150 French fr.). You might get one cheaper. The trip to Genoa isn't expensive provided you do as much as possible of the journey to Turin on foot—up to that point the country is wonderful—via Geneva and Mont Cenis or, more direct, via the Great St Bernhard (Martigny-Ivrea). From Turin you have the railway almost to the foot of the Apennines. Or by footpath (even more direct) via the Reuss Valley, the Furka, the Simplon, straight to Alessandria. These are all very beautiful trips, the weather is now splendid for a sea voyage (easterlies

---

[a] Great Exhibition in 1851

predominating), and the Mediterranean passage most diverting. If possible an English vessel. In my opinion the whole thing could be done on 250 fr., certainly on 300. But whether the people in Cologne[a] will be able to manage this is debatable. But in any case you must get to England. I am on the point of writing to Marx, asking him to write once more to Cologne about the money[b]; if you haven't got it yet, it could do no harm if you, too, were to write again to Daniels or Bürgers.

As regards the fares from England to New York, they are devilish high—'tween-deck passengers often come off very badly, one such case being still before Parliament—1st class cabin usually costs £15-20; this we discovered when we ourselves were proposing to press on further.[406] 2nd class on the Southampton steamers is good and cheap; there are also a few screw-steamers aboard which you could travel 2nd class quickly and cheaply if you chanced on one. But whatever the case, I hope that you will come here and stay here. You would have more opportunities here than in America and it's not so easy, once you're there, to come back again. It's frightful in America where the greatest man is Heinzen and where, too, the prolix Struve is now about to inundate the whole country with his piddle. The devil take the public there. Sooner a galley-slave in Turkey than a journalist in America.

Send us word soon and come soon yourself.

Your
F. E.

F. Engels
Address: Ermen & Engels,
Manchester

First published in: Marx and Engels, *Works,* First Russian Edition, Vol. XXV, Moscow, 1934

Printed according to the original

Published in English for the first time

---

[a] members of the Central Authority of the Communist League in Cologne - [b] See this volume, p. 339.

169

MARX TO ENGELS

IN MANCHESTER

[London,] 3 May 1851

Dear Engels,

Lupus himself has written to tell me that he has received from Cologne a passport to England and the fares for himself and Dronke.[404] Dronke has also sent the people in Cologne[a] an essay on the Italian revolution.

Mais ce qu'il y a de drôle[b]: Dronke's signature is there for all to see—printed by Louis Blanc—beneath the address to the then committee for the celebration of the February Revolution. *Nous lui demanderons des éclaircissements sur ce fait étrange. Dans le meilleur cas, ce n'est pas un trait d'esprit de la part de ce gnome.*[c]

Becker[d] has removed his printing and publishing business to Verviers, and wouldn't appear to be harmed by the government's persecution. An instalment of my stuff has arrived here, but only one copy.[347]

The German Central Democratic Committee[407] here broke up at the very same time as the great Karl Heinzen announced that he would pay it 'military obedience'. The charming Kinkel has withdrawn, since he must, of course, avoid compromising himself on account of his dramatic lectures to respectable City men—12 lectures for 1 guinea: the charmer distributes these tickets through a committee (including Oppenheim of Berlin) to all and sundry, and has an audience of 300 or so. Haug, too, has quarrelled with everybody. Ruge, whose finances seem to be in extreme disarray, intended to buy a daguerreotype establishment and to travel the country as a daguerreotype photographer.

Weerth has written to me today in the highest dudgeon: he is sick of long noses and smoked meat. Besides, he says, he is threatened with 'an excellent situation'—marriage? but is too old to become a philistine. You know our friend Weerth. He soon gets

---

[a] members of the Central Authority of the Communist League in Cologne - [b] But the curious thing is - [c] We shall ask him for an explanation of this strange fact. At very best it is not a bright idea on this gnome's part. - [d] Hermann Becker

bored, and soonest of all when surrounded by bourgeois comforts. His friend Campe, morosely indicating a pile of unsold copies, told him: 'Everything is well received but nothing sells.' And that's how things are generally in Germany.

This place is swarming with PEOPLE of every kind. I don't think that this will inconvenience me IN ANY WAY. For such of the industrialists as are liberal, radical or even simply curious are carefully bagged by Göhringer or the Kinkel clique and then immediately fed with scandal about us two. *Tant mieux pour nous!*[a]

The library has been closed all this week. There's no more news of the red fool.[b]

Daniels writes to say that they are nowhere better represented than in Berlin, where they have at their disposal two 'gentlemen' and 'men of talent' who are very active.

Tupman[c] has the clap very badly. After a violent scene with Madame la baronesse[d] they have partly made it up again but, as a result of his frivolity, his position is now more subordinate than it was.

Foucault's experiment with a pendulum is being demonstrated at the Polytechnical Institute here.

I shall send off the said letter to Daniels tomorrow.[408] Schramm, *mirabile dictu,*[e] has succeeded in obtaining a SEASON TICKET.[f]

In his filthy rag[g] Heinzen has again been chucking his 'NATIVE' mud at me, the *malheureux.*[h] The fellow's so stupid that, under the name Müller, Schramm is acting as a paid correspondent, and surreptitiously introducing all sorts of unsuitable tomfoolery, such as the Blanqui toast, etc., into his journalistic stuff.

A few days ago Willich met Bamberger,[i] whom he had seen once before. Walked up to him. Shook him by the hand: 'I've been very ill for 3 weeks. Couldn't leave the house. The revolution's going famously. We are very active, particularly here in London. Two new branches founded. Schapper's working like a Trojan.'

More another time. Next week I shall really get down to finding your L. Blanc sources at the library.

Your
K. M.

---

a So much the better for us! - b Hermann Becker - c Wilhelm Pieper - d Baroness Rothschild - e wonderful to say - f This seems to refer to a ticket Conrad Schramm received for visiting the Great Exhibition of 1851. - g *Deutsche Schnellpost* - h the wretch - i Louis Bamberger

My wife sends her regards. She was furious at the importunate way in which *Pieper* promptly thrust himself upon us.

By the way, you invariably make the Post Office the present of a STAMP. ONE WILL DO.

First published in *Der Briefwechsel zwischen F. Engels und K. Marx,* Bd. 1, Stuttgart, 1913

Printed according to the original

Published in English for the first time

170

MARX TO ENGELS

IN MANCHESTER

[London,] 5 May [1851]

Dear Engels,

Below you will find in the original English a copy of an article concerning the application of electricity to agriculture.[a] Please be good enough to write by return, telling me

1. What you think of the thing.

2. Explaining the business to me IN PLAIN GERMAN, as I can make little sense of it.

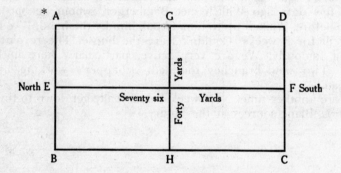

---

[a] 'Remarkable Discovery—Electricity and Agriculture', *The Economist,* Vol. III, Nos. 17 and 18, 26 April and 3 May 1845.

'A field is divided into oblong squares, 76 yards long and 40 yards wide, and containing, therefore, just one acre each.' The above is the plan of such a 'square'.

At each of the points A, B, C and D 'pegs are driven into the ground; the external lines represent strong iron wires, extending from and fastened to each of the 4 pegs, and communicating with each other, so as to form a square of wire, sunk 3 inches below the surface; at the Points E and F poles are fixed in the ground 15 feet high; a wire is connected with the cross wire beneath the surface at the Point E,—carried up the pole and along the centre of the square to the top of the pole at F, down which it is conducted and fixed to the cross wire beneath the surface at that point. We must here remark that the square must be so formed, to run from north to south, so that the wire passing from E to F shall be at right angles with the equator. It is well known that a considerable body of electricity is generated in the atmosphere, and constantly travelling from east to west with the motion of the earth. This electricity is attracted by the wire suspended from E to F, and communicated to the wires forming the square under the surface of the ground, from the points A, B, C and D. ... any quantity of electricity could be generated, that might be required, by placing under the ground at the point G, a bag of charcoal, and plates of zinc at the point H, and to connect the two by a wire passing over two poles similar to those at E and F and crossing the longitudinal wire passing from those points. The cost at which this application can be made is computed at one pound per acre, and it is reckoned to last 10-15 years, the wires being carefully taken up and replaced each year.'

The poles are made of 'dry wood. As the area increases the cost diminishes.... The mode in which the plot is laid out is as follows. With a mariners' compass and measured lengths of common string, lay out the places for the wooden pins, to which the *buried* wire is attached (by passing through a small staple). Care must be taken to lay the length of the buried wire due north and south by compass, and the breadth due east and west. This wire must be placed from two to three inches deep in the soil. The lines of the buried wire are then completed. The *suspended* wire must be attached and in contact with the buried wires at both of its ends. A wooden pin with a staple must therefore be driven in, and the two poles (one 14 feet and the other 15 feet) being placed by the compass due north and south, the wire is placed over them, and fastened to the wooden stake, but touching likewise at this point the buried wire. The suspended wire must not be drawn too tight, otherwise the wind will break it.'*

Voilà l'affaire.[a]

The German Central chaps[b] have reunited for the nth time, and General Haug has accordingly issued an advertisement announcing the appearance on 10 May of his *Kosmos,* with Messrs Ruge, Kinkel, Ronge, etc., for collaborators. That'll be worth seeing.

Tupman[c] has just brought me a letter from Miquel from which it transpires that the German democrats—as well as a number of communists—with Ruge's rotten Bremen rag[d] in the lead, are slandering me indefatigably, that sort of thing being, of course,

---

a There you are - b members of the Committee for German Affairs (see this volume, p. 342) - c Wilhelm Pieper - d *Bremer Tages-Chronik*

greedily lapped up by German philistines and Straubingers.[86] The fellows must really be scared to death of me if, even at this stage, they're employing all available means to make it impossible for me to take up residence in Germany.

Your

K. M.

Jones gave a truly splendid lecture yesterday in which he attacked the COOPERATIVE MOVEMENT and assailed his own public *de front.*[a] He told me that nothing was likely to come of producing a newspaper with Harney, since the latter's wife[b] made it impossible to transact business. For the time being he intends to publish a magazine on his own.[409]

First published in *Der Briefwechsel zwischen F. Engels und K. Marx*, Bd. 1, Stuttgart, 1913

Printed according to the original

Published in English for the first time.

171

ENGELS TO MARX

IN LONDON

[Manchester, about 6 May 1851]

Dear Marx,

You will get the POST OFFICE ORDER tomorrow or the day after. Today our bookkeeper is again without CASH.

Since when have you been using the enclosed beautiful seal on your letters—or has there been a mishap?

Il paraît donc[c] that the whole of the *Neue Rheinische Zeitung* will foregather in London this summer, minus, perhaps, Freiligrath[410] and the *honorarius*[d] Bürgers. I am delighted to hear that Lupus is definitely coming; incidentally, I know for certain that the ALIEN-OFFICES here are far less strict than before and hence all

_____

a head on - b Mary - c It would seem, then - d honourable

that to-do about the ban on sending refugees here is sheer humbug.

The mandrake's signature to the Geneva address is strange indeed—*une bévue inconcevable*[a]—further proof that one must maintain A SHARP LOOK-OUT AFTER THESE YOUNG MEN and that they must be kept on a tight rein. It can only be a *bévue;* the little chap's letters were over-zealous and he may have believed that what he was doing was a wonderful stroke of genius. He must be rigorously questioned, upbraided and told, *surtout pas de zèle!*[b]

I shall shortly tell you of an economic treatise written by Wellington in 1811 on FREE TRADE and monopoly in colonial trade. It's a curious thing and, since it relates to the Spanish and not the English colonies, he can play at being a FREE-TRADER although right at the outset he rails at merchants like the dyed-in-the-wool soldier and aristocrat he is. It never occurred to him that he would later have to help apply these principles in the English colonies. But that's the irony of it. In return for his undeserved victory over Napoleon, the old Irishman subsequently had to yield to Cobden and, *en économie politique,*[c] to pass under the Caudine yoke[411] of FREE-TRADE. World history does indeed give occasion for a great many pleasing reflections!

The dissolution of the Democratic Provisional Government fo Germany in London[d] fills me with sorrow. Such a fine opportunit for the jackasses to hold themselves up to public ridicule will no readily recur. On the other hand the great Franz Raveaux has reopened his cliquish polemic in the *Kölnische Zeitung* with Mr Paul Franck and other jackasses. He is again ripe for election to some national mad-house in which to declare: 'Gentlemen, this is a very great day for the city of Cologne!'[e] The oaf is now in Brussels. Our friend Engels, the Commandant, has become General and First Commandant, and the philistines gave a dinner for him at which 'our Stupp' proposed his health. So you see, you can still get somewhere, even if your name is Engels. And, in returning thanks, that fat old swine, once a lieutenant under Napoleon, expressed his pleasure at the specifically Prussian spirit both of the celebration and of the city of Cologne.[f]

---

[a] an inconceivable blunder (reference to Dronke's signature to the address sent from Geneva to the organisers of the 'banquet of the equal' on 24 February, see this volume, p. 342) - [b] above all no zeal! (words ascribed to Talleyrand) - [c] in political economy - [d] i.e. the Committee for German Affairs (see this volume, p. 342) - [e] This sentence is in a local dialect in the original - [f] 'Köln, 2. Mai', *Kölnische Zeitung*, No. 106, 3 May 1851.

13*

I am, by the way, morally convinced that Willich and Co. are hatching an ambitious plan for the revolutionisation of England during the Exhibition, although it's equally certain that they won't raise a finger. It won't be the first or last time.

The 2nd STAMP on my letters is for late posting. The STAMP enables me to get the letter off by the same train 1 $^1/_2$ hours after the ordinary post office has closed. In any case it's the firm that pays.

Your

F. E.

First published in *Der Briefwechsel zwischen F. Engels und K. Marx,* Bd. 1, Stuttgart, 1913

Printed according to the original

Published in English for the first time

172

ENGELS TO MARX

IN LONDON

[Manchester,] Thursday, 8 May [a] [1851] 10 o'clock at night

Dear Marx,

I sent you today by the first post a POST OFFICE ORDER for £5, which I hope you have received.

Something's *décidément*[b] amiss with the English mails. First, the letter that arrived at your place open. Then your letter to me of the day before yesterday, with the defaced seal, which I returned to you. Now, today, Thursday the 8th, at 7 in the evening, I get your letter of the 5th, i. e. Monday, the one about the electricity business. This letter has three London postmarks dated the 6th (Tuesday), two of which prove that it was posted on Tuesday morning before 10 o'clock. Also a *Manchester* postmark dated the 7th (yesterday) and, finally, two others of today's date. In addition a defaced, badly patched up, unfamiliar seal which I return herewith for your inspection. I am sending the envelope straight

---

[a] The original has: June. - [b] decidedly

off to the postmaster here, demanding an explanation as to why the letter was only delivered this evening instead of yesterday morning. Let me know by return exactly when it was posted and whether the seal is in order. We'll raise such a shindy as will give the scoundrels something to think about. That these fellows are capable of dirty tricks is apparent from today's *Daily News,* which declares outright that Palmerston has asked Vienna and Berlin for spies to keep watch on the refugees, and duly goes on to give the English public a description of Messrs Stieber and Goldheim of Berlin.[a] It would be splendid if we could catch Grey in the act, just as Mazzini once caught Graham.[412]

The fact that something untoward befell the letter is also evident from a mark they have made on it. In the address there is a cross before and after the word Manchester, thus:

$$\times \text{Manchester} \times$$

only with thicker strokes than mine.

Keep any seals I return to you; we may perhaps need them.

Tomorrow I'll write to you about the other points you raised; now I shall go straight out and post this letter and the one to the postmaster. My kindest regards to your wife.

Your
F. E.

The letter has been so clumsily opened that the outline of the original, larger seal is still plainly visible. Sealing-wax is of little avail if, underneath, there's no wafer to secure all four sides of the envelope. As it happens I have none here and, since I want this letter to reach you unopened, I have no alternative but to send it to Schramm,[b] who lives closer to you than Pieper, and through whom you at least have a chance of getting it quickly.

Le tout considéré,[c] it would, perhaps, be better to send it to Pieper, which I shall do.

First published in *MEGA*, Abt. III, Bd. 1, 1929

Printed according to the original

Published in English for the first time

---

[a] 'The Debate in the First Chamber...; Germany. Prussia. Berlin, 4 May', *The Daily News,* 8 May 1851. - [b] Conrad Schramm - [c] All things considered

173

ENGELS TO MARX

IN LONDON

[Manchester,] Friday, 9 May 1851

Dear Marx,

Yesterday I sent you 2 letters, one containing nothing but a Post Office Order, the other through Tupman.[a] I hope you received them both.

As far as the construction goes, the electrical business is simple.[b] At the four corners, A, B, C and D—I assume that you have the drawing before you—pegs are driven into the ground and a stout wire, buried 3 inches below ground, is led from one of these pegs to the next, so that it encompasses the whole field below the surface. At E and F, North and South, two poles are driven into the ground, the tops of which, 15 feet above the surface, are also connected by a wire. The two ends of this wire are carried down the poles and connected below ground with the buried wire, A B C D. Similarly a transverse wire from G to H, on two posts, crossing the wire E F at its centre. I'm not quite clear about the function of the bag of charcoal and the plates of zinc, since I have forgotten the electrical properties of charcoal—but I suspect that, by means of this charcoal at G and zinc at H, both of them also buried and connected to the main buried wire, the fellow intends to polarise the electricity, to establish a positive (zinc) and a negative (charcoal) pole.

The rest is concerned with technical matters, insulation of the wires, etc.

Since you say nothing else about the subject, I assume that the business refers to some sort of experiment; I believe you once told me that it had appeared in *The Economist* or some such paper.[c] I'm a little doubtful about the success of the thing, but maybe something could be made of it if it were expanded and improved. The question remains: 1) how much electricity can be extracted from the air by this means and, 2) how that electricity affects the growth and germination of plants. Anyhow, let me know if the experiment has already been carried out and with what success, and where an account of it may be found.

---

a Wilhelm Pieper - b See this volume, pp. 344-45. - c *The Economist,* Vol. III, Nos. 17 and 18, 26 April and 3 May 1845.

In any case there are two snags about the thing:

1. The fellow wishes the wire, which is to catch the electricity, to lie due north and south, and instructs the FARMERS to lay it out by compass. He makes absolutely no mention of magnetic variation, which here in England is of the order of 20-23 degrees, and he should at least say whether he has taken this into account. The FARMERS, at any rate, know nothing about magnetic variation and would lay the wire according to the compass needle, which, however, would not be pointing from north to south, but from north-north-west to south-south-east.

2. If the effect of the electricity is to encourage the germination and growth of plants, it will cause them to germinate *too early* in the spring, thus exposing them to night frosts, etc. Anyhow, this would inevitably come to light and could be remedied only by disconnecting the overhead and underground wires during the winter. This point, too, the fellow fails to mention. But either the electricity so caught has no effect whatever on growth, or it forces it prematurely. Here again, elucidation is required.

There's no assessing the thing, however, until it's been tried out and the results are available, so let me know where I can find out more about the subject.

I render thanks to the Lord on high that the Central jackasses[a] have come together again, and I don't even begrudge them their *Kosmos*. We shall, after all, have a press organ again soon, so far as we need one, in which we shall be able to repel all attacks without appearing responsible for so doing.[413] That is the advantage the proposed Cologne monthly will have over our *Revue*. We'll lay the entire responsibility on the *bonhomme* Bürgers; after all, he must get something for his profound thinking.

It was only to be expected that vituperation should breed in Germany no less freely than in America and London. You are now in the proud position of being attacked by two worlds at once, something that never happened to Napoleon. Our friends in Germany, incidentally, are jackasses. To ignore mere vituperation, apart from issuing a brief comment once a quarter on the state of this savoury TRADE, may be all very well. But when it comes to slander, when the democratic philistine, no longer content with the simple conviction that one is the blackest of monsters, begins to lay about him with trumped-up and distorted facts, then it would really not be asking too much of these gentlemen that they should send one the document so that one could take steps

---

[a] members of the Committee for German Affairs (see this volume, p. 342)

accordingly. But your German thinks he's done enough if he *simplement*[a] does not *believe* such nonsense. So get Tupman to write to Miquel, telling him that there's no actual need for an immediate reply; rather, having accumulated a few dozen examples of the stuff, one should let fly in earnest and squash the bedbugs *d'un seul coup de pied*.[b] As for their seeking to make it impossible for us to live in Germany— *laissons-leur ce plaisir!*[c] They can't erase from history the *Neue Rheinische Zeitung,* the *Manifesto*[d] and *tutte quante,*[e] and all their howling will avail them nothing. The only people in Germany who might be dangerous to us are hired assassins and, now that Gottschalk's dead, no one there would have the courage to turn such people loose on us. *Et puis*[f] again, in 1848 in Cologne were we not first compelled to fight for our position—and anyway we shall never be *loved* by the democratic, the red, or even the communist mob.

I'm glad that the Exhibition chaps have so far left you in peace. I'm already being plagued by them. Two merchants from Lecco were here yesterday, one of them an old acquaintance of 1841. The Austrians are managing very nicely in Lombardy. After all the levies, the succession of compulsory loans, and thrice yearly tax demands, things are at last becoming regularised. The average merchant in Lecco has to pay 10,000-24,000 zwanzigers (£350-700) a year—in direct, regular taxes, all in HARD CASH. Since Austrian bank-notes are also to be introduced there next year, the government intends to withdraw all metallic currency beforehand. This means that the great aristocracy—*i gran ricchi*[g]—and the peasants will, relatively speaking, be let off *very lightly,* the whole burden falling on *il medio liberale,* the liberal middle classes of the cities. You can see the policy these fellows are pursuing. Under this sort of pressure—in Lecco they have sent the government a signed declaration to the effect that they will pay no more even if it means distraint, but rather emigrate en masse if the system is not abandoned, and already several have suffered distraint—it is understandable that the fellows are waiting for Mazzini and declare that things *must* come to a head because they can stand it no longer, *perchè rovinati siamo e rovinati saremo in ogni caso.*[h] This explains much of the Italians' furious desire to go into the attack. The fellows here are all republicans and highly respected bourgeois at that—one of them is the leading merchant in Lecco

---

[a] simply - [b] with one stamp of the foot - [c] we'll allow them the pleasure! - [d] K. Marx and F. Engels, *Manifesto of the Communist Party.* - [e] all the rest - [f] And then - [g] the exceedingly rich - [h] because we're ruined and shall in any case be ruined

and pays 2,000 zwanzigers a month in taxes. He asked me straight out when the fun was going to begin, since in Lecco—the only place where I'm popular—they had come to the conclusion that I must know the exact day and hour.

Tomorrow Wellington, whom these fellows have kept me from.

Your
F. E.

This letter is sealed with sealing-wax and our firm's seal, E. & E. So you'll be able to see if it's been opened.

First published in *Der Briefwechsel zwischen F. Engels und K. Marx*, Bd. 1, Stuttgart, 1913

Printed according to the original

Published in English for the first time

174

ENGELS TO MARX

IN LONDON

[Manchester,] Thursday [15 May 1851]

Dear Marx,

Last week I sent off a whole SHIP-LOAD of letters to you, among them 1 containing money and 1 through Pieper. Then last Tuesday, yet another, to which I was expecting an answer at least today. *Pas une ligne.*[a] I can only suppose that all the letters went astray, since I had at least expected an answer to the one sent through Pieper; its failure to arrive has put me in an awkward position vis-à-vis the postmaster here. Or else there's been some mishap, in which case, too, *deux mots*[b] would be welcome since I'm *considérablement* worried by the business and, unless I hear from you tomorrow, or the day after tomorrow at the latest, I shan't know what's the matter, or how I should arrange for letters to reach you without going astray.

---

[a] Not a line. - [b] a couple of words

The postmaster here has asked that in future you should not address your letters as up till now, but like this: at the top, the name, beneath it, number and street and, right at the bottom, Manchester. He blames this for the fact that a recent letter of yours made the return journey to London and then back here again. An answer by return, then.

Your
F. E.

First published in: Marx and Engels, *Works,* First Russian Edition, Vol. XXII, Moscow, 1929

Printed according to the original

Published in English for the first time

175

MARX TO ENGELS

IN MANCHESTER

London, 16 May 1851

Dear Engels,

I received your letter, which arrived the day before yesterday,[414] too late for me to answer. I was, as it happens, already at the Museum[a] by the time the POSTMAN arrived, and didn't return home until 7 o'clock in the evening. Even with the best will in the world I couldn't have written to you yesterday since I had such severe abdominal trouble that I felt as though my head would burst like the negro's drum in Freiligrath's poem.[b]

The earlier confusion was due simply to the fact that I immediately gave one of the two idlers (Schramm)[c] a note to post off to you in answer to your first letter. He missed the post, and still had the note in his pocket-book yesterday.[415]

As for the ELECTRICITY, the account appeared in *The Economist* of 1845[d] and contains, besides what I passed on to you, nothing save the statement that the experiment was carried out with great success in Scotland. Even the FARMER is named.

---

[a] British Museum - [b] F. Freiligrath, 'Der Mohrenfürst'. - [c] Conrad Schramm - [d] *The Economist,* Vol. III, Nos. 17 and 18, 26 April and 3 May, 1845.

Freiligrath will be here within the next few days.

Now to the business of the post. I believe the post office to be innocent. At all events I alone am responsible for the poor shape of the seal. The only thing that quite *alienum est*[a] to me is the ×Manchester×.[b]

Did you see how the impertinent Kinkel got his wife to deny in the *Kölnische Zeitung* that he had any connection with the manifesto of the bold 'Provisionals'?[c] and how, in order to titillate the interest of the German philistine, he purports to have a 'serious disease'?

As a result of intervention by my worthy brother-in-law-cum-minister,[d] the printing of my things, as of the *Revue*,[e] has again come to a standstill.[347] It would seem that Becker[f] has run into difficulties in Verviers.

In France *Cavaignac* appears to be making spanking progress. While his election would be the rational solution,[416] it would postpone the revolution for years to come. The meeting between Nicholas, Frederick William and Habsburg[417] is neither more nor less significant than that between General Haug, Ruge and Ronge. Incidentally, to tax incomes was at that particular moment the shrewdest thing the Prussians could do.

Now a look at the émigrés here.

Led by a fellow (a German) whose name I don't know, or rather, along with this fellow, the immortal Faucher, the inevitable E. Meyen, now also here, etc., undertook the editing of the German article for the London (DAILY) *Illustrated News*. As none of the chaps knows English, they asked that a German-Englishman should supervise the editing. The superior allotted to them was an old *woman* who was last in Germany 20 years ago and speaks broken German. Her deletions equalled old Dolleschall's, notably E. Meyen's profound article 'Skulptur'. What this idiot was doing was to reproduce here in London the asinine artistic concoctions that appeared 10 years ago in a Berlin literary gossip sheet.[g] Faucher was also unmercifully blue-pencilled. And a few days ago the editor summoned these louts, who humbly, if reluctantly, suffer the old woman's domination, and told the gentlemen that

---

[a] is incomprehensible - [b] See this volume, p. 349. - [c] The reference is to the manifesto 'To the Germans' issued by the Committee for German Affairs (see this volume, p. 342). An excerpt from Johanna Kinkel's letter about Gottfried Kinkel having nothing to do with the manifesto was published in the *Kölnische Zeitung*, No. 114, 13 May 1851. - [d] Ferdinand von Westphalen - [e] K. Marx, 'Gesammelte Aufsätze' and the *Neue Rheinische Zeitung. Politisch-ökonomische Revue.* - [f] Hermann Becker - [g] *Athenäum*

he couldn't use their concoctions and that they must confine themselves to translating articles from the English. Since the unfortunate pair know not a word of English, this was tantamount to a polite good-bye. And they went. And Meyen will have to wait and while away another decade before he can find a taker for his 'Skulptur'.

What is more, Mr Faucher was unceremoniously jettisoned by the *Kölnische Zeitung* weeks ago on the grounds that the public found his articles boring.

What is your view of the Portuguese revolution?[418]

Mr A. Goegg is here, was immediately taken in tow by Willich & Co., and gives lectures in Windmill Street.[331] Hurrah!

Maintenant, mon cher,[a] farewell. From now on our correspondence will get properly back on the rails again.

Your
K. M.

First published slightly abridged in *Der Briefwechsel zwischen F. Engels und K. Marx,* Bd. 1, Stuttgart, 1913 and in full in *MEGA,* Abt. III, Bd. 1, 1929

Printed according to the original

Published in English for the first time

176

ENGELS TO MARX

IN LONDON

Manchester, Monday, 19 May 1851

Dear Marx,

I'm glad that nothing untoward happened to the letters, it's always better thus. The postmaster here also gave me a satisfactory explanation for the late arrival of the letter. In future, when writing the address, put street and number *above* the name of the town, so that 'Manchester' is right at the bottom. It's what the post office clerks are used to and, because the name of the street was at

---

[a] Now, dear friend

the bottom, they overlooked the 'Manchester' in that particular
letter and ent it back to London as a local London letter.

The latest is that you have been utterly worsted. You believe you
have discovered the correct theory of land rent. You believe you
are the first to demolish Ricardo's theory. *Malheureux que tu es,*[a]
you have been outflanked, destroyed, beaten, overwhelmed, the
whole foundation of your *monumentum aere perennius*[b] has crum-
bled away. Hearken: Mr Rodbertus has just brought out the third
volume of his *Sociale Briefe an v. Kirchmann*—18 sheets. This
volume contains a 'complete refutation of Ricardo's doctrine
of land rent and the exposition of a new theory of rent'—last
week's Leipzig *Illustrierte Zeitung.*[c] That's cooked your goose
for you!

The great Kinkel's efforts to extricate himself from the
disreputable society known as the European Committee without
getting into bad odour are most entertaining.[d] You'll have seen in
Saturday's *Sun*[e] that a handful of wailing democrats have
succeeded in organising a meeting and some little RIOTS near
Elberfeld, at which they distributed these proclamations. This was
made possible through German-Catholic connections[419] of
Ronge's. Neither Kinkel nor any other member of the chorus
would have done anything there.

The Cavaignac business is unfortunate in all respects; if
Girardin regards him as having the best prospects, it must be true.
Besides, the fellows are coming increasingly to realise that a
revision[420] is impossible—by legal means. And, if illegal, it would
be a *coup d'état,* and whoever first embarks on *coups d'état* will be
crushed, the *Débats*[f] declares. Napoleon is beginning to grow
horriblement threadbare. Changarnier's done for, permanently
pensioned off; however nice coalition may be, it can have no
immediate practical results—*il n'y a que Cavaignac.*[g] Whether or
not the fellow postpones the revolution would after all be of no
great moment; a few years of determined industrial development,
a crisis surmounted and a new era of prosperity could do no harm
at all, particularly if accompanied by bourgeois reforms in France,
etc. But in France Cavaignac and bourgeois reform mean tariff
reform and an alliance with England and, at the first opportunity,
war against the Holy Alliance,[271] with English help, with due time

a Wretch that you are - b memorial more enduring than bronze (Horace, *Carmina,*
III, 30, 1) - c *Illustrierte Zeitung,* No. 410, 10 May 1851. - d See this volume, p.
309. - e *The Sun,* 17 May 1851. - f 'France. Paris, 15 May', *Journal des Débats politiques
et littéraires,* 16 May 1851. - g there's no one but Cavaignac

to arm, with a long prepared invasion of Germany, and that might cost us the Rhine frontier which is, in any case, the best means of quieting *crapaud*[a] socialism with a part-payment in *gloire*.[b]

The *Débats*, by the way, has fallen so low that it sees no salvation for society except in upholding the new electoral law.[421]

The Faucher and Meyen affair is truly splendid. All I have seen of the German *Illustrated London News* is the front page of the first number in a SHOP window, so I was RATHER curious to know who the 'leading German writers' of this pompous nonsense might be.

The *Frankfurter Journal* purports to have heard from Cologne[c] that things are now tolerable for the refugees in London, with the exception of those in the barracks, amongst whom is Willich. The Augsburg *Allgemeine* actually believes that the ALIENS BILL[380] is still in force and pictures the refugees—those Wandering Jews of the nineteenth century—creeping round London in mortal terror of this Bill.

I'll say nothing about the Portuguese revolution.[418] Except how remarkable it is that, as a purely *individual* insurgent, as *ôte-toi de là, Costa Cabral, que je m'y mette*,[d] Saldanha should have achieved absolutely nothing, but that from the moment he was compelled to ally himself with the liberal bourgeoisie of Oporto and bring to his side an omnipotent representative of this bourgeois power in the person of Manuel[e] Passos, the whole army should then have rallied to him. The position accorded to Passos, and what happens next, will show whether or not Saldanha and the Queen[f] will immediately set about trying to cheat the bourgeoisie again. Lisbon is nothing, Oporto being the centre of the constitutional bourgeoisie, of Portugal's MANCHESTER SCHOOL.[422]

You can thank your stars that Mr Goegg didn't call on you. *Le diable emporte toutes ces médiocrités gonflées.*[g]

Your
F. E.

First published in *Der Briefwechsel zwischen F. Engels und K. Marx*, Bd. 1, Stuttgart, 1913

Printed according to the original

Published in English for the first time

---

[a] philistine - [b] glory - [c] 'Cologne, 8 May', *Frankfurter Journal*, No. 111, second supplement, 9 May 1851. - [d] get out, Costa Cabral, so I can take your place (Saint-Simon, *Catéchisme politique des industriels*) - [e] The original has: José. - [f] Maria II da Gloria - [g] Devil take all these inflated mediocrities.

177

MARX TO ENGELS

IN MANCHESTER

London, 21 May 1851

Dear Engels,

Freiligrath is here and sends you his regards. He's come to look around for a situation. If he doesn't find one, he intends to go to America.

He brought quite good news from Germany. The people in Cologne[a] are very active. Their agents have been travelling about since September. They have two tolerably good representatives in Berlin and, since the democrats are constantly coming to Cologne to consult them, they as constantly put spokes in those other gentry's wheels. For instance, the Brunswickers were all set to give Schimmelpfennig 2,000 talers for the London Committee (social). But first they sent Dr Lucius to Cologne, and so the matter came to nothing.

Kinkel is seriously discredited in the Rhine Province, particularly in Bonn. The committee there had sent Johanna[b] £200, but after a fortnight she was already asking for more. This greatly displeased the philistines.

In a few weeks' time the people in Cologne will be holding a communist congress.

Sigel, the general-in-chief, is here and has attached himself to Windmill Street.[331]

Further, General Haug has brought out an issue of *Kosmos*. Contains puffs for Willich, Kinkel and Göhringer. The various bands are becoming more and more alike. Never have I seen or heard such inflated and complacent twaddle. Amongst other things it contains a harlequinade by Arnold Winkelried Ruge.[c] This creature pretends to have received a letter from a German 'hospitable friend' in which the latter expresses surprise at everything he reads in the papers about 'English hospitality', and anxiety lest Ruge, 'being overwhelmed by affairs of state', may be

---

[a] members of the Central Authority of the Communist League in Cologne -
[b] Johanna Kinkel (Gottfried Kinkel's wife) - [c] Marx compares Arnold Ruge to Arnold Winkelried, a semi-legendary fourteenth-century Swiss warrior.

prevented from enjoying his fair share of this 'sybaritism of hospitality', and asks him:

'It was not, I take it, the traitor Radowitz who was invited to Windsor, but Mazzini, Ledru-Rollin, Citizen Willich, Kinkel and yourself?'

Ruge then proceeds to disabuse his friend and assure him that English hospitality will not prevent them from returning to Germany torch in hand. *L'imbécile!*

The style of the whole is pretentious, puerile, piffling and of a complacent stupidity unequalled in the annals of world history. To cap it all, an unheard-of want of talent. But I must try and hunt out a copy of this rubbishy sheet for you.

That bedbug Meyen is busily scurrying around here telling everyone who will listen the secret that Marx and Engels have lost all influence and support in Germany. Frightful Meyen!

To give you but one example of the bare-faced forwardness of these blackguards, of their shabby importunities:

Last Sunday[a] I was at John Street where old Owen was giving a lecture on the occasion of his eightieth birthday. Despite his *idées fixes,* the old man was ironical and endearing. When the old gentleman had finished, one of the *Kosmos*'s satellites pushed his way through to him and thrust the *Kosmos* into his hand, saying that the paper expressed his principles. And the old man actually commended it to the audience. *C'est par trop drôle!*[b]

That evening, by the way, I was unable to avoid speaking to Harney again; he came up to me, rather the worse for drink and, with a very ingratiating air, asked after you.

Willich's begging business is doing pretty well. When the Schleswig-Holstein refugees arrived here, he wheedled over £200 'for the latter' (!) out of the CITY-MERCHANTS.

Girardin does indeed say that Cavaignac is now the only serious candidate of the *parti de l'ordre,*[267] of the bourgeois mass. He himself, however, furiously attacks both him and Changarnier, and his polemic recalls once more the best period of his battle with the *National.* This fellow is responsible for more agitation in France than the whole gang of Montagnards[260] and reds[c] put together. Bonaparte would seem to be *hors de question.*[d] However, if the royalist majority in the National Assembly again violates the Constitution and, with a *simple* majority, decides upon its revision, it will finally be compelled—having lost all legal standing—to

---

[a] 18 May - [b] It's really too funny! - [c] i.e. democrats and socialists of various trends - [d] out of the question

conclude a compromise with Bonaparte as the holder of executive power. In which case there could be serious clashes, since Cavaignac is unlikely to let such an opportunity be snatched away under his nose again.

All the *Neue Rheinische Zeitung* lads will be here soon.[410] I'm surprised that Lupus should not have arrived yet, and only hope some misfortune has not befallen him.

I am now spending every day, from 10 in the morning until 7 in the evening, at the library and am saving up the industrial exhibition till you come.[423]

Did you read the bogus and the genuine epistle by Mazzini in the *Débats*[a]?

Your
K. M.

Musch[b] sends his love to 'Friedrich Engels'.

Apropos, Willich and Schimmelpfennig have published the inevitable appeal to 'their brothers in the Prussian Army'.

First published in *Der Briefwechsel zwischen F. Engels und K. Marx*, Bd. 1, Stuttgart, 1913

Printed according to the original

Published in English for the first time

178

ENGELS TO MARX [220]

IN LONDON

Manchester, 23 May 1851

Dear Marx,

I saw with pleasure in the papers that the *Neue Rheinische Zeitung* was represented by you in person also at Soyer's universal press symposium. I hope you enjoyed the *homards*[c] *à la* Washington and the *champagne frappé*.[d] But I am still in the dark about how M. Soyer found your address.

---

[a] G. Mazzini, 'Au Rédacteur', *Journal des Débats politiques et littéraires*, 18 May 1851. - [b] Edgar Marx - [c] lobster - [d] iced champagne

Do you know what has become of that drunkard Laroche of Great Windmill Street[331]? He has, according to German newspaper reports, been caught and sentenced in Berlin to death by hanging. It transpires that this self-styled former Prussian lieutenant of hussars is none other than the shoemaker August Friedrich Gottlieb Lehmann of Triebel near Sorau[a] in Upper Silesian Wasserpolackei,[424] militiaman of the 1st levy, who, on 23 March 1842, had been sentenced to be stripped of military honours and to 16 months' service in a penal detachment for desertion in peacetime, forgery and unauthorised contraction of debts. Yet another ray of light shed on our German revolutionary heroes.

That those great warriors, Willich, Schimmelpfennig and Sigel, should be increasingly consorting with each other is all to the good. This pack of soldiery has an unbelievably sordid *esprit de corps.* They hate each other *à mort*[b] and, like schoolboys, begrudge each other the most paltry marks of distinction, but they are all united against the 'civilians'. Punctilious, as in the first French armies of 1792/93, but scaled down to a dwarfish caricature. They all regard the Windmill Street Society as a battalion, ready, willing and eager to march over here; it's the only one left, since the ones in Switzerland were broken up and deported. Small wonder that they all cleave to this noble corps. It's a very good thing that word of this officers' corps spirit should already have reached us from the old barracks and the officers' mess and that we should already see how this cliquishness prevails as much among the émigré officer material as in the 'glorious army'.[425] In due course we shall show these gentry what '*civilian*' really signifies. All of this goes to show that the very best thing for me to do is to go on with my military studies so that at least one of the 'civilians' is a match for them in theoretical matters. At any rate I want to reach a point where jackasses such as these can't talk me down. I'm delighted, by the way, to hear that they were cheated of 2,000 talers. The news from Cologne is very pleasing, but the people there should be on their guard.

Where begging is concerned that precious Johanna[c] really surpasses anything that has ever been known before. Heinzen is quite eclipsed; he has never attained to the same degree of effrontery as this woman who, moreover, is said to be as ugly as sin.

---

[a] Polish name: Żary - [b] like death - [c] Johanna Kinkel (Gottfried Kinkel's wife)

It is clear even from the English press that Girardin doesn't support Cavaignac. But the very fact that *he* remarked on the brightness of Cavaignac's prospects is enough to characterise the situation. You mentioned the possibility that the majority[a] might conclude an agreement with Bonaparte and endeavour to carry out an illegal revision[420]; if they do so, I think it will go awry. They'll never succeed so long as it's opposed by Thiers, Changarnier and the *Débats*,[b] and their respective adherents. It would be too fine an opportunity for Cavaignac; and in that case he could, I believe, count on the army.

If there's a fracas next year, Germany will be in the devil of a position.[426] France, Italy and Poland all have an interest in her dismemberment. As you'll have seen, Mazzini has even promised the Czechs rehabilitation. Apart from Hungary, Germany would have only one possible ally, Russia—provided that a peasants' revolution had taken place there. Otherwise we shall have a *guerre à mort*[c] with our noble friends from all points of the compass, and it's very questionable how the business will end.

The more I think about it, the more obvious it becomes to me that the Poles are *une nation foutue*[d] who can only continue to serve a purpose until such time as Russia herself becomes caught up into the agrarian revolution. From that moment Poland will have absolutely no *raison d'être* any more. The Poles' sole contribution to history has been to indulge in foolish pranks at once valiant and provocative. Nor can a single moment be cited when Poland, even if only by comparison with Russia, has successfully represented progress or done anything of historical significance. Russia, on the other hand, is truly progressive by comparison with the East. Russian rule, for all its infamy, all its Slavic dirtiness, is civilising for the Black and Caspian Seas and Central Asia, for the Bashkirs and Tatars; and Russia has absorbed far more cultural elements, and especially industrial elements than Poland, which by nature is chivalrously indolent. The very fact that the Russian aristocracy, from the Tsar[e] and Prince Demidov down to the most louse-ridden Boyar, 14th class, who's merely *blagorodno*, well-born, manufactures, haggles, cheats, lays itself open to corruption, engages in all manner of business, Christian and Jewish,—that is in itself an advantage. Poland has never been able to naturalise foreign elements—the Germans in the cities are and will remain Germans. In Russia, every second-generation Russo-German is a

---

[a] the majority in the Legislative Assembly - [b] *Journal des Débats politique et littéraires* - [c] war to the death - [d] a finished nation - [e] Nicholas I

living example of that country's ability to Russify Germans and Jews. There, even the Jews acquire Slav cheekbones.

Napoleon's wars of 1807 and 1812 provide striking examples of Poland's 'immortality'. The only immortal thing about the Poles was their aimless quarrelling. Moreover, the greater part of Poland, what is known as West Russia, i.e. Byelostok, Grodno, Vilna, Smolensk, Minsk, Mogilev, Volhynia and Podolia, has, with minor exceptions, quietly allowed itself to be ruled by Russia since 1772[427]; save for a few scattered members of the bourgeoisie and the nobility, *ils n'ont pas bougé.*[a] A quarter of all Poles speak Lithuanian, one quarter Ruthenian, a small portion semi-Russian, while a good third of the Polish element proper is Germanised.

Fortunately, in the *Neue Rheinische Zeitung*, we assumed no positive obligations towards the Poles, save the unavoidable one of restoration combined with a SUITABLE frontier—and even that only on the condition of there being an agrarian revolution. I'm convinced that such a revolution will sooner be fully effected in Russia than in Poland, because of the national character and because of Russia's more developed bourgeois elements. What are Warsaw and Cracow as compared with Petersburg, Moscow, Odessa, etc., etc.!

Conclusion: To take as much as possible away from the Poles in the West, to man their fortresses, especially Posen, with Germans on the pretext of defence, to let them stew in their own juice, send them into battle, gobble bare their land, fob them off with promises of Riga and Odessa and, should it be possible to get the Russians moving, to ally oneself with the latter and compel the Poles to give way. Every inch of the frontier between Memel[b] and Cracow we cede to the Poles will, militarily speaking, be utterly ruinous to this already wretchedly weak frontier, and will leave exposed the whole of the Baltic coast as far as Stettin.[c]

Besides, I am convinced that, come the next fracas, the entire Polish insurrection will be confined to Poseners and Galician nobility together with a few who have come over from the Kingdom, this having been bled so white that it's capable of nothing more, and that the pretensions of these knights, unless supported by French, Italians and Scandinavians, etc., and bolstered up by rumpuses on the part of the Czechs, will founder on the wretchedness of their performance. A nation which can

---

[a] they didn't stir - [b] Lithuanian name: Klaipeda - [c] Polish name: Szczecin

muster 20,000 to 30,000 men at most, is not entitled to a voice. And Poland certainly could not muster very much more.

Give my regards to Freiligrath when you see him, and also to your family, not forgetting Citizen Musch.[a] I shall be coming to London about a week later than I thought, the thing being dependent on a host of trifling matters.[423]

Apropos, not a word yet from Cologne. Have you written? Unless I get the letter *soon,* it will be no good to me.[b] I don't know why Daniels shouldn't oblige me. Couldn't you write again? Daniels could dash off a line or two and let me have it by return. Otherwise I might find myself in the deuce of a predicament.

Your
F. E.

First published in *Der Briefwechsel zwischen F. Engels und K. Marx,* Bd. 1, Stuttgart, 1913

Printed according to the original

Published in English in full for the first time

179

ENGELS TO MARX

IN LONDON

[Manchester,] Tuesday [27 May 1851]

D. M.,

I shall be coming to London on Saturday if nothing intervenes.[423]

My fears for the people in Cologne have all too soon been realised; the arrests of red Becker[c] and Röser on charges of high treason and attempts to subvert the state system, and the attempted arrest of silent Heinrich[d] are clearly not unconnected with the business of the League.[e] Fortunately no papers whatever, according to the *Frankfurter Journal,*[f] were found on the two who

---

[a] Edgar Marx - [b] See this volume, p. 341. - [c] Hermann Becker - [d] Heinrich Bürgers - [e] the Communist League - [f] 'Cologne, 20 May', *Frankfurter Journal,* No. 123, 23 May 1851.

were arrested—whether any were found on Bürgers is not specified.[428] No doubt Heinrich will be coming to London, to make up
the complement of the *Neue Rheinische Zeitung*.[410] The affair
could take an unpleasant turn if the fellows have acted foolishly.

Your
F. E.

First published in *Der Briefwechsel zwischen F. Engels und K. Marx*, Bd. 1, Stuttgart, 1913

Printed according to the original

Published in English for the first time

180

MARX TO ENGELS

IN MANCHESTER

[London,] 28 May 1851

Dear Engels,

The reasons for Daniels' failure to reply (I shall, by the way,
send him another letter tomorrow if I get none today),[429] are most
disturbing. Nothjung has been arrested in Leipzig, at the station. I
don't know, of course, what papers were found on him.
Thereupon (or simultaneously, I don't know) Becker and Röser
were arrested in Cologne and their houses searched, as was that of
Bürgers, too. The latter is in Berlin with a warrant out against
him; no doubt he will soon turn up here.[430]

The measures adopted by the police against the emissaries, etc.,
can be attributed purely and simply to the wretched braying of the
jackasses in London. These gasbags know that they are neither
conspiring, nor pursuing any real goal, and that they have no
organisation behind them in Germany. All they want is to *seem*
dangerous and set the treadmill of the press turning. In this way
the canaille hamper and imperil the real movement and put the
police on the *qui vive*. Has there ever been a party like this, whose
avowed aim is simply to show off?

Freiligrath instinctively chose the right moment to leave and
thereby avoid capture. No sooner was he here than snares were set

for him by all the émigré cliques, philanthropic Kinkel-lovers,
aestheticising Howitts, etc., in order to lure him into their coterie.
To all these attempts he replied very rudely, saying that he
belonged to the *Rheinische Zeitung*,[a] had nothing to do with
cosmopolitan offal, and would consort only with 'Dr Marx and his
most intimate friends'.

Presently I shall have something to tell you about the *Kosmos*.
But first one more *mot*[b] about the situation in France.

I am becoming *de plus en plus*[c] convinced that, in spite of
everything, Napoleon's chances are, for the present, better than
those of any other candidate. They will *en principe* decide on a
revision but *en pratique*[d] will confine themselves to a revision of the
Article relating to the President.[420] Should the minority kick up
too much fuss, a simple majority [resolution][e] will be taken
whereby the National Assembly will be dissolved and a new one
convoked, which will then function under *auspiciis Faucheri*,[f] of the
telegraph and of the law of 31 May.[431] The bourgeoisie would
prefer Cavaignac; but the threat to the *status quo* of a radical
change of choice seems to them too grave. Already a great many
manufacturers have compelled their HANDS to sign petitions for a
revision of the Constitution and the prolongation of presidential
rule. *En tout cas*[g] the thing must soon be decided and *nous verrons*[h]!

The *Kosmos,* then, has made a prize ass of itself.

Under the heading *Kinkel's Lectures,* and signed 'A Worker', it
carries the following:

'While looking once at Döbler's misty images I was surprised by the whimsical
question of whether it was possible to produce such chaotic creations in "words",
whether it was possible to utter misty images. It is no doubt unpleasant for the
critic to have to confess, at the very outset, that in this case his critical autonomy
will vibrate against the galvanised nerves of a stimulating reminiscence, as the
fading sound of a dying note echoes in the strings. Nevertheless I would prefer to
renounce any attempt at a bewigged and boring analysis of pedantic insensitivity
than to deny that tone which the charming muse of the German refugee caused to
resonate in my receptive imagination. This keynote of Kinkel's paintings, this
sounding board of his chords is the sonorous, creative, formative and gradually
shaping "word"— *modern thought.* The human *"judgment"* of this thought leads
truth out of the chaos of mendacious traditions, and places it, as the inviolable
property of mankind, under the protection of spiritually active, logical minorities
who will lead mankind from a credulous ignorance to a state of more sceptical
science. It is the task of the science of doubt to profane the mysticism of pious
deceit, to undermine the absolutism of a stupefied tradition; through scepticism,

---

[a] *Neue Rheinische Zeitung* - [b] word - [c] more and more - [d] in principle, in practice -
[e] an ink blot in the original - [f] the auspices of Faucher - [g] In any case - [h] we shall
see

that ceaselessly labouring guillotine of philosophy, to decapitate accepted authority and to lead the nations out of the misty regions of theocracy by means of revolution into the luscious meadows of democracy' (of nonsense). 'The sustained, unflagging search in the annals of mankind, and the understanding of man himself, is the great task of all revolutionaries and this had been understood by that proscribed poet-rebel who on three recent Monday evenings uttered his "DISSOLVING VIEWS" before a bourgeois audience in the course of his lectures on the history of the modern theatre.'

'A Worker'[432]

If that's not champion drivel,
Then I really don't know what is.[a]

Vale faveque![b]

Your
K. M.

First published slightly abridged in *Der Briefwechsel zwischen F. Engels und K. Marx*, Bd. 1, Stuttgart, 1913 and in full in *MEGA*, Abt. III, Bd. 1, 1929

Printed according to the original

Published in English for the first time

181

MARX TO ROLAND DANIELS[433]

IN COLOGNE

[London, second half of May 1851]

... Communists must demonstrate that technological truths already attained can only become practicable under communist relations....

First published in: Marx and Engels, *Works*, First Russian Edition, Vol. XXV, Moscow, 1934

Printed according to Daniels' letter to Marx of 1 June 1851

Published in English for the first time

---

[a] Here Marx paraphrases a proverb current in Westphalia (see this volume, p. 249). - [b] Good-bye and farewell.

182

MARX TO ENGELS

IN MANCHESTER

[London,] 16 June 1851
28 Dean Street, Soho

Dear Engels,

Daniels' house has been searched and he himself arrested. I don't think anything was found there.[434]

This morning I received a letter, obviously in Daniels' handwriting but unsigned, informing me of the above and asking me to remove *all* letters since it had been learnt from a 'reliable' (thus in the original) source that house searches would also be taking place here in England.

Whether that is legally possible I don't know. At any rate, I shall remove everything. You, too, would be well-advised to burn all—irrelevant—letters and to deposit the rest, those containing any data and the like, under seal with Mary[a] or your clerk.

It seems probable that an introduction from Daniels was found on Jacobi.

This morning at the same time I received, through a merchant, a letter from Weydemeyer, who is in hiding near Frankfurt. I enclose that letter. Do you happen to know the exact ratio, home to foreign, of Britain's trade, a figure which Weydemeyer wishes to know? The thing has changed significantly of late.

Salut!

Your
K. Marx

First published in *Der Briefwechsel zwischen F. Engels und K. Marx*, Bd. 1, Stuttgart, 1913

Printed according to the original

Published in English for the first time

---

[a] Mary Burns

183

ENGELS TO JOSEPH WEYDEMEYER[435]

IN FRANKFURT AM MAIN

Manchester, 19 June 1851

Dear Hans,

Marx has just communicated to me a letter of yours from which I at last find a definite address for you, which I have been seeking for some time past. For I wish to consult you about the following matter:

Since arriving in Manchester[a] I have been swotting up military affairs, on which—at least to start off with—I found fairly adequate material here. I was prompted to do this by the immense importance which must attach to the *partie militaire*[b] in the next movement, combined with a long-standing inclination on my part, my articles on the Hungarian campaign in the days of the newspaper[c] and finally my glorious exploits in Baden,[264] and I would like to take it at least far enough to be able to join in theoretical discussion without making too much of a fool of myself. Now the material available to me here—on the Napoleonic and, to some extent, revolutionary campaigns—presupposes a mass of detail, my knowledge of which is non-existent or very superficial, and about which only superficial, if any, information can be obtained by dint of laborious research. Autodidacticism, however, is sheer foolishness and, unless one devotes oneself systematically to the thing, one achieves nothing worthwhile. What I now actually need, you will better understand if I remind you that—disregarding, of course, my promotion in Baden—I never rose higher than a Royal Prussian Bombardier in the *Landwehr*[436] and consequently my comprehension of the details of the campaigns—and indeed as regards the various arms of the service—is hampered by the absence of the middle link which, in Prussia, is provided by the subalterns' examination. I am not concerned, of course, with the tedious minutiae of military drill, etc., which would be of little use to me since my eye trouble, as I have now found out once and for all, renders me completely unfit for active service of any sort; rather, I am concerned with an

_____

[a] since mid-November 1850 - [b] military aspect - [c] *Neue Rheinische Zeitung* (see present edition, vols. 8 and 9)

overall survey of the elementary knowledge needed in the various branches, going into detail only in so far as is necessary to enable me to understand and correctly evaluate historical facts of a military nature. Hence, e.g. elementary tactics, the theory of fortification, from a more or less historical point of view, comprising the various systems from Vauban up to the modern *forts détachés*,[a] along with an investigation into field works and other matters associated with the engineering branch, e.g. the various types of bridge, etc.; further, a general history of military science and the changes brought about by the development and perfection both of weapons and of the ways in which they are employed. Then something really sound on artillery, since I have forgotten a great deal and there is much I simply don't know; also other requirements which I can't think of just now, but which will certainly occur to you.

I would ask you to indicate sources on all these elementary matters and this in such a way that I can immediately get hold of the things. Indeed, what I would like best of all would be things from which I could see, on the one hand, the present general average state of individual branches and, on the other, the differences existing between the various modern armies. For instance, the different construction of field-piece carriages, etc., the different methods of sub-dividing and organising divisions, army corps, etc. Again I should be particularly interested in learning about the organisation of armies, commissariat, hospitals, about every aspect of the matériel necessary to any given army.

From this you will be able to gauge approximately what I need and which books you should recommend to me. I would suppose that as regards such manuals German military literature contains more useful matter than does the French or the English. I need hardly say that I am concerned with the knowledge of what is practical and really exists rather than with the systems or quirks of some unrecognised genius. As regards artillery Bem's manual[b] would no doubt be the best.

Anything I am able to find here on more recent military history—earlier periods are of relatively little interest to me and I've got old Montecucculi[c] for those—is naturally in French and English. Among the latter more especially Lieutenant-General William Napier's history of the Peninsular War—by far the best

---

[a] detached forts - [b] J. Bem, *Erfahrungen über die Congrevschen Brand-Raketen...* - [c] This seems to refer to R. Montecucculi's main work *Memorie della guerra ed istruzione d'un generale.*

work of military history I have seen up till now. If you don't know it and are able to get hold of it there, it would be worth your while reading it (*History of the War in the Peninsula and the South of France*, 6 volumes). I have no German stuff and must certainly obtain some; Willisen and Clausewitz immediately spring to mind. What do you think of these two, and what is and what is not worth reading? Theoretical as well as historical. As soon as I have made some progress, I shall mug up properly on the campaigns of 1848/49, especially the Italian and Hungarian. Do you happen to know of a more or less official or otherwise reasonably sober account of the Baden affair from the Prussian side?

In addition can you recommend some good, specialised maps of Germany, not too expensive but adequate for the study of the campaigns since 1792 (in particular maps of Württemberg, Bavaria, Austria for 1801-1809, Saxony, Thuringia, Prussia for 1806/7 and 1813, North-East France for 1814, Lombardy, Hungary, Schleswig-Holstein, Belgium). I have the large Stieler[a] here, which, however, is far from adequate. Though I have here battle-plans for the period 1792-1814 in the atlas to Alison's *History of Europe*[b] since the French Revolution, I have discovered that several of them are inaccurate. Are there similar collections in Germany which, without being too dear, are nevertheless reliable?

Do you know Monsieur Jomini, of whom the French make such a fuss? I know of him only through Mr Thiers who, as everyone is aware, plagiarised him outrageously.[c] This little Thiers is one of the most bare-faced liars in existence; there is not one battle in which the relative strengths are correctly given. Since, however, Mr Jomini later made off to Russia, it may be supposed that he must have had motives for cutting down the *exploits de la bravoure française*[d] to something less than the super-human dimensions vouchsafed them by Mr Thiers, according to whom 1 Frenchman always whacks 2 foes.

Voilà a whole heap of questions. I hope, by the way, that the present persecution of Jews in Germany will spread no further.[437] However, I find Daniels' arrest disquieting. It would seem that they want to make searches here in order to implicate us; that would be no easy matter, however, and would fail dismally since they would find nothing.

---

a *Stieler's Handatlas über alle Theile der Erde...* - b A. Alison, *History of Europe from the Commencement of the French Revolution...* - c A. Thiers, *Histoire du Consulat et de l'Empire.* - d exploits of French bravery

Marx will no doubt be writing to you about the scheme for organising from London a lithographic bureau for America.[a] But if this sort of thing is done properly, it rapidly runs into great expense here, and most of[b] the American papers are by no means sound financially. Lupus is in London and Freiligrath likewise; at the beginning of this month I, too, was there for a fortnight.[423]

Since, by all accounts, you will also be arriving here soon, it would be best for you to come to some arrangement with one or more papers or periodicals to act as correspondent, etc. That sort of thing is very profitable in London, though admittedly most of the best-paying newspapers are already provided for. Another question is what the press is like in Germany just now.

Capitano Willich continues to live in, on, and with his barracks. What do you say to our erecting a magnificent counterpart to it?

Write soon to your

F. E.

Address:
Ermen & Engels,
Manchester

First published slightly abridged in *Die Neue Zeit*, Bd. 2, Nr. 28, 1906-07 and in full in: Marx and Engels, *Works*, First Russian Edition, Vol. XXV, Moscow, 1934

Printed according to the original

Published in English in full for the first time

184

ENGELS TO MARX

IN LONDON

[Manchester,] 27 June 1851

Dear Marx,

It is very *bonasse*[b] of the good Saxon police actually to inform us themselves of what we did not previously know or could not have discovered. Bürgers' didactically dignified circular letter with the

_____
[a] See this volume, pp. 489-90. - [b] kindly

familiar *clair-obscur*[a] of its reasoning must have cost them much fruitless brain-racking [438]; they even picked out all the wrong passages for printing in bold. A pretty figure the great Windmillers [b] cut now, thrown out of their own party before the eyes of the whole world, the great Willich bracketed with Haude, Gebert and other such unknown rabble, with a certain 'Schopper' (derived from 'Schoppen') [c] whose rare services are so little known that even in *Cologne* they can't print his name correctly! So FAR ALL RIGHT. But Article 1 of the Rules bodes ill for the arrested men: 'all methods of revolutionary activity', or however it goes.[439] It removes the business from the sphere of mere prohibited association to that of high treason. To judge, by the way, from an allusion in the *Kölnische Zeitung,* I would seem to be right in supposing that the intention is to arraign the whole company in Berlin before the State tribunal which is to be brought into being specifically for this grandiose occasion.

The utter failure of the government's attempt to make a bogy out of the great Dresden disclosure augurs well for the mood of the bourgeoisie. So little terror does the red spectre now hold for the bourgeois that he refuses to listen to talk of a big communist plot and is already beginning to fear that the system of house searches will ere long be extended to himself.

Not a single paper has taken the bait and the government's frantic endeavour to discover further machinations in gymnastic societies, 'free communities' [350] and among democratically-minded master tailors proves, on the one hand, how much it is vexed by the indifference of the bourgeoisie whose curiosity it is seeking to whet, and, on the other, how little the Rules and the circular letter have led to further disclosures. It would seem that Miquel's house also was searched in vain.

Qu'y a-t-il de nouveau à Londres?[d]

Your
F. E.

First published in *Der Briefwechsel zwischen F. Engels und K. Marx,* Bd. 1, Stuttgart, 1913

Printed according to the original

Published in English for the first time

---

[a] half-light - [b] members of the London German Workers' Educational Society - [c] 'Der communistische Bund', *Kölnische Zeitung*, No. 150, 24 June 1851. Instead of 'Schapper' the paper had 'Schopper', on which Engels made a pun by deriving it from 'Schoppen'—'a pint pot'. - [d] What's new in London?

185

MARX TO JOSEPH WEYDEMEYER[435]

IN FRANKFURT AM MAIN

[London,] 27 June 1851

Dear Hans,

I am not at all sure whether I am doing the right thing in sending you a letter with Fabricius. What assurance have I that this man won't be nabbed at the border, since he is letting people here burden him with a veritable valiseful of letters?

As your proposed American plan—Engels may have already written to you about this[a]—has come to nothing, you will have no alternative but to come and reinforce us here. Something might even turn up that would enable us to collaborate—for payment, of course, *car il faut vivre.*[b]

I have now heard from a *reliable* source that betrayal and denunciation are playing a part in the arrests of our friends. I am *morally* convinced that Messrs Willich and Schapper and their good-for-nothing pack of rascally curs are directly taking part in this infamy. You will appreciate how important it is to these 'great men' *in partibus*[c] to remove such people in Germany as they believe to be directly in the way of their accession to the throne. The jackasses fail to comprehend that we regard them as jackasses and accord them at best our disdain.

Despite his respectably high-minded, broth-without-bread, non-commissioned officer's moral hypocrisy, Willich is a thoroughly common, mark well, *thoroughly common chevalier d'industrie, pillier d'estaminet*[d] and—or so I am told by a respectable philistine, though I cannot myself vouch for it—also *cardsharper.* The lad loafs around all day at the pub, a *democratic* pub, naturally, where he drinks *gratis,* bringing customers in lieu of payment and entertaining them with his stereotyped phrases about a future revolution in which the chevalier himself no longer believes, so often has he reiterated them under such widely disparate circumstances, and always with the same result. The fellow is a *parasite* of the basest kind—invariably, of course, under patriotic pretences.

---

[a] See this volume, p. 373. - [b] for one has to live - [c] *in partibus infidelium* - in parts inhabited by infidels. Here: abroad, far from the fray - [d] adventurer, pillar of the taproom

All this individual's communism amounts to is a determination to tread the primrose path, always at the public expense, in communion with other footloose chevaliers. This man's activities consist solely in gossiping and lying about us in pubs, and boasting of connections in Germany which, though non-existent, are nevertheless taken for gospel by the Central clown A. Ruge,[440] the ideological boor Heinzen and by the stagey, coquettish, theologising belletrist Kinkel, connections of which he also boasts to the French.

Apropos, while this last-named sanctimonious Adonis runs off his legs in bourgeois *cercles,* permitting himself to be fed, cosseted, etc., etc., by them, he associates secretly and illicitly with Schapper and Willich in order to keep in touch with the 'Workers' Party' as well. This lad would greatly like to be all things to all men. In every respect he bears a most striking resemblance to Frederick William IV who is nothing more than a Kinkel enthroned and is afflicted with the same rhetorical leucorrhoea.

Were you to ask me how you are to subsist here, my answer would be: follow in the footsteps of the doughty Willich. He sows not neither does he reap, and yet the heavenly Father feeds him.[a]

But now *au sérieux!* If living in Germany is becoming too dangerous for you, it might be good for you to come here. If you could remain in Germany unmolested, that would, of course, be preferable, since it's more useful to have people there than here.

Your

K. M.

Apropos, Britain's overseas trade amounts to at least $1/3$ of its entire trade—more, since the repeal of the corn duties.[270] There is, by the by, no sense at all in Mr Christ's arguments.[b] Pinto[c] has already pointed out that, if $10/10$ are necessary to something, the final $1/10$ is as important as the previous $9/10$. Granted that Britain's overseas trade amounts to only $1/4$ (which is wrong), there can be no doubt that without that, the other $3/4$ would not exist, and still less the $4/4$ which alone can produce the numeral 1.

---

[a] Matthew 6:26. - [b] The original has: Christmann. Marx refers to A. Christ, *Ueber den gegenwärtigen Stand der Frage der Schutzzölle.* - [c] I. Pinto, *Traité de la circulation et du crédit.*

The democrats have long been accustomed to miss no opportunity of compromising themselves, making themselves *ridicules,* and risking their own skins. But never has the impotence of the *infiniment petits*[a] succeeded in demonstrating itself so strikingly as in the paper which the local Central democrats—Ruge, Haug, Ronge, etc.—are bringing out. Under the presumptuous title *Der Kosmos* (or *Das Kosmos* as Freiligrath aptly calls it)[b] there appears a weekly scrawl the like of which, in its brazen and insipid insignificance, the German language—and that is saying a great deal—has never, perhaps, produced before. Not even one of little-German democratic parish magazines has ever brought forth such evil-smelling wind as this.

It would perhaps be as well if things were to remain quiet for a few years yet, so that all this 1848 democracy has time to moulder away. Untalented as our governments may be, they are veritable *lumina mundi*[c] as compared with these bumptious mediocre jackasses.

Adieu!

I am usually at the British Museum from 9 in the morning until 7 in the evening. The material I am working on is so damnably involved that, no matter how I exert myself, I shall not finish for another 6-8 weeks. There are, moreover, constant interruptions of a practical kind, inevitable in the wretched circumstances in which we are vegetating here. But for all that, for all that,[d] the thing is rapidly approaching completion. There comes a time when one has forcibly to break off. The democratic 'SIMPLETONS' to whom inspiration comes 'from above' need not, of course, exert themselves thus. Why should these people, born under a lucky star, bother their heads with economic and historical material? It's really all *so simple,* as the doughty Willich used to tell me. All so simple to these addled brains!—Ultra-simple fellows!

First published in: Marx and Engels, *Works,* First Russian Edition, Vol. XXV, Moscow, 1934

Printed according to the original

Published in English in full for the first time

---

[a] infinitely small (an expression used by P.-J. Béranger to describe the men of the Restoration in France, see present edition, Vol. 5, p. 514) - [b] Freiligrath apparently used the neutral instead of masculine gender to stress the amorphous and shallow character of this publication. - [c] lights of the world - [d] F. Freiligrath, 'Trotz alledem!'

186

ENGELS TO MARX

IN LONDON

[Manchester, about 6 July 1851]

Dear Marx,

After trailing around here for a week with my old man, I have happily sent him on his way again and today am at last able to send you the enclosed POST OFFICE ORDER for 5 pounds. On the whole I can declare myself satisfied with the results of my encounter with the old man. He will need me here for three years at least, and I have entered into no long-term obligations, not even for 3 years, nor was I asked for any, either with regard to my writing, or to my staying here in case of a revolution.

This last would appear to be far from his mind, so secure do these people now feel! On the other hand, I stipulated at the very start what my expense and entertainment allowance was to be—approx. £200 a year, which was agreed without over-much difficulty. With such a salary, all should be well, and if there are no ructions before the next balance sheet and if business prospers here, he'll have quite a different bill to foot—even this year I'll exceed the two hundred pounds by far. Moreover, he has acquainted me with every aspect of his business, both here and over there and, since business has been very good and he is now more than twice as wealthy as he was in 1837, it goes without saying that I shan't be needlessly scrupulous.

Besides, the old man is artful enough, too. His plan, which, however, can only be executed very gradually and laboriously and, indeed, is unlikely to go through on account of the trouble with the Ermens, is that Peter Ermen should be moved to Liverpool, as he himself wishes, and that I should be left solely responsible for the office here—G. Ermen would then look after the mill. Thus I would be completely tied down. I, of course, feigned modesty, claiming that this was beyond my capabilities. Had my old man stayed here a few days longer, however, we'd have been at each other's throats; good fortune seems to upset the chap; he gets above himself, reverts to his old schoolmasterly habits and becomes provocative. What's more, he's so stupid and tactless that, on the last day of his visit, for example, he sought to take advantage of the presence of one of the Ermens, before whom he thought I would keep my mouth shut and behave myself, to indulge himself at my expense by intoning a dithyramb in praise of Prussia's institutions. A word or two and a furious look were, of course, enough to bring him back to heel, but also just enough to place us suddenly on a less cordial footing—just at the moment of parting—and I can be quite sure that, one way or another, he will seek to avenge himself for this CHECK. *Nous allons voir.*[a] So long as the affair has no immediate, practical repercussions, i.e. on my financial situation, a dispassionate business relationship is obviously preferable to any kind of emotional humbug.

Ceci entre nous.[b]

The *Kölner Zeitung* hasn't been seen here since the beginning of July, perhaps because the subscription has been allowed to lapse, so I don't know whether anything further has happened. If you have any news, do pass it on to me. I shall at long last be able to start working properly again, now that the interruptions caused by the Exhibition[c] are more or less over and the Athenaeum catalogue[d] is finally complete. It is also my intention to move out into the country soon, so that I shall be completely undisturbed. Since I shan't see my old man within the year, I can arrange things to suit myself and use the expense allowance largely for other purposes.

Give my regards to your wife and write soon,

Your
F. E.

First published abridged in *Der Briefwechsel zwischen F. Engels und K. Marx,* Bd. 1, Stuttgart, 1913 and in full in *MEGA,* Abt. III, Bd. 1, 1929

Printed according to the original

Published in English for the first time

---

a We shall see. - b This between ourselves. - c the Great Exhibition in London in 1851 - d See this volume, p. 316.

14*

187

ENGELS TO ERNST DRONKE

IN GENEVA

Manchester, 9 July 1851

Dear Dronke,

You have heard nothing from us for some considerable time—firstly because, since Galeer's death, we haven't had any address, and then because, after you had given us Schuster's address, news reached us that you yourself would soon be coming to England. But, since Lupus has now been in London for almost a month and we have heard nothing from you, we can only suppose that you will be remaining where you are for the time being.

You will have been informed of the happenings in London last autumn.[441] What you did not hear from this quarter you will have seen in the documents published since then. So to put you *au fait* I need only tell you about a few of the things that have happened in the meantime.

As I have been stuck here in Manchester since Nov. '50 and as Marx speaks little English, our connection with Harney and the Chartists was making little or no headway. This was exploited by Schapper, Willich, L. Blanc, Barthélemy, etc.,—in short, the whole Franco-German caboodle, displeased on the one hand with us and on the other with the Ledru-Mazzini Committee[442]—to get Harney involved in a banquet planned for 24 February; in this they succeeded. During that banquet the following curious things happened:

1. Two of our people who were present, one of them Schramm,[a] were thrown out by the German refugee rabble—the thing took a serious turn and legal proceedings might have ensued had we not been able to settle it well enough to satisfy the injured parties; on the other hand it led—momentarily—to somewhat strained relations with Harney, who showed weakness on that occasion. Jones, however, a fellow quite unlike Harney, is wholly on our side and is at present expounding the *Manifesto*[b] to the English.

---

[a] Conrad Schramm and Wilhelm Pieper - [b] K. Marx and F. Engels, *Manifesto of the Communist Party.*

2. Mr Willich, for want of an address from Germany, read out one from Switzerland, beneath which was *your* signature among others. By what deception or forgery your name found its way onto such a document we here cannot of course know; at all events, you must duly investigate the matter, and let us have the necessary information. The address, by the way, is printed in the *compte rendu*[a] of the banquet with your name under it, and you can imagine the glee occasion by the name of someone from the *Neue Rheinische Zeitung* appearing at its foot.

3. The business of Blanqui's toast.[382] As a professed Blanquist, Barthélemy transmitted a request to Blanqui for a toast and Blanqui obliged with a splendid attack on the entire prov. government, Blanc and Co. included. Thunderstruck, Barthélemy laid it before the Committee, who resolved to suppress it. Blanqui, however, knew his men, the toast was published in the Paris papers[b] to coincide with the banquet and quite spoiled the dramatic effect. That pious little swindler, L. Blanc, now asserted in *The Times,* as did the Committee—Willich, Schapper, L. Blanc, Barthélemy, Vidil, etc.,—in the *Patrie,* that they knew nothing whatever about the toast.[c] The *Patrie,* however, added the comment that, in reply to their inquiries, Blanqui's brother-in-law, Antoine, had told them he had sent the toast to Mr Barthélemy and was in possession of an acknowledgment from the latter—one of the co-signatories of the statement. Barthélemy thereupon declared that this was so, that he accepted full responsibility, had lied, had received the toast but, in the interests of concord, had suppressed it.[d] Unfortunately, however, the ex-*capitaine de dragons* Vidil simultaneously declared that he wished to confess everything: the toast had been submitted by Barthélemy to the Committee and suppressed by a resolution of the latter.[e] Can one imagine a more horrid fiasco for the whole band? We translated the toast into German[f] and had 30,000 copies distributed in Germany and England.

During the November mobilisation [443] Willich, transported to the height of ecstasy by bogus letters, wanted to revolutionise the

---

[a] account - [b] 'Toste envoyé par le citoyen L. A. Blanqui à la commission près les réfugiés de Londres, pour le banquet anniversaire du 24 février', *La Patrie,* No. 58, 27 February 1851. - [c] L. Blanc, 'To the Editor of *The Times*', *The Times,* No. 20741, 5 March 1851; ['La déclaration de la commission du Banquet des Egaux du 1 mars 1851'], *La Patrie,* No. 66, 7 March 1851. - [d] E. Barthélemy, 'Au rédacteur en chef du journal *La Patrie*', *La Patrie,* No. 71, 12 March 1851. - [e] J. Vidil, ['Letter to the editors of *La Patrie*,] *La Patrie,* No. 69, 10 March 1851. - [f] K. Marx and F. Engels, 'Introduction to the Leaflet of L. A. Blanqui's Toast Sent to the Refugee Committee'.

world with the Prussian *Landwehr*.[385] We have in our hands some exceedingly comical documents and revolutionary plans relating to this.[a] They will be put to use in due course. First and foremost, all 'quill-pushing elements' were to be extirpated, root and branch, and the dictatorship of the mobilised Eifel peasants proclaimed. *Malheureusement il n'en fut rien.*[b]

Since then the associated great men, amidst mutual assurances of power and immortality, have been fruitlessly attempting to gain a footing somewhere. All in vain. And they have the gratification of knowing that, of all the house searches and arrests that have taken place in Germany, not one has been due to connections with themselves.

We, on the other hand, have the satisfaction of being rid of the entire loud-mouthed, muddle-headed, impotent émigré rabble in London, and of being at long last able to work again undisturbed. The innumerable private iniquities of that gang need not concern us. We have always been superior to the riff-raff and, in any serious movement, have dominated them; but we have, mean-while, learnt an enormous amount from our experiences since 1848, and have made good use of the lull since 1850 to resume our swotting. If anything should blow up again, the advantage we shall have over them will this time be of quite a different order, and in fields, furthermore, of which they have small inkling. Apart from all that, we have the enormous advantage that, unlike us, they are place-seekers to a man. It is beyond comprehension that there should still be jackasses whose supreme ambition, after the experiences they have been through, is to join some government or other, *le lendemain même de la première insurrection victorieuse*[c]—as they call revolution—only to be spurned or thrown out in disgrace 4 weeks later, as were Blanc and Flocon in 1848! And a Schapper-Gebert-Meyen-Haude-Willich government to boot! Alas, the poor devils will never achieve this satisfaction; they will, alas, revert to being mere appendages and, as such, may continue to sow confusion in the small towns and among the peasantry.

What are you actually doing in Geneva? They say you are a husband and a father, and that you are also on very friendly terms with Moses[d]—with an eye to Mrs Moses.[e] Others have it that all this is sheer calumny but—at a distance of 10 degrees of latitude—that would be difficult to judge. Freiligrath, too, is in London and is bringing out a new volume of poetry. Weerth is in

---

[a] See this volume, p. 320. - [b] Unfortunately, nothing came of it. - [c] on the very morrow of the first victorious insurrection - [d] Hess - [e] Sibylle Hess

Hamburg and, like myself, is writing business letters pending the next set-to. He brought nothing back from his travels in Spain, not even the clap. He is, by the way, coming to London this month. Red Wolff[a] has gone through various phases of being an Irishman, a worthy bourgeois, a madman and other interesting states, and has completely abandoned *Schnaps* in favour of HALF-AND-HALF. *Père* Marx goes daily to the library and is adding amazingly to his knowledge—but also to his family. Finally, as to myself, I drink rum and water, swot and spend my time 'twixt TWIST and tedium. So much for the Personal Column.

Since we over here have been compelled by the arrests in Germany to provide in many respects for the re-establishment of contacts, and to resume responsibility for much of the work we had delegated, it is essential that you write and tell us as soon as possible how things are in Switzerland. Reply at once, therefore, and should you want further elucidation, let us know upon what points. Write to me—CARE OF MESSRS Ermen & Engels, Manchester—via Calais.

Your
F. Engels

First published in: Marx and Engels, *Works,* First Russian Edition, Vol. XXV, Moscow, 1934

Printed according to the original

Published in English for the first time

188

MARX TO ENGELS [220]

IN MANCHESTER

[London,] 13 July 1851
28 Dean Street, Soho

Dear Engels,

I have put off writing from day to day so as to send you complete the documents communicated below. But as they won't be complete for several days, I am writing today so as not to keep you waiting any longer for an answer.

---

[a] Ferdinand Wolff

D'abord.[a] From your letter it would seem that, during your old man's visit to Manchester, you did not hear that a second document had appeared in the *Kölnische Zeitung* under the heading 'Der Bund der Kommunisten'.[b] This was the piece we wrote jointly, 'Ansprache an den Bund'[c]—*au fond,*[d] nothing less than a plan of campaign against democracy. From one point of view its publication was desirable, unlike Bürgers' document,[438] of which the form was absurd, *plus ou moins,*[e] and the content not very reassuring. On the other hand, certain passages will make the present prisoners' position more difficult.

From Louis Schulz[f] in Cologne I have heard that Bürgers writes most dolefully from Dresden. On the other hand it is generally believed in Cologne that Daniels will be released, since there is nothing against him, and all the wailers[300] in the Holy City have reacted in his favour. Naturally they consider him to be incapable of such 'foolery'.

Miquel has written from Göttingen. Has been subjected to several house searches. Nothing was found. Wasn't locked up. Five new emissaries—GENTLEMEN—have left Göttingen for Berlin, etc. The persecution of the Jews[437] has, of course, stimulated both zeal and interest.

The funniest thing is that that fatuous sheet, the Augsburg *Allgemeine Zeitung,* attributes paternity of our document to Messrs Mazzini and Ruge, beats its breast over and over again and can find no better way of expressing its shock at the enormity than by crying at intervals, 'Madness! Madness! Madness!'[g]

The *Trier'sche Zeitung*—i.e. K. Grün—has, of course, climbed onto its high horse and used the first document to prove the material, and the second, the 'intellectual' impotence of the party.[h] Needless to say, neither the stock phrases of the friends of light[350] nor the most extreme 'anarchist' catch-words are wanting. Everything to be done from above! Police state! All dissenters literally to be proscribed and expelled. *Mon Dieu!* That really is the limit.

Now for the local storms—which customarily take place in a tea-cup.

First. Father Willich has bolted from the barracks—the demise

---

a First of all. - b 'Der Communisten-Bund', *Kölnische Zeitung,* No. 156, 1 July 1851, supplement. - c K. Marx and F. Engels, 'Address of the Central Authority to the League', March 1850. - d basically - e more or less - f The original has: Schüler. - g 'Der Communistenbund', *Allgemeine Zeitung,* No. 186, 5 July 1851, supplement. - h 'Eine Polizei-Ente?', *Trier'sche Zeitung,* No. 158, 6 July 1851.

of which, it seems, has been decided—and has become deeply involved in squabbles with most of his bodyguard.

Second. The great Fickler has arrived here. A few days before he came to England he was in Strassburg with Lupus. Liebknecht has long been an intimate of his. Both, therefore, went to see him on 5 July. He chatted away most affably, spoke of the need for reconciling the parties, etc. Then they were joined by the great A. Goegg. He called Willich a 'mere fantasist', Schapper a 'disgusting character'—having several times heard the fellows blustering in the Windmill,[331] he had disassociated himself from them and hadn't darkened their door again. Fickler and Goegg inveighed with exceptional vigour against the great Kinkel, who here plays the role of happy parvenu, thus bringing down on his head the ire of the other great men. Ruge, on the other hand, was regarded as a kind of *lumen*.[a]

Fickler asked for my address and Lupus and Liebknecht departed, duped by the worthies and their striving for 'concord'.

A few days later Freiligrath sent me the following letter which he had received:

4 Brunswick Place, North Brighton,
4 July 1851

Dear Freiligrath,

We are planning a kind of club or society which does away with the privacy of such organisations and excludes no one from the revolutionary social democratic party save him who desires to be exclusive or is debarred by his own character and antecedents.

Fickler, Goegg, Sigel, Ronge and Ruge are promoting the affair and I have undertaken to inform you, and to invite you if, as I suppose, you are interested, to a meeting to be held for this purpose on 14 July (Monday week) at 11 in the morning at *Fickler's* lodgings, 26 York Buildings, which form part of New Road[b] at the lower end of Baker Street. We have invited about 24 people whom we know to be reliable and to have remained true. At present we know of no more.

I would have liked to talk to you. If the plan comes off, this will be possible in any case. Even if you are not going to remain in London, you still ought to come.

With regards and a handshake.

Your
A. Ruge

Qu'en dis-tu?[c]

Freiligrath has made the great mistake of not sending off his answer until yesterday, 12 July, so that Ruge won't even get it

---

[a] luminary - [b] Now Marylebone Road - [c] What do you make of that?

before leaving Brighton for London. Freiligrath was altogether too lackadaisical over the matter. *Mais enfin chacun a sa manière d'agir.*[a] Lupus, to whom I communicated the letter, immediately wrote to Fickler:

10 July 1851

Citizen Fickler,

On the 5th of this month Liebknecht and I came to visit you. From the manner in which you addressed us, I could not possibly have inferred that only the previous day the following letter had been sent to Freiligrath. (The above letter follows.)

If, on the 5th of this month, I had so much as remotely suspected that such a connection existed between yourself and A. Ruge, that fatuous, insolent, rapscallion, I would certainly not have set foot inside your lodgings.

Since I perceive from the above, however, that you consort with a person *'who is debarred by his own character and antecedents'* (e.g. by his own cowardly flight from Berlin, etc.) from any truly revolutionary party, and who has already been sent to coventry by the whole communist party in Germany, I would hereby inform you that I neither will nor can have anything to do with people who move so intimately within the orbit of an individual such as Ruge.

W. Wolff

3 Broad Street, Golden Square

P.S. You can make whatever use you like of this note. I for my part shall bring it to the notice of my comrades in the party.

The above

To this Lupus received the following answer:

London, 11 July 1851

Dear Citizen Wolff,

So feeble indeed are my powers of prescience that they never remotely led me to fear the loss of your goodwill and of your company, should I associate with that 'rapscallion' Ruge.—More, I was not even aware of being subject in this respect to the tutelage of one section of the party and to police rule by the men of the future. It is to this want of percipience as also to what I have learned in twenty years of political activity, namely that there is not *one* political party able to avoid co-operating with rapscallions—that I owe my resolve to offer my hand to any qualified man desirous of treading the same revolutionary path as myself;—whether he goes no more than half way to the goal I have set myself; —whether he accompanies me all the way there, or whether he continues beyond it.

---

[a] But after all, everyone has his own way of doing things.

Anathemas, whether political or religious, are anachronisms, even if emanating from Emperor or Pope;—how infinitely more ridiculous do they appear when hurled by the kinglets and popelets of a party which, to judge by public avowals, is as inconsistent as your own, and which today transforms into 'rapscallions' those in its own midst to whom only yesterday it accorded almost divine honours!

In the course of my life I have encountered disproportionately more 'rapscallions' than upright people, and have been disproportionately less deceived by the former than by the latter. I therefore waste no time in drawing distinctions of this kind, but rather look for those qualities which may be put to use in the most diverse ways.

Should you desire, therefore, together with Marx and Liebknecht—whom I would beg you to inform—to take part in the said 'meeting', I hereby invite you to it, only pointing out that it will be no more than a preliminary discussion and that the chief disadvantage for you, as for half the company in general, will probably be the absence of accommodation for the grosser portions of the anatomy—a fact which, however, should contribute materially to expediting the proceedings.

With warm regards

Yours
Fickler, etc.

The most comical thing about the whole business is and will remain the unending efforts of Ruge and his clique to thrust themselves on the public by constantly changing the combination. If it doesn't work as ABCDEF, it will assuredly do so as FEDCBA. Just try calculating how many variations and permutations of this kind are possible. Has there ever been a more impotent, ludicrously pretentious clique of barren jackasses?

Your
K. M.

Apropos, have received the 5 pounds. They arrived like a *deus ex machina*,[a] for CIRCUMSTANCES are ''orrible', and it's hard to see how to extricate oneself. Write *direct* to Klose (6 Upper Rupert Street, NEAR Princes Street, Soho), since the jackass will otherwise think that the letter he addressed to you, the one about the £10, remember? hasn't reached you.

First published in *Der Briefwechsel zwischen F. Engels und K. Marx,* Bd. 1, Stuttgart, 1913

Printed according to the original

Published in English in full for the first time

---

[a] a god from the machine (by which in ancient theatre gods were shown in the air); a power or an event that comes in the nick of time to solve difficulty.

189

MARX TO ENGELS

IN MANCHESTER

[London, about 17 July 1851]
28 Dean Street, Soho

Dear Engels,

Be so kind as to post enclosed letter for Schulz[444] in Manchester without delay.

Herewith you will find Freiligrath's letter to Ruge, which I would ask you to return, and Bermbach's letter to me. Also a letter from Miquel.

A certain 'Ulmer', a shoemaker, fled from Cologne at the time of the recent house searches. He gave a Straubinger[86] at Schärttner's a letter to take to his relations. Immediately afterwards this Straubinger was caught with the letter at the Dutch border. The only people to be compromised by this are those who set him free. So well organised are the police at the Schärttner place.

Weydemeyer has got across the border. We are expecting him here.

That wretched pair, Heinzen and Ruge, claim to have received all kinds of stupid tittle-tattle about the events in Cologne, allegedly from Germany. To judge by the total inaccuracy of the contents they are acting as their own correspondents.

Let me hear from you soon.

Your
K. M.

P.S. It has just occurred to me that it would be better if you were to send the letter to Bermbach yourself. On the outside namely: Louis Schulz, 2 Schildergasse, Cologne. Inside, the sealed letter to Bermbach. Of course you will see to it that the inside address is quite invisible, and seal the letter as a merchant does.

First published in *Der Briefwechsel zwischen F. Engels und K. Marx*, Bd. 1, Stuttgart, 1913

Printed according to the original

Published in English for the first time

190

ENGELS TO MARX [220]

IN LONDON

Manchester, 17 July 1851

Dear Marx,

I'll write to Klose this very day [445]—I'm glad you included his address, which I hadn't got.

That you're in a pretty tight corner, I can readily conceive, and this is all the more vexatious as I shan't be able to lay my hands on another centime until the beginning of next month. If you can't wait so long, could it not be arranged for Weerth to advance you something until then? I can repay £5 on 1 August, and another £5 on 1 September, and that is as safe as cash.

The newspaper subscriptions here are at last in order again, and thus I have at last set eyes on our old document[a] in the *Kölnische Zeitung*. By the way, in an otherwise apparently well-informed article entitled 'Dresden', the Augsburg paper relates that, as a result of browbeating during interrogation, Nothjung eventually made the most sweeping confessions.[b] However, I think it more than probable that skilled interrogators can soon corner him and get him embroiled in the wildest contradictions. A Prussian official is said to have gone there to squeeze still more out of him. Apparently the King of Hanover[c] has refused to engage in persecution in his domains, at least in the crude manner usual in Prussia, Hamburg, etc., etc. Miquel's letter seems to bear this out. As you know, Martens has been arrested in Hamburg.[446] Incidentally, nowhere has the stupidity of the Prussians been more in evidence than during the house search at Carl am Rhein's, who was also suspected of belonging to the Communist League, and was found to have only letters from Raveaux!

The only passage in the old document that could harm the arrested men is the one about 'excesses',[447] all the rest is directed against the democrats and would aggravate their position only if they were to appear before a semi-democratic jury; but it seems

---

[a] K. Marx and F. Engels, 'Address of the Central Authority to the League, March 1850'. - [b] 'Noch umfassendere Haussuchungen in Aussicht. Umfassende Geständnisse des Schneiders Nothjung', *Allgemeine Zeitung*, No. 189, 8 July 1851 (a report from Leipzig with reference to the *Dresdner Journal und Anzeiger*). - [c] Ernst August

likely that, if they come before a jury at all, it will be a
hand-picked special, or federal, jury. And even these matters had
been largely restated in the Bürgers document,[438] which was
seized at the very start. In all other respects, however, it is of
enormous advantage that the thing has been published and has
appeared in all the newspapers. It will tremendously encourage
the mute, isolated groups of aspiring communists of which one
knows nothing and which, to judge by past experience, must exist
all over Germany, and even the article in the Augsburg paper
betrays that the thing has affected it in quite a different way from
the first disclosures. Its arrangement of the material shows that it
has understood the 'madness' only too well—*en effet il n'y avait pas
moyen de s'y méprendre.*[a]

Moreover, so madly and recklessly is feudal reaction galloping
into the fray that the bogy that had been raised is not having the
slightest effect on the bourgeoisie. It is too amusing to see how the
Kölnische Zeitung daily preaches that *il faut passer par la mer rouge*[b]
and admits all the mistakes made by the Constitutionalists of 1848.
But in truth, with a Kleist-Retzow as Oberpräsident in Coblenz
and with the impertinent *Kreuz-Zeitung's*[c] flat jokes and doggerel
becoming ever more insulting, what can the cultured and sober
constitutional opposition do? It's a pity we don't have the
Kreuz-Zeitung over here. I see sundry excerpts from it. You can
have no conception of the excessively vulgar, guttersnipish,
cretinously Prussian manner in which that rag is now belabouring
the decent, well-to-do and respectable constitutional bigwigs. If
fellows such as Beckerath and Co. possessed even so much as an
ounce of self-respect and resilience, they would be bound to
prefer the maltreatment and abuse of a *Père Duchesne,* in the rude
Rhenish manner and the entire *terreur rouge,*[d] to the treatment they
have to endure daily at the hands of the Junkers and the
Kreuz-Zeitung.

> Then spake the donkey: 'Furthermore
> Wesel has a councillor.
> And were I not a moke,' quoth he,
> 'A Wesel councillor I'd be'[e]

—such are the witty verses with which the *Kreuz-Zeitung* is now
bespattering each of the great constitutional figures *seriatim* and

---

[a] indeed, there could be no mistake about it - [b] the Red Sea must be
crossed (see Exodus 13:18; 15:22). - [c] *Neue Preussische Zeitung* - [d] red terror -
[e] 'Kreistags-Lieder, II', *Neue Preussische Zeitung,* No. 137, 17 June 1851. (In the
original the rhyme is based on the words 'Esel' (donkey) and 'Wesel', the name of the
councillor.)

the fellows meekly put up with it. But it serves these dogs right, who once decried the best articles in the *Neue Rheinische Zeitung* as 'vulgar abuse', to have the difference knocked into their cowardly skulls. They will look back nostalgically to what was, by comparison, the infinitely Attic raillery of the *N.Rh.Z.*

The Willich business[a] is like a ray of sunshine on a cloudy day. So the 'most popular of men' has reached the zenith of his popularity and may now, as unrecognised saviour of humanity, console himself for the world's ingratitude with a pot of beer and Schapper's friendship. I can imagine his distress, now that the army of the future, the 'nucleus' round which the whole of Europe was to gather, has been destroyed. Where will the noble fellow find his new 'men of principle'?

I can't quite make sense of the Fickler business.[b] Why did Lupus go straight to Fickler instead of first getting Liebknecht to take soundings, *puisque celui-ce n'aurait compromis que lui-même*[c]? It looks as though they were trying to win Fickler over. And then, after Lupus had been there, his letter was altogether too brutal. Either it was not worth taking any trouble at all with Fickler, or—after Ruge had been set up as a kind of *lumen*[d] during the actual conversation that took place between Fickler and Goegg—it would have been enough to break with him without doing it so thoroughly and brutally. It was a mean trick on Fickler's part, *c'est clair,*[e] but should it not have been assumed from the outset that South German worthies are capable of such things? And he had certainly made no secret of his respect for Ruge. Ruge's importunity is, of course, unspeakable. But these ever new variations are in themselves proof enough that not one of them can have any appeal whatsoever, and that the '*comité allemand*'[f] to which Mazzini sends his Roman Epistles[g] is still no more than a figment of Ruge's imagination.

See to it that Weerth comes here, and write again soon.

Your
F. E.

First published in *Der Briefwechsel zwischen F. Engels und K. Marx,* Bd. 1, Stuttgart, 1913

Printed according to the original

Published in English in full for the first time

---

[a] See this volume, p. 385. - [b] ibid. - [c] since the latter would have compromised no one but himself - [d] luminary - [e] that's clear - [f] the German Committee (i.e. the Committee for German Affairs) - [g] An ironical comparison of Mazzini's appeal to the Epistle of Paul the Apostle to the Romans (New Testament).

191

ENGELS TO MARX[448]

IN LONDON

[Manchester, about 20 July 1851]

Dear Marx,

I return the documents herewith. I like the letter from Miquel. The fellow does at least think, and would assuredly turn out very well if he were to spend some time abroad. His fears concerning the ill-effects of our document,[a] now published, on the democrats are without doubt perfectly correct as regards his own district; this primitive, Lower Saxon, middle peasant democracy, whose arse the *Kölnische Zeitung* has recently been licking and to whom it has offered an alliance, is just what one might expect and is greatly inferior to the philistine democracy of the larger towns by which, after all, it is dominated. And this humdrum, petty-bourgeois democracy, although obviously much piqued by the document, is itself so pinched and oppressed that it is far more likely, in common with the big bourgeoisie, to come round to the necessity of *passer par la mer rouge.*[b] The fellows will increasingly resign themselves to the need for a short reign of terror by the proletariat—it can't, of course, last very long, for so nonsensical, indeed, is the actual tenor of the document that there can be no question of permanent rule by such people or of the eventual implementation of such principles! On the other hand the Hanoverian big and middle peasant, who has nothing but his land, and whose house, farm, barn, etc., are exposed, with the prospective ruin of all the assurance companies, to every kind of peril, and who in any case, since the accession of Ernst August, has tasted all the sweets of lawful resistance—this STURDY German YEOMAN will take good care not to enter the Red Sea any sooner than he has to.

According to Bermbach's letter, the traitor was Haupt—which I cannot believe.[449] The business must in any case be investigated. It

---

[a] K. Marx and F. Engels, 'Address of the Central Authority to the League, March 1850'. - [b] crossing the Red Sea (see Exodus 13:18; 15:22)

may of course seem suspicious that Haupt, at least so far as I know, is still free. The possibility of travelling to Hamburg from Göttingen or Cologne cannot be entertained. What sort of explanation will emerge, and when, from the record of the trial or from the proceedings is impossible to say. *S'il y a trahison*,[a] it must not be forgotten, and it would be most desirable, given the opportunity, were an example to be made.

I hope that Daniels will be released soon, *après tout c'est la seule tête politique, qu'il y ait dans Cologne*[b] and, despite surveillance by the police, he would still be in a position to keep the business on the right track.

To come back to the effect of our document on the democrats: Miquel should not forget that we have continuously and uninterruptedly harried the gentry in writings which were, after all, more or less party manifestos. Why, then, the present outcry about a programme that merely sums up in a very calm and, above all, quite impersonal manner, what has already long been in print? Did our disciples on the continent, then, deny us? Did they involve themselves more deeply with the democrats than party policy and party honour permitted? If it was because of freedom from contradiction that the democrats shouted in such revolutionary tones, who was it that freed them from contradiction? Not we, to be sure, but in all likelihood the German communists in Germany. And there, it would seem, lies the snag. Any democrat with a modicum of intelligence must have known from the start what was to be expected of our party—the document cannot have taught him much that was new. In so far as they allied themselves *pro tempore* with the communists, they were fully *au fait* with the conditions and duration of the alliance, and no one but Hanoverian middle peasants and lawyers could have ever believed that the communists had, after 1850, turned away from the principles and the policy of the *Neue Rheinische Zeitung*. The thought certainly never occurred to Waldeck and Jacoby. Anyhow, in the long run publications of this kind can have no effect either on the 'nature of things' or on the 'concept of relation', to use Stirner's expressions,[c] and the democrats will soon be in full cry again, wire-pulling as busily as ever and proceeding hand in hand with the communists. And we have long known that, on the *lendemain*[d] of the movement, the fellows are bound to

---

[a] If there is treason - [b] after all, he's the only political brain in Cologne - [c] See M. Stirner, *Der Einzige und sein Eigenthum* - [d] morrow

play us some dirty tricks. No amount of diplomacy will prevent this.

On the other hand, I am delighted that, as I anticipated, small communist groups are being formed everywhere on the basis of the *Manifesto*.[a] This is just what we lacked, the General Staff having hitherto been so weak. There'll never be any shortage of rank and file when it comes to the point, but it is agreeable indeed to have in prospect a General Staff not consisting of Straubinger[86] elements, and admitting of a wider selection of men with a modicum of education than does the existing staff of 25. It would be a good idea to issue a general recommendation to carry out propaganda among office workers everywhere. In the event of having to set up an administration, such fellows would be indispensable—they are accustomed to hard work and intelligible book-keeping, and commerce is the only practical school for reliable clerks. Our jurists, etc., are no good for that. Clerks for book-keeping and accounts, talented, well-educated men for preparing dispatches, letters, and documents, *voilà ce qu'il faut*.[b] I could organise an administrative office infinitely more simply, practically and more conveniently with 6 office workers than with 60 government advisers and financial experts. The latter cannot even write legibly, and make such a mess of one's books that the devil himself couldn't make head or tail of them. Since we are increasingly obliged to prepare for this eventuality, the matter is not without importance. Besides, these office workers, being accustomed to sustained mechanical activity, are less exacting, more easily kept from loafing about, and easier to get rid of in case of inefficiency.

The letter to Cologne has gone off—all nicely taken care of[c]; if it doesn't arrive safely, I don't know why. Otherwise Schulz's address isn't to be recommended—ex-co-publisher[d]!

First published in *Der Briefwechsel zwischen F. Engels und K. Marx*, Bd. 1, Stuttgart, 1913

Printed according to the original

---

[a] K. Marx and F. Engels, *Manifesto of the Communist Party*.- [b] that's what is needed - [c] See this volume, p. 388. - [d] Schulz was responsible editor of the *Neue Rheinische Zeitung* at one time.

192

ENGELS TO MARX

IN LONDON

[Manchester,] 30 July 1851

Dear Marx,

I am surprised not to have heard from you for a fortnight.

Our predictions in the last *Revue* of an enormous expansion in ocean-going steam shipping are already being borne out.[a] Apart from several small lines, there are now two new, large and highly important lines in operation: 1. the screw-vessels from Liverpool to Philadelphia—every fortnight—4 vessels in the line; 2. the steamers between Liverpool, Rio de Janeiro and Valparaiso, etc., every 7 weeks, 4 vessels in the line. Furthermore, in a month or two there will be regular overland journeys to California—New York, to San Juan, from there by steamer to Lake Nicaragua—overland to Léon, thence direct to San Francisco; the journey to California cut by a week at least.

Next month a train will be running between London and Aberdeen—550 English miles, or 8 degrees of latitude, in one day.

One can now travel from Leeds to London and back for five shillings with one railway company and four and sixpence with another. Next Saturday the fares are going to be reduced here as well. If they get as low as that, I shall come to London at least once a fortnight.

Provided nothing untoward happens within the next 6 weeks, this year's cotton crop will amount to 3,000,000 bales or 1,200 million to 1,350 million lbs in weight. *Jamais on n'a vu la plante aussi florissante.*[b] At the same time symptoms of declining trade: East India is overstocked and is crying out for a STOPPAGE of imports of cotton goods, in this country the market for yarn and cloth still upset by fluctuating cotton prices—if the CRASH in the market coincides with such a gigantic crop, things will be cheery indeed. Peter Ermen

---

[a] K. Marx and F. Engels, 'Review, May to October 1850'. - [b] Never has the plant appeared more flourishing.

is already fouling his breeches at the very thought of it, and the little tree-frog's a pretty good barometer.

Voilà[a] the industrial potpourri for today.

Your
F. E.

First published in *Der Briefwechsel zwischen F. Engels und K. Marx,* Bd. 1, Stuttgart, 1913

Printed according to the original

Published in English for the first time

193

MARX TO ENGELS[450]

IN MANCHESTER

[London,] 31 July 1851
28 Dean Street, Soho

Dear Engels,

I have just received your letter which opens up very pleasing prospects of a trade crisis.

I haven't written for about a fortnight because during such time as I haven't spent at the library, I've been harried from pillar to post and hence, despite the best will in the world, have constantly been deflected from writing.

After I'd been put off from week to week—at first, from month to month—by the two Bambergers, father and son,[b] with the promise that they'd discount a bill for me, after I had at length been summoned to the Jew's place for that purpose last Monday,[c] and had actually brought the STAMPED PAPER with me, the younger one explained that the old one, who was also present, could not ect., etc.

It was highly regrettable that I couldn't give those two Jews a box on the ears for such infamous stalling and wasting of time and for putting me in a *fausse*[d] position vis-à-vis other people.

Incidentally, I have Mr Conrad Schramm to thank, if not in *fact*, then in *principle*, for my having been bamboozled, truly *à la*

---

a there's - b Simon and Louis Bamberger - c 28 July 1851 - d false

Sancho, first for months on end, and then again for the past 6 weeks.

As you know, that individual left for Paris four or five weeks ago. In their usual fashion, our precious friends here—e.g. that booby Hain—have only just divulged what they have long known about the blackguard. But I am now forbidding them to raise an 'outcry', as it could only do more harm than good. Well, one evening—I don't know whether I've written to you about this before—I was told by Mr Schramm that he intended to leave in 2×24 hours. I therefore decided to take the necessary steps regarding League[a] documents and other papers still in Mr Conrad's possession. That same evening I learned through Liebknecht that Mr Conrad refused to hand over these documents, but had given them to Mr Louis Bamberger under sealed cover. And what made rapid action even more necessary was my discovery, upon emerging from the Museum[b] the *following* day, that Mr Vagabond wasn't leaving in 2×24 hours,but actually within the first 24 hours, i.e. at 2 o'clock the following morning. The precious Conrad had asked for a private rendezvous with me that evening, but I thwarted him by taking Lupus, Liebknecht and Pieper with me. Hardly had we SETTLED down in an INSULATED pub, when I called on Mr Conrad to account for his doings over the documents, etc. As always when he makes a *faux pas*,[c] the fellow flew off the handle, declaring that he wouldn't hand over the documents since *he* needed them to vindicate himself, and other inanities. He was, he said, as much the League as you and me, he too was capable of deeds of deliverance. He had no idea, he went on, whether or not I was head of the district in London. Then Stirnerisms about his uniqueness in the party.[d] Some of the others, particularly Lupus, flared up; he threatened to make off, shouted, raved—all *connu*.[e] Once again I quelled the tumult, and since I know how to handle the lad, and no purpose could be served by a rumpus, the point being to get hold of the documents and that without delay—I succeeded with threats and smooth talk in persuading Mr Conrad to give me a note for Bamberger instructing the latter to hand over the sealed package to me.

This I obtained the following day. It contained everything, even including your and my statement against A. Ruge,[f] which the precious Conrad had not after all sent to the *Staatszeitung*,

[a] the Communist League - [b] the British Museum - [c] false move - [d] A pun on M. Stirner's *Der Einzige und sein Eigenthum* - [e] familiar stuff - [f] K. Marx and F. Engels, 'Statement, 27 January 1851'.

probably because he had told his brother [a] so many lies that he was afraid of any—public—explanation.

At the same time this blackguard—thinking to further his own business thereby—had warned the Bambergers against me, telling them that I had exhausted the last of my credit to meet the last bill etc., etc. In general he has intrigued against and calumniated us, etc., in the meanest fashion.

Now—all this being a *fait accompli*—we mustn't, as the boobies here wanted to do and in fact did, cry out in self-righteous indignation, but rather let the vagabond continue for a while to believe he's still connected with us, until such time as we have the power and the opportunity to dispose of the fellow, *d'une manière ou de l'autre*.[b] If we were in any way to confront him with our knowledge of his dishonourable scoundrelly conduct, he might at this moment constitute a real danger to our German comrades.

You will believe, by the by, without my insisting, that I am damned sick of my situation. I've written to America to find out whether there's any possibility of setting up, in collaboration with Lupus, as correspondent here for a couple of dozen of journals. It is IMPOSSIBLE to go on living like this.

As to the negotiations with Ebner in Frankfurt, he writes to say that Cotta will probably take my Political Economy—of which I sent an outline—and that, if not, he will find another publisher. I should have finished at the library long ago. But there have been too many interruptions and disturbances and at home everything's always in a state of siege. For nights on end, I am set on edge and infuriated by floods of tears. So I cannot of course do very much. I feel sorry for my wife. The main burden falls on her and, *au fond*,[c] she is right. *Il faut que l'industrie soit plus productive que le mariage*.[d] For all that[e] you must remember that by nature I am *très peu endurant*[f] and even *quelque peu dur*,[g] so that from time to time I lose my equanimity.

Julius was buried about a week ago. I was present at the funeral. The precious Kinkel delivered a few platitudes at the grave-side. Julius was the only one of the émigrés who applied himself to study and was progressively moving away from idealism into our own sphere.

The precious Dulon is here.

---

[a] Rudolf Schramm - [b] one way or another - [c] at bottom - [d] Industry ought to be more productive than marriage. - [e] F. Freiligrath, 'Trotz alledem!' - [f] not at all patient - [g] rather hard

Heinzen and Ruge are still thundering in the New York *Schnellpost* against the communists and against ourselves in particular. But the stuff's so abysmally stupid that it's impossible to deal with it other than by selecting, at some opportune moment, the funniest bits in Ruge's concoctions and thereby revealing to the Germans by whom, *malgré eux*,[a] they are ruled.

Have you by any chance read Proudhon's latest book[b]?

Weydemeyer has written to me from Zurich. Karstens[c] is jailed in Mainz. He made an unsuccessful attempt to escape.[451]

Vale faveque.[d]

Your
K. M.

It would, by the by, be a very good idea if you were to write a signed article for Jones. He is making progress with his paper. He is learning. *Ce n'est pas un* Harney.[e] The *Notes to the People* is, accordingly, on the up and up, while *The Friend of the People* is going to pot.

First published abridged in *Der Briefwechsel zwischen F. Engels und K. Marx*, Bd. 1, Stuttgart, 1913 and in full in *MEGA*, Abt. III, Bd. 1, 1929

Printed according to the original

Published in English in full for the first time

194

ENGELS TO MARX

IN LONDON

[Manchester, about 1 August 1851]

Dear Marx,

Enclosed the 2nd half of the 5 pound note.

I didn't know that Schramm had gone off to Paris.[f] You had told me nothing about it. Hence it was with the utmost astonishment that I read in the *Kölnische Zeitung* that he had been drowned—it can't, alas, be true. The cur is very obtrusive—we

---

[a] against their will - [b] P. J. Proudhon, *Idée générale de la Révolution au XIXᵉ siècle*. - [c] Friedrich Lessner - [d] Good-bye and farewell - [e] He's not a Harney. - [f] Reference to Conrad Schramm (see this volume, p. 397).

have allowed him to become too familiar—and he's a complete blackguard. However, you're perfectly right in saying that protests and recriminations are useless; we must just leave the fellow to go his own way until we have him in our power. As I said, it would have been quite a good thing if he really had been drowned in the Channel; but as likely as not he spread the rumour himself— *c'est une manière comme une autre de faire parler de soi*.[a]

So Weydemeyer's going to America to see whether he can take over the New York *Arbeiterzeitung* presently being run by Fenner von Fenneberg. If he can stay in New York he will be more useful to us there than in London, where the *embarras*[b] would only be made worse. A reliable chap like him is just what we've been wanting in New York and after all, New York isn't the back of beyond and with Weydemeyer one can be sure that, *le cas échéant,*[c] he would immediately be to hand.

The lithographic correspondence[d] scheme is quite a good one. Only you must keep it completely under your hat. Should little Bamberger[e] and others ever get hold of the idea, they would immediately steal a march on you. As soon as the initial arrangements have been made I should, if I were you, advertise in the German-American papers and, indeed, sign the thing myself, as director, to give it appeal. If it can be done on your responsibility and you think it might help in some way to name me as collaborator, you are, of course, entirely at liberty to do so. If, however, you want to keep your name out of the affair, although I see absolutely no need for this, *car enfin,*[f] why shouldn't you, too, be entitled to set up an industrial firm and carry on the *Neue Rheinische Zeitung* in lithograph—the man to set up the firm is Lupus. In this connection Weydemeyer could be of great service to you in New York, especially as regards the collection of money, which is the main thing. I'm convinced the thing will have enormous appeal and that the many American correspondents in London, etc., will soon become aware of it.

If you name yourself as a director there can be no question but that the thing will attract more custom, and this right from the outset; if you choose to name only Lupus, there's no longer any moral responsibility, and his Silesian tirades *à la* Luther, which are very well suited to the German Americans,—better than your style, which compels them to think—can be given free rein.[452] In

---

[a] it's as good a way as any other of getting oneself talked about - [b] confusion - [c] should the occasion arise - [d] See this volume, pp. 373, 489-90. - [e] Louis Bamberger - [f] for after all

any case you must make a point of writing as badly and as *décousu*[a] as possible, otherwise you'd soon be in hot water with your readers.

What's this new thing of Proudhon's you mention[b]?

I shall write a signed article for Jones[453]; I only wish that he would send me as complete a run as possible of his *Notes*,[c] which isn't to be had here. What is his address? I've forgotten it.

From America, too, reports on the cotton goods trade sound bad. The markets are OVERSTOCKED, and the YANKEES themselves are producing too much, given the present state of the market.

Write again soon, I am bored to death here.

Your
F. E.

N.B. Always keep your papers well away from home; for some time now I've been under very close observation here and can't move a step without having 2-3 INFORMERS at my heels. Mr Bunsen will not have missed the opportunity of providing the British government with new and important disclosures about how dangerous we are.[454]

First published slightly abridged in *Der Briefwechsel zwischen F. Engels und K. Marx*, Bd. 1, Stuttgart, 1913 and in full in *MEGA*, Abt. III, Bd. 1, 1929

Printed according to the original

Published in English for the first time

195

MARX TO JOSEPH WEYDEMEYER[43]

IN ZURICH

[London,] 2 August 1851
28 Dean Street, Soho

Dear Weydemeyer,

Engels has just sent me your letter, which I hasten to answer. I would, of course, have liked very much—if it was impossible to keep you here—at least to see and talk to you before you left.

---

[a] disjointedly - [b] See this volume, pp. 409-16. - [c] *Notes to the People*

But if you are really going to America you couldn't have chosen a better moment, both as regards finding a source of livelihood there and being of service to our party.

For it is almost as good as certain that you will obtain a position as editor with the *New-Yorker Staatszeitung.* It was previously offered to Lupus. Enclosed is a letter from him to Reichhelm, the co-proprietor of the paper. So much for the industrial aspect. But you have no time to lose.

On the other hand, Mr Heinzen, and with him the worthy Ruge, sounds weekly trumpet blasts against the communists, especially myself, Engels, etc., in the New York *Schnellpost.* Our local democratic riff-raff have a pit over there where they deposit their guano which forces neither seed nor fruit but rather a luxuriant growth of weeds. Finally Heinzen is harrying the *Staatszeitung,* which is no match even for this opponent.

Whatever the attitude of the *Staatszeitung* to American politics, you will have *la voix libre*[a] as regards European politics. Heinzen goes around posing as a great writer. The American press will be delighted by the arrival of someone who will rap this loud-mouthed poltroon over the knuckles.

If you become editor, we shall give your department every support. Unfortunately that blackguard and jackass, Seiler, is the *Staatszeitung*'s London correspondent. In addition, the member of the European government,[b] Ruge, needs to have his mouth stopped.

Your article against Christ[c] is good. I have no alterations to suggest but would simply remark, by way of parenthesis, that the workers in the manufacturing areas do indeed marry in order to coin *money* out of the children. It's a sad fact but a true one.

As you can imagine, my circumstances are very dismal. My wife will go under if things continue like this much longer. The constant worries, the slightest everyday struggle wears her out; and on top of that, there are the infamies of my opponents who have *never yet* so much as attempted to attack me as to the substance, who seek to avenge their impotence by casting suspicions on my civil character and by disseminating the most unspeakable infamies about me. Willich, Schapper, Ruge and countless other democratic rabble make this their business. No

---

[a] a free say - [b] i.e. the Central Committee of European Democracy - [c] Probably Weydemeyer's critical article on A. Christ's *Ueber den gegenwärtigen Stand der Frage der Schutzzölle*

sooner does someone arrive from the Continent than he is collared and worked upon so that he in turn takes up the self-same handiwork.

A few days ago the 'famous' referendary Schramm,[a] on meeting an acquaintance in the street, at once whispered in his ear: Whatever the outcome of the revolution, everyone is agreed that Marx is *perdu*.[b] Rodbertus, who has the best prospects, will have him shot outright—and all the rest likewise. I, of course, would make a joke of the whole dirty business; not for one moment do I allow it to interfere with my work but, as you will understand, my wife, who is poorly and caught up from morning till night in the most disagreeable of domestic quandaries, and whose nervous system is impaired, is not revived by the exhalations from the pestiferous democratic cloaca daily administered to her by stupid tell-tales. The tactlessness of some individuals in this respect can often be colossal.

By the by, there's no question of parties here. The great men, despite their *professed* disparity of views, do nothing except mutually underwrite one another's importance. Never has revolution brought a hollower crew to the surface.

When you reach New York, go and see A. Dana of the *New-York Tribune* and give him my and Freiligrath's regards. He may be of use to you. As soon as you arrive, write to me at once, but still care of Engels, who is better able to afford the postage than any of us. At any rate I expect a line or two from you before you actually put to sea. When your wife[c] arrives, convey to her the warm regards of myself and my wife.

If you are able to remain in New York, you will not be very far from Europe and, with the wholesale suppression of newspapers in Germany, it is only over there that we can conduct the struggle in the press.

Your
K. Marx

P.S. I have just learnt that the great men, Ruge and clique, Kinkel and clique, Schapper, Willich and clique, and these great ones' go-betweens, Fickler, Goegg and clique, have combined to form a spongey mass.[455] Remember the story of the peasant who sold a dozen bushels a time at below cost price. But, he said, it's

---

a Rudolf Schramm - b lost - c Louise

the volume that does it; and that's what these weaklings also say: it's the volume that will do it. The cement, by the by, which has kneaded this dough together, is hatred of the 'Neue Rheinische Zeitung clique', and in particular of myself. When there's a dozen of them together, they're proper fellows.

If you don't become master of the Arbeiterzeitung in New York—which would undoubtedly be best—if, that is, you are compelled to negotiate with the Staatszeitung, beware of your friend Kapp, who's always in and out of the place. We have proof to hand that this individual—for what reason I know not—is one of the main intriguers against us.

Adieu mon cher.

First published slightly abridged in Die Neue Zeit, Bd. 2, No. 28, 1906-07 and in full in: Marx and Engels, Works, First Russian Edition, Vol. XXV, Moscow, 1934

Printed according to the original

196

ENGELS TO WILHELM WOLFF

IN LONDON

Manchester, 6 August 1851

Dear Lupus,

I shall make inquiries here about Mr Kendall this very day, and let you know tomorrow what I find out about him. Were I to approach him myself at this stage, before he has given you an answer, and some indication that he is considering you, the only result would be that he would dismiss me very coolly and with inadequate information. These GENTLEMEN are extremely formal. Not long ago Hain also applied to this same Kendall for a post and promptly mentioned my name, yet Kendall did not think it worth the trouble to approach me for information about him—if, after this incident, I were to importune Kendall, this could only do you harm. As soon as you have an answer from Kendall, let me know and tell me what he writes; I'll then at once go to him and find out everything I can, and shall do my best to make him well disposed towards you. Of course, if it were not for Hassenpflug's warrants against you, you would be engaged straight away. But even so, all will probably be well. If I could somehow procure you a position here it would be splendid, but unfortunately I have too few acquaintances in this LINE, and only in modern languages is there permanent employment for private tutors, and of these there are enough. I shall see, by the way, about setting Watts in motion—the fellow is in the EDUCATIONAL MOVEMENT [339] and now has a mass of connections.

Your
F. E.

In future, wet the glue on your ENVELOPES more thoroughly— your letter arrived ± [a] open.

First published in: Marx and Engels, *Works*, First Russian Edition, Vol. XXV, Moscow, 1934

Printed according to the original

Published in English for the first time

197

ENGELS TO JOSEPH WEYDEMEYER [293]

IN ZURICH

Manchester, 7 August 1851

Dear Weydemeyer,

Many thanks for your information. If you can get anything further out of Hoffstetter, [456] I would be much obliged to you. I should, by the way, have thought that you might still remember from earlier days the titles of a few manuals and other military text-books; what I need particularly is precisely the utterly commonplace and ordinary stuff required for the ensign's and lieutenant's examination, and which for that reason is generally assumed to be common knowledge. I had already acquired a Decker in Switzerland, in a bad French translation and without

---

[a] more or less

plans,[a] but Marx has mislaid it, and will hardly be able to find it again. I will get hold of the atlas myself, but must also have a map of Hungary. I see that the Austrian General Staff has published several works on the subject; tell me whether your map is of this kind and how much it costs; at the very worst, it's bound to be more serviceable than the large Stieler.[b] As regards Baden and the Rhine frontier between Baden and Switzerland, I salvaged sufficient maps from the campaign.[457] I shall now find out about prices, etc., from Weerth, who is back in Hamburg, and then see what to buy. But as I said, any further information you can obtain for me will be most welcome.

It is bad that you should be going to America, and yet I honestly don't know what other advice I should give you if you can't find anything in Switzerland. There's nothing much doing in London, and Lupus still hasn't found anything here. He's looking round for a position, and I am trying to obtain one for him here, but so far without success. As regards music, the competition here is enormous. Après tout,[c] looked at from England and particularly from here, New York does not seem so very far away, when you see STEAMERS regularly making the passage, which begins on a Wednesday and ends on the Saturday of the following week, and seldom taking the full 10 days. In New York you will also find little red Becker[d]; he was recently in the dispatch department of the Arbeiterzeitung, but whether he is still there I don't know, since I have not heard from him for a long time. His last address was 24 North William Street, UPSTAIRS, but should you not be able to discover his present one, you can certainly find out where he is from Lièvre, Shakespeare Hotel, or at the Staatszeitung. In New York, by the way, there's a great deal to be done, and a proper representative of our party, who has also had a theoretical training, is badly needed there. You'll find enough material there, your greatest obstacle, however, being the fact that reliable Germans, those who are worth anything, readily become Americanised and give up all idea of returning; and then there are the special American circumstances to be considered—the ease with which the surplus population can drain off into the country, the necessarily rapid, indeed ever more rapid, increase in the country's prosperity—which cause them to regard bourgeois conditions as the beau idéal, etc. Such of the Germans there as are

---

[a] C. Decker, La Petite guerre, ou Traité des opérations secondaires de la guerre (see this volume, p. 331). - [b] Stieler's Handatlas über alle Theile der Erde... - [c] After all - [d] apparently Max Joseph Becker

minded to return are mostly good-for-nothing individuals, exploiters of revolution—à la Metternich or Heinzen—, who are the more pitiful the more subordinate they are. You will, incidentally, find the fatherland's imperial rabble [458] in New York. That you'll be able to support yourself there, I have no doubt—besides New York, the only place that is at all tolerable is St Louis; Philadelphia and Boston are ghastly holes.

If you could win the paper over, that would be splendid. Otherwise, make sure that you approach the *New-Yorker Staatszeitung,* which is very favourable to us and whose European reports were constantly under our supervision.

The best thing would be for correspondence from there to go through me, I can then get the postage paid by the firm.

I hear very little about the barracks now, save that Willich has quarrelled with that crew and no longer lives in barracks. The nucleus of the army of the future has been disbanded,[a] so Marx informs me, and Willich is without a Besançon.[459] *Quelle horreur!* This Willich, by the way, is not merely a fool but an infinitely perfidious, malicious fellow, whose wickedness—serving as tool for the most colossally and unimaginably puffed-up vanity and self-adulation—knows absolutely no bounds. Never have I seen a creature who is so consummate a liar. I can assure you that I have literally never heard a true word fall from his lips. You can hardly conceive the figure cut by this fellow as a result of the *idée fixe* that, thanks to his genius as soldier, politician and organiser of societies, he is destined to lead the revolution to victory and completion. This folly has, of course, come upon him only by degrees. While considering him capable of any dirty trick, no matter how base, I do not, by the way, believe him guilty of actual betrayal on this occasion. The Hamburg affair has resolved itself in a different fashion; Bruhn, the only agent Willich and Schapper have there, is not the traitor. Haupt is said to have blabbed, but this I cannot believe.[460]

We, naturally, leave the whole crew to their own devices—their activity being, of course, confined to rodomontade, the forging of crazy schemes, and abuse of ourselves—and leaves us indifferent. We have no need to keep them under observation, this being done for us by the Prussian police. Not a word is spoken in Schärttner's pub, where they meet, that isn't reported.

Anyhow, write to me again before you leave and give me the

---

[a] See this volume, p. 391.

name of the vessel on which you are sailing—I can see from the papers here when it is due in New York. Once in New York, let us have your address straight away.—Marx's is 28 Dean Street, Soho Square, London.

All my regards,

Your
F. Engels

Have you heard anything of Dronke? He's stuck in Geneva; Schuster will have given you his address.

First published slightly abridged in *Die Neue Zeit,* Bd. 2, No. 28, 1906-07 and in full in: Marx and Engels, *Works,* First Russian Edition, Vol. XXV, Moscow, 1934

Printed according to the original

Published in English in full for the first time

198

MARX TO ENGELS

IN MANCHESTER

[London,] 8 August 1851
28 Dean Street, Soho

Dear Engels,

You'll excuse me for not having written sooner, and at the same time acknowledging receipt of the £5. So great was the PRESSURE FROM WITHOUT this week that I didn't get round to writing. For the time being I've saved myself from being thrown out of the house by signing a BILL on the LANDLORD.

I enclose herewith a copy of the *Schnellpost* in which you'll be able to see how infamously inane are the doings and chatterings of that bunch of old women, Ruge & Co. As soon as you've read the muck, sent it back. About the letter from which the boorish Heinzen cites extracts—and which in any case, originates from Fickler—a word of explanation: for some 2-3 weeks the jackasses—the émigrés—have been holding MEETINGS in order to 'settle their differences', constitute themselves a round 'dozen' and mutually 'set each other up' as the great men of the future. Today they held their definitive sitting. I shall be hearing the result and shall inform you of it.[a] But already the seed of dissension has grown so prolific that Mr Sigel has sent me a message through Schabelitz, who is here for the Exhibition,[b] saying he would call on me.

The *New-York Tribune* has invited me and Freiligrath to work as paid collaborators.[461] It's the most widely disseminated journal in North America. If you could possibly let me have an article in English on conditions in *Germany* by *Friday morning* (15 August), that would make a splendid beginning.

As to Schramm, we know that he corresponds regularly with his brother.[c] He wrote and told Bamberger not to give us his address. Fresh reports come in daily of his infamous doings here.

Red Wolff has once again become an 'Irishman'.[d]

Now for the *Idée générale de la Révolution au XIX siècle par* P. J. Proudhon. The first time I wrote to you about this book,[e] I had read no more than extracts from it—often misquoted, to boot. Now I can send you the σκελετόν.[f] First of all, the book contains well-written attacks on Rousseau, Robespierre, the Montagne,[260] etc. The force of the true sequence, to use the words of the immortal Ruge, is generated as follows:

I. Étude.[g] It was reaction that first brought about the development of the revolution.

II. Étude. Y a-t-il raison suffisante de la Révolution au XIX siècle?[h] The revolution of 1789 overthrew the *ancien régime.* But it omitted to create a new society or to create society anew. It was concerned only with *politique*[i] instead of with *économie politique.*[j] At present *'anarchie des forces économiques'*[k] prevails, hence *'tendance de la société à la misère!'*[l] This manifests itself in the division of labour, machinery, competition, the credit system. Increase in pauperism and crime. Again, the *State (l'état)* becomes ever greater, endowed with all the attributes of absolutism, acquires ever more independence and power. Increase in the national debt. The State sides with wealth against poverty. Corruption. The State subjugates society. There is a need for the new revolution. The task of the revolution consists *à changer, à redresser la mauvaise tendance de la société.*[m] Society itself must not be touched. In its case there can be no question of *reconstitution arbitraire.*[n]

---

[a] See this volume, pp. 436-38. - [b] the Great Exhibition of 1851 - [c] Conrad and Rudolf Schramm - [d] See this volume, p. 383. - [e] ibid., p. 399. - [f] skeleton - [g] *First Essay.* - [h] *Second Essay. Is there sufficient reason for revolution in the nineteenth century?* - [i] politics - [j] political economy - [k] anarchy of economic forces - [l] the tendency of society towards poverty - [m] in changing, in redressing the evil tendency of society - [n] arbitrary reconstruction

III. Étude. Du Principe d'Association.[a]

Association is a dogma, but not a *force économique*. Association is in no way organic or productive, as are the division of labour, commerce, exchange, etc. Association should not be confused with *force collective.*

La force collective est un acte impersonnel, l'association un engagement volontaire. L'association est de sa nature stérile, nuisible même, car elle est une entrave à la liberté du travailleur. [b]

The force that has been ascribed to the *contrat de société*[c] belongs solely to the division of labour, to exchange, to the *force collective.* When an association is founded for the purpose of carrying out great works, these must be ascribed to its *means* rather than to the *principe* of association. A man submits to an association only if it offers him *une indemnité suffisante.*[d] Only to the *associé faible* or *paresseux*[e] is the association *productive d'utilité.*[f] It is *solidarité, responsabilité commune*[g] vis-à-vis third parties. As a rule an association is only feasible *dans des conditions spéciales, dépendantes de ses moyens.*[h]

L'association, formée en vue du lien de famille et de la loi du dévouement, et en dehors de toute considération économique extérieure—l'association pour elle même, est un acte de pure réligion, un lien surnaturel, sans valeur positive, un mythe.[i]

Association should not be confused with the

rapports nouveaux que se propose de développer la réciprocité entre les producteurs et les consommateurs. L'association met de niveau les contractants, subordonne leur liberté au devoir social, les dépersonnalise.[j]

---

[a] *Third Essay. On the Principle of Association.* - [b] Collective force is an impersonal act, association is voluntary commitment. Association is by its nature sterile, even harmful, since it impedes the freedom of the worker. - [c] social contract - [d] adequate compensation - [e] the associate who is weak or lazy - [f] production association of any utility - [g] solidarity, joint responsibility - [h] in special conditions, depending on the means employed - [i] Association established with a view to the family tie and the law of dedication, and apart from any external economic consideration—association for its own sake, is purely an act of religion, a supernatural bond, devoid of positive value, a myth. - [j] new relations which are intended to evolve from reciprocity between producers and consumers. Association puts the contracting parties on an equal footing, subordinates their freedom to social duty, depersonalises them.

IV. Étude. Du Principe d'Autorité.[a]

The idée gouvernementale naquit des mœurs de famille et de l'expérience domestique. The démocratie is the dernier terme of évolution gouvernementale.[b]

The idea of government is in opposition to that of contract. The true revolutionary motto is: *Plus de Gouvernement!*[c] The *autorité absolue*[d] is soon compelled to negate itself and to circumscribe itself with *lois*[e] and *institutions.* The laws enacted are as innumerable as the interests which they outwardly determine. They have an ominous tendency to multiply. The law is a fetter forced on me from without. *Constitutional monarchy.* A contradiction in terms. *Suffrage universel.* The *intuition divinatoire de la multitude*[f] is nonsense. *Qu'ai-je besoin de mandataires, pas plus que de représentants!*[g] Votes, even though unanimous, decide nothing. According to *suffrage universel,* Bonaparte would be the right man, etc. *La démocratie pure ou le gouvernement direct*[h]—figments in the minds of Rittinghausen, Considérant, Ledru-Rollin—*aboutit à l'impossible et à l'absurde.*[i] In being carried to extremes this idea of the State is revealed for the *nonsense* it is.

V. Étude. Liquidation sociale.

1. *Banque nationale.* The liquidation of the Bank of France is decreed. It is not declared a national bank, but rather an *'établissement d'utilité publique'.*[j] Interest is reduced to $1/2$ or $1/4$ per cent.

2. *The national debt.* The *capitaux particuliers,*[k] having been deprived of the *industrie de l'escompte,*[l] flows into the Bourse, the State no longer pays more than $1/2$ or $1/4$ per cent, and thus interest ceases to be of interest. Instead of interest, the State pays annuities, i.e. it repays in yearly quotas the capital it has been loaned. Or in other words, a decree to the effect that the interest on the debt paid by the State be deemed annuities and deducted from the principal.

3. *Dettes hypothécaires. Obligations simples.*

'Les intérêts te toutes créances, hypothécaires, chirographaires, actions de commandite, sont fixés à $1/4$ or $1/2$%. Les remboursements ne pourront être exigés

---

[a] *Fourth Essay. On the Principle of Authority.* - [b] The idea of government was born of family custom and domestic experience. The final stage of governmental evolution is democracy. - [c] No more government! - [d] absolute authority - [e] laws - [f] Universal suffrage. The prophetic intuition of the masses - [g] What need have I of mandatories, any more than of representatives! - [h] Pure democracy or direct government - [i] leads to impossibility and absurdity - [j] establishment of public utility - [k] private capital - [l] discount industry

que par annuités. L'annuité, pour toutes les sommes au-dessous de 2000frs. sera de 10%; pour les sommes au-dessus de 2000frs., 5%. Pour faciliter le remboursement des créances et suppléer à la fonction des anciens prêteurs, une division des bureaux de la banque nationale d'escompte deviendra Banque foncière; le maximum de ses avances sera, par année, de 500 millions.'ᵃ [op. cit., p. 213.]

4. *Propriété immobilière: Bâtiments.*

Decree: 'Tout payement fait à titre de loyer sera porté en *à compte de la propriété*, celle-ci estimée au vingtuple du prix de location. Tout acquittement de terme vaudra au locataire part proportionelle et indivise dans la maison par lui habitée, et dans la totalité des constructions exploitées à loyer, et servant à la demeure des citoyens. La propriété ainsi remboursée passera à fur et mesure au droit de l'administration communale qui, par le fait du remboursement, prendra hypothè- que et privilége de premier ordre, au nom de la masse des locataires, et leur garantira à tous, à perpétuité, le domicile, au prix de revient du bâtiment. Les communes pourront traiter de gré à gré avec les propriétaires, pour la liquidation et le remboursement immédiat des propriétés louées. Dans ce cas, et afin de faire jouir la génération présente de la réduction des prix de loyer, les dites communes pourront opérer immédiatement une diminution sur le loyer des maisons pour lesquelles elles auront traité, de manière que l'amortissement en soit opéré seulement en trente ans. Pour les réparations, l'agencement et l'entretien des édifices, comme pour les constructions nouvelles, les communes traiteront avec les Compagnies maçonnes ou associations d'ouvriers en bâtiment, d'après les principes et les règles du nouveau contrat social. Les propriétaires, occupant seuls leurs propres maisons, en conserveront la propriété aussi longtemps qu'ils le jugeront utile à leurs intérêts.'ᵇ [op. cit., pp. 221-22.]

ᵃ 3. *Mortgage Debts. Simple Bonds.* 'Interest on all debts, mortgages, simple contract debts, joint-stock shares, is fixed at ¹/₄ or ¹/₂ per cent. Repayment claims can be met only by annual instalments. The annual instalment for all sums below 2,000 fr. will be 10 per cent, for sums above 2,000 fr. 5 per cent. In order to facilitate the repayment and replace the function of the former money-lenders a section of the offices of the National Discount Bank will become a mortgage bank, the maximum of its advances will be 500 million per annum.' - ᵇ 4. *Real estate: Buildings.* Decree: 'Every payment made in respect of rent shall be entered to *the account of the property* reckoned as twenty times the rent. With every instalment of rent the tenant will acquire a proportional and joint share in the house he occupies and in the totality of all buildings let for rent and serving as dwellings for the citizens. Property thus paid for will pass by degrees into the hands of the communal administration, which by the fact of the payment will take over the mortgages and prerogatives in the name of the mass of tenants, and will guarantee their domicile to all of them in perpetuity at the cost price of the building. The communes will be able to negotiate separate agreements with the owners for the immediate liquidation and repayment of the leased properties. In this case, and in order that the present generations shall enjoy reduced rents, the said communes will be able immediately to reduce the rent of houses for which they have concluded agreements, in such a way that amortisation be completed only in thirty years. For repairs, fittings and upkeep of the buildings, as in the case of new constructions, the communes will negotiate with the companies of masons or associations of building workers according to the principles and rules of the new social contract. The owners, sole occupiers of their own houses, will retain the property as long as they judge this advantageous to their interests.'

5. *Propriété foncière.*

'Tout payement de redevance pour l'exploitation d'un immeuble acquerra au fermier une part de propriété dans l'immeuble, et lui vaudra hypothèque. La propriété, intégralement remboursée, relèvera immédiotement de la commune, laquelle succèdera à l'ancien propriétaire et partagera avec le fermier la nue-propriété et le produit net. Les communes pourront traiter de gré à gré avec les propriétaires qui le désireront, pour le rachat des rentes et le remboursement immédiat des propriétés. Dans ce cas il sera pourvu, à la diligence des communes, à l'installation des cultivateurs et à la délimitation des possessions, en ayant soin de compenser autant que possible l'étendue superficiaire avec la qualité du fonds, et de proportionner la redevance au produit. Aussitôt que la propriété foncière aura été intégralement remboursée, toutes les communes de la République devront s'entendre pour égaliser entre elles les différences de qualité des terrains, ainsi que les accidents de la culture. La part de redevance à laquelle elles ont droits sur les fractions de leurs territoires respectifs, servira à cette compensation et assurance générale. A partir de la même époque, les anciens propriétaires qui, faisant valoir par eux-mêmes leurs propriétés, auront conservé leur titre, seront assimilés aux nouveaux, soumis à la même redevance et investis des mêmes droits, de manière que le hasard des localités et des successions ne favorise personne, et que les conditions de culture soient pour tous égales. L'impôt foncier sera aboli. La police agricole est dévolue aux conseils municipaux.'[a] [op. cit., p. 228.]

VI. *Étude. Organisation des forces economiques.*

1. *Crédit.* The above-mentioned *banque nationale,* together with its branches. Gradual withdrawal of gold and silver from circulation. Substitution of paper. *Quant au* crédit personnel, *c'est dans les compagnies ouvrières et les sociétés agricoles et industrielles qu'il doit trouver son exercise.*[b]

---

[a] 5. *Landed property.* 'Every payment of rent for the use of a piece of real estate will make the farmer part-proprietor of it and will count as a mortgage payment by him. When the property has been entirely paid for it will be immediately taken over by the commune, which will take the place of the former owner and will share with the farmer the ownership and the net product. The communes will be able to negotiate separate agreements with the owners who desire it for the redemption of the rents and the immediate repayment of the properties. In that case at the request of the communes steps shall be taken to instal the cultivators, and to delimit their properties, taking care that as far as possible the size of the area shall make up for the quality of the land, and that the rent shall be proportional to the product. As soon as the property has been entirely paid for, all the communes of the Republic will have to reach agreement among themselves to equalise the differences in the quality of the strips of land, and also the contingencies of farming. The part of the rent due to them from the plots in their particular area will be used for this compensation and general insurance. Dating from the same period the old owners who worked themselves on their properties, will retain their title, and will be treated in the same way as the new owners, will have to pay the same rent and will be granted the same rights in such a way that no one is favoured by the chance of location and inheritance and that the conditions of cultivation are equal for all. The land tax will be abolished. The functions of the rural police will devolve on the municipal councils. - [b] As for *personal credit,* it should be operated in the workers' companies and the agricultural and industrial societies.

2. *Propriété*. See 'Propriété foncière' cited above. Under the above conditions it is possible

sans la moindre inquiétude, permettre au propriétaire de vendre, transmettre, aliéner, faire circuler à volonté la propriété ... Avec les facilités du remboursement par annuités, la valeur de l'immeuble peut être indéfiniment partagée, échangée, subir toutes les mutations imaginables, sans que l'immeuble soit entamé jamais. Le travail agricole repousse la forme sociétaire.[a]

3. *Division du travail, forces collectives, machines. Compagnies ouvrières.*

Toute industrie, exploitation ou entreprise qui par sa nature exige l'emploi combiné d'un grand nombre d'ouvriers de spécialités différentes, est destinée à devenir le foyer d'une société ou compagnie de travailleurs. Mais là où le produit peut s'obtenir sans un concours de facultés spéciales, par l'action d'un individu ou d'une famille, il n'y a pas lieu à l'association.[b]

Hence no associations in small workshops, among artisans, shoemakers, tailors, etc., *marchands*,[c] etc. Association in *big industry*. Here, then, *compagnies ouvrières*.

Tout individu employé dans l'association a un droit indivisé dans la propriété de la compagnie; il a le droit d'en remplir successivement toutes les fonctions; son éducation, son instruction et son apprentissage, doivent être dirigés de telle sorte, qu'en lui faisant supporter sa part des corvées répugnantes et pénibles, ils lui fassent parcourir une série de travaux et de connaissances, et lui assurent, à l'époque de la maturité, une aptitude encyclopédique et un revenu suffisant; les fonctions sont électives et les règlements soumis à l'adoption des associés; le salaire est proportionné à la nature de la fonction, à l'importance du talent, à l'étendue de la responsabilité; tout associé participe aux bénéfices comme aux charges de la compagnie, dans la proportion de ses services; chacun est libre de quitter à volonté l'association, de faire régler son compte et liquider ses droits, et réciproquement la compagnie maîtresse de s'adjoindre toujours de nouveaux membres[d]...

---

[a] without the slightest misgiving, to permit the owner to sell, transfer, alienate or otherwise dispose of his property as he pleases... Given the facility of repayment by annual instalments, the value of a piece of real estate can be indefinitely divided, exchanged, and undergo any conceivable change, without the real estate being in the least affected. Agricultural labour rejects associatory forms. - [b] 3. *Division of labour, collective forces, machinery. Companies of workers.* Every industry, enterprise or undertaking which by its nature requires the combined employment of a large number of workers with different skills is bound to become the basis for an association or company of workers. But where a product may be obtained without a combination of special skills, through the activity of an individual or family, there is no need for association. - [c] shopkeepers - [d] Every person working in the association possesses an indivisible right in the property of the company; he has the right to perform successively all duties. His education, training and apprenticeship ought therefore to be conducted in such a way that, while he is made to take his share of disagreeable and arduous tasks, he will acquire experience in various sorts of work and fields of

This is the solution to the *deux problèmes: celui de la force collective, et celui de la division du travail...*[a] In the transitional period these workshops will be managed by the manufacturers, etc.

4. *Constitution de la valeur: organisation du bon marché.*[b] To combat *cherté de la marchandise*[c] and the *arbitraire du prix.*[d] The *juste prix représente avec exactitude:* a) *le montant des frais de production, d'après la moyenne officielle des libres producteurs;* b) *le salaire du commerçant, ou l'indemnité de l'avantage dont le vendeur se prive en se dessaisissant de la chose.*[e] To induce the merchant so to do, he must be given a guarantee. This may be

de plusieures manières: soit que les consommateurs qui veulent jouir du juste prix, et qui sont en même temps producteurs, s'obligent à leur tour envers le marchand à lui livrer, à des conditions égales, leurs propres produits, comme cela se pratique entre les différentes associations ouvrières parisiennes; soit que les dits consommateurs se contentent d'assurer au débitant une prime ou bien encore une vente assez considérable pour lui assurer une revenue.[f]

E.g., the State

au nom des intérêts que provisoirement il représente, les départements et communes, au nom de leurs habitants respectifs, voulant assurer à tous le juste prix et la bonne qualité des produits et services, offrent de garantir aux entrepreneurs qui offriront les conditions les plus avantageuses, soit un intérêt pour les capitaux et le matériel engagé dans leurs entreprises, soit un traitement fixe, soit, s'il y a lieu, une masse suffisante de commandes. Les soumissionnaires s'obligeront, en retour, à fournir les produits et services pour lesquels ils s'engagent, à toute réquisition des consommateurs. Toute latitude réservée, du reste, à la concurrence. Ils devront indiquer les éléments de leurs prix, le mode des

---

knowledge, so that when he reaches mature age he will have a wide range of qualifications and a sufficient income. Posts are subject to election and the rules are adopted by the members of the association. The size of the recompense depends on the nature of the work, the degree of the proficiency, and the amount of responsibility. Every member of the association shares both in the profits and in the expenses of the company in proportion to his services. Everyone is free to resign from the association whenever he wishes, and therefore to settle his accounts and renounce his rights; conversely the company is entitled to recruit new members at any time.

[a] two problems: that of collective force, and that of the division of labour - [b] *The Determination of Value; the Establishment of a Cheap Market.* - [c] the high price of goods - [d] arbitrariness of prices - [e] The *fair price* accurately reflects: a) a total production cost according to the official average for free producers, b) the merchant's salary or the compensation for the advantages which the seller forgoes by parting with the article. - [f] of several kinds: either the consumers, who wish to have the benefit of a fair price and who are at the same time producers themselves, undertake in their turn to supply the merchant with their own products on equal terms, as is done by the various workers' associations in Paris; or else the said consumers confine themselves to guaranteeing the dealer either a premium, or a sale large enough to guarantee him an income.

livraisons, la durée de leurs engagements, leurs moyens d'exécution. Les soumissions déposées, sous cachet, dans les délais prescrits, seront ensuite ouvertes et publiées, 8 jours, 15 jours, 1 mois, 3 mois, selon l'importance des traités, avant l'adjudication. A l'expiration de chaque engagement, il sera procédé à de nouvelles enchères.[a]

5. *Commerce extérieur*.[b] As soon as the interest falls, it is necessary to *abaisser les tarifs*[c] and, if it be depressed or standing between $^1/_4$ and $^1/_2$ per cent, the Customs must be abolished.

VII. Étude. Dissolution du gouvernement dans l'organisme économique.

La société sans l'autorité. Elimination des cultes, Justice, administration, police, Instruction publique, Guerre, Marine etc.[d], the whole with appropriate Stirnerian stock phrases.

Write and tell me in detail what you think of this formula. Salut.

Your
K. Marx

First published in *Der Briefwechsel zwischen F. Engels und K. Marx*, Bd. 1, Stuttgart, 1913

Printed according to the original

Translated from the German and French

Published in English for the first time

---

[a] on behalf of the interests which it temporarily represents, and the departments and communes on behalf of their respective inhabitants, being desirous of ensuring a fair price and a high standard of goods and services for all, propose to guarantee that the entrepreneurs who offer the most advantageous conditions will receive either interest on the capital and material invested in their enterprises, or a fixed salary, or in appropriate cases a sufficient quantity of orders. In return, the tendering parties will pledge themselves to meet all consumers' requests for the goods and services they have undertaken to supply. Apart from that, full scope is left for competition. They must state the component parts of their prices, the method of delivery, the duration·of their commitments, and their means of fulfilment. The tenders submitted under seal within the periods prescribed will subsequently be opened and made public 8 days, 15 days, 1 month or 3 months before the contracts are allocated depending on the importance of the contracts. At the expiry of each contract, new tenders will be invited. - [b] External trade. - [c] to lower the tariffs - [d] *Seventh Essay. The Merging of Government in the Economic Organism*. Society without authority. Elimination of cults, Justice, Administration, police, Public Education, War, the Navy.

199

ENGELS TO MARX

IN LONDON

[Manchester, about 10 August 1851]

Dear Marx,

I was very much tickled by the *Schnellpost*. It's a long time since I've read such consummate balderdash as 'A. Ruge an K. Heinzen'.[a] I couldn't have believed that even two jackasses such as Ruge and Heinzen could emerge from three years of revolutionary tumult so completely unchanged and still so encumbered with the same old stock phrases, absurd mannerisms, turns of speech, etc. It's like the clown in the circus riders' troupe who, after performing the most hair-raising leaps, makes yet another bow, says: 'HERE WE ARE AGAIN!' and then, without the least compunction, proceeds to repeat every item in his all-too familiar repertoire. I can just see Ruge, that egregious literary laxative, as he seriously declares that

'the fundamental answer to tyranny, anarchy and high treason ... is precisely the bull's-eye which it behoves us to hit',

and then himself hits the bull's-eye with the discovery that the modern class struggle is the *secessio plebis*,[b] whence, by a process of effortless association, he goes on to the Roman schoolmaster[c] whose name I forget, his fable of the stomach and the hands [462] and other such charming fourth form pedagogic recollections. The chap's *impayable*[d] when he comes to speak of 'circumstances',

'As you know ... by "circumstances" all I mean are the thoughts which are presently uppermost in men's minds!'

His lame attempts at making wittily malicious allusions were a dismal failure. The fellow is adroit enough; his malice is plain for all to see, but nobody has the faintest idea of its object nor of the general why and wherefore. And whereas the great Ruge is turning out to be a buffoon pure and simple, the great Heinzen excels no less as a boor, a condition now become chronic. The manner in which the

---

[a] See this volume, p. 408. - [b] secession of the plebs - [c] Menenius Agrippa - [d] priceless

fellow seeks, in his note of 23 July 1851, to fob off on his readers his old nonsense about communism couched in the very same terms as those he used in the *Deutsche-Brüsseler-Zeitung* in the summer of 1847, is impudent beyond words.[a]

Et pourtant,[b] the fellows are compelled to recognise the superiority of our stuff, not only by their constant preoccupation with it, but even more by its influence on them of which despite their stubbornness and rage they are quite unaware. In all this scribble, there is not a single phrase that does not contain a plagiarism, an uncomprehending distortion of our stuff, or something suggested by it.

Mr Meyen or Faucher has published a fatuous article in Manteuffel's semi-official *Lithographische Correspondenz* in Berlin about the attempted conciliation in London[c]; only we two still stick to one another, etc.—all the rest being united and opposed to us. No mention of Freiligrath or Wolff. It would seem that, following the disbandment of the army of the future, the great Willich finds himself obliged to gain recognition as 'a character'[d] among the great men of all parties; he is even said to have attended their meetings. *A quoi tous ces coups de désespoir ont-ils abouti?*[e] And has the great Sigel been to see you?

I have just been assured by a German social jackass who arrived from Dessau with an introduction from Julius, that the gentlemen there have been circulating the rumour that, by your own confession—you yourself are alleged to have told Mr Louis Drucker (!) so—you are writing for the *Neue Preussische Zeitung*. *En voilà une bonne!*[f]

As for Proudhon,[g] the man seems to be making progress. The phases of development through which his nonsense passes are at least assuming a more tolerable form and these *'hérésies'* are something for Mr Louis Blanc to break his teeth on. Thus, *au bout du compte*,[h] Mr Proudhon has now also come to the conclusion that the true meaning of property rights lies in the disguised confiscation of all property by a more or less disguised State, and that what abolition of the State really means is intensified state centralisation. What else are

---

a 'Karl Heinzen und die Kommunisten', *Deutsche-Brüsseler-Zeitung*, No. 77, 26 September 1847. Engels' reply to it were articles 'The Communists and Karl Heinzen'. - b Nevertheless - c See this volume, p. 425. - d Cf. H. Heine, *Atta Troll*, XXIV—'no talent but a character' (description of the bear-hero Atta Troll). - e What have all these acts of despair led to? - f That's a good one! - g P. J. Proudhon, *Idée générale de la Révolution au XIXᵉ siècle* - h in the final analysis

'toutes les communes de la république qui s'entendent pour égaliser entre elles les différences de qualité des terrains ainsi que les accidents de la culture',[a]

with all the appurtenances and consequences this would entail?

More about this old character tomorrow, provided I have the time. I can't possibly let you have Friday's article this week.[b] But write and tell me soon what sort of thing it should be—whether you wish it to stand on its own or to be one of a series, and 2) what attitude I should adopt, as I know nothing about the POLITICS of the *New-York Tribune* beyond the fact that they are American Whigs.[463] Also, any other available information that may help me find my bearings.

Your
F. E.

First published in *Der Briefwechsel zwischen F. Engels und K. Marx,* Bd. 1, Stuttgart, 1913

Printed according to the original

Published in English for the first time

200

ENGELS TO MARX

IN LONDON

[Manchester, about 11 August 1851]

Dear Marx,

Today I shall continue the glosses on Proudhon[c] which were interrupted yesterday. For the time being I shall disregard the many gaps in the formula, e.g. the fact that one cannot see how the factories are to be transferred from the hands of the manufacturers to the *compagnies ouvrières*,[d] since interest and land rent are to be abolished, but not profit (for there will still be competition); further, what is to become of the big landowners who exploit their land by means of hired labour, and other such deficiencies. In order to assess the thing as a theoretical whole, I should have to have the actual book in front of me. Hence I can give an opinion only in so far as I consider the feasibility, *le cas échéant*,[e] of the individual measures and at the same time examine the extent to which they lend themselves to the centralisation of all

---

[a] all the communes in the Republic which come to an agreement regarding mutual compensation for the difference in the quality of their lands, and for the hazards of agriculture - [b] See this volume, pp. 408-09. - [c] P. J. Proudhon, *Idée générale de la Révolution au XIX*e *siècle*.- [d] workers' associations - [e] should the occasion arise

the productive forces. And even then, I really ought to have the book in order to see all the *développements.*

The fact that Mr Proudhon has at last come to realise the need for more or less covert confiscation is, as I have already said, a step forward. The question is, however, whether his pretext for confiscation will serve, for, as always with these blinkered fellows who persuade themselves that compulsory measures of this kind are not confiscation, the whole thing hinges on that pretext. 'Interest is reduced to $\frac{1}{2}$ or $\frac{1}{4}$ per cent.' But your extracts say nothing of how this is done, save that the State, or the Bank which secretly and under another name is part and parcel of the State, must make an annual loan on mortgage of 500 mill. fr. at that rate of interest. From this I conclude that the reduction is intended to take place gradually. Once interest was as low as that, the annual liquidation of all debts etc., etc., at a rate of 5 to 10 per cent per annum would, of course, be easy. But Mr Proudhon fails to indicate by what means this is to be attained. In this connection I recall our recent discussion about your scheme for reducing the interest rate by setting up a national bank with exclusive privileges and a monopoly of paper CURRENCY, gold and silver being excluded from circulation.[a] I believe that any attempt to lower the interest rate rapidly and steadily would inevitably fail because of the growing need, at a time of revolution and stagnating business, for usury, for the granting of credit to people who are momentarily in a tight corner, at a loss what to do, in other words, momentarily unsound financially. Even if that portion of the interest rate intended for the actual repayment of the loan can be depressed by weight of capital, there still remains the portion representing the guarantee of repayment, which, at times of crisis, rises enormously. In any revolution merchants are grateful to a government which lends to them, not at $\frac{1}{4}$ or $\frac{1}{2}$ per cent, but at 5 per cent. Cf. 1848, loan offices, etc., etc. The State, and any large, centralised state bank, unless it operates branches in the most out-of-the-way places and has given its officials a long training in commercial practice, can lend to large businesses only, otherwise it would be lending at random. And small businesses cannot pledge their goods like large ones. *Donc,*[b] 1. the consequence of any reduction in interest rate for government loans=increased profits for big businessmen and a general advancement of that class.

Small businesses would, as before, be compelled to have recourse to middlemen to whom the government had advanced

---

[a] See this volume, pp. 299-300. - [b] Hence

money at $^1/_2$ per cent so that they could lend it again at 5-10 per cent. That is inevitable. Small businesses furnish no guarantees, and can offer no pledges. Hence in this respect, too, advancement of the big bourgeoisie—indirect creation of a large usurer class, bankers at a lower level.

The constant harping by the socialists and Proudhon on the reduction of interest is, in my opinion, no more than a glorified pious wish of the bourgeoisie and petty bourgeoisie. So long as interest and profit remain in inverse proportion, a reduction of interest can only lead to an increase in profit. And so long as there are people who are financially unsound, unable to provide a guarantee and for that very reason truly in need of money, state lending cannot supersede private lending, i.e. cannot bring down interest rates in respect of all transactions. The State, which lends at $^1/_2$ per cent, would be in precisely the same position vis-à-vis the usurer whom it provides with money as was the French Government of 1795 vis-à-vis the property speculators and stock jobbers of that time when it collected taxes to the tune of 500 mill. in *assignats*[a] and reissued them for 3 mill. and, simply to maintain its 'credit' which had already collapsed, accepted the *assignats* used for tax payments at their face value, or 200 times their real value.

Proudhon is altogether too naive. *Le crédit personnel trouve* or *doit trouver son exercice dans les compagnies ouvrières.*[b] Hence the dilemma: either management and finally administration and regulation of these companies by the State, which Proudhon doesn't want, or the organisation of the most splendid association fraud, the fraud of 1825 and 1845, reproduced at the level of the proletariat, *Lumpenproletariat* and petty bourgeoisie.

To seek to place the main emphasis on the gradual reduction of the interest rate by commercial and compulsory measures so that all debts etc., etc., are liquidated by converting interest payments into repayments, all real wealth being concentrated in the hands of the State or the communes, seems to me utterly impracticable, 1) on the grounds already cited; 2) because it takes far too long; 3) because the only consequences, if state paper maintained its credit, would necessarily be the country's indebtedness to foreigners, since all money repaid would find its way abroad; 4) because, even if the feasibility of the thing were accepted in principle, it would be nonsense to believe that *France, la République,* could carry this out in the teeth of England and America; 5) because war abroad and the PRESSURE OF THE MOMENT generally, make sheer nonsense of

_____
[a] paper money issued at the time of the French Revolution - [b] Personal credit finds or should find its application in the workers' associations

such systematically protracted measures, extending over 20 or 30 years and more especially of money payments.

The only practical significance of the thing would seem to be that it is indeed possible, at a certain point of revolutionary development, and with the help of a monopolist state bank, to decree: Art. 1: interest is abolished or limited to $^1/_4$ per cent; Art. 2: interest will continue to be paid as hitherto, being regarded as repayment; Art. 3: the State is empowered to purchase all real estate, etc., at current tax value and pay for it over 20 years at 5 per cent. Such *might* perhaps one day serve as the final and immediate precursor of undisguised confiscation; but it would be pure speculation to ponder on the when, where and how.

In any case it would seem that this book of Proudhon's is much more down-to-earth than his earlier ones—even the *constitution de la valeur* assumed a more fleshly aspect: that of the *juste prix des boutiquiers. Quatre francs, Monsieur, c'est le plus juste prix!*[a] What there is in common between the abolition of customs and that of interest is not clear. The fact that, since 1847, Proudhon should have made so complete a transition from Hegel to Stirner is another step forward. Be it said, however, that he won't understand German philosophy even should he persist with it until his corpse is in the final stage of decomposition.

Write soon and tell me what you think of the foregoing.

Your
F. E.

First published in *Der Briefwechsel zwischen F. Engels und K. Marx*, Bd. 1, Stuttgart, 1913

Printed according to the original

Published in English for the first time

201

MARX TO ENGELS

IN MANCHESTER

[London,] 14 August 1851
28 Dean Street, Soho

Dear Engels,

In a day or two I shall be sending you the Proudhon itself,[b] but send it back as soon as you've read it. For I intend—for the

---

[a] fair price of the shopkeepers. Four francs, sir, that's the fairest price! -
[b] P. J. Proudhon, *Idée générale de la Révolution au XIXe siècle*.

money—to publish 2-3 sheets about the book. So let me have your views in greater detail than your hasty letter-writing generally allows.[464]

The Proudhon business—and the whole is first and foremost a polemic against communism, however much he may filch from it and however much it may appear to him in the light of the Cabet-Blanc transfiguration—boils down, in my opinion, to the following line of reasoning:

The real enemy to be combatted is capital. The pure economic affirmation of capital is interest. So-called profit is nothing but a particular form of wage. We abolish interest by transforming it into an annuity, i.e. repayment of capital by annual instalments. Thus the working class—read *industrial* class—will be assured precedence for ever, while the actual capitalist class will be condemned to an ever-diminishing existence. The various forms of interest are money interest, rent interest and lease interest. In this way bourgeois society is retained, justified, and divested only of its *mauvaise tendance*.[a]

Liquidation sociale is simply a means of building anew a 'healthy' bourgeois society. Quick or slow, *peu nous importe*.[b] I want first to hear your views on the contradictions, uncertainties and obscurities of this liquidation as such. The truly healing balm of the newly built society, however, consists in the abolition of interest, i.e. in the yearly transformation of interest into an *annuité*. This, introduced not as a means but as an *economic law* of the reformed bourgeois society, has, of course, a twofold result:

1. The transformation of small, non-industrial capitalists into industrial capitalists. 2. The perpetuation of the big capitalist class, for *au fond*[c] if one takes an overall view of the thing, it becomes apparent that, *by and large,*—and aside from industrial profits—society never pays anything except the *annuité*. Were the converse true, Dr Price's compound interest calculations[d] would become a reality and the entire globe would not suffice to *pay interest* on a capital, however tiny, invested at the time of Christ. In fact, however, it may be confidently said that the capital invested, whether in land or otherwise, over the past 50 or 100 years e.g. in England—the most tranquil and bourgeois of countries, that is—has never as yet paid interest, at least in terms of price, which is what we are concerned with here. Let us assume, e.g., that at the highest estimate, England's national wealth amounts to e.g. 5

---

[a] evil tendency - [b] it matters little to us - [c] basically - [d] The reference is to R. Price's *An Appeal to the Public on the Subject of the National Debt* and *Observations on Reversionary Payments...*

thousand million. Suppose England produces 500 millions each year. Hence England's entire wealth merely=England's annual labour×10. Hence, not only is this capital not paying interest, it is not even *reproducing* itself in terms of value. And this by reason of the simple law. Value originally determined by the original production costs, in terms of the working time originally needed to manufacture the object. But once the product is produced, its price is determined by the costs necessarily incurred in *reproducing* it. And reproduction costs fall steadily and at a speed proportionate to the current state of industrialisation. Hence the law of the continuous depreciation of capital value itself, through which the law *des rentes*[a] and of interest, which would otherwise lead to absurdity, is nullified. This also explains the thesis you yourself put forward that no factory covers its production costs. Thus Proudhon cannot refashion society by introducing a law which, *au fond,* is already being observed without his counsel.

The means by which Proudhon proposes to achieve all this is the bank. *Il y a ici un qui pro quo.*[b] The bank's business is divisible into two parts: 1. The *conversion* of capital *into cash.* Here *money* is simply substituted for *capital,* which can, of course, be done simply at production cost, i.e. at $1/2$ to $1/4$ per cent. 2. *Advances of capital* in the form of money, and here the interest rate will adjust itself in accordance with the amount of capital. All that credit can do here is to convert by means of concentration, etc., etc., existing but unproductive wealth into truly active capital. Proudhon considers No. 2 to be as easy as No. 1, and *au bout du compte*[c] he will find that by making over an illusory mass of capital in the form of money he will at best reduce the *interest* on the capital, only to increase its *price* in like proportion. Whereby nothing is gained but the discrediting of his paper.

I shall allow you to savour in the original the correlation between customs and interest. The thing's too delicious to spoil it by mutilation. Mr Proudhon entirely fails to elucidate either the commune's share in the houses and land—something he certainly should have done as regards the communists—or how the workers come into possession of the factories. At any rate, while anxious to have '*des compagnies ouvrières puissantes*',[d] he is so afraid of these industrial 'guilds' that he reserves the right, if not for the State, then for *société, to dissolve* them. As a true Frenchman who knows neither a Moses & Son[e] nor a MIDLOTHIAN FARMER, he confines

---

[a] of rents - [b] Here there is a quid pro quo. - [c] in the final analysis - [d] powerful workers' associations - [e] a large firm of men's clothiers in London

association to the factory. To him, the French peasant and the French shoemaker, tailor, MERCHANT appear as *des données éternelles et qu'il faut accepter*.[a] But the more I go into the stuff, the more I become convinced that the reform of agriculture, and hence the question of property based on it, is the alpha and omega of the coming upheaval. Without that, Father Malthus will turn out to be right.

So far as Louis Blanc, etc., are concerned the piece is capital, notably because of its cheeky outpourings about Rousseau, Robespierre, God, *fraternité* and similar twaddle.

As to the *New-York Tribune,* you've got to help me, now that I'm so busy with political economy. Write a series of articles on Germany, from 1848 onwards.[465] Witty and uninhibited. The gentlemen of the foreign department are exceedingly *uppish.*

In a few days' time I'll send you 2 volumes of Roman stuff. To wit *Économie politique des Romains.* Par Dureau de la Malle. I sent to Paris for the book (very erudite). It will open your eyes to, amongst other things, the economic backing of the Roman way of waging war, which was nothing else than the— *cadastre.* What's the cheapest way of sending the thing to you? There are 2 fat volumes.

You must pinch the *Lithographische Correspondenz* article[b] or try to get hold of a copy. As soon as Weydemeyer gets there, he must make the jackasses in New York run the gauntlet. For that all the documents are needed. Faucher *is* correspondent of the *Neue Preussische Zeitung.* Sigel has not yet turned up. Willich, of course, is a unifying member of the *Emigré Fraternity.* They held their first general meeting on Friday. We had a spy there.[c] The proceedings opened with a reading (by *General* Haug) of the *Lithographische Correspondenz* article in which we are attacked. For because of us they live and move and have their being. Next, a resolution in favour of all manner of undesirable and contentious lectures. Mr Meyen undertook to do Prussia; Oppenheim, England; Ruge, France; and Kinkel, America—and the future. I very much look forward, by the way, to hearing what you think about all this.

First published in *Der Briefwechsel zwischen F. Engels und K. Marx,* Bd. 1, Stuttgart, 1913

Printed according to the original

Published in English for the first time

---

[a] eternal data that must be accepted - [b] See this volume, p. 418. - [c] Jakob Schabelitz (the meeting of émigrés was held on 8 August 1851—see this volume, pp. 436-38)

202

MARX TO HERMANN EBNER[466]

IN FRANKFURT AM MAIN

[Copy]

[London, 15-22 August 1851]

...You will have read, in various German papers, the *semi-ministerial Lithographische Correspondenz*[a] article in which the official German emigration in London notifies the public of its fraternal unification, its constitution as a joint body. The agreement-seeking united democrats fall into 3 cliques: the Ruge clique, the Kinkel clique, and the indescribable Willich clique. Between the three hover the intercalated deities, minor *literati* such as Meyen, Faucher, Oppenheim, etc., erstwhile Berlin agreers[467] and, finally, Tausenau along with a few Austrians.

Let us begin, as is fitting, with A. Ruge, the 5th wheel of European Central Democracy's[468] state coach. A. Ruge arrived in London, not exactly weighed down with laurels. All that was known of him was that, at the critical moment, he had cut and run from Berlin and had later vainly applied to Brentano for the post of Ambassador in Paris, that throughout the period of revolution he had espoused, always with the same unshakable conviction, whatever illusion happened to be in vogue and, at one inspired moment, had even discovered that the simplest way of resolving modern conflicts was 'after the *Dessau* pattern'. For that is what he called this little model state's royalist-constitutional-democratic farce. Meanwhile he was firmly determined to become a great man in London. As always, he had prudently arranged to maintain contact with a democratic local paper in Germany so that he could, without constraint, regale the German public with talk of his important person. This time the lot fell to the *Bremer Tages-Chronik*. Now Ruge could embark on further operations. Since he speaks only very broken French, no one could stop him presenting himself to foreigners as Germany's most important man, and Mazzini aptly summed him up at first glance as a *homme sans conséquence*[b] whom he could, without hesitation, call on to supply the German counter-signature to his manifesto. In this way A. Ruge became the 5th wheel of the Provisional Government of

---

[a] Note in the margin: from Berlin (see this volume, p. 418) - [b] man of no consequence

Europe and, as Ledru-Rollin once said, *l'homme de Mazzini.* He found himself outdone in his own ideal. However, it now behoved him to make himself appear a power in the eyes of Mazzini and Ledru-Rollin, and to prove that there was more to be thrown onto the scales than an equivocal name. A. Ruge set himself to perform three great deeds. In company with Messrs Haug, Ronge, Struve and Kinkel, he founded a so-called German Central Committee,[469] he founded a journal modestly entitled *Der Kosmos* and, finally, he sought to extract a loan of 10 millions from the German people, the *quid pro quo* being that he would gain them their liberty. The 10 millions never came in, but the *Kosmos* came to an end and the Central Committee came apart, disintegrating into its original elements. The *Kosmos* had appeared only three times. Ruge's classical style put his profane readers to flight, but nevertheless this much had been achieved: A. Ruge had been able to place on record his amazement at the fact that the Queen should have invited Herr von Radowitz to Windsor Castle rather than himself[470]; and in letters of his own fabrication he had had himself hailed from Germany 'as provisional government' and condoled with in advance by gullible friends on the score that, after his return to the fatherland, 'affairs of state' would debar him from all companionable intercourse.

Hardly had the invitation to subscribe to the loan of 10 millions appeared, signed by Messrs Ruge, Ronge, Haug, Struve and Kinkel,[a] when the rumour was suddenly put round that a subscription list was circulating in the City for the purpose of dispatching Struve to America, while at the same time the *Kölnische Zeitung* carried a statement by Mrs Johanna Kinkel to the effect that her husband had not signed that appeal and had resigned from the newly formed Central Committee.[b]

Mr Struve's entire political wisdom before and after the March revolution had notoriously confined itself to preaching 'hatred of princes'. Nevertheless in London he found himself compelled to contribute articles for cash to Duke Karl of Brunswick's German paper[c] and even to submit to the ducal blue pencil wielded by His Grace himself. Mazzini had been secretly informed of this and, when Mr Struve wished to see his name appear in splendour beneath the European circular letter, Mazzini pronounced an interdict. His heart filled with rage against the Central Committee, Struve shook the dust off his feet and sailed for New York,

---

a 'An die Deutschen', *Bremer Tages-Chronik,* No. 534, 28 March 1851. - b 'Bonn, 10 May', *Kölnische Zeitung,* No. 114, 13 May 1851. - c *Deutsche Londoner Zeitung*

there to acclimatise his *idée fixe,* his inevitable *Deutscher Zuschauer.*

Now as for Kinkel, he had not, if the gossip of A. Ruge and the New York *Schnellpost* are to be believed, actually signed that appeal but had approved it, the scheme had been hatched in his own room, he had himself undertaken to dispatch a number of copies to Germany and had only resigned because the Central Committee had elected General Haug chairman instead of himself. A. Ruge accompanied this explanation with angry attacks upon the 'vanity' of Kinkel whom he described as a *democratic Beckerath* and with aspersions upon Mrs Johanna Kinkel for having access to newspapers as execrated as the *Kölnische Zeitung.*

Thus the democratic Central Committee was reduced to Messrs Ruge, Ronge and Haug; even A. Ruge realised that this trinity was incapable of creating anything at all, let alone a world. However, the tireless fellow by no means threw up the sponge. All this great man was really concerned about was that something or other should be always afoot, which would lend him an air of activity, of being engaged in deep political combinations, and, above all, afford him material for self-important chitchat, for comings and goings, negotiations, complacent gossip and notices in the press. Luckily for him, Fickler now arrived in London. Like his fellow South Germans, Goegg and Sigel, he was repelled by Kinkel's pretentious mannerisms. Sigel felt no inclination whatever to place himself under the supreme command of Willich, any more than did Goegg to accept his plans for world improvement. Finally, all 3 were too little acquainted with the history of German philosophy not to mistake Ruge for a significant thinker, too naive not to be taken in by his false bonhomie, and too gullible not to take *au sérieux*[a] all the doings of the so-called emigration. They decided, as one of them[b] writes in the New York *Schnellpost,* upon union with the other coteries for the purpose of restoring the reputation of the moribund Central Committee. But, the same correspondent complains, there was little prospect for this pious and well-intentioned task; Kinkel was continuing to intrigue; he had formed a committee consisting of his saviour,[c] his biographer[d] and several Prussian lieutenants; it was to work unseen, expand in secret, if possible attract democratic funds and then, suddenly, emerge into the light of day as the mighty Kinkel party. This was neither honourable, nor just, nor sensible. In the same issue of the

---

[a] seriously - [b] Amand Goegg - [c] Karl Schurz (helped Kinkel to escape from prison in 1850) - [d] Adolf Strodtmann

paper Ruge was unable to resist a few innuendoes at the expense of the 'absolute martyr'. On the very same day that the New York *Schnellpost* brought this gossip to London, the hostile coteries for the first time officially celebrated their fraternal unification. But that is not all. A. Ruge is making propaganda in America through the New York *Schnellpost* on behalf of the unfortunate European loan. But Kinkel, who disavowed this absurd undertaking in the *Kölnische Zeitung*, is now, off his own bat, calling for a loan in the transatlantic papers, with the comment that the money should be sent to the man who enjoys the greatest confidence; that he is that man, goes without saying.

For the present he is demanding an instalment of £500 sterling in order to manufacture revolutionary paper money. Ruge, no sluggard, lets it be known through the *Schnellpost* that he, A. Ruge, is the treasurer of the democratic Central Committee and the notes, ready and to hand, are to be had from him; anybody with £500 sterling to lose would do better to exchange it for already printed notes than as yet non-existent ones. And the editorial department of the *Schnellpost* has stated pretty plainly that, if Mr Kinkel does not desist from his machinations, he will be treated as an enemy of the revolution. Finally, while Ruge disposes of his weekly gossip in the *Schnellpost,* cuts his capers here as man of the future and has himself accorded all the honours due to a 5th wheel, Kinkel writes in the *New-Yorker Staatszeitung*, the direct antagonist of the *Schnellpost:*

'So you see that, on the other side of the Atlantic Ocean, war is waged in due form, whereas on this side Judas kisses are exchanged.'

If you were to ask me how an A. Ruge—a man who, almost from the start, has been quite useless, who in theory has long departed this life and distinguished himself only by his classically confused style—how he can continue to play any role at all, I would first remark that that role is a pure newspaper fiction which he tries, with a unique and persistent diligence and by the most mean-minded methods, to disseminate and convince himself and others. As regards his position among the so-called emigration here, it is a fitting one, be it only as a gutter for the reception of all the contradictions, inconsistencies and limitations of the united democrats. As the classic representative of their general confusion and woolly state of mind, he rightly claims his place as their Confucius.[a]

---

[a] A pun on the name of the Chinese philosopher Confucius and the word 'confusion'.

From the foregoing you will have seen how Kinkel now advances, now retreats, now embarks on an undertaking, now disavows it, always in accordance with the way he believes the popular wind to be blowing. In a piece for the short-lived *Kosmos,* he expressed particular admiration for a gigantic mirror exhibited in the Crystal Palace.[a] That's Kinkel for you; the mirror is the element in which he exists. He is first and foremost an actor. As the martyr *par excellence* of the German revolution, he has received here in London the honours due to the other battle victims. But while, officially, he allows himself to be paid and fêted by the liberal-aesthetic bourgeoisie, he engages behind the latter's back in illicit dealings with the most extreme fraction of the agreement-seeking émigrés represented by Willich, thinking thereby to assure himself both the delights of the bourgeois present and a title to the revolutionary future. While the conditions in which he lives here might be called splendid by comparison with his former position in Bonn, he nonetheless writes to St Louis saying he lodges and lives as befits the representative of the poor.[b] Thus he simultaneously complies with the required etiquette vis-à-vis the bourgeoisie, while making the obeisance that is due to the proletariat. However, as a man in whom imagination far outweighs intelligence, he has been unable to avoid succumbing to some of the vices and pretensions of the parvenu, and this has alienated from him many a pompous émigré worthy. At this moment he apparently intends to make a tour of England to lecture in various towns to audiences of German merchants, receive homage and extend to the North of England the privilege of the double harvest normally confined to southern climes. It is self-delusion on Kinkel's part if he regards himself as ambitious. He is a man of vain appetites, and fate could play this otherwise innocuous speechifier no worse trick than to permit him to attain the goal of his desires and a responsible position. He would be a complete and irretrievable failure.

Finally, as to Willich, I need do no more than apprise you of the opinion of his acquaintances, all of whom regard him as an uninspired visionary. They doubt his talent but, for that very reason, declare him to be a character.[c] He is happy in this

---

[a] The Crystal Palace was built of metal and glass for the first world trade and industrial exhibition in London in 1851. - [b] G. Kinkel, 'Der Brief an die Bürger von St. Louis', *Bremer Tages-Chronik,* No. 507, 25 February 1851. - [c] Cf. H. Heine, *Atta Troll,* XXIV—'no talent but a character' (description of the bear-hero Atta Troll).

situation and exploits it with more Prussian cunning than he is generally credited with. Now you know who the great men of the future are.

The vast majority of the official emigration consists with very few exceptions of noughts, each of whom thinks to become the number one by combining with others to form a dozen. Hence their constant attempts at uniting and conglomerating, which are constantly being undone by the petty jealousies, intrigues, basenesses and rivalries of these *petits grands hommes*,[a] and as ceaselessly entered into again. While slinging mud at each other in the North American papers they believe that, vis-à-vis Germany, they form a front, and that by coagulating to form a great gossiping cheese-pat they will inevitably produce the effect of being a power and a *corpus venerabile*.[b] They are always under the impression that there is still something they lack if they are to impress, hence their organised courtship of every new arrival. Their efforts to win over Freiligrath, whom they have now sent to Coventry, and to lure him away from Marx, were as importunate as they were, of course, fruitless. Kinkel left no stone unturned, and A. Ruge actually wrote him a letter to induce him to join the League of the Just. He does not now, of course, belong to '*the* emigration' any more than W. Wolff and other refugees who remain aloof from these goings-on. *One* more name! If these capuchins of the revolution, these mendicant friars of the same, had anything at all to give away, they would give a kingdom for one more name,[c] especially a name as popular as Freiligrath's. Place-seekers and popularity-mongers, that's what all this crowd amounts to. These gentlemen believe that the revolution is at hand and that they must naturally make their dispositions. In like manner did the Imperial Assembly[d] men in Switzerland form themselves into an association in which future posts were shared out hierarchically by number. And it bred bitter strife as to who should represent No. 17 or 18.

You express surprise that these gentlemen should make the semi-ministerial *Lithographische Correspondenz* their monitor. Your surprise will be at an end when I tell you that one of its scribes regularly scribbles in the *Neue Preussische Zeitung*,[e] another serves as general factotum to the Russian *Morning Chronicle*, etc., etc. Nor does this take place behind the backs of the official emigration—

---

[a] petty panjandrums - [b] a venerable body - [c] Cf. Shakespeare, *Richard III*, Act V, 4. - [d] Frankfurt - [e] A reference to Julius Faucher

far from it. Indeed, their first general assembly opened with a reading of the article from the *Lithographische Correspondenz*. They mustered some 50 men, a number which, at the second sitting, dwindled to less than half.[a] The seed of discord had already begun to germinate freely among those craving agreement, who, by the by, as one of them remarked in confidence, consisted solely of *'superior refugees'*. Of the profane *vulgus*[b] of the refugee working men, none was to be seen.

If there is one point upon which the fraternising emigration are all unanimous, it is their common and fanatical hatred of Marx, a hatred which regards no fatuity, no baseness, no intrigue as too high a price to pay for the gratification of their ill-humour towards this, their *bête noire*. For these gentlemen have not even thought it beneath their dignity to make contact with Beta or Bettziech, a former collaborator on Gubitz's *Gesellschafter*, and through that great author and patriot writing in the organ of the merry vintner, Louis Drucker,[c] to insinuate that Marx is a spy because he is brother-in-law to the Prussian minister, von Westphalen.[471] The only connection Herr von Westphalen ever had with Marx lay in the former's confiscation of Becker's printing works and the incarceration of H. Becker in Cologne, by which he frustrated the publication of Marx's *Gesammelte Aufsätze* which Becker had undertaken and of which the first volume had already appeared,[347] and likewise prevented the publication of a *Revue* then actually printing. Their hatred of Marx was further intensified by the Saxon Government's publication of the communist address,[d] since he was held to be its author. Marx, however, being wholly engaged in working out his critique and history of political economy, begun years before, had no more time or inclination than Freiligrath and their mutual friends to attend to the tittle-tattle of the fraternising emigration.

But the more one ignores them, the more frantic the yapping of these pug-dogs of the future becomes. Gustav Julius, a man with a thoroughly critical and scientifically trained intellect, who died all too young and is now being claimed by the emigration for their own, grew so weary of their shallow and preposterous goings-on

---

[a] The reference is to emigrant meetings in London on 8 and 15 August. -
[b] common people - [c] *How Do You Do?* - [d] K. Marx and F. Engels, 'Address of the Central Authority to the League. March 1850'.

that he wrote a full and detailed description of the same and, only a few weeks before his death, sent it to a North German newspaper[a] which, however, rejected it....

First published in *Mitteilungen des öster-reichischen Staatsarchivs*, Bd. 9, Wien, 1956

Printed according to a copy in an unknown hand

Published in English for the first time

203

MARX TO ENGELS

IN MANCHESTER

[London, about 20 August 1851]

Dear Engels,

It would be best if you read the Proudhon[b] first, since I must have it back. I have made as many notes as I need from the Dureau.[c]

Apropos, *do for goodness' sake write to Fischer in New Orleans.* (Liebknecht is at present his regular correspondent). This is all the more important because it is precisely from New Orleans that the Kinkels, Ruges, etc., are hoping to draw subsidies. So don't forget to write to the man who complained in a letter to Liebknecht about your silence.

Your

K. M.

First published in *Der Briefwechsel zwischen F. Engels und K. Marx*, Bd. 1, Stuttgart, 1913

Printed according to the original

Published in English for the first time

---

[a] At this point the words 'of Magdeburg' have been added in the margin. -
[b] P. J. Proudhon, *Idée générale de la Révolution au XIXe siècle*. - [c] Dureau de la Malle, *Économie politique des Romains*.

204

ENGELS TO MARX

IN LONDON

Manchester, 21 August 1851

Dear Marx,

Herewith an article of a sort.[a] Various circumstances have conspired to spoil the thing. In the first place I have, for a change, been unwell ever since Saturday. Then there was the total absence of material—all I could do was scrape the bottom of the barrel, and rely on memory. Then the shortness of time and working to order, almost total ignorance of the paper[b] and its readership, precluding any proper plan. Finally, the impossibility of keeping the manuscript of the whole series for comparison, hence the need for a *plus ou moins*[c] pedantically methodical beginning to obviate repetitions in subsequent articles. All this, combined with the fact that I have quite got out of the habit of writing, has made the piece very dry and, if there's anything to be said in its favour, it is the greater fluency of the English, which I owe to the fact that for the past eight months I have been accustomed to speak and read practically nothing but English. *Enfin, tu en feras ce que tu voudras.*[d]

I am half way through the Proudhon and heartily endorse your view. His appeal to the bourgeoisie, his reversion to Saint-Simon and a hundred and one other matters in the critical section alone, provide confirmation that he regards the industrial class, the bourgeoisie and the proletariat as virtually identical and as having been brought into opposition only by the fact that the revolution was never completed. The pseudo-philosophical nature of the historical construction is plain for all to see: before the revolution, the industrial class an entity in itself, 1789-1848 in opposition: negation; Proudhonian synthesis TO WIND UP THE WHOLE WITH A FLOURISH. The whole thing seems to me a last attempt to maintain the bourgeoisie in theory; our premises on the decisive historical initiative of material production, class struggle, etc., largely adopted, for the most part distorted and used as the basis for the endeavour apparently to reincorporate the proletariat in the

---

a F. Engels, *Revolution and Counter-Revolution in Germany*, Article I. - b *New-York Daily Tribune* - c more or less - d Anyhow, you can do what you please with it.

bourgeoisie by a pseudo-Hegelian sleight-of-hand. I have not yet read the synthetic part. There are one or two nice things in the attacks on L. Blanc, Robespierre, and Rousseau, but on the whole it would be hard to find anything more pretentiously insipid than his critique of politics, e.g. in the case of democracy, in which, like the *Neue Preussische Zeitung* and all the old historical school,[472] he comes up with head-counting, and in which, without a blush, he builds up systems out of small, practical deliberations worthy of a schoolboy. And what a great idea that *pouvoir* and *liberté*[a] are irreconcilably opposed, and that no form of government can provide him with sufficient moral grounds why *he* should obey it! *Par Dieu!*[b] Then what does one need *pouvoir* for?

I'm convinced, by the way, that Mr Ewerbeck let him have his translation of the *Manifesto*[c] and also, perhaps, in an underhand manner, passages translated from your articles in the *Revue.*[d] A number of points were indubitably lifted from them—e.g. that a *gouvernement* is nothing but the power of one class to repress the other, and will disappear with the disappearance of the contradiction between classes. Then, a number of points concerning the French movement since 1848. I don't think he can have found all that in your book against him.[e]

In a few days' time, as soon as I've read the whole thing, I'll write about it in greater detail. Meanwhile, Weerth, who is making one of his sudden visits to Bradford, is likely to turn up here any day, in which case I may be obliged to keep the Proudhon for another two or three days.

Tell Lupus that I've spoken to Watts, who is going to make every effort, and with every prospect of success, to obtain a position for him here. Watts believes that his having been a member of the National Assembly[f] will be quite sufficient here. He knows the whole genus of schoolmasters and clergy of liberal complexion and, once he gets moving, will certainly be able to arrange something. I shall therefore keep him in good humour; as soon as I hear anything further, I shall let him know. By the way, Watts is, all things considered, no less tolerable than the usual type of philistine. Since the man lives the life of an Englishman, socialist, doctor and paterfamilias, allowance must be made for the fact that he's been a TEETOTALLER for the past 7 years—and has even

---

[a] power and liberty - [b] By God! - [c] K. Marx and F. Engels, *Manifesto of the Communist Party* (the French translation, made in 1848, was not published). - [d] K. Marx, *The Class Struggles in France, 1848 to 1850* (published in the *Neue Rheinische Zeitung. Politisch-ökonomische Revue*). - [e] K. Marx, *The Poverty of Philosophy.-* [f] in Frankfurt in 1848-49

felt a yearning to become a Struvian herbivore. His wife,[a] on the other hand, tipples and guzzles enough for two. It's regrettable, but a fact, that here in Manchester your ordinary little man is, by and large, more congenial than anyone else; he tipples, talks smut, is a repooblican (like Martens), and you can laugh about him.

What news have you from Germany? In Hamburg 3 have been released and one re-arrested. So all the journeyman tailor Nothjung's confessions amount to is that he's the emissary of a propagandist secret society—*quelle découverte!*[b]

Your
F. E.

First published in *Der Briefwechsel zwischen F. Engels und K. Marx*, Bd. 1, Stuttgart, 1913

Printed according to the original

Published in English for the first time

205

MARX TO ENGELS

IN MANCHESTER

[London,] 25 August 1851
28 Dean Street, Soho

Dear Engels,

D'abord mes remercîments pour ton article.[c] Despite all the bad things you say about it, it was splendid and has set sail unaltered for New York. You hit just the right note for the *Tribune*. As soon as we get the first number of it, I'll send it to you, and continue to do so regularly from then on.

Maintenant,[d] I've got a whole load of émigré dung to forward to you and, should you know a farmer in the neighbourhood who requires the guano of these cleanly birds for manure, you can do a deal with him.

Well, then, as you already know, the first *official* meeting of the fraternising émigrés took place on Friday, 8 August, the leading lights being: The 'Damm', who presided; Schurz, secretary, Goegg, two Sigels,[e] Fickler, Tausenau, Franck (the Austrian worthy),

---

[a] Catherine Shaw - [b] what a revelation! - [c] First, many thanks for your article (the reference is to F. Engels, *Revolution and Counter-Revolution in Germany*. Article I). - [d] Now - [e] Albert and Franz Sigel

Willich, Borkheim, Schimmelpfennig, Johannes Ronge, Meyen, Count Reichenbach, Oppenheim, Bauer (Stolpe),[a] the intolerable Lüders, Haug, A. Ruge, Techow, Schmolze (Bavarian lieutenant), Petzler, Böhler, Gehrke, Schärttner, Göhringer, etc., not, of course, forgetting Kinkel and Strodtmann. Thus the main cliques: 1. Ruge-Fickler, 2. Kinkel, 3. Tausenau. Interspersed with other independent literary loafers and agreers.[467] The real issue with which this great historical event[371] was concerned was the following: Ruge-Fickler-Tausenau-Goegg-Sigel-Haug, etc., sought the election of an official committee, partly to denounce the misdeeds of the reactionaries, partly to represent the émigrés, partly for 'Action'—agitation as regards Germany. A further snag about that idiot, Ruge, was that he had been recognised as plenipotentiary vis-à-vis Ledru-Mazzini and, in addition to his name, was now in fact able to place an army at their disposal in the shape of the German refugee corps. Mr Kinkel (and with him, besides his saviour Schurz and his biographer Furz,[b] more esp. Willich, Techow, Schmolze, Schimmelpfenning), on the other hand, did not want a public institution of this kind, partly so as not to imperil his position vis-à-vis the bourgeoisie here in London—since it's the guineas that count—partly so as not to have to more or less recognise Ruge vis-à-vis Mazzini-Ledru.

From the start the Ruge-Fickler clique was furious to see that the meeting-room was full to overflowing. It had been agreed at a secret sitting that only notables were to be asked to attend. But the Kinkel clique had brought in *le menu peuple*[c] so as to assure themselves of a majority.

The sitting opened with the reading of a piece of rubbish from the *Lithographische Correspondenz* by General Haug, who at the same time declared that there must be spies present, that the document might be abused, etc. Willich, his pathos as yet unimpaired, seconded this and called on the miscreants to declare themselves. Thereupon Bauer of Stolpe (whom, by the way, I hold to be a regular spy) rose to his feet and declared he was unable to understand Willich's virtuous horror since, at the first preparatory sitting, he had introduced Mr Scheidler without any opposition as editor of the *Lithographische Correspondenz*.

This incident settled, Tausenau, with much cosily emotional grunting and groaning, doubtless under the impression that he was before a Viennese audience, made his proposal for nomina-

---

[a] Ludwig Bauer - [b] Adolf Strodtmann—a pun in the original: Schurz and Furz (fart) - [c] the small fry

tions to the committee. In reply, Mr Meyen said that what he wanted was not deeds but voluntary lectures. As prearranged, Kinkel at once undertook to deal with America and its future, Oppenheim England, Schurz France, and Meyen Prussia. Tausenau's proposal having met with a resounding defeat, he declared with emotion that, despite his failure, he would sacrifice his righteous anger on the altar of the fatherland and remain in the bosom of the fraternising.

But the Fickler-Ruge clique immediately assumed the menacing and injured air of beautiful souls who've been cheated.

At the end of the sitting Kinkel went up to Schabelitz (who was there purely in the capacity of our agent—and a very useful agent, too, since he enjoyed the confidence of all those worthies), declared him to be an honest democrat, declared the *Basler National-Zeitung* to be an excellent democratic paper and asked, among other things, about the state of its finances. Schabelitz: Poor. Kinkel: But aren't the working men doing anything? *Schabelitz*: Everything we ask of them; they read the paper. *Kinkel*: The workers should do more. They don't support us either as they ought to. And you know, we really do so much for the workers. We do everything we can to make them into 'respectable',—you understand me, of course,—'honourable citizens'. *En voilà une bonne!*[a]

The agreers' meeting on the 15th was not well attended and was, as the English say, INDIFFERENT.

Meanwhile great things were taking place—on the 17th—and the true course of the affair assumed, as our great A. Ruge would say, the following course:

Mr Kinkel summoned Willich, Techow, Goegg, Sigel and a few others, and revealed to them that he had received £160 through Fischer from New Orleans and had been charged with disposing of this money in consultation with the above-named and with Mr '*Fr. Engels*'. Instead of the latter, he had invited Fickler who, however, had declared that he had nothing to do with the 'scoundrels'. Mr Kinkel was forced to show the letter from which it transpired that, anonymous and incognito, this money had already been at his lodgings for three weeks, unable to decide whether or not it should generously unbosom itself to the profane world. Though Kinkel spake with the tongues of angels, it availed him nothing. The Fickler clique realised that the Kinkel clique was doing some considerable angling on the side and would merely

---

[a] That's a good one!

exploit the storm in the émigrés' communal tea-cup to lure the 'goldfish' away by stealth. And thus it was in vain that the great Heinzen had cast such lovelorn and plain-speaking glances at the £s collected in New Orleans! Goegg and Sigel left the conclave. A separate sitting of the Fickler-Ruge-Tausenau clique took place.

For the South Germans had privily discovered that A. Ruge was an imbecile. They need him because he provides a channel to Ledru-Mazzini, and this patronage is of great importance to the South Germans. Tausenau appears to have opened their eyes for them and is now their real LEADER alongside Fickler. Tausenau is, in general, very much a wiseacre and intriguer, dabbling in diplomacy and equipped with the petty Jew's flair for calculation; he believes in the imminence of the revolution. Hence his presence in this League.

Ruge, in a tremendous rage over the lost £160, now revealed to his friends that, more than 12 months previously, Willich-Kinkel had sent Schimmelpfennig to Mazzini, saying that he was an emissary and had come for money so that he could travel to Germany for the purpose of agitation. Mazzini gave him 1,000 fr. in cash and 5,000 fr. in his Italian notes on condition that in 12 months' time he would return the 1,000 fr. and $^2/_3$ of the Italian notes provided. On these Schimmelpfennig travelled round France and Germany. The 12 months elapsed but nothing more was heard of either Kinkel-Schimmelpfennig, or the 1,000 fr., or the Italian notes. Now, when the money had arrived from New Orleans, Kinkel had once more sent his envoys to Mazzini, not to pay, but to blow their own trumpets and enter into an alliance with, him. Mazzini had too much delicacy to remind them of their debt but told them that, since he had connections in Germany, he could not enter into any new ones. These gentlemen, A. Ruge went on, had also betaken themselves to Ledru-Rollin. But here Ruge had stolen a march on them: since Ledru-Rollin already considers himself President of the French Republic and has determined to wage war abroad forthwith, Ruge had presented Sigel to him as commander-in-chief of the German revolutionary army, whereupon Ledru-Rollin had embarked on a strategical discussion with Sigel. Another snub, then, for Kinkel-Willich.

After these revelations of Ruge's, therefore, the turpitude of the Kinkel-Willich clique was laid bare before the eyes of the bemused beautiful souls. Now was the time for action, but what action is Ruge capable of other than new combinations and permutations of his mouldy old Central Committee? Hence it was resolved to form an *agitation club*,[473] not for debating, but *'essentially for working'*, productive not of WORDS but of WORKS, and above all for inducing like-minded comrades to make financial contributions. To be composed of: Fickler, Tausenau, Franck, Goegg, Sigel, Hertle, J. Ronge, Haug, Ruge. You will immediately note the reconstruction Ruge-Ronge-Haug. But closer inspection reveals that the main components of the club are 1. the western South German worthies, Fickler, Goegg, Sigel, Hertle, 2. the eastern South Germans, Tausenau, Haug, and Franck, and hence that the club has been formed mainly as a *South German* one in opposition to the '*Prussians*', and Ruge is only the umbilical cord maintaining the connection with the European Central Committee.[338] In fact, they now call the other societies simply '*the Prussians*'. This agitation club nominated Tausenau to its executive authority and simultaneously made him its Minister of the Exterior. This meant that the Central Ruge was *completely ousted.* But in order to sugar the pill for him, he was given a *douceur* in the shape of an acknowledgment that his position on the Central Committee was recognised, as also his previous activities and his representation of the German people in accordance with the wishes of the German people. You'll have seen this *testimonium paupertatis*[a] in print since it appeared in a notice, published in almost every English newspaper, in which the agitation society most humbly announces its birth to the European public and solicits its custom. Even this *douceur* was soured for poor Ruge by the fact that Bauer-Fickler imposed the intolerable *conditio sine qua non*[b] that Ruge should desist 'from writing and publishing his stupid stuff'.

Before I go on, I should observe that, *all unbeknown to the others,* we are represented in the united democratic club by a working man called *Ulmer* who has fled from Cologne to join our League[c]; he's a man who, when he's with us, is very quiet and taciturn and of whom we would never have believed that he would hold the united democrats in check. But *indignatio facit poetam,*[d] and the silent Ulmer, or so he told me, has a 'genius' for flaring up easily, whereupon he shakes all over and lets fly like a Berserk. Despite his weedy tailor's build, he is the best gymnast in Mainz, and has a considerable awareness of his physical strength and agility. In addition a communist's pride in infallibility.

On 22 August, then, the 3rd sitting was held. Meeting very well attended in anticipation of great row over the highly treasonable

---

[a] certificate of poverty - [b] indispensable condition - [c] the Communist League - [d] indignation makes the poet—adaptation of *facit indignatio versum* (indignation makes the verse), Juvenal, *Satires,* I

agitation club. President: Meyen. Also present: R. Schramm and Bucher. The Kinkel clique proposed that a refugee committee be set up. For Mr Kinkel has no wish to make his exit from the public stage. Nor does he wish to compromise himself in the eyes of England's aesthetic-liberal bourgeoisie. A refugee committee, besides being politico-philanthropic, is a source of funds, and thus combines all the desirable prerequisites. On the other hand, Ulmer and a certain Hollinger put forward a proposal that the refugee committee be elected at a general meeting of refugees, whereat the Kinkel clique began to harp on the danger that people (namely we, the unnamed) would kick up a row behind the backs of the assembly. But they also had enemies *before* them. Goegg, Sigel and his brother were the only members of the agitation club present. Goegg was elected to the refugee committee. This provided an opportunity, 1) to announce Tausenau's resignation, 2) to reject the agitation club's statement, 3) finally, after the conclusion of the debate, to announce their resignation in a body. Uproar. *Techow and Schramm gave A. Ruge a fearsome dressing down.* Altogether a great deal of *abuse* was hurled. Goegg replied to the others with assurance, launched a bitter attack on the ambivalent Kinkel, who, replying only through his satellites, stroked his beard like the Great Mogul and dictated to Schurz, who was constantly dancing attendance on him, notes which he then, like the agreers in Berlin, caused to be circulated among his trusties and, after the circulation, recorded his final vote. Only when Goegg said that the agitation club would publish its declaration in the English papers, did *Kinkel* answer *majestically that he already controlled the whole of the American press and that steps had been taken to bring the whole of the French press likewise under his control within a very short space of time.*

Besides this scandal-laden theme, others were mooted which stirred up the most almighty turmoil in the bosom of the fraternising democrats. Fists were shaken and there was a great clamour and hullaballoo until, at 2 o'clock in the morning, the landlord put out the lamps, thus plunging the agreement-seekers into impenetrable darkness. The row pivoted on two people, Schramm and Ulmer. For in his diatribe against Ruge, Schramm simultaneously vented his wrath on the communists, which received much acclaim, launched a most virulent attack on Willich, and called the workers cowards. To this Ulmer replied; but, for his part and in company with Hollinger—Sigel's friend— demanded the convening of a general meeting of refugees to elect a relief committee. He accused Willich, etc., outright of dissipating and squandéring refugee funds. Indescribable tumult. Up sprang Dietz, the cockroach, stated that he was the treasurer of the Great Windmill Street[331] refugee committee[292] and demanded that the allegation be withdrawn. Ulmer declared that, should the gentlemen so desire, he would provide proof. He would withdraw nothing. Willich, in his usual manner, tried to mollify him and invited him to his lodgings for a private discussion. But Cato Ulmer stood his ground and would say nothing without witnesses. By the by, during Goegg's speech Schimmelpfennig, who was sitting behind Ulmer, had kept on grunting and making noises until Ulmer, suddenly seized by his 'genius', turned round with clenched fist and roared at Schimmelpfennig: 'If you don't keep your mouth shut, you miserable penny-pincher, I'll chuck you out of the window.' Schimmelpfennig turned white as a sheet but, discretion getting the better of a Prussian officer's valour, he betook himself to the farthest corner of the room.

Time and again in the course of this memorable *séance* Willich was so savagely assailed from all sides—by Goegg, Schramm, Hollinger, Ulmer, etc.—that on 6 occasions he declared he would have to resign if they refused to leave his worthy person alone.

But now a new element enters the row which was all our doing. For, the 'superior refugees' as these gentlemen call themselves, had left the 'inferior émigrés' completely out of account. We had got Ulmer, Rumpf and Liebknecht to give these 'inferior émigrés', who are faring very badly, a spicy account of the fact that the Great Windmill Street refugee committee had received 800 gulden from Württemberg, and that they were being well and truly diddled. So yesterday, there was a row at the sitting of the Windmill Street committee, *praesidio Schapperi*.[a] The refugees demanded to see the letters, accounts, etc. Willich, who had made the same demands as these jackasses' when he was opposing us, tells them curtly that he and co. are answerable only to the Workers' Society.[52] When a refugee comes too close, he tells him to stand back and keep his lice to himself. In return the man calls him an 'empty-headed half-wit'. Schapper is asked to account for his hippopotamus's belly and addressed as 'Snapper'. Willich calls the landlord and asks him to eject one of the refugees. The latter says he will leave if they call a POLICEMAN. The gents, he states, are rascals, and there the matter rests. Willich and Schapper declare that in the circumstances they will resign.

These 'inferior émigrés' have now been told by Rumpf and

---

[a] chaired by Schapper

Ulmer that next Friday their interests will be placed before the general emigration society. They will proceed there *en masse* armed with clubs in order to assert their claims. I then let them know through Ulmer that Kinkel has received £160 on their behalf which he has secreted for weeks and is now proposing to share with Willich, and that in any case they are simply being used—*et c'est vrai*[a]—as a trade-mark to bolster up the finances of these statesmen. Ulmer is to be the speaker and since Schramm, etc., are completely unaware of this surprise—the row should be edifying from every point of view.

You may write a—belated but necessary—letter to Kinkel as soon as I have informed you about Friday's sitting. What you must do forthwith, however, is write to *Fischer* in New Orleans, explaining the whole dirty business to him and letting him know that henceforward he should collect money only under the '*Freiligrath*' trade-mark, which is quite popular. Our party of course needs it. It is the only active one, the only one to be in direct confrontation with the Federal Diet,[474] God and the devil, and we have no money whatever for agitation. Again, money must be raised for our people in prison who are, for the most part, quite penniless. These two aspects, it seems to me, should be easy to explain to the man. If possible, by the way, he should make the collections in *secret*, since our efficiency can only be impaired by newspaper gossip.

Vale faveque.[b]

Your

K. Marx

25 August

I should further remark that Schapper, that orthodox ox, is by no means prepared to consort with 'unbelievers'; rather he has told Willich that he'd sooner have his skull split open than betake himself to 'the curs'.

If a few days sometimes elapse between letters, it is because I want to send you a fuller report.

First published in *Der Briefwechsel zwischen F. Engels und K. Marx*, Bd. 1, Stuttgart, 1913

Printed according to the original

Published in English for the first time

---

[a] and it's true - [b] Good-bye and farewell.

16*

206

ENGELS TO MARX

[Manchester, about 27 August 1851]

Dear Marx,

The homeric struggles of these great men in their striving after unity have cheered me up wonderfully. What an Iliad!

I have written to Fischer.[475] But is it absolutely certain that my name appears in the letter to Kinkel? For I don't want to make an ass of myself with Fischer. The Freiligrath idea is a splendid one; it must surely have been thought up by your wife. A request to Fischer to raise money specifically for *our* party purposes is altogether inappropriate; but if any should be forthcoming— which to judge by the experience of the people in America, I rather doubt—I think my letter will be enough to channel it into Freiligrath's hands *et cela suffit*.[a]

Write to me immediately about the upshot of Friday's scene so that I can take the necessary steps against Kinkel. To begin with I can do no more than ask for information and to be sent the records and then, after their receipt or non-receipt, take further steps. But do you know Kinkel's address?

It would have been a good idea had you let me have Freiligrath's address, too, so that I could have passed it to Fischer immediately. It's now too late for this steamer and, by the time his answer arrives, 4 weeks will have gone by during which we ought not to bombard him overmuch with letters.

My letter will have cooked Kinkel's and Willich's goose over there. It will give them something to think about.

More on Proudhon tomorrow or the day after.[b] Weerth's presence and then this mummery, combined with office rubbish, have prevented me from tackling the thing seriously. At all events the charlatanry of it is superb. Part 2, from liquidation onwards, is to be marvelled at for its blend of Girardin display and Stirner braggadocio. Moreover, both grammatically and logically much of it is pure galimatias, of which he himself knows that it is totally

---

[a] and that is sufficient - [b] F. Engels, 'Critical Review of Proudhon's Book *Idée générale de la Révolution au XIXe siècle*'.

devoid of meaning. This second part is really not to be treated seriously; with the best will in the world one couldn't do so.

I have not, of course, been able to do anything for the *Tribune*—shall resume next week.[a] In great haste.

Your
F. E.

First published slightly abridged in *Der Briefwechsel zwischen F. Engels und K. Marx*, Bd. 1, Stuttgart, 1913 and in full in *MEGA*, Abt. III, Bd. 1, 1929

Printed according to the original

Published in English for the first time

207

MARX TO ENGELS

IN MANCHESTER

[London,] 31 August 1851
28 Dean Street, Soho

Dear Engels,

One always miscalculates badly if one reckons on a definitive crisis among the democratic heroes. A row like the one a fortnight ago demands a recuperation of several weeks for these PERFORMERS. Hence nothing of any moment happened the day before yesterday, Friday the 29th.

D'abord.[b] On Monday, 25 August, as I have already told you, Willich and Schapper threatened to resign from the Great Windmill refugee committee.[292] The following Tuesday they did in fact resign during an official sitting, and all in all the committee came to a satisfactory end. Harsh words were exchanged on this occasion. Willich moralised and pontificated, whereupon he was confronted with his iniquities. The main charge against him was that on this, as on an earlier occasion, when account had to be given of the twenty or so pounds invested in the brush-making business, matters had been so arranged that Mr Lüssel, the manager responsible for same, had absconded.

On Friday General Sigel[c] had attended the general meeting of the agreement-seekers. He had counted on the appearance of the

---

[a] A series of articles *Revolution and Counter-Revolution in Germany.*- [b] First of all. - [c] Franz Sigel

'inferior émigrés', on whose behalf he broke a few mighty lances with Willich, who gave free rein to his indignation over the herd of immoral louts he had once apotheosised vis-à-vis ourselves. Conspicuous by their absence, however, were the lumpen-proletariat. Those who had presented themselves before the gates of the Areopagus were too few in number to be able to count on success, and therefore withdrew. You know that they are cowardly rascals, and that every one of the rapscallions has too bad a conscience to appear before a gathering of any size and take the floor as public prosecutor.

A few Rugians such as Ronge, 4 in number, had been elected to the refugee committee of the 'united democrats'. These men announced their resignation. So the committee was dissolved. A new, *provisional,* one was elected, consisting of Mr Kinkel, Count Reichenbach,[a] Mr Bucher and Mr Semper from Saxony.

From this you will see that they have entered a new phase. They have thrown themselves into the arms of the respectable *'hommes d'état',*[b] since the former leaders are now compromised as being bourgeois scum. The *'hommes d'état'*—their nucleus—are the 'doughty men of the people' *Bucher* (Berlin agreer[467]), *Count Reichenbach* (Knight of the Spirit and compromised deputy to the Frankfurt Assembly, not the Berlin beard of the party[c]) and that eminent stutterer *'Rudolf Schramm' (connu*[d]).

Because of his long-standing friendship with Countess Reichenbach and her brother—also now in this country—Lupus now and again frequents the Reichenbach's house, and yesterday found there Mr Techow, whom he had known in Switzerland. Not long afterwards Willich himself appeared, in company with the melancholy Eduard Meyen. Lupus left when these two great ones took their seats.

Voilà tout ce que j'ai à rapporter pour le moment.[e] With the help of the 160 pounds from America, Kinkel has clearly succeeded—partly himself and partly through his followers—in inducing in the 'respectables' and *'hommes d'état'* a tremendous opinion of his power and connections. But with the dissolution of the Windmill committee, the precious Willich has broken the stoutest link that bound him to the 'rascals'.

Maintenant,[f] as to yourself, there is no doubt whatever that *Fischer* expressly named you as one of the godfathers of the £160. General Sigel and Goegg told their friend Schabelitz about this,

---

[a] Oskar Reichenbach - [b] statesmen - [c] Eduard Reichenbach - [d] well-known - [e] That's all I have to report for the present. - [f] Now

ostensibly *au secret*,[a] but in fact, I believe, in order that it should come to your ears. In my opinion, all you should do is write to Mr Kinkel saying you have heard from New Orleans about the remittance and your role as co-advisor as to its disposal. You *simplement*[b] ask him what has happened to the money, or what it is intended to do with it. Kinkel's address is: Dr. phil. (that's how he describes himself on his visiting cards) Kinkel, 1, Henstridge Villas, St. Johns Wood. Some time, just for fun, I'll send you one of these visiting cards, in form and content exactly like a London advertisement for corn cures AND SO FORTH.

Lest I forget the big event. In the issue[c] of 13 August, the unfortunate Heinzen announces that Otto has withdrawn his capital, thus leaving him on his own with his mental capital which will not, in industrial America, keep a newspaper going. Hence he writes an elegy on the premature fall of Hector. And in the same issue Hoff and Kapp invite readers to subscribe for shares in a newspaper which is to take the place of the *Schnellpost*. And, fate having strange quirks, the *Staatszeitung* has at the same time begun proceedings against the precious Heinzen—incidentally disclosing many of his financial villainies—for libel, proceedings which, he anticipates, will land him up in a 'house of correction'. *Le pauvre*[d] Heinzen! Moreover this great man is now morally outraged at America and the 'unemotional Yankees' and at the German Americans who take after them, instead of working for the 'humanisation of society' and going into raptures over A. Ruge's politico-social revelations.

In the said issue we read, for example:

'That free German spirit, which is to fill the world ... that spring which, for almost two millennia now, and in ever richer spiritual measure, has been flowing over the continents of the earth.'

'For what purpose, then, are there Germans in the world? For what purpose a German heart, for what purpose the German tongue? To what purpose, e.g., this instrument, invented by the German Gutenberg, for the education and enlightenment of the mind? All this exists, and so does the very soil on which it is coming or should come to pass, this America, **discovered by A German**.'

'The free communities,[350] lusty German philosophy, magnificent German literature, transposed and brought into intellectual interaction with everything excellent and enduring that the country and its inhabitants possess,—from factors such as these there must arise an *American-ness* [Amerikanertum] *of world-historical importance*, an all-powerfully humane, spiritual and moral greatness, whose heart is activated by a never-ceasing influx of Teuton-ness [Teutschtum], its head by a refined Yankee-ness [Yankeetum] and its arm by both combined.'

---

[a] in confidence - [b] simply - [c] of the *Deutsche Schnellpost* - [d] Poor

'Indeed, I maintain that the German people are more ripe for a democratic republic than the American.... Verily, were Germany to be freed of her fetters and bloodsuckers, she would be better equipped to "fix", as the Americans say, a purely democratic republic and to bring it about more successfully than the Yankees, for in as much as even the politically most educated section of the Americans is still so much a prey to superstition, so unfree intellectually, and so remote from any humane education, how can the final goal of democracy, true humanity, the harmonious development of mankind, be realised politically, socially and morally or spiritually?'

Thus writes the German buffoon,[a] or gets someone to write, at the very time when the Americans have successfully made their way across the isthmus.[476] In the same issue the hooligan has himself addressed as follows:

'So aptly do you castigate American conditions, notably the German Americans, that any discriminating and unbiassed person must agree with you. You would be doing really praiseworthy work were you, through your paper, to help assure the refinement and education of Germans in America, and even if your voice should elude the untutored masses, enough would be achieved if you freed the individual German of the simian and pernicious urge to ape the Americans.'

And then, with all stops pulled out, the churl proceeds to vent the foul, morning-after-the-night—before pecuniary jeremiads.

You'll have undoubtedly long since learnt from the papers that Girardin has allied himself with Ledru-Rollin. He was already convinced he was the future Great Mogul of France. But now a Lamennais-Michel (de Bourges)-Schoelcher rival committee has been set up in Paris whose intention is to bring into being the 'United States of Europe' with the help of the *Romance* peoples— French, Spanish and Italians—round whom the Germans, etc., will then crystallise. So the Spanish! are to civilise us! *Mon Dieu,*[b] that even outdoes K. Heinzen, who wants to introduce Feuerbach and A. Ruge among the Yankees in order to 'humanise' them. Ledru's *Proscrit* bitterly attacked the rival committee.[c] They replied in the same coin. But what was still more bitter for the Great Mogul *in partibus*[d] was this: a conclave of the entire press was held in Paris. The *Proscrit,* too, was represented by a delegate.[e] Purpose: to agree on a common President. The rejection of all the *Proscrit's* proposals was followed by the unequivocal declaration that, let the gentlemen in London chatter as they would, what was necessary for France must emanate from France herself; Ledru was very much mistaken if he regarded himself as 'the important personage' Mazzini made him out to be.

---

[a] Karl Heinzen - [b] My God - [c] 'Cronique de l'intérieur', *La Voix du Proscrit,* No 18, 23 August 1851. - [d] *In partibus infidelium*—literally: in parts inhabited by infidels; figuratively; without any real power. - [e] Ch. Delescluze [see Ch. Delescluze, 'Le conclave démocratique', *La Voix du Proscrit,* No. 19, 30 August 1851]

For the rest, the conclave broke up amidst much uproar without having achieved anything. Unity-seeking democrats are everywhere as like as two peas.

Adieu.

Your

K. M.

First published slightly abridged in *Der Briefwechsel zwischen F. Engels und K. Marx*, Bd. 1, Stuttgart, 1913 and in full in *MEGA*, Abt. III, Bd. 1, 1929

Printed according to the original

Published in English for the first time

208

ENGELS TO MARX

IN LONDON

[Manchester,] Monday, 1 September [1851]

Dear Marx,

Once again you must excuse me.

1. I still haven't been able to make a start on the Proudhon,[a] having for the past 4 days been plagued by the most atrocious toothache, which has rendered me quite incapable of anything. On top of that my brother[b] (whom you know) is arriving this evening from London and will keep me from my work for heaven knows how long. *Que le diable emporte l'exposition!*[c]

2. I can't send the £5 I promised for today until tomorrow, since there is absolutely no money at all in the firm's cash box, and so I won't be able to get it until tomorrow.

The triumphant article in the *Lithographische Correspondenz* on the unity finally achieved by the honest émigrés is belied by another lament and the attacks by the 'Prussians' on the 'South Germans' and on Ruge the 'Pomeranian' in the very same number of the *Lithographische Correspondenz*. *Sic transit gloria*[d]—their joy was short-lived. It's a good thing that, having so many friends in both the new societies,[e] we'll be molested by neither.

---

[a] Reference to Engels' 'Critical Review of Proudhon's Book *Idée générale de la Révolution au XIXe siècle*'. - [b] probably Hermann - [c] Confound the Exhibition! (i.e. the Great Exhibition in London in 1851.) - [d] Thus passes away the glory - [e] the German Agitation Society and the Refugee club

Have you read the edifying article in today's *Daily News* about that genuine whore and putative baroness Beck, who breathed her last in Birmingham, in the midst of her swindles, whilst in the hands of the English police[a]? A delightful business, the more so since it revealed that that importunate mendicant, 'Dr' Heinemann was also a spy in the direct pay of the 'newly established foreign department of the British police'. You will remember how suspect that base creature has always seemed to us. Again, the handing over of documents 'concerning a German communist association existing in London' explains the chicanery of the police last summer, and I should like to know to what extent Mr Christian Joseph Esser is involved in this affair. Do you know the 'Baron Soden' who vouches for these stories and offers to provide proof? It would be a good thing if we could have this man secretly investigated. There would be no difficulty in finding a pretext and much would emerge about the rascally elements among the émigrés which might later come in useful. I shall get hold of this number of the *Daily News* and keep it; it's a document that may be of use some time or other.

In Liverpool and London the bankruptcies have already begun and *The Economist,* despite the evidence it adduces that the country's TRADE is exceptionally healthy, i.e. that most of the surplus capital is invested in soundly based production, has to admit that East India is again over-stocked and that the old story of consignment goods and cash advances is once again the rule rather than the exception in Indian trade.[b] Next week it proposes to tell us how to run the consignment business on a sound basis—to which I much look forward. In the meantime the spinners and weavers here are making an enormous amount of money—most of them are booked up until the New Year, and in the country they generally work until at least 8 o'clock in the evening, that is, between 12 and $12^{1}/_{2}$ hours, and often longer. They are spinning yarn at 7-8d a pound from cotton at $3^{3}/_{4}$ to $4^{1}/_{2}$d per pound; the cost of spinning these coarse counts is barely $1^{1}/_{2}$-2d per pound, hence, with a weekly production of 12 million pounds (with 600,000,000 pounds of raw cotton imports) and taking the coarse counts as the norm, English spinners as a whole are earning £75,000 a week, $3^{3}/_{4}$ million

---

a 'Remarkable Case of Fraud by an Austrian Spy.—Sudden Death of the Impostor', *the Daily News,* 1 September 1851. - b 'Indigo', *The Economist,* No. 417, 23 August 1851.

pounds a year net. The same holds good if, instead of Nos. 6-12, we take an average yarn count of 18-24 and many of those who can use inferior cotton on good machines earn, not $1\,^{1}/_{2}$d per pound of yarn, but $2\,^{1}/_{2}$d. All this dates back to the fall in cotton prices in April and May, and the people who buy relatively more twist than anyone else are the Germans. When the trouble starts—and the present state of TRADE will certainly not persist beyond March at the latest—and if at the same time the fun begins in France, it will be keenly felt by the Germans, with all that unsaleable yarn on their hands, and in this way, too, the country will be well prepared.

Let us dedicate a silent tear to the shade of Brüggemann.[477] Never before, perhaps, has a worthy citizen met with more undeserved misfortune—*sit illi terra levis.*[a]

Your
F. E.

First published slightly abridged in *Der Briefwechsel zwischen F. Engels und K. Marx*, Bd. 1, Stuttgart, 1913 and in full in *MEGA*, Abt. III, Bd. 1, 1929

Printed according to the original

Published in English for the first time

209

ENGELS TO MARX

IN LONDON

[Manchester,] Monday, 8 September [1851]

Dear Marx,

My brother[b] is going away tomorrow and then I shall at last get some peace again. All this while I haven't had a moment to myself, and it was quite impossible to get the banknote off to you before Saturday, both pieces going by the same post, since there's only one DELIVERY on Sundays. As this involves the risk of its misappropriation, herewith the PARTICULARS of the note—its number was E/X 01780 and it was dated Leeds, 15 July 1850. So if it hasn't reached

---

[a] may the earth lie lightly upon him - [b] probably Hermann

you, go at once to the bank and STOP PAYMENT; there's still time enough. It was a five pound note.

On Friday evening I suddenly got a letter from my old man in which he tells me that I'm spending far too much money and must make do with £150. Naturally I shan't stand for this ludicrous imposition, all the less so that it is accompanied by the threat that, if necessary, the Ermens will be instructed not to pay me more than that amount. I shall, of course, at once write and tell him that the moment he attempts to put his scandalous plan into practice, I shall turn my back on the office for ever and immediately hie me to London again. The man's completely mad. The whole thing's all the more absurd and preposterous in that this point was agreed verbally between us long ago, and I have given him absolutely no pretext for it. I think that, with the help of my brother and mater, I shall be able to settle the matter, but at first shall have to retrench a little, having already spent £230 *summa summarum* and, from now until November when I shall have been here a year, I had better not to go too far beyond that sum. Anyhow this fresh piece of knavery is most disagreeable and vexes me considerably, the more so because of the mean attitude my old man has adopted. Admittedly he is making far less money here than he did last year, but that's due entirely to the bad MANAGEMENT of his partners over whom I have no control.

What's this fresh piece of knavery in Paris[478]? This time it's the hippopotamus[a] clique that seems to have got into trouble; to judge by the names of the Germans arrested, they are all former Weitlingians from the 1847 period and earlier.[479] A number of little betrayals seem to have been involved. The Swabian saviour appears to be one of the lucky ones. *Tant mieux pour lui.*[b] If you hear anything, let me know.

According to the German papers, the Cologne people[c] will *not* be brought before the next—October—assizes.

More tomorrow or the day after.

Your
F. E.

First published in *Der Briefwechsel zwischen F. Engels und K. Marx,* Bd. 1, Stuttgart, 1913

Printed according to the original

Published in English for the first time

---

[a] Karl Schapper - [b] So much the better for him. The reference is probably to Willich. - [c] i.e. the arrested members of the Central Authority of the Communist League set up in Cologne in October 1850

210

ENGELS TO MARX

IN LONDON

[Manchester,] Thursday, 11 September [1851]

Dear Marx,

Today I had hoped to be able to finish an article for you to send to America.[a] I still have about 3-4 pages to do. So I must give up all idea of tomorrow's post but, unless I'm mistaken, a Collins steamer is leaving on Wednesday—the article can go by that, to be followed by the 3rd on Friday. I shall make inquiries about it. IN THE PRESENT MOMENT I consider this American business, which definitely brings in money, to be more urgent than the Proudhon,[b] of which I can't tell whether it will bring so certain and rapid a return; that is why I have tackled the former first. If you should think otherwise, write and say so.

You'll have got my Monday's letter.

En attendant tes nouvelles.[c]

Your
F. E.

First published in *Der Briefwechsel zwischen F. Engels und K. Marx,* Bd. 1, Stuttgart, 1913

Printed according to the original

Published in English for the first time

211

MARX TO JOSEPH WEYDEMEYER[220]

IN ZURICH

[London,] 11 September [1851]
28 Dean Street, Soho

Dear Weydemeyer,

Lupus has written to his acquaintance on the *Staatszeitung* about your affairs. The only cause for regret is that Mr Kinkel has

---

[a] F. Engels, *Revolution and Counter-Revolution in Germany.* Article II. - [b] F. Engels, 'Critical Review of Proudhon's Book *Idée générale de la Révolution au XIXe siècle'.* - [c] Waiting to hear from you.

recently ensconced himself there. On the other hand, there is cause for rejoicing that Mr Heinzen's paper, the New-York *Schnellpost*, has been compelled to declare itself insolvent. Messrs Hoff and Kapp are now trying to found a new paper by issuing shares. At any rate, this is a favourable moment for speculating in newspapers.

Our local great men are now completely at loggerheads. They are behaving as though they were Alexander's successors and were having to share out the Macedonian-Asiatic Empire between them, *les drôles.*[a]

If only I knew more people here, I would have tried to get you a post as an engineer, railroad surveyor or the like. Unfortunately I have no contacts whatever. Otherwise I feel sure that employment is to be found here in that LINE. The pity of it is that we are all SO SHORT OF MONEY and that you haven't the means to spend some time here and take a look around. But if you really succeed in carrying out your plans in New York, you will at all events find it easier, in case of revolution, to return to Europe from there than we from here.

And yet I rack my brains trying to think of ways for you to SETTLE here, for once over there, who can say that you won't lose yourself in the FAR WEST! And we have so few people and have to be so sparing of the talent we have.

Besides, you are choosing a bad and uncomfortable time to travel. However, *il n'y a rien à faire contre la nécessité des choses.*[b] And if there is one thing of which I am convinced, it is that, once you are over there, you will not have to go through the same *misère* as all of us here. And that prospect, at least, has to be taken into account.

That this is a time of dissolution for 'democratic' provisional governments, Mr Mazzini, too, has had to learn. After some violent clashes the minority has resigned from the Italian Committee.[480] It is said that they are the more advanced ones.

I regard Mazzini's policy as basically wrong. He is working wholly in the Austrian interest by inciting Italy to the present secession. On the other hand, by failing to turn to the part of Italy that has been repressed for centuries, to the peasants, he is laying up fresh resources for the counter-revolution. Mr Mazzini knows only the towns with their liberal nobility and their *citoyens éclairés.*[c]

---

[a] the queer fellows - [b] needs must when the devil drives - [c] enlightened citizens

The material needs of the Italian country folk—bled white and systematically enervated and stultified just like their Irish counter-parts—are, of course, too lowly for the platitudinous paradise of his cosmopolitan-neo-catholic-ideological manifestos. But admittedly it required some courage to tell the bourgeoisie and the nobility that the first step towards gaining Italy's independence was the complete emancipation of the peasants and the transformation of their métayage system into bourgeois freeholdings. Mazzini would seem to regard a loan of 10 million francs as more revolutionary than a gain of 10 million human beings. I very much fear that, if the worst comes to the worst, the Austrian Government *itself* will alter the state of tenure in Italy and effect 'Galician' reforms.[481]

Tell Dronke that I shall write to him in a few days' time. Warm regards to you and your wife from my wife and myself. Consider once again whether you mightn't give it a try here.

Your
K. Marx

First published abridged in *Die Neue Zeit*, Bd. 2, No. 28, 1906-07 and in full in: Marx and Engels, *Works*, First Russian Edition, Vol. XXV, Moscow, 1934

Printed according to the original

Published in English in full for the first time

212

MARX TO ENGELS[482]

IN MANCHESTER

[London,] Saturday, 13 September 1851
28 Dean Street, Soho

Dear Engels,

Did you in fact—while your brother[a] was there—get a letter from me? I ask, because you don't mention it, not on account of its contents. It contained only gossip, although even that might as

---

[a] probably Hermann Engels

well be kept on record. But I would rather it didn't fall into the hands of strangers.

Your various letters, including the one with the five pounds, have arrived here safely.

Kinkel is now making his tour of northern England. Hasn't he been to Manchester yet?

Little has happened here since the matter referred to in my last letter. A week ago yesterday (Friday), Count Reichenbach[a] announced his resignation from the general refugee society. You, too, Brutus? Sigel,[b] etc., who had still not definitively resigned, have now done so. Willich, however, is conducting a campaign against the *'Lumpenproletariat'* among the refugees. As yet I've had no report of the sitting held yesterday evening.

There has also been a split in the Italian committee.[480] An appreciable minority has resigned. Mazzini gives a sorrowful account of the event in the *Voix du Peuple*.[c] The main causes would appear to be:

D'abord Dio. Ils ne veulent pas de dieu. Ensuite, et c'est plus grave, ils reprochent à Maître Mazzini de travailler dans l'intérêt autrichien en prêchant l'insurrection, d. h. en la précipitant. Enfin: Ils insistent sur un appel direct aux intérêts matériels des paysans italiens, ce qui ne peut se faire sans attaquer de l'autre côté les intérêts matériels des bourgeois et de la noblesse libérale qui forment la grande phalange mazzinienne.[d]

This last matter is exceedingly important. If Mazzini, or anyone else puts himself at the head of the Italian agitators and fails this time to transform the peasants, *franchement* and *immédiatement*,[e] from *métaires*[f] into free landowners,—the condition of the Italian peasants is atrocious, I have thoroughly mugged up the beastly subject—, the Austrian government will, in the event of revolution, have recourse to Galician methods.[481] In the *Lloyd* it has already threatened 'a complete transformation of the state of tenure' and the 'extermination of the turbulent nobility'. If Mazzini's eyes have not yet been opened, then he's a dunderhead. Admittedly certain agitational interests are involved here. Where will he find the 10 million fr. if he

---

[a] Oskar Reichenbach - [b] Franz Sigel - [c] Marx probably means *La Voix du Proscrit* - [d] 'Firstly, Dio. They don't want a god. Next, and more serious, they blame Maître Mazzini for working for the Austrian interest by preaching insurrection, i.e. by precipitating it. Finally, they insist on a direct appeal to the material interests of the Italian peasants, and this cannot be made without a corresponding attack on the material interests of the bourgeoisie and liberal nobility, who form the great Mazzinian phalanx. - [e] outright and immediately - [f] tenant share-croppers

antagonises the bourgeoisie? How retain the services of the nobility, if he informs them that their expropriation comes first on the agenda? Such are the difficulties encountered by a demagogue of the old school.

Unfortunately those arrested in Paris include that rascal Schramm.[483] The day before yesterday Liebknecht had a letter from the rogue, and we are faced with the agreeable prospect of having this dissolute character once again in our midst. But he'll get a bit of a shock, *ce monsieur là!*[a] You would greatly oblige me by *sending me the essay for Dana by Tuesday morning.*[b]

Herewith letter from Dronke. By the by, should you write him a letter, you must send it direct to his address. Schuster's is by no means safe. In a day or two I'll send you a note for him, to which you can add something before forwarding it to the little fellow.

First published in *Der Briefwechsel zwischen F. Engels und K. Marx*, Bd. 1, Stuttgart, 1913

Printed according to the original

Published in English in full for the first time

213

ENGELS TO MARX

IN LONDON

[Manchester,] Friday, 19 September [1851]

Dear Marx,

Yesterday, in the greatest haste, I managed to finish the American article[c] — *tel quel,*[d] with many interruptions over the past 3 weeks and finally the remainder thrown together in haste. *Tu en feras ce que tu pourras.*[e] At all events you'll get it by the first post today.

The only letter I got after my brother's[f] arrival was yours of 31

---

a will that gentleman - b F. Engels, *Revolution and Counter-Revolution in Germany.* Article II. - c F. Engels, *Revolution and Counter-Revolution in Germany.* Article II. - d such as it is - e You'll have to do what you can with it. - f probably Hermann

August, which I only received on 2 September and in which you quoted the passages from Heinzen (in the *Schnellpost* concerning the refinement of Yankee-ness).

My laziness was due to:

1. a business trip to Bradford,

2. our clerk's departure for London, whence he won't be returning till Monday,

3. the sudden dismissal of our WAREHOUSEMAN and assistant, leaving me with my hands full.

Tomorrow or Monday I shall devote myself to the 3rd American article, which will definitely reach you in time for the next steamer—by Tuesday if there's a sailing on Wednesday, otherwise by Friday. More tomorrow; the office is now closing, and as yet we have no gas, so that I am writing virtually in darkness.

Your
F. E.

The Willich document in the *Débats* is superb [484]!

First published in *Der Briefwechsel zwischen F. Engels und K. Marx*, Bd. 1, Stuttgart, 1913

Printed according to the original

Published in English for the first time

214

ENGELS TO MARX [482]

IN LONDON

Manchester, 23 September 1851

Dear Marx,

At last I think I've reached the point at which, after so many deplorable interruptions, I can settle down to regular work again. Article No. 3 for America[a] will be finished by this evening and

---

[a] F. Engels, *Revolution and Counter-Revolution in Germany*. Article III.

dispatched to you forthwith, and then I will at once get down to the Proudhon.[a]

I have heard nothing more about Kinkel's tour. The split among the Italians is wonderful. It's excellent that that astute visionary, Mazzini, should at last find himself thwarted by material interests, and in his own country to boot. One advantage of the Italian revolution has been that there, too, ít has swept the most isolated classes into the movement, and that a new party, more radical than the old Mazzinian emigration, is now being formed, and is gradually displacing Mr Mazzini. Newspaper reports would also seem to indicate that *il Mazzinismo*[b] is falling into disrepute even among people who are neither constitutionally nor reactionarily minded, and that what remains of the freedom of the press in Piedmont is being used by them for attacks on Mazzini, the *portée*[c] of which the government fails to grasp. In other respects the Italian revolution far outdoes the German in poverty of ideas and wealth of hot air. It is fortunate that a country which, instead of proletarians, has virtually nothing but *lazzaroni*,[485] should at least possess *métayers*. The other reasons given by the Italian dissidents are delightful too, and, finally, it is really splendid that the only émigrés to have remained united, at least in public, should now be at each other's throats.

The little man's[d] report pleased me greatly. Pompous tittle-tattle, a duel, a bit of money to be collected in Hamburg, Piedmontese plans—DODGE, DODGE and DODGE again[486]! There are two things one can never understand about the little fellow, firstly what he's up to, and secondly what he lives on. I return the letter herewith, send me the answer and I shall forward it to him post free. I have noted his own address—much good Schuster's would be, now that his house has been searched.

It was only to be expected that the precious Schramm[e] should be one of the first to fall into the clutches of the Parisian police. He must have been vociferating in cafés and been nabbed for it. But since he has no connection with the Willich-Schapper conspiracy, you'll no doubt have him back in London again by now.[483] The excerpts from the Willich document[484] in the *Kölnische Zeitung*[f] are much nicer than in the French papers, the original German text being given, and the great all-rounder's vigorous arguments emerge here quite unadulterated. E. g. where he says

---

[a] F. Engels, 'Critical Review of Proudhon's Book *Idée générale de la Révolution au XIX* *siècle*'. - [b] Mazzinism - [c] import - [d] Ernst Dronke - [e] Conrad Schramm - [f] 'Maßregeln vor, während und nach der Revolution', *Kölnische Zeitung*, No. 225, 19 September 1851.

that, in the next revolution, 'the League' and the 'fourth estate' (not, of course, to be confused with the bogus article from the Marx-Engels factory, placed on the market under the label 'proletariat') 'are to bring the historical developments of the economic question to a conclusive conclusion'!! The poor translation by the French police has altogether spoilt this incomparable document. The age-old *idées fixes* of this crazy martial clod, the hoary fatuities about social revolution stemming from the village commune, the cunningly calculated little schemes, which, as long ago as last November, were to have stood the world on its head through the agency of the Rhenish *Landwehr*,[385] none of this really comes through. But the most infuriating thing about it is that this poor translation almost completely spoils one's pleasure in observing how the ideas we instilled have gradually, after 12 months of independent cerebration within this misshapen skull, been finally converted into pompous nonsense. In the translation the provenance is everywhere discernible, but precisely the accretion of underived craziness, the distortion, is not in evidence. And are we to be deprived of the pleasure of at last being able to read in the vernacular a piece of unalloyed Willich which has assuredly been long chewed over by the noble man? One sees nothing but the most appalling dearth of ideas and the attempt to conceal the same beneath an immense heap of revolutionary admonition as brought forth of a gloomy evening in the inglenook by Mr Willich and Mr Barthélemy. Unsurpassed, too, the financial measures: first you make paper money, *n'importe combien,*[a] second you confiscate, third you requisition. Then the social ones, which are equally simple: 1) you organise, *tellement quellement,*[b] 2) you guzzle, guzzle a great deal, until you get to 3) when there's nothing left to guzzle, which is fortunate, for you then reach the point at which, 4) you start all over again, since the most radical *tabula rasa*[c] consists in leaving not a crumb on the table, by which time the hour will have come for the word of the prophet Willich to be fulfilled: 'We must march into Germany as into a waste land that we are to colonise and render fertile'. From the beginning the fellow's one idea has been to conquer the communist Canaan from without, exterminating the original inhabitants, with the help of '5,000 men', hand-picked from the 'people of the Lord'. Moses and Joshua rolled into one; alas, during their exile in Egypt the Children of Israel had already dispersed in all directions.

One must hope the Australian gold business won't interfere with

---

[a] no matter how much - [b] as best you can - [c] clean sweep

the trade crisis.[487] At any rate it has momentarily created a new, largely fictitious market, sending wool sky-high, since the flocks are being neglected. Otherwise it's a splendid thing. In six months' time the circumnavigation of the world by steam will be fully under way and our predictions concerning the supremacy of the Pacific Ocean will be fulfilled even more quickly than we could have anticipated.[a] When this happens the British will be thrown out and the united states of deported murderers, burglars, rapists and pickpockets[b] will startle the world by demonstrating what wonders can be performed by a state consisting of undisguised rascals. THEY WILL BEAT CALIFORNIA HOLLOW. But whereas in California rascals are still lynched, in Australia they'll lynch the *honnêtes gens*,[c] and Carlyle will see his ARISTOCRACY OF ROGUES established in all its glory.

The numerous asseverations in the press to the effect that, notwithstanding the recent bankruptcies and the depression prevailing in Liverpool and elsewhere, the country's TRADE has never been healthier, are most suspect. What is certain is that East India is OVERSTOCKED and that for months past sales there have been made at a loss. I am not clear about where the mass of stuff manufactured in Manchester and district is going; a great deal, a very great deal, of speculation must be involved, for as soon as cotton had reached its lowest point in July, and the spinners began to lay in a stock of raw material, all the spinners and weavers were immediately given long-term contracts by the local commission houses, which were very far from having orders for all the goods they were ordering from manufacturers. In the case of the East Indian houses, the old cash advance system is obviously in full swing again; this has already come to light in a few cases, and in others there will sooner or later be a fine old CRASH. As the manufacturers here are working at full stretch, and productive power, particularly within a 5-20 mile radius of Manchester, has increased by at least 30 per cent since 1847 (in Lancashire it was 30,000 in 1842, 40,000 in 1845; now certainly 55,000-60,000 horsepower), this brisk activity has only to continue until March or April and we shall have such overproduction as will warm the cockles of your heart.

The following information, prepared by the Liverpool Cotton Brokers Corporation, may not have come to your notice in so detailed a form. First I should explain that delivery to the ports of

---

[a] K. Marx and F. Engels, 'Review. January-February 1850'. - [b] Australia was formerly a place of deportation for criminals - [c] honest folk

each year's cotton crop is completed by 1 September of the following year, so that the cotton year runs from one 1 September to the next. Hence it follows that what is here described e. g. as the 1851 crop was grown in the summer of 1850, harvested in the autumn of 1850 and conveyed to the ports between September '50 and September '51. The crop now ripening which, by the way, will be poorer as the result of drought and storms, and will amount to about $2^1/_2$ millions, would thus figure as that of 1852.

Cotton crop in the year:		American domestic consumption:	
1846 2,110,537	bales	not given	
1847 1,778,651	"	427,967	bales
1848 2,347,634	"	531,772	"
1849 2,728,596	"	518,039	"
1850 2,096,706	"	487,769	"
1851 2,355,257	"	404,108	"

The Americans, therefore, have consumed between $1/_5$ and $1/_4$ of their entire crop themselves. I have not yet any information concerning exports and imports of other types of cotton besides those from the United States. Exports from the US to Britain amounted to about 55-60 per cent of the crop, to France, $1/_8$. But both countries in their turn export fairly heavily, Britain to France, Germany and Russia, France to Switzerland.

At the present moment the Russians are no longer taking so much as a pound of twist from Britain, very few finished cotton goods, a great deal of raw cotton—2,000-3,000 bales per week and, despite the reduction in duty on yarn from 7d to 5d a pound, new spinning mills are going up daily. Nicholas seems at last to be growing apprehensive about this industry and wants to reduce the duty even further. But since all his rich nobility and all the bourgeoisie have an interest in this business, the affair might become serious should he insist on it.

Your
F. E.

First published slightly abridged in *Der Briefwechsel zwischen F. Engels und K. Marx*, Bd. 1, Stuttgart, 1913 and in full in *MEGA*, Abt. III, Bd. 1, 1929

Printed according to the original

Published in English in full for the first time

215

MARX TO ENGELS

IN MANCHESTER

[London,] 23 September 1851
28 Dean Street, Soho

Dear Engels,

This business of the Paris document[484] is quite stupid. The German papers, the *Kölnische* and the *Augsburg*,[a] as might be expected of such undiscerning curs, attribute it to us. On the other hand, the wretched Willich & Co. are putting it about that we had had the rubbish denounced by acquaintances of ours in Paris. *Qu'en dis-tu?*[b]

C. Schramm is also in jug. *Habeat sibi.*[c] Next time—when I've gleaned some further news—I'll write and tell you more about the dirty business here. Today I shall regale you with the following résumé of Citizen Techow's manifesto which occupies several columns in the *New-Yorker Staatszeitung*,[d] and is entitled: '*Umrisse des kommenden Kriegs. London, 7. August.*' (Ill-written, doctrinaire, sundry echoes of our *Revue*,[e] seemingly intelligently developed, but insipid in content, undynamic in form, nothing striking.) I shall spare you Techow's initial narrative of the revolution of 1849. These, for a start, are the general lessons he draws from it:

1. Force can be resisted only by force.

2. A revolution can only be victorious if it becomes general, i. e. if it is kindled in the larger centres of the movement (Bavaria-Palatinate, Baden) and if, furthermore, it is not the expression of *one single oppositional faction.* (Example: the June insurrection of 1848.[488])

3. National struggles cannot be decisive because they are divisive.

4. Fighting on the barricades has no significance other than to signal a population's resistance and to put the power of governments, i. e. the troops' frame of mind, to the test by confronting them with that resistance. Whatever the outcome of this test, the first and most important step in revolution always remains organisation for war, the raising of disciplined armies. For this alone makes an offensive possible and it is only in the offensive that victory lies.

---

[a] *Kölnische Zeitung* and *Allgemeine Zeitung* - [b] What do you make of that? - [c] Serve him right. See this volume, p. 459. - [d] of 6 September - [e] *Neue Rheinische Zeitung. Politisch-ökonomische Revue*

5. National constituent assemblies are not capable of organising for war. *They invariably waste time* on *questions of internal politics,* the *time* for whose *solution* does not come till *after victory has been won.*

6. In order to be able to organise for war, a revolution must gain time and space. Hence it must attack politically, i. e. bring into its domain as many stretches of country as possible, since militarily it is at first always restricted to the defensive.

7. In the republican, no less than in the royalist, camp organisation for war can only be based on compulsion. No pitched battle has ever been won by political enthusiasm or fantastically bedizened volunteers against disciplined and well-led soldiers. Military enthusiasm only sets in after a series of successes.— Initially there can be no better basis for such successes than the iron rigour of discipline. In armies, even more so than in the internal organisation of a country, democratic principles can only apply after the victory of the revolution.

8. By its nature the coming war will be a war of extermination— of peoples or princes. From this follows the recognition of the political and military solidarity of all peoples, i. e. of intervention.

9. Spatially the area of the coming revolution falls within the boundaries of that of the defeated ones: France, Germany, Italy, Hungary, Poland.

From all this it follows that the question of the coming revolution is equally as important as that of a European war. Object of the war: a Cossack or republican Europe.[a] Theatre of the war—as before: Northern Italy and Germany.

Mr Techow now enumerates: 1. the armed forces of the counter-revolution; 2. the armed forces of revolution.

I. Armed Forces of the Counter-Revolution

1. *Russia.* Suppose that it could bring its armed forces up to 300,000. That would be a great deal. How quickly and at what strength could it then appear on the Rhine or in Italy? At the best, in 2 months. Deduct at least $\frac{1}{3}$ for sickness and for manning the lines of communication. That leaves 200,000 men who, 2 months after the action has begun, will make their appearance at the crucial points in the theatre of war.

2. *Austria.* Estimates the strength of its army at 600,000 men. In 1848 and '49 employed 150,000 men in Italy. Radetzky is demanding that number even now, in time of peace. In Hungary

---

[a] In *Mémorial de Sainte-Hélène* by Las Cases Napoleon is reported to have said: 'Dans cinquante ans l'Europe sera républicaine ou cosaque' (In fifty years Europe will be republican or Cossack).

he now requires, in peacetime, 90,000 men. During the last war, 200,000 were not enough. $1/3$ of this army consists of Hungarians and Italians, who will defect. At best, if the uprising does not take place simultaneously in Hungary and Italy, she will be able to reach the Rhine in 6 weeks with 50,000 men, having been delayed by sundry battles at the barricades.

3. *Prussia.* Numbers 500,000 men, incl. of the replacement battalions and the *Landwehr*[385] of the First Levy, which do not accompany the army into the field. For operations in the field, 300,000 men, $1/2$ line, $1/2$ *Landwehr*. Mobilisation: 2 to 3 weeks. The officers' corps in the Prussian army aristocratic, the non-commissioned officers bureaucratic, the masses 'democratic' through and through. The revolution has further opportunities in the mobilisation of the *Landwehr*. Disorganisation of the Prussian army by the revolution which will be mastered by the King[a] only under the protection of the Russian army and in order to lead the remnants of his army, in company with the Russians, against the rebels. Rhine Province, Westphalia, Saxony lost to him, thus the most important fortified lines and at least $1/3$ of his army. He will need $1/3$ against the uprisings in Berlin, Breslau,[b] the province of Posen and West Prussia. This leaves at most 100,000 who will be unable to appear on the battlefield any earlier than the Russians themselves.

4. The *German Federal Army.* The regiments of Baden, Schleswig-Holstein, the Electorate of Hesse, and the Palatinate belong to the revolution. Only the remnants of the German Federal Army, following the fleeing princes, will reinforce the armies of reaction. Of no military significance.

5. *Italy.* Italy's only military force, the Sardinian army, belongs to the revolution.

To sum up, then:

Theatre of war in Germany

150,000 Russians	
100,000 Prussians	
50,000 Austrians	300,000 men

Theatre of war in Italy

150,000[c] Austrians	
50,000 Russians	200,000 men
	Total: 500,000 men

---

[a] Frederick William IV - [b] Polish name: Wrocław - [c] In the original: 110,000

II. Armed Forces of the Revolution

1. *France.* 500,000 men at the disposal of the revolution from the very start. Of these, 200,000 on the Rhine, 100,000 in Italy (North) ensure that the revolution in Italy and Germany has time and space to organise itself.

2. *Prussia.* 50,000 ⎫   i.e. half the defecting armies
3. *Austria.* 100,000 ⎭   organised.

4. Small German armies: 100,000.

This adds up as follows:

Active French Army 300,000   men
German revolutionary army 150,000   ”
Italy and Hungary 200,000   ”
                                                    ─────────
                                                    650,000   ”

Thus the revolution will lead 650,000 men against absolutism's 500,000.

He concludes:

'Whatever differences of nationality or principle may, after all, split the great party of the revolution—we have all of us learnt that the time to combat these different views amongst ourselves will only come after victory has been won', etc., etc.

What do you make of these calculations? Techow presupposes that there will be disorganisation on the part of the regular armies and organisation on the part of the revolutionary armed forces. That forms the basis of his calculation. However, you'll be better able than I to judge these statistics.

But the essay's actual political tendency, which emerges even more clearly in the exposition, is as follows: No revolution ever breaks out, i. e. there is no party struggle, no civil war, no class dissension, until after the *ending of the war* and the collapse of Russia. But in order to organise these armies for this war, *force* is needed. And where is the *force to come from?* From General Cavaignac, or some similar military dictator in France, who has his generals in Germany and Northern Italy. *Voilà la solution,*[a] which is not very far removed from Willich's ideas. World war, i. e. as understood by your revolutionary Prussian lieutenant, domination,

───────────

[a] There is the solution

at least temporarily, of civilians by the military. But how any general, even were the old Napoleon himself to rise up out of his grave, is to get, not only the means, but also so much influence without preliminary and simultaneous *internal* struggles, without those damned 'internal politics', is not vouchsafed by the oracle. At least this future world-warrior's 'pious wish', which finds its due political expression precisely in the classless politicians and democrats as such, has been clearly and frankly stated.

Farewell.

Your

K. M.

I have just received your letter which I acknowledge herewith.

NB. You know, of course, that Stechahn or Steckhahn[a] has been arrested in Hanover and, before he joined our association, was corresponding with the Schapper committee, etc. Well, 2 letters which he wrote to the secretary of this committee—Dietz, the cockroach—and which the latter received, are at present in the police inspector's office in Hanover. We then entrusted Ulmer with the task of questioning Messrs Dietz & Co. on the subject at next Friday's public sitting of the 'refugee or émigré society'. This we countermanded again. Stechan has done a bunk and is, therefore, either on his way to London or already here. And who's to say that Stechan won't go to our enemies rather than to us?

The Straubingers[86] are *capables de tout.*[b] Further proof: Mr Paul Stumpf who, during his short visit to London, did not come to see either myself or Lupus but consorted exclusively with the blackguards.

I found your trade news exceedingly interesting.

As for C. Schramm, he was carrying in his pocket-book a brief note from me establishing his *bona fides.* Those lines could have been as fatal Uriah's letter.[c] They were originally given to him to make him think he was trusted and to disarm him, since the fellow could do us considerable damage. But at the same time a letter went off to Reinhardt warning him to be on his guard should he

---

[a] should read Stechan - [b] capable of anything - [c] The bible relates that David sent a letter by Uriah condemning the bearer to death (2 Samuel 11:14, 15).

(Schramm) present himself with the note, which was couched in *general* terms. The worst of it is that my name is at the bottom. It could earn Schramm 6 months.

  Addio!

First published in *Der Briefwechsel zwischen F. Engels und K. Marx*, Bd. 1, Stuttgart, 1913

Printed according to the original

Published in English for the first time

216

ENGELS TO MARX

IN LONDON

[Manchester,] [25][a] September 1851

Dear Marx,

  Your letter has arrived. Will write about Techow's erudition tomorrow. Kinkel's begging letter to New Orleans is very charming, but unfortunately I only saw the French version. Mr Stechan must also be in London by now; should he fail to announce himself, you will be absolutely right to leave the fellow to his own devices and to wait and see what happens before allowing anyone to take his side. Those released in Paris, of whom there is word in today's papers, will doubtless include Mr Conrad.[b] I, too, was much annoyed by the stupidity of the German newspapers in laying Willich's document[484] at our door. However, it will soon transpire that we have nothing to do with this wretched screed. *Par dieu, nous en avons assez sur les bras*[c] with other people's documents, as regards both style and content. Herewith article No. 3[d] for New York, at least a little less trashy than No. 2. I shall shortly be tackling No. 4.

---

[a] Manuscript damaged - [b] Conrad Schramm - [c] By God, we have enough on our hands - [d] F. Engels, *Revolution and Counter-Revolution in Germany*. Article III.

You might from time to time send me an American paper *sous bande*,[a] it being occasionally desirable to see the muck *in natura*. I shall shortly be sending you another LOT OF STAMPS for this purpose. *Adieu!*

Your
F. E.

First published in *Der Briefwechsel zwischen F. Engels und K. Marx*, Bd. 1, Stuttgart, 1913

Printed according to the original

Published in English for the first time

217

ENGELS TO MARX

IN LONDON

[Manchester, 26 September 1851]

Dear Marx,

As regards Techow's war story,[b] from a military standpoint too, it is tremendously superficial and in parts downright wrong. Apart from the profound verities that only force avails against force and from the absurd discovery that revolution can only be victorious if it is general (i.e. literally if it meets no resistance and, by inference, if it is a bourgeois revolution), apart from the well-meaning intention to suppress those awkward 'internal politics', that is, the revolution itself through the agency of a military dictator as yet to be discovered, *pace* Cavaignac and Willich, and apart from this very significant political formulation of the views on revolution held by these gentlemen, it should, militarily speaking, be noted that:

1. The iron discipline which alone can procure victory is the exact obverse of the 'postponement of internal politics' and of military dictatorship. Whence is that discipline to come? The gentlemen really should have gleaned some experience in Baden and the Palatinate.[c] It is a manifest fact that the disorganisation of

---

[a] in a wrapper - [b] See this volume, p. 463. - [c] i.e. during the uprising of May-July 1849 there

armies and a total relaxation of discipline have been both precondition and consequence of all successful revolutions hitherto. It took France from 1789 to 1792 to reorganise an army—Dumouriez's—of only about 60,000-80,000 men, and even that disintegrated again and there was no organised army to speak of in France until the end of 1793. It took Hungary from March 1848 to the middle of 1849 to create a properly organised army. And who brought discipline to the army in the first French Revolution? Not the generals who, at a time of revolution, do not acquire influence and authority in improvised armies until a few victories have been won, but rather the *terreur* of internal politics, of the civil power.

Armed forces of the Coalition:

1. Russia. The estimate of an effective force of 300,000 men, 200,000 of them under arms in the theatre of war, is on the high side. *Passe encore*.[a] But they could not be on the Rhine (at most an advance guard on the Lower Rhine, at Cologne), or in Northern Italy in 2 months. In order to act in concert, to co-ordinate their movements adequately with those of Prussia, Austria, etc., etc., they would require 3 months—a Russian army does not cover more than 2-$2^1/_2$ German miles[b] a day, and rests every third. It took them almost 2 months to reach the theatre of war in Hungary.

2. Prussia. Mobilisation: at least 4-6 weeks. The speculation regarding defections, uprisings, etc., etc., very uncertain. At best can make 150,000 men available, at worst maybe less than 50,000. This being so, to count on $^1/_3$ or $^1/_4$ is sheer humbug, since everything depends on chance.

3. Austria. Equally *chanceux*[c] and even more complex. No possibility here of estimating probabilities *à la* Techow. At best it could, as Techow supposes, put some 200,000 men into the field against France, at worst it would not succeed in detaching one man, and might *at the very outside* pit 100,000 men against the French at Trieste.

4. Federal army—of the Bavarian, $^2/_3$ would certainly march against the revolution, and here and there even a bit more. At all events a corps 30,000-50,000 strong could be raised within 3 months, and against revolutionary soldiers this is enough to start off with.

5. Denmark would immediately put 40,000-50,000 good troops into the field and, as in 1813, the Swedes and also the Norwegians

---

[a] But let that pass - [b] 1 German mile is roughly 4-$4^1/_2$ statute miles - [c] risky

would have to accompany it on the great crusade. Techow has overlooked this, as he has overlooked Belgium and Holland.

Armed forces of the revolution:

1. France. Has 430,000 men under arms. Of these, 100,000 in Algiers. 90,000 not *présent sous les armes*[a]—$^1/_4$ of the remainder. This leaves 240,000—of whom not more than 100,000 could reach the Belgo-German and 80,000 the Savoyard-Piedmontese frontier in 4-6 weeks, despite the now largely completed railways. This time Sardinia will try, like Belgium in 1848, to be the firm rock in the turbulent sea; hence whether the Piedmontese army, crammed as it is with bigoted Sardinian peasant lads, is—at least in its present form, officered by aristocrats—as committed to the revolution as Techow imagines is highly questionable. Victor Emmanuel has taken Leopold for his model, *c'est dangereux*.[b]

2. Prussia—? 3. Austria—?; i.e. so far as regular organised soldiers are concerned. As regards volunteers, they will turn up in their thousands, useless, of course. If in the first months 50,000-60,000 useful soldiers can be made out of troops who have defected, that's a great deal. Where are the officers to come from in so short a time?

Judging by all this, it is more likely that since any revolution (even in France) is bound to lack the very thing which enabled Napoleon to muster vast armies rapidly, to wit, good cadres, the revolution, if it takes place next year, will first either have to remain on the defensive or else confine itself to empty proclamations from Paris and highly inadequate, reprehensible and damaging Risquons-Tout expeditions [489] on a larger scale. Unless, of course, the Rhine fortresses come over during the first attack and the Piedmontese army responds to Citizen Techow's call; or unless the disorganisation of the Prussian and Austrian troops immediately centres on Berlin and Vienna, thus placing Russia on the defensive; or unless something else happens which cannot be foreseen. And to speculate on this and to calculate probabilities *à la* Techow is both otiose and arbitrary, as I know well enough from my own experience. All that can be said in this connection is that a very great deal depends on the Rhine Province.

First published in *Der Briefwechsel zwischen F. Engels und K. Marx*, Bd. 1, Stuttgart, 1913

Printed according to the original

Published in English for the first time

---

[a] under arms - [b] it's dangerous

218

MARX TO AMALIE DANIELS[490]

IN COLOGNE

[London, between 4 and 8 October 1851]

My dear Mrs Daniels,

I believe it is hardly necessary for me to mention the deep concern I feel about your husband's[a] arrest and your own separation from him. I console myself with the conviction that the courts will not be able to allow his detention to drag on much longer without bringing the case before a jury, and that you and your husband possess fortitude enough to defy adversity. I should be much obliged to you if you would hand over to the bearer of these lines the following books for me....

First published in the *Kölnische Zeitung*, No. 275, 27 October 1852

Printed according to the newspaper

Published in English for the first time

219

MARX TO ENGELS[491]

IN MANCHESTER

[London,] 13 October 1851
28 Dean Street, Soho

Dear Engels,

You'll have seen in the *Kölnische Zeitung* that I've made a statement[b] refuting the Augsburg *Allgemeine Zeitung*'s nonsense.[c] The tittle-tattle was becoming altogether too wild. The ruffians'

---

[a] Roland - [b] K. Marx, 'Statement and Accompanying Letter to the Editorial Board of the Augsburg *Allgemeine Zeitung*, 4 October 1851'. - [c] *Allgemeine Zeitung*, No. 273, 30

intention, in launching the recent series of prolonged attacks in all the German newspapers, was, I am quite sure, to place me on the horns of a dilemma. Either I must publicly disown the conspiracy and hence our party friends, or I must publicly acknowledge it, thus committing an act of treason 'in law'. However, these gentlemen are too clumsy to catch us out.

On 29 September Weydemeyer sailed for New York from Le Havre. There he met Reich, who was also crossing the ocean to the Atlantic regions. Reich had been arrested with Schramm[a] and reports that the police found Schramm in possession of a copy of the minutes containing the transaction which caused his duel with Willich, the minutes, that is, of that same evening when he insulted Willich and walked out of the meeting.[379] The thing was written in his own hand and was unsigned. In this way the police found out that his name was Schramm and not 'Bamberger' on whose passport he was staying in Paris. On the other hand the minutes have added to the confusion of Messrs Chief of the City Police Weiss & Co. in that our names thus became mixed up in the dirty business. Since it was Schramm who committed this blunder, it is at least gratifying that this man of honour is himself being punished for it.

So the £160 sent from America has been used by Kinkel to go collecting in America in person, accompanied by his saviour, Schurz.[b] Whether he's going at the right time, in view of the present PRESSURE ON THE AMERICAN MONEY-MARKET, would seem doubtful. He chose the moment so as to arrive *before* Kossuth, and likes to imagine that he will have some opportunity of publicly embracing the latter in the land of the future and of seeing the legend 'Kossuth and Kinkel!' in all the newspapers.

On the strength of his clamour over the emancipation of slaves, Mr Heinzen succeeded in forming a new joint-stock company in New York and is continuing to run his paper[c] under a somewhat modified title.

Stechan—never trust a Straubinger[86]—has been here for several weeks in Willich-Schapper's retinue. While the fact remains that the letters he wrote to the cockroach Dietz are now in the possession of the Hanover police, Stechan has written an article

---

September 1851 carried in a supplement an item datelined 'Cologne, 26 September' in which the arrests of the Communist League members in Cologne were linked with information allegedly received by Baroness von Beck from Marx.

[a] See this volume, p. 457. - [b] ibid., p. 439. - [c] *Deutsche Schnellpost*

for the *Norddeutsche Zeitung*[a] in which he reports that Mr Dietz's desk was broken into (*quelle bêtise!*)[b] and that was how the letters were purloined. The spy, as has now been established, was Haupt of Hamburg, who had long been in the service of the police. How fortunate that a few weeks ago I forestalled any overt moves in the Dietz-Stechan affair. As for Haupt, I've heard nothing more of him, and am vainly racking my brains to find some way of having a letter conveyed to him in person, for Haupt has got to declare himself. I've already tried to do so through Weerth but Haupt's fellow lodgers always turned him away on the pretext that he wasn't in. *Que penses-tu de Haupt?*[c] I'm convinced that he isn't a spy and never has been.

Edgar Bauer is also said to be here. I have not yet seen him. A week ago Blind and his wife (Madame Cohen) arrived to visit the exhibition and left again on Sunday last. I didn't see him again after the Monday, and this because of the following absurd incident, which will show you how very much henpecked the wretched man is. Today I received a locally posted letter in which he announces his departure. Now, the previous Monday he had come to see me with his wife. Others present were Freiligrath, red Wolff[d] (who, be it said in passing, has crept back again all unobtrusively and has, moreover, *married* an English bluestocking), Liebknecht, and the luckless Pieper. The wife is a vivacious Jewess and we were laughing and chatting quite merrily when the father of all lies[e] brought the conversation round to religion. She was showing off on atheism, Feuerbach, etc. I attacked Feuerbachus, but very civilly, of course, and in a most affable way. At first it seemed to me that the Jewess was enjoying the discussion which, of course, was the only reason why I had engaged in this boring topic. In between whiles my dogmatically obtrusive echo, Mr Pieper, held forth—but not exactly in a tactful manner. Suddenly I noticed that the woman was in floods of tears. Blind was casting sorrowfully expressive glances in my direction, she decamped—and was not seen again,[f] *ni lui non plus*.[g] It was something the like of which I had never seen before in all my long experience.

Pieper has set sail for Frankfurt am Main with the house of Rothschild. He has acquired a most disagreeable habit of butting

---

[a] G. L. Stechan, 'Hannover, 28 September', *Zeitung für Norddeutschland*, No. 544, 29 September 1851. - [b] what a stupidity! - [c] What do you think of Haupt? - [d] Ferdinand Wolff - [e] the devil—see Dante, *The Divine Comedy*, 'Hell', XXIII. - [f] Goethe, 'Der Fischer'. - [g] and neither was he

in on my conversations with other people in a very fatuous, pedantic tone.

> What they have just learnt, they must needs teach others forthwith.
> Ah me, what a short gut these gentry have! [a]

The honourable Göhringer has sent me a SUMMONS for the 22nd of this month because of the old demand. At the same time the great man set off for Southampton to welcome Kossuth. It would seem that I am to pay for the reception ceremonies.

I have had 2 letters from Paris, one from Ewerbeck and one from Sasonow. Mr Ewerbeck is publishing an immortal work: *L'Allemagne et les Allemands.* Ranging from Arminius the Cheruscan (his actual words) to the year of Our Lord 1850. He asks me for biographical-literary-historical notes on 3 men: F. Engels, K. Marx and B. Bauer. The muck's already printing. *Que faire?* [b] I fear that if we don't send the fellow any answer at all, he will spread the most arrant nonsense about us. Write and tell me what you think about this.

The most interesting thing about Sasonow's letter at any rate is the postmark, 'Paris'. How does Sasonow come to be in Paris just when things are so difficult? I shall ask him to explain this *mystère*. He, for his part, goes into long complaints about Dronke's being a *fainéant* [c] and allowing himself to be *enjôler* [d] by a few bourgeois. He says he has translated half the *Manifesto*. [e] Dronke had apparently undertaken to translate the other half but, because of his customary negligence and idleness, the whole thing had come to naught. This last is, indeed, just like our Dronke.

After the rejection by Mr Campe of my offer regarding the anti-Proudhon pamphlet, and by Mr Cotta and, later, Löwenthal of the one (transmitted through Ebner in Frankfurt) concerning my Economy, there would at last appear to be some prospect for the latter. [492] I shall know in a week whether anything will come of it. It's a publisher in Dessau [f] and through Ebner too. This man Ebner is a friend of Freiligrath's.

I haven't yet had a letter from the *Tribune*, which I have not so much as seen, but I don't doubt that the thing is going ahead. [g] At any rate it's bound to resolve itself in a few days' time.

By the way, you must at long last let me have your *vues* [h] on

---

[a] F. Schiller, 'Die Sonntagskinder'. - [b] What's to be done? - [c] lazybones - [d] cajoled - [e] K. Marx and F. Engels, *Manifesto of the Communist Party*. - [f] Friedrich Suchsland - [g] the publishing of Engels' *Revolution and Counter-Revolution in Germany*. - [h] views

Proudhon,[a] however brief. They are of particular interest to me since I am now in the throes of working out the Economy. Incidentally, during my recent visits to the library, which I continue to frequent, I have been delving mainly into technology, the history thereof, and agronomy, so that I can form at least some sort of an opinion of the stuff.

Qu'est ce que fait la crise commerciale?[b] The *Economist* is full of the anodynes, assurances and appeals which regularly precede a crisis. However, one senses its fear as it seeks to dispel the fears of others. If you happen to come upon the following book: Johnston, *Notes on North America,* 2 vols., 1851, you will find all manner of interesting information in it. For this Johnston is the English Liebig. An atlas of physical geography by 'Johnston', not to be confused with the above, may perhaps be had from one of Manchester's lending libraries. It is a compilation of all the most recent as well as earlier research in this field. Costs 10 guineas. Thus not meant for private individuals. Not a word from our DEAR Harney. He would seem to be still living in Scotland.

The English admit that, at the industrial exhibition, the Americans carried off the prize and beat them at everything. 1. Gutta-percha. New materials and new industries. 2. Weapons. Revolvers. 3. Machines. Reapers, seed drills and sewing-machines. 4. Daguerreotypes, used for the first time on a large scale. 5. Shipping, with their yacht. Finally, to show that they are also capable of producing luxury articles, they exhibited an enormous lump of Californian gold ore and beside it a golden SERVICE of VIRGIN gold.

Salut!

Your
K. Marx

First published in *Der Briefwechsel zwischen F. Engels und K. Marx,* Bd. 1, Stuttgart, 1913

Printed according to the original

Published in English in full for the first time

---

[a] P. J. Proudhon, *Idée générale de la Révolution au XIXe siècle.* - [b] How is the commercial crisis going?

220

ENGELS TO MARX

IN LONDON

[Manchester,] Wednesday, 15 October 1851

Dear Marx,

Herewith POST OFFICE ORDER for two pounds. PARTICULARS as before. The business with Göhringer is a great nuisance. You'll have to pay; the GENTLEMEN of the COUNTY COURT make short work of it, and the handwriting is there. If I were you, I'd raise the money along with the cost of the SUMMONS as soon as possible, and send it to the fellow. *Il n'y à rien à faire*,[a] and to go to court and be sentenced only increases the costs and isn't exactly pleasant. What is the total amount, and how much can you raise? Let me have as exact a figure as possible and I shall certainly do everything in my power to keep the BROKERS away from your door, short though I myself am just now.

The business with Schramm is not very pleasant[b] and it would have been better had we been kept out of this beastly mess altogether. That the minutes concerning those edifying squabbles over Bauer's and Pfänder's trust funds[328] should be in the hands of these gentlemen is far from pleasant, and Schramm deserves to have his backside kicked for carting such things around with him. At any rate, it serves him right if, as a result, he's locked up for a time and gets six months for using a false passport.

As for Haupt, I shall not regard him as a spy until I have the actual proof before my eyes. The fellow may have done some stupid things while in clink and there's admittedly something fishy about the business with Daniels, who is said to have been arrested on the strength of his denunciation. But all this journeymen's club chatter from Windmill Street[331] is the more fatuous for coinciding with the story of the forcing of Dietz's desk. Doubtless it was actually from Hamburg that Haupt broke into the cockroach's desk! And then, why doesn't the precious Dietz complain to the English police? It would, by the way, be a very good idea if Haupt could be induced to make a statement about the matter. If you send Weerth a letter for him, I would imagine that Weerth would be bound to find some opportunity of handing

---

[a] There's nothing you can do - [b] See this volume, p. 473.

it to him personally within the fortnight and, if needs be, could even call on him at the office. A merchant can always be found.

The affair of Blind and spouse[a] is truly inimitable. To shed tears and push off because Monsieur Pieper maligned Feuerbach, *c'est fort*.[b]

When you use the word *'married'* of red Wolff,[c] is it in the English, respectably bourgeois sense? I'm inclined to believe this, since you underline it. That would really beat everything hollow. M. Wolff *bon époux, peut-être même bon père de famille!*[d]

I think you'd be well-advised to fob Ewerbeck off with a few meagre notes and keep him in tolerably good humour; no purpose would be served by the fellow's spreading something altogether too idiotic about us in France. By the way, the tenacity this fellow evinces in his endeavours to become a great man is unbelievable considering that it actually gets the better of his avarice; for this new piece of 'immortality'[e] is undoubtedly again being paid for out of his own pocket, with a sale of 50 copies in prospect.

I'd like to hear more about Sasonow should you hear from him. This episode is piquant and Mr Sasonow is becoming extremely suspect.

I am at present engaged in making what summaries I need from the Proudhon. Wait until the end of this week, and it'll be returned to you, with my comments.[f] Once again the fellow's calculations are capital. Wherever there's a figure there's a howler.

What course the crisis will take here cannot be foreseen. Nothing was done last week because of the Queen.[g] Not much this week either. But the market has a DOWNWARD TENDENCY, with raw material prices still firm. Both will fall considerably within a few weeks and probably, to go by current prospects, the industrial product relatively further than the raw material; hence the spinners, weavers and printers will have to work on lower margins. That in itself is suspect enough. But the American market threatens to expire, the reports from Germany are not too favourable and, if markets continue moribund, we might see the beginning of the end in a few weeks' time. In America it's hard to say whether PRESSURE and bankruptcies (debts of 16 million dollars in all) really are the beginning, or are merely straws in the wind. Here, at all events, there are already some very significant straws.

---

[a] Cohen - [b] is preposterous - [c] Ferdinand Wolff - [d] a good husband, perhaps even a good pater familias! - [e] H. Ewerbeck, *L'Allemagne et les Allemands*. - [f] F. Engels, 'Critical Review of Proudhon's Book *Idée générale de la Révolution au XIX*e *siècle*'. - [g] In mid-October 1851 Queen Victoria visited Manchester.

The IRON TRADE is totally paralysed, and 2 of the main banks which supply it with money—those in Newport—have gone broke; now, besides the recent FAILURES in London and Liverpool, a tallow speculator in Glasgow and, on the London STOCK EXCHANGE, Mr Thomas Allsop, a friend of O'Connor's and Harney's. I haven't seen today's reports from the woollen, silk and hardware districts, *cela ne sera pas trop brillant non plus.*[a] At any rate there will no longer be any question of mistaking present indications, and there is the prospect, if not actually the certainty, of next spring's convulsions on the Continent coinciding with quite a nice little crisis. Even Australia seems incapable of doing very much; since California, the discovery of gold has become an old story and the world has grown *blasé* about it; it's beginning to be a REGULAR TRADE and the surrounding markets are themselves so overstocked that, without making very much impression on their own GLUT, they are capable of bringing about an EXTRA GLUT among the 150,000 inhabitants of New South Wales.

So Mr Louis Napoleon has *enfin*[b] decided to give Mr Faucher the boot. It was only to be expected that, this time, he would not allow the prorogation to go by without repeating the previous year's coup with Changarnier—whether with equal success, we shall see. He has, to use an expression from the hunting field, at last been BROUGHT TO BAY by the royalists, has turned on them and is threatening them with his antlers. It remains to be seen, however, when he will tuck his tail between his legs again. At all events, the miserable adventurer is fallen so low that, do what he will, *il est foutu;*[c] but the affair is now beginning to become interesting.In one respect it's a pity that the splendid Faucher-Carlier repression, the progressive state of siege, the gendarmerie's tyranny, etc., is so soon threatened with interruption and, should the cowardly Napoleon really be brave enough to launch a serious attack on the electoral law,[d] he could even now bring about its repeal, which would also be a pity as it would again provide a lawful basis for these jackasses, the legal progressives of 13 June[493]—but who knows what is good and what is bad where these Frenchmen are concerned? What do you make of the dirty business? You see more newspapers there.

Your
F. E.

---

[a] they won't be very wonderful either - [b] at last - [c] he is done for - [d] A law of 31 May 1850 which abrogated universal suffrage.

I have had a circular from Jones; he must either get 600 more subscribers or go broke,[a] *mais que puis-je faire?*[b]

<table>
<tr><td>First published slightly abridged in Der Briefwechsel zwischen F. Engels und K. Marx, Bd. 1, Stuttgart, 1913 and in full in MEGA, Abt. III, Bd. 1, 1929</td><td>Printed according to the original

Published in English for the first time</td></tr>
</table>

221

MARX TO JOSEPH WEYDEMEYER[494]

IN NEW YORK

London, 16 October 1851
28 Dean Street, Soho

Dear Weydemeyer,

Not only have I myself written to A. Charles Dana,[495] one of the editors of the *New-York Tribune,* but I have sent him a letter of introduction for you from Freiligrath. So all you have to do is to call on him and mention our names.

You ask about a statistical manual. I would recommend—since it also contains economic expositions—the *Commercial Dictionary* by MacCulloch, 1845. There are more recent things, e.g., by MacGregor, whose works on statistics are, generally speaking, probably the best so far as Europe as a whole is concerned.[c] But they are very dear. However, you will certainly find them in one of the New York libraries. MacCulloch, on the other hand, is a manual which every journalist ought to possess.

On England, specially to be recommended: Porter, *The Progress of the Nation.* New edition, 1851.

On the history of commerce generally:

Tooke: *History of Prices.* 3 vols. Up to 1848. On North America, especially MacGregor, who has written a statistical study of the United States.

---

[a] Reference to the terms for publication of *Notes to the People.* - [b] but what can I do? - [c] J. MacGregor, *Commercial Tariffs and Regulations, Resources, and Trade of the Several States of Europe and America; The Resources and Statistics of Nations.*

On Germany: Freiherr von Reden: *Vergleichende Kulturstatistik.*
On France: Moreau.[a]

Now I have another commission for you. At the request of
Koch, a former German Catholic priest, whom you may inquire
after at the *Staatszeitung,* for which he writes from time to time, I
sent him 20 *Manifestos*[b] (in German) and one English translation of
the same, instructing him to have it—the English translation—
printed in pamphlet form, along with Harney's introductory note.[c]
Since that time there hasn't been a word from Mr Koch. Please ask
him, 1) for an explanation of this most suspect silence, after he
had written to me so urgently, and 2) get him to give you the
English translation and see if you can dispose of it in pamphlet
form, i.e. if you can publish, distribute and sell it. Needless to say,
any proceeds there may be will go to you, but we should like to
have 20-50 copies for ourselves.

Dronke is coming here on the 23rd inst.[496]

Write soon. Regards to you and your wife[d] from my wife,
myself and all friends.

I hope that you have weathered the voyage successfully and that
things will go well with you in the United States.

Your
K. Marx

[From Mrs Jenny Marx]

Tell your dear wife that, during this time, I have been thinking of her with
heartfelt sympathy and concern. What must she have endured on the long sea
voyage with two small children! I hope these lines will not reach New York too
long before yourselves. I feel sure that you will manage to make a provisional
home for yourselves there.

We have had no news of Edgar[e] since his departure in April. He left Bremen
on the sailing vessel *Reform,* Captain Ammerman, intending to disembark at
Galveston and stay, to begin with, in New Braunfels. Perhaps, dear Mr
Weydemeyer, it might be possible for you to track him down somewhere from New
York. His silence is all the more incomprehensible as he knows that, because of the

---

a A. Moreau de Jonnès, *Statistique générale de la France.* - b K. Marx and F. Engels,
Manifesto of the Communist Party. - c [G. J. Harney, Introduction to the *Manifesto of the
Communist Party,*] *The Red Republican,* No. 21, 9 November 1850. - d Louise - e Edgar
von Westphalen

paralysis of her right hand, our poor, lonely little mama[a] has been deprived of the last solace fate has left her—to communicate in writing with those she loves most.
Farewell, and warm regards from

Jenny Marx

First published (without Jenny Marx's postscript) in: Marx and Engels, *Works,* First Russian Edition, Vol. XXV, Moscow, 1934 and in full in: Marx and Engels, *Works,* Second Russian Edition, Vol. 27, Moscow, 1962

Printed according to the original

Published in English in full for the first time

222

MARX TO ENGELS

IN MANCHESTER

[London,] 19 October 1851
28 Dean Street, Soho

Dear Engels,

A few days ago I received a letter from Dronke wherein—ostensibly on account of his expulsion—he announces that he will be arriving in London on the 23rd or 24th of this month.[486] The question of subsistence will loom larger for him here than ever before.

A still more baleful piece of news is this: Of late my correspondence with Cologne has been carried on in such a way that letters for me are brought to Liège by Schmidt, a railway guard, and I, for my part, sent a letter to him in Liège under cover through a third person. Well, this man Schmidt was arrested and later released, but the investigation is still going on. This would seem to be a case of outright betrayal. In accordance with the arrangement, Pieper should, by the way, have long since sent news from Cologne, where the Rothschilds stopped for a day, and from Frankfurt. Instead, I see from one of Ebner's letters (from Frankfurt) to Freiligrath that, although he has already spent a week in Frankfurt, he has not yet been to see Ebner, to whom he was to deliver a letter from me. It is our great misfortune that our agents should always go about their business in so very slipshod a

---

[a] Caroline von Westphalen

manner, and invariably as though it were of secondary importance. The others are unquestionably better served.

Kinkel, to whom it seemed that the ground had been cut away
under his feet by that boor Heinzen, and who in any case feels
able to take the floor only when unanimously hailed as a saviour,
did not hold a meeting in New York, nor did he sell any
'interest-bearing notes' on the future German republic.[497] In
Philadelphia, on the other hand, as he writes and tells the
emigration club, he sold 4,000 dollars' worth. Throughout
Pennsylvania he found the inevitable crowd of light-loving
German-Catholics.[498] All Kinkel did was to enter into the
inheritance of Johannes Ronge. The latter was John.[a] He is Christ.

This evening I shall be meeting Göhringer. The whole thing's
the fault of Willich & Co. For at the urgent request of these oafs,
he allegedly gave them the sum I owed him. I shall give him a
promissory note payable in 4 weeks' time. I think he will agree to
this. If not, let him go to court. I have, in the interim, every
prospect of concluding the contract with the Dessau publisher,[b]
who will, of course, have to pay me a sum in advance.

Weerth is in Bradford again. Il importe[c] that you should write
and ask him whether he can take a letter to Haupt in person. The
entire calumny seems to me to emanate from 2 sources, on the
one hand, Stechan-Dietz, on the other, Willich the beadle, who was
the first person here to bruit it about among Schärttner's
customers that Haupt might be a spy. For Willich associated
regularly with Berthold, the ex-Prussian corporal. Haupt had
managed to place this beast with a merchant in Hamburg.
Berthold stole from the merchant and was charged by the police.
Haupt, of course, gave evidence against the rascal, who may,
perhaps, have shared the proceeds with his friend Willich.
Whereupon the latter began to yelp about the betrayal of 'a poor,
fugitive patriot'. If this story is made public, the 'noble' Willich will
be all eyes. Now it would be important, not only for us
to call on Haupt for an explanation regarding the suspicions
overtly and covertly cast upon him, but for him, if innocent, to
make a public statement, declaring that the whole business is based
on Willich's calumny and at the same time hinting at the latter's
association, maybe as partner, with the rascally Berthold. For
Haupt doesn't yet know about this dirty trick of Willich's, which
was the actual source of the suspicions cast upon him. If Weerth is
willing, you could give him a letter to Haupt couched in these

---

[a] the Baptist - [b] Friedrich Suchsland (see this volume, p. 475) - [c] It's important

terms. *La chose presse.*[a] In his statement Haupt should also refer to 'Dietz' and the equivocal matter of the forcing of his desk.

Now, as regards Ewerbeck, you must let me have a line or two concerning yourself, at least up to the year 1845.[b]

Mr Louis Bonaparte's sudden about-face, whatever its consequences may be, is a master-stroke of Girardin's. As you know, this gent had allied himself in London with Ledru-Rollin and his paper[c] really became, for a time, as stupid as might be expected from an ally of Ledru's and Mazzini's. Unexpectedly he adopted the ploy of *suffrage universel,* determining Bonaparte in its favour with the aid of his articles, Dr Véron and personal *entrevues.*[d] In this way the royalist conspiracy was smashed. The fury of the normally so diplomatic *Journal des Débats* is the clearest proof of this. The whole lot were hand-in-glove, Faucher, Carlier, Changarnier, and even the noble Berryer and Broglie, who had ostensibly rallied to Bonaparte. At any rate the 'revolution'—in the sense of triggering it off—has been juggled away. With *suffrage universel* there can be no question of it. But Mr Girardin doesn't care for a revolutionary *mise en scène.* He has duped both royalists and professional revolutionaries, and it may even be asked whether he is not intentionally duping Louis Bonaparte. For *suffrage universel* once restored, who will guarantee Bonaparte revision, and revision once achieved, who will guarantee that it will turn out as he wants?[420] Nevertheless, in view of the native stupidity of the French peasantry, the question arises whether the *elu du suffrage universel*[e] will not be re-elected out of gratitude for having restored the said suffrage, more especially if, BY AND BY, he nominates liberal ministers and with the help of ingenious pamphlets, puts the blame for all the mischief on the royalist conspirators, who kept him prisoner for 3 years. It will depend on his ingenuity. At all events, Bonaparte now knows that, with the *parti de l'ordre,*[267] he's not in clover.

One of the most comical interludes in this game of intrigue is the melancholy mien of the *National* and the *Siècle* which, as every one knows, have for some considerable time been howling for *suffrage universel.* Now that France is in danger of being presented with it again, they cannot conceal their chagrin. For as the royalists had counted on *suffrage restreint,*[f] for Changarnier's election, so they counted on the same for Cavaignac's. Girardin told them bluntly that he knew that beneath their republican horror of

---

[a] The matter is urgent. - [b] See this volume, pp. 475, 478. - [c] *La Presse* - [d] interviews - [e] electee of universal suffrage - [f] limited suffrage

revision—with its prospect of re-election for Bonaparte—they were merely concealing their hatred of *suffrage universel,* which would exclude their man, Cavaignac, and their entire coterie. The *National,* poor thing, *s'était déjà consolé du départ du suffrage universel.*[a]

So much is certain. This coup will have thwarted the May 1852 uprising,[499] which at best might now break out earlier should one of the ruling coteries attempt a coup d'état.

Your

K. M.

First published abridged in *Der Briefwechsel zwischen F. Engels und K. Marx,* Bd. 1, Stuttgart, 1913 and in full in *MEGA,* Abt. III, Bd. 1, 1929

Printed according to the original

Published in English for the first time

223

MARX TO ENGELS

IN MANCHESTER

[London,] 25 October 1851

Dear Engels,

Did you get my letter of last Monday? You're so meticulous about writing that your silence disturbs me.

I have heard nothing from Pieper up to the present. If nothing has happened to him, he is being unpardonably irresponsible. Dronke has not yet arrived. Have heard nothing from Cologne.

Enclosed a letter from Fischer who writes like a true democratic philistine. For the time being, *il faut le laisser faire,*[b] since nothing further can be done about it. If only he doesn't do anything silly where Kinkel is concerned. His letter rather gives the impression that he might.

Well, as we now learn, Kinkel had arranged matters as follows. Part of the £160 sterling was used to send Schurz on a secret mission to Belgium, France and Switzerland. He induced all the

---

[a] had already consoled itself for the demise of universal suffrage - [b] he must be given his head

great men there, including the Parliamentarians[a] (and not excluding the LATE Raveaux), to confer plenary powers on Kinkel and, at the same time, to guarantee the debt to be contracted in respect of the future German republic.[497] Hence the vast majority are now united and E. Meyen was able to promulgate in the *New-Yorker Staatszeitung* the great secret that the meaning of the future movement in Germany had now been discovered, namely, the principle of nationhood. Even at the time of his finest flowering, this individual never wrote as foolishly as he does now. Intellectually, these fellows are completely bankrupt.

Addio!

Your
K. M.

I have for the time being postponed the Göhringer business. Unfortunately the jackass is leaving for Spain on 1 November, having sold his public house here. Meanwhile, I need not fear any further hostile moves from him.

First published in *Der Briefwechsel zwischen F. Engels und K. Marx*, Bd. 1, Stuttgart, 1913

Printed according to the original

Published in English for the first time

224

ENGELS TO MARX

IN LONDON

[Manchester, about 27 October 1851]

Dear Marx,

If I didn't at once reply to your letter of the 19th inst., this was because I was expecting Weerth here within a few days and wanted to settle matters with regard to Haupt; and also because I wanted to be done with the Proudhon screed.[b] That will be today

---

[a] i.e. the members of the Frankfurt National Assembly - [b] F. Engels, 'Critical Review of Proudhon's Book *Idée générale de la Révolution au XIX[e] siècle*'.

and tomorrow evening, and Weerth was here on Saturday and Sunday; he will be remaining in Bradford for some time yet, and hence cannot take the letter over himself and refuses to do so even if he could, present conditions in Germany being so brilliant that one is liable to summary arrest on the slightest provocation, and he has no desire to be in any way mixed up in this League matter.[a] This cannot *au fond*[b] be held against him. He will, however, certainly see for me that a letter reaches Haupt, and only asks to be kept out of the thing completely. He told me, moreover, that he had come across Haupt on several occasions of late, but that, each time he had gone up to him, the man had, with a considerable show of embarrassment, suddenly avoided him and made off. It could be that, while in jug, Haupt was to some extent talked round by his family, etc., etc., and made certain admissions which now weigh heavily upon him. For the rest, Weerth is also of the opinion that those other stories emanating from Willich-Stechan are downright calumnies, since Haupt could have had no reason to sell himself.

I shall now write to Haupt anonymously,[500] since he knows my hand, and leave the conveyance of the letter to Weerth. I shall call upon him to declare himself openly and shall suggest that the Berthold business may well have been the cause of all the rumours. However, I shall omit the further suggestion that Willich might have gone shares with Berthold, because 1) Haupt will take care not to put his name to such insinuations, 2) the story is too improbable, Mr Berthold not being the man to go shares with distant acquaintances, particularly with Willich whom *au fond*[c] he detests, and 3) within the week the others would write to all the newspapers, describing this as a fresh calumny put about by Mr Marx, and appealing to philistine sentiment on behalf of that calumniated worthy Willich. The fellow's already enough of a rogue without our trying to make him into a greater one, or spreading lies about him which he can refute.

I must say that the Fischer letter is the stupidest thing I have seen in a long while. But I was expecting something of the kind and believe, moreover, that it will get no further than *promises* of money. The democratic jackasses can hardly be asked to send *us* money when their own people are coming in person to beg it from them, and the most they can be persuaded to do is, as Fischer himself says, to accord us some say in the disposal of the money, if

---

[a] the impending trial of the Communist League members - [b] really - [c] at bottom

we are prepared to consent to sit in conclave with such rabble and as a minority at that. The borrowing scheme *à la* Mazzini, with an imperial guarantee[a] (the German Empire guarantees the Republic!), isn't bad at all, and it did at least require the combined efforts of all the most exemplary mendicants to produce it. Now that this has been invented, no other course remains open to our party than to withdraw completely from the democratic money market. THIS IMPUDENCE BEATS US HOLLOW. Such money as we have received from the democrats for political purposes has in any case come our way purely *per abusum*[b] and, now that the great men have themselves appeared on the market as a JOINT STOCK COMPANY, this illusion entirely ceases to be. All we should incur by our requests would be *refus*[c] and humiliation unless, of course, Weydemeyer should succeed in achieving something in New York, and even then it would only be among the workers.

Weerth will be writing to you shortly. He is very undecided about what he should do. He has had some splendid offers, but none of them really suit him.

Like the Apostle Paul, Mr Kossuth is all things to all men.[d] In Marseilles he shouts *Vive la République,* in Southampton GOD SAVE THE QUEEN. What remarkable and hyper-constitutional moderation the fellow now parades! But Mr Pettie and the Harney clique are happy enough that he should have no intention whatever of attending their banquet. Even Mr Mazzini would be given a very cool reception—at least in public. Yet another one about whom we weren't mistaken. Should there be no *secousses*[e] next year, how long before Mr Kossuth, too, stoops to common, tub-thumping demagogy *à la* Mazzini?

Proudhon tomorrow or the day after. If possible, I shall send Fischer the *Revue* but only of the last issue have I more than one copy. Can you still get hold of Nos. 1-4 for me?

Your

F. E.

First published in *Der Briefwechsel zwischen F. Engels und K. Marx,* Bd. 1, Stuttgart, 1913

Printed according to the original

Published in English for the first time

---

[a] See this volume, p. 486. - [b] here: irregularly - [c] refusals - [d] 1 Corinthians 9:22 - [e] convulsions

225

MARX TO JOSEPH WEYDEMEYER[310]

IN NEW YORK

London, 31 October 1851
28 Dean Street, Soho

Dear Weydemeyer,

I am sending yet another letter to America in your wake. For after mature consideration with Lupus, I believe that we might do some business together.

Firstly. The erstwhile *Neue Rheinische Zeitung* was not widely distributed in America. If you could manage to ferret out some bourgeois or other, or even just the necessary credit with a printer and paper merchant, I believe it would pay to create out of the *N.Rh.Z.* a kind of pocket library in the form of small booklets such as those produced by Becker in Cologne.[501] E.g. the *Schlesische Milliarde* by W. Wolff, Hungary by Engels,[a] the Prussian bourgeoisie by myself[b] and some of Weerth's feuilletons, etc. I would send you the things from here if they are not to be found there, at the same time indicating the most suitable for selection. You would have to write a short general introduction to this '*N.Rh.Z.* Pocket Library', and notes or a postcript to individual volumes where circumstances seemed to demand it.

Secondly. Similarly, you could bring out in the same form and with explanatory remarks Engels' and my anti-Heinzen pieces from the *Deutsche-Brüsseler-Zeitung.*[c] I think they should sell well.

We would share the profits after deducting production costs.

Thirdly. I have had all kinds of inquiries and orders from America for the 6 numbers of my *Revue* that have appeared, but have not responded to any of them as I could not trust the rascals there. You could announce that the thing is to be had from you, but obviously a fair number of orders would have to be received before we would dispatch anything from here.

Fourthly. You as well as ourselves could, if the moment demanded it, include in the small library referred to above

---

[a] F. Engels, 'The Magyar Struggle', 'Hungary' and other articles. - [b] K. Marx, 'The Bourgeoisie and the Counter-Revolution'. - [c] F. Engels, 'The Communists and Karl Heinzen'; K. Marx, 'Moralising Criticism and Critical Morality'.

pamphlets written in response to that demand. Commercially it is, of course, safer and more convenient to start off with material that is ready to hand. In your short forewords and postscripts you could conduct the necessary polemic, both to the left and to the right.

I therefore suggest that you should turn publisher. There's less to it than to a newspaper, and politically you achieve the same end. You avoid the long, time-consuming preparations attaching to a journal.

I believe that if you put the matter properly to Reich, who has money, he will join you in the enterprise.

Warm regards to your family from my family, Freiligrath, Lupus, etc.

Your
K. Marx

First published in: Marx and Engels, *Works,* First Russian Edition, Vol. XXV, Moscow, 1934

Printed according to the original

226

MARX TO ENGELS

IN MANCHESTER

[London,] 24 November 1851

Dear Frederick,

You must understand that, if I have not written to you before, it is because my household is all at sixes and sevens.

You will remember that in his last letter Pieper wrote that the contract for my anti-Proudhon was about to be concluded.[a] From his letter, enclosed herewith, you will see that there is no further mention of *this manuscript.* This is typical of the way in which I have been kept on tenterhooks by our dear henchmen these six months past. On the other hand, Ebner has written to say that

---

[a] K. Marx, *The Poverty of Philosophy*—German translation planned but not then published.

Löwenthal is willing to try out one volume but didn't mention whether I am to start with the *'history* of economy'.[a] If so, it would mean upsetting my whole scheme. Ebner further said that Löwenthal could only pay 'a little'. This I am prepared to accept, provided he publishes what I want published first. But if he forces me to ruin my whole scheme, he will have to pay me as though I were directly commissioned by him. However, I shall for the time being let Ebner do as he thinks fit. He has informed me that he won't conclude anything without my consent. *Qu'en penses-tu?*[b]

I am glad that our people in Cologne[c] are at last to appear before the assizes and indeed, or so I was assured yesterday by Schüller, the Düsseldorf publisher, will do so this very December when there are to be extraordinary assizes.

Apropos, don't forget to let me have the New York *Schnellpost* back *by return*. Bamberger is pressing me, and it's the only way of extracting from him the subsequent numbers which are said to contain all manner of curious things.

I know that you yourself are now feeling the pinch and that my sudden descent, my razzia, on Manchester[502] has made things even tighter for you, at least so far as this month is concerned. Nevertheless, I must ask you whether, in an emergency, you could lay your hands on another £2. For before leaving London I borrowed £2 and at the same time stated *in writing* that I'd repay it *before* December. At all events I would ask you to write by return to let me know whether or not this is possible.

Eccarius' brother[d] has arrived here. He and all the other Straubingers[86] arrested in Hamburg have been set free and given their marching orders. That Haupt originally had no treacherous intentions is apparent from the following: Bürgers' letter to him fell into the hands of his old man, who taxed him with it and proposed to hand it over to the police. This he prevented, tore the thing up and later took the pieces to Eccarius, etc., first to reassemble and read them, and then to burn them in their presence. This fact is important. It is pressure from his family that *has ruined the unfortunate* fellow.

A few days ago at the library I read Mr Proudhon's lucubrations on *Gratuité du crédit* against Bastiat. In terms of charlatanism, poltroonery, bluster and ineffectuality it exceeds anything this man has done before. *Exempli gratia,*[e] the French believe that on

---

[a] See this volume, p. 476. - [b] What do you think? - [c] the Communist League members arrested and under investigation - [d] Johann Friedrich Eccarius - [e] For example

average they are paying 5-6 per cent interest. They are paying 160 per cent. *Comment donc?*[a] Well, like this. Interest on mortgage, unsecured, state, etc., debts amounts to 1,600 millions. Now in France there is only 1 thousand million of capital in existence, i.e. gold and silver. Hence, q.e.d. A further example: When the Banque de France was set up, its capital amounted to 90 millions. At that time it was legally empowered to take 5 per cent on this sum. It is now operating (deposits, etc., included) on a capital of 450-460 millions, of which $^3/_4$ belong not to it, but to the PUBLIC. If the bank, therefore, (90:450=1:5) takes only 1 per cent instead of 5, it will be making a legitimate profit. And because the Banque de France could, in an emergency (2), content itself (i.e. the *stockholders*) with 1 per cent, the interest rate for *France* can therefore be reduced to 1 per cent. And 1 per cent, *c'est la presque gratuité du crédit.*[b]

And you should see how the fellow flaunts his *dialectique hégelienne*[c] vis-à-vis Bastiat.

I have been through your critique again here.[d] It's a pity *qu'il n'y a pas moyen*[e] of getting it printed. If my own twaddle were added to it, we could bring it out under both our names, provided this didn't upset your firm in any way.

As you know, Kossuth left on the 20th, but what you don't know is that he was accompanied by Lola Montez and *caballero* Göhringer.

Schramm,[f] with an officious obstinacy wholly *sans pareil*[g] is endeavouring to attach himself to me again. *Il n'y parviendra pas.*[h]

How goes it with K. Schnapper's[i] 'tippling jaunts'?[503]

Your
K.M.

First published in *Der Briefwechsel zwischen F. Engels und K. Marx*, Bd. 1, Stuttgart, 1913

Printed according to the original

Published in English for the first time

---

a How so? - b is almost free credit. - c Hegelian dialectics - d F. Engels, 'Critical Review of Proudhon's Book *Idée générale de la Révolution au XIXe siècle*'. - e that there's no means - f Conrad Schramm - g unparalleled - h He won't succeed. - i Snapper, i.e. Schapper

227

ENGELS TO MARX

IN LONDON

[Manchester,] 27 November 1851

Dear Marx,

You will have received the few lines I wrote you the day before yesterday.[504] If Weerth can't raise the necessary forthwith, I shall see to it that the thing's cleared up the day after tomorrow or by Monday at the latest. In any case you will be able if needs must to keep the matter in suspense until Tuesday.

I return Master Pieper's letter herewith. Heine seems to have come in very handy in helping him fill up the requisite 4 pages.[505] You have, I hope, written him a letter about the Proudhon[a] that will spur him on to action, for once he's back here again you'll neither see nor hear anything of the manuscript for some time to come. Pieper and Ebner give very conflicting reports about Löwenthal, but the second is at any rate the more trustworthy. As regards what Pieper says about starting off with the history of economy, I believe that, if Löwenthal really has this in mind, it would be best for Ebner to object that it wouldn't do to upset your whole scheme, that you had already begun to elaborate the critique, etc. But if there's no other alternative, Löwenthal should undertake to contract for two volumes and, indeed, you would need something of this length, partly on account of the critical section to be anticipated, partly to make the proposition reasonably economic for you, the fee being in no way commensurate with the price of things in London. Next would come the socialists as 3rd volume, and as 4th the critique— *ce qu'il en resterait*[b]—and the much-vaunted 'positive', being what you 'really' want. In such a form the thing may have its difficulties, but it has the advantage of not divulging the much coveted secret until the very last and of keeping bourgeois curiosity whetted throughout 3 volumes before revealing the fact that what one is producing isn't Morison's Pills.[506] For those with a modicum of intelligence the allusions in

---

[a] See this volume, p. 490. - [b] what would remain of it

the first volumes, the anti-Proudhon[a] and the *Manifesto*,[b] will suffice to put them on the right track; the common run of buyers and readers will lose interest in the history, etc., if the great mystery has already been revealed to them in Volume I; they will, as Hegel says in his *Phänomenologie,* have read the 'preamble', where the general outline is to be found.

Undoubtedly your best course is to conclude an agreement with Löwenthal in any case—with decorum, but on any acceptable terms, and to strike while the iron is hot. The best for you would be to do the opposite of the Sibyl. For every *louis d'or* he cuts you down per sheet, you force him to take the number of extra sheets required to extract it from him again, and you fill those additional sheets with quotations, etc., which cost you nothing. 20 sheets at £3, or 30 sheets at £2 amount after all to £60, and to put together 10 sheets, at no expense in time or money, from Petty, Stewart, Culpeper and other such fellows is, after all, easy enough and your book will be all the more 'instructive'...

The main thing is that you should once again make a public debut with a substantial book, and preferably with the most harmless, the history. Germany's mediocre and lamentable literati know perfectly well that they would be ruined if they did not present the public with some kind of trash 2 or 3 times yearly. Their tenacity sees them through; although their books sell only moderately, the booksellers finally end up by believing that they must be great men because their names appear several times in every Fair catalogue. Again, it's absolutely essential to break the spell created by your prolonged absence from the German book market and, later, by funk on the part of the booksellers. But once one or two instructive, erudite, well-grounded and withal interesting things of yours have appeared, *alors c'est tout autre chose,*[c] and you can snap your fingers at booksellers who offer you too little.

Another thing is that you can do this *history* only in London, whereas you can do the socialists and the critique anywhere. Hence it would be a good idea if you were to take advantage of the opportunity now, before the *crapauds*[d] get up to some sort of nonsense and again deposit us on the *theatrum mundi.*[e]

The New York *Schnellpost* will arrive tomorrow.

---

[a] K. Marx, *The Poverty of Philosophy.* - [b] K. Marx and F. Engels, *Manifesto of the Communist Party.* - [c] then it will be quite a different matter - [d] philistines (here: French political circles) - [e] world stage

As I have already said, stick to Löwenthal so long as circumstances are at all propitious. If it's no go with him, then Ebner's resources, Pieper writes, will be exhausted. In any case, we should subsequently be able to do more with Löwenthal than with the others, because we have Ebner in Frankfurt who can be for ever at his heels. Should he fail to achieve anything with Löwenthal, upon whom he can bring pressure to bear day in day out, the thing becomes much more problematical in the case of the other ones who are not in Frankfurt. You should write to Ebner telling him that he has full authority to act and should at once conclude an agreement; the longer the thing drags on, the sooner Löwenthal will tire of it, and political fears about 1852 intervene. Should there be the slightest curtain raiser in Paris, any prospect of a publisher will go to pot, and if the Federal Diet passes press laws before a contract has been drawn up in black and white, it will also be all up with you. You must cast a sprat to catch a mackerel, or else— *te résigner, ce qui n'est pas trop agréable*.[a]

The more I think about the matter, the more practical it seems to me to start off with the history. *Sois donc un peu commerçant, cette fois!*[b]

So far as my Proudhon commentaries[c] are concerned, they are too insignificant to warrant much being done with them. The same thing would happen as in the case of the *Critical Criticism*[d] for which I similarly wrote a few sheets because a pamphlet was envisaged, and you turned it into a full-blown book of 20 sheets in which my trifle looked strange indeed. Once again you would assuredly do so much to it that my contribution, in any case hardly worth mentioning, would quite disappear before your heavy artillery. Otherwise I should have no objection, save that your business with Löwenthal is far more important and urgent.

Your
F. E.

First published in *Der Briefwechsel zwischen F. Engels und K. Marx*, Bd. 1, Stuttgart, 1913

Printed according to the original

Published in English for the first time

228

MARX TO ADOLF CLUSS[507]

IN WASHINGTON

[London, beginning of December 1851]

... One of our best friends, Joseph Weydemeyer, has now arrived in New York. Make contact with him straight away; I do not yet know his address. But if you send a letter to the *Staatszeitung* or the *Abendzeitung* it will no doubt reach him. He can enlighten you on all matters relating to the party. He will be useful to you in the gathering in New York[508] and you can help him to arrange his living in America. Write and tell him that I asked you to write to him....

First published in: Marx and Engels, *Works*, First Russian Edition, Vol. XXV, Moscow, 1934

Printed according to Adolf Cluss' letter to Joseph Weydemeyer of 20 December 1851

Published in English for the first time

229

MARX TO ENGELS

IN MANCHESTER

[London,] 1 December 1851
28 Dean Street, Soho

Dear Engels,

I enclose herewith: 1. Extract from Cluss' letter (from Washington) to Wolff[a]; 2. Letter from Pieper from Brussels.

As to No. 1, Lupus forgot to extract two more items of information which you will find not uninteresting. *Firstly:* the

---

[a] Wilhelm Wolff (Lupus)

article 'Revolution and Counter-Revolution in Germany' has appeared in *German* in the *New-Yorker Abendzeitung,* has been reprinted in various papers and has created a furore. Cluss doesn't say whether or not this is a translation from the *Tribune.* I've written direct to Dana about it.[509] *Secondly:* Mr Wiss, Kinkel's principal tool, has publicly declared that 'economically' he shares our views. You can see how the curs operate.

As for Mr Tupman,[a] he mentions neither our letter from Manchester nor a subsequent letter written him from here by my wife at my behest.[510]

But as to the *people in Cologne,*[b] it is typical of these dastardly émigré swine, who root about in all the cess-pits of the press, that they should maintain *la conspiration du silence* in this matter so as not to detract from their own importance. This must now be counteracted. Today I have sent letters to Paris attacking Prussian justice, in order to raise the matter in the press there.[511] Lupus has undertaken to do the articles for America and Switzerland. *Maintenant*[c] you must hammer out for me something for England, along with a private letter to the EDITOR of *The Times,* to which the thing must tentatively be sent. If *The Times,* which at present is seeking to regain its popularity and would certainly feel flattered if treated as the only influential paper on the Continent and which is in any case hostile to Prussia—if *The Times* were to accept the thing, we could exert some influence in Germany. Stress should be laid on the state of the judicial system generally in Prussia.

Should this attempt not succeed—it can in any case do no harm—then write from Manchester direct to *The Sun.* If they receive the thing *before The Times,* the latter would not accept it under any circumstances.[512]

You can hardly be aware that addresses have reached O'Connor from almost every city in England and have been published in *The Northern Star* and *Reynolds's Newspaper* in which Thornton Hunt was described as 'INFAMOUS' and the scene at 'Copenhagen Fields' roundly denounced.[513] In addition there was a meeting of all the Chartist sections in London at which abuse was heaped upon Th. Hunt, who was present. When the executive committee is renewed, he will definitely be thrown out. In his desperation, this *allié* of the great Ruge now publicly proclaims himself a '*communist*'.

---

[a] Wilhelm Pieper - [b] the Communist League members arrested and under investigation - [c] Now

E. Jones—drawing on my letter[514]—has attacked Kossuth *sans miséricorde.*[a]

* 'I tell him that the revolutions of Europe mean the crusade of labour against capital, and I tell him they are not to be cut down to the intellectual and social standard of an obscure semi-barbarous people, like the Magyars, still standing in the half-civilisation of the 16th century, who actually presume to dictate to the great enlightenment of Germany and France, and to gain a false won cheer from the gullibility of England.'*[b]

You'll have seen that Kinkel will, *tout bonnement,*[c] set himself up here, after the pattern of the provisional government in France. I, for my part, believe it would be a good idea if, as soon as we know that Weydemeyer is editor of the *Abendzeitung,* you were to communicate, initially in the form of pamphlets, fragments from K. Schnapper,[d][503] whose first confessions I long to see. (See continuation after Pieper's letter.[e])

Apropos! I'd almost forgotten an important item in the *chronique scandaleuse.* Stechan, Hirsch, Gümpel, etc., in short the working men who have arrived from Germany, have announced their intention of calling on me. I shall receive them today. They have already considerably fallen out with Schapper and Willich. Stechan has publicly denounced Dietz as a spy before the Workers' Society[331] and, though a few voices declared him to be an agent of Marx, effected the establishment of a committee in which, however, the chief role is played by the friends and patrons of Dietz-Schapper and Willich. At all events I shall use these Straubingers[86] to precipitate fresh crises in the wretched hostel for tailors and idlers.

I herewith acknowledge receipt of the £3.
Salut.

Your
K.M.

First published slightly abridged in *Der Briefwechsel zwischen F. Engels und K. Marx,* Bd. 1, Stuttgart, 1913 and in full in *MEGA,* Abt. III, Bd. 1, 1929

Printed according to the original

Published in English for the first time

---

[a] mercilessly - [b] E. Jones, 'What is Kossuth', *Notes to the People,* Vol. II, No. 31, 1851. - [c] quite simply - [d] Snapper, i.e. Schapper - [e] The continuation is on the third page of Pieper's letter to Marx sent from Brussels on 27 November 1851.

230

MARX TO HERMANN EBNER[515]

IN FRANKFURT AM MAIN

[London, 2 December 1851]

...You know that Mr Kinkel is continuing his tour of the United States.[497] So far he has raised some 12,000 dollars, but has taken very good care not to give any inkling of the true party positions of the various émigré fractions, as you will realise if only from the fact that he even addresses himself to personal friends of mine and has even inveigled them into collaborating with him. He has sent the press the following fatuous manifesto:

*'To the friends of the People

'The shameful tyranny and injustice of the German despots have reached the highest point. Every free institution gained during the revolutionary struggle of 1848, has been destroyed by the brutal power of the Monarchs. The time has arrived when it becomes a right as well as a duty of the oppressed people to draw their swords and fight for the most sacred rights which the supreme being has granted all men alike. The hatred against the despots who cowardly murder or imprison every man, whoever raised his arm or tongue for a republican reform and for the freedom of the downtrodden, is on the point of a tremendous outbreak, and it is most likely that next spring the sun will rise over the most desperate struggle ever waged by men against their oppressors. Italy will set the ball in motion, until tyranny is swept away and liberty proclaimed in every province of the Old World. America having set the noble example in 1776, Europe is ready to follow in the footsteps of her young and noble sister on Columbia's shores. To bring about this much desired aim, more especially in Germany, the leading German republicans (?), now refugees in London, have united for the purpose of creating a national loan, with the promise to use every effort, after the establishment of the republic, to liquidate the same with full interest. All friends of liberty in this country are now called upon to lend their willing aid for this purpose. Without money nothing can be accomplished. It rests in a high degree with the sympathisers of Republicanism whether the project shall be accomplished. 'Baltimore, October, 1851. Dr. *G. Kinkel.* In behalf of the London Committee.'*

In the United States Mr Gottfried found only one ardent adversary, namely K. Heinzen, who represents the Ruge-Fickler clique. But the enmity of a base blusterer like Heinzen cannot but be beneficial to anyone against whom it is directed. Among those who figure *publicly* as guarantors of Kinkel's loan are the 3 Prussian ex-lieutenants, Schimmelpfennig, Willich, Techow, the *studiosus*[a] Schurz, Count Oskar Reichenbach and the mediocre

---

[a] student

Berlin literatus, Meyen. *Privately,* however, Kinkel has also secured the signature of *Löwe of Calbe* (better named *Kalb* of Löwe[a]), ex-President of the Imperial Rump Parliament in Stuttgart.[516] This Löwe is in possession of a document from Stuttgart empowering him to convene the Imperial Parliament when and where he will. To Kinkel, who hopes to move into Germany as provisional government, the *accaparation*[b] of this man, in order to place his 'rule' on a 'legal basis', was therefore of moment.

The second secret guarantor is Dr *d'Ester.* His numerous *creditors* in Germany will assuredly learn with satisfaction that he is guaranteeing the interest on Kinkel's 2 million loan and that, as Finance Minister, he will at the same time administer the 20,000 dollars so far received. Mr d'Ester, as a country doctor in Switzerland, intends to go on fleecing the peasants (he is said to be in better circumstances there than in Cologne where he was swamped, not by patients, but by debts) while at the same time keeping a foot in the great door that leads to the heaven of revolutionary government. That is why he would give his guarantee only under the seal of secrecy. It could do no harm if he were compelled to advocate *in public* what he is, after his usual fashion, 'adumbrating in private'.[c]

From the material once sent to you by Freiligrath,[d] you will be familiar enough with Mr Gottfried Kinkel's character. Hence it will not surprise you to learn that 'lies' were his 'chief' and, come to that, his sole recourse in the United States. Thus a friend writes, *inter alia*:

'Kinkel is vigorously coquetting with Ledru-Rollin who has promised some esteemed friends from Germany that, as soon as Kinkel takes over the helm and, with him, Löwe, he will send armies across the border to wage a war of propaganda. Kinkel, he says, will establish contact with Mazzini as soon as he is flush and thereby (!) has become his *equal* (!).'

Now, as you know, Ledru maintains contact with the committee *hostile* to Kinkel, and he sent Kinkel's emissary away *with a flea in his ear.* But as for Mazzini, the following will be explanation enough: Some 14-15 months ago the great Gottfried Kinkel sent the very insignificant Prussian ex-lieutenant Schimmelpfennig to Mazzini to say that he, Schimmelpfennig, would be undertaking a missionary tour of Germany on Kinkel's behalf. For this, much

[a] *Kalb*—calf - [b] monopolising - [c] Goethe, 'Die Spinnerin'. - [d] See this volume, pp. 426-33.

was wanting, money included. Mazzini gave him 1,000 fr. in cash, and 4,000 fr. in Mazzinian government bonds on condition that the 1,000 fr. be paid back without 12 months and half the placed government bonds within the same period. Schimmelpfennig returned from Germany where he had downed a great many bottles of wine but scarcely one 'tyrant'. The 12 months went by. Whoever may have visited Mazzini, it was not Kinkel or Kinkel's emissary. A few weeks later this same Schimmelpfennig again presented himself to Mazzini, not in order to pay up, but rather to invite Mazzini yet again to ally himself with Gottfried. For Gottfried had just received £160 sterling from New Orleans and since, in his view, only a few more pounds were needed to make him a 'great man', he *now* believed himself to be Mazzini's equal. Mazzini was of a different opinion and declared that he had *his own* people (Ruge & Co.) in Germany and that he would have none of Mr Gottfried's alliance. Kinkel, however, is imperturbable and *profondément convaincu*[a] that, if £160 were still not enough to make him Mazzini's 'equal', this miracle could not fail to be effected by 20,000 dollars. Blessed are they that ... have believed.[b]

Kinkel's success in the United States is explained partly by the fact that he was no less hazy about the movement than the masses over there, and hence is sympathetic to them, and partly by his lies and prevarications about what he *really* stands for. Messrs Kinkel & Co. want to elect a revolutionary committee of 7 men, each of whom will be given a special ministry, e.g. d'Ester finance, Kinkel the ministry of rhetoric and higher politics, Techow ministry of war, Willich minister for *requisitioning*, at which he is a past master, Meyen minister for education, etc. One of the seven will occupy a seat on one of these committees in order to keep the supreme body, the Septarchy, thoroughly posted on with everything. Exactly after the pattern of the French provisional government, you see, except that the Septarchy have their seat outside Germany while their people consists of a club[c] 50-100 strong.

Mr Kinkel has expressly stated that he will *not* use for the support of refugees the money raised in America. He has actually entered into an obligation to that effect. As you will understand, this is no more than a way of *dodging* the obligation to allow *inferior* refugees to share the cash, and of gobbling it up *oneself* instead. This is already happening now and, as the hoard

---

[a] deeply convinced - [b] John 20:29 - [c] the Refugee Club in London

increases, will happen to an ever greater extent, and in the following way:

1. The 7 septarchs and their 7 ministries, i.e. all the creatures of Kinkel, Willich, etc., must be paid, and thus these gentlemen, on the pretext of working for the revolution, secure for themselves the lion's share of the funds. Mr Willich, for one, who for the past two years has been living here by public begging.

2. The gentlemen publish lithographed reports and distribute them *free* to the newspapers. A further share of the funds goes to those wretched literati, Meyen, Oppenheim, *studiosus* Schurz, etc., for their services as writers.

3. Others of the great men such as Schimmelpfennig, Schurz, etc., receive further payment as 'emissaries'.

Thus, you see, the whole plan has a twofold aim: to exclude the mass of exceedingly needy refugees (workers, etc.) from a share in the funds and, on the other hand, to provide Mr Kinkel and his creatures with safe, and at the same time politically profitable, *sinecures,* all this on the pretext of using the money *solely* for revolutionary purposes. It would certainly be very fitting if these financial speculations, cooked up by *studiosus* Schurz, were brought *to the knowledge of the public at large.*

Before I close, I have a few brief comments to make about *Kossuth.* Kossuth gave evidence of considerable talent and generally showed tact in handling the British public. However, the situation was not as simple as the man from the East had supposed. On the one hand he fawned over-much on the MIDDLE-CLASS and was oriental in his praise of institutions such as, for example, the City of London and its *municipal constitution* which even *The Times* castigates daily as PUBLIC NUISANCES. On the other hand he has made an enemy of the Chartist party which, through its most talented representative, Ernest Jones, is attacking him with all the virulence they might accord a Haynau. And it was, indeed, tactless of Kossuth, after forbidding all demonstrations of *partisanship,* to turn *partisan* himself. Finally Kossuth has become convinced that enthusiasm and ready cash are in inverse proportion to one another. So far, no amount of enthusiasm for *his* loan has succeeded in bringing him in more than £800 sterling.

On this occasion our democratic emigration has yet again made a fool of itself as is its wont. Kossuth has not deigned to answer its addresses. That foppishly vain and importunate dwarf, L. Blanc, was lucky enough to receive a reply to his address, but it was a reply in which Kossuth disavowed socialism outright.

I remain your truly

K. Marx

First published in *Mitteilungen des öster-reichischen Staatsarchivs*, Bd. 9, Wien, 1956

Printed according to the original

Published in English for the first time

231

ENGELS TO MARX [517]

IN LONDON

[Manchester,] 3 December 1851

'*Représentants de la France, délibérez en paix!*'[a] And where can the gentlemen deliberate more peacefully than in the Caserne d'Orsay, guarded by a battalion of *chasseurs de Vincennes!*

The history of France has entered a stage of utmost comicality. Can one imagine anything funnier than this travesty of the 18th Brumaire, effected in peacetime with the help of discontented soldiers by the most insignificant man in the world without, so far as it has hitherto been possible to judge, any opposition whatsoever? And how beautifully have all the old jackasses been caught! The slyest fox in the whole of France, old Thiers, the astutest advocate of the *barreau*,[b] Mr Dupin, caught in the trap set for them by the most notorious blockhead of the century; caught as easily as Mr Cavaignac's inflexible republican virtue and as that braggart of a Changarnier! And to complete the tableau, a rump parliament with Odilon Barrot as 'Löwe of Calbe' [518]; and, in view of this violation of the Constitution, the said Odilon demands to be arrested and cannot contrive to get himself hauled off to Vincennes! The whole thing is as if expressly invented for the

---

[a] 'Representatives of France, hold your deliberations in peace!'—from Changarnier's speech in the Legislative Assembly on 3 June 1851 in reply to one by President Louis Bonaparte in Dijon on 1 June containing concealed threats to the Assembly. - [b] at the Bar

benefit of red Wolff[a]; henceforward he alone will be capable of writing the history of France. Has ever a coup been effected with more fatuous proclamations than this one? And the ludicrous Napoleonic apparatus, the anniversary of the coronation and of Austerlitz,[519] the provocation against the consular Constitution and so on—the fact that anything of this kind could succeed even for a day—does indeed lower *Messieurs les Français* to a level of puerility that is without parallel.

Wonderful, the arrest of those great, loud-mouthed advocates of order,[364] of little Thiers first and foremost, and of the bold Changarnier. Wonderful, the sitting of the rump parliament in the 10th Arrondissement, with Mr Berryer yelling '*Vive la République*', out of the window, until finally the whole lot were apprehended and shut up in a barrack square among the soldiers. And then the stupid Napoleon, who at once packed his bags to move into the Tuileries. Even though one racked one's brains for a whole year, one couldn't think up a prettier comedy.

And that evening, when the stupid Napoleon at last flung himself down on the long coveted bed in the Tuileries, the numskull must really have been at a loss to know what he was about. *Le consulat sans premier consul!*[b] Internal difficulties no greater than they had been, generally speaking, for the past three years, no exceptional financial straits, not even as regards his private purse, no coalition on the borders, no St Bernard to be crossed, no Marengo to be won.[396] It's enough to make one despair. And now there's no longer even a National Assembly to foil the great schemes of this unappreciated man; nay, for the time being at least the jackass is as free, as untrammelled, as absolute as the old man on the night of the 18th Brumaire, so completely unrestrained that he can't help coming the jackass on each and every occasion. Appalling, a prospect devoid of conflict!

Mais le peuple, le peuple!—*Le peuple se fiche pas mal de toute cette boutique,*[c] are happy as children over the franchise accorded to them and which, indeed, they will probably make use of like children.[520] What can result from these ridiculous elections a week on Sunday, if in fact it ever comes to that? No press, no meetings, martial law enough and to spare and, on top of it all, the order to produce a deputy within 14 days.

---

[a] Ferdinand Wolff - [b] The consulate without the First Consul! - [c] But the people, the people! The people don't care a damn for all this business

What is to come of the whole business? 'If we adopt the standpoint of world history',[a] we are presented with a splendid subject for declamation. Thus, e.g.: it remains to be seen whether the Praetorian regime of the time of the Roman Empire, for which the prerequisite was an extensive state organised on strictly military lines, a depopulated Italy and the absence of a modern proletariat, is possible in a geographically compact, densely populated country such as France, which has a large industrial proletariat. Either: Louis Napoleon has no party of his own; having spurned the Orleanists and Legitimists, he must now turn towards the left. Turning towards the left implies an amnesty, an amnesty implies a collision, etc. Or else: Universal suffrage is the basis of Louis Napoleon's power, he cannot attack it, and universal suffrage is *now* incompatible with a Louis Napoleon. And other suchlike conjectural theses which would lend themselves splendidly to prolixity. But, after what we saw yesterday, there can be no counting on the *peuple,* and it really seems as though old Hegel, in the guise of the World Spirit, were directing history from the grave and, with the greatest conscientiousness, causing everything to be re-enacted twice over, once as grand tragedy and the second time as rotten farce,[521] Caussidière for Danton, L. Blanc for Robespierre, Barthélemy for Saint-Just, Flocon for Carnot, and the moon-calf[b] together with the first available dozen debt-encumbered lieutenants for the little corporal[c] and his band of marshals. Thus the 18th Brumaire would already be upon us.

The people of Paris have behaved with childish stupidity. *Cela ne nous regarde pas; que le président et l'assemblée s'entre-tuent, peu nous importe!*[d] But that the army should presume to foist a government—and what a government!—on France, *that* undoubtedly does concern them, and the mob will wonder what kind of a 'free' universal suffrage it is they are now to exercise 'for the first time since 1804'!

How much longer the World Spirit, clearly much incensed at mankind, is going to continue this farce, whether within the year we shall see Consulate, Empire, Restoration and all pass by before our eyes, whether, too, the Napoleonic dynasty must first be thrashed in the streets of Paris before it is deemed impossible in

---

[a] Engels quotes the Left-wing deputy Wilhelm Jordan (cf. also Engels' article 'The Frankfurt Assembly Debates the Polish Question'). - [b] Louis Bonaparte - [c] Napoleon Bonaparte - [d] That is no concern of ours; that the President and the Assembly should massacre each other is of small moment to us!

France, the devil only knows. But it strikes me that things are taking a remarkably lunatic turn and that the *crapauds*[a] are heading for an astonishing humiliation.

Even assuming that Louis Napoleon momentarily consolidates his position, such stuff and nonsense can hardly endure, despite the fathomless depths to which the French have sunk. But what then? There's damned little red in prospect, that much is clear, and if Mr Blanc and Ledru packed their bags at midday yesterday, they may as well begin unpacking them again. *La voix tonnante du peuple ne les rappelle pas encore.*[b]

Here and in Liverpool the affair suddenly brought business to a standstill, but today in Liverpool they are already briskly speculating again. And French funds have only fallen by 2 per cent.

In the circumstances any attempt to intercede for the Cologne people[c] in the British press must, of course, be postponed.

With regard to the articles for the *Tribune*,[d] which have obviously already appeared in it, write to the EDITOR of the *Tribune* in *English*. Dana may well be away, and a BUSINESS LETTER will certainly be answered. *Tell him that he must distinctly state per next returning steamer what has become of these papers, and in case they have been made use of, he is requested to send by the same opportunity copies of the *Tribune* containing them, as no copy has been kept here and without having the articles already sent, again before our eyes, we cannot, after such a lapse of time, undertake to go on with the following numbers of the series.*

The news from France must have had a jolly effect on the European émigré rabble. I'd like to have witnessed it.

En attendant tes nouvelles[e]

Your
F. E.

First published in *Der Briefwechsel zwischen F. Engels und K. Marx*, Bd. 1, Stuttgart, 1913

Printed according to the original

---

[a] philistines - [b] The thunderous voice of the people is not recalling them yet. - [c] the Communist League members arrested and under investigation (see this volume, p. 497) - [d] F. Engels, *Revolution and Counter-Revolution in Germany* - [e] Awaiting your news

232

MARX TO ENGELS [115]

IN MANCHESTER

[London,] 9 December 1851
28 Dean Street, Soho

Dear Frederic,

I have kept you waiting for an answer, QUITE BEWILDERED by the tragi-comic sequence of events in Paris. Unlike Willich, I couldn't say: 'Strange, we've had no advice from Paris!' Nor, like Schapper, declare myself and my pot of beer a permanent fixture at Schärttner's. To save the fatherland, Schapper and a few of his satellites slept two nights at Schärttner's on the pretext of holding a vigil. These gentlemen, like Löwe of Calbe and his like, had packed their *malles*[a] but, discretion being the better part of valour,[b] decided not to move there until the issue had been 'decided'.

Have you read Louis Blanc's Miserere[c]? The other day Bernard le Clubiste protested that he had not been a co-signatory of this jeremiad.

Enclosed a letter from Reinhardt from Paris and the 'drunken gossip' I spoke to you about when I was in Manchester.[d]

Pieper is here again, highly delighted with himself. He is leaving the Rothschilds but continuing to give German lessons there; Madame has given him notice as resident private tutor. Since writing to me last he has done nothing, seen nothing and heard nothing in connection with my Proudhon business.[e] It seems to me that he has treated the translation as *his own* work, *ce qui n'est pas.*[f]

Maintenant,[g] what can I tell you about the situation? This much is clear, the proletariat has spared its strength. For the time being Bonaparte is victorious because, overnight, he transformed the open ballot into a secret one. With the million £ sterling purloined, despite all d'Argout's posthumous protestations, from the bank, he has bought the army. Will his coup again succeed if the vote goes against him? Will the majority vote at all? The Orléans have left for France. It is difficult, indeed impossible, to

---

[a] trunks - [b] Cf. Shakespeare, *Henry IV,* Part One, Act 5, Scene 4. - [c] Address of the French Exiles to Their Countrymen, by Bernard le Clubiste, Louis Blanc and others, *The Daily News,* 5 December 1851. - [d] See this volume, p. 492. - [e] The planned publication of *The Poverty of Philosophy* in German - [f] which is not so - [g] Now

18*

make any prognostication in a drama with Krapülinski[a] for its hero. At all events it seems to me that the situation has improved rather than deteriorated as a result of the coup d'état. It is easier to deal with Bonaparte than it would have been with the National Assembly and its generals. And the dictatorship of the National Assembly was imminent.

Capital, the disappointment of Techow & Co., who, without more ado, saw in the French army *les apôtres de la trinité démocratique, de la liberté, de l'égalité, de la fraternité. Les pauvres hommes!*[b] And Messrs Mazzini and Ledru can also now sleep easy. The catastrophe was the DOWNFALL of the émigrés. It has been shown that they are *pour rien*[c] in the revolution. For these gentlemen had *resolved* to suspend world history until Kossuth's return. Apropos, the penny subscription for the latter in London yielded exactly 100d., pronounced pence.

Salut.

Your
K. M.

Apropos, didn't I send you a letter from Pieper to me, written in *French?* If so, let me have it back by return.

First published in *Der Briefwechsel zwischen F. Engels und K. Marx,* Bd. 1, Stuttgart, 1913

Printed according to the original

Published in English in full for the first time

233

ENGELS TO MARX

IN LONDON

Manchester, 10 December 1851

Dear Marx,

What are the great men doing in this EVENTFUL CRISIS? It is said that L. Blanc has been arrested in France, but this cannot alas be true; *nous connaissons notre petit bonhomme.*[d] By the way, since nothing has

---

[a] a character in Heine's 'Zwei Ritter', here Louis Bonaparte - [b] the apostles of the democratic trinity, of liberty, equality, fraternity. The poor chaps! - [c] of no account - [d] we know our little fellow

come of the Paris insurrection,[522] I'm glad that the first storm is over. On such occasions, *tout blasé qu'on est,*[a] one is always to some extent gripped by the old political fever and one always has some personal interest in the upshot of such a business. Now I can at least resume my ethnological study [132] upon which I was engaged at the onset of this great coup.

By the way, in spite of all this there's no sign of a return of *confiance,*[b] either here or in Liverpool, and P. Ermen alone is as cocksure and as faithful to Napoleon as 4 days ago he was DEJECTED and CHAPFALLEN. By and large the bourgeois here are too shrewd to regard this Napoleonic farce as anything other than ephemeral. But what is to come of the whole dirty business? Napoleon will be elected, no question of that, the bourgeoisie has no choice, and who is to verify the ballot-papers? To make a wrong count in favour of the adventurer is too much of a temptation, and the full measure of the French property-owning class's turpitude, its servile abjection in the face of the slightest success, its habit of crawling before a *pouvoir quelconque,*[c] have this time come more splendidly to light than ever before. But how does the jackass propose to rule? He will receive fewer votes than in 1848, *c'est clair,*[d] perhaps 3 to $3\frac{1}{2}$ million in all; that is already a dangerous setback so far as credit is concerned. Any financial and taxation reform is impossible 1. because of shortage of money, 2. because it can only be effected by a military dictator who wages successful wars abroad, *où la guerre paie la guerre,*[e] whereas in peacetime any surplus, and a great deal more besides, inevitably finds its way into the pockets of the army, 3. because Napoleon is too stupid. What remains for him? *La guerre?*[f] Against whom, against England perhaps? Or simple military despotism, which in peacetime must necessarily lead to a fresh military revolution and call into being the parties of the National Assembly within the army itself? Here there is no way out, the farce is bound to collapse. And what if a trade crisis comes!

That Louis Napoleon has something 'big' up his sleeve, I do not for a moment doubt. But I shall be curious to see what sort of foolishness it will be. The *developpement* of the Napoleonic ideas[g] will fly exceeding high and come a cropper over the most ordinary obstacles.

What emerges pretty clearly from the whole transaction is that

---

[a] however blase one may be - [b] confidence - [c] any kind of power - [d] that's clear - [e] where war pays for war - [f] War? - [g] An allusion to Louis Napoleon Bonaparte's *Des idées napoléoniennes.*

the reds[a] have abdicated, completely abdicated. To attempt to vindicate them now for not having defended themselves *en masse* would be nonsensical. The next few months will show whether prostration in France is such that several years' peace and quiet will be needed before the reds are capable of another '48. But where, on the other hand, is that peace and quiet to come from?

I see only 2 ways out of this beastly mess:

Either the factions of the party of order, as reflected in the army, now take the place of the 'anarchists', i.e. bring about such a state of anarchy that ultimately the reds and Ledru-Rollin will appear as saviours just as now Louis Napoleon; or Louis Napoleon abolishes the tax on drinks and lets himself be inveigled into introducing one or two bourgeois reforms—though where the money and power are to come from is hard to say. In this highly unlikely event he might be able to maintain his position.

Qu'en penses-tu?[b]

Your
F. E.

First published in *Der Briefwechsel zwischen F. Engels und K. Marx*, Bd. 1, Stuttgart, 1913

Printed according to the original

Published in English for the first time

234

ENGELS TO MARX[523]

IN LONDON

Manchester, 11 December 1851

Dear Marx,

Herewith I return Reinhardt's letter as well as the one from Pieper which I had been keeping for a time because of the happenings in Cologne.

It seems that the 700 vagabonds' great expedition to Paris, so loudly proclaimed by the press, will not take place; and little L. Blanc, too, to judge by his renewed groans of pain in today's

---

[a] i.e. democrats and socialists of various trends - [b] What do you think?

Daily News[a] is, even if allegedly not in London, at least for the time being in safety. The first jeremiad[b] was divine by comparison with today's. *Peuple français—noble fierté—courage indomptable— éternel amour de la liberté—honneur au courage malheureux*[c]—and thereupon the little fellow makes a *demi-tour à droite*[d] and preaches trust and union between the people and the bourgeoisie. *Vide* Proudhon: Appel à la bourgeoisie, page 2.[e] And such reasoning! If the insurgents were beaten, it was due to the fact that they were not the *vrai peuple*[f]; the *vrai peuple* cannot be beaten; and if the *vrai peuple* failed to fight, this was due to the fact that it didn't wish to fight for the National Assembly; true, it may be objected that, once victorious, the *vrai peuple* would itself have been a dictator, but it was taken so much by surprise that it could never have thought of that and, after all, it had so often been duped before!

It's the old, vulgar, democratic logic of the kind disseminated whenever the revolutionary party suffers defeat. *Le fait est,*[g] in my opinion, that if, this time, the proletariat failed to fight *en masse*, it was because it was fully aware of its own prostration and impotence and was prepared to submit with fatalistic resignation to a renewed cycle of Republic, Empire, restoration and fresh revolution, until such time as it regained fresh strength from a few years of *misère* under a rule of maximum order. I'm not saying that this will be so, but it seems to me to have been at bottom the instinctive attitude which prevailed among the people of Paris on Tuesday and Wednesday,[h] and after the introduction of the secret ballot and the resulting retreat of the bourgeoisie on Friday. It is nonsense to say that this was not an opportunity for the people. If the proletariat wants to wait until confronted by the government with its own question, until a collision occurs in which the conflict will assume a sharper and more definite form than in June 1848,[488] it may have to wait a long time. The last time the question between proletariat and bourgeoisie was posed with any degree of precision was on the occasion of the 1850 electoral law, and then the people chose not to fight. This and the perpetual references to 1852 were of themselves proof enough of inertia for us to make a

[a] L. Blanc, 'To the Editor of *The Daily News*', *The Daily News*, 11 December 1851. - [b] Address of the French Exiles to Their Countrymen, by Bernard le Clubiste, Louis Blanc and others, *The Daily News*, 5 December 1851. - [c] French people—noble pride—indomitable courage—eternal love of liberty—all honour to courage in adversity - [d] right-about turn - [e] A reference to the section 'Appeal to the Bourgeoisie' in the introduction to Proudhon's *Idée générale de la Révolution au XIXe siècle*. - [f] true people - [g] The fact is - [h] 2 and 3 December 1851

fairly gloomy prognostication for 1852 also, always assuming that no trade crisis supervened. Universal suffrage having been abolished and the proletariat elbowed off the official stage, it is asking rather too much to expect the official parties to pose the question in a way that will suit the proletariat. And how did matters stand in February[a]? At that time the people were just as *hors de cause*[b] as they are now. And there can be no denying that if, at a time of revolutionary development, a revolutionary party begins by allowing things to take a decisive turn without itself having any say in them, or if it does intervene and fails to win, it can be regarded with some certainty as temporarily done for. WITNESS the insurrections after Thermidor and after 1830.[524] And the gentlemen who now so loudly maintain that the *vrai peuple* is biding its time, are in danger of gradually finding themselves in the same boat as the powerless Jacobins of 1795-99 and the Republicans of 1831-39, and of making thorough fools of themselves.

Nor is there any denying that the effect which the establishment of the secret ballot has had on the bourgeoisie, the petty bourgeoisie and, *au bout du compte*,[c] *upon many proletarians as well* (as all the reports go to show), casts a curious light on the courage and insight of the Parisians. It has clearly never occurred to many of them how fatuous is the question posed by Louis Napoleon, or to ask what guarantees there were that the votes would be correctly recorded, yet the majority must have seen through this humbug and have nevertheless persuaded themselves that everything was now ALL RIGHT, *merely in order to have a pretext for not fighting*.

According to Reinhardt's letter, according to the fresh revelations each day brings about the infamies perpetrated by the soldiery and in particular their outrages on the boulevards against any and every *pékin quelconque, n'importe*[d] whether worker or bourgeois, red or Bonapartist—according to the accumulating reports of local insurrections even in the remotest places where no one expected any resistance,[522] according to the letter in yesterday's *Daily News* from a French ex-deputy and *commerçant*,[e] it would indeed seem that the *appel au peuple*[f] is taking an undesirable turn for Bonaparte. The mass of the bourgeoisie in Paris would not appear very much to RELISH this new régime and the deportation laws it has imposed. Military terrorism is increasing too rapidly and too brazenly. $^2/_3$ of France is in a state

---

[a] February 1848 - [b] uninvolved - [c] in the end - [d] civilian of any description, no matter - [e] businessman - [f] appeal to the people

of siege. I believe that after all this the bulk of the bourgeoisie won't vote at all, that the whole electoral farce will come to nothing; for in all the doubtful localities, where Louis Napoleon's opponents will turn up in crowds to vote, the gendarmes will stir up trouble with the voters, and then the whole electoral procedure will be declared null and void there. Then Louis Napoleon will declare France to be *en état d'aliénation mentale*[a] and proclaim the army the sole saviour of society and then the whole dungheap will be plain to all and Louis Napoleon in the middle of it. Yet it is precisely through this business of elections that things could take a very nasty turn, if *by then* any really serious resistance to an established government could still be expected.

The fellow's assured of a million votes from officials and soldiers. There are also half a million Bonapartists in the country, maybe more. Half a million, maybe more, irresolute townspeople will vote for him. Half a million stupid peasants, a million mistakes in adding up, that makes $3\,^1/_2$ millions already—more than the old Napoleon could boast in an empire which included the entire left bank of the Rhine and Belgium, i.e. certainly 32 million inhabitants. Why shouldn't he be content with that to start off with? And were he to get them with, perhaps, 1 million against him, the bourgeois would soon fall into his lap. But maybe he won't get the $2^1/_2$ millions and maybe—though this might be asking too much of the probity of French officials—he will not succeed in having himself credited with mistakes in adding up to the tune of 1 million. At all events a great deal depends on the measures he is forced to take in the meantime. Anyhow, what's to prevent the officials from chucking a few hundred *oui's*[b] into the ballot box before the voting starts? *Il n'y a plus de presse*[c]—nobody can verify it.

At any rate it's unfortunate for Krapülinski[d] that funds should be falling again, and for L. Blanc that he should now have to recognise England as a free country.

In a few months' time the reds are bound to be given another opportunity of proving their mettle, perhaps actually when the voting takes place; but if they again hang back, then I shall give them up, and then, even with the finest of trade crises, all that they can hope for is a sound thrashing which will most assuredly eliminate them for several years to come. What is the rabble worth if it has forgotten how to fight?

---

[a] non compos mentis - [b] Ayes - [c] There's no longer any press - [d] a character in Heine's 'Zwei Ritter', here Louis Bonaparte

Is Pieper back in London? I wanted him to do something for me about books in Frankfurt and don't know whether he is still in Brighton.

The worst of it is that you will now run into difficulties with Löwenthal. It would have been best had the contract already been concluded.

* Liverpool Market—quiet at yesterday's prices; Manchester Market—firm. Some overtrading going on to the Levant. German buyers continue keeping out of the Market.*

Your
F. E.

First published in *Der Briefwechsel zwischen F. Engels und K. Marx*, Bd. 1, Stuttgart, 1913   Printed according to the original

235

ENGELS TO MARIE BLANK

IN LONDON

Manchester, Monday, 15 December 1851

Dear Marie,

I got your letter on Saturday, the only day of the week on which I can never manage to write a private letter because we then shut up the office as early as noon; otherwise you'd have had an answer sooner.

I'm sorry that you should have had so much illness in the house of late, but am glad to hear that things are now taking a better turn; I hope to see Hermann as well as little Titi fully recovered by the time I arrive. You should really have written to tell me all about it for, so long as I don't hear, I have to assume that all is well; and besides you also owed me a letter in reply to the one in which I returned you your latch-key last summer.[525]

I have as usual been well all this while, and am merely somewhat vexed by the onset of bad weather which prevents me going out into the country, this being a real necessity here in Manchester. For the past few days I have been aware of certain premonitory symptoms which lead me to believe that there may be a recurrence of the disagreeable tooth-ache I suffered from last winter, the more disagreeable in that it interferes with my customary bathing, etc. I hope, however, that the thing will pass off without too much inconvenience—at any rate I don't intend to fret in advance about pain which I'm not yet suffering.

By the end of this week I shall probably have put my current business in order and, this being a quiet time for us anyway, I shall see to it that I leave here on Saturday evening[526] and, since the trains all arrive in London either too late at night or too early in the morning for one to drive across to Camberwell directly, I shall recuperate a while in the Euston Hotel and arrive at your place BEFORE DINNER TIME on Sunday. At any rate you can expect me at the Grove for dinner on Sunday, unless you get a letter to the contrary from me on Saturday morning.

As for the French, the jackasses can do what they like, it's all one to me.

My warm regards to Emil and Hermann and your children. Your description of your new maids has made me eager to see them. *Nota bene,* should you have too much BOTHER in the house on Sunday, thus making my company and any further inconvenience seem undesirable just now, you have only to write and send me an army order instructing me when to present myself, and I shall not fail to be punctual.

Toujours[a] your

Friedrich

First published in: Marx and Engels, *Works,* Second Russian Edition, Vol. 27, Moscow, 1962

Printed according to the original

Published in English for the first time

236

ENGELS TO MARX

IN LONDON

[Manchester,] 16 December 1851

Dear Marx,

Herewith a letter from Weydemeyer which reached me at midday today. So far, the news is quite good, Heinzen's paper[b] about to expire and Weydemeyer already in a position to bring

---

[a] Ever - [b] *Deutsche Schnellpost*

out a weekly.[527] But the demand to send off an article to him by Friday evening is rather too much—particularly under present circumstances. And yet this is just the moment when people there are pining for arguments and cogent facts about the French business, and if one could say something sensational about the situation, the success of the enterprise would be assured in the very first number. But that's just the snag, and as usual I shall again pass on the difficulty to you and, whatever I may write, it will not at any rate be about Krapülinski's *coup de tête*.[a] You, at any rate, can write a diplomatic non-committal-epoch-making article for him.[528] What I shall do, I don't know yet, but shall at any rate attempt something or other. I cannot send the Schnapper,[503] firstly because the first chapter is weak, and secondly because I have dropped the thing altogether now that History is starting to write comic novels—a rather too dangerous form of competition. Meanwhile I'll introduce a few more comic scenes into the plot and then begin the thing again—but it would be quite unsuitable for them over there and in any case Weydemeyer wants stuff with our names at the bottom. Write and tell me by return what you propose to do; *le temps presse*,[b] Saturday's steamer won't reach New York before the New Year and that's bad; even worse is the short respite still left us.

Weydemeyer must really keep his fingers out of the American pie until he is able to get the local names right. It's a pity he hasn't the time to orient himself first and learn a little English. The 'abolutionists'[c] would make a splendid tidbit for Heinzen. As for Weerth, I shall see him here tomorrow or the day after and find out what he can do. Next week, or maybe even on Saturday evening, I shall be in London,[526] when we can discuss matters further; meanwhile there remains only the question of what is to be done for the first number; this cannot be put off, so you must write and tell me by return what you propose to do.

To judge by this letter Weydemeyer certainly appears to be still somewhat 'green' in regard to business matters; I shall drop him such hints on the subject as are necessary. As yet he knows nothing whatever about his readers.

Lupus might also bestir himself and see what he can produce for the first number. Weydemeyer will be very hard put to it to find material.

What do you think of the French funds, which yesterday were

---

[a] impulsive act of Louis Bonaparte (called Krapülinski after a character in Heine's 'Zwei Ritter') - [b] time is short - [c] Engels refers to a mistake made by Weydemeyer when he used this word instead of 'abolitionists.'

standing at 101.50 c.,—1 $\frac{1}{2}$ per cent above par—and which, better than any venal lies in the press, will pull in a mass of votes for Louis Napoleon. He's even being helped by the excesses of the peasantry in the south and central parts of France.[a] Some did undoubtedly occur, nor could anything else be expected of this race of barbarians. The fellows don't give a rap for the government, etc., etc., but think only of tearing down the tax collector's or notary's house, raping his wife and killing the man himself if they can lay hands on him. In itself the matter is *au fond*[b] of scant significance and serves these gentlemen perfectly right, but it drives into Napoleon's camp everyone who has anything to lose. In fact, the invasion of native barbarians, should it ever come to pass, promises to be an amusing spectacle, and happy are those under whose governance such agreeable events take place. The *present* rise in the funds is assuredly no longer a mere government manoeuvre but the expression of the fear— translated into confidence in Louis Napoleon—felt by *haute finance*[c] of being flayed alive, as depicted in such vivid colours by the truthful *Constitutionnel*.

Write to me at once, then, about Weydemeyer.

Your
F. E.

First published in *Der Briefwechsel zwischen F. Engels und K. Marx*, Bd. 1, Stuttgart, 1913

Printed according to the original

Published in English for the first time

237

ENGELS TO JENNY MARX

IN LONDON

[Manchester,] Thursday evening
[18 December 1851]

Dear Mrs Marx,

I have received both your letters[d] and hasten to write and tell you that it goes without saying that each of us will send off his article separately, as there is otherwise every prospect of none of

---

[a] See this volume, pp. 512-13. - [b] basically - [c] high finance - [d] See this volume, pp. 562 and 563.

them catching the steamer.[529] In London the letters should be at the post office by 5 or 6 o'clock on Friday evening. I shall see what I can do—for some time now the fatherland has bored me so dreadfully that I know nothing about anything. Anyway I shall send off something. The English *Manifesto*[a] together with such New York *Schnellposts* as are still available here, I shall be bringing with me. Tell Marx to be sure not to forget to write to Weydemeyer, asking him to obtain the relevant numbers of the *Tribune* immediately from Dana and send them on to me here so that I may proceed.[b]

When I shall be able to leave—maybe not until Saturday morning—I don't yet know exactly.[526] But I think I shall arrive at the latest at 6 o'clock on Saturday evening, perhaps as early as 11 in the morning. Until then, my warm regards to you and all your family from your

F. Engels

First published in *MEGA,* Abt. III, Bd. 1, 1929

Printed according to the original

Published in English for the first time

238

MARX TO JOSEPH WEYDEMEYER[435]

IN NEW YORK

[London,] 19 December 1851
28 Dean Street, Soho

DEAR Weydemeyer,

The day before yesterday I received your letter, sent on to me by Engels.

First, my best New Year wishes to your wife[c] and yourself. Ditto from my wife.

---

[a] the English translation of the *Manifesto of the Communist Party* - [b] with the *Revolution and Counter-Revolution in Germany* - [c] Louise

I am at this moment sitting here working on an article for you. Your commission arrived too late for me to be able to carry it out today. On Tuesday *(23 December)* the following will go off to you 1. *Der 18te Brumaire des Louis Bonaparte* by K. Marx. 2. *Der Staatsstreich in Frankreich* by F. Wolff. 3. *Nemesis* by Wilhelm Wolff. *Engels* will send you his article—on Prussia, I believe— possibly even by today's mail. *Freiligrath* has nothing ready but authorises you to name him as one of your collaborators. We are negotiating with *Weerth.* Likewise with *Eccarius.*

You can now settle down in the United States for *du moins*[a] a year. *'It'* is not going to begin on 2 May 1852.[530]

I suppose that you will hold back your first number[b] until the above articles arrive. After all, it will only make a difference of 5 days. For the following numbers you can announce a serialised work of mine, to appear article by article, namely, *Neuste Offenbarungen des Sozialismus, oder 'Idée générale de la Révolution au XIX*[e] *siècle' par J. P. Proudhon.— Kritik von K.M.*[531]

Write forthwith to 'Adolf Cluss, U.S. Navy Yard, Washington D.C.' We've already told him you are coming.[c] He is one of our best and most talented men and could be of the greatest use to you both generally and for the preparation and founding of your paper in particular.

Don't forget the following:

Go and see Dana; ask him to give you the numbers of the *Tribune* in which my articles appeared,[d] and send them to me *forthwith.* Hearing nothing from him, I had stopped writing, and there's been such a long interval that I must see the paper itself in order to write the sequel, which I must do, if only for pecuniary reasons.

As soon as your paper appears you must not only send it to us regularly, but let us have a sufficient number of copies so that we can send them out as samples.

Tout à toi[e]

K. Marx

Unless you are contractually committed, don't buy the *Arbeiter-republik*[f] from the wretched Weitling. While you might gain 200

---

[a] at least - [b] of *Die Revolution* - [c] See this volume, p. 496. - [d] first articles from *Revolution and Counter-Revolution in Germany* by Engels - [e] All yours - [f] *Die Republik der Arbeiter*

Straubingers,[86] you would lose a wider readership. Write only under the old name. *Règle générale.*[a]

First published abridged in *Die Neue Zeit,* Bd. 2, No. 29, 1906-07 and in full in: Marx and Engels, *Works,* First Russian Edition, Vol. XXV, Moscow, 1934

Printed according to the original

Published in English in full for the first time

239

MARX TO FERDINAND FREILIGRATH

IN LONDON

[London,] 27 December 1851
28 Dean Street, Soho

Moorish Prince[b]!

Enclosed a letter from Ebner.

Today I also received another letter from Weydemeyer in which, among other things, he says:

'Not long ago an emissary arrived from the London "agitation club"[473] for the purpose of opposing Kinkel's loan.[497] These people probably imagine that here in America all are split into Kinkelians and anti-Kinkelians simply because a handful of refugees have made much ado about nothing. The stir over Kossuth has long consigned Kinkel to oblivion and the couple of thousand dollars he is collecting are, indeed, hardly worth making a fuss about.

'In any case, I can see to the sale of the *Revue* for you over here. Similarly it would be possible to dispose of some more of Freiligrath's more recent poetry.'

After dunning us once again Weydemeyer goes on:

'But above all, a poem from Freiligrath: that is the most popular of all.'

Take that to heart and hammer out a New Year's ode to the New World. As things are now, it seems to me really more feasible to write in verse than in prose, whether sentimental or humorous. If, by the by, you were some time to attempt to render as art the humour that is peculiar to Your African Majesty in private life, I

---

a General rule - b From the title of Freiligrath's ballad 'Der Mohrenfürst'.

feel sure you would play a role in this genre also, since you are, as your wife[a] has rightly remarked, rather a rogue.

I would enclose Weydemeyer's letter if I hadn't first to show it to Engels, who will probably be staying here until Thursday and who had hoped last Tuesday to find you ensconced in the 'synagogue'.

The Association has now moved its quarters to 'Farringdon Street, City, Market House, c/o W. J. Masters. Wine and Spirit Merchant.' Meetings henceforward on Thursdays, 9 o'clock. The Association rightly claims that its quarters are now within your district.[532]

Palmerston has been dismissed by Russell,[533] 1) in order that the latter may act the constitutional hero vis-à-vis Bonaparte, 2) in order to make a concession to Russia and Austria. While I do not share the view that this FACT will in any way affect the fate of the refugees generally or our own in particular, I believe that for Britain it presages a most lively year politically. From what Engels tells me, the CITY MERCHANTS now also share our view that the crisis, held in check by all kinds of factors (including, e.g., political misgivings, the high price of cotton last year), etc., must blow up at the latest next autumn. And, *après les derniers événements je suis plus convaincu que jamais, qu'il n'y aura pas de révolution sérieuse sans crise commerciale.*[b]

Regards from my family to yours.

Expiring,
The Moor

First published abridged in *Die Neue Zeit*, Ergänzungshefte, No. 12, 12 April 1912 and in full in: Marx and Engels, *Works*, First Russian Edition, Vol. XXV, Moscow, 1934

Printed according to the original

Published in English for the first time

---

[a] Ida - [b] since the latest events I am more than ever convinced that there will be no serious revolution without a trade crisis.

APPENDICES

1

JENNY MARX TO KARL MARX [534]

IN BRUSSELS

[Paris,] 10 February [1845]

...partment. He is coming tomorrow to give the order to the *concierge*. It was a terrible blow and I leave you to imagine what I'm going to do with my 200 francs, now that I've had to give him 380 fr. as a deposit, half of which he will return when he has found a tenant.

Such are the delightful consequences of that governmental, Guizotian, Humboldtian disgraceful trick. I don't know what we're going to do. This morning I traipsed all over Paris. The Mint was closed and I shall have to go again. Then I visited the carriers and the agent of a furniture auctioneer. I had no success anywhere. And in the course of these wearisome excursions, what's more, Ewerbeck forced me to call on Mme Glaise, who, however, is quite an amiable, artless and kindly woman who pleased me much. At this moment I'm amusing myself with the infant and the grumbler while writing to you. Little Jenny never stops saying papa. She still has a very bad cold and her little teeth are very painful. However I hope she'll soon be herself again. The *person* is in good spirits, though this morning she felt quite 'lausig'.[a] I heard from mama[b] today. Edgar[c] will be sitting his exam shortly. Aren't you astonished, my good Karl, at my addressing you in French? But it happened without my thinking about it. I intended to start off with a few sentences in French and then, just as the appetite comes with eating, I was unable to part company with this language. I find it so easy to write to you and chat with you. I am writing as fast as I would in German and, although it may not be classical French, I trust it will amuse you to read it, faults,

---

[a] rotten - [b] Caroline von Westphalen - [c] Jenny Marx's brother

inexpressible beauties and all. I shall not send off these lines until I get your first letter. Say lots of nice things to our good friend Bürgers on my behalf. A thousand kisses from mama to papa, and a little kiss from Munsterchen. Adieu my friend. I long to see you again. By now you will already be in Brussels. Best greetings to our new fatherland. Adieu.

10 February

Heine was at the Ministry of the Interior where he was told they knew nothing at all about it; Ledru-Rollin will be raising the matter in the Chamber as soon as everyone has escaped. Have you read the *Réforme*? What a silly, pitiful thing it is. Everything it says is offensive, more so than the most violent attacks launched by the others. There you have the work of that great man, such as he should be—Mr Bakunin, who, however, came and gave me a lesson in rhetoric and drama in order to unbosom himself to me. Herwegh is playing with the child. Ewerbeck is talking incessantly about the continual distractions of Mr Bürgers and the son of the people. Mr Weill, my special protector, came to my aid....

First published in *MEGA*$_2$, Abt. III, Bd. 1, Berlin, 1975

Printed according to the original

Translated from the French

Published in English for the first time

2

JENNY MARX TO KARL MARX [535]

IN BRUSSELS

[Trier, after 24 August 1845]

Although our letters may have crossed on this occasion, my beloved Karl, I nevertheless look on yours as furnishing a reply to my last letter, since it in fact anticipates and answers in advance all the questions concerning which my mind was unsettled and in doubt.[536]

Only one big vital question, the one of the tailor's and dressmaker's bills, still awaits a favourable solution, which I hope will soon be forthcoming. You, sweetheart, weigh up every circumstance with such loving concern that when I read your dear letter I felt quite comforted. But my heart is still irresolute in the matter of leaving or staying or at any rate of fixing a definite date and, if I am to be honest, it inclines more and more toward staying. If only I could draw out each day to twice its length, if only I could attach leaden wings to the hours that they might not hasten by so fast—oh, if only you knew what bliss it is for my mother, our living together, what unending happiness and joy of life she derives from the contemplation of the lovely child, and what consoling elation from my presence! And am I to deprive her of all this with one cold word, am I to take all this away, leaving her with nothing but the forlorn loneliness of long, dreary winter days, anxious worry concerning my life and Edgar's future, nothing save gentle, kindly memories? She herself urges me with rare courage to depart but, having one day secretly fixed the date, I vacillate again on the morrow and grant myself one day more—and then another and still another. And yet my days here are already numbered and it will soon behove me to eke out the time, for it is drawing inexorably closer. Besides, I feel altogether too much at ease here in little Germany! Though to say so in the face of you arch anti-Germans calls for a deal of courage, does it not? But that courage I have and, for all that and all that,[a] one can live quite happily in this old land of sinners. At all events it was in glorious France and Belgium that I first made acquaintance with the pettiest and meanest of conditions. People are petty here, infinitely so, life as a whole is a pocket edition, but there heroes are not giants either, nor is the individual one jot better off. For men it may be different, but for a woman, whose destiny it is to have children, to sew, to cook and to mend, I commend miserable Germany. There, it still does one credit to have a child, the needle and the kitchen spoon still lend one a modicum of grace and, on top of that, and by way of reward for the days spent washing, sewing and child-minding, one has the comfort of knowing in one's heart of hearts that one has done one's duty. But now that old-fashioned things such as duty, honour and the like no longer mean anything, now that we are so advanced as to consider even old watchwords such as these outmoded, now that we actually feel in ourselves an urge towards sentiments of positively Stirnerian egoism, we no longer feel any inclination for the lowlier duties of life. We, too, want to enjoy ourselves, to do things and to

---

[a] An allusion to Freiligrath's 'Trotz alledem!'

experience THE HAPPINESS OF MANKIND in our own persons. But for me, what really turns the scales in favour of Germany is my having seen, *me Hercule*,[a] that prince of men, the model man—let no one say a word against a Germany in which men such as these stand up on their little legs and turn somersaults. But now joking apart. I shall probably be leaving after the middle of September. Weydemeyer may accompany me as far as Cologne; Schleicher is also going to Brussels and told me yesterday that he might manage to be there at the right moment for me. Fiddlesticks, stout Sir, nothing will come of it. We shall probably have to stick to Breyer. The little house should do. In winter one does not need much room anyhow. My mother thought it might be best if we were to lodge Edgar elsewhere throughout that period, perhaps in the *bois sauvage*.[b] Anyhow that would be cheapest. Then, having concluded my important business[c] on the upper floor, I shall remove downstairs again. Then you could sleep in what is now your study and pitch your tent in the *salon immense*[d]—that would present no difficulty. The children's noise downstairs would then be completely shut off, you would not be disturbed upstairs, I could join you when things were quiet and the living-room could, after all, always be kept reasonably tidy. The two rooms on the second floor would be of little or no use to us. At all events we must instal a good, warm stove and appurtenances in the living-room at the earliest opportunity. That again is Breyer's business, for one doesn't let out unheatable rooms. It would be as well to tackle Master Braggart in really good time, otherwise it will be the same as in the case of the kitchen table of hallowed memory. After that I shall see to everything else. Such preparations as could be made here, have been made. It would be wonderful for me if you could come and meet me. It is too far to Verviers and there wouldn't be any point. Maybe as far as Liège. Do make inquiries about an inn there at which we could meet. Wilhelm the Pacific, anti-pauper and metal-hard, strongly advised me against making the trip from here to Cologne in óne day. It's simply that I detest the idea of spending the night at Coblenz. Nor should I like to spend a whole day at Cologne, but shall travel on to Aix. Then on to Liège the following day. However, I shall have to break the train journeys often for the joggling might well have unpleasant consequences. But I shall let you know more definitely about the journey itself later. What a colony of paupers there is going to be in Brussels!

---

[a] by Hercules - [b] the Bois Sauvage boarding house - [c] forthcoming labours; in September 1845 Jenny Marx gave birth to Laura - [d] immense drawing room

Has Engels come back alone or *à deux*[a]? Hess has written and told Weydemeyer he intends to marry. Is Bourgeois[b] living in Cologne, or does he have to be in Elberfeld on account of the *Spiegel*? I should also like to ask Daniels to come and see me, but how? Little Jenny is sitting beside me and is also writing to her papa about whom she constantly talks. She is too sweet for words. Mrs Worbs gave her such a lovely little blue frock. Everyone is quite besotted with the child who has become the talk of the town, so that every day people come to see her. Her favourite is the chimney sweep, by whom she insists on being picked up. Tell Edgar that the woollen stockings are in the big box on the right in the attic, not immediately beneath the window. He will probably find them if he rummages about a bit amongst the children's clothes. If only the great catastrophe did not take place at the very time when you are finishing off your book,[5] the publication of which I anxiously await. More about this and one or two personal *rencontres*[c] with your mother when we meet. Such things are better talked of than written about. Goodbye, sweetheart. Give my love to Edgar and the others, and cherish fond thoughts of mother and daughter. Write again soon. I am so happy when you write.

Your
Jenny

First published in *MEGA*₂, Abt. III, Bd. 1, Berlin, 1975

Printed according to the original

Published in English for the first time

3

JENNY MARX TO KARL MARX [537]

IN BRUSSELS

Trier, 24 [March 1846]

A thousand thanks, my dearly beloved Karl, for your long, dear letter of yesterday.[538] How I longed for news of you all during those days of anxiety and sorrow when my heart scarcely dared to

---

[a] in company - [b] Heinrich Bürgers - [c] encounters

hope any more, and how long, how very long, did my yearning breast remain unsatisfied. Every hour contained in itself an eternity of fear and worry. Your letters are the only gleams of light in my life just now. Dear Karl, pray let them shine for me more often and cheer me. But maybe I shall not need them much longer, for my dear mother's condition has taken such a turn for the better that the *possibility* of her recovery has become almost a *probability*. This time we all of us hope that the improvement that has set in is not an illusory one as is so often the case in insidious afflictions such as nervous disorders. She is recovering her strength and her mind is no longer oppressed by worries and fears, real or imaginary. I had composed myself for any eventuality and, had the worst happened, should have found comfort and solace enough, but nevertheless my heart is now jubilant with all the joy and rapture of spring. It's a strange thing about the life of someone you love. It is not so readily relinquished. You cling to it with every fibre of your being and, when the other's breathing falters, feel as though those fibres have been abruptly severed. I believe that recovery is now on the way and will rapidly accomplish its task. Now it is a matter of banishing all gloomy thoughts while constantly conjuring up cheerful images before her mind's eye. I now have to think up all kinds of tales which must nonetheless have about them some semblance of truth. All this is most difficult and is rendered easier only by the love I bear my dear mother and the blessed hope that, when all this is over, I shall be able to hasten back again and rejoin you, my darling, and my dear, sweet, little ones.[a] Stay fit and well, all you my dear ones, and keep a careful watch over their sweet little heads. How I look forward to seeing the children's little faces again!

It seems that murder and mayhem has broken loose among you! I am glad that this radical breach should not have taken place until after my departure. Much of it would have been attributed to the machinations of that ambitious woman, Lady Macbeth,[b] and not without reason. For I have, to be sure, for too long again been carping at circumstances and exercising *la petite critique*.[c] But it is better thus. Now as regards this critical woman, Engels was perfectly right, as opposed to yourselves, in finding such a woman '*as she ought to be*',[d] as the eternal antithesis, very arrogant and hence in

---

[a] Jenny and Laura - [b] i. e. Mary Burns - [c] petty criticism - [d] an adaptation of Weitling's *Die Menschheit, wie sie ist und wie sie sein sollte* (Mankind as it is and as it ought to be)

making a great fuss about very LITTLE. I myself, when confronted with this abstract model, appear truly repulsive in my own eyes and would like to be sure of finding out all its faults and weaknesses in return. Moreover, it is quite false, or at any rate very mistaken, to speak, in respect of Engels, of a 'rare exemplar'. Then he is right in maintaining that 'such is not to be found'. But that is precisely where the argument falls to the ground. There is an abundance of lovely, charming, capable women, they are to be found all over the world and are only waiting for a man to liberate and redeem them. Any man can become the redeemer of a woman.

Present-day women, in particular, are receptive to all things and very capable of self-sacrifice. True, one would have to acquire a somewhat wider knowledge of one's wares if one was not to renounce all taste which, more than anything else, is reprehensible in a salesman who has long been dealing in such articles. Who could accuse Rabbi Rabuni[a] of a blunder, a display of ignorance, in respect of a commercial transaction? To him, all cats are of the same colour and he is satisfied at that. On the other hand, when he sees rosy tints appear in far-away Poland, he forgets that the colour of these blood-red roses is not genuine; they are pleasing to the eye and necessary and have, 'for all that and all that',[b] created a great stir, but how can one establish any connection between this attempt and attempts to attempt an attempt? Who can understand that? Things have come to such a pass that, along with the perfectly justified aim and intention of conceiving the real flesh-and-blood human being, with all his needs and desires, as the be-all and end-all, of seeing man as humankind—that, along with this, almost all idealism has gone by the board and been replaced by nothing but fantasticism. Once again the mania for practical reality is firmly in the saddle. And when men like Hess, who are, in fact, nothing but ideologists, who actually have no real flesh and blood but only, as it were, an abstraction of the same, when such men suddenly parade the knife and fork question as their mission in life, then they are bound to plunge neck and crop into fantasticism. Hess will constantly beguile himself with bogus projects while still continuing to exercise a mysterious, inexplicable, magical, personal sway over the weak. Such is indeed his calling—to act, as it were, the prophet and high priest. So let him go to Babel-Jerusalem-Elberfeld if he will. Weitling's hullaballoo about his fantastical projects is also quite

---

[a] A reference to Móses Hess. - [b] An allusion to Freiligrath's 'Trotz alledem!'

explicable. Just as he, coming from the artisan class, is perforce incapable of anything more elevated than to herald drinking bouts in popular poetry, so too he is capable of nothing more elevated than ill-fated undertakings which are obviously foolhardy and fail. He has no sense of the ridiculous, and what a fiasco it would have been on this occasion. That is now plain for all to see. I am happy beyond words, my dear Karl, that you are still keeping your spirits up and continuing to master your impatience and your longings. How I love you for this courage of yours. You are my husband, and I am still thankful for this! To remain calm and clear-headed in the midst of the hurly-burly and to be in harmony with the times! The most repulsive thing about the ill-starred insurrection [539] is that wretched Prussia, with its spinelessness and pseudo-humanism, is again acclaimed by those idiots the French and all the rest of its admirers as against crude, brutish Austria. This besottedness with progress is truly repulsive. But now, my beloved Karl, I shall dwell on the subject of progress and enlarge on it as regards you, my dear master. How are you getting on with Stirner and what progress have you made?[a] Above all, apply yourself to your book.[5] Time marches inexorably on. I myself am besieged with inquiries here. Schleicher has already asked after it twice and complained bitterly about the literature that comes their way. And it's true, they are very badly off.

They are all having to grapple with Grün and Ruge and do not know which way to turn. Schleicher asked whether the Rabbi was by any chance Hess.[b] Even Schleicher is prepared to swallow anything. But there is altogether too great a lack of knowledge. The false prophets have done so much to queer the pitch....

First published in *MEGA*$_2$, Abt. III, Bd. 1, Berlin, 1975

Printed according to the original

Published in English for the first time

4

GEORGE JULIAN HARNEY TO FREDERICK ENGELS[540]

IN BRUSSELS

For Engels   London, March 30, 1846

My dear E.,

I am your debtor for two or three letters, and I fear must have offended you by my silence, particularly through not answering before this time the one very important letter to which I shall presently more particularly allude. I am always busy, but the Polish Insurrection[539] has found for me additional occupation. Night and day I have been working to rouse public feeling—not altogether without success. At length the great London meeting has been accomplished[541]—I breathe again, and devote the first moment to write to you.

I first notice a very long letter I received through *Weerth* several weeks ago, the letter was without a date. I was glad to hear of your arrangements for the publication of your *Quarterly*.[57] Has the result answered your expectations [?] When I informed my wife[a] of your very philosophical system of writing in couples till 3 or 4 o'clock in the morning,[542] she protested that such philosophy would not suit her, and that if she was in Brussels she would get up a 'pronunciamento' amongst your wives. My wife has no objection to the manufacturing of Revolutions, provided the work is done on the *short time* system. She recommends your wives to form an 'Anti-3- or 4 o'clock-in the morning-Association', she will volunteer her services as 'English Correspondent' and she thinks that *Mrs Caudle*[b] might also be induced to join the sister-hood.

Your speculations as to the speedy coming of a revolution in England, I doubt. Revolutionary changes in Germany I think certain and likely to come soon. Such changes are not less certain in France and likely to ensue soon after the death of that old scoundrel Louis Philippe, but I confess I cannot see the likelihood of such changes in England, at least until England is moved from *without* as well as within. Your prediction that we will get the Charter[543] in the course of the present year, and the abolition of

---

[a] Mary - [b] A character in Douglas Jerrold's *Mrs Caudle's Curtain Lectures,* a series of humorous sketches published in *Punch* in 1845.

private property within three years will certainly not be realized;—
indeed as regards the latter, although it may and I hope will come,
it is my belief that neither you nor I will see it. As to what
O'Connor has been saying lately about 'physical force',[544] I think
nothing of it. The English people will not adopt Cooper's slavish
notions about peace and non-resistance, but neither would they *act*
upon the opposite doctrine. They applaud it at public meetings,
but that is all. Notwithstanding all the talk in 1839 about
'arming',[545] the people did not arm, and they will not arm. A long
immunity from the presence of war in their own country and the
long suspension of the militia has created a general distaste for
arms, which year by year is becoming more extensive and more
intense. The *body* of the English people, without becoming a
slavish people, are becoming an eminently pacific people. I do not
say that our fighting propensities are gone, on the contrary, I
believe that the trained English soldiery is the most powerful
soldiery in the world, that is, that a given number will, ninety
times out of a hundred, vanquish a similar number of the *trained
troops* of any nation in the world (I hope I shall not offend your
Prussian nationality). Wanting, however, military training, the
English *people* are the most unmilitary, indeed anti-military people
on the face of the earth. To attempt a 'physical-force' agitation at
the present time would be productive of no good, but on the
contrary of some evil—the evil of exciting suspicion against the
agitators. I do not suppose that the great changes which will come
in this country, will come altogether without violence, but
organised combats such as we may look for in France, Germany,
Italy and Spain, cannot take place in this country. To organise, to
conspire a revolution in this country would be a vain and foolish
project and the men who with their eyes open could take part in
so absurd an attempt would be worse than foolish, would be
highly culpable.

I must next notice what you say about my '*leadership*'. First let
me remark that you are too hard upon O' Con. You find fault
with his 'leaders',[a] but you say the 'week's summary' affords you
entertainment—fun. You speak as though you credited me with
the 'summary', but the 'summary' is prepared by O'Connor, as you
might have known by the Irish jokes and very Irish poetry
continually introduced into the commentary. You are wrong in
supposing that he prevented my continuing the remarks on Cabet.
The discontinuance was the result first of my own neglect, and

---

[a] in *The Northern Star*

second that Hetherington has never completed the translation,[a] and I have deferred further comment until the publication was complete. I must do O'C. the justice to say that he never interferes with what I write in the paper, nor does he know what I write until he gets the paper. You have thought proper in the letter I am now commenting on to credit me with all the revolutionary virtues. You say I am 'anti-national', 'revolutionary', 'energetical', 'proletarian', 'more of a Frenchman than an Englishman', 'Atheistical, Republican, and Communist'. I am too old a soldier to blush at this accumulation of virtues credited to my account, but supposing it to be even as you say, it does not follow that I am qualified for 'leadership'. A popular chief should be possessed of a magnificent bodily appearance, an iron frame, eloquence, or at least a ready fluency of tongue. I have none of these. O'C. has them all—at least in a degree. A popular leader should possess great animal courage, contempt of pain and death, and be not altogether ignorant of arms and military science. No chief or leader that has hitherto appeared in the English movement has these qualifications, we have never had a B a r b é s for instance. In these qualifications I am decidedly deficient, I know nothing of arms, have no stomach for fighting, and would rather die after some other fashion than by bullet or rope. From a knowledge of myself and all the men who have, and do figure in the Chartist movement, I am convinced that even in this respect was O'C. thrown overboard, we might go further and fare worse. Amongst my revolutionary virtues you give me credit for *'energy'*. I know I do possess a sort of energy, which when occasion demands enables me to rouse others to exertion and direct their exertions, myself setting the example, but this is *moral energy*, the physical energy which makes Cromwells, Napoleons, etc. I possess, I fear, not an atom of. Placed in certain circumstances I should, I fear, fall like Robespierre, through want of the necessary courage to save myself. This is not all, the very qualities you give me the credit for possessing, and which you emphatically sum up in the sentence 'You are the *only* Englishman who is really free of *all* prejudices that distinguish the Englishman from the Continental man', are sufficient of themselves to prevent my being a leader. If I am 'the *only* Englishman, etc.', it follows that I would be a chief without an army, a leader without followers. To myself my proper position appears clear, I am a 'pioneer', the teacher of 'strange doctrines', the proclaimer of principles which startle the many, and are but

---

[a] into English of Cabet's *Voyage en Icarie*

timidly acknowledged even by the few; and the office of the pioneer is surely useful, and as surely not inglorious. You see I am perfectly candid, I speak of myself as perhaps few men would speak, but I wish you not to be deceived, not to deceive yourself, not to deceive others. I am but one of the humble workers in the great movement of progress, as such I desire to be considered.

The letter I am commenting on came to me through W[eerth] opened. Now I have every confidence in W. but it is possible that, without meaning any harm, some points of your letter might come to be known, particularly as W. wrote me that he approved and agreed with all you had said about my leadership. Now if what you did say had become known it would place me in a very awkward position with O'C. I do not wish to prevent you criticising O'C. in your letters, or any other person (myself included), only I would wish that every necessary precaution should be taken by you in transmitting your letters.

If you find fault with this egotism, this talk about myself, you have only yourself to blame for it.

I now come to your letter of the 5th of March, which letter exists not, it has *gone the way of all flesh,* in accordance with your expressed wishes.

It is not necessary that I should go through all the points of your (5th of March) letter seriatim. I cannot pretend to judge of the policy and practicability of your scheme,[546] of these you and your compatriots must be the best judges. For myself I have confidence in your discretion as well as your zeal, and as far as my humble abilities, and time will permit I am willing to aid you in the manner you suggest, you bearing in mind what I have said of my own deficiencies, and consequently that while competent to serve the cause in some ways, I am not competent to do so in others. But before I regularly commence the duties you expect of me, there is one point I must be assured of,—namely,—that your scheme has the sanction of the long-trusted, incorruptible, and martyr men of the German movement. I must inform you that I have been a member of the German Society[a] for some weeks past (several Englishmen have joined the Society lately which adds to its members every week), now should your scheme not be made known to the Society, or at least to one or two of its most trusted members, I should hesitate to join you, because if your arrangements came to be known I should be placed in a false position,

---

[a] the London German Workers' Educational Society

perhaps regarded as a conspirator against the popular interests. I have great faith in Schapper, and if he is not consulted I do not see how I could join you. But are you sure your scheme is not already known in London? I have acted as you directed, no one but myself knows the contents of your letter of the 5th March, but two or three weeks before that letter reached me, I heard that *you* (the literary characters in Brussels) *had formed a society, confined to yourselves into which you admitted no working man.*[547] If by this society is meant the society respecting which you have written to me, you will see that it is already known and has excited prejudice amongst the good men. If this 'society' be not your present scheme but something else, still whatever it may be it has excited prejudice here which you must endeavour to dispel before you can hope to have the views expressed in your 5th of March letter adopted by the Germans here. As regards *Weitling* he may have friends in the London Society, but certainly not the majority. *S.* is the man who leads, and properly so. He repudiates 'leadership', but nature forms some men for chiefs and she has given him the necessary qualifications.

On Saturday[a] I received a long letter from you through Weerth, or rather two letters. The one for the *Star* I like very much, it will appear this week.[b] I have altered the date from February 20 to March 20th, it will thereby not look so stale.

The private letter accompanying your public letter I read with much interest, the facts connected with France are very important, and down to the line you indicate I shall use them in the *Star* though perhaps not this week. Do not be surprised if I use those facts in a 'leader'. All that you say about the middle-class in England and France I fully accord with. All that you say about 'Merry England' is true. You say 'I am just in time to include some resolutions which we thought proper to pass against Cooper'.[548] There are no 'resolutions' in the letter I received from you.

A few words on the state of things in England. The anti-Corn Law[270] agitation is drawing to a close. Whether or no Peel carries his measure through the Lords, the Corn Laws are doomed and the day of their final extinction is drawing nigh. Then comes complete middle-class domination, an increased agitation for the Charter, complete estrangement between the proletarians and the middle-class, and the beginning of that conflict which will be a social as well as a political one.

---

[a] 28 March - [b] F. Engels, 'The State of Germany. Letter III'.

The Chartists as Chartists are doing nothing, the 'Chartist Convention' at Manchester, and the 'Chartist Message' resulted in nothing—a mere flash in the pan. The Land Society[549] goes on prospering, at least so I learn by the account of monies received, for I am not a member. Some land has been purchased and more will be almost immediately. The Land scheme may do as a passing experiment but is unworthy of the energies of a national movement. I have told you that the German Society is advancing, I am glad that the report of their annual supper[a] pleased your friends. I have seen the German paper published in New York.[b] You will have seen that the 'Fraternal Democrats'[122] are progressing. After a deal of trouble and discouragement I think I shall succeed in this. We were for some time regarded with much prejudice and jealousy by the Chartists but this is wearing away. The Polish affair has done a good deal towards bringing this about. Seeing that no other party would move, we determined to begin. Our efforts excited the Chartist-Executive, who feared we would take the popular leadership out of their hands. Hence they came to us. As soon as they came, we said 'You lead, we will follow'. Our policy is not to push ourselves, but our principles, and compel others to adopt them. Thus the two parties worked harmoniously, forming a joint committee to get up the meeting. To me was left the drawing up of the resolutions and petition, and I determined to make both ultra-democratic. I had all my own way in the Committee and at the public meeting the resolutions were passed *unanimously*. Schapper was received with great enthusiasm, and just in proportion as we were democratic in our sentiments we were applauded. Several Polish aristocrats present left the meeting in a rage, grinding their teeth, and denouncing me as a *'sans-culotte'* for my onslaught on them. The meeting was a glorious one, at least three thousand persons present. The humbugs (Lovett and Co.) were plotting to get up a *genteel* Polish-*nationality* meeting, when we stepped in and settled their hash for them. It is not likely that they will now hold a meeting at all. The meeting was reported in the *Times*,[c] *Chronicle*, *Advertiser*, *D. News*, *Globe*, and *Sun*. It was editorially praised by the *Advertiser*, and *Sun*, and denounced by the *Times*, and *D. News*. Did you see the *Times* denunciation? It was capital, especially as

---

[a] 'Annual Banquet of the German Democratic Society for the Education of the Working Classes', *The Northern Star*, No. 431, 14 February 1846. - [b] *Der Volks-Tribun*. - [c] 'Meeting of the Friends of Poland', *The Times*, No. 19194, 26 March 1846.

following within a few days a 'leader' in which the *Times* man had asserted that the 'delusion of Chartism' was dead and gone.[a] This meeting will be the commencement of a new era in English agitation, henceforth mere Chartism will not do, ultra democracy, social as well as political, will be the object of our propaganda. Tonight a meeting is to be holden in South London, but that of course [will] not be reported in the daily papers. I must conclude. Write again soon. I will myself write again in a week or two. Mary's love to Mrs E.[b] [and] yourself. Remember me to Marx, Gigot, etc.

Thine fraternally—

Julian

(Henceforth 'J.')

First published in *The Harney Papers,*   Reproduced from the original
Assen, 1969

5

JENNY MARX TO JOSEPH WEYDEMEYER [310]

IN HAMM

Paris, on Thursday[c] [17 March 1848]
Hotel Manchester, rue Grammont No. 1

Dear Mr Weydemeyer,

   My husband, being again so caught up in the work and pother here in this huge city, has asked me to suggest that you announce in the *Westphälisches Dampfboot* that several German societies have been formed here, particulars of which will be known to Mr Lüning; but that the *German* Workers' Club[550] under the leadership of the Germans in London, Schapper, Bauer, Moll, and the Germans in Brussels, Marx, Wolff, Engels, Wallau, Born, that these (who are also in direct touch with the Chartists in England via Harney and Jones) have nothing in common with the

---

[a] 'The painful impression...', *The Times,* No. 19188, 19 March 1846. - [b] Mary Burns - [c] Judging by the mention made in the second paragraph of the Paris workers' demonstration, which took place on Friday, 17 March, the letter must also have been written on that date.

19*

German Democratic Society headed by Börnstein, Bornstedt, Herwegh, Volk, Decker, etc., a society which flies the black, red and gold flag[205] (wherein it had already been anticipated by the Federal Diet[474]) and babbles of Father Blücher and is drilled in sections by retired Prussian officers. It is of the utmost importance that, in the eyes of *France* and Germany, one should dissociate oneself completely from that society, since it will bring the Germans into disrepute. If the *Dampfboot* comes out too late, use the information provided above for a short article in any German newspapers you choose, these being more readily at your command in the South. Try and get as much as you can into German papers.

I would like to write and tell you a great deal more about the interesting goings-on here which grow livelier by the minute (tonight 400,000 workers are meeting in front of the Hôtel de Ville[a]), while *attroupements*[b] are again on the increase; however I am so busy with house and home and the three mites[c] that all I have time for is to hail you and your dear wife[d] from afar with a few friendly words of greeting.

Greeting and fraternity.

Your *Citoyenne* and *Vagabonde*

Jenny Marx

First published in: Marx and Engels, *Works,* First Russian Edition, Vol. XXV, Moscow, 1934

Printed according to the original

6

ELISABETH ENGELS TO FREDERICK ENGELS

IN BRUSSELS

Barmen [after 4 October 1848]

Dear Friedrich,

You will have received your father's letter; I should have liked to add a few words to it, but I felt too sick at heart. Now you have really gone too far. So often have I begged you to proceed no

---

[a] town hall - [b] unlawful assemblies - [c] Jenny, Laura and Edgar - [d] Louise

further, but you have paid more heed to other people, to strangers, and have taken no account of your mother's pleas. God alone knows what I have felt and suffered of late. I was trembling when I picked up the newspaper[a] and saw therein that a warrant was out for my son's arrest.[233]

I can think of nothing else but you and then I often see you as a little boy still, playing near me. How happy I used to be then and what hopes did I not pin upon you. Dear Friedrich, if the words of a poor, sorrowing mother still mean anything to you, then follow your father's advice, go to America and abandon the course you have pursued hitherto. With your knowledge you will surely succeed in finding a position in a good firm and if, later on, you should not like it, you could always take to something else. For so many years now I have never been able to think of you without a pang; pray send me for once some piece of news that will gladden my heart a little. You are now separated from your friends—why not break away from them too now and go your own way for once, or listen for once to what your mother has to say. Nobody, surely, can mean so well by you as I do, so why have you refused to listen to my plea?

Do write to me soon, dear Friedrich, and let me have good news of you, I beseech you. May God have mercy on you and not forsake you.

But believe me when I say that your father, no less than I, will bless the day when you return to us again and once more consent to be our child and walk the same path with us. May God soon grant us that joy. Then we shall forget all the worry and distress we have endured on account of you.

Write soon to your deeply grieving mother

Elise Engels

First published in *Zeitschrift für Geschichtswissenschaft*, Jg. 18, Heft 10, Berlin, 1970

Printed according to the original

Published in English for the first time

---

[a] 'Steckbrief', *Kölnische Zeitung*, No. 271, 4 October 1848 (see present edition, Vol. 7, p. 593).

7

HERMANN EWERBECK TO MOSES HESS

IN PARIS

Cologne, 14 November 1848

My dear Hess,

Here I sit—not in a bower of roses, far from it—at half past one in the morning side by side with Marx at the newspaper's[a] editorial table correcting proof-sheets, but still find time to write to you, especially since, newly arrived and due (I hope) to depart for Paris tomorrow, I have heard that the philosopher Wolf[b] is in Paris. There is, I presume, no need for me to advise you as to how our club[551] should act vis-à-vis this man. My presence in Paris might be needed at this moment, lest the philosopher should prove troublesome with his nagging and taunting. So I am hastening thither. I could not come any sooner. Berlin has held me in thrall and I have got to spend *one* day in Cologne, especially since Marx has been summoned to appear in court tomorrow and is in danger of being *arrested.*[236]

The city of Berlin, in state of siege, will be severely wrangled.[c] It is a matter either of a republic or of Cossack rule.[d]

Do not let Wolf exert any influence. Neither Worcell nor anyone else must be allowed to listen to him. He seems to be corresponding with Marx. The latter is very enthusiastic about Engels, whom he describes as outstanding 'intellectually, morally and from the point of view of character'. The said Engels is in Switzerland for *the good cause,* says Marx.[233]

Farewell.

NB. Post the enclosed without delay.

First published in: M. Hess, *Briefwechsel,* 's-Gravenhage, 1959

Printed according to the original

Published in English for the first time

---

[a] *Neue Rheinische Zeitung* - [b] Probably Ferdinand Wolff - [c] Ewerbeck coins a verb from the name Wrangel. - [d] A pun on Napoleon's words: 'In fifty years Europe will be republican or Cossack', cited by Las Cases in *Mémorial de Sainte-Hélène.*

8

ELISABETH ENGELS TO FREDERICK ENGELS

IN BERNE

Barmen, 5 December 1848

Dear Friedrich,

Yesterday a letter arrived from you at long last [552] and although I was grieved by the tone in which it was written, I was nevertheless glad to hear that all was well with you and that you had received the money. I shall not hark back to your speech at the Eiser Hall except to say that we first read it in the *Deutsche Zeitung*,[a] which they take at the Concordia,[553] and only later did it also appear in the *Elberfelder*.[554]

Now as to the suspicions your friends have incurred, let me tell you quite simply how matters stood. When the disturbances broke out in Cologne and the *Rheinische Zeitung*[b] was suspended,[233] we heard immediately that you had already earlier left for Verviers. For what reason, no one knew. But nobody, ourselves included, doubted that the meetings at which you and your friends spoke, and also the language of the *Rh. Z.*, were largely the cause of these disturbances. You, too, will be perfectly well aware that this led to bitter feeling, since most of the country desires a return to peaceful and orderly conditions. We then got your letter from Liège and I could not but agree with your father when he expressed the hope that, if you were compelled to fend for yourself, you might perhaps decide, or have to decide, to turn to activities other than those which you have been pursuing in recent years and which have already caused us so much distress. You must not imagine, dear Friedrich, that, when your father made his proposals to you in the letter he sent to Brussels, he did so without my assent. I was in complete agreement with him and hoped that you would either fall in with the proposal that you go to America or, should you cease to receive money from us, that you would make up your mind to take up something else so as to be able to exist.

Just at the time when we received your letter from Liège, our Emil arrived here from Engelskirchen via Cologne, where he had inquired at the editorial office of the *Rh. Z.* whether they knew

---

[a] 'Eine demokratische Volksversammlung', *Deutsche Zeitung*, No. 262, Supplement, 27 September 1848. - [b] *Neue Rheinische Zeitung*

anything about you, and was told in reply that the editors were all expected back on the following day and that the paper would be reappearing within the next few days.[a] As you yourself know, it was not long before this happened, so what could be more natural than that I should imagine that Marx and the others were back in Cologne? A little later, your father went to Cologne where he heard from Plasmann, as I told you in my letter, that several letters had arrived from you, in which you asked for money but that none had yet been sent to you—I mentioned this in an earlier letter. A few days later Plasmann actually sent us a letter of yours, addressed to one Schulz and written, if I am not mistaken, in Brussels, in which you complain that they have not replied to your letters, including one to Mrs Marx. About this time we read of your expulsion from Brussels and, not having heard at all whether you had received the money in Brussels, we grew anxious and your father wrote to Gigot, who soon replied, saying he had handed you the money and giving us the address to which I wrote to you in Paris. We then got your letter from Geneva in which you told us that, for the first fortnight, you could expect nothing from your friends as 'they had all been dispersed'. Was I not forced to conclude from this that you did not know that the *Rh. Z.* was again appearing and hence that the editors must also be there?

I do not wish to say anything further about Marx; if he acted in the way you describe, and I do not doubt this for one moment, he did what he could and in my heart I thank him for it. As to your other Cologne friends, I do not wish to discuss them further, for you yourself say little about them, so we shall let the matter rest. Time will tell who is most dependable. They were, by the way, at great pains to send us your address when they heard from Gigot that we had been making inquiries about it. We got it from three sources[b] at the very time your letter arrived from Geneva.

I am sorry to see from your letter that you imagine us to be responsible for the hard time you had in Geneva. But that often happens to people. They willingly blame others for things for which they are themselves responsible. Why did you have to leave Cologne? You know yourself, dear Friedrich, how often I expressed concern that one day you might again come to such a pass, but you always said that that was out of the question. We

---

[a] The *Neue Rheinische Zeitung* suspended on 26 September, when the state of siege was introduced in Cologne, resumed publication on 12 October 1848. - [b] Marx, Gigot and Dronke

then had no word from you for five weeks, neither a letter nor your address, so how could you expect us to send you money? No sooner did we receive word from you, than we sent you some. It is surely not our fault if you received it so belatedly.

There is many a thing I could say in reply to your letter, but what purpose would it serve? We cannot, after all, agree on everything, so it is better to hold one's peace. Except for one thing, dear Friedrich. I have learned from a fairly reliable source a thing or two about your plans in Cologne, and I must say that when one plans to build barricades one is not so far from murder. Thank God such plans are not all carried out. Later, perhaps, we can discuss this affair, you had best not reply concerning it. Now for another matter. Plasmann sent us your things, which arrived, I am happy to say, while your father was still away, for amongst them I discovered various letters which I would rather did not find their way into your father's hands. I prefer to withhold from him matters which may distress him or cause him anxiety, for I consider it unnecessary to tell him everything I know, but if asked I do not knowingly tell anything but the *truth,* as you too will have discovered. Amongst the letters in your trunk I found one addressed to 'Madame Engels' and one from a lady to yourself, written in French though from Cologne. Both these letters I burnt unread and at once put all the other letters together in the leather brief-case, so that there is little probability of your father seeing them. Those two letters might perhaps have given me the explanation why last spring,[a] when we had that talk together in the garden, you were *not* being *truthful* with me. Whatever your relations may have been at the time and may perhaps still be, it is as well to let the matter rest. Do not write to me about it, for I am most anxious that your father should hear nothing of the matter. Later on, perhaps, you might give me an explanation by word of mouth. But I only wish to hear the truth. If you cannot tell me that, it would be better for us not to speak at all on the subject.

Now that you have got the money from us, I entreat you to buy yourself a warm overcoat so that you will have it when the weather turns colder, as it soon will; also to provide yourself with drawers and a bed jacket so that you will be warmly clad should you catch a cold, as can very easily happen. I only wish I had occasion to send you some warm socks. Your father, however, thinks it would cost more than they are worth and says I ought to keep them and everything else until you are closer to us again.

---

[a] during Engels' stay in Barmen from mid-April to 20 May 1848

What more can I say to you, dear Friedrich? That I love you as only a mother can love her child, you know. May God shine His light upon your heart that you may know what will bring you peace. It is already one o'clock in the morning and I too shall now go to bed. May God's grace and mercy go with you.

With much love
Your mother Elise

Your father returned from his trip last Friday[a] but left again today for Engelskirchen.

Hermann, Hedwig, Rudolf and Elise send their love.

First published in extracts in *Archiv für Sozialgeschichte*, Bd. 9, Hannover, 1969 and in full in *Zeitschrift für Geschichtswissenschaft*, Jg. 18, Heft 10, Berlin, 1970

Printed according to the original

Published in English for the first time

9

JENNY MARX TO CAROLINE SCHÖLER

IN COLOGNE

Paris, 14 July 1849
rue de Lille, No. 45

My dear Lina,

You will have received my two letters from Trier and will have seen from them that on this occasion I did not feel at ease there. Everything has changed too much there and one does not, of course, always remain the same oneself. I felt an intense nostalgia for Paris and so, together with all my baggage, I returned posthaste via Aix and Brussels; we got back here last Saturday, fit and well.[263] I found very pretty, convenient lodgings in a salubrious district where we have already set up house, including kitchen, quite cosily.

At this moment Paris is splendid and luxurious in the extreme. The aristocracy and bourgeoisie suppose themselves safe since the ill-starred 13th of June and the fresh victories their party has

---

[a] 1 December 1848

won.[260] On the 14th all the grandees, together with their carriages and their liveried retainers, were already creeping out of the holes in which they had been hiding and thus the marvellous streets are awash with magnificence and splendour of every description. Paris is a gorgeous city. How often during the past few days have I not wished you were here beside me as, filled with admiration and amazement, I walked along streets that were alive with people. Once we have settled in properly you must pay us a visit here and see for yourself how lovely it is.

Until 15 August we shall remain in these lodgings which, however, are too dear for us to stay in for any length of time. In Passy, a very pretty place an hour's distance from Paris, we have been offered a whole cottage with garden, 6-10 rooms, elegantly furnished throughout, and having four beds, at the unbelievable rent of eleven thalers a month. If it were not too remote we should remove there at once.

We have still not made up our minds whether we should have our things sent or not. So I shall have to make yet further calls upon your kindness and good nature.

Could you not find out from Johann and my packing-case maker, Hansen [Kunibert], *approximately* how many cwt. the whole amounts to, i.e. including only one of the boxes of books, No. 4, and how much it costs to transport a cwt. from Cologne to Paris? That would enable us to make an estimate of sorts. Before winter sets in you would in any case have to unpack out of the trunks and dispatch to me here some of the linen, clothing, etc. I shall be sending you further details later on. Johann would be of very great service to you in this.

At the end of August our things will have to be removed from the place where they are now. Perhaps you could have a word with Johann or Faulenbach about cheap storage for them later on. These are all very tiresome affairs, but unavoidable in view of our vagabond existence. I am only sorry that I should have to place this additional burden on you, the more so since you yourself will surely have had a great deal to arrange and see to of late. For I feel sure that your next dear letter will bring me the joyous tidings of Bertha's[a] marriage. Whether that day is already past or whether it is yet to come, do please convey to her my most cordial wishes for her future prosperity and happiness. I wish it were within my power to make you all really happy and more than anything else I should like to see you, my dear Lina, as cheerful and contented as

---

[a] Caroline Schöler's sister

you deserve and have every right to be, considering the many cares, troubles and disappointed expectations that have already clouded and embittered your young life. Rest assured that in me you will always find a loyal and loving friend.

I shall not write anything about politics today. There is no telling what may happen to a letter.

My dear husband sends you his warm regards and wonders whether you could, perhaps, find out from Stein, the banker in the Neumarkt, or from his mother, etc., etc., the address of Jung, the assessor, and then forward the enclosed letter to him,[555] the matter is one of some urgency. I am not franking these letters because the franking office is much too far away—I beg you not to frank your letters either and, in fact, to get yourself a cash book for your outlays on my behalf. If you fail to keep strict accounts, I shall have to have recourse to coercive measures.

The children,[a] who can hardly open their eyes wide enough to take in all these marvels, often babble about their dear Aunt Lina and send you their love, so does Lenchen,[b] *qui est toujours la même.*[c]

My love to your sisters, to Roland *et femme*[d] and to the Eschweilers should you happen to see them, etc., etc.

Yours ever
Jenny[e]

First published in: Marx and Engels, *Works,* Second Russian Edition, Vol. 50, Moscow, 1981

Printed according to the original

Published in English for the first time

10

CONRAD SCHRAMM TO JOSEPH WEYDEMEYER

IN FRANKFURT AM MAIN

London, 8 January 1850

Dear Weydemeyer,

I am writing to you at the request of Marx, who is up to his eyes in work completing the first issue of the *Revue*. The *Revue* will be distributed through booksellers and besides, in larger cities,

---

[a] Jenny, Laura and Edgar - [b] Helene Demuth - [c] who is still the same as ever - [d] Roland Daniels and his wife (Amalie) - [e] Postscript by Marx see on p. 202.

through agents. It will be printed, etc., in Hamburg and dispatched from there to the agents. The first issue will come out a bit late, but will be quickly followed by the next ones, so that the March issue will probably appear at the beginning of the month. If the *Revue* does at all well, it will appear twice a month. I would urge you to insert the announcement *straight away*,[a] even supposing the *Kölnerin*[b] has not yet had it. As regards your South German article,[295] Marx would like to have it as soon as possible for the February issue; the point is not so much to report the most up-to-date facts, which is not in any case feasible; it would be best, I think, to conclude the reports on the 15th of each month; and send off the manuscript soon enough for it to get here by the 19th or 20th of each month. One more thing; please alter the price in the announcement from 24 to 25 Sgr.[c] or 20 ggr.,[d] this latter price having been suggested by the booksellers as being more convenient. It is to be hoped that in Frankfurt you will take the lead in promoting the *Revue,* in which case you must charge to us the cost of sub-agents, delivery boys, etc. How many copies should I let you have?

Little that's new today over here. Struve and Heinzen are doing all they can to create a commotion and are, to the best of their ability, making asses of themselves and the German emigration. These two dictators, by the by, have fallen out, Struve having allegedly stolen an idea (?) of Heinzen's! I shall shortly be writing to Bruhn, to whom kindly give my regards, and shall then provide a detailed account of what is going on here.

Do you not require a correspondent over here? I could always send you prompt reports on the most important events in Parliament, which, in any case, promises to be interesting. I regularly follow the English movement for financial reform[284] and can keep you *au courant.* In the next day or two I shall send you a sample article and you could then let me know at your convenience whether you would like to have my letters and what you would give for them. Here in England one has got to have something with which to pay for one's STEAKS and beer.

The young communist who has installed himself *chez* Marx is called Henry Edward Guy Fawkes. He was born on the anniversary of the Gun Powder Plot, 5th Nov., and for that reason

---

[a] K. Marx and F. Engels, 'Announcement of the *Neue Rheinische Zeitung. Politisch-ökonomische Revue'* (The *Neue Deutsche Zeitung,* edited by Weydemeyer, carried it in Nos. 14, 23 and 31, 16 and 26 January and 5 February 1850). - [b] The *Kölnische Zeitung* published the announcement in the supplement to No. 24, 27 January 1850. - [c] silver groschen - [d] good groschen

has been named Guy Fawkes.[324] Just now the little fellow is getting on everyone's nerves with his bawling; however, he will no doubt become more reasonable in due course.

All your acquaintances send their kind regards.

With cordial regards,

Yours

C. Schramm[a]

First published in: Marx and Engels, *Works,* Second Russian Edition, Vol. 27, Moscow, 1962

Printed according to the original

Published in English for the first time

11

FROM PETER RÖSER'S EVIDENCE[556]

... Immediately after the New Year of 1850 *I* received a letter from *Marx* in which he asked me to set up a community[b] in Cologne and to do my utmost *to start communities in other Rhine towns,* because, now that freedom of speech and of the press has been all but suppressed, he too considers it necessary to reorganise the League, as in the near future, clandestine propaganda will alone be possible. I replied that I was prepared to do this but demanded, before proceeding further, Rules to which we [must] conform and such as would preclude any kind of conspiracy. Marx replied that the Rules of 1847[c] were no longer in keeping with the times, that the Rules of 1848 were no longer approved in London[557] and that new Rules were to be drafted; also that, as soon as the League had been organised, a Congress was to be held to which the Rules would be submitted for approval. Up till then, he said, I was to organise things on the basis of the *Manifesto*[d] of 1847 which was sold openly in Cologne in 1848 as printed in The Hague and had been in my possession ever since. In both letters he urgently recommended that I hold discussions with *Dr Daniels* and *Bürgers* with a view to recruiting them into the League...

---

[a] Postscript by Marx see on p. 224. - [b] of the Communist League - [c] Rules of the Communist League (see present edition, Vol. 6, pp. 633-38). - [d] *Manifesto of the Communist Party.*

...In the letter I received from Marx, he repeated that his brother-in-law, *von Westphalen*,[a] a lawyer resident in Trier, had formerly been admitted by him into the League and had subsequently set up a community in Trier, but that he was a lazy man and had of late failed to reply to his letters. Marx asked me to write to this von Westphalen, since it was less dangerous for me to correspond with him from Cologne.

I received no reply to two letters conveyed to von Westphalen through Schlegel...

...At the end of July[b] *Wilhelm Klein, a knife grinder* and a native of Solingen, who had hitherto lived in London as a refugee, having been compromised by his participation in the uprising in Elberfeld in 1849,[286] returned from London to Germany after the trial relating to the Elberfeld uprising was over and there was no longer any fear of his being prosecuted. I had known Klein since the time of the 1848 and 1849 congresses in Cologne.[558] He arrived in Cologne at the end of July 1850, lodged there with his uncle, whose name and address I do not know, and brought me a letter from Marx in which the latter gave vent to his anger at Willich & Company and said it was a great pity that Schapper should have attached himself to this bunch of frauds. He said that during the winter of 1849/50 he had lectured to the London Workers' Society[52] on the *Manifesto* and had explained that communism could only be introduced after a number of years, that it would have to go through several phases and that generally its introduction could only be effected by a process of education and gradual development, but that Willich had violently opposed him with his rubbish—as Marx called it—saying that it would be introduced in the next revolution, if only by the might of the guillotine, that the hostility between them was already great and he [Marx] feared it would lead to a split in the League, General Willich having got it firmly into his head that, come the next revolution, he and his brave men from the Palatinate would introduce communism on their own and against the will of everyone in Germany. Finally he recommended the said Klein to me as a capable worker who did not as yet have any clear idea of social and communist principles. Here I must repeat what I said during the trial[c]—that we did not receive the second London Address,[d] or at any rate I was not given it by the said Klein...

---

[a] Edgar von Westphalen - [b] 1850 - [c] the communist trial in Cologne in the autumn of 1852 - [d] K. Marx and F. Engels, 'Address of the Central Authority to the League. June 1850'.

...One afternoon during the second half of September 1850 *Dr Daniels* and *Bürgers* turned up at my lodgings accompanied by a young man whom they described as *Haupt*, a *salesman* and native of Hamburg, who was on his way home from London. Whether it was Daniels or Bürgers who told me that Haupt had brought with him a letter from Marx addressed to Daniels, I cannot recollect, but either one or the other told me this. We went together to Bürgers' lodgings which Daniels left immediately afterwards and where I remained alone with Bürgers and Haupt. At this point the letter was handed to me and, having read it, I found that the contents tallied with the letter previously received from Marx. In it Marx said that it was no longer possible to go along with Schapper and Willich, that there had been a formal split and that the majority of the London Central Authority had decided to remove the Central Authority to Cologne and that, should the people in Cologne accept that resolution, they, as the new Central Authority, would shortly have to draft new Rules, which might possibly have to remain provisionally in force until the next Congress, and that they would have to communicate the said Rules to the districts and communities [342]...

Haupt gave us detailed information on the London conflict and stressed in particular that the split had occurred because Marx and Engels, the opposing party maintained, were not going forward resolutely enough and refused to abandon the illusion that it would not be possible to introduce communism already in the next revolution. The conflict had become so embittered that Schramm called Willich a liar at a committee sitting. The result was that Willich challenged Schramm to a duel, which took place on Belgian territory.[379] Willich is said to have left Schramm lying severely wounded at the place of the duel while he himself returned to London and said that he had bumped Schramm off. There were no seconds at the duel, Schramm was found by a peasant, in whose house he was attended to, and later he returned to London. This Schramm is a Krefeld merchant.

We explained to Haupt that we would submit the resolutions of the Central Authority to the community for discussion, but must first await the arrival of the relevant minutes which, Haupt had said, would follow. Haupt told us that he had fought in the Baden campaign[a] and had taken refuge in Switzerland, and had gone from there to London. It was only very recently that he had been

---

[a] of the insurgent Baden-Palatinate army in the summer of 1849

admitted into the League by Marx. I was surprised at his admittance and subsequently also expressed my disapproval of it to Bürgers, because I did not trust Haupt.

...A few days later, I received through the cashier Zimmermann a *letter from Eccarius* together with a copy of the London minutes, if I am not mistaken, of the 15th of September 1850.[a] I had recommended Zimmermann to Marx as a reliable man. I gave him the letters and took the letters from him. Police Sergeant Quelting of Cologne saw me frequently visit Zimmermann at his tax collector's office. Through whom Zimmermann forwarded the letters I do not know, but at all events through guards or other employees of the Cologne-Aix-la-Chapelle Railway. Marx must have had similar connections in Belgium and on the Calais-Dover or Ostend-London crossings, through whom letters were forwarded.

The letter was signed by Eccarius. At that time Engels must already have been living in Manchester and Eccarius have been secretary of the Central Authority. I knew of Eccarius, partly through Moll and partly from an earlier letter which, as secretary of the London Workers' Society, he had addressed to the Cologne Workers' Association[559] in the autumn of 1848. This last-mentioned letter is among the documents relating to the case. I obtained the most reliable information on Eccarius during a visit I paid to Schapper in Cologne in February 1850.

There was nothing in Eccarius' letter save a note to the effect that the minutes of the London Central Authority were enclosed. The minutes contained the resolutions already communicated to us by Marx, namely the removal of the Central Authority to Cologne and the drafting of new Rules. The minutes had been signed by the majority of the now dissolved London Central Authority—that is, if I am not mistaken, by Marx, Eccarius, Schramm, Harry Bauer, Pfänder and by Engels or else by Friedrich[b] Wolf (Lupus)—I can no longer say for certain—and the signatures were, moreover, original ones. Hence I cannot say whether the minutes sent to Cologne were the original ones, or a duplicate of the same, or a copy with original signatures. This document remained in Bürgers' possession and only after we had been arrested was it burnt with all the other papers, as stated by

---

[a] Meeting of the Central Authority. 15 September 1850 (see present edition, Vol. 10, pp. 625-29). - [b] Röser was wrong here, it should be Wilhelm Wolff; but he was in Switzerland at the time and did not sign the minutes.

Bürgers during the final hearing. Bürgers had placed the said papers in safe hands—whose, I do not know, nor could I hazard a guess...

...Finally, I would further remark that we—both parties, that of Marx as well as that of Schapper—have been reproached for wanting communism. Yet it was on the question of the introduction of communism that the two parties became declared opponents, even enemies. Schapper-Willich propose to introduce communism on the basis of the present state of education, if necessary in the next revolution and by force of arms. Marx considers it to be feasible only by a process of education and gradual development and, in a letter to us, cites four phases through which it must pass before it is introduced. He says that as things are now, the petty bourgeoisie and proletariat will combine against the monarchy until the next revolution. That revolution will not be of their making but will arise out of the force of circumstances, of the general distress. It will be accelerated by periodically recurring trade crises. Only after the next revolution, when the petty bourgeoisie is at the helm, will the communists' activities and opposition really begin. This will be followed by a social and then a socio-communist republic which will finally make way for the purely communist republic...

After the Central Authority had removed to Cologne, Marx told me in a letter that there was a very good community in Göttingen and that Liebknecht, a student, maintained correspondence with it, for which there were very favourable opportunities. For this reason he held that it was better for the time being to correspond with this community from London. I presume that this community consisted or still consists of students. Liebknecht studied in Giessen and Göttingen and does not come from Hanau, as I mistakenly testified today. My testimony in this instance must therefore be corrected. But one of the members of the London League is from Hanau, his name will be easy to ascertain. I can give no further testimony on the community in Göttingen, we never corresponded with it...

First published in extracts in German in *International Review of Social History*, Vol. IX, Part 1, 1964 and in *Soyuz Kommunistov*, Russian edition, Moscow, 1964

Printed according to the original

Published in English for the first time

12

JENNY MARX TO JOSEPH WEYDEMEYER

IN FRANKFURT AM MAIN

London, 20 May [1850]

Dear Mr Weydemeyer,

Almost a year has gone by since I was accorded such a kind and cordial reception by you and your dear wife,[a] since I felt so happy and at home in your house,[263] and throughout that long time I have sent you no word; I remained silent when your wife wrote to me so kindly, I even remained mute when news reached us of the birth of your child. I have myself often felt oppressed by this silence, but for much of the time I have been incapable of writing, and even today find it difficult, very difficult.

Circumstances, however, compel me to take up my pen—I beg you to *send us as soon as possible any money that has come in or comes in* from the *Revue*. We are in *dire need of it*. No one, I am sure, could reproach us with having made much ado about what we have been obliged to renounce and put up with for years; the public has never, or hardly ever, been importuned with our private affairs, for my husband is very sensitive about such matters and would sooner sacrifice all he has left rather than demean himself by passing round the democratic begging-bowl, as is done by the official great men. But what he was entitled to expect of his friends, especially in Cologne, was active and energetic concern for his *Revue*. He was above all entitled to expect such concern from those who were aware of the sacrifices he had made for the *Rh. Ztg.*[b] Instead, the business has been utterly ruined by the negligent, slovenly way in which it was run, nor can one really say which did most harm—the bookseller's procrastination, or that of acquaintances and those managing the business in Cologne, or again the whole attitude of the democrats generally.

Over here my husband has been all but crushed by the most trivial worries of bourgeois existence, and so exasperating a form have these taken that it required all the energy, all the calm, lucid, quiet self-confidence he was able to muster to keep him going during these daily, hourly struggles. You, dear Mr Weydemeyer, are aware of the sacrifices made by my husband for the sake of

---

[a] Louise - [b] *Neue Rheinische Zeitung*

the paper; he put thousands in cash into it, he took over the paper's property, talked into doing so by democratic worthies who otherwise must themselves have assumed responsibility for the debts, at a time when there was already small prospect of being able to carry on. To save the paper's political honour and the bourgeois honour of his Cologne acquaintances, he shouldered every burden, he gave up his machinery, he gave up the entire proceeds and, on his departure, even borrowed 300 Reichstalers so as to pay the rent for newly hired premises, the editors' arrears of salary, etc.—and he was forcibly expelled.

As you know, we saved nothing out of all this for ourselves, for I came to Frankfurt to pawn my silver—all that we had left; I sold my furniture in Cologne because I was in danger of seeing my linen and everything else placed under distraint. As the unhappy era of counter-revolution dawned, my husband went to Paris where I followed him with my three children.[a] Hardly had we settled down in Paris than he was expelled, I and my children being refused permission to stay for any length of time. Again I followed him across the sea. A month later our 4th child[b] was born. You would have to know London and what conditions are like here to realise what that means—3 children and the birth of a 4th. We had to pay 42 talers a month in rent alone. All this we were in a position to defray with our own realised assets. But our slender resources ran out with the appearance of the *Revue*. Agreements or no agreements, the money failed to come in, or only by dribs and drabs, so that we found ourselves faced with the most frightful situations here.

Let me describe for you, as it really was, just *one* day in our lives, and you will realise that few refugees are likely to have gone through a similar experience. Since wet-nurses here are exorbitantly expensive, I was determined to feed my child myself, however frightful the pain in my breast and back. But the poor little angel absorbed with my milk so many anxieties and unspoken sorrows that he was always ailing and in severe pain by day and by night. Since coming into the world, he has never slept a whole night through—at most two or three hours. Latterly, too, there have been violent convulsions, so that the child has been hovering constantly between death and a miserable life. In his pain he sucked so hard that I got a sore on my breast—an open sore; often blood would spurt into his little, trembling mouth. I was sitting thus one day when suddenly in came our landlady, to

---

[a] Jenny, Laura and Edgar - [b] Heinrich Guido

whom we had paid over 250 Reichstalers in the course of the winter, and with whom we had contractually agreed that we should subsequently pay, not her, but her LANDLORD by whom she had formerly been placed under distraint; she now denied the existence of the contract, demanded the £5 we still owed her and, since this was not ready to hand (Naut's letter arrived too late), two bailiffs entered the house and placed under distraint what little I possessed—beds, linen, clothes, everything, even my poor infant's cradle, and the best of the toys belonging to the girls, who burst into tears. They threatened to take everything away within 2 hours—leaving me lying on the bare boards with my shivering children and my sore breast. Our friend Schramm[a] left hurriedly for town in search of help. He climbed into a cab, the horses took fright, he jumped out of the vehicle and was brought bleeding back to the house where I was lamenting in company with my poor, trembling children.

The following day we had to leave the house, it was cold, wet and overcast, my husband went to look for lodgings; on his mentioning 4 children no one wanted to take us in. At last a friend came to our aid, we paid and I hurriedly sold all my beds so as to settle with the apothecaries, bakers, butchers, and milkman who, their fears aroused by the scandal of the bailiffs, had suddenly besieged me with their bills. The beds I had sold were brought out on to the pavement and loaded on to a barrow—and then what happens? It was long after sunset, English law prohibits this, the landlord bears down on us with constables in attendance, declares we might have included some of his stuff with our own, that we are doing a flit and going abroad. In less than five minutes a crowd of two or three hundred people stands gaping outside our door, all the riff-raff of Chelsea. In go the beds again; they cannot be handed over to the purchaser until tomorrow morning after sunrise; having thus been enabled, by the sale of everything we possessed, to pay every farthing, I removed with my little darlings into the two little rooms we now occupy in the German Hotel, 1 Leicester Street, Leicester Square, where we were given a humane reception in return for £5.10 a week.

You will forgive me, dear friend, for describing to you so exhaustively and at such length just one day in our lives over here. It is, I know, immodest, but this evening my heart has flowed over into my trembling hands and for once I must pour out that heart to one of our oldest, best and most faithful friends. Do not

---

[a] Conrad Schramm

suppose that I am bowed down by these petty sufferings, for I know only too well that our struggle is not an isolated one and that, furthermore, I am among the happiest and most favoured few in that my beloved husband, the mainstay of my life, is still at my side. But what really shatters me to the very core of my being, and makes my heart bleed is that my husband has to endure so much pettiness, that so little would have been needed to help him and that he, who gladly and joyously helped so many, has been so bereft of help over here. But as I have said, do not suppose, dear Mr Weydemeyer, that we are making demands on anyone; *if money is advanced to us by anyone,* my husband *is still in a position to repay it out of his assets.* The only thing, perhaps, my husband was entitled to ask of those who owe him many an idea, many a preferment, and much support was that they should evince more commercial zeal, greater concern for his *Revue.* That modicum, I am proud and bold enough to maintain, that modicum was his due. Nor do I even know whether my husband ever earned by his labours 10 silver groschen to which he was not fully entitled. *And I don't believe that anyone was the worse off for it.* That grieves me. But my husband is of a different mind. Never, even in the most frightful moments, has he lost his confidence in the future, nor yet a mite of his good humour, being perfectly content to see me cheerful, and our dear children affectionately caressing their dear mama. He is unaware, dear Mr Weydemeyer, that I have written to you at such length about our situation, so do not make any use of this letter. All he knows is that I have asked you on his behalf to expedite as best you can the collection and remittance of the money. I know that the use you make of this letter will be wholly dictated by the *tact* and *discretion* of your friendship for us.

Farewell, dear friend. Convey my most sincere affection to your wife and give your little angel a kiss from a mother who has shed many a tear upon the infant at her breast. Should your wife be suckling her child herself, do not tell her anything of this letter. I know what ravages are made by any kind of upset and how bad it is for the little mites. Our three eldest children are doing wonderfully well, for all that and for all that.[a] The girls are pretty, blooming, cheerful and in good spirits, and our fat boy is a paragon of comical humour and full of the drollest ideas. All day the little imp sings funny songs with tremendous feeling and at the top of his voice, and when he sings the verse from Freiligrath's Marseillaise

---

[a] Freiligrath, 'Trotz alledem!'

> Come, o June, and bring us deeds,
> Fresh deeds for which our hearts do yearn[a]

in a deafening voice, the whole house reverberates. Like its two unfortunate precursors, that month may be destined by world history to see the opening of the gigantic struggle during which we shall all clasp one another's hands again.

Fare well.

First published in *Die Neue Zeit*, Bd. 2, No. 27, 1906-07

Printed according to the original

Published in English for the first time

13

JENNY MARX TO JOSEPH WEYDEMEYER

IN FRANKFURT AM MAIN

[London, about 20 June 1850]

Dear Mr Weydemeyer,

My husband is not a little astonished that you could send the money to Naut, and likewise that from the red number[b] to anyone but himself.

There will, of course, have to be a complete overhaul of the way in which the *Revue* is distributed. Meanwhile my husband requests you not to send anything more to Mr Naut, but rather all of it here, even the smallest amount (in Prussian talers). Conditions here are not as they are in Germany. We live, all six of us, in one small room and a very small closet, for which we pay more than for the largest house in Germany, and pay weekly at that. Hence you can imagine what a position one finds oneself in if so much as 1 Reichstaler arrives a day too late. For all of us here, without exception, it's a question of our daily bread. So do not await Mr Naut's orders and so forth. Another thing my husband wishes me to say is that it really is not desirable for Lüning to write a critique, a strong attack would do, only no praise. Nor has my husband ever expected a profound critique, but only a straightforward piece such as all newspapers accord to reviews and

---

[a] Freiligrath, 'Reveille'. - [b] *Neue Rheinische Zeitung* of 19 May 1849

pamphlets, and what your paper[a] also does when it wants to make works known and promote them, namely, publish short excerpts of a suitable kind. This involves little work.

Many regards to your dear wife,[b] and my cordial regards to yourself.

Yours
Jenny Marx

First published in: Marx and Engels, *Works,* First Russian Edition, Vol. XXV, Moscow, 1934

Printed according to the original

Published in English for the first time

14

JENNY MARX TO FREDERICK ENGELS

IN MANCHESTER

London, 19 December [1850]

Dear Mr Engels,

On Karl's request I send you herewith six copies of the *Neue Rheinische Zeitung.*[c] Harney, who is a little better, wishes you to send one to Helen Macfarlane. Just imagine, that rascal Schuberth will only let Eisen have the 300 copies if he is paid in cash and Naut, the jackass, is now quite beside himself. Hence Karl has masses of letters to write, and you know what that means where he is concerned. The Cologne anathema against Willich and Co. arrived yesterday, together with new Rules,[560] circulars, etc. This time the Cologne people were exceptionally active and energetic and adopted a firm stand vis-à-vis the rotten band. Just imagine, it wasn't enough for Willich to have put his foot in it once, with the Fanon-Caperon manifesto[d]—the leviathans must needs issue another epistle, while Willich has gone so far as to send red Becker[e] 3 decrees for forwarding to the Cologne *Landwehr*[385] in which he gives them orders from here to

---

mutiny, to nominate a provisional government in every company and to overthrow all civil and military authorities and have them shot if need be. And the Cologne *Landwehr,* at that, who are now quite happily talking pot politics in the city of their fathers on the Rhine's cool strand. If Willich is not ripe for the lunatic asylum, then I don't know who is. Schapper has obtained a passport from Hamburg, to enable him to take over in person Haude's occupation of emissary. Good luck to the hippopotamus!

We have also heard from Dronke. Mrs Moses[a] has again persuaded her husband that he is 'poss' of the 'gommunists'. But you'll soon be here[345] and can hear and see for yourself everything that's been going on. The Caperonians set upon and beat up red Wolff[b] one night, and our red friend had Wengler taken into custody. The next morning, when he had been sentenced, Willich ransomed him for 20 shillings.

We are all looking forward to seeing you here soon.

Yours

Jenny Marx

[On the back of the letter]

Frederic Engels, Esquire
70 Great Ducie Street, Manchester

First published in *MEGA*, Abt. III, Bd. 1, 1929

Printed according to the original

Published in English for the first time

15

JENNY MARX TO FREDERICK ENGELS

IN MANCHESTER

[London, 11] January 1851

Dear Mr Engels,

On my husband's request I am sending you herewith a letter for Weerth.[561] You had agreed to forward it along with your own. Red Wolff has made a new pair of shoes by machine, citizen

---

[a] Sibylle Hess - [b] Ferdinand Wolff

Liebknecht grows daily more earnest and virtuous, Schramm[a] is down in the dumps and no one has seen anything of him. The children send their love to Engels, and my husband is at the library[b] whiling away his time.

With my warm regards,

Jenny Marx

First published in *MEGA*, Abt. III, Bd. 1, 1929

Printed according to the original

Published in English for the first time

16

JENNY MARX TO FREDERICK ENGELS

IN MANCHESTER

London, 17 December 1851

Dear Mr Engels,

Moor has just asked me to send you in great haste a few words in reply to Weydemeyer's letter,[c] just received. He will himself let you have an article on the French *misère*[d] by Friday[e] and wonders whether you might not be able to dispatch to America a humorous essay on the German nonsense, notably the hoaxing of Prussia by Austria, etc.[562] I am also, on the orders of the powers that be, sending Freiligrath a reminder. We all look forward very much to seeing you here soon.[526] Colonel Musch and the young ladies, his sisters,[f] send you their warm regards as does your

Jenny Marx

First published in: Marx and Engels, *Works,* Second Russian Edition, Vol. 27, Moscow, 1962

Printed according to the original

Published in English for the first time

---

[a] Conrad Schramm - [b] of the British Museum - [c] See this volume, pp. 518-20. [d] K. Marx, *The Eighteenth Brumaire of Louis Bonaparte* - [e] 19 December 1851 - [f] Edgar, Jenny and Laura

17

JENNY MARX TO FREDERICK ENGELS

IN MANCHESTER

[London, 17 December 1851]

Dear Mr Engels,

Hardly had I posted my letter to you (yours[a] not having arrived until four o'clock in the afternoon) when Moor returned from the Museum[b] and began 'burning his fingers' over the French stuff.[c] Now he asks me to send you at once this second epistle to tell you that, as he would not be able to post his article until late on Thursday evening,[d] he proposes to send it off from here, and that, supposing you were in fact to leave on Friday,[526] everything would cross. If you can send your article[562] here by Friday, it could travel in company with the rest; but you might consider it preferable to send yours off from Liverpool. So *comme il vous plaira.*[e] How do you like my husband creating a stir with your article[f] throughout western, eastern and southern America—and mutilated at that, and what's more under another name? For the rest the whole article is nothing but a source of mystification.

Should you have the English version of the *Manifesto*[g] to hand, please bring it with you.

Colonel Musch[h] writes three letters a day to Frederick in Manchester, sticking used stamps thereon with the utmost conscientiousness. The whole tribe sends its love. Until Saturday, then.

Farewell.

Yours

Jenny Marx

First published in: Marx and Engels, *Works*, Second Russian Edition, Vol. 50, Moscow, 1981

Printed according to the original

Published in English for the first time

---

a See this volume, pp. 515-17. - b the library of the British Museum - c *The Eighteenth Brumaire of Louis Bonaparte* - d 18 December - e as you please - f Presumably Engels' series of articles *Revolution and Counter-Revolution in Germany* published in the *New-York Daily Tribune* over Marx's signature. - g K. Marx and F. Engels, *Manifesto of the Communist Party.* - h Edgar Marx

NOTES
AND
INDEXES

NOTES

[1] This is the earliest extant letter of Engels to Marx, written soon after Engels' return to Germany from England. On his way back to Germany at the end of August 1844, he stopped in Paris, where he met Marx. During the days they spent together they discovered that their theoretical views coincided, and they immediately began their first joint work, directed against the Young Hegelians. Engels finished his part before leaving Paris, while Marx continued to write his. At first they intended to call the book *A Critique of Critical Criticism. Against Bruno Bauer and Co.* But while it was being printed Marx added *The Holy Family* to the title.

This meeting of Marx and Engels in Paris marked the beginning of their friendship, joint scientific work and revolutionary struggle.

The extant original of this letter bears no date. The approximate time of its writing was determined on the basis of Engels' letter to Marx of 19 November 1844 (see this volume, pp. 9-14).

This letter was published in English in full for the first time in: Marx and Engels, *Selected Correspondence*, Foreign Languages Publishing House, Moscow, 1955.—3

[2] Karl Bernays, one of the editors of the German newspaper *Vorwärts!*, published in Paris, was sued by the French authorities in September 1844 at the request of the Prussian Government for not having paid the caution-money required for the publication of a political newspaper. The real reason, however, was the article 'Attentat auf den König von Preußen' published in *Vorwärts!*, No. 62, 3 August 1844. On 13 December 1844 Bernays was sentenced to two months' imprisonment and a fine.—4

[3] Engels left Germany in November 1842 and lived for nearly two years in England, working in the office of a Manchester cotton-mill of which his father was co-proprietor.—4

[4] In July 1844 Marx began to contribute to the newspaper *Vorwärts!*, which prior to that—from early 1844 to the summer of the same year—reflected the moderate liberalism of its publisher, the German businessman H. Börnstein, and its editor A. Bornstedt. However, when Karl Bernays, a friend of Marx, became its editor in the summer of 1844, the newspaper assumed a democratic

character. By contributing to the newspaper, Marx began to influence its policy and in September became one of its editors. Other contributors were Engels, Heine, Herwegh, Ewerbeck and Bakunin. Under Marx's influence the newspaper came to express communist views, and attacked Prussian absolutism and moderate German liberalism. At the behest of the Prussian Government, the Guizot ministry took repressive measures against its editors and contributors in January 1845, when publication ceased.—5

5 Engels is referring to *Kritik der Politik und National-Ökonomie*, a work which Marx planned to write. Marx began to study political economy at the end of 1843 and by spring 1844 he set himself the task of writing a criticism of bourgeois political economy from the standpoint of materialism and communism. The draft 'Economic and Philosophic Manuscripts of 1844' (see present edition, Vol. 3), written at that time, have reached us incomplete. Work on *The Holy Family* forced Marx temporarily to interrupt his study of political economy until December 1844. In February 1845, just before his expulsion from Paris, he signed a contract for his *Kritik der Politik und National-Ökonomie* with the publisher Leske (see Note 27). In Brussels Marx continued to study the works of English, French, German, Italian and other economists and added several more notebooks of excerpts to those compiled in Paris, although his original plan for the book was not carried out.—6, 27, 94, 105, 532

6 *The Holy Family* by Marx and Engels was published not in Hamburg by Hoffmann and Campe, but in Frankfurt am Main by Z. Löwenthal, founder of the Literarische Anstalt publishing house (owned by Joseph Rütten since the autumn of 1844).—7

7 Heinrich Heine wrote to Marx from Hamburg on 21 September 1844 (see the new *Marx-Engels Gesamtausgabe*—referred to in future as *MEGA*₂—Abt. III, Bd. 1, S. 443-44) telling him that a new collection of his poems, *Neue Gedichte*, had been published there. It contained romances, ballads and other poems including the satirical poem *Deutschland. Ein Wintermärchen*, which was also published separately by Hoffmann and Campe. Heine sent Marx a copy of this poem for simultaneous publication in *Vorwärts!* and announcement of his new collection of verse in this and other newspapers (he promised to bring the ballads and other poems to Paris himself).

On 19 October 1844 *Vorwärts!*, No. 84, carried Heine's preface to the separate edition of his poem. It was dated 17 October 1844 and entitled 'H. Heines neue Gedichte'. It was preceded by an editorial introduction which accorded high praise to the poet's new work and in fact expressed Marx's point of view. The poem was published in full in *Vorwärts!* in late October-November 1844.—7

8 L. Feuerbach's *Das Wesen des Glaubens im Sinne Luther's* was published in instalments in *Vorwärts!* from the middle of August to the end of October 1844.—8

9 This letter without an address on the back of it was published in English for the first time in: K. Marx and F. Engels, *On Britain*, Foreign Languages Publishing House, Moscow, 1953 and in full in *Letters of the Young Engels, 1838-1845*, Progress Publishers, Moscow, 1976.—9

10 The letter written by Marx and Bürgers to Engels on 8 October 1844 has not been found.—9

[11] The disagreements between Marx and Engels on the one hand and Arnold Ruge on the other dated back to the time of the publication of the *Deutsch-Französische Jahrbücher,* under the editorship of Marx and Ruge. These disagreements were due to Ruge's negative attitude towards communism and the revolutionary proletarian movement, the fundamental difference between Marx's views and those of the Young Hegelian Ruge, who was an adherent of philosophical idealism. The final break between Marx and Ruge occurred in March 1844. Ruge's condemnation of the Silesian weavers' rising in June 1844 impelled Marx to criticise his views in the article 'Critical Marginal Notes on the Article "The King of Prussia and Social Reform. By a Prussian"' (see present edition, Vol. 3, pp. 189-206).— 10

[12] A reference to the Associations for the Benefit of the Working Classes formed in a number of Prussian towns in 1844 and 1845 on the initiative of the German liberal bourgeoisie, who were alarmed at the rising of the Silesian weavers in the summer of 1844, and hoped that the associations would help to divert the German workers from militant struggle. Despite the efforts of the bourgeoisie and the government authorities to give these associations a harmless philanthropic appearance, they gave a fresh impulse to the growing political activity of the urban masses and drew the attention of broad sections of German society to social questions. The movement to establish such associations was particularly widespread in the towns of the industrial Rhine Province.

Seeing that the associations had taken such an unexpected direction, the Prussian Government hastily cut short their activity in the spring of 1845 by refusing to approve their statutes and forbidding them to continue their work.— 10

[13] *Rationalists*—representatives of a Protestant trend which tried to combine theology with philosophy and to prove that 'divine truths' can be explained by reason. Rationalism opposed pietism, an extremely mystical trend in Lutheranism.— 10

[14] At the meeting held in *Cologne* on 10 November 1844 and attended by former shareholders of and contributors to the *Rheinische Zeitung,* liberals Ludolf Camphausen, Gustav Mevissen, radicals Georg Jung, Karl d'Ester, Franz Raveaux and others among them, a General Association for Relief and Education was set up with the aim of improving the workers' condition (the measures to be taken included raising funds for mutual assistance and relief to the sick, etc.). Despite the opposition of the liberals, the meeting adopted democratic rules which provided for the workers' active participation in the work of the Association. Subsequently a definitive split took place between the radical-democratic elements and the liberals. The latter headed by Camphausen withdrew from the Association, which was soon prohibited by the authorities.

In November 1844 an Educational Society was set up in Elberfeld. Its founders had from the very start to fight against the local clergy, who attempted to bring the Society under their influence and give its activity a religious colouring. Engels and his friends wished to use the Society's meetings and its committee to spread communist views (see F. Engels, 'Speeches in Elberfeld', present edition, Vol. 4, pp. 243-64). As Engels had expected, the statute of the Society was not approved by the authorities, and the Society itself ceased to exist in the spring of 1845. (On the meetings in Cologne and Elberfeld, see F. Engels, 'Rapid Progress of Communism in Germany', present edition, Vol. 4, pp. 229-42).— 10

15 Originally Engels planned to write a work on the social history of England and
   to devote one of its chapters to the condition of the working class in England
   (see present edition, Vol. 4, p. 302). But realising the special role played by the
   proletariat in bourgeois society, he decided to deal with this problem in a
   separate book, which he wrote on his return to Germany, between September
   1844 and March 1845. Excerpts in Engels' notebooks made in July and August
   1845, and the letters of the publisher Leske to Marx of 14 May and 7 June
   1845 (see *MEGA*₂, Abt. III, Bd. 1, S. 465, 469) show that in the spring and
   summer of 1845 Engels continued to work on the social history of England.
   Though he did not abandon his plan up to the end of 1847, as is seen from an
   item in the *Deutsche-Brüsseler-Zeitung*, No. 91 of 14 November 1847, he failed to
   put it into effect.— 11

16 Engels did not write a pamphlet on Friedrich List's book *Das nationale System der
   politischen Oekonomie* (Stuttgart und Tübingen, 1841) though later he continued
   to discuss this idea with Marx (see this volume, pp. 28 and 79), who in his turn
   intended to publish a critical analysis of List's views (see K. Marx, 'Draft of an
   Article on Friedrich List's Book *Das nationale System der politischen Oekonomie*',
   present edition, Vol. 4, pp. 265-93). Engels criticised the German advocates of
   protectionism, and List above all, in one of his 'Speeches in Elberfeld' (see
   present edition, Vol. 4, pp. 256-64).— 11

17 *'The Free'*—a Berlin group of Young Hegelians formed early in 1842. Among
   its prominent members were Edgar Bauer, Eduard Meyen, Ludwig Buhl and
   Max Stirner (pseudonym of Kaspar Schmidt). Their criticism of the prevailing
   conditions was abstract, devoid of real revolutionary content and ultra-radical in
   form. The fact that 'The Free' lacked any positive programme and ignored the
   realities of political struggle soon led to differences between them and the
   representatives of the revolutionary-democratic wing of the German opposition
   movement. A sharp conflict arose between 'The Free' and Marx in the autumn
   of 1842, when Marx had become editor of the *Rheinische Zeitung* (see present
   edition, Vol. 1, pp. 393-95).
       During the two years which had elapsed since Marx's clash with 'The Free'
   (1843-44), Marx's and Engels' disagreement with the Young Hegelians on
   questions of theory and politics had deepened still more. This was accounted
   for not only by Marx's and Engels' transition to materialism and communism,
   but also by the evolution in the ideas of the Bauer brothers and their
   fellow-thinkers. In the *Allgemeine Literatur-Zeitung* Bauer and his group
   renounced the 'radicalism of 1842' and, besides professing subjective idealist
   views and counterposing chosen personalities, the bearers of 'pure Criticism', to
   the allegedly sluggish and inert masses, they began spreading the ideas of
   moderate liberal philanthropy.
       It was to the exposure of the Young Hegelians' views in the form which
   they had acquired in 1844 and to the defence of their own new materialistic
   and communistic outlook that Marx and Engels decided to devote their first
   joint work *The Holy Family, or Critique of Critical Criticism. Against Bruno Bauer
   and Co.* (present edition, Vol. 4, pp. 3-211).— 13, 19

18 Here Marx writes about the *Vorwärts! Pariser Deutsche Monatsschrift* which
   Heinrich Börnstein planned to publish instead of the newspaper *Vorwärts!* The
   prospectus of the monthly published in German and French on 1 January 1845
   (its publication date helps in determining the approximate date of this letter)
   stated that one of the reasons for the reformation of *Vorwärts!* was that no
   caution-money was needed for publishing a journal as distinct from a

newspaper. The journal of eight printed sheets was to appear on the 16th of each month. The expulsion of Marx and other contributors to *Vorwärts!* from France (see notes 4 and 19) prevented the publication of the first issue, the proof sheets of which had already been printed.

As is seen from this letter and that of Engels to Marx written approximately 20 January 1845 (see this volume, p. 16), Marx intended to write a critical review of Stirner's *Der Einzige und sein Eigenthum* at the end of December 1844 and originally wanted to publish it in the monthly *Vorwärts!* There is no information on whether this plan materialised. It is only known that two years later Marx and Engels scathingly criticised Stirner's book in their *German Ideology* (see present edition, Vol. 5, pp. 117-443).— 14, 18

19 Marx, Ruge and Bernays were expelled from France for contributing to the newspaper *Vorwärts!* The French authorities issued the expulsion decree on 11 January 1845, under pressure from the Prussian Government. Hearing about this, Marx hastened to warn Ruge despite the ideological conflict between them (the postmark on the envelope shows that the letter was written on 15 January). The expulsion decree was handed to Marx together with the order to leave Paris within a week. Marx prepared to leave for Brussels on 3 February (see this volume, p. 21).— 15

20 The letter is not dated. The postmark shows that it was sent on 20 January 1845, but its contents prove that Engels wrote it over several days.

An excerpt from this letter was published in English for the first time in: Marx and Engels, *Selected Correspondence*, Foreign Languages Publishing House, Moscow, 1955; published in English in full for the first time in *Letters of the Young Engels. 1838-1845*, Progress Publishers, Moscow, 1976.— 15

21 This letter of Marx has not been found.— 16

22 Engels took part in preparing the publication of the Elberfeld journal *Gesellschaftsspiegel*, in drawing up its programme and in compiling the prospectus published in the first issue in the form of the editorial address (see present edition, Vol. 4, pp. 671-74). The prospectus reflected Engels' intention that the journal should expose the evils of the capitalist system and defend the interests of the workers by criticising half-measures and advocating a radical transformation of the social system. But at the same time, not a few abstract philanthropic sentiments in the spirit of 'true socialism', emanating from Hess, found a place in the prospectus. Dissatisfaction with the position adopted by Hess was apparently one reason why Engels refused to become one of the editors. Under the editorship of Hess the journal very soon became a mouthpiece of the reformist and sentimental ideas of 'true socialism'.— 16, 23

23 *Ein Handwerker* (An Artisan) was the pseudonym under which *Lebenslieder*, a cycle of poems by J. F. Martens, was published in *Vorwärts!* on 24 August, 4 September and 20 October 1844, and the article 'Über Handwerksunterricht' on 25 December.— 16

24 Under the press laws existing in a number of German states, only publications exceeding 20 printed sheets were exempted from preliminary censorship. The size of the *Rheinische Jahrbücher* exempted it from censorship, but the police of the Grand Duchy of Hesse nevertheless confiscated the first volume of the journal which was published in Darmstadt in August 1845 and banned its publication altogether. The second volume was published in Belle-Vue, Switzerland, at the end of 1846.— 16

25 On Engels' intention to write a book on the social history of England (it was also to deal with the history of English social thought) see Note 15.—17

26 Engels' reference is to the Berlin confectioner who owned a shop in the Gendarmenmarkt where 'The Free' used to have their meetings.—19

27 The letter has no date. The approximate date of its writing is established on the basis of Marx's mentioning in it his imminent departure from Paris due to the expulsion decree issued against him by the French authorities (see Note 19), and also his meeting with the publisher Leske during which he probably concluded the contract for publishing his *Kritik der Politik und National-Ökonomie* (for the text of the contract see present edition, Vol. 4, p. 675) which was signed on 1 February 1845.

This letter was first published in English in full in *The Letters of Karl Marx*, selected and translated with explanatory notes and an introduction by Saul K. Padover, Prentice-Hall, Inc., Englewood Cliff, New Jersey, 1979.—21

28 The first English translation of this letter was published in *Letters of the Young Engels. 1838-1845*, Progress Publishers, Moscow, 1976.—21, 26, 32, 34

29 On Marx's expulsion, see Note 19.

Soon after his arrival in Brussels from Paris Marx was followed by his wife Jenny Marx and daughter Jenny (born on 1 May 1844). It was with great difficulty that Jenny Marx had managed to get the money for the journey.—21

30 Engels' apprehensions proved to be well founded. When Marx arrived in Brussels the Belgian authorities demanded that Marx should undertake not to publish anything concerning current politics in Belgium. Marx was compelled to undertake such an obligation on 22 March 1845 (see present edition, Vol. 4, p. 677 and this volume, p. 31). The Prussian Government, too, did not leave Marx in peace and pressed for his expulsion from Belgium. To deprive the Prussian authorities of the pretext for interfering in his life, Marx officially renounced his Prussian citizenship in December 1845.—22

31 Feuerbach's letter to Engels and that of Marx and Engels to Feuerbach have not been found.—22

32 The meetings in Elberfeld on 8, 15 and 22 February 1845 were described by Engels in the third article of the series 'Rapid Progress of Communism in Germany' published in *The New Moral World* in May 1845 (see present edition, Vol. 4, pp. 237-42). Engels' speeches at the first two meetings were published in the *Rheinische Jahrbücher zur gesellschaftlichen Reform* (ibid., pp. 243-64). Further meetings were banned by the police.—22, 24, 28

33 The socialist circle in Westphalia and the Rhine Province, with which Engels maintained close contacts and whose members were Otto Lüning and Julius Meyer, was mentioned in the report of the Prussian police superintendent Duncker to the Minister of the Interior Bodelschwingh of 18 October 1845. This report contains the following remark concerning Engels: 'Friedrich Engels of Barmen is a quite reliable man, but he has a son who is a rabid communist and wanders about as a man of letters; it is possible that his name is Frederick.'—23

34 This refers to the General Association for Relief and Education founded in Cologne in November 1844 (see Note 14).—24

35 *Cabinets noirs* (secret offices or black offices) were established under the postal departments in France, Prussia, Austria and a number of other countries to deal with the inspection of correspondence. They had been in existence since the time of the absolute monarchies in Europe.—25

36 *The Holy Family* by Marx and Engels was published about 24 February 1845.—25

37 The projected publication in Germany of the. 'Library of the Best Foreign Socialist Writers' was also discussed by Marx and Engels in their subsequent letters (see this volume, pp. 27-28). Engels mentioned it in the third article of his series 'Rapid Progress of Communism in Germany' published in May 1845 in *The New Moral World.* In early March 1845 Marx drew up a list of authors to be included in the 'Library' (see present edition, Vol. 4, pp. 241 and 667). This list shows that 'Library' was intended to be an extensive publication in German of works by French and English utopian socialists. The project was not realised because of publishing difficulties. The only work completed was 'A Fragment of Fourier's on Trade' compiled by Engels and published with his introduction and conclusion in the *Deutsches Bürgerbuch für 1846* (see present edition, Vol. 4, pp. 613-44).—25

38 Here Engels has in mind Marx's *Kritik der Politik und National-Ökonomie* and probably his own work on the social history of England (see notes 5 and 15).—25

39 Marx's letter mentioned here has not been found. Judging by this letter of Engels, Marx expressed there his thoughts about the 'Library of the Best Foreign Socialist Writers'.—26

40 Engels means the translation of Charles Fourier's unfinished work *Section ébauchée des trois unités externes* published posthumously in the journal *La Phalange* for 1845. The same journal published Fourier's manuscripts on cosmogony. Excerpts from his first work in Engels' translation made up the core of the latter's 'A Fragment of Fourier's on Trade' (see present edition, Vol. 4, pp. 613-44).—26

41 This letter adds new aspects to the intention of Marx and Engels to criticise in the press List's book *Das nationale System der politischen Oekonomie* (see Note 16). Judging by the publisher Leske's letter to Marx of 14 May 1845, at the latter's request conveyed to him by Püttmann, Leske had sent Marx the book he needed for this purpose: K. H. Rau, *Zur Kritik über F. List's nationales System der politischen Oekonomie,* Heidelberg, 1843 (see *MEGA*₂, Abt. III, Bd. 1, S. 465). However, the intention of Marx and Engels to criticise List in Püttmann's *Rheinische Jahrbücher* did not materialise.—28

42 Engels left Barmen for Brussels early in April 1845.—30

43 This letter was first published in English in full in *The Letters of Karl Marx*. selected and translated with explanatory notes and an introduction by Saul K. Padover, Prentice-Hall, Inc., Englewood Cliff, New Jersey, 1979.—30, 207, 212, 216, 285, 297, 322, 401

44 Julius Campe's letter to Engels mentioned here has not been found.—34

45 The available sources do not allow us to establish what publication is meant here. It can only be supposed that it was connected with the intention of Marx and Engels to write a critical work against List (see notes 16 and 41). Many

years later Engels recalled in his letter to Hermann Schlüter of 29 January
1891 that in the forties or some years later they simulated a dispute in which
Marx defended free trade and Engels protective tariffs. This recollection may
have been a late reflection of that intention.—34

46 Queen Victoria already had five children by that time.—35

47 During his trip to England with Marx in July-August 1845 Engels again met in
Manchester Mary Burns, an Irish working woman with whom he had become
acquainted as far back as 1843. They now began their life together and Mary
also left for Brussels.—37

48 This letter has no date. The approximate time of its writing was established on
the basis of a letter written to Marx on 8 May 1846 by P. V. Annenkov (see
$MEGA_2$, Abt. III, Bd. 2, S. 187) who had brought this particular letter from
Brussels to Paris. Annenkov wrote that he had already been in Paris over a
month.
   This letter was first published in English in full in *The Letters of Karl Marx*,
selected and translated with explanatory notes and an introduction by Saul
K. Padover, Prentice-Hall, Inc., Englewood Cliff, New Jersey, 1979.—37

49 The bulk of the letter was compiled by Marx, copied by Gigot and signed by
Marx. Without the P.S. by Marx and the additions by Gigot and Engels, it was
first published in English in: Marx and Engels, *Selected Correspondence*, Foreign
Languages Publishing House, Moscow, 1955.—38

50 Having left Paris (see Note 19) Marx arrived in Brussels at the beginning of
February. During his three-year stay there he lived mostly in the Hotel Bois
Sauvage, where he and his family moved at the beginning of May 1846.—38

51 A reference to the Communist Correspondence Committee formed by Marx
and Engels at the beginning of 1846 in Brussels. Its aim was to prepare the
ground for the creation of an international proletarian party. The Committee
had no strictly defined composition. Besides the Belgian communist Philippe
Gigot, Joseph Weydemeyer, Wilhelm Wolff, Edgar von Westphalen and others
were equal members at various times. As a rule, the Committee discussed
problems of communist propaganda, corresponded with the leaders of existing
proletarian organisations (the League of the Just, Chartist organisations), tried
to draw Proudhon, Cabet and other socialists into its work, and issued
lithographed circulars. On the initiative of Marx and Engels, correspondence
committees and groups connected with the Brussels Committee were set up in
Silesia, Westphalia and the Rhine Province, Paris and London. These
committees played an important role in the development of international
proletarian contacts and the organisation of the Communist League in 1847.—39,
53.

52 Marx has in mind members of the League of the Just in Paris and the German
Workers' Educational Society in London.
   The *League of the Just*—the first political organisation of German workers
and artisans—was formed between 1836 and 1838 as a result of a split in the
Outlaws' League, which consisted of artisans led by petty-bourgeois democrats.
The League of the Just, whose supreme body—the People's Chamber—was in
Paris, and from the autumn of 1846 in London, was connected with French
secret conspiratorial societies and had groups in Germany, Switzerland and
England. Besides Germans it included workers of other nationalities. The views

of the League's members showed the influence of various utopian socialist ideas, primarily those of Wilhelm Weitling.

The *German Workers' Educational Society* in London was founded in February 1840 by Karl Schapper, Joseph Moll and other members of the League of the Just, its aim being political education of workers and dissemination of socialist ideas among them. After the Communist League had been founded the leading role in the Society belonged to the League's local communities. In 1847 and 1849-50 Marx and Engels took an active part in the Society's work.—39, 551

53 In his reply to Marx of 17 May 1846 Proudhon refused to collaborate and declared that he was opposed to revolutionary methods of struggle and to communism (see *MEGA*$_2$, Abt. III, Bd. 2, S. 205-07).—39

54 A reference to the fee due to Bernays for an article which seems to have been an extract from his manuscript on crimes and criminal law, then being prepared for printing by the publisher Leske but was demanded back by the author because of careless typesetting. Marx wanted to include this article in the quarterly journal the planned publication of which was discussed with Westphalian publishers in 1845 and 1846 (see Note 57). Thanks to Marx's mediation, Bernays, who was in need of money, received two advances on his article. But as the planned publication of the quarterly did not take place, Bernays' work, in the form he had conceived it, was not published.—40, 43

55 The visit to Liège in the first half of May 1846 mentioned here by Marx seems to have been his second visit there; there is some evidence that Marx stopped in Liège at the beginning of February 1845 on his way from Paris to Brussels.—41

56 This seems to refer to the undiscovered reply by the Brussels Communist Correspondence Committee to Weydemeyer's letter of 30 April 1846.—41

57 A reference to the two volumes of a quarterly journal the publication of which was negotiated in 1845 and 1846 with a number of Westphalian socialists, the publishers Julius Meyer and Rudolph Rempel among others. Marx and Engels intended to publish in it their criticism of the German ideology which they started to write in the autumn of 1845. It was also planned to publish a number of polemical works by their fellow-thinkers, in the first place those containing criticism of German philosophical literature and the works of the 'true socialists'.

In November 1845 Hess reached an agreement with Meyer and Rempel on financing the publication of two volumes of the quarterly. Further negotiations were conducted by Weydemeyer, who visited Brussels in February 1846 and returned to Germany in April on the instruction of the Brussels Communist Correspondence Committee. In a letter to the Committee of 30 April 1846 from Schildesche (Westphalia) he wrote that no headway was being made and that he proposed that Meyer should form a joint-stock company in Limburg (Holland), as in Germany manuscripts of less than 20 printed sheets were subject to preliminary censorship. He also recommended that Marx should sign a contract with the Brussels publisher and bookseller C. G. Vogler for the distribution of the quarterly and other publications. The contract was not concluded because Vogler could not assume even part of the expenses.

Weydemeyer continued his efforts, but succeeded only in getting from Meyer a guarantee for the publication of one volume. But as early as July 1846 Meyer and Rempel refused their promised assistance on the pretext of financial difficulties, the actual reason being differences in principle between Marx and

Engels on the one hand and the champions of 'true socialism' on the other, whose views both publishers shared.

Marx and Engels did not abandon their hopes of publishing the works ready for the quarterly, if only by instalments, but their attempts failed. The extant manuscript of *The German Ideology* was first published in full in the Soviet Union in 1932.—41, 533

58 The reference is to Joseph Weydemeyer's letters to Engels and Gigot of 13 May, and to Marx of 14 May 1846 with the current information on the negotiations with the publishers Meyer and Rempel on the publication of a quarterly. Weydemeyer wrote to Marx that because of the financial difficulties the Westphalian publishers would be able to pay in the near future only a limited sum of his fee on account.

Engels' reply mentioned here to Weydemeyer's first letter has not been found.—42

59 On 1 February 1845 Marx signed a contract with the publisher Leske (see notes 5 and 27) for the publication of his *Kritik der Politik und National-Ökonomie*. But as early as March 1846 Leske suggested that Marx find another publisher and, in case he did find one, return him the advance received. Therefore Marx hoped to repay Leske either when he signed a contract with a new publisher or out of the sum received for financing the planned publication. But Marx was unable either to sign a new contract or to fulfil his intention to write a work on economics, and in February 1847 the contract with Leske was cancelled.—43

60 Marx has in mind a group of bourgeois-democratic intellectuals, Georg Jung among others, who contributed to the *Rheinische Zeitung* and were already enthusiastic about socialist ideas in 1842. Georg Jung, however, who was on friendly terms with Marx and supported his criticism of the Young Hegelians, left the socialist movement in 1846.—43

61 Marx's letter to Herwegh has not been found.—43

62 Marx writes here about the advance which Hess had probably already received from Meyer and Rempel for his collaboration in preparing the quarterly planned by Marx and Engels. Hess wrote articles on A. Ruge ('Dottore Graziano, der Bajazzo der deutschen Philosophie') and G. Kuhlmann ('Der Dr. Georg Kuhlmann aus Holstein oder die Prophetie des wahren Sozialismus') for the first two volumes of the quarterly. Later Hess tried in vain to have the first article published separately, and finally, on 5 and 8 August 1847, it was printed in the *Deutsche-Brüsseler-Zeitung* under the title 'Dottore Grazianos Werke. Zwei Jahre in Paris. Studien und Erinnerungen von A. Ruge'. The article on G. Kuhlmann, edited by Marx and Engels, was included in *The German Ideology* and published as Chapter V of Volume II (see present edition, Vol. 5, pp. 531-39).—44, 48

63 In 1846 the Government of Frederick William IV began the transformation of the Prussian Bank into a joint-stock company in order to draw private capital to redeem the state debts. The management of the Bank was left in the hands of the Government (see F. Engels, 'The Prussian Bank Question', present edition, Vol. 6, p. 57). The reorganisation of the Bank was completed by 1 January 1847 on the basis of a decree of 5 October 1846.—46

64 Judging by Marx's letter to Leske of 1 August 1846 (see this volume, pp. 49-52), it may be assumed that in the first half of August Marx had a 12 or 14 days' holiday with Engels at Ostend.—46

[65] This letter of Marx has not been found.—48

[66] C. F. J. Leske, with whom Marx had signed a contract for the publication of his *Kritik der Politik und National-Ökonomie* on 1 February 1845 (see Note 5; the text of the contract is published in the present edition, Vol. 4, p. 675), wrote to Marx on 16 March 1846 that he doubted the possibility of publishing the book owing to the growing repression in Prussia against opposition literature. Marx's reply (presumably of 18 March 1846) to this letter and his other letters to Leske mentioned below have not been found.

On 31 March 1846 Leske sent Marx a second letter proposing to him to find another publisher who would agree to redeem the advance received by the author. In a letter of 29 July 1846 he asked Marx whether he had found such a publisher and informed him that, if he had not, he could publish the book with the imprint of another publishing house. He stressed the necessity of giving the book a strictly academic character. In reply Marx wrote the letter which is published here according to the extant draft, which has many author's corrections and stylistic improvements. On 19 September 1846 Leske informed Marx that he could not publish the book because of the severe censorship.

This letter was first published in English in full in *The Letters of Karl Marx*. selected and translated with explanatory notes and an introduction by Saul K. Padover, Prentice-Hall, Inc., Englewood Cliff, New Jersey, 1979.—48

[67] See Notes 57 and 62.—49

[68] On the formation of a joint-stock company for the publication and distribution of socialist and communist literature, see Note 57.

In the summer of 1846 the project found support among the members of the socialist movement in Cologne (Bürgers, d'Ester, Hess). Some German bourgeois sympathising with socialism were also expected to finance the publication. This and other similar projects were repeatedly discussed by Marx and Engels in their correspondence. The present letter also deals with this below.—50

[69] During his trip to England with Engels in July-August 1845, Marx studied works by the English economists and utopian socialists in the library of the Athenaeum in Manchester.—51

[70] Engels arrived in Paris on 15 August 1846 entrusted by the Brussels Communist Correspondence Committee with communist propaganda among the workers, primarily among the members of the Paris communities of the League of the Just (see Note 52), and with founding a correspondence committee. After failing to draw Weitling into the activities of the Brussels Communist Correspondence Committee, Marx and Engels broke with him in the spring of 1846, and particular importance was attached to the struggle against the sectarian views of his followers, who advocated crude egalitarian communism, and against 'true socialism', a petty-bourgeois socialist trend which spread between 1844 and 1846 among German intellectuals and artisans, including emigrants in France. 'True socialism' was a mixture of the idealistic aspects of Feuerbachianism with French utopian socialism in an emasculated form. As a result, socialist teaching was turned into abstract sentimental moralising divorced from real needs.—52

[71] A reference to the negotiations which Weydemeyer helped to conduct with Meyer and Rempel on the publication of a quarterly. Marx and Engels wanted to publish in it their manuscripts which later appeared under the title of *The*

German Ideology (see Note 57). During the negotiations the Westphalian publishers continually twisted and turned, and finally refused to finance the publication.

Joseph Weydemeyer was an artillery lieutenant dismissed from the Prussian army for political reasons.—53

72 Engels refers here to the critical work against L. Feuerbach which Marx was still writing in the second half of 1846 and which was to be included in the first volume of the planned two-volume edition of polemical works directed also against Bauer, Stirner, Ruge and Grün (see Note 57). Marx did not finish this work and later it became Chapter I of *The German Ideology* written jointly by him and Engels.—54

73 The letter of Engels and Ewerbeck to Bernays has not been found.—55

74 Apart from the letters to Marx containing information on his activities in Paris, in the autumn of 1846 Engels sent several letters to other members of the Brussels Communist Correspondence Committee (Ph. Gigot, W. Wolff, et al.) c/o Marx, marked 'Comité' and numbered. They differed from official reports to an organisation and rather recalled private correspondence between close friends.—56

75 On the struggle against the Weitlingians in the League of the Just, particularly in its Paris communities, see Note 70.—56

76 A reference to a machine invented by Weitling for making ladies' straw hats.—57

77 The congress of liberal press representatives was held in Paris in 1846. The committee it elected drew up a draft electoral reform which became the main demand of the liberal opposition to the July monarchy. The sponsors of the congress did their utmost to prevent more radical circles, including the workers who supported *L'Atelier* (a journal of Christian socialists), from attending it and taking part in drafting a constitution. At the same time they simulated its 'unanimous' approval by all opposition press organs.—58

78 This letter has reached us in the form of an extract quoted in Bernays' reply to Marx of August 1846. Bernays touches on criticism of various alien trends, including 'true socialism', as an ideological prerequisite for the creation of a revolutionary party (see *MEGA*$_2$, Abt. III, Bd. 2, S. 294).—60

79 The letter of Marx and other members of the Brussels Communist Correspondence Committee to Engels mentioned here has not been found.—60

80 A reference to the Paris communities of the League of the Just (see Note 52).—61

81 *Barrière meetings* were Sunday assemblies of members of the League of the Just held at the Paris city gates (barrières). As a police agent reported on 1 February 1845, 30 to 200 German emigrants gathered in premises rented for this purpose from a wine-merchant in avenue de Vincennes near the city gate.—61, 83

82 By 'tailors' communism' Engels means the utopian communism of W. Weitling and his followers (see Note 70).

Karl Grün, who visited Paris in 1846-47, preached 'true socialism' (see Note 70) and Proudhon's petty-bourgeois reformist ideas among the German workers.—61

83 Adolph Junge, a cabinet-maker from Düsseldorf, was a notable figure in the Paris communities of the League of the Just in the early 1840s. At the end of June 1846, after a short visit to Cologne, he returned to Paris via Brussels where he met Marx and Engels. In Paris he vigorously opposed Grün and other advocates of 'true socialism' and became an associate of Engels when the latter was in Paris. At the end of March 1847, the French police expelled Junge from the country.—62

84 Grün's German translation of Proudhon's book was published in Darmstadt in February (Volume I) and in May (Volume II) 1847 under the title *Philosophie der Staatsökonomie oder Notwendigkeit des Elends.*—62

85 By *labour-bazars* or *labour markets* Engels means equitable-labour exchange bazars which were organised by the Owenites and Ricardian socialists (John Gray, William Thompson, John Bray) in various towns of England in the 1830s for fair exchange without a capitalist intermediary. The products were exchanged for labour notes, or labour money, certificates showing the cost of the products delivered, calculated on the basis of the amount of labour necessary for their production. The organisers considered these bazars as a means for publicising the advantages of a non-capitalist form of exchange and a peaceful way—together with cooperatives—of transition to socialism. The subsequent and invariable bankruptcy of such enterprises proved their utopian character.—63

86 *Straubingers*—travelling journeymen in Germany. Marx and Engels used this term for German artisans, including some participants in the working-class movement of that time, who were still largely swayed by guild prejudices and cherished the petty-bourgeois illusion that it was possible to return from capitalist large-scale industry to petty handicraft production.—63, 80, 138, 154, 161, 249, 346, 388, 394, 467, 471, 491, 498, 520

87 Engels refers to Proudhon's letter to Marx of 17 May 1846, in which he turned down a proposal to work in the correspondence committees (see Note 53).—63

88 Engels had been misled by Karl Bernays and Heinrich Börnstein as he later pointed out in his letter to Marx of 15 January 1847 (see this volume, p. 109). The item in the *Allgemeine Zeitung* dealt with the tsarist spy Y. N. Tolstoy and not with the Russian liberal landowner G. M. Tolstoy whose acquaintance Marx and Engels had made in Paris.—64

89 During the campaign for the elections to the local councils in Cologne which started at the end of June 1846, it was obvious at the very first meetings that the Cologne communists had a considerable influence on the petty-bourgeois electors (the Prussian workers were virtually deprived of suffrage). In the course of the election campaign, disorders took place in Cologne on 3 and 4 August, and were suppressed by the army. The people indignantly demanded that the troops should be withdrawn to their barracks and a civic militia organised. Karl d'Ester, a Cologne communist, described these disturbances in an unsigned pamphlet *Bericht über die Ereignisse zu Köln vom 3. und 4. August und den folgenden Tagen,* published in Mannheim in 1846.—65

90 By *materialists* Engels meant associates of Théodore Dézamy and other revolutionary representatives of French utopian communism who drew their socialist conclusions from the teaching of the eighteenth-century French materialist philosophers. In the 1840s there existed in France a society of

materialist communists which consisted of workers; in July 1847 eleven of its members were brought to trial by the French authorities.—66

91 By *spiritualists* Engels must have meant the editors of the *Fraternité* who were influenced by the religious-socialist ideas of Pierre Leroux, and by the 'Christian socialism' of Philippe Buchez and Félicité Lamennais.—66

92 An extract from this letter was published in English for the first time in: Marx and Engels, *Selected Correspondence*, Foreign Languages Publishing House, Moscow, 1955.—67

93 When the Westphalian publishers Meyer and Rempel finally refused to help in the publication of the polemical works of Marx and Engels (*The German Ideology*), of Hess and other authors (see Note 57), Marx demanded, through Weydemeyer, that the manuscripts ready for publication should be dispatched from Westphalia to Roland Daniels in Cologne. This decision was taken because there was a project to start a joint-stock company for the publication of socialist literature, which was supported by a group of Cologne communists (see Note 68). Here Engels asks Marx how the project was faring.—68

94 In July 1846 *Das Westphälische Dampfboot* published 'Circular Against Kriege' written by Marx and Engels. However, the editor of the journal, Otto Lüning, a representative of 'true socialism' criticised in the circular, subjected the text to tendentious editing and in a number of places glossed over the sharp principled criticism of this trend. Yet he had to admit in the conclusion that in publishing the circular the journal was criticising itself.—68

95 Engels' letter to Püttmann has not been found.
   In the summer of 1846 Hermann Püttmann, a radical journalist and 'true socialist', put out a prospectus of the journal *Prometheus,* whose publication was planned. Among its probable contributors he included 'people in Brussels', i.e. members of the Brussels Communist Correspondence Committee. The only issue—a double one—of *Prometheus* appeared at the end of 1846. Neither Marx nor Engels contributed to it.—69

96 A reference to the joint address of the German Readers' Society and German Workers' Educational Society in London (see Note 52) on the Schleswig-Holstein problem. When the Educational Society passed it on 13 September 1846, it was printed as a leaflet; then it was published in the *Deutsche Londoner Zeitung*, No. 77, 18 September 1846 and, translated into English, in *The Northern Star,* No. 463, 27 September 1846.
   As early as 17 September the leaflets were delivered to Paris and distributed by the members of the League of the Just. It was then that Engels acquainted himself with the address.
   The address to the working people of Schleswig and Holstein emphasised the interests common to the workers of all countries. But the attempt to contrast proletarian internationalism with bourgeois nationalism did not escape the influence of 'true socialism', which opposed the struggle for bourgeois-democratic freedoms and the bourgeois-democratic national movements.—69

97 The *Customs Union* (Zollverein) of German states (initially including 18 states), establishing a common customs frontier, was founded in 1834 and headed by Prussia. By the 1840s the Union embraced all the German states except Austria, the Hanseatic towns (Bremen, Lübeck, Hamburg) and some small states. Formed owing to the necessity for an all-German market, the Customs Union subsequently promoted Germany's political unification.—69

98 An allusion to the *Berliner Zeitungs-Halle* published by Gustav Julius from 1846 and used by him to attack the liberal bourgeoisie using typically 'true socialist' arguments. By these tactics the Prussian ruling circles wanted to cause clashes between the different opposition groups.

During the 1848-49 revolution, however, the *Berliner Zeitungs-Halle* expressed the views of the left democratic forces.—69

99 The government of Christian VIII tried in all possible ways to strengthen its rule over the German population in the duchies of Schleswig and Holstein which had been ceded to Denmark by decision of the Vienna Congress of 1815. On the other hand, up to 1848 the national movement in Schleswig-Holstein did not go beyond the bounds of moderate liberal opposition and pursued the separatist aim of setting up another small German state. Influenced by the revolutionary events of 1848, however, it assumed a liberation character. The struggle for the secession of Schleswig and Holstein from Denmark became a part of the progressive struggle in Germany for the national unification of the country and was supported by Marx and Engels.—70

100 *Dithmarschen*—a district in the south-west of present-day Schleswig-Holstein. It was remarkable for its peculiar historical development; in particular, up to the second half of the nineteenth century there were still survivals of patriarchal customs and the communal system preserved among the peasants even after the conquest by Danish and Holstein feudal lords in the sixteenth century.—70

101 A reference to the Cologne citizens' protest against the official report of the War Minister von Boyen, the Minister of the Interior von Bodelschwingh and the Chief Counsellor of Justice Ruppenthal on the Cologne disturbances of 3 and 4 August 1846 (see Note 89).—70

102 A reference to the General Synod convened in Berlin in the summer of 1846 on the initiative of Frederick William IV, at which an unsuccessful attempt was made to reduce the differences between the Lutheran and Reformist (Calvinist) trends of Protestantism, the contradictions between which grew more acute despite their forced union in 1817.—70

103 *Droit d'aubaine* (the right of escheat)—a feudal custom widespread in France and other countries during the Middle Ages, according to which the property of aliens dying without heirs reverted to the crown.—71

104 From 1841 Friedrich Walthr published the radical *Trier'sche Zeitung*, which during the period dealt with was a mouthpiece of the 'true socialists', but he had no influence on the paper's political line.—72

105 A reference to the numerous anonymous pamphlets (about thirty, as Engels pointed out in his 'Government and Opposition in France', see present edition, Vol. 6, pp. 61-63) published in France against Rothschild (one of the authors was the French worker Dairnvaell). Directed against one of the biggest bankers of France, they testified to the growing opposition to the July monarchy regime which relied on financial tycoons.—73

106 Only an extract of this letter has survived. In it Engels discusses the project of starting a company for the publication of socialist and communist literature (see notes 57 and 68).

The date of this letter was established by the fact that this extract and Engels' letter to Marx of 18 September 1846 deal with the same project.—73

107 A reference to *assemblies of the estates* introduced in Prussia in 1823. They embraced the heads of princely families, representatives of the knightly estate, i.e. the nobility, of towns and rural communities. The election system based on the principle of landownership provided for a majority of the nobility in the assemblies. The competency of the assemblies was restricted to questions of local economy and administration. They also had the right to express their desires on government bills submitted for discussion.—75

108 This letter is not dated. The time of its writing was established by the fact that at the end of the letter Engels mentions a meeting of the Paris communities of the League of the Just which was to take place 'this evening'. Judging by his letter to the Brussels Communist Correspondence Committee of 23 October 1846 that meeting was held on Sunday, 18 October (see this volume, p. 82).—75

109 A reference to the following passage in the preface mentioned: 'The evil is not in the head or the heart, but in the stomach of mankind. But of what help is all the clarity and healthiness of the head and the heart, when the stomach is ill, the basis of human existence spoilt' (L. Feuerbach, *Sämtliche Werke*, Bd. 1, Leipzig, 1846, S. XV).—79

110 Marx's letter to Engels mentioned here has not been found.—79

111 Engels probably means a special pamphlet (see p. 28 and notes 16 and 41) in which he intended to develop the criticism of the German protectionists, particularly List, which he had made in his second 'Elberfeld speech' (see present edition, Vol. 4, pp. 256-64). The manuscript of the pamphlet has not been found.—79

112 A reference to the polemical material against the Brussels Communist Correspondence Committee published in the *Volks-Tribun* by its editor Hermann Kriege in reply to the 'Circular Against Kriege' by Marx and Engels. On the demand of the Committee the 'Circular' was published in the newspaper under the title 'Eine Bannbulle' but was accompanied by insinuations against its authors (*Der Volks-Tribun*, Nos. 23 and 24, 6 and 13 June 1846).—79

113 In October 1846 Marx wrote a second circular against Kriege, but it has not been found so far.—80

114 Engels' intention to use the projected journal *Die Pariser Horen* for communist propaganda did not materialise. The journal appeared from January to June 1847 and carried works by Herwegh, Heine, Freiligrath, Mäurer and other authors; in general, it was influenced by 'true socialism' and that this would be its line had already been proved by the editorial introduction to the first issue.—81

115 This letter was published in English in part for the first time in: Marx and Engels, *Selected Correspondence*, Foreign Languages Publishing House, Moscow, 1955.—81

116 At the beginning of this letter Engels gives the name *Straubingers* (see Note 86) to the members of the Paris communities of the League of the Just (see Note 52) who supported the 'true socialist' Karl Grün. Further on he uses it to denote advocates of 'true socialism' among the German artisans, including those living in the USA.—81

117 A reference to an uprising in Geneva which began in October 1846; as a result the radical bourgeoisie came to power and rallied the advanced Swiss cantons in their struggle against the Sonderbund, the separatist union of Catholic cantons.—83

118 A reference to the civil war in Portugal which was caused by the actions taken by the dictatorial ruling Coburg dynasty against the popular uprising. It broke out in the spring of 1846 and was crushed in the summer of 1847 with the help of British and Spanish interventionists.—85

119 This letter is not dated. The time of its writing is ascertained by Engels' reference to a letter he wrote almost at the same time to the Brussels Communist Correspondence Committee on 23 October 1846 and by the Brussels postmark of 24 October.

The letter was published in English in part for the first time in: Marx and Engels, *Selected Correspondence*, Foreign Languages Publishing House, Moscow, 1955.—86

120 Engels refers to the second (October) circular against Kriege (see Note 113).—86

121 Weitling was in Brussels with intervals from February to December 1846, when he left for France and later to the USA.—87

122 *Fraternal Democrats*—an international democratic society founded in London on 22 September 1845. It embraced representatives of Left Chartists, German workers and craftsmen—members of the League of the Just—and revolutionary emigrants of other nationalities. During their stay in England in the summer of 1845, Marx and Engels helped in preparing for the meeting at which the society was formed, but did not attend it as they had by then left London. Later they kept in constant touch with the Fraternal Democrats trying to influence the proletarian core of the society, which joined the Communist League in 1847, and through it the Chartist movement. The society ceased its activities in 1859.

Engels' letter to Harney mentioned here has not been found.—88, 289

123 This is a postscript by Engels to the letter Bernays wrote to Marx on 2 November 1846 (see text of the letter in *MEGA*$_2$, Abt. III, Bd. 2, S. 62-63).—88

124 A reference to Bernays' article on crimes and criminal law (see Note 54). When speaking about printed stuff, Engels seems to have in mind proofs of Bernays' work on the above subject, which the latter demanded back from the publisher Leske.—88

125 Engels' letter to the Swiss publisher J. M. Schläpfer who printed works by opposition writers (F. Freiligrath, K. Heinzen and others), written prior to 2 November 1846, has not been found.—88

126 This letter is not dated. The approximate time of its writing is established from reference to the London Correspondence Committee's letter to the Brussels Communist Correspondence Committee of 11 November 1846, which was probably sent to Engels in Paris in mid-November. Other evidence for establishing the date of the letter is that it mentions Proudhon's *Philosophie de la misère*, which Marx received in Brussels not earlier than 15 December 1846 (see this volume, p. 96). Judging by this letter, Engels did not yet know that Marx had obtained Proudhon's book.—89

127 Disturbances among workers took place in the Faubourg St. Antoine in Paris from 30 September to 2 October 1846. They were caused by the intended raising of the price of bread. The workers stormed bakers' shops and raised barricades, there were clashes with troops. Paris members of the League of the Just were suspected by police of participating in the disturbances.
   Engels' letter to Gigot mentioned above has not been found.
   Straubingers—see notes 86 and 116.—89

128 Ewerbeck had left for Lyons at that time.—90

129 A reference to the complications which arose in the relations of Marx and Engels with the leaders of the League of the Just in London (Karl Schapper, Joseph Moll, Heinrich Bauer). The latter maintained contacts with the Brussels Communist Correspondence Committee and together with Harney formed a correspondence committee in London (below Engels writes about Harney's correspondence with Brussels and his letter of 11 November 1846 in particular). However, Schapper, Moll and Bauer, influenced by certain immature ideas of utopian 'working-class communism', including those of Weitling, were still very cautious at that time in regard to revolutionary theoreticians—'scholars'. They did not approve of Marx's and Engels' attacks on Kriege and other 'true socialists', sought ways of reconciling various trends and, with this aim in view, planned to convene a congress of participants in the communist movement early in May 1847. In this connection they issued an address to the League of the Just members in November 1846. Marx and Engels considered that to convene such a congress without thorough preparation and dissociation from the trends hostile to the proletariat would be premature. The effect of scientific communist ideas, however, proved stronger than sectarian and backward tendencies. At the beginning of 1847 the London leaders of the League of the Just themselves took a step to remove their differences and draw closer to Marx and Engels.—91

130 The address of the German Workers' Educational Society in London to Johannes Ronge, leader of the bourgeois trend of German Catholics, was drawn up by Weitling in March 1845 and testified to the immature views of the leaders of the Society and the League of the Just. The document developed the idea that the Christian religion, 'purified' and reformed, could serve communism.
   On the address of the Educational Society in London about Schleswig-Holstein, see Note 96.—91

131 At that time the Verlagsbuchhandlung zu Belle-Vue was owned by Johann Marmor and August Schmid. It is impossible to establish which of the two Engels means. In December 1846 the firm moved to Constance.—93

132 As is seen from the publisher Löwenthal's letter to Engels of 11 March 1847 (included in *MEGA*₂, Abt. III, Bd. 2, S. 330), Engels intended to have his 'Die Gegenwart der blonden Race' printed by J. Rütten of Literarische Anstalt publishers. Judging by Engels' letter to Marx of 10 December 1851, Engels returned to this subject after the 1848-49 revolution, which had interrupted his studies (see this volume, p. 509). However, there is no information as to whether he realised his intention.—93, 509

133 The *Order of the Dannebrog* (Order of the Danish State Banner)—an Order of Danish knights founded in 1671.—94

134 Engels' report to the Brussels Communist Correspondence Committee has not been found.—94

135 Marx wrote this letter in reply to the request of his Russian acquaintance Pavel Vasilyevich Annenkov for his opinion on Proudhon's *Système des contradictions économiques, ou Philosophie de la misère*. On 1 November 1846 Annenkov wrote to Marx, concerning Proudhon's book: 'I admit that the actual plan of the work seems to be a *jeu d'esprit,* designed to give a glimpse of German philosophy, rather than something grown naturally out of the subject and requirements of its logical development.'

Marx's profound and precise criticism of Proudhon's views, and his exposition of dialectical and materialist views to counterbalance them, produced a strong impression even on Annenkov, who was far from materialism and communism. He wrote to Marx on 6 January 1847: 'Your opinion of Proudhon's book produced a truly invigorating effect on me by its preciseness, its clarity, and above all its tendency to keep within the bounds of reality' (*MEGA*$_2$, Abt. III, Bd. 2, S. 321).

When in 1880 Annenkov published his reminiscences 'Remarkable Decade 1838-1848' in the *Vestnik Yevropy,* he included in them long extracts from Marx's letter. In 1883, the year when Marx died, these extracts, translated into German, were published in *Die Neue Zeit* and *New-Yorker Volkszeitung.*

The original has not been found. The first English translation of this letter was published in: Karl Marx and Friedrich Engels, *Correspondence. 1846-1895,* Martin Lawrence Ltd., London, 1934.—95

136 Here Marx uses the word 'cacadauphin' by which during the French Revolution opponents of the absolutist regime derisively described the mustard-coloured cloth, recalling the colour of the Dauphin's napkins, made fashionable by Queen Marie Antoinette.—103

137 *Parliaments*—juridical institutions which arose in France in the Middle Ages. They enjoyed the right to remonstrate government decrees. In the seventeenth and eighteenth centuries their members were officials of high birth called *noblesse de robe* (the nobility of the mantle). The parliaments, which finally became the bulwark of feudal opposition to absolutism and impeded the implementation of even moderate reforms, were abolished in 1790, during the French Revolution.—104

138 The letter was dated 1845 by mistake. The correct date was established on the basis of the contents and the postmark: 'Paris 60, 15. Janv. 47'.

An extract from this letter was published in English for the first time in: K. Marx and F. Engels, *Literature and Art,* International Publishers, N. Y., p. 81, 1947.—107

139 The reference here and below is to Marx's possible removal to Paris and the documents he needed for that move. The text below shows that Marx had the permission of the Belgian authorities to stay in Belgium. It was issued to him after his expulsion from France in February 1845 and signed on 22 March 1845 on condition that Marx would not publish anything concerning current politics. Besides, on 1 December 1845 Marx received a certificate of renunciation of his Prussian citizenship and perhaps permission to emigrate to America for which he had applied in order to deprive the Prussian authorities of any pretext for interfering in his future.

However, Marx was not able to go to Paris until after the February 1848 revolution.—107

[140] An allusion to relations with Hess which deteriorated in February and March 1846 when Marx and Engels started a decisive struggle against 'true socialism' and Weitling's utopian egalitarian communism. In an effort to avoid an open break, Marx and Engels persuaded Hess to leave Brussels in March 1846.—108

[141] The reference is to *The Poverty of Philosophy* by Marx. He worked on it from the end of December 1846 to the beginning of April 1847. It came out early in July 1847 in Brussels and Paris. In it Marx compared Proudhon's views and the theory of the British utopian communist John Bray. The latter advocated exchange of the products of labour without money as a method of transition to a society free from exploitation (see present edition, Vol. 6, pp. 138-44). Bray expounded his theory in his *Labour's Wrongs and Labour's Remedy*, Leeds, 1839.

By 'our publication' Engels meant the manuscripts of *The German Ideology* intended for publication.—109

[142] Here Engels refers to the second part of his and Marx's joint work *The German Ideology* devoted to the critique of 'true socialism' (see present edition, Vol. 5, pp. 453-539). Engels continued his work on this section up to April 1847 and its results have reached us in the form of an unfinished manuscript 'The True Socialists' supplementing *The German Ideology* (see present edition, Vol. 5, pp. 540-81).—109

[143] As is seen from this letter Engels originally intended to work up the article he had apparently written in the autumn of 1846 or early in 1847 on Grün's *Über Goethe* for the second part of *The German Ideology*, devoted to the critique of 'true socialism'. Later this article served as a basis for the second essay in the series *German Socialism in Verse and Prose* (see present edition, Vol. 6, pp. 249-73). It is quite possible that Engels also used the manuscripts of *The German Ideology* for the first essay in that series. The essays on Grün were published in the *Deutsche-Brüsseler-Zeitung*, Nos. 93-98 of 21, 25 and 28 November and 2, 5 and 9 December 1847.—110

[144] Engels has in mind the time the young Goethe spent among the burghers of his native town Frankfurt am Main, and his service at the Duke of Weimar's court: from 1782 to 1786 Goethe held several high administrative posts, was a member of the Privy Council, Minister of Education, etc.—110

[145] Marx's letter to Zulauff has not been found. Like the letter published here, it apparently concerned the tasks facing the Brussels Communist Correspondence Committee and the communist groups close to it when Marx and Engels joined the League of the Just as a result of their negotiations at the end of January and the beginning of February 1847 with Joseph Moll, a representative of the London leaders of the League who was sent to Brussels and Paris specially for this purpose. The negotiations showed that the League leaders were prepared to recognise the principles of scientific communism as a basis when drawing up its programme and carrying out its reorganisation. Marx and Engels, therefore, called on their followers grouped around the Brussels Communist Correspondence Committee not only to join the League of the Just but also to take an active part in its reorganisation.—111

[146] See Note 86. Here the reference is to the members of the Paris communities of the League of the Just.—112

[147] The reference is to Engels' as yet unfound satirical pamphlet about Lola Montez, a favourite of King Ludwig I of Bavaria. The scandalous influence of

this Spanish dancer on the policy of the Bavarian Government caused in 1847-48 the appearance of numerous pamphlets, articles, cartoons, etc. Further on, the text (see p. 114) shows that Engels tried to have this pamphlet published by Vogler in Brussels and by the Belle-Vue publishers in Switzerland. A letter has survived which Vogler wrote on 3 April 1847 in reply to Engels' letter of 28 March which has not been found. Engels' proposal was rejected because of the censorship existing in the Great Duchy of Baden where the publishers had moved by that time.—112

148 The reference is to the rescripts by Frederick William IV of 3 February 1847 convening the United Diet—a united assembly of the eight provincial diets. The United Diet as well as the provincial diets consisted of representatives of the estates: the curia of high aristocracy and the curia of the other three estates (nobility, representatives of the towns and the peasantry). Its powers were limited to authorising new taxes and loans, to voice without vote during the discussion of Bills, and to the right to present petitions to the King.

The *United Diet* opened on 11 April 1847, but it was dissolved as early as June because the majority refused to vote a new loan.—112

149 Engels intended to have this work published as a pamphlet by Vogler in Brussels who was printing Marx's *The Poverty of Philosophy*. However, when Marx received the manuscript, Vogler had been arrested in Aachen (see this volume, p. 117). The part of the pamphlet which has reached us was first published in Russian in the USSR in 1929.—114

150 *Communistes matérialistes*—members of the secret society of materialist communists founded in the 1840s (see Note 90). The members of this society were tried in July 1847 and sentenced to long terms of imprisonment.—114

151 The persecution of the Paris members of the League of the Just by the French police was reported in an item datelined Paris, 2 April 1847, published in the *Berliner Zeitungs-Halle*, No. 81, 8 April 1847. It said of Engels: "Several police agents have also been to Fr. Engels, who lives here in great retirement and devotes himself only to economic and historical studies; naturally they could find nothing against him."—115

152 Marx's letter to Bakunin has not been found.—116

153 The reference is to a cartoon by Engels of Frederick William IV of Prussia delivering the speech from the throne at the opening of the United Diet in Berlin on 11 April 1847 (see present edition, Vol. 6, p. 67). This cartoon was published as a special supplement to the *Deutsche-Brüsseler-Zeitung* of 6 May 1847.—117

154 The reference is to the congress of the League of the Just at which, as agreed between the League leaders in London (H. Bauer, J. Moll, K. Schapper) and Marx and Engels early in 1847, the League was to be reorganised. The congress was held between 2 and 9 June 1847. Engels represented the Paris communities, and Wilhelm Wolff, briefed by Marx, was a delegate of the Brussels communists.

Engels' active participation in the work of the congress affected the course and the results of its proceedings. The League was renamed the Communist League, the old motto of the League of the Just 'All men are brothers' was replaced by a new, Marxist one: 'Working Men of All Countries, Unite!' The congress expelled the Weitlingians from the League. The last sitting on 9 June approved the draft programme and the draft Rules of the League, which had been drawn up either by Engels or with his help (see present edition, Vol. 6, pp. 96-103 and 585-88). Both documents and the congress circular to the League members were sent to the local communities and districts for discussion to be finally approved at the next, second congress.

This congress laid the foundation for the first international proletarian communist organisation in history.— 117

155 Engels arrived in Brussels about 27 July 1847 and stayed there up to mid-October. He actively contributed to enhancing the influence of the Communist League among the German workers residing in Belgium and to the establishment of international contacts between representatives of the proletarian movement and progressive democratic circles.— 118

155a This letter was first published in English abridged in *The Letters of Karl Marx*, selected and translated with explanatory notes and an introduction by Saul K. Padover, Prentice-Hall, Inc., Englewood Cliff, New Jersey, 1979.— 119

156 Marx refers here to the prospects of his and Engels' regular collaboration in the *Deutsche-Brüsseler-Zeitung*. Previously they had only occasionally contributed to this emigrant newspaper, though they approved of the collaboration in it of W. Wolff, G. Weerth and others of their followers. On the whole up to that time the newspaper's line had reflected the desire of its editor-in-chief, the petty-bourgeois democrat A. Bornstedt, to combine eclectic ideological trends in opposition. But financial and other difficulties compelled him to agree to the collaboration of the proletarian revolutionaries in the newspaper. From 9 September 1847 Marx and Engels were its regular contributors, directly influenced its line and at the end of 1847 concentrated editorial affairs in their own hands. During this period the newspaper became a mouthpiece of the proletarian party then being formed, virtually the press organ of the Communist League.— 120

157 Engels wrote this letter to Marx when the latter was on a visit to his relatives in Holland to settle his financial affairs. At the end of September 1847 Marx spent a few days in Zalt-Bommel at his uncle's (on his mother's side), Lion Philips, and returned to Brussels early in October.— 122

158 The *German Workers' Society* was founded by Marx and Engels in Brussels at the end of August 1847, its aim being the political education of the German workers who lived in Belgium and dissemination of the ideas of scientific communism among them. With Marx, Engels and their followers at its head, the Society became the legal centre rallying the revolutionary proletarian forces in Belgium. Its most active members belonged to the Communist League. The Society played an important part in founding the Brussels Democratic Association. After the February 1848 revolution in France, the Belgian authorities arrested and banished many of its members.— 122, 141, 153

159 The international banquet of democrats in Brussels on 27 September 1847, of which Engels speaks here, adopted the decision to found a Democratic Association. Engels was elected to its Organising Committee.

The *Democratic Association* united proletarian revolutionaries, mainly German refugees and advanced bourgeois and petty-bourgeois democrats. Marx and Engels took an active part in its establishment. On 15 November 1847 Marx was elected its Vice-President (the President was Lucien Jottrand, a Belgian democrat) and under his influence it became a centre of the international democratic movement. During the February 1848 revolution in

France, the proletarian wing of the Brussels Democratic Association sought to arm the Belgian workers and to intensify the struggle for a democratic republic. However, when Marx was expelled from Brussels in March 1848 and the most revolutionary elements were repressed by the Belgian authorities, its activity assumed a narrow, purely local character and in 1849 the Association ceased to exist.— 123, 132, 141

160 The text of Engels' speech at the democratic banquet on 27 September 1847 is not extant. The recorded speeches of some speakers were published in the *Deutsche-Brüsseler-Zeitung*, No. 80, 7 October 1847.— 124

161 The reference is to the newspaper Correspondence Bureau (Deutsche Zeitungs-Correspondenzbureau), set up by S. Seiler and K. Reinhardt in the spring of 1845. It supplied information and correspondence material to the German newspapers.— 125

162 The reference is to Georg Weerth's speech at the International Congress of Economists held in Brussels on 16-18 September 1847 to discuss free trade. Marx, Engels and Wilhelm Wolff also attended the congress, intending to make use of it to criticise bourgeois economics (the free trade doctrine, in particular) and to defend working-class interests. When Weerth made a speech along these lines the congress organisers closed the discussion on 18 September without allowing Marx to speak. Excerpts from Weerth's speech were published in a few German, British and French newspapers. It was published in full in the Belgian *Atelier Démocratique* on 29 September 1847. A report on the proceedings of the congress is given by Engels in his articles 'The Economic Congress' and 'The Free Trade Congress at Brussels' (see present edition, Vol. 6, pp. 274-78 and 282-90).— 125

163 This refers to the agreement reached with Bornstedt in September 1847 concerning Marx's and Engels' regular contribution to the *Deutsche-Brüsseler-Zeitung* (see Note 156).— 126

164 The discussion of protective tariffs and free trade which had begun before Marx went on a visit to Holland continued at a meeting of the German Workers' Society on 29 September 1847. To enliven this discussion Marx and Engels started a 'sham battle' which Engels later recalled in a letter to Hermann Schlüter of 29 January 1891: '...I remember only that when the debates in the German Workers' Society in Brussels became dull Marx and I agreed to start a sham discussion in which he defended free trade and I protective tariffs....'— 126

165 Engels means the meeting of the Brussels community of the Communist League. The community and the Brussels District Committee of the League were formed on the basis of the Communist Correspondence Committee on 5 August 1847. The District Committee included Marx, Engels, Junge and Wolff (see present edition, Vol. 6, p. 601).— 129

166 Marx seems to have in mind primarily literary works reflecting local peculiarities in the various shades of 'true socialism' (cf. F. Engels, 'The True Socialists', present edition, Vol. 5, pp. 540-81).— 131

167 Marx's intention to start a joint-stock company for the publication of a communist monthly in 1847, about which he also wrote to Herwegh on 26 October 1847 (see this volume, p. 141) like similar earlier plans did not materialise.— 132, 141

168 Engels' letter to Louis Blanc presumably written soon after his arrival in Paris from Brussels in mid-October 1847 has not been found.— 133

169 At that time a civil war was imminent in Switzerland between the Sonderbund (a separatist union formed by seven economically backward cantons which opposed progressive bourgeois reforms and defended the privileges of the Church and the Jesuits) and the other cantons which persuaded the Swiss Diet to declare the dissolution of the Sonderbund in July 1847. Hostilities began early in November, and the Sonderbund army was defeated by the federal forces on 23 November 1847.

Johann Jacoby, a representative of the German radicals since the convocation of the United Diet in Prussia in 1847 (see Note 148), criticised it as a substitute for people's representation. In April and June 1847 he made a trip to Saxony, South Germany, Switzerland, visited Cologne and Brussels where he established contact with the *Deutsche-Brüsseler-Zeitung.*

A radical programme of political reforms was adopted at a meeting of representatives of the democratic wing of the opposition movement (F. Hecker, G. Struve, etc.) in Offenburg (Grand Duchy of Baden) on 12 September 1847.— 133

170 The Prussian United Diet (see Note 148) was dissolved in June 1847.

In calling A. Ruge the panegyrist of the Diet Engels refers to the 'Adresse an die Opposition des vereinigten Landtages in Berlin' of 11 June 1847 included by Ruge in the *Polemische Briefe* published in Mannheim that year.— 135

171 Engels' first article in *La Réforme,* 'The Commercial Crisis in England.— The Chartist Movement.— Ireland' (see present edition, Vol. 6, pp. 307-09), appeared as early as 26 October 1847. After that the newspaper regularly carried his articles, or summaries of *The Northern Star* reports on the Chartist movement which he translated into French. As a rule they were published under the headings 'Mouvement chartiste' and 'Agitation chartiste' and introduced by the editorial 'On nous écrit de Londres'. Engels contributed to *La Réforme* till January 1848. Though Engels' views differed from those of the newspaper's editors (especially Louis Blanc and Ledru-Rollin), his articles on the Chartist movement to some extent helped to overcome the national exclusiveness of *La Réforme* and exerted a revolutionary influence on its readers—the French workers and the radical middle classes.— 135

172 Engels contributed to the Chartist *Northern Star* from the end of 1843 to 1848. From May 1844 he sent in regular reports about European events, primarily about the political and social movement.— 135

173 Here Engels refers to the speech on free trade Marx intended to deliver at the International Congress of Economists in Brussels held between 16 and 18 September 1847 (see Note 162). Not being allowed to speak, Marx published it in the *Atelier Démocratique* on 29 September. Part of the speech was also published by Joseph Weydemeyer in 1848 under the title 'The Protectionists, the Free Traders and the Working Class' and excerpts from it were quoted by Engels in his article 'The Free Trade Congress at Brussels' in *The Northern Star,* No. 520, 9 October 1847 (see present edition, Vol. 6, pp. 279-90).

As is seen from this letter the version sent to *La Réforme* was not printed, and it is not extant.— 135, 143

174 Engels alludes to the case of the Duke of Praslin. In August 1847 the Duchess of Praslin was found murdered in her house. Suspicion fell on her husband and he was arrested. A political scandal broke out which caused the Duke of Praslin to take poison during the investigation.—135

175 The management referred to is that of the Correspondence Bureau of S. Seiler and K. Reinhardt (see Note 161).—138

176 In the summer of 1847 the London Central Authority of the Communist League distributed for discussion in the League's local communities and districts the 'Draft of a Communist Confession of Faith' drawn up by Engels and approved by the First Congress (see Note 154). In mid-October, when Engels returned to Paris from Brussels, the League's draft programme written in the form of a catechism was already being discussed in the Paris communities. Hess proposed to the Paris District Committee his own version of the draft, which was rejected after sharp criticism by Engels. But Engels was no longer satisfied with his own version because in drafting it he had to take into account the fact that the delegates to the League's First Congress were still influenced by utopian communism. In a new version—'Principles of Communism'—drawn up by Engels this shortcoming was eliminated and the programme principles of the working-class movement were elaborated in greater detail, but still in the form of a catechism. This new document was later approved by the Paris communities as the draft programme for the Second Congress of the Communist League.—138

177 Engels refers to Born's intended participation in the Second Congress of the Communist League, but Born did not go to the congress.—139

178 Neither Engels' letter to the Elberfeld communists nor their reply to it has been found. Presumably they were about the possibilities for publishing Marx's and Engels' works on free trade and protective tariffs (see Note 173).—140

179 Marx alludes here to Countess Hatzfeldt's divorce case which lasted from 1846 to 1854.—140

180 Marx presumably has in mind here the refusal of Baron Arnim, Prussian Ambassador to Paris, to give Emma Herwegh, Georg Herwegh's wife, a visa for Berlin. The fact was reported in the *Deutsche-Brüsseler-Zeitung* on 21 October 1847. Later Emma Herwegh set out with a Swiss passport without a visa.—141

181 Marx's *The Poverty of Philosophy* was published simultaneously by Vogler in Brussels and by Frank in Paris. As is seen from Marx's letter to Engels of 15 October 1868, both Vogler and Frank were mere 'commissioners' (agents de vente), all printing expenses being paid by the author.—142

182 The reference is to the election of delegates from the Paris district to the Second Congress of the Communist League which was to meet in London on 29 November 1847.—143

183 The *Lille Banquet* took place on 7 November 1847 during the campaign for an election reform in France which revealed the extremely anti-democratic stand of the liberal opposition to the July monarchy and of the moderate republicans of the *National* party (see Engels' 'Split in the Camp.—The *Réforme* and the *National.*—March of Democracy', present edition, Vol. 6, pp. 385-87).—144

184 An international meeting organised by the Fraternal Democrats (see Note 122) took place in London on 29 November 1847 to mark the anniversary of the

Polish insurrection of 1830. Marx and Engels, who had come to London for the Second Congress of the Communist League, made speeches about Poland. The report on the meeting and accounts of the speeches made by Marx and Engels appeared in the *Deutsche Londoner Zeitung*, No. 140, 3 December 1847, *The Northern Star*, No. 528, 4 December 1847, and the *Deutsche-Brüsseler-Zeitung*, No. 98, 9 December 1847. Engels wrote a special item on this subject for *La Réforme*, which published it on 5 December 1847 (see present edition, Vol. 6, pp. 391-92).—144

[185] Proposals to convene an international democratic congress were made both by the Fraternal Democrats and the Brussels Democratic Association. During his stay in London at the end of November 1847, Marx had talks on the subject with the Chartist leaders and representatives of the proletarian and democratic emigrants. Engels had similar talks with French socialists and democrats. In the beginning of 1848 it was agreed to convene the congress in Brussels. It was scheduled for 25 August 1848, the eighteenth anniversary of the Belgian revolution. However, these plans did not materialise because in February 1848 a revolution began in Europe.—145

[186] Engels sent this letter to Marx on the eve of the Second Congress of the Communist League for which they both made thorough preparations and expected to reach a final agreement concerning their stand during their meeting on the way to London. What Engels writes here on certain points, e.g. a Communist League programme not in the form of a catechism or confession of faith (see notes 154 and 176) but of a manifesto, found expression in the congress decisions.

The *Second Congress of the Communist League* was held in London from 29 November to 8 December 1847. It was attended by delegates from Germany, France, Belgium, Switzerland, Poland and Denmark. Marx represented the League's Brussels communities, Engels the Paris communities and Victor Tedesco the Liège communities. During many days of discussion Marx and Engels defended the principles of scientific communism on which the congress based its decisions. It was resolved that in all its external relations the League would come out openly as a communist party. The congress adopted the previously drawn up Rules in an improved form, a clause clearly defining the League's communist aim being included. On the instruction of the Second Congress Marx and Engels wrote as the League's programme the *Manifesto of the Communist Party*, which was published in February 1848 (see present edition, Vol. 6, pp. 477-519).

An excerpt from this letter was published in English for the first time in: Karl Marx and Friedrich Engels, *Correspondence, 1846-1895*. A Selection with Commentary and Notes, Martin Lawrence Ltd., London, 1934, and International Publishers, New York, 1935.—146

[187] Marx's letter to Engels written about 22 November 1847 has not been found.—149

[188] The working man referred to was Stephan Born, who was to speak at the meeting of the Democratic Association in Brussels held to mark the seventeenth anniversary of the Polish revolution of 1830 instead of Marx who at that time was to take part in the Second Congress of the Communist League in London. Below Engels mentions Wilhelm Wolff (Lupus) and Georg Weerth as possible representatives, with Born, of the German Workers' Society at the Brussels meeting. It was held on 29 November 1847, and Born spoke on behalf of the German workers.

A report on the meeting was published in the *Deutsche-Brüsseler-Zeitung*, No. 96, 2 December 1847.— 149

189 Engels refers to the Congress of Economists in Brussels where Georg Weerth made a speech on 18 September (see Note 162).— 150

190 The reason for Marx's visit to London was to attend the Second Congress of the Communist League. Marx and Engels profited by this occasion to attend the international meeting (mentioned in this letter) held in London to mark the anniversary of the Polish insurrection of 1830 (see Note 184).— 150

191 Engels returned to Paris at the end of December 1847 after a few days' stay in Brussels, where he had arrived from England soon after Marx, on about 17 December (Marx and Engels had gone to England to participate in the Second Congress of the Communist League—see Note 186). In Brussels Engels worked with Marx on the *Manifesto of the Communist Party*. On his arrival in Paris, Engels wished to meet Louis Blanc, as he writes at the beginning of the letter, to get him to write a review of Marx's *The Poverty of Philosophy* for *La Réforme.*— 152

192 In 1843 Jules Michelet was dismissed from his teaching post for his democratic and anti-clerical convictions; his right to teach history at the Paris University was not restored till after the February 1848 revolution.— 154

193 Here Engels means the United commissions, an advisory social-estate body in Prussia elected by the Provincial Diets from their own members. Engels' article on Prussian finances, mentioned in the letter, has not been found.— 155

194 It is not known whether Engels carried out his intention. The review of Marx's *The Poverty of Philosophy* did not appear in *La Réforme.*— 156

195. Engels' letter to Bernays has not been found.— 157

196 At the end of February 1848 a revolution took place in France which was enthusiastically welcomed in Belgium. Alarmed by the scope of the democratic movement in the country, the Belgian authorities resorted to arrests and expulsion of German revolutionary emigrants. They arrested the Communist League members Wilhelm Wolff and Victor Tedesco. On 3 March Marx was ordered to leave Belgium in twenty-four hours. However, in the night of 3 March, when he was preparing to leave, the police burst into Marx's flat, arrested him and then his wife. After 18 hours of imprisonment Marx and his family were forced to leave Belgium at once. On the invitation of Flocon, who had been elected member of the Provisional Government of the French Republic, Marx moved to Paris.

Engels, expelled from Paris at the end of January 1848 for his revolutionary activity, was in Brussels from 31 January.

The time of writing of this letter, as well as of many other undated ones, is established on the basis of the chronology of events mentioned, in particular the constitution of the new Central Authority of the Communist League on 7 March 1848, and of Jones' departure for England, where he arrived not later than 12 March, etc.

An excerpt from this letter was published in English for the first time in *Labour Monthly*, 1948, No. 3, III.— 158

197 The Second Congress of the Communist League retained the seat of the Central Authority in London. However, as a revolution had broken out in

France, Schapper, Bauer, Moll and other members of the London Central
Authority intended to move to the Continent and decided to transfer their
powers of general direction of the League to the Brussels District Committee
headed by Marx. But the persecution of revolutionaries by the Belgian
authorities impelled the Brussels Central Authority that had been formed to
adopt on 3 March 1848 a decision to dissolve itself and to empower Marx to
form a new Central Authority in Paris. Marx arrived in Paris on 5 March and
took up this appointment. On 7 March the Paris Central Authority mentioned
by Marx was formed. Engels was elected in his absence.— 158

[198] The reference is to the arrest of Marx and his wife by the Belgian police (see
Note 196).— 159

[199] The interpellation on the arrest and expulsion of Marx and his family was
made by Bricourt at the sitting of the Chamber of Representatives of the
Belgian Parliament on 11 March 1848.— 159, 164

[200] Marx's notes on Wilhelm Wolff's arrest on 27 February 1848, his maltreatment
by the police and prison authorities and his expulsion from Belgium on
5 March have survived. Marx published an article on the persecution of
revolutionary emigrants in Belgium in La Réforme, 12 March 1848 (see present
edition, Vol. 6, pp. 567-68 and 581-82).— 159

[201] The news of the victory of the February revolution in France caused a
widespread popular movement in the Rhine Province of Prussia and other
parts of Germany. A demonstration of about five thousand workers and
artisans, organised by the local community of the Communist League, was held
in Cologne on 3 March before the town hall. A petition demanding universal
suffrage, freedom of speech, press and assembly, armament of the people,
labour protection, children's education at the public expense, etc., was
presented to the magistrate. The meeting following the demonstration was
dispersed by troops, and the leaders of the demonstration—Andreas
Gottschalk, August Willich and Friedrich Anneke—were arrested and brought
to trial (they were set free on 21 March when a revolution began in Prussia).
Gottschalk, Willich and Anneke belonged to a group in the local community of
the Communist League which was under the influence of 'true socialism' and,
in contrast to Karl d'Ester, Roland Daniels and Heinrich Bürgers (below Engels
calls them 'old friends'), displayed sectarian tendencies.— 159

[202] The information received by Engels concerning d'Ester was inaccurate. D'Ester
was present at the sitting of the Cologne city council on 3 March 1848 and
spoke for the inclusion of a number of the people's demands in the liberal
memorandum under discussion to be presented to the Berlin authorities. His
proposals were rejected.— 159

[203] A movement for definitive secession from the German Empire and for
bourgeois-democratic reforms arose in 1797 in the territories along the left
bank of the Rhine seized by the armies of the French Republic. With the
approval of the French commander-in-chief, General Hoche, a plan was drawn
up in September 1797 to form a filial left-bank Rhine Republic (Cisrhenanische
Republik) allied to France. However, as a result of General Bonaparte's victory
over Austria the territories along the left bank of the Rhine were directly
attached to France by the Campo Formio Treaty (November 1797).— 160

[204] An extract from this letter was published in English for the first time in
Labour Monthly, 1948, No. 3, III.— 161

205 The *German Democratic Society* was formed in Paris after the February 1848 revolution. The Society was headed by petty-bourgeois democrats, Herwegh, Bornstedt and others, who campaigned to raise a volunteer legion of German refugees, with the intention of marching into Germany. In this way they hoped to carry out a revolution in Germany and establish a republic there. Marx and his followers in the Communist League opposed to this adventurist plan the tactics of uniting the German emigrants and organising their return to Germany individually to take part in the revolutionary struggle that was developing there. Late in April 1848 the volunteer legion moved to Baden, where it was dispersed by government troops.

Black, red and gold were the colours symbolising German unity; the unity slogan was interpreted by the petty-bourgeois democrats as a call to establish in Germany a federation of autonomous provinces on the pattern of the Swiss Confederation.— 162, 540

206 There is no further information about the letters Marx intended to write to Maynz and Jottrand.— 162

207 Engels moved to Paris from Brussels about 21 March 1848.— 164

208 Neither Engels' letter to his mother nor his mother's letter quoted by Engels below has been found.— 166

209 On 24 February 1848 the people of Paris revolted, overthrew the monarchy and formed a Provisional Government, with the party of the *National* in the majority. Under pressure from the armed masses, however, the bourgeois republicans were compelled to include in the government four ministers from the list compiled by *La Réforme*, among them Louis Blanc and a worker Albert, a leader of secret republican societies and participant in the street fighting.

On 17 March there was a 100,000-strong demonstration of Paris workers demanding postponement of the elections to the Constituent Assembly (see Note 214).— 166

210 The reference is to the organisation of a legion of German refugees to march into Germany (see Note 205).— 166

211 This letter was published in English for the first time in *Science and Society*, New York, 1940, Vol. IV, No. 2.— 167

212 The reference is to the attempts of Ledru-Rollin, Minister of the Interior, to renew the administrative staff of municipal councils and his decree of 14 March to abolish the privileged National Guard units of bourgeois and aristocrats.— 168

213 This refers to the utopian plans for the 'organisation of labour' with the help of a bourgeois state proposed by Louis Blanc as president of the Labour Commission set up by the Provisional Government on 28 February 1848 (it held its meetings in the Luxembourg Palace). The Commission was dissolved by the Government after the popular action of 15 May 1848.— 168

214 The reference is to the elections to the National Guard, fixed for 18 March, and to the Constituent Assembly of the Republic, which originally were to be held on 5 April 1848. To hold the elections in a short time would have benefited the anti-revolutionary forces. That is why the demonstration of the Paris workers on 17 March, of which Engels writes above, demanded that the Provisional Government, besides withdrawing the troops from the capital,

should postpone the elections to the National Guard till 5 April and to the Constituent Assembly till 31 May 1848. The Government was compelled to comply with these demands, but the elections to the Constituent Assembly were postponed only till 23 April.—168

215 About 6 April 1848 Marx and Engels returned to Germany from emigration to take part in the revolution that was developing there. On their way to Cologne, the centre of the Rhine Province—the most economically developed region in Germany—which they chose as the place for the planned publication of a revolutionary newspaper, they made a stop at Mainz on 8 April. Here they discussed with the local communists (Karl Wallau who had arrived from Paris earlier, Adolf Cluss and others) the plan of actions to prepare for the creation of a mass party of the German proletariat, with the Communist League as its nucleus. Marx and Engels arrived at Cologne about 11 April.

There is no information about the letters which Marx and Engels promised to write to Cabet from Germany.—170

216 In mid-April Engels left Cologne and made a trip to towns of the Rhine Province of Prussia—Barmen, Elberfeld and others—to organise a subscription to the shares for the publication of the *Neue Rheinische Zeitung*. During the trip he also acted as an emissary of the Communist League's Central Authority. He returned to Cologne on 20 May 1848.—170

217 On 10 April 1848 a Chartist demonstration in London was dispersed by troops and special constables; the purpose of the demonstration was to present the third Chartist Petition to Parliament.

Engels' letter to Harney has not been found.—171

218 The subject is the prospects of the planned *Neue Rheinische Zeitung*, the first issue of which appeared on 31 May but was dated 1 June 1848.

Marx and Engels began to prepare for the publication of a German revolutionary newspaper as early as March 1848 when they were in Paris (see this volume, p. 173). They regarded a proletarian periodical as an important step towards creating a mass party of the German proletariat based on the Communist League. Soon after their return to Germany, however, they realised that the conditions for the creation of such a party had not yet matured. Disunity and lack of political awareness made the German workers susceptible to the artisan and petty-bourgeois influences and particularist aspirations. Moreover it was senseless for the League to continue to work underground in the context of the revolution but the League was too weak and numerically small to serve as a rallying centre. Under these conditions the newspaper was to play an especially important role in the ideological and political education of the masses. It was also to become an organ of political guidance for the Communist League members, whom Marx and Engels advised to take an active part in the workers' organisations and democratic societies then being set up in Germany.

It was decided to call the newspaper the *Neue Rheinische Zeitung* in order to stress that it was to continue the revolutionary-democratic traditions of the *Rheinische Zeitung* which was edited by Marx in 1842 and early 1843. In view of the specific conditions and the absence of an independent proletarian party, Marx, Engels and their followers entered the political scene as the Left, in fact proletarian, wing of the democratic movement. This predetermined the stand adopted by the *Neue Rheinische Zeitung*, which had as its subtitle *Organ der Demokratie* (Organ of Democracy). The editorial board included Karl Marx (editor-in-chief), Frederick Engels, Wilhelm Wolff, Georg Weerth, Ferdinand Wolff, Ernst Dronke and Heinrich Bürgers. In October 1848 Ferdinand Freiligrath also became an editor.

The consistent revolutionary line of the *Neue Rheinische Zeitung*, its militant internationalism, its articles containing political accusations against the Government aroused the displeasure of its bourgeois shareholders in the first months of its existence and led to attacks in the feudal monarchist and liberal bourgeois press. The editors were persecuted by the police and judicial authorities. On 26 September 1848, when a state of siege was declared in Cologne, the publication of the newspaper was suspended and was resumed only on 12 October. Despite all this, the *Neue Rheinische Zeitung* courageously defended the interests of revolutionary democracy and the proletariat. In May 1849, against the background of the general counter-revolutionary offensive, the Prussian Government issued an expulsion order against Marx on the grounds that he had not obtained Prussian citizenship. This arbitrary act and repressions against other editors led to the paper ceasing publication. The last issue, No. 301, printed in red ink, appeared on 19 May 1849. In their farewell address to the workers the editors wrote that 'their last word everywhere and always will be: *emancipation of the working class*' (see present edition, Vol. 9, p. 467).— 171

219 On 6 May 1848 Marx and Weerth arrived in Elberfeld to discuss with Engels problems connected with the publication of the *Neue Rheinische Zeitung* and the activity of the Communist League.— 172

220 An extract from this letter was published in English for the first time in: Karl Marx and Friedrich Engels, *Correspondence. 1846-1895*. A Selection with Commentary and Notes, Martin Lawrence Ltd., London, 1934, and International Publishers, New York, 1935.— 172, 270, 278, 291, 325, 361, 383, 389, 453

221 Engels' letter to Wilhelm Blank has not been found.— 172

222 Moses Hess, Friedrich Anneke and other sectarians in the Communist League attempted to start a new paper in Cologne to succeed the *Rheinische Zeitung* of the early 1840s. The newspaper's programme, published by Hess and Anneke on 7 April, was very vague and narrowed the tasks of the planned publication, which they conceived as a local, provincial newssheet. Hess and his followers were prevented from realising their plan by the return of Marx and Engels to Cologne.— 173

223 There is no other information about the Italian and Spanish translations mentioned here of the *Manifesto of the Communist Party*. The first Spanish and Italian translations of the *Manifesto* appeared in 1872 and 1889 respectively.— 173

224 Engels did not finish this translation. In the autumn of 1850 he helped Helen Macfarlane translate the *Manifesto* into English and it appeared in *The Red Republican*, Nos. 21-24, in November 1850.— 173

225 The *Elberfeld political club*, which was formed soon after the March revolution in Prussia, advocated a constitutional monarchy and gradual reforms.— 173

226 Presumably Engels means Marx's letter to Ewerbeck concerning the Paris communities of the Communist League; this letter has not been found.— 174

227 The shareholders of the *Neue Rheinische Zeitung* were to meet in Cologne in May 1848, before the newspaper started publication. The shareholders from

other towns who could not attend the meeting in person sent in proxies for the
newspaper's editors or other persons in Cologne.—174

228 An extract from this letter was published in English for the first time in: Karl
Marx and Frederick Engels, *Selected Correspondence*, Progress Publishers,
Moscow, 1975.—175, 210

229 Here and below Engels gives the addresses of the editorial office and the
dispatch department of the *Neue Rheinische Zeitung* which at the beginning was
printed by Clouth (12 St Agatha) and from 30 August 1848 by Dietz (17 Unter
Hutmacher).—175

230 In the spring of 1848 the Polish national liberation uprising broke out in the
Grand Duchy of Posen subject to Prussia. The Prussian General Pfuel ordered
that all the insurgents who had been taken prisoner should be shaved and their
hands and ears branded with silver nitrate.
   In May 1848 a clash took place between the soldiers and the civic militia in
Mainz, which the fortress commander Hüser used as a pretext to send troops
to disarm the latter. The conflict was discussed in the Frankfurt National
Assembly which, however, did not take any serious measures to stop the
arbitrary actions of the Prussian military authorities.—176

231 The all-German *National Assembly*, which opened on 18 May 1848 in Frankfurt
am Main, was convened for the purpose of unifying the country and drawing
up its constitution. The liberal majority of the Assembly turned it into a
debating club engaged in fruitless discussions such as on the disarmament of
the civic militia in Mainz.—176

232 The editorial office of the *Neue Rheinische Zeitung* was removed at the end of
August to 17 Unter Hutmacher (see Note 229).
   There is no information about the article by Köppen who might have sent it
in after meeting Marx in Berlin in August 1848 when Marx went there on
business connected with the *Neue Rheinische Zeitung*.
   By the 'sleepless night of exile' Engels presumably meant the time Marx
and he spent abroad before the 1848 revolution.—177

233 On 26 September 1848 the Prussian authorities, fearing the growing
revolutionary-democratic movement, declared a state of siege in Cologne (it was
lifted on 2 October). By order of the military command political organisations
and associations were banned, the civic militia disbanded, democratic newspapers, including the *Neue Rheinische Zeitung*, suspended, and an order issued for
the arrest of Engels and a few other editors. Engels and Dronke had to leave
Cologne. For a time Engels lived in hiding in Barmen. On 5 October Engels
and Dronke arrived in Paris after a short stay in Belgium whence they were
expelled by the police. Dronke remained in the French capital and wrote to the
Neue Rheinische Zeitung from there, while Engels started on foot for
Switzerland via the south-west of France. About 24 October he arrived in
Geneva and at the beginning of November moved to Lausanne (these facts
served as a basis for establishing the date of this letter and those by Marx which
followed and were not dated); Engels arrived in Neuchâtel on 7 November and
in Berne on 9 November. He stayed there until mid-January 1849 when it was
possible for him to return to Germany.
   Engels' letter written to Marx from Geneva has not been found.—177, 185,
192, 541, 542, 543

234 In 1848 Engels lived at Plasmann's, owner of a stationery firm and a shareholder of the *Neue Rheinische Zeitung*. His address was: Köln, In der Höhle, 14.—178

235 The discontent of the bourgeois shareholders over the political line of the *Neue Rheinische Zeitung* grew particularly strong after it defended the June proletarian insurgents in Paris. These shareholders refused to finance and support the newspaper any longer. So in August and September 1848 Marx made a trip to Berlin and Vienna to raise funds for the further publication of the *Neue Rheinische Zeitung*. Wladislaw Kóscielski gave him about 2,000 talers on behalf of the Polish democrats.

The interruption in publication caused by the state of siege in Cologne aggravated the newspaper's financial position. Marx was practically compelled to take upon himself most of the expenses and he spent his share of the inheritance from his father—about 7,000 talers—to purchase an expensive quick printing press.—179

236 Early in July 1848 legal proceedings were instituted against Marx because of his article 'Arrests' published in the *Neue Rheinische Zeitung* (see present edition, Vol. 7, pp. 176-79), exposing the arbitrary actions of the Prussian authorities. At the beginning of October 1848 the Cologne Public Prosecutor started an investigation against Marx and other newspaper editors for publishing anonymously Georg Weerth's series of feuilletons *Leben und Taten des berühmten Ritters Schnapphanski*. At the end of October 1848 the Cologne Public Prosecutor began another investigation against Marx as the newspaper's editor-in-chief for publishing the proclamation of the republican Friedrich Hecker. The 'insult' to the Public Prosecutor and 'libel' against the police officers contained in the article 'Arrests' were the main accusations levelled at Marx and Engels at the trial held on 7 February 1849. The jury acquitted them.—179, 542

237 On 1 November 1848 the King of Prussia transferred power to the openly counter-revolutionary Brandenburg-Manteuffel Government. It decided on a coup d'état which was successful and led to the dissolution of the National Assembly on 5 December. The very first steps of this government aroused a protest campaign in democratic circles, especially in the Rhine Province, which sought to unite the opposition forces. In Düsseldorf, in particular, for 14 November a joint meeting was announced for this purpose of the local People's Club, the Union for the establishment of a democratic monarchy, the General Civil Union, and the civic militia (it was probably this meeting that Marx called the democratic-monarchist club). At this meeting Lassalle put forward Marx's plan of actions.—180

238 The Central Committee of German Democrats was set up in June 1848 at the first democratic congress in Frankfurt am Main convened with the aim of uniting the local democratic associations. The second all-German democratic congress in Berlin (26-30 October 1848) elected a new Central Committee.—180

239 This refers to the *Rhenish District Committee of Democrats* set up at the first district congress of democrats of the Rhine Province and Westphalia (13-14 August 1848). The committee directed the activity of the democratic organisations in the Rhineland, Marx playing a prominent role in it.—180

[240] On 14 November 1848 Marx was summoned to the examining magistrate for 'insulting' the Cologne Public Prosecutor Hecker in the article 'Public Prosecutor "Hecker"' and the *Neue Rheinische Zeitung*' published in the *Neue Rheinische Zeitung*, No. 129, 29 October 1848 (see present edition, Vol. 7, pp. 485-89).—180

[241] The *Code pénal* was adopted in France in 1810 and introduced into the regions of West and South-West Germany conquered by the French. It remained in force in the Rhine Province even after its incorporation into Prussia in 1815.—181

[242] In order to give its readers prompt information on events, the editors of the *Neue Rheinische Zeitung* often put out supplements to the main issue or a second edition. If the news was very important they printed special supplements and special editions in the form of posters.—181

[243] Marx probably made the acquaintance of Eduard von Müller-Tellering during his stay in Vienna in August and September 1848. In October and November the *Neue Rheinische Zeitung* published a number of articles marked Q which were sent by E. von Müller-Tellering from Vienna. They described the situation in the city after the suppression of the popular rising in October.—182

[244] The arrest of Andreas Gottschalk and Friedrich Anneke, the leaders of the Cologne Workers' Association, on 3 July 1848 was the subject of Marx's article 'Arrests' which served as a pretext for accusing Marx and other editors of the *Neue Rheinische Zeitung* of insulting the Public Prosecutor and libelling police officers (see Note 236). On 23 December 1848, Gottschalk and Anneke were acquitted by a Cologne jury.—183

[245] The reference is to the state of siege declared in Cologne on 26 September 1848 and the persecution of the *Neue Rheinische Zeitung*'s editors, Engels among them (see Note 233). On 3 October, though the state of siege had been lifted, the Public Prosecutor issued a warrant for Engels' arrest. Engels was able to return to Cologne only in mid-January 1849.—183

[246] This is a draft reply to the letter sent from Berlin on 26 December 1848 by Wilhelm Stieber to the *Neue Rheinische Zeitung*. In it Stieber tried to disprove information on his spying activities in Silesia during and after the Silesian weavers' uprising in 1844 (he went there disguised as an artist, under the name Schmidt), and on his secret mission to Frankfurt am Main in September 1848 in connection with a popular uprising there. This information was given in a report from Frankfurt am Main published in the *Neue Rheinische Zeitung*, No. 177, 24 December. Marx agreed to make a correction as regards Stieber's visit to Frankfurt (the supplement to No. 182 stated that he went there on private business) but did not disavow the information on his spying in Silesia. Later, in his *Revelations Concerning the Communist Trial in Cologne* (end of 1852), exposing Stieber as an organiser of police persecution of the Communist League members and disclosing his attempts to blacken the *Neue Rheinische Zeitung*, Marx quoted in full Stieber's letter to the newspaper editors of 26 December 1848. Marx stressed that the reply to Stieber was sent by another editor (see present edition, Vol. 11, pp. 435-36). It may be assumed that the final version of the letter was signed by Wilhelm Wolff, who was well aware of Stieber's activities in Silesia.—183

247 On the *Code pénal* see Note 241. The reference is to 'Livre troisième. Titre II. Chapitre I. Section VII. 2. Calomnies....'—184

248 Engels received news, probably on 11 or 12 January, that he could return to Germany without running the risk of being arrested. He immediately undertook all the formalities necessary to obtain an exit permit from Switzerland, and obtained it on 18 January 1849 (see present edition, Vol. 8, p. 515). Shortly after this Engels returned to Cologne and resumed work as editor of the *Neue Rheinische Zeitung.*—185

249 By 'grace and favour (*oktroyierte*) Prussia' Engels means Prussia after the counter-revolutionary coup d'état which resulted in the dissolution of the National Assembly on 5 December 1848 and the proclamation of the so-called imposed constitution. The Constitution introduced a two-chamber parliament: the First Chamber consisting of privileged aristocrats and the Second Chamber elected in two stages. Under the law of 6 December a considerable proportion of the workers had no right to vote. The King was invested with wide powers, including the right to convene and dissolve both Chambers, to repeal their decisions, to appoint Cabinets and to revise the Constitution itself.—186

250 The *March Association*, thus named after the March 1848 revolution, was founded in Frankfurt am Main at the end of November 1848 by the Left-wing deputies of the Frankfurt National Assembly and had branches in various towns of Germany. Fröbel, Simon, Ruge, Vogt and other petty-bourgeois democratic leaders of March associations confined themselves to revolutionary phrase-mongering and showed indecision and inconsistency in the struggle against the counter-revolutionaries, for which Marx and Engels sharply criticised them.—186

251 Marx's letter to Eduard von Müller-Tellering has not been found.
    At the beginning of January von Müller-Tellering was arrested and banished from Vienna (on his reports from that city published in the *Neue Rheinische Zeitung* see Note 243). Later Tellering sent reports from Silesia and Saxony on the situation in Vienna based on the letters of his Vienna acquaintances, and also reports from Leipzig and Dresden (these were marked △).—189

252 Threatened with arrest after the state of siege was declared in Cologne on 26 September 1848 (see Note 233), Dronke emigrated to Paris but persisted in the desire to return to Germany. He was kept in Paris only by categorical directions from Marx, who had grounds to fear he would be arrested. It was not till March 1849 that Dronke returned to Cologne and began to work on the *Neue Rheinische Zeitung.*
    Neither Marx's previous letter to Dronke nor his other letters mentioned below have been found.—190

253 An anonymous item published in the supplement to No. 233 of the *Neue Rheinische Zeitung* for 28 February 1849 accused von Uttenhoven, a Captain in the 8th Company of the 16th Infantry Regiment, known for his reactionary views, of misuse of and speculation in army fuel.—193

254 This refers to two lawsuits held in Cologne on 7 and 8 February 1849. The first was instituted by the Cologne Public Prosecutor's office against the *Neue Rheinische Zeitung*, its editors Marx and Engels and the responsible editor Hermann Korff for publishing the article 'Arrests' (see notes 236 and 244).

The pretext for the second was the charge against Marx, Karl Schapper and the lawyer Schneider II of incitement to mutiny in connection with the call of the Rhenish District Committee of Democrats (see Note 239) of 18 November 1848 for refusal to pay taxes. In both cases the juries acquitted the defendants.— 194

255 From mid-April to 9 May 1849 Marx made a trip to North-Western Germany. He visited Bremen, Hamburg and the neighbouring towns, including Harburg. On his way back to Cologne Marx stopped at Bielefeld and Hamm. The purpose of the trip was to strengthen contacts between the Communist League members and workers' associations in preparation for the creation of a mass proletarian party, to discuss problems of revolutionary tactics with members of the working-class and democratic movements, and to raise funds for the continued publication of the *Neue Rheinische Zeitung*. In Marx's absence Engels directed the newspaper.

Engels' letter to Marx mentioned here has not been found.— 195

256 Karl Bruhn participated in the Baden republican uprising in April 1849 and played an active role in the popular uprising in Frankfurt am Main (September 1848) in protest against the ratification by the Frankfurt National Assembly of the capitulatory truce of Malmö. Concluded between Prussia and Denmark, this truce preserved Danish rule in Schleswig-Holstein. Since the end of 1848 Bruhn had been working in Hamburg and Schleswig-Holstein on the instruction of the Communist League and sending reports to the *Neue Rheinische Zeitung* from there.— 196

257 An allusion to the cruel suppression of the popular uprising in Vienna in October 1848 by the Austrian counter-revolution. Marx made Andreas Stifft's acquaintance in August 1848 during his visit to Vienna (see Note 235), where he made a speech at a meeting of the Democratic Society and delivered a report and a lecture at the Vienna Workers' Society. Stifft was member of both these organisations and a contributor to the *Neue Rheinische Zeitung.*— 197

258 After the *Neue Rheinische Zeitung* had ceased publication on 19 May 1849, Marx and Engels left for Frankfurt am Main where they tried to persuade the Left-wing deputies to the all-German National Assembly to take decisive action in support of the uprising in South-Western Germany at the time in defence of the Imperial Constitution drawn up by the Assembly but rejected by the German sovereigns. Having failed to achieve their aim they left for Karlsruhe and then Kaiserslautern—capitals of insurgent Baden and the Palatinate. Convinced that the petty-bourgeois democratic leaders of the Provisional Governments in Baden and the Palatinate lacked revolutionary energy and were helpless, Marx and Engels left at the end of May for Bingen, where they parted. Early in June Marx went to Paris, and Engels returned to Kaiserslautern to join the Baden-Palatinate revolutionary army.— 198

259 Marx arrived in Paris about 2 June 1849 with the mandate from the Central Committee of German Democrats (see Note 238) issued to him in Kaiserslautern by d'Ester, a member of the Committee and of the Palatinate Provisional Government. Marx decided to go to France when he realised that the petty-bourgeois democrats of Baden and the Palatinate were unable to make the struggle all-German in scale, to launch a resolute offensive and bring the Frankfurt Assembly openly to join the uprising. New great events were expected in France, where the conflict between the democratic party—the so-called Montagne (Mountain)—and the ruling circles was coming to a head.

In Paris Marx hoped to strengthen international contacts between the German and French democrats, for this would have been of major importance in the event of a new revolutionary upsurge in both countries.— 198

260 *Montagnards*—during the French revolution of 1848-49 representatives in the Constituent and subsequently Legislative Assembly of a bloc of democrats and petty-bourgeois socialists grouped around the newspaper *La Réforme.* They called themselves the Montagne by analogy with the Montagne in the Convention of 1792-94.

On *13 June 1849* the Montagne staged a peaceful demonstration to protest against the sending of French troops to suppress the Roman Republic. The demonstration was dispersed by the army and the bourgeois detachments of the National Guards and there followed a counter-revolutionary offensive, persecution of democrats and proletarian activists, including emigrants. Many Montagnards were arrested or emigrated.— 199, 211, 283, 309, 360, 409, 547

261 Engels' 'article in French' on the national liberation struggle in Hungary was probably never written.— 200

262 The last issue, No. 301, of the *Neue Rheinische Zeitung* for 19 May 1849, printed in red, was published in a greater number of copies than usual. Later it was reprinted several times and used by the Communist League members, who remained in Germany, for propaganda purposes.— 201, 237

263 Jenny Marx spent June 1849 in her native town of Trier. On July 7 she joined her husband in Paris accompanied by her three children and Hélène Demuth (the Marxes' housekeeper).— 201, 207, 546, 555

264 At the beginning of June 1849, when in Kaiserslautern, Engels entered into close contact with d'Ester, the most energetic member of the Palatinate Provisional Government, but refused, however, to accept any civil or military post.

On 13 June Engels left for Offenburg, where he joined Willich's volunteer corps of 800 men, mostly workers, which was part of the Baden-Palatinate insurgent army. Engels fought the whole campaign as Willich's adjutant. Willich's corps covered the retreat of this army under pressure from numerically superior counter-revolutionary forces and was among the last units to cross the Swiss border on 12 July 1849. On 24 July Engels arrived at Vevey (Canton Vaud) where he stayed for a month. He described the operations of the insurgent army in *The Campaign for the German Imperial Constitution* (see present edition, Vol. 10, pp. 147-239).

Engels' letter to Marx from Kaiserslautern has not survived.

An extract from Engels' letter to Jenny Marx was published in English for the first time in: K. Marx and F. Engels, *Correspondence. 1846-1895*, Martin Lawrence Ltd., London, 1934, and International Publishers, New York, 1935.— 202, 370

265 On 17 June 1849 Engels fought in the battle of *Rinnthal*. He commanded a flank group of Willich's corps which covered the retreat of the Palatinate army and fought the advance guard of an enemy division for many hours.

On 21 June Willich's men, with the active participation of Engels, checked the advance of a Prussian battalion at *Neuchart* near Karlsdorf and forced it to retreat.

On 28 June 1849 Engels took part in an engagement at *Michelbach* in which the advance guard of the division to which Willich's corps belonged after the reorganisation of the insurgent army defeated a Prussian force.

On 29 and 30 June at *Rastatt* the Baden-Palatinate insurgent army fought and lost its last battle against the Prussian army. At certain critical moments of the battle Engels assumed command of the vanguard.—203, 215

266 The subject is Lassalle's intention to raise funds to help Marx.

The letters to Lassalle mentioned by Marx have not been found.

An extract from this letter was published in English for the first time in: K. Marx and F. Engels, *On Britain,* Foreign Languages Publishing House, Moscow, 1954.—204

267 These were the two factions in the so-called Party of Order—a conservative bloc of the monarchist groups formed in 1848 which had the majority in the Legislative Assembly of the French Republic (opened at the end of May 1849).

The *Philippists* or *Orleanists* were supporters of the House of Orleans (a lateral branch of the Bourbon dynasty) overthrown by the February revolution of 1848; they represented the interests of the financial aristocracy and the big industrial bourgeoisie; their candidate for the throne was Louis Philippe Albert, Count of Paris and grandson of Louis Philippe.

The *Legitimists,* supporters of the main branch of the Bourbon dynasty overthrown in 1830, upheld the interests of the big hereditary landowners and the claim to the French throne of the Count of Chambord, King Charles X's grandson, who called himself Henry V. Some of the Legitimists remained outside the bloc of monarchist groups.—205, 360, 484

268 According to a decision of the Constituent Assembly the wine tax was to be abolished before 1 January 1850. But, as Marx predicted, it was retained by a decision of the Legislative Assembly on 20 December 1849 (see present edition, Vol. 10, pp. 117-19).—205, 211

269 The *Peace Society*—a pacifist organisation founded by the Quakers in 1816 in London. It was actively supported by the Free Traders who assumed that in peace time free trade would enable Britain to make better use of its industrial superiority and win economic and political supremacy.—205, 211, 219

270 The *Corn Laws* (first introduced in the fifteenth century) imposed high import duties on agricultural produce in the interests of landowners in order to maintain high prices for these products on the home market. In 1838 the Manchester factory owners Cobden and Bright founded the Anti-Corn Law League, which demanded the lifting of the corn tariffs and urged unlimited freedom of trade for the purpose of weakening the economic and political power of the landed aristocracy and reducing worker's wages. The struggle between the industrial bourgeoisie and the landed aristocracy over the Corn Laws ended in 1846 with their repeal.

The *Navigation Acts* were passed by the British Parliament in 1651 and subsequent years to protect British shipping companies against foreign rivals. They were repealed in 1849.—205, 211, 261, 376, 537

271 Marx mentions the *Holy Alliance* in connection with the attempts of feudal-monarchical circles in Prussia, Austria and tsarist Russia to form a coalition similar to the counter-revolutionary Holy Alliance founded in 1815 by the European monarchs, and which ceased to exist after the 1830 revolution in France.—205, 288, 329, 357

272 On 19 July 1849 in an atmosphere of repression against democrats and socialists following the events of 13 June in Paris (see Note 260), the French

authorities notified Marx that an order had been issued for his expulsion from Paris to Morbihan, a swampy and unhealthy département in Brittany. Marx protested and the expulsion was delayed, but on 23 August he again was ordered by the police to leave Paris within 24 hours.

Marx compares the département of Morbihan with the Pontine marshes in Italy, mentioned by Strabo in his *Geography*, Book 5, Ch. 3, § 5, and other ancient authors, which are a breeding-ground of malaria and other diseases.— 207, 212

273 Marx's suggestion was approved and subsequently put into practice by Engels. However, Engels started writing his work, which was later published under the heading, *The Campaign for the German Imperial Constitution* (see present edition, Vol. 10), not earlier than mid-August 1849 after he had moved to Lausanne (see this volume, p. 215) and did not finish it until February 1850, after his arrival in London from Switzerland.—207

274 The negotiations mentioned here ended in December 1849 in the foundation of the *Neue Rheinische Zeitung. Politisch-ökonomische Revue*. The periodical was planned as a continuation of the *Neue Rheinische Zeitung* published by Marx and Engels during the 1848-49 revolution. Altogether six issues appeared from March to November 1850, one of them a double one (5-6). The journal was edited in London and published in Hamburg. Most of the articles and literary and international reviews were written by Marx and Engels, who got their followers Wilhelm Wolff, Joseph Weydemeyer and Johann Georg Eccarius to contribute to the *Revue*. The works published in the journal assessed the results of the 1848-49 revolution and developed further the theory and tactics of the revolutionary proletarian party. The publication of the *Revue* was discontinued due to police persecution in Germany and lack of funds.—207

275 The date of writing of this letter was established on the basis of Marx's mentioning in it the receipt of Engels' letter to Jenny Marx of 25 July 1849.

In English this letter was first published abridged in: K. Marx and F. Engels, *Letters to Americans. 1848-1895*, International Publishers, New York, 1953.—208

276 The reference is to a contract signed between Leske and Marx on 1 February 1845 for the publication of Marx's work *Kritik der Politik und National-Ökonomie* (see Note 59).—208

277 An allusion to the setback of the Montagne on 13 June 1849 (see Note 260).

In the battle of *Waterloo* (18 June 1815) Napoleon's army was defeated by the Anglo-Dutch and Prussian forces commanded by Wellington and Blücher.—209, 332

278 There is no information about this article except a mention in Marx's next letter to Weydemeyer.—209

279 This seems to refer to Rühl's offer to participate in publishing a series of pamphlets (see this volume, p. 208) planned by Marx. The offer was conveyed through Weydemeyer on the basis of whose letter to Marx of 28 August 1849 the approximate date of this letter was established.—209

280 It is not known whether Marx wrote to Naut or not.—210

281 This letter written in the first half of August 1849 has not been found.—210

282 Marx's protest to the French Ministry of the Interior against the decision to expel him from Paris has not been found. When he wrote this letter Marx did not know that his protest had been rejected. But he soon received a notification by the commissioner of police, dated 16 August 1849, stating that Minister of the Interior Dufaure had upheld the decision on Marx's expulsion (see present edition, Vol. 9, p. 527).—211

283 The reference is to the home situation in France in the summer of 1849 which was characterised by intensified repressions against democrats and socialists and by discord and friction within the ruling circles themselves—between the various factions in the Assembly majority (see Note 267), between these factions and the Government, and between the Assembly and Louis Bonaparte's entourage.

The addition of *45 centimes* to every franc of all direct taxes was introduced by the Provisional Government on 16 March 1848. It aroused particular discontent among the peasants, who formed the bulk of tax-payers.

In mid-August 1849 under pressure from the monarchist deputies, a two months' adjournment of the French Legislative Assembly was decreed. The Assembly met again in October 1849.—211

284 At the meeting on 13 August 1849 in the London Drury Lane Theatre of the *National Association for Parliamentary and Financial Reform* (founded by the bourgeois radicals in 1849 with the aim of achieving a democratic electoral system and changes in the tax system) O'Connor advocated a union of the middle and working classes. His speech was supported by the Free Trader Thomas Thompson.—211, 219, 272, 279, 549

285 On 23 August 1849 Marx and his wife were ordered by the police to leave Paris within 24 hours. Jenny Marx got permission to stay in Paris till 15 September with her children, but Marx was obliged to make leave in haste. According to the Boulogne stamp in the passport issued to him by the French police on 24 August, he was in this port on his way to London on 26 August (see present edition, Vol. 9, pp. 529-30). Presumably he arrived on the same day in London, where he was based for the rest of his life.

Meanwhile Engels had left Vevey for Lausanne.—212

286 The Elberfeld uprising of workers and petty bourgeoisie in defence of the Imperial Constitution, which flared up on 8 May 1849, served as a signal for armed struggle in a number of towns in the Rhine Province (Düsseldorf, Iserlohn, Solingen and others). Engels arrived in Elberfeld on 11 May and took an active part in the uprising, in particular directing the erection of street barricades. However, his efforts to secure the disarmament of the bourgeois civic militia, the imposition of a war tax on the bourgeoisie, the formation of the nucleus of a Rhenish revolutionary army out of armed workers' detachments and to unite localised uprisings, met with opposition from the bourgeois and petty-bourgeois leaders of the movement. Under pressure from bourgeois circles Engels was expelled from the town on 15 May. The uprising in Elberfeld, as in other towns of the Rhine Province, was a failure.

On Engels' participation in the revolutionary struggle in Baden and the Palatinate see notes 264 and 265.—213, 551

287 In English this letter was first published abridged and datelined '25 August 1849' in: K. Marx and F. Engels, *Letters to Americans. 1848-1895,* International Publishers, New York, 1953.

The date of writing has been corrected after a more exact deciphering of the original.—213

288 At the end of May 1849, returning from insurgent Baden and the Palatinate (see Note 258), Marx and Engels were arrested on the way to Bingen by Hesse soldiers, who suspected them of being insurgents, and were deported to Darmstadt and thence to Frankfurt am Main. There they were released and resumed their journey to Bingen.

Early in June 1849 Engels was arrested in Kirchheimbolanden by the Palatinate Provisional Government on a charge of anti-government propaganda. The day after his arrest he was released on the insistence of d'Ester, a member of the Provisional Government.—213

289 Jenny Marx and her three children arrived in London about 17 September 1849.—216

290 Accepting Marx's suggestion to move to London Engels had to go via Piedmont, as he risked being arrested in France and more so in Germany. On 5 October 1849 he arrived in Genoa, and on the following day left for England on a British schooner via Gibraltar and the Bay of Biscay. The voyage lasted nearly five weeks. About 12 November, Engels arrived in London as was reported in the item: 'London, 14. Nov.' by the *Westdeutsche Zeitung*, No. 154, 20 November 1849.

The English original of the present letter was first printed in the *Harney Papers*, Assen, 1969.—217

291 This letter has not been found.—217

292 Societies referred to are the *German Workers' Educational Society* (London) (see Note 52) and the *Democratic Association* formed by a group of petty-bourgeois democrats headed by Kallenberg in London early in November 1849, and joined later by some former members of the Educational Society, Ludwig Bauer among them. Engels also wrote to Jakob Schabelitz on the collision between the two organisations (see this volume, p. 222).

The *German Political Refugee Committee* was set up on Marx's initiative under the auspices of the German Workers' Educational Society in London on 18 September 1849. Besides Marx and other members of the Communist League it included some petty-bourgeois democrats. At the meeting of the Educational Society on 18 November the Committee was transformed into the *Social-Democratic Refugee Committee,* the aim being to dissociate the proletarian section of the London refugees from the petty-bourgeois elements. The new Committee included only members of the Communist League. Marx was elected its chairman. Engels, who after his arrival in London was included in the Central Authority of the Communist League restored by Marx, also became a member of the Social-Democratic Refugee Committee.

Besides rendering material aid to the proletarian refugees, the Committee played an important role in reorganising the Communist League and reestablishing ties between its members. In September 1850, Marx, Engels and their adherents withdrew from the Committee because the followers of the Willich-Schapper sectarian group were in the majority in the Educational Society to which the Refugee Committee was accountable.

Early in November 1849, the petty-bourgeois democrats of the Democratic Association formed their own Refugee Committee headed by Ludwig Bauer, Friedrich Bobzin and Gustav Struve.—218, 442, 445

293 In English this letter was first published abridged in: K. Marx and F. Engels, *Letters to Americans. 1848-1895,* International Publishers, New York, 1953.— 218, 405

294 On Marx's plans to write and publish a work on political economy see notes 5 and 59.—219

295 Marx's intention to enlist Joseph Weydemeyer as a regular contributor to the *Neue Rheinische Zeitung. Politisch-ökonomische Revue* was never realised. About mid-January Weydemeyer wrote his first article 'From South Germany' but it was not published in the first issue of the *Revue* owing to lack of space, and later lost its topical interest.—219, 225, 228, 549

296 In a series of articles published in the *Voix du Peuple* from 10 November 1849 to 18 January 1850 Proudhon polemicised bitterly with Louis Blanc, particularly against the latter's idea of using the existing State for solving the social problem, and censured his activity as a member of the Provisional Government of the French Republic (see Note 213) calling him a pseudo-socialist and pseudo-democrat.

    Proudhon criticised from anarcho-reformist positions Louis Blanc's 'state socialism' and other French socialists' ideas close to Blanc's.—219

297 After their defeat in 1848 (dispersal of their demonstration of 10 April, etc.) the Chartists resumed agitation in the autumn of 1849: mass meetings in factory districts were held in support of the imprisoned Chartists and an amnesty of political prisoners was demanded. At the beginning of December 1849 a new wave of meetings swept over London and the towns of Northern England on the occasion of the nomination of delegates to the Chartist Convention which was to reorganise the movement.—220

298 Karl Heinzen's statements in his pamphlet, *Lehren der Revolution,* that during the future revolution millions of reactionaries would be beaten up, were used by some conservative European press organs for launching a campaign against political refugees. As *The Times* of 23 November 1849 tried to lay the responsibility for these 'hellish doctrines' on all German socialists and described Heinzen as one of their leading figures, Marx and Engels deemed it necessary to dissociate themselves from his utterances. With this aim in view Engels published a note 'The German Social Democrats and *The Times'* in the Chartist *Northern Star,* 1 December 1849 (see present edition, Vol. 10, pp. 3-4).—220

299 The first issue of the *Neue Rheinische Zeitung. Politisch-ökonomische Revue* published on 8 March 1850 carried the first part of Marx's *The Class Struggles in France, 1848 to 1850* (see present edition, Vol. 10, pp. 45-70), two chapters of Engels' *The Campaign for the German Imperial Constitution* (see present edition, Vol. 10, pp. 147-85) and Karl Blind's article 'Österreichische und preussische Parteien in Baden'.

    The general introduction mentioned in this letter was not published. The review of events written by Marx and Engels appeared only in the second issue of the journal (see present edition, Vol. 10, pp. 257-70). Wilhelm Wolff's article was only published in the fourth issue under the heading 'Nachträgliches "aus dem Reich"'; it discussed the final stage in the work of the Frankfurt National Assembly (see Note 231) after the majority of the liberal deputies had withdrawn and it had been transferred to Stuttgart (end of May 1849).

    The lectures on political economy which Marx delivered in the London German Workers' Educational Society (see Note 52) at the end of 1849 and in 1850 were not published in the *Revue.*—222

300 The club referred to by Engels is the emigrant *Democratic Association* (see Note 292).

In 1848-49 the republican democrats in Germany called the moderate bourgeois constitutionalists 'wailers' (Heuler). In this particular instance the reference is to petty-bourgeois democrats who left the London German Workers' Educational Society and took part in setting up the Democratic Association.—222, 384

301 In a letter of 30 December 1849 addressed to Marx and Engels and other refugees, Louis Bamberger (editor of the *Deutsche Londoner Zeitung*), Eduard von Müller-Tellering and Rudolf Schramm invited them to attend a German refugees' meeting which was to be held on 3 January 1850 with the alleged aim of uniting the German refugees. Actually the organisers wanted to bring the proletarian elements under petty-bourgeois influence.—223

302 Marx's letter to Jung has not been found.

Besides raising funds for the publication of the *Neue Rheinische Zeitung. Politisch-ökonomische Revue* and the projected resumption of the *Neue Rheinische Zeitung,* Conrad Schramm's trip to the USA was aimed at raising funds for other activities of the Communist League, which was being reorganised by Marx and Engels. The trip did not take place for lack of funds.

For his participation in the revolutionary movement Conrad Schramm (presumably a Communist League member since the beginning of 1849) was sentenced in Cologne on 15 June 1849 to two years' imprisonment in the fortress of Jülich. On 8 September 1849 he escaped from prison and emigrated to London, where he was elected to the Central Authority of the Communist League.—225

303 In his note of 5 February 1850 Eduard von Müller-Tellering asked for a ticket to the ball organised by the London German Workers' Educational Society. Engels' refusal was used by Tellering as a pretext for intrigues against Marx and Engels. See also this volume, pp. 229-30, 234.—227

304 The printing of the first issue of the *Neue Rheinische Zeitung. Politisch-ökonomische Revue* by Köhler's printshop in Hamburg turned to be of poor quality. Because of this and of the disagreements between Köhler and the publisher Schuberth, from the second issue the *Revue* was printed at H. G. Voigt's in Wandsbeck near Hamburg.—229

305 While the *Revue* was being printed, disagreements arose between the proof-reader Theodor Hagen and the publisher Schuberth, who wanted to accommodate the *Revue* to the censorship standards existing in Germany at the time. Hagen proposed to assume responsibility to the censors for the content, and Marx and Engels insisted that Hagen's name should appear as 'responsible editor' on the title page. However Schuberth succeeded in having Hagen's proposal rejected.—229

306 On 3 March 1850 the court of honour, presided by Willich, expelled Tellering from the London German Workers' Educational Society. Tellering wrote a new letter of protest, slandering Engels. This letter of Marx was in reply to Müller-Tellering's intrigues and slander (see also Note 303).—229

307 Marx presumably has in mind Müller-Tellering's unprincipled behaviour in connection with a translation of the memoirs of György Klapka, a participant in the 1848-49 Hungarian revolution. When Klapka had declined Tellering's offer

to translate the memoirs, early in January 1850 Tellering tried in vain to have material compromising the Hungarian general published in the *Neue Rheinische Zeitung. Politisch-ökonomische Revue* of which Marx was an editor. At the same time Tellering proposed his services to Klapka in the struggle against Karl Heinzen, but having been exposed in this intrigue, he helped Heinzen to spread insinuations against Marx and Engels.—230

308 The Refugee Committee in Frankfurt am Main was founded by the Frankfurt Workers' Association at the end of 1849. At its meeting on 28 September 1849, presided by Joseph Weydemeyer, the Association decided to make weekly allocations to refugees.—231, 236

309 In April 1850 the petty-bourgeois democrats Gustav Struve, Rudolf Schramm and others tried to gain influence among the German political refugees in London to counterbalance the Social-Democratic Refugee Committee. They spread false rumours, which got into the German press, alleging a biased approach on the part of the Committee in distributing material aid among the refugees. The London Refugee Committee's statement mentioned at the beginning of this letter refuted the rumours.—232

310 This letter was published in English for the first time in: K. Marx and F. Engels, *Letters to Americans. 1848-1895,* International Publishers, New York, 1953.—233, 489, 539

311 Engels' letter to Dronke has not been found.—233

312 The letter of Marx and Engels to Naut has not been found.—234

313 The society referred to is that of the French Blanquist refugees in London (Société des proscrits démocrates socialistes) with whom Marx and Engels, and also representatives of the revolutionary wing of the Chartists, concluded an agreement in mid-April 1850 (see present edition, Vol. 10, pp. 614-15) to set up a Universal Society of Revolutionary Communists (Société universelle des communistes révolutionnaires). However, the Blanquists soon violated the agreement by contacting the emigrant 'Society in Greek Street'—the petty-bourgeois Democratic Association (on this see Note 292). Subsequently, the leaders of the Blanquist refugees took an openly hostile stand towards Marx and Engels and their supporters by making a bloc with a sectarian faction within the Communist League. In these circumstances Marx and Engels considered it appropriate to cancel their agreement with the Blanquists early in October 1850 (see present edition, Vol. 10, p. 484).—235

314 This is an allusion to the campaign against German political refugees launched by the Prussian conservative newspapers and taken up by the English press. This campaign grew in intensity especially after an attempt on the life of King Frederick William IV of Prussia in Berlin on 22 May 1850 by the retired non-commissioned officer Max Sefeloge (he died in a lunatic asylum). The reactionary press, the *Neue Preussische Zeitung* in particular, spread the lie that the attempt had been prepared by Marx and other leaders in London of an extensive conspiracy. The Prussian authorities urged the British Government to deport the political refugees. Marx and Engels unmasked the organisers of this slander campaign in their letter to the Prussian Ambassador in London Bunsen and in other statements in the press (see present edition, Vol. 10, pp. 370, 378 and 386).—237

315 Two excerpts of this letter are extant: one is quoted by Roland Daniels in his letter to Marx of 28 June 1850, the other in the letter of 10 July 1850 from the Cologne leading district of the Communist League to the London Central Authority of the League.

The letter reflects the disagreement which arose in the summer of 1850 between the London Central Authority and the leaders of the Cologne organisations of the Communist League (Heinrich Bürgers, Roland Daniels, Peter Röser and others). The Cologne people's claim to become the Communist League's leading centre for the whole of Germany was contrary to the League's Rules, which were inspired by democratic centralism and provided for equality of the district organisations in individual provinces and countries and their equal responsibility to the Central Authority.—237

316 This letter was first published in English with abridgments in: K. Marx and F. Engels, *Letters to Americans. 1848-1895*, New York, 1953.

However, a slip of the pen on the part of the author, substituting July for June, was not taken into account and in the present edition it has been corrected on the basis of Weydemeyer's reply to Marx of 3 July 1850.—238

317 Marx's intention to reply to Lüning's criticism remained unfulfilled. However, in a statement to the editor of the *Neue Deutsche Zeitung* (published on 4 July 1850) Marx and Engels protested against Lüning's attempts to distort their views on the dictatorship of the proletariat and the role of the *Neue Rheinische Zeitung* as the mouthpiece of the working class.—238

318 The foreign policy of the Russell cabinet was debated in the House of Commons on 24-27 June 1850. Despite strong Tory opposition the Whig Government was given a vote of confidence by majority of 46.—238

319 This refers to the proposed convocation of a congress of the Communist League (see also present edition, Vol. 10, pp. 375-76) which did not take place, however, owing to the split in the League in September 1850 caused by the disruptive activity of the Willich-Schapper separatist group.—239

320 Marx may have had in mind the situation in the Duchy of Schleswig-Holstein in the summer of 1850, when Communist League members conducted intense propaganda among the military units there. During the 1848 revolution the population of the duchy staged a national liberation uprising against Danish rule, demanding union with Germany. Prussian circles launched a phoney war against Denmark, but a truce was signed on 26 August 1848. The Prusso-Danish war was resumed at the end of March 1849 and it ended with a new betrayal by Prussia signing a peace treaty with the Danish monarchy on 2 July 1850. As a result the insurgents were compelled to continue the war on their own and on 24-25 July 1850 the Schleswig-Holstein army was defeated by Danish troops, and ceased resistance.—239

321 In the summer of 1849, after the closing down of the *Neue Rheinische Zeitung*, Jenny Marx on her way to Trier with her children stopped for a few days in Frankfurt am Main where, badly needing money to continue her journey, she pawned, with the help of Joseph and Louise Weydemeyer, the silver plate she had inherited from her family's Scottish relations.—240

322 Weydemeyer did not carry out his plan to write a popular outline of political economy until after his arrival in the USA in October 1851. This work was published in New York in April-August 1853 in the German newspaper *Die Reform* under the title 'National-ökonomische Skizzen'.—241

323 In mid-November 1850 Engels left London for Manchester, where he worked
in the Ermen and Engels firm first as a clerk and later as a partner until June
1869. He took up this work, in spite of his dislike for it, mainly to provide
material assistance for Marx and his family, so that Marx could continue to
work on the theory of political economy. Henceforth Marx and Engels
maintained regular and frequent correspondence.

This letter was first published in English in full in *The Letters of Karl Marx*,
selected and translated with explanatory notes and an introduction by Saul
K. Padover, Prentice-Hall, Inc., Englewood Cliff, New Jersey, 1979.—241

324 Marx's son Heinrich Guido was nicknamed Fawksy by the family because he
was born on 5 November 1849, the anniversary of the Gunpowder Plot of
1605. The conspirators, Guy Fawkes among them, wanted to blow up the
Houses of Parliament and James I on 5 November. In Britain this anniversary
is celebrated with fireworks.—241, 550

325 Engels' letter to Jenny Marx mentioned here has not been found.—242

326 *Stamp duty* on newspapers introduced in 1712 was a source of state revenue
and the means of fighting the opposition press. In 1836 Parliament was
compelled to reduce it and in 1855 to abolish it altogether.

Harney was accused of not paying stamp duty on *The Red Republican*.—243

327 The reference is to the legal proceedings against the weekly *Household Words*
founded by Charles Dickens in March 1849. They ended on 1 December 1851
in favour of the weekly.—243

328 In mid-September 1850 the Communist League split due to the adventurist
activities of the Willich-Schapper separatist group, which, contrary to the
majority of the League's Central Authority, stood for the tactics of immediately
launching a revolution without due consideration of the real conditions in
Europe. On 17 September Marx, Engels and their followers withdrew from the
London German Workers' Educational Society which fell under the influence
of the group. The spokesmen of the Willich-Schapper group brought a suit on
behalf of the Society against Heinrich Bauer and Karl Pfänder, supporters of
the majority of the League's Central Authority, who held some of the Society's
money as trustees to cover the needs of the League and help political refugees.
Bauer and Pfänder were willing to return the money in instalments, provided it
was not spent by the separatists to the detriment of the Communist League.
However, the separatists insisted on the immediate return of the entire sum.
On 20 November 1850 the court rejected the Society's suit, but the followers of
Willich and Schapper did not halt their insinuations and started a press
campaign against Bauer and Pfänder, accusing them of embezzlement. Marx
and Engels helped to refute this slander (see present edition, Vol. 10,
p. 533).—243, 245, 477

329 Engels' letter to Marx mentioned here has not been found.—243

330 *Pulteney Stores*—apparently the premises where the members of the London
district of the Communist League held their meetings. At the meeting of the
Central Authority held on 15 September 1850 Marx, in an effort to avert a
split and with the support of the majority, suggested to transfer the seat of the
Central Authority to Cologne, to authorise the Cologne district committee to
form a new Central Authority, and to set up in London two independent
district committees, one of the followers of Marx and Engels, and the other of
those of Willich and Schapper. The separatists refused to submit to this

decision and formed their own Central Committee in London. Marx's followers in London grouped around the London district committee, while a new Central Authority was formed in Cologne in October 1850, and expelled the members of the separatist organisation from the Communist League.—245

331 The London German Workers' Educational Society (see Note 52) had its premises in *Great Windmill Street.*—245, 280, 283, 285, 287, 289, 298, 334, 356, 359, 362, 385, 442, 477, 498

332 The meeting between the Russian Emperor Nicholas I, the Austrian Emperor Francis Joseph and the head of the Prussian Government, the Count of Brandenburg, took place in Warsaw on 28 October 1850. At it Nicholas I resolutely took the side of Austria in the Austro-Prussian conflict and brought pressure to bear upon the Prussian Prime Minister, demanding that Prussia should abandon all plans to unite Germany under her hegemony.—246

333 The leaders of the refugee organisations listed signed this document. Among them were in particular the organisation of the French Blanquist refugees— Société des proscrits démocrates socialistes (see Note 313), the London German Workers' Educational Society and the Social-Democratic Refugee Committee (see Note 292). The last two fell after the split in the Communist League under the influence of the Willich-Schapper separatist group.

Subsequently, in their satirical pamphlet *The Great Men of the Exile,* Marx and Engels noted that this group was formed from the lower strata of the emigrants and took part in the squabbles among the political refugees. They also made fun of its *Fanon-Caperon manifesto,* as the conservative press called it (see present edition, Vol. 11, p. 294).—247

334 Haude went to Germany as an emissary of the Willich-Schapper group after the split in the Communist League.—250

335 Marx apparently has in mind Engels' work for a quarterly planned by him as a continuation of the *Neue Rheinische Zeitung. Politisch-ökonomische Revue* whose publication was discontinued after the double No. 5-6 issue (see pp. 257, 266 of this volume). The plans of publishing a quarterly were never realised.—250

336 This, presumably, refers to a refugee meeting held in London on 20 November 1850.—251

337 The German translation of *The Poverty of Philosophy* was not published during Marx's lifetime. It appeared only in 1885.—252

338 Engels compares the grouping of refugee organisations whose representatives signed the address 'To the Democrats of All Nations!' with the Central Committee of European Democracy set up in London in June 1850 on the initiative of Giuseppe Mazzini. The Committee included, besides Mazzini, Ledru-Rollin from the French democrats, Arnold Ruge from the German, and Albert Darasz from the Polish democrats. The Central Committee members held sharply differing ideological views, and the strained relations between the Italian and French democrats led to its dissolution in March 1852.—255, 309, 440

339 By *educational movement* Engels means the attempts of the Christian socialists and bourgeois radicals in Britain in the late 1840s and early 1850s to divert the working class from independent political struggle by means of various educational and associated institutions (schools, libraries, etc.).

Moral force—the name given in the political vocabulary of the time to peaceful, non-revolutionary methods of carrying out social and political reforms. From the 1830s to the 1850s the moral force supporters included Right-wing Chartists oriented towards collaboration with the bourgeois radicals.

Engels made the acquaintance of John Watts during his stay in England in 1842-44 and assessed his part in disseminating Robert Owen's socialist ideas in his 'Letters from London' (see present edition, Vol. 3, pp. 385-89).—255, 405

340 Dissenters were members of Protestant religious sects and trends in England who rejected the dogmas and rites of the official Anglican Church.—255

341 Engels' letter to Dronke mentioned here has not been found.—256

342 This refers to the Communist League Rules drawn up by the Cologne Central Authority in the autumn of 1850 after the split in the League (see present edition, Vol. 10, pp. 634-36). The Rules were received in London on 18 December 1850 and were approved on 5 January 1851 by a London district committee meeting, at which Marx was present.—257, 552

343 An extract from this letter was published in English for the first time in: Karl Marx and Friedrich Engels, *Correspondence. 1846-1895*, London, 1934. The letter was published in fuller form but without the last paragraph in: K. Marx and F. Engels, *Selected Correspondence*, Foreign Languages Publishing House, Moscow, 1955.—258

344 At the end of 1850 the German democratic refugees Gross, Hine and Wilhelmi in Cincinnati wrote to Marx and Engels asking them to contribute free of charge to so-called 'progressive pamphlets' and to the planned periodicals *Social-Demokrat* and *Republik der Bauern*. However, Marx and Engels ignored their offer because of their differences of views with the petty-bourgeois democrats and the commercial interests behind the offer.—262, 271

345 At the end of 1850 Engels stayed with Marx's family in London for a whole week and on 30 December he made a speech at a New Year party organised by the Fraternal Democrats. Marx and his wife were also present (see present edition, Vol. 10, p. 637).—263, 561

346 On 5 January 1851 a public meeting was organised at the People's Institute by the Manchester Chartist Council in which reformist elements (James Leach, Daniel Donovan), supporters of O'Connor, who had favoured collaboration with the bourgeois radicals since 1848, were in the majority. The initiators of the meeting wanted to counteract the influence of Ernest Jones and George Harney, representatives of the revolutionary wing of the Chartists, who played the leading role in the London Executive of the National Charter Association and were working to reorganise the Chartist Party on the basis of open recognition of the movement's socialist aims. On learning of the proposed meeting Ernest Jones went to Manchester. On Harney's request Engels attended the meeting and supported Jones.

A bitterly contested issue at the meeting on 5 January 1851 was that of the relations between the Manchester Council and the London Executive to which Harney and Jones had been reelected in December 1850. Despite opposition from the reformist leaders, half of those present supported the new Executive.—263

347 Marx has in mind negotiations concerning publication of his works started with Hermann Becker in December 1850. The first issue of *Gesammelte Aufsätze von*

Karl Marx was published in Cologne in April 1851. It contained the article 'Comments on the Latest Prussian Censorship Instruction' and part of the first article 'Proceedings of the Sixth Rhine Province Assembly' (see present edition, Vol. 1, pp. 109-31 and 132-81), written by Marx in 1842. The edition was discontinued owing to Becker's arrest.—266, 342, 355, 432

348 Marx intended to bring an action against the Hamburg publisher Julius Schuberth to make him continue publication of the *Neue Rheinische Zeitung. Politisch-ökonomische Revue.*—266

349 This refers to the manifesto of the Central Committee of European Democracy (see Note 338) 'Aux peuples! Organisation de la démocratie' published in *Le Proscrit,* No. 2, 6 August 1850 and signed by Mazzini, Ledru-Rollin, Darasz and Ruge. Ruge, who posed as an atheist, signed the manifesto, despite the religious slogans it contained. For criticism of the manifesto see: K. Marx and F. Engels, 'Review (May to October [1850])' (present edition, Vol. 10, pp. 528-32).—267

350 *Friends of Light*—a religious trend which arose in 1841. It was directed against pietism which, supported by Junker circles and predominant in the official Protestant Church, was distinguished by extreme mysticism and bigotry. The 'Friends of Light' movement was an expression of bourgeois discontent with the reactionary order in Germany in the 1840s, which led in 1846-47 to the formation of so-called *free communities,* which broke away from the official Protestant Church.—267, 374, 384, 447

351 Jenny Marx who was extremely grieved by the death of her son Heinrich Guido (Fawksy) was soon to have a baby. On 28 March 1851 she gave birth to a daughter, Franziska, the Marxes' fifth child.—268

352 At this time Engels was working on a series of articles on the European petty-bourgeois democratic leaders which he intended for *The Friend of the People,* a weekly edited by G. J. Harney. His intention did not materialise, however, owing to disagreements with Harney because of the latter's sympathising with opponents of Marx and Engels—petty-bourgeois emigrants and sectarian elements. Later Marx and Engels used this material in *The Great Men of the Exile* (see present edition, Vol. 11).—268, 278, 287

353 Marx's and Engels' statement on Ruge's article in the *Bremer Tages-Chronik* was not published either in the *Weser-Zeitung* or in the *New-Yorker Staatszeitung* (see this volume, p. 397).—269

354 Marx's letter to Georg Weerth, sent through Engels, has not been found.—269

355 An allusion to what Siegfried Weiss, a petty-bourgeois democrat, wrote to Marx on 2 April 1850, offering to contribute to the *Neue Rheinische Zeitung. Politisch-ökonomische Revue:* 'My pen is sharp and spicy.' Below Engels, presumably, plays on words from this letter.—272

356 This refers to the Chartist Conference held in Manchester on 26-30 January 1851 by O'Connor's supporters, despite opposition from the Executive of the National Charter Association. At Harney's request Engels attended the conference in order to inform the revolutionary wing of the Chartists of its proceedings and results. The majority of the participants took a conciliatory reformist stand on the attitude to be adopted towards other parties and the organisation of cooperative societies, etc. However, at the Chartist Convention

which took place in London from 31 March to 10 April the supporters of the revolutionary line of Harney and Jones were in the majority. The Convention adopted the programme of the National Charter Association, which openly proclaimed socialist aims.—272

357 The original of the letter is not extant. The excerpt published here was quoted in the indictment of Hermann Becker and others at the Cologne communist trial (1852).—273, 282, 308, 331

358 Marx's reference to Joseph, the carpenter, husband of Mary, the mother of Christ, is an ironical allusion to August Willich who resigned his commission in the Prussian army just before the 1848 revolution and worked as a carpenter in Cologne.—273, 282, 284

359 By *currency chaps* Marx presumably meant the Birmingham school of 'little shilling men', so called after the Birmingham banker Thomas Attwood who founded it. This school's views were expounded in *The Currency Question. The Gemini Letters,* London, 1844 written anonymously by Thomas Wright and John Harlow, calling themselves the 'Gemini'.—275

360 *Papal aggression* here means Pope Pius IX's interference in Anglican Church matters. On 30 September 1850 the Pope issued a bull establishing several Catholic bishoprics in England and appointing Nicholas Wiseman Archbishop of Westminster and Cardinal. In reply to this, the Whig Prime Minister, Lord John Russell, carried a bill through Parliament in 1851 forbidding any clergyman not belonging to the Anglican Church to assume the title of bishop. The bill in fact remained a dead letter.—279

361 The reference is to the commission of 17 Orleanist and Legitimist deputies to the Legislative Assembly appointed by the Minister of the Interior on 1 May 1850 to draft a new electoral law. Its members were nicknamed burgraves, a name borrowed from the title of Victor Hugo's historical drama as an allusion to their unwarranted claims to power and their reactionary aspirations. The drama is set in medieval Germany where a *Burggraf* was governor of a *Burg* (city) or a district, appointed by the Emperor.—280

362 *Church Street*—a street in London where the Fraternal Society of French Socialist Democrats had its seat. The Society included different elements of the French emigration in London, Ledru-Rollin and Louis Blanc were among its members. The Society was founded in the autumn of 1850 for the purpose of providing material assistance to French political emigrants (see also this volume, p. 292).
    24 February was the anniversary of the February 1848 revolution in France.—283, 292, 309, 312, 314

363 A reference to Eccarius' contribution to Harney's journal *The Friend of the People;* Nos. 4-7 of 4, 11, 18 and 25 January 1851 carried Eccarius' article 'The Last Stage of Bourgeois Society'.—285

364 In February 1851 the Party of Order (a bloc of monarchist parties of Legitimists and Orleanists) in coalition with the Mountain party in the Legislative Assembly rejected by a majority of 102 votes a motion to grant President Louis Napoleon a supplementary provision of 1,800,000 francs.—286, 504

365 A reference to a conflict between Prussia and Switzerland over the principality of Neuchâtel and Valangin which prior to 1848 was under Prussian rule, but

which since 1815 had been incorporated into the Swiss Confederation as a canton. In February 1848 a bourgeois revolution broke out in Neuchâtel and a republic was proclaimed. However only in 1857 under pressure from France did Prussia give up its claims to Neuchâtel and Valangin.—288

366 An allusion to Montalembert, a representative of the monarchist coalition (the Party of Order), who in February 1851 supported in the Legislative Assembly the motion to grant Louis Napoleon a supplementary provision of 1,800,000 francs. The majority of the Party of Order voted against (see also Note 364).—288

367 The letter Engels intended to send to Harney on 14 February 1851 has not been found.
   On Engels' planned articles, see Note 352.—289

368 A reference to the Central Committee of European Democracy (see Note 338).—292

369 The reference is to the *Labour Commission* which sat at the Luxembourg Palace from 28 February to 16 May 1848 and was presided over by Louis Blanc (see Note 213).
   The *Pre-parliament,* which sat at Frankfurt am Main from 31 March to 4 April 1848, consisted of representatives of the German states, mostly constitutional monarchists. On a motion of the Pre-parliament a *Committee of Fifty* was formed which was to provide, in agreement with the United Diet, for the convocation of an all-German National Assembly. The Pre-parliament worked out the 'Fundamental Rights and Demands of the German People'. This document proclaimed some rights and freedoms, but it did not actually affect the foundation of the semi-feudal absolutist regime prevalent in Germany at the time.—293

370 An allusion to a governmental crisis in Britain. In February 1851 the Prime Minister, Lord John Russell, resigned after failing in his opposition to M.P. Locke King's motion to assimilate the county to the borough franchise. However, the Tory leader Stanley failed to form a cabinet and in March Russell again became Prime Minister.—296

371 In the original Marx used the term *Haupt- und Staatsaktion* ('principal and spectacular action', 'main and state action') which has a double meaning. First, in the seventeenth and the first half of the eighteenth century, it denoted plays performed by German touring companies. Second, this term can denote major political events. It was used in this sense by a trend in German historical writing known as 'objective historiography', of which Leopold Ranke was one of the chief representatives, regarding *Haupt- und Staatsaktion* as history's main subject-matter.—297, 437

372 These cries were used at the meeting to get those present to deal with Pieper and Schramm in the same way as the workers of the Barclay, Perkins & Co. did with the Austrian Field Marshal Julius Haynau, who directed the suppression of the revolution in Italy and Hungary. Haynau was attacked by workers during a visit to Britain in September 1850.—298, 309

373 Engels' letters to Wilhelm Wolff, who was in Zurich (Switzerland) at the time and did not come to London till early July 1851, have not been found.—301

374 This may mean *Le Constitutionnel,* the issue No. 58 of which on 27 February 1851 carried a report of the so-called 'banquet of the equals' held on 24 February on the initiative of Louis Blanc, Willich, Schapper and other emigrants to mark the anniversary of the February 1848 revolution.—303

375 Harney joined Marx and Engels in officially breaking with the Blanquists and the members of the Willich-Schapper separatist group who supported them. The result was the cancellation of the previously concluded agreement to establish a Universal Society of Revolutionary Communists (see Note 313).—304

376 A reference to Ferdinand Wolff's letter sent to Engels from London on 25 February 1851. Wolff wrote about the clearly unrealistic plans to publish, in order to make money, a guide-book in Russian for the Great Exhibition which was to open in May 1851, and asked for Engels' advice.—305

377 Neither of the two versions—of 26 and 27 February 1851—of Engels' letter to Harney has been found.—306

378 An allusion to the false accusation made against Marx's and Engels' associates, Heinrich Bauer and Karl Pfänder, of appropriating money belonging to the German Workers' Educational Society in London (see Note 328).—307

379 An allusion to a duel between Conrad Schramm and August Willich on 11 September 1850 in Belgium in which Schramm was slightly wounded. Schramm challenged Willich because the latter had insulted him at a meeting of the Communist League Central Authority at the end of August 1850 during heated disputes between supporters of Marx and Engels and adherents of the Willich-Schapper separatist group.—307, 473, 552

380 The *Aliens Bill,* enacted by the British Parliament in 1793, was renewed in 1802, 1803, 1816, 1818 and, finally, in 1848 (An Act to Authorise for One Year, and to the End of the Then Next Session of Parliament, the Removal of Aliens from the Realm). In 1850 public opinion obstructed the renewal of this Bill despite Conservative efforts.—308, 312, 358

381 Marx's invitation to Ernest Jones of 27 February 1851 and another note mentioned earlier have not been found.—312

382 Early in March 1851 Engels went to London for a few days to improve relations with the Chartists which deteriorated after Conrad Schramm and Wilhelm Pieper had been man-handled at the 'banquet of the equals' (see Note 374). Simultaneously, Marx and Engels took steps to expose Louis Blanc, Willich, Schapper and other organisers of the banquet. By that time it had transpired that the latter had deliberately kept secret the text of the toast sent by Auguste Blanqui from the Belle-Isle prison, in which he exposed Louis Blanc, Ledru-Rollin and other members of the Provisional Government of the French Republic as traitors to the revolution. However, the text of the toast was published in *La Patrie* (No. 58, 27 February 1851) and other newspapers. Marx and Engels translated it into German and English. The German version with a short preface written by them was sent to Cologne and printed in leaflet form, giving Berne as the place of publication (see present edition, Vol. 10, pp. 537-39).

  During his stay in London, on 5 March, Engels apparently wrote a letter to the editor of *The Times* refuting a false declaration of Louis Blanc, published in that day's issue of the paper, that Blanqui's toast was never received by the organisers of the 'banquet of the equals'. Engels enclosed the English translation of Blanqui's toast for publication in *The Times*. But neither the letter nor the translation was published.—312, 381

[383] This refers to the banquet organised in London on 13 March 1851 by a group of emigrants to mark the anniversary of the March revolution in Vienna. Marx and Engels gave their assessment of the banquet in *The Great Men of the Exile* (see present edition, Vol. 11, p. 297).—317

[384] Vidil was one of the six members of the organising committee of the banquet held on 24 February 1851 who voted for Blanqui's toast to be read out. Seven committee members voted against. Yet the statement in *La Patrie*, No. 67 of 7 March, denying reception of Blanqui's toast, was also signed by six committee members, including Vidil. Marx drew attention to this in his letter to Engels of 22 March 1851 (see this volume, p. 321). Later Marx and Engels described in detail in *The Great Men of the Exile* how the attempts to keep Blanqui's toast secret had been exposed. They also included in the pamphlet a passage from *La Patrie*, No. 71 of 12 March 1851 (see present edition, Vol. 11, p. 296) which Marx quoted in his letter of 17 March.—319

[385] *Landwehr* (the army reserve) in Prussia was formed at the time of the struggle against Napoleonic rule. In the 1840s it was made up of persons up to forty years of age who had served three years in the army and been on the reserve list for at least two years. As distinct from the regular troops, the army reserve was mobilised only in special emergencies (war or threat of war). In the autumn of 1850, in connection with the aggravation of the Austro-Prussian conflict, the Prussian Government mobilised the army reserve.—320, 382, 460, 560

[386] During the liberation war of the Spanish people against Napoleonic rule the French twice laid siege to Saragossa: from 15 June to 14 August 1808 and from 20 December 1808 to 20 February 1809. The city withstood the first siege but fell after resisting the second heroically for two months.

Engels' remark about the second siege of Saragossa is his own interpretation of an episode described by W.F.P. Napier in his *History of the War in the Peninsula...*, Vol. II, London, 1832, p. 51.—320

[387] The beginning of this letter was written on the last page of Wilhelm Pieper's letter to Engels of 22 March 1851 in which Pieper on Marx's request cites the full text of the proclamation 'To the Germans' issued by Ruge, Struve, Haug, Ronge and Kinkel on 13 March 1851 on behalf of the Committee for German Affairs ('Der Ausschuss für die deutschen Gelegenheiten') set up by them at the time.

An abridged version of the proclamation was quoted by Marx and Engels in *The Great Men of the Exile* (see present edition, Vol. 11, pp. 297-98).—321

[388] Marx has in mind the *Weltgeschichte* which Struve was working upon at the time and which was published by him in 9 volumes in New York, beginning in 1856. In 1864 it was published in 6 volumes in Coburg.—322

[389] Neither of Marx's two letters to his mother mentioned here, or the notification of the bill on her he had made out to Simon Bamberger, has been found.—323

[390] This presumably refers to the will of Jenny Marx's Scottish relative who died in the early 1850s. Under this will Jenny inherited about £200.—324

[391] An ironical allusion to Proudhon's assertion in *La philosophie de la misère* that 'since in society time is value itself, the railway would, prices being equal,

present an advantage of 400 per cent over road transport'. For criticism of this proposition see Marx's *The Poverty of Philosophy* (present edition, Vol. 6, pp. 153-55).—325

392 Marx visited Engels in Manchester in the second half of April 1851 and stayed from about 17 to 26 April.—325, 335

393 Exactly what was Marx's plan mentioned here and in Engels' letter to Marx of 3 April 1851 has not been established. Most likely Marx intended to prepare publication in two volumes of works summing up the experience of the 1848-49 revolution in Europe. This seems to emerge from Marx's suggestion that Engels should write a survey of the revolutionary war in Hungary in 1848-49 for this publication.
    Blue Books—periodical collections of documents of the British Parliament and Foreign Office. The first were published in the seventeenth century.—325

394 The letter to Roland Daniels, containing Marx's analysis of Daniels' manuscript *Mikrokosmos. Entwurf einer physiologischen Anthropologie* which the author sent to Marx in mid-February 1851 requesting his opinion of it and a preface to it, is not extant. Judging by Daniels' reply of 25 March 1851 (which Marx forwarded to Engels), Marx's letter containing critical notes on the manuscript was dated 20 March.—326

395 In the battle of Jena on 14 October 1806 a considerable Prussian force was defeated by Napoleon's army and another was beaten on the same day at Auerstadt by Marshal Davu's army.—329

396 In the battle at Marengo (Northern Italy) on 14 June 1800 the French army under Napoleon Bonaparte defeated the Austrians. This battle decided France's victory over the forces of the second anti-French coalition (1798-1801).—329, 504

397 The *Thirty Years' War*, 1618-48—a European war, in which the Pope, the Spanish and Austrian Habsburgs and the German Catholic princes rallied under the banner of Catholicism and fought against the Protestant countries: Bohemia, Denmark, Sweden, the Republic of the Netherlands and a number of German states. The rulers of Catholic France—rivals of the Habsburgs—supported the Protestant camp.—329

398 Engels compares the policy of some Tory leaders who made forced concessions to the bourgeoisie, with the military tactics of Wellington in the Peninsular war of 1808-14, when the Anglo-Portuguese army under his command retreated to the fortified line at Torres Vedras (near Lisbon) in the autumn of 1810. Wellington left covering forces along the French line of advance which the enemy could overcome only after stubborn fighting. As a result, when the French troops reached Torres Vedras they were so exhausted that they could not attack the fortifications and were compelled to withdraw to the Spanish border in March 1811.—333

399 Marx's letter to Wilhelm Wolff of 11 April 1851 has not been found.—333

400 *Parliamentary trains*—name given in England in the nineteenth century to trains, which under a law of 1844 each railway company had to run once a day at a speed of twelve miles per hour, fares not exceeding one penny per mile.—335

401 On Marx's stay in Manchester see Note 392.—336

402 In the battle of Austerlitz (now Slavkow in Czechoslovakia) on 2 December 1805 the French army under Napoleon defeated the allied Russo-Austrian forces thus predetermining the defeat of the third anti-French coalition.—336

403 On 25 April 1851 Cologne's deputy burgomaster Schenk, welcoming Prince William of Prussia on his arrival there, expressed gratitude on behalf of the City Council for suppression of the 1848-49 revolution in Prussia. In reply the Prince declared that his army was prepared to suppress any revolutionary movement at any time, but that the Cologne press should 'reform'. Schenk's speech aroused the dissatisfaction of the City Council.—337

404 Engels refers to Wolff's plans to emigrate from Switzerland to the USA. In March 1851 Wolff received through Anneke an offer of a post as editor of the *Illinois Staats-Zeitung*, while his Silesian friend Voidechovsky invited him to teach at a high school for girls at St. Louis (Missouri). Meanwhile, on 13 March an expulsion order was issued against him. In his letter to Marx of 5 April Wolff asked for assistance in getting a passport and money to go to England and on to the USA via Liverpool. Engels did his utmost to get passports and money for Wolff and Dronke through the Cologne Central Authority of the Communist League. About 9 June 1851 Wolff arrived in London and remained in England.—339, 342

405 On Engels' journey from Switzerland to England see Note 290.—340

406 Engels may have in mind Marx's and his prospective crossing the Atlantic to settle in the USA. No documents have been found to prove this, but the perspective may have occurred to them in the summer of 1850. That was when Marx wrote to Joseph Weydemeyer that if the Whig ministry were to fall they would be 'the Tories' first victims', in which case 'long-intended expulsion' would become a probability (see this volume, p. 240).—341

407 This apparently refers to the so-called Committee for German Affairs (see Note 387).—342

408 Marx's letter to Roland Daniels written on about 4 May 1851 has not been found.—343

409 A reference to *Notes to the People* (at first the title was intended to be *Poems and Notes to the People*)—the Chartist weekly published in London from 1851 to 1852 and edited by Ernest Jones. Since Harney had then drawn closer to the petty-bourgeois democrats, the publication of this periodical—the mouthpiece of the revolutionary proletarian wing of the Chartists—assumed exceptional importance.—346

410 Despite this conjecture Freiligrath moved from Cologne to London in the second half of May 1851 (see this volume, pp. 355, 359). Of the other members of the *Neue Rheinische Zeitung* editorial board (not counting Heinrich Bürgers, who was only so in name), Marx and Ferdinand Wolff were already in London; Wilhelm Wolff and Ernst Dronke were expected and Engels planned to go to London in the second half of May, and as emerges from his letters he did arrive there at the end of the month (see this volume, pp. 365, 373). Georg Weerth, then in England, also intended to go to London but did not do so until July.—346, 361, 366

411 Engels suggests that Wellington, a supporter of the Corn Laws (see Note 270), was compelled, as a minister without portfolio in Peel's Government, to promote their repeal in 1846. Engels compares Wellington's defeat with that of

the Roman legions in the Caudine pass during the second Samnite war in 321 B.C. The Romans were compelled to pass under the yoke which was the greatest disgrace for a defeated army. Hence the expression 'to pass under the Caudine yoke', meaning to undergo extreme humiliation.—347

412 An allusion to Mazzini's exposure of Sir James Graham, the British Home Secretary, on whose order letters of Italian revolutionary emigrants, including the Bandiera brothers and Mazzini, were opened. The letters of the Bandiera brothers contained the plan of their expedition to Calabria to spark off an insurrection in Italy against the Bourbons of Naples and Austrian rule. In June 1844 the participants in the expedition were arrested. The Bandiera brothers were shot.—349

413 The members of the Cologne Central Authority of the Communist League planned to start a periodical in Cologne. On 5 April 1851 Hermann Becker informed Marx that he, Bürgers, Daniels, Weydemeyer and others intended to publish a monthly, the *Neue Zeitschrift,* and asked for articles. Marx agreed to contribute and on 8 April he asked Georg Weerth (who was in Hamburg at the time) to write an article against Gottfried Kinkel. Early in May, on Becker's request, Marx sent his *Poverty of Philosophy* for him to publish excerpts from it in the *Neue Zeitschrift.* But as early as mid-May Becker was compelled to abandon the idea of starting a periodical because of lack of funds and harassment by the police. The subsequent arrests of Communist League members in Germany made its publication impossible.—351

414 Engels' letter written on about 12-13 May 1851 has not been found.—354

415 Marx's letter to Engels apparently in reply to Engels' letter of 9 May 1851 (see this volume, pp. 350-53) has not been found.—354

416 In this letter and the reply to it written on 19 May 1851, Marx and Engels discussed the situation in France and noted that there were two ways in which the bourgeoisie could succeed in its attempt to maintain the existing very unstable state of affairs: either by prolonging Louis Bonaparte's powers, which were to expire in May 1852 or by electing Cavaignac, another pretender to dictatorship, to the presidency. A section of the bourgeoisie favoured the second solution (see present edition, Vol. 11, p. 172).—355

417 Nicholas I, Emperor of Russia, Prince William of Prussia and Emperor Francis Joseph I of Austria and their ministers met in Warsaw in October 1850 (see Note 332).—355

418 The reference is to an uprising which began in April 1851 against the reactionary dictatorial regime established in Portugal by the Costa Cabral Government representing the extreme monarchist bourgeoisie and the land-owners. The uprising ended in May, with Costa Cabral fleeing from the country and Marshal Saldanha, a representative of the liberal-constitutional section of the big bourgeoisie, coming to power.—356, 358

419 'German Catholicism'—a religious movement which arose in a number of German states in 1844 and spread to a considerable section of the middle and petty bourgeoisie. 'German Catholicism' did not recognise the supremacy of the Pope, rejected many dogmas and rites of the Roman Catholic Church and sought to adapt Catholicism to the needs of the German bourgeoisie.—357

420 In 1851 Bonapartist circles strongly advocated a revision of the Constitution of
     the French Republic adopted on 4 November 1848, in particular the articles
     defining the presidential powers. Under that Constitution the president of the
     Republic was elected for four years and could not be reelected till four years
     after his term of office had expired. For details see Marx's 'The Constitution of
     the French Republic Adopted November 4, 1848' (present edition, Vol. 10,
     pp. 567-80).—357, 363, 367, 484

421 This refers to the law adopted by the French Legislative Assembly on 31 May
     1850 abolishing universal suffrage. It introduced a veiled property qualification
     of three years' permanent residence in the given locality and payment of
     personal tax.—358

422 The *Manchester School*—a trend in economic thinking which reflected the
     interests of the industrial bourgeoisie. Its supporters, known as Free Traders
     (the centre of their agitation was Manchester), advocated free trade and
     non-interference by government in the economy. In the 1840s and 1850s the
     Free Traders formed a separate political group which later constituted the Left
     wing of the Liberal Party.—358

423 Engels visited Marx in London presumably on 31 May 1851 and stayed for two
     weeks, till about 15 June.—361, 365, 373

424 *Wasserpolackei*—a name denoting Silesia, and derived from *Wasserpolacken*—
     original name of the Oder ferrymen who were mainly natives of Upper Silesia;
     subsequently it became widespread in Germany as a nickname for Silesian
     Poles.—362

425 Frederick William IV in his New-Year Greeting 'To My Army' (1 January 1849)
     gave this name to the troops who suppressed the 1848-49 revolution and
     helped to carry out the coup d'état in Prussia on 5 December 1848 (see
     K. Marx, 'A New-Year Greeting', present edition, Vol. 8, pp. 222-26).—362

426 Below Engels analyses German policy towards Poland not in an abstract way
     but from a definite perspective which might have opened up if a revolutionary
     democratic movement had taken shape and prevailed in Germany, and a
     people's revolution against tsarism had simultaneously developed in Russia. It is
     clear from the letter that Engels considered the political line he recommends
     here to be appropriate only on condition that the national movement in Poland
     proper did not go beyond the limits of landowners' (szlachta) demands and, as
     had often happened in the past, ignored the task of emancipating the
     peasantry from the feudal yoke. This letter therefore reflects the striving of
     Marx and Engels to consider the nationalities question from the concrete
     historical standpoint and to link its solution with the general interests of the
     revolutionary movement.
        When, some years later, Marx and Engels realised that the situation in
     Central and Eastern Europe had not changed and that counter-revolutionary
     regimes continued to reign supreme in Germany and Russia, whereas in the
     Polish national movement there was a continual strengthening of the influence
     of the revolutionary-democratic elements which had played a prominent part in
     the 1863-64 uprising, they were as Lenin put it 'treating the Polish movement
     with the most profound and ardent sympathy' (V. I. Lenin, *Collected Works*,
     Vol. 20, p. 436).—363

427 Engels enumerates here Byelorussian, Lithuanian and Ukrainian lands which
     formed part of the Polish state (Rzecz Pospolita) and were ceded to Russia after

the three partitions of Poland in 1772, 1793 and 1795, between Russia, Prussia and—apart from the second partition—Austria.

Below Engels uses the term by which West-European scholars denoted the Ukrainian population of Galicia and Bukovina who came under the Habsburg rule as a result of Poland's partitions. In this particular case Engels calls all Ukrainians Ruthenians.— 364

428 For details on the arrest of Hermann Becker and Heinrich Bürgers see Note 430.— 366

429 Marx's letters to Daniels mentioned here have not been found.— 366

430 Peter Nothjung was arrested in Leipzig on 10 May 1851 during his tour of Northern Germany as emissary of the Cologne Central Authority of the Communist League. Marx was informed of this by Hermann Haupt in a letter from Hamburg of 22 May 1851. Haupt for his part referred to information sent to him by Heinrich Bürgers in Berlin. The police discovered on Nothjung a mandate of the Central Authority, the March 1850 Address of the Central Authority and the new Rules of the Communist League (see present edition, Vol. 10, pp. 277-87 and 634-36). In the same letter Haupt wrote about the arrest of Hermann Becker and Peter Röser in Cologne on 19 May 1851. Documents compromising Heinrich Bürgers were found on them. At the time Bürgers was away, having gone to Hamburg and then on to Berlin. The police did not find anything incriminating when they searched his apartment in Cologne on 19 May. Bürgers was arrested in Dresden on 23 May 1851 according to a report in the *Kölnische Zeitung* on 27 May, to which Freiligrath drew Marx's attention.

Arrests of the League's Central Authority members in Germany were followed by police repression against participants in the working-class movement.— 366

431 The reference is to the false information which Minister of the Interior Léon Faucher sent by telegraph to the prefects during the elections to the Legislative Assembly in May 1849. In it he intimidated the voters with a possible repetition of the events of June 1848 to make them vote for the Right-wing candidates.

On the law of 31 May 1850 see Note 421.— 367

432 In *The Great Men of the Exile,* in which this article from *Der Kosmos* was quoted, Marx and Engels note that it was written by Johanna Mockel, Kinkel's wife (see present edition, Vol. 11, p. 258).— 368

433 All that remains of this letter is an excerpt quoted by Roland Daniels in his letter to Marx of 1 June 1851.— 368

434 Roland Daniels was arrested on 13 June 1851. During the search the police did not find any documents compromising him.— 369

435 An excerpt from this letter was published in English for the first time in: K. Marx and F. Engels, *Letters to Americans. 1848-1895,* New York, 1953.— 370, 375, 518

436 Engels was promoted to bombardier in the autumn of 1841 when he was doing his twelve months military service as a volunteer in an artillery brigade in Berlin.

Landwehr—see Note 385.— 370

437 Engels uses the words 'persecution of Jews' here, for security reasons, meaning the arrests of Communist League members which had begun in Germany. Marx uses the same formulation with the same meaning in his letter to Engels of 13 July 1851. Similarly, Freiligrath when writing to Marx called the London district of the League the 'synagogue'.—372, 384

438 The reference is to the Address of the Cologne Central Authority of the Communist League of 1 December 1850, which was discovered by the police during the arrests of Communist League members in Dresden and published in the *Kölnische Zeitung* and other bourgeois papers in June 1851. On the whole, the authors of the Address, especially Bürgers, supported Marx and Engels in their condemnation of the splitting activities of the Willich-Schapper group. They stated in the Address that the Cologne Central Authority was expelling from the League all the members of the separatist union set up by Willich and Schapper. However, instead of disclosing the real causes of the split in the League, the Address put the blame partially on Marx and his followers. Some propositions set forth in the Address were vague and obscure.—374, 384, 390

439 On the new Rules of the Communist League see Note 342. The first paragraph of the Rules said: 'The *aim* of the Communist League is to bring about the destruction of the old society—and *the overthrow of the bourgeoisie*—the spiritual, political and economic emancipation of the proletariat, the communist revolution, using all the resources of propaganda and political struggle towards this goal...' (see present edition, Vol. 10, p. 634).—374

440 Marx hints that Ruge was a member of the Central Committee of European Democracy (see Note 338).—376

441 Engels has in mind the split in the Communist League and Marx's, his own and their followers' withdrawal from the German Workers' Educational Society in London (see Note 328).—380

442 This refers to the Central Committee of European Democracy (see Note 338).—380

443 In the autumn of 1850 the struggle between Austria and Prussia for supremacy in Germany was aggravated as a result of a conflict between them over Hesse-Cassel. Revolutionary actions in Hesse-Cassel were used by Austria and Prussia as a pretext for interfering in the electorate's internal affairs each party claiming the right to suppress them. The Prussian Government reacted to the entry of Austrian troops into Hesse-Cassel by mobilising and sending its own troops there in November 1850. But under pressure from Nicholas I Prussia yielded to Austria without offering any serious resistance.—381

444 Marx's letter to Louis Schulz, written on about 17 July 1851, has not been found. It follows from the text below that Marx may have used this address when writing to the lawyer Adolph Bermbach on matters concerning the Cologne accused.—388

445 No information is available on Engels' letter to Klose, presumably written on 17 July 1851.—389

446 J. F. Martens was soon released for lack of evidence and emigrated to London.—389

447 Engels has in mind the following passage from the March (1850) Address of the Central Authority to the League: 'Far from opposing so-called excesses,

instances of popular revenge against hated individuals or public buildings that
are associated only with hateful recollections, such instances must not only be
tolerated but the lead in them must be taken' (see present edition, Vol. 10,
p. 282).—389

448 This letter was published in English for the first time with abridgments in: Karl
Marx and Friedrich Engels, *Correspondence. 1846-1895*, London, 1934, and in
full in: K. Marx and F. Engels, *Selected Correspondence,* Foreign Languages
Publishing House, Moscow, 1955.—392

449 Haupt in fact played an unseemly role in the legal proceedings against the
Communist League members in Germany. Arrested on 22 or 23 May 1851, he
gave evidence which was used as incriminating material against the accused by
investigators and the police, who were preparing a case of 'communist
conspiracy' (it came up for trial in Cologne in the autumn of 1852).—392

450 This letter was first published in English abridged in *The Letters of Karl Marx*,
selected and translated with explanatory notes and an introduction by Saul
K. Padover, Prentice-Hall, Inc., Englewood Cliff, New Jersey, 1979.—396, 397

451 Friedrich Lessner was arrested in his tailor's shop in Mainz on 18 June 1851,
and made an abortive attempt to escape. While searching his flat the police
discovered a large library of communist literature including such books as the
Manifesto of the Communist Party, 'Demands of the Communist Party in
Germany' and the Rules of the workers' educational societies in London,
Cologne, Mainz. Lessner was detained in the Mainz prison till July 1852, when
he was transferred to Cologne and soon included in the group of the accused
in the Cologne communist trial.—399

452 An allusion to Wilhelm Wolff's articles and statements of the 1848-49
revolution period in which he castigated the enemies of the revolution, and also
to the series of articles *Die Schlesische Milliarde*, published in the *Neue Rheinische
Zeitung* from 22 March to 25 April 1849, in which he exposed the plundering
of the peasants by the Junkers in his native Silesia, which he represented at the
Frankfurt National Assembly.
     Marx and Engels did not carry out their plan to put out lithographed
bulletins.—400

453 Engels could prepare an article for Ernest Jones only in the beginning of 1852.
His article 'Real Causes Why the French Proletarians Remained Comparatively
Inactive in December Last' was published in *Notes to the People*, Nos. 43, 48 and
50 of 21 February, 27 March and 10 April 1852 (see present edition, Vol. 11,
pp. 212-22).—401

454 In May and June 1850 the Prussian Government tried through Baron Bunsen,
its envoy in London, to get the British Government to deport Marx, Engels and
other emigrants it considered hostile to its interests. For this purpose Prussian
police agents organised the shadowing of emigrants (see K. Marx and
F. Engels, 'The Prussian Refugees', 'Prussian Spies in London', present edition,
Vol. 10, pp. 378-79, 381-84). In 1851 the Prussian Government again tried to
get the *Hauptrevolutionäre* ('chief revolutionaries') deported from Britain to the
colonies. In March 1851, at the request of the Minister of the Interior—
Ferdinand von Westphalen, Jenny Marx's stepbrother—the Prussian Prime
Minister, Otto Manteuffel, inquired of Bunsen whether the British Government
would consent to such a deportation. Bunsen replied that, fearing public
opinion, the English authorities hesitated to take such measures. Nevertheless,

Ferdinand von Westphalen did not abandon his intention to persuade the British Government to deport the emigrants, in the first place Prussians, and continued using police agents to collect material compromising them.—401

455 An allusion to the German Emigration Club set up in London on 27 July 1851 on the initiative of Kinkel, Willich and the groups of refugees supporting them. In August 1851 the rival German Agitation Club, headed by Ruge, Tausenau, Fickler, Haug and others, was set up to counter it. The rivalry between these two refugee associations and the vain attempts to achieve agreement between them are described in satirical form in Marx's and Engels' *The Great Men of the Exile* (see present edition, Vol. 11, pp. 317-25).—403

456 Weydemeyer met the Swiss officer Gustav Hoffstetter, author of *Tagebuch aus Italien 1849* (Zurich-Stuttgart, 1851), in Zurich at the time.—405

457 On the Baden-Palatinate military campaign in the summer of 1849 and Engels' participation in it see notes 264 and 265.—406

458 Engels ironically gave this name to the deputies of the all-German Frankfurt National Assembly, who took part in drawing up the Imperial Constitution which was adopted by the Assembly on 27 March 1849, but was rejected by the German princes and their governments.—407

459 Informing Weydemeyer of the break-up of the community of Willich's supporters formed according to the principles of barracks communism, Engels hinted at Willich's earlier experiments along this line in forming a military unit out of German émigré workers and artisans in Besançon (France) in November 1848. The members of this unit received an allowance from the French Government but it was stopped at the beginning of 1849. Later the unit was incorporated in Willich's detachment which took part in the Baden-Palatinate uprising in May-June 1849.—407

460 On the Hamburg affair and Haupt's unseemly behaviour during the investigation see notes 430 and 449.—407

461 About 8 August 1851 Marx was invited by Charles Dana, editor of the *New-York Daily Tribune*, to contribute to that paper. Because of the progressive orientation of the newspaper and its wide circulation Marx agreed. He contributed from August 1851 till March 1862; at Marx's request many of the articles for the *New-York Daily Tribune* were written by Engels (beginning with the series *Revolution and Counter-Revolution in Germany*, the first of which was dispatched to New York in August 1851). Marx began to send his own articles to the newspaper in August 1852.

Marx's and Engels' articles in the *New-York Daily Tribune* dealt with major questions of foreign and home policy, the working-class movement, economic development in the European countries, colonial expansion, and the national liberation movement in oppressed and dependent countries. The articles at once attracted attention by the amount of information they conveyed, the clarity of their political analysis and their literary qualities. Many of the articles were reprinted in the *Tribune*'s special editions, the *New-York Weekly Tribune* and the *New-York Semi-Weekly Tribune*, and were quoted by other American newspapers.

The editors of the *New-York Daily Tribune* arbitrarily printed some of Marx's and Engels' articles without the author's signature as editorial leading articles, and occasionally made insertions and additions which were sometimes at variance with their content. Marx repeatedly protested against this. In the autumn of 1857, as a result of the economic crisis in the USA, which also affected the newspaper's finances, Marx had to reduce the number of his contributions. His final break with the newspaper occurred during the Civil War in the United States, and was largely due to the fact that its editorial policies increasingly supported compromise with the slave-owning states, and to its decline in support for progressive views.—409

462 An allusion to an episode in the struggle between the plebeians and patricians in Ancient Rome described by Livy in his *Ab urbe condita libri*. Tradition has it that Menenius Agrippa persuaded the plebeians who had rebelled and withdrawn to the Mons Sacer in 494 B.C. to submit by telling them the fable about the other parts of the human body revolting against the stomach because, they said, it consumed food and did no work, but afterwards realising that they could not exist without it.—417

463 *American Whigs* were members of a political party in the USA mainly representing the interests of the industrial and financial bourgeoisie and supported by some of the plantation owners. The American Whig Party existed from 1838 to 1854, when the intensified struggle over slavery gave rise to splits and regroupings in the political parties of the country. In 1854 the majority of the Whigs, together with a section of the Democratic Party and the farmers' party (Free-Soilers), formed the Republican Party, which opposed slavery. The Right-wing Whigs joined the Democratic Party, which defended the interests of the slave-owning planters.—419

464 At Marx's request Engels prepared the 'Critical Review of Proudhon's Book *Idée générale de la révolution au XIXᵉ siècle*' (see present edition, Vol. 11, pp. 545-70). Engels worked on it in August (approximately from 16 to 21) and from mid-October. He sent the material to Marx at the end of October 1851 (see this volume, pp. 488, 495). Marx's attempt to publish a pamphlet against Proudhon with Hoffmann and Campe, book-sellers in Hamburg, failed but he did not give up his plans to produce a critique of Proudhon's work. At the end of 1851 he hoped to publish this in the USA, because in the autumn of 1851 Weydemeyer moved to the United States and intended to publish the weekly *Die Revolution* in New York from January 1852 (see this volume, p. 519). But Marx's plans did not materialise because publication of the journal ceased.—423

465 At Marx's request Engels wrote in thirteen months (from August 1851 to September 1852) a series of 19 articles about the 1848-49 German revolution—*Revolution and Counter-Revolution in Germany*—for the *New-York Daily Tribune* (see present edition, Vol. 11, pp. 3-96). Engels used a file of the *Neue Rheinische Zeitung* as the main source apart from some additional material given to him by Marx, whom he constantly consulted. Marx read all the articles before mailing them to the newspaper.

The series of articles, *Revolution and Counter-Revolution in Germany*, was printed in the *New-York Daily Tribune* from 25 October 1851 to 23 October 1852 over the signature of Karl Marx, the paper's official correspondent. Only in 1913, when the correspondence of Marx and Engels was published, did it become known that this work was written by Engels.—425

466 Marx sent this document to the German journalist Hermann Ebner, apparently through Freiligrath. A copy with the beginning and the end missing and written in an unknown hand is extant. Ebner, it transpired later, was a secret agent of the Austrian police to whom he delivered material emanating from

Marx, including this letter and that of 2 December 1851 published below, the original of which has survived but with the beginning missing (see this volume, pp. 499-503). Both documents found their way, via the Ministry of the Interior and the Ministry of Foreign Affairs, into the Austrian state archives where they were discovered in the mid-1950s.

In his letter to Ebner of 2 December 1851 Marx called this document a 'communication' and in fact in some passages it is more like an article than a private letter. Marx chose this form purposely. Having no idea of Ebner's spying activities he hoped to use the latter's journalistic connections to have published in the German press documents revealing the intrigues of the German and other petty-bourgeois emigrants, refuting their slander of the proletarian revolutionaries. The letters to Ebner, especially the first one, were therefore written so as to form parts of articles for eventual publication. For Marx himself these letters were the first draft of *The Great Men of the Exile* which he later wrote together with Engels; in some places the texts coincide.

The extant part of the letter has no date. The approximate date of writing has been established by the mention made in the letter of the emigrants' meetings in London on 8 and 15 August 1851 but not of the third meeting, which took place on 22 August and about which Marx wrote to Engels on 25 August 1851 (see this volume, pp. 440-42).—426

467 An allusion to the former deputies to the Prussian National Assembly convened in Berlin during the revolution in May 1848 to draft a constitution by 'agreement with the Crown'. The Prussian liberal bourgeoisie and the moderate democrats used the 'theory of agreement' in an attempt to justify their policy of compromise during the revolution.—426, 437, 446

468 An allusion to Ruge's participation in the Central Committee of European Democracy (see Note 338).—426

469 The reference is to the Committee for German Affairs (see Note 387).—427

470 From the end of 1850 to February 1851 Joseph Radowitz, then Prussian Minister of Foreign Affairs, was in London trying to conclude an official alliance between Prussia and Britain. His attempts met with no sympathy among British ruling circles.—427

471 The London German weekly *How Do You Do?* published insulting allusions to Marx's family connection with the Prussian Minister of the Interior, Ferdinand von Westphalen (Jenny Marx's stepbrother). On 19 August 1851 Marx, accompanied by Freiligrath and Wilhelm Wolff, went to the office of the paper and demanded satisfaction of the publisher Louis Drucker and the editor Heinrich Beta.—432

472 The *Historical School of Law*—a trend in German historiography and jurisprudence which emerged in the late eighteenth century. The representatives of this school—Gustav Hugo, Friedrich Karl Savigny and others—sought to justify feudal institutions and the privileges of the nobility on the grounds of the inviolability of historical tradition.—435

473 A reference to an emigrant organisation—the German Agitation Club—set up in London in August 1851 by Ruge, Fickler, Tausenau and others to counter the Emigration Club (see Note 455) directed by Kinkel and his followers.—439, 520

474 The *Federal Diet*—a representative body of the German Confederation, an ephemeral union of German states, founded in 1815 by decision of the Congress of Vienna. Though it had no real power, it was nevertheless a vehicle for feudal and monarchical reaction. During the 1848-49 revolution in Germany, reactionary circles made vain attempts to revive the Federal Diet, intending to use it to prevent the democratic unification of Germany. After the defeat of the revolution, the Federal Diet was reestablished in its former rights in 1850 and survived till 1866.—443, 540

475 Engels' letter to Fischer has not been found.—444

476 Marx apparently has in mind the treaty between the USA and Britain (known as the Clayton-Bulwer treaty), signed in Washington on 19 April 1850, on the cutting of a navigable canal from the Atlantic to the Pacific across Nicaragua. On 30 August 1851, a day before this letter was written, *The Economist* (No. 418) carried an item on the project 'New Route Between the Atlantic and the Pacific'.—448

477 At the end of August 1851 German newspapers reported that the editor of the *Kölnische Zeitung*, Brüggemann, had been deported from Cologne for opposition articles published in his newspaper. But these reports, based on rumours, turned out to be false.—451

478 In September 1851 arrests were made in France among the members of local communities belonging to the separatist Willich-Schapper group, which was responsible for the split in the Communist League in September 1850. The group's petty-bourgeois conspiratorial tactics, ignoring realities and aiming at an immediate uprising, enabled the French and Prussian police, with the help of the agent-provocateur Cherval (real name Crämer), who headed one of the local communities in Paris, to fabricate the case of the so-called Franco-German conspiracy. In February 1852 the accused were sentenced on a charge of plotting a coup d'état. Cherval was allowed to escape from prison.

The provocative character of the trial was exposed by Marx in *Revelations Concerning the Communist Trial in Cologne* and *Herr Vogt* (see present edition, vols. 11 and 17).—452

479 The reference is to the supporters of Weitling's utopian egalitarian communism in the Paris communities of the League of the Just (later, the Communist League), whose sectarian tendencies Engels had to fight (on this see Note 70).—452

480 This refers to the split in the provisional Italian National Committee formed after the fall of the Roman Republic (July 1849) by members of its Constituent Assembly who had emigrated to England. Mazzini and his followers were in the majority. The Committee was empowered among other things to organise a national movement and to float loans for Italy's liberation.—454, 456

481 In February-March 1846, simultaneously with the national liberation insurrection in the free city of Cracow, which had been under the joint control of Austria, Prussia and Russia since 1815, a big peasant revolt flared up in Galicia. Taking advantage of class contradictions, the Austrian authorities provoked clashes between the insurgent Galician peasants and the Polish nobility who sought to help Cracow. After quelling the insurgent movement of the nobility, the Austrian Government also suppressed the peasant uprising in Galicia.

In the spring of 1848 in another effort to gain the support of the Galician peasants against the Polish national liberation movement, the Austrian Government abolished corvée and some other services. However, this half-hearted reform did not affect the big landed estates and the whole burden of the redemption payment fell on the peasants.—455, 456

482 An excerpt from this letter was published in English in: Karl Marx and Friedrich Engels, *Correspondence. 1846-1895,* London, 1934 and also in: K. Marx, F. Engels, *Selected Correspondence,* Foreign Languages Publishing House, Moscow, 1955.—455, 458

483 Conrad Schramm left for Paris at the end of June 1851 on Louis Bamberger's passport. This journey, the purpose and cause of which cannot be established by the available documents, met with Marx's disapproval. On 3 September 1851 Conrad Schramm was arrested in Paris on a charge of participation in the so-called Franco-German conspiracy (see Note 478). However, he was released from prison for lack of evidence at the end of October 1851 and expelled from France. The Prussian police's attempts to use Schramm's arrest in order to incriminate the followers of Marx and Engels in the Communist League failed.—457, 459

484 The reference is to the appeal to the members of the separatist organisation set up by Willich and Schapper after the split in the Communist League. (Marx and Engels called this organisation the Sonderbund by analogy with the separatist union of the Swiss Catholic cantons formed in the 1840s.) The appeal adopted at the congress of this organisation in the summer of 1851 was pervaded with adventuristic tendencies and voluntaristic-sectarian ideas of carrying out a revolution without any regard for objective conditions. In September 1851 the appeal fell into the hands of the police when they arrested members of local communities of this organisation in France (see Note 478). It was published in French papers under the heading: 'Instructions pour la Ligue, avant, pendant et après la révolution'. Excerpts were also published in the *Kölnische Zeitung,* No. 225, 19 September 1851.—458, 459, 463, 468

485 *Lazzaroni*—a contemptuous nickname for declassed proletarians, primarily in the Kingdom of Naples, who were repeatedly used by the Government in the struggle against liberal and democratic movements.—459

486 An allusion to Dronke's letter to Marx written from Geneva in August 1851 and sent by Marx to Engels on 13 September same year (see this volume, p. 459). Among other things Dronke wrote about his duel with a Russian refugee, the journalist N. I. Sazonov, his plans to move to Piedmont because the Swiss authorities wanted to expel him from the country, and his intention to get certain sums of money from his debtors in Hamburg with the help of Weerth, who was there at the time.

As is evident from Marx's letters to Weydemeyer of 11 September and to Engels of 13 December 1851 and also from this particular letter of Engels, Marx intended to reply to Dronke jointly with Engels. But it is not known whether he did so. In mid-October 1851 Marx received news that Dronke intended going to London (see this volume, p. 481), but he did not arrive there until April 1852.—459, 482

487 In 1851 gold was found in the South Australian colony of Victoria. The Australian 'gold rush', like the discovery of gold in California in 1848, led to a

greater inflow of colonists, the opening of new markets, the development of sea routes, and a growth in world trade and credit.—461

[488] The reference is to the uprising of the Paris workers on 22-25 June 1848. Marx assessed its historical importance in *The Class Struggles in France, 1848 to 1850* (see present edition, Vol. 10, pp. 67-70).—463, 511

[489] The reference is to the clash on 29 March 1848 between the Belgian Republican Legion bound home from France and a detachment of soldiers near the village of Risquons-Tout not far from the French border. The Republican Legion was dispersed by the soldiers. The Government of King Leopold used this incident as a pretext for legal proceedings against the Belgian democrats. The case lasted from 9 to 30 August 1848. Seventeen of the accused received the death sentence, which was later commuted to long-term imprisonment; subsequently the accused were pardoned (see Engels' article 'The Antwerp Death Sentences', present edition, Vol. 7, pp. 404-06).—471

[490] This was a postscript written by Marx to Jenny Marx's letter to Amalie Daniels. It may be assumed that the reference is to books from Marx's library left in Cologne in Daniels' care when Marx was compelled to leave the Rhine Province after the suppression of the *Neue Rheinische Zeitung*. In the autumn of 1850 Daniels sent a list of these books to Marx in London. Marx marked with asterisks those in which he was most interested and which he wished to be sent to him in England. They included grammar books, dictionaries, works by Hegel, Holbach, and Vico, and books on the history of political economy, and a considerable number of works by utopian thinkers and socialists—Campanella, Morelly, Saint-Simon, Fourier, Owen, Dézamy, Louis Blanc, Cabet, Weitling and others.

The end of the letter, where Marx enumerated the books he needed, did not appear in the *Kölnische Zeitung*. The text of the letter, which got into the hands of the police, as well as of Marx's postscript has survived only as published in the *Kölnische Zeitung* together with other material concerning the communist trial in Cologne in October 1852.—472

[491] An extract from this letter was published in English for the first time in: Marx and Engels, *On the United States*, Progress Publishers, Moscow, 1979.—472

[492] Hoffmann and Campe in Hamburg rejected Marx's request made in August 1851 to publish a pamphlet containing Marx's criticism of Proudhon's *Idée générale de la Révolution au XIXe siècle* (see Note 464).

Marx had been trying since the spring of 1851 to find a German publisher for his work on political economy. In particular he asked Freiligrath, while the latter was still in Germany, to act as a go-between. As emerges from Roland Daniels' letter to Marx of 12 April 1851, Freiligrath's attempts to get the book published by J. G. Cotta proved abortive and Freiligrath requested H. Ebner's assistance. Neither Freiligrath nor Marx had any idea of Ebner's secret activities as an informer (see Note 466) and Freiligrath hoped to use his publishing connections in Marx's interest. In August 1851 Freiligrath moved to London and continued to keep Marx abreast of negotiations Ebner was carrying on with various publishers on Freiligrath's instructions. On 2 October he wrote to Marx that Ebner had had a refusal from Löwenthal, but was not abandoning attempts to have the book published by someone else, Suchsland in particular. In early October 1851 Marx asked Pieper, who was going to Frankfurt, to get in touch with Ebner and find out whether there was any possibility of publishing his work. But all efforts up to December 1851 remained fruitless.—475

493 This refers to French bourgeois and petty-bourgeois democrats who still harboured constitutional illusions and believed exclusively in peaceful means of political struggle despite the lessons of the defeat suffered by the petty-bourgeois Mountain party who, on 13 June 1849, called upon the masses to organise a peaceful demonstration instead of taking the lead in revolutionary resistance to reaction. On the 13 June 1849 events, see Note 260.—479

494 This letter was published in English for the first time slightly abridged and without the postscript by Jenny Marx in: K. Marx and F. Engels, *Letters to Americans. 1848-1895*, International Publishers, New York, 1953.—480

495 Marx's letter to Charles Dana has not been found.—480

496 Dronke's arrival in London from Switzerland was delayed till the end of April 1852.—481

497 A reference to the attempts by Gottfried Kinkel and other leaders of the Emigration Club to organise a so-called German-American revolutionary loan, for which purpose Kinkel went to the USA in September 1851. The loan was to be subscribed to by German-born Americans and used to begin an immediate revolution in Germany. The rival Agitation Union headed by Arnold Ruge also sent a representative to the USA to raise money for the revolution. In a number of works and letters Marx and Engels denounced the undertaking as an adventurist attempt to produce a revolution artificially in a period when the revolutionary movement was on the wane.—483, 486, 499, 520

498 See notes 350 and 419.—483

499 In May 1852 Louis Bonaparte's presidential powers were to expire and according to the Constitution of the French Republic of 1848 new elections were to be held on the second Sunday in May. Major events, popular unrest and attempts at a coup d'état were expected on that occasion owing to the acute struggle between different political groups and the growing contradictions between the president and the royalist majority in the Legislative Assembly. However Bonapartist circles carried out a coup d'état earlier, on 2 December 1851.—485

500 It is not known whether Engels actually wrote an anonymous letter to Haupt.—487

501 Apparently the reference is to the publication of *Gesammelte Aufsätze von Karl Marx* (see Note 347) started by Hermann Becker in Cologne and interrupted by his arrest. The first issues were to contain Marx's articles from the *Rheinische Zeitung.*—489

502 Marx arrived in Manchester to visit Engels on about 5 November 1851 and stayed some ten days.—491

503 Despite a temporary break with Harney in whose journal *The Friend of the People* Engels intended at one time to publish a series of articles criticising the petty-bourgeois emigrants and the Willich-Schapper sectarian adventurist group (see Note 352), he did not give up the idea of denouncing in the press the pseudo-revolutionary illusions and voluntarism of the petty-bourgeois emigrants. At the end of November and beginning of December 1851, Engels was

working on a satirical essay, one of the main characters of which was to be Karl
Schapper. It occurred to Marx to have this work published in the USA, in *Die
Revolution*, a weekly planned by Weydemeyer, who had moved to New York by
that time. But Marx and Engels were busy writing other works until the spring
of 1852 and the publication of *Die Revolution* was soon discontinued. By that
time the differences between Willich and Schapper had become apparent; the
latter was disillusioned with sectarianism and wanted to be reconciled with
Marx. So when in May-June 1852 Marx and Engels returned to the subject and
started writing *The Great Men of the Exile* (see present edition, Vol. 11), they
thought it inexpedient to give a special characterisation of Schapper and
concentrated their criticism on Kinkel, Ruge, Heinzen, Struve, Willich and
others.—492, 498, 516

504 Engels' letter to Marx written about 25 November 1851 has not been
found.—493

505 An allusion to the fact that Pieper's letter to Marx of 17 November 1851
contained excerpts from Heinrich Heine's poems.—493

506 *Morison pills*—pills invented by the English quack James Morison and widely
advertised as a cure for all illnesses in the mid-1820s. Their main ingredient
was the juice of certain tropical plants.—493

507 The original of Marx's letter to Cluss is not extant. The excerpt published here
is translated from Cluss' letter to Weydemeyer of 20 December 1851.—496

508 In his letter to Weydemeyer of 20 December 1851 Cluss explains this passage
as follows: 'Kinkel's loan, in which I let myself become involved through lack of
knowledge of the state of affairs, and in which, in Marx's view, I should maintain
my position for the present.'
    On the so-called German-American revolutionary loan see Note 497.—496

509 Marx's letter to Charles Dana has not been found.—497

510 Neither the letter Marx and Engels wrote to Pieper from Manchester during
Marx's stay there from 5 to 15 November 1851, nor the letter Jenny Marx
wrote to him on her husband's request has been found.—497

511 The statements Marx sent to Paris to be published in the French press did not
appear in the papers and their originals have not survived.—497

512 Engels supported Marx's initiative of denouncing in the English press the
Prussian Government's arbitrary treatment of the arrested Cologne communists
under investigation. At Marx's request he wrote a letter to the editor of *The
Times* at the end of January 1852 and prepared a similar letter for *The Daily
News*, but the newspapers did not publish them. Only a rough copy of the letter
'To the Editor of *The Times*' written by Marx and Engels is extant (see present
edition, Vol. 11, pp. 210-11).—497

513 On 2 November 1851 a meeting was held at Copenhagen House (Copenhagen
Fields) in London to mark Kossuth's arrival (in October 1851) in England.
The reformist Thornton Hunt, chairman of the Chartist committee responsible
for organising the meeting, tried to prevent O'Connor from attending on the
pretext that he was insane. This aroused violent protests on the part of the
Chartists and O'Connor was admitted to the meeting. To justify himself Hunt
made a demagogic declaration in *The Northern Star* on 29 November describing
himself as a zealous defender of people's interests and calling himself a

communist. As Marx foresaw, Hunt was not elected to the new Executive of the National Charter Association.—497

514 Marx's letter to Ernest Jones has not survived.—498

515 This letter, the beginning of which has not survived, and the one written between 15 and 22 August 1851 (see this volume, pp. 426-33) and also sent by Marx to Ebner, show that Marx intended to use the Frankfurt journalist's connections with a view to publishing in the German press material denouncing the pseudo-revolutionary schemes of the petty-bourgeois emigrant leaders. Both letters fell into the hands of the Austrian police through the secret police agent Ebner (see Note 466).—499

516 An ironical allusion to the Frankfurt National Assembly after it had moved to Stuttgart in early June 1849. On 18 June the remnants of the National Assembly were dispersed by troops.—500

517 This letter was written by Engels on the occasion of the coup d'état of 2 December 1851 carried out by the supporters of Louis Bonaparte, President of the French Republic, which led to the dissolution of the Legislative Assembly and the establishment of the Bonapartist regime (from December 1852—the Second Empire under Napoleon III). Some ideas expressed by Engels in this letter were developed by Marx in *The Eighteenth Brumaire of Louis Bonaparte* (see present edition, Vol. 11), in particular the ironical comparison of Louis Bonaparte's coup with that of 9 November (18th Brumaire according to the Republican calendar) 1799, which resulted in the establishment of Napoleon Bonaparte's dictatorship, and also the thought that Hegel was right in saying that historical events occur first as tragedy and then as farce.

An excerpt from this letter was published in English for the first time in: Karl Marx and Friedrich Engels, *Correspondence. 1846-1895*, London, 1934; the letter was published in full in: K. Marx and F. Engels, *Selected Correspondence*, Foreign Languages Publishing House, Moscow, 1955.—503

518 An allusion to the fact that during the coup d'état some of the deputies to the Legislative Assembly who belonged to the conservative Party of Order gathered in Odilon Barrot's mansion, others went to the municipal hall of the 10th arrondissement about which Engels writes below. In both cases the deputies confined themselves to merely protesting at the president's actions and formally removing Louis Bonaparte from his post. Engels compares Barrot with Löwe von Calbe who was elected chairman of the German Frankfurt National Assembly after its remnants had moved to Stuttgart early in June 1849 (see Note 516) and remained in office until the Assembly was dispersed by Württemberg troops.—503

519 The Bonapartist coup d'état was timed to coincide with the anniversary of two events in the history of the First Empire—the coronation of Napoleon I in Notre-Dame de Paris on 2 December 1804 and the victory of Austerlitz a year later, on 2 December 1805 (see Note 402).—504

520 The Bonapartist circles exploited for demagogical purposes the popular discontent over the abrogation by the Legislative Assembly of the universal suffrage law of 31 May 1849. The suffrage was restored by a presidential decree. The initial system of open ballot was replaced by secret ballot because of the popular discontent. A plebiscite on the new political system proposed by the president was announced for the period 14-21 December 1851. It took place on 21 December 1851 in an atmosphere of Bonapartist terror and

suppression of all opposition and was actually only a show to produce an impression of popular support for the military and police regime.—504

521 Hegel expressed this idea of the recurrence of historical events in his work *Vorlesungen über die Philosophie der Geschichte* (the first edition was published in Berlin in 1837). In the third part of this work, at the end of Section 2, entitled 'Rom vom zweiten punischen Krieg bis zum Kaiserthum', Hegel wrote, in particular, that 'a coup d'état is sanctioned as it were in the opinion of people if it is repeated. Thus, Napoleon was defeated twice and twice the Bourbons were driven out. Through repetition, what at the beginning seemed to be merely accidental and possible becomes real and established'.

Hegel also repeatedly expressed the idea that in the process of dialectical development there is bound to be a transition from the stage of formation and efflorescence to that of disintegration and ruin (see, in particular, G. W. F. Hegel, *Grundlinien der Philosophie des Rechts*, Th. 3, Abt. 3, § 347).

Hegel's idea was developed by Marx in *The Eighteenth Brumaire of Louis Bonaparte* (see present edition, Vol. 11, p. 103), 'Contribution to the Critique of Hegel's Philosophy of Law. Introduction' (Vol. 3, p. 179) and 'The Deeds of the Hohenzollern Dynasty' (Vol. 9, p. 421).—505

522 An allusion to the attempts of the Left republicans and democrats, supported by certain leaders of the workers' organisations, to offer armed resistance to the Bonapartist coup d'état. A thirty-thousand-strong army was sent against the not more than 1,200 defenders of the barricades erected on 3 and 4 December 1851. Not only insurgents, but all those who happened to be in the streets, were massacred. Scattered uprisings of republicans in the south-eastern, south-western and central départements of France, in which local democratic intelligentsia, artisans, workers, peasants and small traders participated, were also crushed.—509, 512

523 This letter was published in English for the first time in: K. Marx and F. Engels, *Selected Correspondence*, Foreign Languages Publishing House, Moscow, 1955.—510

524 An allusion to the workers' uprisings in Paris on 1 April (12 Germinal according to the Republican calendar) 1795 and 20-23 May (1-4 Prairial) the same year against the Thermidor reactionary regime set up on 27 and 28 July 1794 (after the overthrow of the Jacobin revolutionary dictatorship on 9-10 Thermidor), and to the proletarian uprisings in Lyons in 1831 and 1834 after the July 1830 bourgeois revolution in France.—512

525 Engels' letter to his sister Marie Blank has not been found.—514

526 Engels went to London on 20 December 1851. He stayed there for about a fortnight, mostly in Marx's company, and returned to Manchester on about 4 January 1852.—515, 516, 518, 562, 563

527 This refers to Joseph Weydemeyer's intention to publish a communist weekly *Die Revolution* in New York. Marx and Engels agreed to contribute regularly and intended to get some of their party friends to work for it. Weydemeyer managed to produce only two issues in January 1852, following which publication ceased for lack of funds. In May and June 1852 with the help of Adolph Cluss, Weydemeyer published two more issues of the 'non-periodic journal' *Die Revolution;* the first issue carried K. Marx's *The Eighteenth Brumaire of Louis Bonaparte,* the second Freiligrath's poems against Kinkel.—516

528 This apparently refers to the first in a series of articles on the coup d'état of 2 December 1851 in France, conceived by Marx and intended for Joseph Weydemeyer's weekly *Die Revolution* published in America. The articles arrived too late for inclusion in the two January 1852 issues of the weekly. They were published in May in a non-periodic issue under the title *The Eighteenth Brumaire of Louis Bonaparte.—516*

529 The reference is to material intended for Joseph Weydemeyer's *Die Revolution* (see Note 527). Engels wrote four articles on England for it in December 1851-January 1852; only two, written at the end of January 1852 (see present edition, Vol. 11, pp. 198-209), reached Weydemeyer; the other two got lost on the way. Even the two which reached Weydemeyer were not published in *Die Revolution,* since it had ceased publication.—518

530 The Bonapartist coup d'état of 2 December 1851 shattered all earlier expectations of major revolutionary events in France in May 1852 based on the expiry of the presidential powers that month (see Note 499).—519

531 In the first issue of *Die Revolution* Weydemeyer announced Marx's work on Proudhon. But since publication of the weekly was discontinued and there were no other possibilities for publishing the work, Marx did not write it. Other plans connected with the weekly as set forth at the beginning of the letter were not carried out either. *The Eighteenth Brumaire of Louis Bonaparte* which Marx finished only in March 1852 exceeded the limits of a mere article. Engels sent Weydemeyer articles on England and not on Prussia; some of them got lost on the way, some arrived too late (see Note 529). The two issues of *Die Revolution* carried excerpts from Marx's and Engels' 'Review, May to October 1850' published earlier in the *Neue Rheinische Zeitung. Politisch-ökonomische Revue,* No. 5-6, and (in issue No. 2) part of Chapter Two of the *Manifesto of the Communist Party.—519*

532 This refers to the change in the place and time of the meetings of the London district of the Communist League which Marx above calls the 'synagogue' partly jokingly, partly for reasons of secrecy. Early in 1852 the meetings were moved to premises in Crown Street and were held on Wednesdays, because of suspicions aroused by the appearance in London Communist League circles of Hirsch, a shop assistant, who later turned out to be a police spy (see present edition, Vol. 11, p. 426).—521

533 The British Foreign Secretary, Lord Palmerston, in a conversation with the French Ambassador in London shortly after the coup d'état of 2 December 1851 in France, approved of Louis Bonaparte's usurpation. He did this without consulting the other members of the Whig Ministry, which led to his dismissal. The British Government was nevertheless the first to recognise the Bonapartist regime.—521

534 Only part of this letter is extant; the beginning and the end are missing. The year of its writing has been established by the fact that it deals with the expulsion of Marx from Paris by the French authorities early in February 1845 and the worries of his wife, who was forced to sell family heirlooms in a hurry to raise money for her journey with her small child to join Marx in Brussels.

As emerges from the letter, Jenny Marx was convinced that the German scientist, Alexander Humboldt, relative of the Prussian Foreign Minister, had played an unseemly role in Marx's expulsion from Paris, acting as mediator between the Prussian authorities and the Guizot Government on this issue. Subsequently, Engels confirmed this version in his obituary of Jenny Marx (1881).—525

[535] The letter has no date. The date of writing has been established by its mentioning Engels' return to Brussels from England (he had gone there with Marx in the second half of July 1845) on about 24 August 1845. Jenny Marx, who was expecting a second child, was in Trier at the time with her mother, Caroline von Westphalen.—526

[536] Marx's letter to Jenny written in August 1845 has not been found.—526

[537] Only part of the letter is extant, the end is missing, and neither month nor year of writing is given. Judging by Joseph Weydemeyer's letter to his future wife Louise Lüning of 21 February 1846, Marx accompanied his wife to Arlon on her way to Trier to visit her sick mother. Jenny Marx returned to Brussels in April 1846.—529

[538] Marx's letter to his wife written some time before 23 March 1846 has not been found.—529

[539] The reference is to the national liberation uprising in the Cracow republic which by the decision of the Congress of Vienna was controlled jointly by Austria, Russia and Prussia. The seizure of power in Cracow by the insurgents on 22 February 1846 and the establishment of a National Government of the Polish Republic, which issued a manifesto abolishing feudal services, were part of the plan for a general uprising in the Polish lands. In March the Cracow uprising was crushed by the forces of Austria and Russia; in November 1846, Austria, Prussia and Russia signed a treaty incorporating the 'free town of Cracow' into the Austrian Empire.—532, 533

[540] George Julian Harney's letter was in reply to several letters Engels wrote to him on his own behalf and that of the Brussels Communist Correspondence Committee (see Note 51); these letters have not survived but Harney's reply gives some idea of their contents.—533

[541] On 15 and 17 March 1846 meetings of the Fraternal Democrats (see Note 122) in support of the Cracow uprising (see Note 539) took place in London. A report on them was published in *The Northern Star,* No. 436, 21 March 1846.—533

[542] Engels recalled this period of joint work with Marx on *The German Ideology* in a letter to Laura Lafargue of 2 June 1883 (see present edition, Volume 47). He wrote that when he read passages from the manuscript to Hélène Demuth who kept house for him after Marx's death, she said: 'Now at last I know why that time in Brussels you two laughed at night so much that nobody in the house could sleep.' To this Engels added: 'We were bold devils then, Heine's poetry is childlike innocence compared with our prose.'—533

[543] The *People's Charter* containing the demands of the Chartists was published on 8 May 1838 in the form of a Bill to be submitted to Parliament. It consisted of six points: universal suffrage (for men of 21 years of age), annual elections to Parliament, secret ballot, equal constituencies, abolition of property qualifications for candidates to Parliament, and salaries for M.P.s. In 1839 and 1842, petitions for the Charter were rejected by Parliament.—533

544 Unlike the supporters of 'moral force' in the Chartist movement (see Note 339), O'Connor called in his speeches not only for peaceful means of struggle but for the use of 'physical force' as well.— 534

545 Presumably an allusion to a resolution adopted by the Chartist Convention in 1839 confirming the people's right to support their demands by force of arms. But the Convention showed inconsistency and lack of determination by failing to organise the masses for energetic action when the Chartist petition was rejected by Parliament on 12 July.— 534

546 Harney refers to plans for establishing an international communist organisation to unite by means of correspondence committees the advanced workers and the revolutionary intellectuals in various countries of Europe, primarily England, France and Germany.— 536

547 The false rumours that when the Brussels Communist Correspondence Committee was being formed Marx and Engels intended to restrict the organisers of the international proletarian party to intellectuals were spread by Weitling. This emerges from the letter of the London Communist Correspondence Committee to Marx of 6 June 1846 (*MEGA*$_2$, Abt. III, Bd. 2, Berlin, 1980).— 537

548 This refers to a resolution of the Brussels Communist Correspondence Committee censuring Thomas Cooper for disavowing the Chartist movement and preaching the anti-revolutionary doctrine of non-resistance to evil by force (the text of the resolution has not survived). Marx and Engels also censured Cooper in their 'Address of the German Democratic Communists of Brussels to Mr Feargus O'Connor' in July 1846 (see present edition, Vol. 6, p. 59).— 537

549 The reference is to the Chartist Land Cooperative Society founded on the initiative of O'Connor in 1845 (later the National Land Company, which lasted till 1848). The aim of the Society was to buy plots of land with the money collected, and to lease them to worker shareholders on easy terms. Among the positive aspects of the Society were its petitions to Parliament and printed propaganda against the aristocracy's monopoly of land. (These aspects were emphasised by Engels in 1847 in his article 'The Agrarian Programme of the Chartists', see present edition, Vol. 6.) However, the idea of liberating the workers from exploitation, of reducing unemployment, etc., by a return to the land proved utopian. The Society's activities were not successful in practice.— 538

550 The *German Workers' Club* was founded in Paris on 8 and 9 March 1848 on the initiative of the Communist League leaders. The leading role in it belonged to Marx. The Club's aim was to unite the German emigrant workers in Paris, explain to them the tactics of the proletariat in a bourgeois-democratic revolution and also to counter the attempts of the bourgeois and petty-bourgeois democrats to stir up the German workers by nationalist propaganda and make them join the adventurist march of volunteer legions into Germany. The Club was successful in arranging the return of German workers one by one to their own country to take part in the revolutionary struggle there.— 539

551 Presumably an allusion to the émigré German Union (Réunion allemande) organised in Paris in August 1848. Although it occupied the left flank of the democratic movement and followed on the whole the political line charted by the Communist League, this organisation was not free from petty-bourgeois

influence. Moses Hess, who was in Paris at the time, tried to use it against Marx, Engels and their followers. On his initiative an attempt was made to split and change the organisation directed by the Communist League, in particular to set Marx and Engels at loggerheads. Ewerbeck, who came to Germany to attend the Second Congress of Democrats in Berlin, was to a certain extent involved by Hess in his political intrigues.—542

552 Neither Engels' letter to his mother written about 30 November 1848 nor his letters to his parents from Liège and Brussels mentioned below have been found.—543

553 *Concordia*—publishers in Vienna, apparently had an office in Berlin.—543

554 Engels and other editors of the *Neue Rheinische Zeitung* attended the open meeting in the Eiser Hall, Cologne, on 20 September 1848 and he made a speech the text of which has not survived. From newspaper reports of the meeting it emerges that Engels branded as treachery the decision of the all-German Frankfurt National Assembly to ratify the treaty on the Danish-Prussian armistice.—543

555 Marx's letter to Georg Jung has not been found.—548

556 Peter Röser, a member of the Communist League Central Authority in Cologne, was sentenced to six years' imprisonment at the Cologne communist trial in November 1852. From December 1853 to February 1854 he was in prison first in Berlin and then in Stettin. Hoping to ease his lot he gave written evidence, which survived in the Prussian police archives, concerning mainly the Communist League activity and the Cologne communities' contacts with Marx and other leaders in London. In particular, he quoted from memory some letters Marx sent to Cologne, which are not extant. Some of the information he gave was inexact, perhaps owing partly to the fact that he himself was not well informed and partly to a deliberate attempt on his part to give a more moderate impression of the Communist League's activity. So he gave an oversimplified account of Marx's idea about the stages of transition to communism, as though Marx reduced the whole process of revolutionary transformation passing through various stages merely to education. Contrary to Röser's assertion, the Cologne community of the Communist League already existed before it received Marx's letter early in 1850 suggesting that organisational activity in the Rhine Province should be intensified. Schramm was slightly and not seriously wounded in the duel with Willich, and seconds from both parties were present.

Despite these and some other inaccuracies, Röser's evidence on the whole presents an objective picture of the state of affairs in the Communist League at the time and throws additional light on the struggle by Marx and his associates against the sectarian adventurists.—550

557 The reference is to the Statute of the Revolutionary Party drafted by the London members of the Communist League at the end of 1848. Marx and his adherents criticised it sharply as early as the spring of 1849. The Statute reflected sectarian and conspiratorial tendencies, while the communist nature of the organisation and the communist aims of the movement were obscured by vague phrases about a 'social republic', etc. The document got no farther than the stage of draft rules, not being approved in Communist League circles.—550

558 Presumably this refers to the district congresses of democrats of the Rhine Province and Westphalia held in Cologne on 13-14 August and 23 November 1848 and also to the district congresses of democratic societies and workers' unions of the province held in Cologne on 6 May 1849.—551

559 The *Cologne Workers' Association*—a workers' organisation founded on 13 April 1848 by Andreas Gottschalk. Most of the leading figures in the Workers' Association were members of the Communist League. After Gottschalk's arrest on 6 July, Moll was elected President of the Association, and on 16 October the presidency was temporarily assumed by Marx at the request of the Association members. From February to May 1849 the post was held by Schapper.

From the very outset, Gottschalk's sectarian position was opposed by the supporters of Marx and Engels. Under their impact the Workers' Association became a centre of revolutionary agitation among the workers and the peasants. It maintained contacts with other workers' and democratic organisations. After the *Neue Rheinische Zeitung* was suppressed and Marx, Schapper and other leaders left Cologne, the Association gradually turned into an ordinary workers' educational society.—553

560 The reference is to the Address of the Cologne Central Authority of the Communist League to the League of 1 December 1850 censuring the splitting activities of the Willich-Schapper group. Together with the Address and other documents, the Central Authority also sent to the London district the Communist League Rules which had been drawn up in Cologne (see notes 342 and 438).—560

561 Jenny Marx's letter to Georg Weerth written at Marx's request has not survived.—561

562 Instead of an article on Prussia, Engels soon wrote a series of articles on England for Joseph Weydemeyer's weekly *Die Revolution*; however, they were not published (see Note 529).—562, 563

NAME INDEX*

A

Adam—French worker, Blanquist; member of the Committee of the Société des proscrits démocrates et socialistes in London, supported the sectarian Willich-Schapper group.— 247, 251, 283, 292

Adelung, Johann Christoph (1732-1806)—German philologist, author of a number of works on German etymology and grammar.—62

Albert (Martin, Alexandre) (1815-1895)—French worker; a leader of secret revolutionary societies during the July monarchy; member of the Provisional Government (1848).— 168

Alexander I (1777-1825)—Emperor of Russia (1801-25).—337

Alexander of Macedon (Alexander the Great) (356-323 B.C.)—general and statesman of antiquity.—454

Alison, Sir Archibald (1792-1867)—Scottish historian and economist; Tory.—372

Allard, Jean Baptiste Pierre (1798-1877)—French democrat.—158

Allsop, Thomas (1795-1880)—English journalist, sided with the Chartists.—479

Ammerman—captain of the sailing vessel *Reform.*—481

André, Félicité—an acquaintance of Engels in Paris in the 1840s.—153, 166

Anneke, Friedrich (1818-1872)—Prussian ex-artillery officer; member of the Communist League, a founder of the Cologne Workers' Association (1848), lieutenant-colonel in the Baden-Palatinate revolutionary army; later emigrated to the USA.—159, 183, 224

Annenkov, Pavel Vasilyevich (1812-1887)—Russian liberal critic and journalist.—37, 64, 95-106, 150-51

Antoine, Gustave—French refugee in London in the early 1850s; son-in-law of Auguste Blanqui.—313, 381

Arago, Dominique François Jean (1786-1853)—French astronomer, physicist and mathematician; republican politician, member of the Provisional Government (1848).—168

Arends (Ahrens), Heinrich—a German worker from Riga, a leader of the League of the Just in Paris, emigrated to the USA early in 1843.—59

Argout, Antoine Maurice Apollinaire, comte d' (1782-1858)—Director-General of the Bank of France (1834-57).—507

---

member of the Communist League until his expulsion in March 1848; a secret agent of the Prussian police in the 1840s.—120, 122, 123, 125, 126, 127, 128, 130, 138, 145, 153, 154, 155, 156, 162, 165, 540

Börnstein, Arnold Bernhard Karl (1808-1849)—German democrat; a leader of the volunteer legion of German refugees in Paris.—540

Börnstein, Heinrich (1805-1892)—German democratic journalist; founder and editor of *Vorwärts!* (Paris); emigrated to the USA in 1849, editor of the *Anzeiger des Westens* (St. Louis).—8, 14, 15, 31, 55, 88, 107, 108, 114, 115, 135

Bourbons—royal dynasty in France (1589-1792, 1814-15 and 1815-30).—116

Boyen, Leopold Hermann Ludwig von (1771-1848)—Prussian general, Minister of War (1814-19 and 1841-47).—70

Bracht—member of a political club in Elberfeld (1848).—175

Bray, John Francis (1809-1897)—English economist; utopian socialist, follower of Robert Owen, developed the theory of 'labour money'.—109

Brehmer, Hermann—founder of the Workers' Association in Breslau in 1848-49; correspondent of the *Neue Rheinische Zeitung;* editor of the *Schlesische Volkszeitung* (October 1849-March 1850).—196

Bremer, Fredrika (1801-1865)—Swedish novelist.—94

Brentano, Lorenz Peter (1813-1891)—Baden lawyer, democrat; deputy to the Frankfurt National Assembly (Left wing) in 1848; headed the Baden Provisional Government in 1849; emigrated to Switzerland and then to the USA.—426

Breyer, Friedrich Albert (1812-1876)—German liberal; physician in Brussels in the 1840s, member of the Brussels Democratic Association.—118, 162, 164, 528

Bricourt, Jean Joseph (1805-1857)—Belgian legal officer; democrat;

member of the Chamber of Representatives (1847-48).—164

Brockhaus, Heinrich (1804-1874)—publisher and bookseller, owned a big publishing and bookselling business in Leipzig from 1850.—68

Broglie, Achille Charles Léonce Victor, duc de (1785-1870)—French statesman, Prime Minister (1835-36), deputy to the Legislative Assembly (1849-51), Orleanist.—484

Brüggemann, Karl Heinrich (1810-1887)—German journalist, moderate liberal; editor-in-chief of the *Kölnische Zeitung* (1846-55).—337, 451

Bruhn, Karl von (b. 1803)—German journalist, member of the League of Outlaws and subsequently of the Communist League, from which he was expelled in 1850; belonged to the sectarian Willich-Schapper group, later a Lassallean.—196, 197, 407, 549

Brunswick, Duke of—see *Karl Friedrich August Wilhelm*

Brutus, Marcus Junius (c. 85-42 B.C.)—Roman politician, republican; an initiator of the conspiracy against Julius Caesar.—285, 338, 456

Bucher, Lothar (1817-1892)—Prussian official and journalist; deputy to the Prussian National Assembly (Left Centre) in 1848; a refugee in London; later a national-liberal and supporter of Bismark.—296, 317, 321, 440, 446

Buchez, Philippe Joseph Benjamin (1796-1865)—French politician, historian, Christian socialist.—58

Bugeaud de la Piconnerie, Thomas Robert (1784-1849)—Marshal of France, Orleanist.—169

Buhl, Ludwig Heinrich Franz (1814-c.1882)—German journalist; Young Hegelian; editor of the *Berliner Monatsschrift* in Mannheim (1844).—11

Bülow, Dietrich Heinrich, Baron von (1757-1808)—Prussian officer and military writer.—329

Bülow, Friedrich Wilhelm, Count von Dennewiss (1755-1816)—Prussian general, took part in the wars against Napoleonic France.—329

Bunsen, Christian Karl Josias, Baron von (1791-1860)—Prussian diplomat, writer and theologian; ambassador to London (1842-54).—401

Bürgers, Heinrich (1820-1878)— German journalist, an editor of the *Neue Rheinische Zeitung*, member of the Communist League and of its Central Authority (from 1850); one of the accused in the Cologne communist trial (1852).—9, 14, 25, 28, 49, 61, 69, 111, 128, 159, 171, 185-86, 251, 341, 346, 351, 365, 366, 373, 384, 390, 491, 526, 529

Burns, Lydia (Lizzy, Lizzie) (1827-1878)—Irish working woman, sister of Mary Burns; Frederick Engels' second wife.—266

Burns, Mary (c. 1823-1863)—Irish working woman, Frederick Engels' first wife.—37, 153, 266, 273, 369, 530

Butz, Gustav—publisher in Hagen in the 1840s.—16

C

Cabet, Étienne (1788-1856)—French writer, utopian communist, author of *Voyage en Icarie.*—53, 114, 136, 169, 423, 534

Caesar, Gaius Julius (c. 100-44 B.C.)— Roman general and statesman.—288

Campe, Johann Julius Wilhelm (1792-1867)—German publisher and bookseller, from 1823 co-proprietor of the Hoffman & Campe Publishing House, Hamburg.—7, 34, 343, 475

Camphausen, Ludolf (1803-1890)— German banker; a Rhenish liberal bourgeois leader; Prime Minister of Prussia (March-June 1848).—176

Canute (Cnut), 'Canute the Great' (c. 995-1035)—King of Denmark (1014-35) and also of England (from 1017) and of Norway (from 1028).—93

Capefigue, Jean Baptiste Honoré Raymond (1801-1872)—French journalist and historian; monarchist.—116

Caperon, Paulin—French émigré, member of the Société des proscrits démocrates et socialistes in London in the early 1850s.—247, 249, 254, 560

Carlier, Pierre Charles Joseph (1799-1858)—Prefect of the Paris police (1849-51); Bonapartist.—479, 484

Carlyle, Thomas (1795-1881)—British writer, historian, philosopher, Tory; preached views bordering on feudal socialism up to 1848; later a relentless opponent of the working-class movement.—4, 461

Carnap, Johann Adolph von (born c. 1793)—Prussian official, Chief Burgomaster of Elberfeld from 1837 to 1851.—24

Carnot, Lazare Nicolas (1753-1823)— French mathematician; political and military figure in the French Revolution, Jacobin; took part in the Thermidor coup in 1794.—505

Cassel—Brussels banker.—158, 164

Castiau, Adelson (1804-1879)—Belgian lawyer and politician; democrat; member of the Chamber of Representatives (1843-48).—159, 164

Cato, Marcus Porcius (Cato the Elder) (234-149 B.C.)—Roman statesman and writer.—442

Caussidière, Marc (1808-1861)—French democrat, took part in the Lyons uprising of 1834; Prefect of the Paris police after the February 1848 revolution; deputy to the Constituent Assembly; emigrated to England in June 1848.—337, 505

Cavaignac, Louis Eugène (1802-1857)— French general, moderate republican; took part in the conquest of Algeria; War Minister of France from May 1848; directed the suppression of the June uprising; head of the executive (June-December 1848).—355, 357, 360-61, 363, 367, 466, 469, 484-85, 503

Cervantes Saavedra, Miguel de (1547-1616)—Spanish writer.—397

Changarnier, Nicolas Anne Théodule (1793-1877)—French general and politician, monarchist; deputy to the Constituent and Legislative Assemblies; commander of the Paris garrison and the National Guard after June 1848; took part in dispersing the demonstration of 13 June 1849 in Paris.—357, 360, 363, 479, 484, 503, 504

Christ, A.—German journalist, author of a pamphlet on protective tariffs.—376, 402

Christian VIII (1786-1848)—King of Denmark (1839-48).—70

Cicero (Marcus Tullius Cicero) (106-43 B.C.)—Roman orator, statesman and philosopher.—316

Clark, Thomas (d. 1857)—a Chartist leader, Fraternal Democrat (1847), reformist after 1848.—272, 285

Clausewitz, Karl von (1780-1831)—Prussian general and military theoretician.—372

Clouth, Wilhelm—owner of the Cologne printshop where the *Neue Rheinische Zeitung* was printed from 1 June to 27 August 1848.—175

Cluss, Adolph (1825-1905)—German engineer; member of the Communist League; emigrated in 1848 to the USA, where he was a member of German-American workers' organisations; one of the first propagandists of scientific communism in America.—496, 519

Cobbett, William (c. 1762-1835)—English politician and radical writer.—140

Cobden, Richard (1804-1865)—English manufacturer and politician; a leader of the Free Traders and founder of the Anti-Corn Law League.—205-06, 211, 281, 347

Cohen—wife of Karl Blind.—474, 478

Confucius (550 or 551-479 B.C.)—Chinese philosopher and statesman.—429

Considérant, Victor Prosper (1808-1893)—French journalist, utopian socialist, disciple and follower of Fourier.—94, 411

Cooper, Thomas (1805-1892)—English poet and journalist; Chartist in the early 1840s; subsequently a nonconformist preacher.—537

Costa Cabral, António Bernardo da (1803-1889)—Portuguese statesman, leader of the bourgeois-monarchist party, head of government (1842-46 and 1849-51).—358

Cotta, Johann Georg (1796-1863)—German publisher.—398, 476

Crémieux, Isaac Moïse (called *Adolphe*) (1796-1880)—French lawyer and politician; liberal; member of the Provisional Government (February-May 1848); deputy to the Constituent and Legislative Assemblies.—167

Cromwell, Oliver (1599-1658)—leader of the English revolution; Protector of England, Scotland and Ireland from 1653.—284, 323, 535

Crüger, Friedrich (1820-c. 1857)—member of the Communist League and the German Workers' Society in Brussels.—122, 123, 124, 127-28

Culpeper, Sir Thomas (1578-1662)—English economist, advocate of mercantilism.—494

D

Damm—German democrat; President of the Baden Constituent Assembly in 1849; emigrated to England.—436

Dana, Charles Anderson (1819-1897)—American journalist, an editor and editor-in-chief (1849-62) of the *New-York Daily Tribune.*—403, 457, 480, 497, 506, 518, 519

Daniels, Amalie (née *Müller*) (1820-1895)—wife of Roland Daniels.—472, 548

Daniels, Roland (1819-1855)—German physician; member of the Communist League and of its Cologne Central Authority from 1850; one of the accused in the Cologne communist

Name Index

Fickler, Joseph (1808-1865)—German democratic journalist; member of the Baden Provisional Government (1849); emigrated to Switzerland and then to England and the USA.—385, 386, 391, 403, 408, 428, 436, 437, 438, 439-40, 499

Fieschi—refugee in London in the 1850s.—251

Fischer—German democratic journalist, took part in the Baden-Palatinate uprising of 1849, emigrated to the USA.—334, 336, 339, 433, 438, 443, 444, 446, 485, 487, 488

Fischer, F.—member of the Communist League and the German Workers' Society in Brussels.—127

Fix, Théodore (1800-1846)—French economist and journalist, contributor to the *Journal des Économistes.*—66, 67

Flocon, Ferdinand (1800-1866)—French politician and journalist, democrat; an editor of *La Réforme;* member of the Provisional Government in 1848.—135, 136, 137, 139, 143, 152, 156, 158, 161, 166, 168, 169, 382, 505

Florencourt, Franz von (François Chassot de) (1803-1886)—German writer, editor of a number of periodicals; first liberal and later conservative.—338

Foucault, Léon (1819-1868)—French physicist.—343

Fould, Achille (1800-1867)—French banker and politician, Orleanist, subsequently Bonapartist; Minister of Finance several times from 1849 to 1867.—166

Fourier, François Marie Charles (1772-1837)—French utopian socialist.—13, 25, 26, 27, 55, 57, 95, 104

Francis Joseph I (1830-1916)—Emperor of Austria (1848-1916).—355

Franck, Gustav (d. 1860)—Austrian democrat, a refugee in London in the early 1850s.—436, 440

Franck, Paul—German democratic journalist; emigrated to the USA in the early 1850s.—347

Frank, A.—Paris publisher.—8, 142, 143, 144, 149

Frederick II (the Great) (1712-1786)—King of Prussia (1740-86).—329

Frederick William IV (1795-1861)—King of Prussia (1840-61).—70, 141, 160, 249, 355, 376

Freiligrath, Ferdinand (1810-1876)—German revolutionary poet, member of the Communist League, an editor of the *Neue Rheinische Zeitung* in 1848-49.—178, 191, 198, 204, 205, 206, 207, 216, 217, 224, 225, 230, 346, 354, 359, 365, 366, 373, 377, 382, 385-86, 388, 403, 409, 418, 431, 432, 443, 444, 474, 480, 482, 490, 500, 520, 521, 531, 558, 562

Freiligrath, Ida (1817-1899)—wife of Ferdinand Freiligrath.—206, 217, 521

Fröbel, Julius (1805-1893)—German radical writer and publisher.—19, 49, 74

G

Galeer, Albert Frédéric Jean (1813-1851)—Swiss teacher and man of letters, democrat; took part in the war against the Sonderbund (1847) and in the Baden-Palatinate uprising of 1849.—319, 380

Garnier-Pagès, Louis Antoine (1803-1878)—French politician, moderate republican; member of the Provisional Government and Mayor of Paris in 1848.—167

Gebert, August—Mecklenburg joiner, member of the Communist League in Switzerland and later in London, belonged to the sectarian Willich-Schapper group in 1850.—247, 320, 334, 374, 382

Gehrke—German refugee in London in the 1850s.—437

Geiger, Wilhelm Arnold—Prussian police official; in 1848 examining magistrate, then Chief of Police in Cologne.—189, 192

Gigot, Charles Philippe (1819-1860)—participant in the Belgian working-class and democratic movement, member of the Communist League and of the Brussels Communist Correspondence Committee.—38, 39, 89, 118, 126, 130, 153, 158, 159, 162, 165, 178, 179, 544

Girardin, Émile de (1806-1881)—French journalist and politician, editor of *La Presse;* notorious for his lack of principles in politics; moderate republican during the 1848-49 revolution, later Bonapartist.—357, 360, 363, 444, 448, 484

Glaise—an acquaintance of Mrs Marx.—525

Godwin, William (1756-1836)—English writer and philosopher, one of the founders of anarchism.—27

Goegg, Amand (1820-1897)—German democratic journalist; member of the Baden Provisional Government (1849); emigrated after the defeat of the revolution.—240, 356, 358, 385, 391, 403, 428, 436, 438, 439, 440, 441, 442, 446

Goethe, Johann Wolfgang von (1749-1832)—German poet.—18, 68, 110, 264, 474, 500

Göhringer, Carl (born c. 1808)—Baden innkeeper, member of the Communist League, belonged to the sectarian Willich-Schapper group.—334, 343, 359, 437, 475, 477, 483, 486, 492

Goldheim—Prussian police officer, a secret agent of the Prussian police in London in the early 1850s.—349

Görgey, Arthur (1818-1916)—a commander and, from April to June 1849, commander-in-chief of the Hungarian revolutionary army; War Minister from May 1849; voiced the conservative sentiments of the nobility; advocated agreement with the Habsburgs, and later capitulation.—206, 328

Gottfried—see *Kinkel, Gottfried*

Gottschalk, Andreas (1815-1849)—German physician; member of the Cologne community of the Communist League; President of the Cologne Workers' Association (April-June 1848); exponent of 'Left' sectarian tendencies in the German working-class movement.—142, 159, 183, 352

Gouté—French émigré, member of the Committee of the Société des proscrits démocrates et socialistes in London in the early 1850s.—247, 249, 254

Graham, Sir James Robert George (1792-1861)—British statesman, a Whig at the beginning of his career and later a Peelite; Home Secretary in Peel's Cabinet (1841-46).—349

Greppo, Jean Louis (1810-1888)—French socialist, took part in the Lyons uprisings in 1831 and 1834; deputy to the Constituent and Legislative Assemblies during the Second Republic.—310

Grey, Sir George (1799-1882)—British Whig statesman, Home Secretary (1846-52, 1855-58 and 1861-66) and Secretary of State for the Colonies (1854-55).—349

Gross, Magnus—German democratic journalist; emigrated to the USA in the 1850s.—262, 269, 271

Grouchy, Emmanuel, marquis de (1766-1847)—Marshal of France, took part in the Napoleonic wars.—169

Grün, Karl Theodor Ferdinand (penname *Ernst von der Haide*) (1817-1887)—German journalist, 'true socialist' in the mid-1840s; petty-bourgeois democrat during the 1848-49 revolution; deputy to the Prussian National Assembly.—9, 39, 52, 53, 59, 61, 62, 63, 65, 71, 72, 80, 81, 82, 83, 85, 86, 110, 112, 115, 116, 117, 384, 532

Gsell—the Marxes' landlady in Paris.—56, 65, 161

Gubitz, Friedrich Wilhelm (1786-1870)—German writer and wood engraver; editor of *Gesellschafter* from 1817.—432

Guerrier—French socialist.—6, 18

Guizot, François Pierre Guillaume (1787-1874)—French historian and statesman; practically directed France's foreign and home policy

tailor, member of the Communist League; took part in the Elberfeld uprising in 1849.—306

Hunt, Thornton Leigh (1810-1873)— English radical journalist; took part in the Chartist movement in the 1840s-50s.—497

Hurst, Ambrose—Chartist; a reformist after 1848.—272

I

Imandt, Peter (b. 1824)—German teacher; took part in the 1848-49 revolution; member of the Communist League; emigrated to London in 1852; supporter of Marx and Engels.—191

Imbert, Jacques (1793-1851)—French socialist, took part in the Lyons uprising of 1834; a refugee in Belgium in the 1840s; Vice-President of the Brussels Democratic Association; commandant of the Tuileries after the February 1848 revolution.— 123, 124, 126, 129, 169

J

Jacobi, Abraham (1830-1919)—German physician, member of the Communist League; one of the accused in the Cologne communist trial (1852), acquitted; later emigrated to the USA.—369

Jacoby, Johann (1805-1877)—German radical writer and politician; a Left wing leader in the Prussian National Assembly (1848).—133, 393

James I (1566-1625)—King of Great Britain and Ireland (1603-25).—70

Jenni, Samuel Friedrich (1809-1849)— radical journalist and publisher in Bern.—88

Jerrold, Douglas William (1803-1857)— English writer and dramatist.—533

Johnston, Alexander Keith (1804-1871)— British traveller, geographer and cartographer.—476

Johnston, James Finlay Wier (1796-1855)—British chemist, author of works on agricultural chemistry.— 476

Joinville, François Ferdinand Philippe Louis Marie, Prince de (1818-1900)— Duke of Orleans, son of Louis Philippe; emigrated to England after the February revolution of 1848.— 169

Jomini, Antoine Henri, baron de (1779-1869)—Swiss-born general in the service of France and then Russia; military theoretician and historian.— 372

Jones, Ernest Charles (1819-1869)— prominent figure in the English working-class movement, proletarian poet and journalist, Left-wing Chartist leader; friend of Marx and Engels.—158, 243, 244, 251, 263-65, 272, 285, 294, 297, 304, 307, 312, 322, 346, 380, 399, 401, 498, 502, 539

Jottrand, Lucien Léopold (1804-1877)— Belgian lawyer and journalist, President of the Brussels Democratic Association (1847).—123, 124, 129, 132-33, 160, 162

Julius, Gustav (1810-1851)—German democratic journalist, publisher of the daily *Berliner Zeitungs-Halle* (1846-49).—67, 69, 296, 317, 398, 432

Jung, Georg Gottlob (1814-1886)— German democratic writer, Young Hegelian, a manager of the *Rheinische Zeitung*; deputy to the Prussian National Assembly (Left wing) in 1848.—9, 21, 22, 225, 548

Junge (Jungen), Adolph Friedrich— German worker, member of the League of the Just in Paris, member of the Communist League (from 1847); emigrated to the USA early in 1848.—62, 71, 83, 85, 90, 111, 126, 127, 130

Juvenal (Decimus Junius Juvenalis) (c. 60-c. 140)—Roman satirical poet.—285, 440

M

N

O

the early 1850s, supporter of Marx and Engels.—251

Rittinghausen, Moritz (1814-1890)—German democratic journalist; took part in the 1848-49 revolution; later member of the German Social-Democratic Party.—411

Roberts, William Prowting (1806-1871)—English lawyer; connected with the Chartist and the trade union movement.—243

Robertson—English Chartist, friend of George Julian Harney.—264

Robespierre, Maximilien François Marie Isidore de (1758-1794)—prominent figure in the French Revolution, Jacobin leader, head of the revolutionary government (1793-94).—409, 425, 435, 505, 535

Rodbertus-Jagetzow, Johann Karl (1805-1875)—German economist; Left Centre leader in the Prussian National Assembly (1848); subsequently theoretician of 'state socialism'.—357, 403

Rogier, Charles Latour (1800-1885)—Belgian statesman, moderate liberal; Minister of the Interior (1848-52).—160

Rohde, Johann Karl Adolph (b. 1818)—German merchant, participant in the democratic and working-class movement in Hamburg in 1848-49.—196

Rollin—see Ledru-Rollin, Alexandre Auguste

Ronge, Johannes (1813-1887)—German clergyman, initiator of the 'German Catholics'' movement; participant in the revolution of 1848-49, after its defeat emigrated to England.—91, 267, 345, 355, 357, 377, 385, 427, 428, 437, 440, 446, 483

Röser, Peter Gerhard (1814-1865)—German cigar-maker; Vice-President of the Cologne Workers' Association (1848-49); member of the Communist League and from 1850 of its Cologne Central Authority; one of the accused in the Cologne communist trial in 1852; later a Lassallean.—365, 366

Rösing, Johannes (b. 1791)—Bremen merchant; leader of the Democratic Society in Bremen from 1848.—195

Roth, Richard (1821-1858)—Elberfeld friend of the young Engels, later a factory owner.—5

Rothacker, Wilhelm (1828-1889)—German democratic journalist; member of the Communist League; emigrated to the USA in 1850; an editor of Der Hochwächter and from 1853 of the weekly Die Menschenrechte (Cincinnati).—334

Rother, Christian von (1778-1849)—Prussian statesman, Minister of Finance (1836-48).—69

Rothschild, Jacob (James), baron de (1792-1868)—head of the Rothschild banking house in Paris.—71, 73, 109, 144

Rothschilds—dynasty of bankers with branches in many European countries.—474, 482, 507

Rotteck, Karl Wenzeslaus Rodecker von (1775-1840)—German historian and politician, liberal.—322

Rousseau, Jean Jacques (1712-1778)—French philosopher and writer of the Enlightenment.—409, 425, 435

Rovigo, Duke of—see Savary, Anne Jean Marie René, duc de Rovigo

Ruge, Arnold (1802-1880)—German radical journalist and Young Hegelian philosopher; deputy to the Frankfurt National Assembly (Left Centre) in 1848; a leader of the German petty-bourgeois refugees in England in the 1850s.—10, 15, 18, 48, 58, 109, 135, 200, 249, 255, 265-68, 279, 285, 287, 296, 317, 321, 334, 342, 345, 355, 359-60, 376, 377, 384-88, 391, 397, 399, 402, 403, 408, 409, 417, 425, 426-31, 433, 437-41, 446, 447-48, 449, 497, 499, 501, 532

Rühl—acquaintance of Joseph Weydemeyer in Frankfurt.—209

Rumigny, Marie Hippolyte Gueilly, marquis de (1784-1871)—French diplomat, envoy to Switzerland, Piedmont and Belgium.—115

INDEX OF LITERARY AND MYTHOLOGICAL NAMES

Sancho Panza—character in Cervantes' Don Quixote.—397

Sapphira (also Saphira) (Bib.)—wife and accomplice of Ananias.—84

Sarastro—character in Mozart's opera Die Zauberflöte; a good magician.—109

Sibyl—a prophetess in ancient times.—494

Siegfried—one of the main characters in an ancient German epic and in the medieval epic Nibelungenlied.—153

Tuck—a monk in the Robin Hood ballads.—245

Tupman, Tracy—character in Dickens' Posthumous Papers of the Pickwick Club.—343, 350, 352, 497

Uriah (also Urias) (Bib.)—a Hittite officer in the army of David; husband of Bathsheba. David ordered Joab, his general, to secure Uriah's death by abandoning him in the heart of battle.—467

INDEX OF QUOTED
AND MENTIONED LITERATURE

WORKS BY KARL MARX AND FREDERICK ENGELS

Marx, Karl

The Bourgeoisie and the Counter-Revolution (present edition, Vol. 8)
— Die Bourgeoisie und die Contrrevolution. In: *Neue Rheinische Zeitung,*
Nr. 165, 169, 170, 183; 10., 15., 16., 31. Dezember 1848.—489

The Class Struggles in France, 1848 to 1850 (present edition, Vol. 10)
— Die Klassenkämpfe in Frankreich, 1848 bis 1850. In: *Neue Rheinische Zeitung.
Politisch-ökonomische Revue,* Nr. 1, Januar 1850; Nr. 2, Februar 1850; Nr. 3,
März 1850; Nr. 5-6, Mai-Oktober 1850.—435

Contribution to the Critique of Hegel's Philosophy of Law. Introduction (present edition,
Vol. 3)
— Zur Kritik der Hegelschen Rechtsphilosophie. Einleitung. In: *Deutsch-
Französische Jahrbücher,* hrsg. von A. Ruge und K. Marx, 1-ste und 2-te
Lieferung. Paris, 1844.—19, 34, 59

[Editorial Statement Concerning the Reappearance of the 'Neue Rheinische Zeitung']
(present edition, Vol. 7). In: *Neue Rheinische Zeitung,* Nr. 114, 12. Oktober
1848.—179

The Eighteenth Brumaire of Louis Bonaparte (present edition, Vol. 11)
— Der achtzehnte Brumaire des Louis Bonaparte. In: *Die Revolution,* Erstes
Heft, New York, 1852.—519, 562, 563

Gesammelte Aufsätze. Heft I. Köln, 1851.—266, 342, 355, 432

[Letters Opened] (present edition, Vol. 8). In: *Neue Rheinische Zeitung,* Nr. 155,
Extrablatt, 29. November 1848.—181

*Moralising Criticism and Critical Morality. A Contribution to German Cultural History.
Contra Karl Heinzen* (present edition, Vol. 6)

---

* The asterisk denotes articles which originally had no title or were not published in the
authors' lifetime.

— Die Moralisierende Kritik und die Kritisierende Moral. Beitrag zur deutschen Kulturgeschichte. Gegen Karl Heinzen. In: *Deutsche-Brüsseler-Zeitung*, Nr. 86, 87, 90, 92, 94; 28., 31. Oktober; 11., 18., 25. November 1847.—139, 489

On the Jewish Question (present edition, Vol. 3)
— Zur Judenfrage. In: *Deutsch-Französische Jahrbücher*, hrsg. von A. Ruge und K. Marx, 1-ste und 2-te Lieferung. Paris, 1844.—19, 34, 59

The Poverty of Philosophy. Answer to the 'Philosophy of Poverty' by M. Proudhon (present edition, Vol. 6)
— Misère de la philosophie. Réponse à la philosophie de la misère de M. Proudhon. Paris-Bruxelles, 1847.—109, 112, 114, 121, 124, 134, 135, 137, 142-44, 146, 151, 156, 181, 201, 252, 435, 490, 494

The Protectionists, the Free Traders and the Working Class (present edition, Vol. 6)
— Die Schutzzöllner, die Freihandelsmänner und die arbeitende Klasse. In: *Zwei Reden über die Freihandels- und Schutzzollfrage.* Hamm, 1848.—135, 136, 143-44, 145

Speech on the Question of Free Trade (present edition, Vol. 6)
— Discours sur la question du libre échange. Bruxelles, 1848.—156, 219

* [*Statement and Accompanying Letter to the Editorial Board of the Augsburg 'Allgemeine Zeitung'. October 4, 1851*] (present edition, Vol. 11). In: *Kölnische Zeitung*, Nr. 242, 9. Oktober 1851.—472

*[*To the Editor of 'La Réforme'*] (present edition, Vol. 6). In: *La Réforme*, 8 mars 1848.—161

Wage Labour and Capital (present edition, Vol. 9)
— Lohnarbeit und Kapital. In: *Neue Rheinische Zeitung*, Nr. 264, 265, 266, 267, 269; 5., 6., 7., 8., 11. April 1849.—208

Engels, Frederick
The Campaign for the German Imperial Constitution (present edition, Vol. 10)
— Die deutsche Reichsverfassungs-Campagne. In: *Neue Rheinische Zeitung. Politisch-ökonomische Revue*, Nr. 1, 2, 3, 1850.—207, 214, 215, 221, 228, 234

The Chartist Movement [*The Fraternal Democrats to the Working Classes of Great Britain and Ireland*] (present edition, Vol. 6)
— Mouvement chartiste. In: *La Réforme*, 10 janvier 1848.—156

*[*The Commercial Crisis in England.—The Chartist Movement.—Ireland*] (present edition, Vol. 6). In: *La Réforme*, 26 octobre 1847.—139

The Communists and Karl Heinzen (present edition, Vol. 6)
— Die Kommunisten und Karl Heinzen. In: *Deutsche-Brüsseler-Zeitung*, Nr. 79, 80; 3. und 7. October 1847.—126, 489

The Condition of England. 'Past and Present' by Thomas Carlyle, London, 1843 (present edition, Vol. 3)
— Die Lage Englands. 'Past and Present' by Thomas Carlyle. London, 1843. In: *Deutsch-Französische Jahrbücher*, 1844.—4, 19, 34

The Condition of the Working-Class in England. From Personal Observation and Authentic Sources (present edition, Vol. 4)
— Die Lage der arbeitenden Klasse in England. Nach einer Anschauung und authentischen Quellen. Leipzig, 1845.— 10, 17, 22, 25, 26, 34, 67

[Conditions and Prospects of a War of the Holy Alliance against France in 1852] (present edition, Vol. 10).— 329, 332

[The Constitutional Question in Germany] (present edition, Vol. 6).— 113, 117-18

[Critical Review of Proudhon's Book 'Idée générale de la Révolution au XIXᵉ siècle'] (present edition, Vol. 11).— 444, 449, 453, 459, 478, 486, 488, 492, 495

Description of Recently Founded Communist Colonies Still in Existence (present edition, Vol. 4)
— Beschreibung der in neuer Zeit entstandenen und noch bestehenden Kommunistischen Ansiedlungen. In: *Deutsches Bürgerbuch für 1845,* Darmstadt, 1845.— 6, 23, 69, 87

The English Ten Hours' Bill (present edition, Vol. 10)
— Die englische Zehnstundenbill. In: *Neue Rheinische Zeitung. Politisch-ökonomische Revue,* Nr. 4, April 1850.— 250

The Festival of Nations in London (present edition, Vol. 6)
— Das Fest der Nationen in London. In: *Rheinische Jahrbücher zur gesellschaftlichen Reform.* Bd. II, Belle-Vue, 1846.— 69

The Frankfurt Assembly Debates the Polish Question (present edition, Vol. 7)
— Die Polendebate in Frankfurt. In: *Neue Rheinische Zeitung,* Nr. 70, 73, 81, 82, 86, 90, 91, 93, 96; 9., 12., 20., 22., 26., 31. August, 1., 3., 7. September 1848.— 505

German Socialism in Verse and Prose (present edition, Vol. 6)
— Deutscher Socialismus in Versen und Prosa. In: *Deutsche-Brüsseler-Zeitung,* Nr. 73, 74, 93, 94, 95, 96, 97, 98; 12., 16. September, 21., 25., 28. November, 2., 5., 9. Dezember 1847.— 110, 145

Herr Müller.—Radetzky's Chicanery towards Tessin.—The Federal Council.—Lohbauer (present edition, Vol. 8)
— Hr. Müller.—Radetzki's Chikanen gegen Tessin.—Der Bundesrath.—Lohbauer. In: *Neue Rheinische Zeitung,* Nr. 194, 13. Januar 1849.— 185

[Hungary] (present edition, Vol. 9). In: *Neue Rheinische Zeitung,* Nr. 301, 19. Mai 1849.— 489

The 'Kölnische Zeitung' on the Magyar Struggle (present edition, Vol. 8)
— Die "Kölnische Zeitung" über den magyarischen Kampf. In: *Neue Rheinische Zeitung,* Nr. 225, 18. Februar 1849.— 489

The Magyar Struggle (present edition, Vol. 8)
— Der magyarische Kampf. In: *Neue Rheinische Zeitung,* Nr. 194, 13. Januar 1849.— 181, 185, 189, 489

The Masters and the Workers in England. To the Worker Editors of 'L'Aletier' (present edition, Vol. 6)
— Les maîtres et les ouvriers en Angleterre. In: *L'Atelier,* No. 2, novembre 1847.— 137

The Movements of 1847 (present edition, Vol. 6)
— Die Bewegungen von 1847. In: *Deutsche-Brüsseler-Zeitung*, Nr. 7, 23. Januar 1848.—155

Müller.—The Freiburg Government.—Ochsenbein (present edition, Vol. 8)
— Müller.—Die Freiburger Regierung.—Ochsenbein. In: *Neue Rheinische Zeitung*, Nr. 197, 17. Januar 1849.—185

The National Council (present edition, Vol. 8)
— Der Nationalrath. In: *Neue Rheinische Zeitung*, Nr. 165 und 165 (2. Ausgabe), 10. Dezember 1848.—181

Outlines of a Critique of Political Economy (present edition, Vol. 3)
— Umrisse zu einer Kritik der Nationalökonomie. In: *Deutsch-Französische Jahrbücher*, 1-2. Lfg. Paris, 1844.—4, 19, 34, 61, 271

* *Principles of Communism* (present edition, Vol. 6).—139, 149

Protectionist Agitation.—Recruiting into the Neapolitan Army (present edition, Vol. 8)
— Schutzzollagitation.—Neapolitanische Werbungen. In: *Neue Rheinische Zeitung*, Nr. 197, 17. Januar 1849.—185

[Proudhon] (present edition, Vol. 8).—181

The Prussian Warrant for the Arrest of Kossuth (present edition, Vol. 8)
— Preußischer Steckbrief gegen Kossuth. In: *Neue Rheinische Zeitung*, Nr. 207, 28. Januar 1849.—488

Reform Movement in France.—Banquet of Dijon (present edition, Vol. 6). In: *The Northern Star*, No. 530, 18. December 1847.—152

The 'Réforme' and the 'National' (present edition, Vol. 6)
— Die Réform und der National. In: *Deutsche-Brüsseler-Zeitung*, Nr. 104, 30. Dezember 1847.—152

Revolution and Counter-Revolution in Germany (present edition, Vol. 11). In: *New-York Daily Tribune*, Nos. 3282, 3284, 3292, 3293, 3297, 3311, 3389, 3395, 3403, 3406, 3407, 3425, 3432, 3438, 3517, 3537, 3564, 3576, 3594; 25 and 28 October, 6, 7, 12 and 28 November 1851, 27 February, 5, 15, 18 and 19 March, 9, 17 and 24 April, 27 July, 19 August, 18 September, 2 and 23 October 1852.—434, 436, 445, 453, 457, 458, 468, 497, 506, 518, 519, 563

The 'Satisfied' Majority.—Guizot's Scheme of 'Reform'.—Queer Notions of M. Garnier-Pages.—Democratic Banquet at Châlon.—Speech of M. Ledru-Rollin.—A Democratic Congress.—Speech of M. Flocon.—The 'Réforme' and the 'National' (present edition, Vol. 6). In: *The Northern Star*, No. 533, 8 January 1848.—152

[The Situation in Belgium] (present edition, Vol. 6).—164

Speeches in Elberfeld (present edition, Vol. 4)
— [Zwei Reden in Elberfeld.] In: *Rheinische Jahrbücher zur gesellschaftlichen Reform*. 1. Bd. Darmstadt, 1845.—28

Split in the Camp.—The 'Réforme' and the 'National'.—March of Democracy (present edition, Vol. 6). In: *The Northern Star*, No. 528, 4 December 1847.—152

The State of Germany. Letter III (present edition, Vol. 6). In: *The Northern Star*, No. 438, 4 April 1846.—537

The Swiss Press (present edition, Vol. 8)

— Die Schweizer Presse. In: *Neue Rheinische Zeitung,* Nr. 197, 17. Januar 1849.—185

To the Editor of *'The Northern Star'* (present edition, Vol. 6). In: *The Northern Star,* No. 544, 25 March 1848.—160

* To the Editor of *'The Times'* (present edition, Vol. 10).—313, 314

To the Working-Classes of Great-Britain [address] (present edition, Vol. 4). In: *Der Lage der arbeitenden Klasse in England.* Leipzig, 1845.—10

Marx, Karl and Engels, Frederick

Address of the Central Authority to the League, March 1850 (present edition, Vol. 10)
— Die Zentralbehörde an den Bund, London im März 1850 (distributed as handwritten copies).—384, 389, 392, 432

Address of the Central Authority to the League, June 1850 (present edition, Vol. 10)
— Die Zentralbehörde an den Bund. [London, Juni 1850] (distributed as handwritten copies).—239, 551

*[*Announcement of the *'Neue Rheinische Zeitung. Politisch-ökonomische Revue'*] (present edition, Vol. 10). In: *Kölnische Zeitung,* Nr. 24, erste Beilage, 27. Januar 1850; *Neue Deutsche Zeitung,* Nr. 14, 23, 31; 16., 26. Januar, 5. Februar 1850; *Schweizerische National-Zeitung,* Nr. 8, 10. Januar 1850.—219, 222, 549

[*Circular Against Kriege*] (present edition, Vol. 6)
— Zirkular gegen Kriege. May 1846.—68, 84, 86

Demands of the Communist Party in Germany (present edition, Vol. 7)
— Forderungen der Kommunistischen Partei in Deutschland, gedruckt als Flugblatt, Köln, 1848.—173

The German Ideology. Critique of Modern German Philosophy According to Its Representatives Feuerbach, Bruno Bauer and Stirner, and of German Socialism According to Its Various Prophets (present edition, Vol. 5)
— Die deutsche Ideologie. Kritik der neuesten deutschen Philosophie, in ihren Repräsentanten, Feuerbach, B. Bauer und Stirner, und des deutschen Sozialismus in seinen verschiedenen Propheten.—41, 50, 54, 68, 76, 79, 88, 93, 105, 109, 110, 112-13, 120, 151, 532

The Holy Family, or Critique of Critical Criticism. Against Bruno Bauer and Company (present edition, Vol. 4)
— Die heilige Familie oder Kritik der kritischen Kritik. Gegen Bruno Bauer und Konsorten, Frankfurt a. M., 1845.—4, 7, 8, 13, 16, 18, 25, 28, 31, 34, 495

Introduction to the Leaflet of L. A. Blanqui's Toast Sent to the Refugee Committee (present edition, Vol. 10)
— Vorbemerkung. In: *Trinkspruch gesandt durch den Bürger L. A. Blanqui an die Kommission der Flüchtlinge zu London für die Jahresfeier des 24. Februar 1851.* Bern, 1851.—334, 381

*[*A Letter to Adam, Barthélemy and Vidil] (present edition, Vol. 10).—304

Manifesto of the Communist Party (present edition, Vol. 6)
— Manifest der Kommunistischen Partei, London, 1848.—149, 173, 264

[*On Poland*] (present edition, Vol. 6)
— Reden von Marx und Engels über Polen in London am 29. November 1847.
   In: *Deutsche-Brüsseler-Zeitung*, Nr 98, 9. Dezember 1817.—150

Review [January-February 1850] (present edition, Vol. 10)
— Revue [Januar/Februar 1850]. In: *Neue Rheinische Zeitung. Politisch-
   ökonomische Revue*, Nr. 2, Februar 1850.—222, 461

Review, May to October [1850] (present edition, Vol. 10)
— Revue, Mai bis Oktober [1850]. In: *Neue Rheinische Zeitung. Politisch-
   ökonomische Revue*, Nr. 5-6, Mai-Oktober 1850.—250, 395

Statement [April 20, 1850] (present edition, Vol. 10)
— Erklärung. 20. April 1850. In: *Neue Deutsche Zeitung*, Nr. 102, 28. April
   1850.—232, 233

* *Statement* [27 January 1851, against A. Ruge] (present edition, Vol. 10).—267,
   268-69, 272, 397

* *To the Editor of 'The Times'* (present edition, Vol. 11).—497

WORKS BY DIFFERENT AUTHORS

Alison, A. *History of Europe from the Commencement of the French Revolution in
MDCCLXXXIX to the Restoration of the Bourbons in MDCCCXV*. Vol. 1-10,
Edinburgh, 1833-1842.—372

Antoine, G. *À M. le rédacteur du journal 'La Patrie'*. In: *La Patrie*, No. 66, 7 mars
1851.—313, 381

Ariosto, L. *L'Orlando furioso.*—202

Barthélemy. E. *Au rédacteur en chef du journal 'La Patrie'*. In: *La Patrie*, No. 71, 12
mars 1851.—318, 381

Becker, J. Ph. und Esselen, Ch. *Geschichte der süddeutschen Mai-Revolution des Jahres
1849.* Genf, 1849.—222

Bem, J. *Erfahrungen über die Congrevschen Brand-Raketen, bis zum Jahre 1819 in der
Königl. Poln. Artillerie gesammelt.* Weimar, 1820.—371

Bernays, K. L. *Die Ermordung der Herzogin von Praslin. Ein Beitrag zur Geschichte des
Kampfes der Leidenschaften mit den modernen Gesellschafts-Elementen.* Flawyl,
1847.—135, 157

[Bernays, K. L.] *Affaire Martin du Nord.* In: *Kölnische Zeitung*, Nr. 67, 8. März
1847.—114
— *Das entschleierte Geheimniß der Criminal-Justiz. Eine kommunistische
   Anschauungsweise.* In: *Der Volks-Tribun*, Nr. 26, 27; 27. Juni, 4. Juli
   1846.—88
— *Jugement rendu contre J. Rothschild et Georges Dairnvaell, auteur de l'Histoire de
   Rothschild 1er par le Tribunal de la Seine, accompagné d'un jugement sur l'accident
   de Fampoux.* Paris, 1846.—73
— *Rothschild. Ein Urtheilsspruch vom menschlichen Standpunkte aus.* Herisau,
   1846.—73, 89, 109

Bible
  The Old Testament
    Exodus—390, 392
    2 Samuel—61, 290, 467
    Psalms—273, 280
    Ecclesiastes—382
  The New Testament
    Matthew—376
    John—501
    The Acts—84
    1 Corinthians—488
    Galatians—13
    Revelation—13
Biedermann, K. *Unsre Gegenwart und Zukunft.* Leipzig, 1846.—66

Blanc, L. *Histoire de dix ans. 1830-1840.* T. 1-5, Paris, 1841-1844.—279, 294, 302
— *Histoire de la révolution française.* T. 1-2, Paris, 1847.—115, 137, 154, 157, 302
— *Organisation du travail.* 5-éd. Paris, 1847.—19, 134, 302
— *Pages d'histoire de la révolution de février 1848.* Bruxelles, 1850.—302
— *Programme de M. Lamartine.* In: *La Réforme,* Paris, 27 octobre 1847.—134, 137
— *To the Editor of 'The Daily News'.* In: *The Daily News,* 11 December 1851.—511
— *To the Editor of 'The Times'.* London, March 3. In: *The Times,* No. 20741, 5 March 1851.—381

[Blanqui, L.-A.] *Toste envoyé par le citoyen L.-A. Blanqui à la commission près les réfugiés de Londres, pour le banquet anniversaire du 24 février.* In: *La Patrie,* No. 58, 27 fevrier 1851.—313, 314, 318, 334, 343, 381

Bonaparte, N.-L. *Des idées napoléoniennes.* Paris, 1839.—509

Börne, L. *Urtheil über H. Heine. Ungedruckte Stellen aus den Pariser Briefen. Als Anfang: Stimmen über H. Heine's letztes Buch, aus Zeitblättern.* Frankfurt a.-M., 1840.—38

[Bornstedt, A.] *La dernière assemblée de la société démocratique du Bruxelles...* In: *La Réforme,* 19 janvier 1848.—156

Bürgers, H. *Prospekt zur Gründung der Neuen Rheinischen Zeitung.* In: *Das Westphälische Dampfboot.* Paclertorn, Nr. 12, 17. Mai 1848.—171, 172

[Bürgers, H.] *Hr. v. Ladenberg und die Volksschullehrer.* In: *Neue Rheinische Zeitung,* Nr. 182, 30. Dezember 1848.—186

Cabet, [E.] *Voyage en Icarie, roman philosophique et social.* Paris, 1842.—535

Capefigue, [J.-B.-H.-R.] *Les cent jours.* T. I-II, Paris, 1841.—116

Carlyle, Th. *Past and Present.* London, 1843.—4

Cervantes Saavedra, M. de. *Don Quixote.*—397

Chemnitz, [M. F.] *Schleswig-Holsteinische Bundeslied.* In: *Rheinischer Beobachter,* Nr. 259, 16. September, 1846.—70

Christ, A. *Ueber den gegenwärtigen Stand der Frage der Schutzzölle.* Frankfurt a. M., 1851.—376, 402

Cicero, Marcus Tullius. *Epistolae.*—316

Cobden, R. [Speech at a meeting in London in support of Hungary. 23 July 1849.] In: *The Times*, No. 20236, 24 July 1849 (in the article 'Hungarian Independence') and *The Northern Star*, No. 614, 28 July 1849.—206

Crüger, F. [Speech at a democratic banquet in Brussels on 27 September 1847.] In: *Deutsche-Brüsseler-Zeitung*, Nr. 83, 17. Oktober 1847.—127

Daniels, R. *Mikrokosmos. Entwurf einer physiologischen Anthropologie.* Manuscript.— 326, 330

Dante, Alighieri. *La Divina Commedia. Inferno.*—474

Daul, A. *Tagebuch eines politischen Flüchtlings während des Freiheitskampfes in der Rheinpfalz und Baden.* St. Gallen, 1849.—222

Decker, C. von. *La Petite guerre, ou Traité des opérations secondaires de la guerre.* Paris, 1827.—331, 406

Delescluze, Ch. *Le conclave démocratique.* In: *La Voix du Proscrit*, No. 19, 30 août 1851.—448

Dietz, O. *An die deutschen Arbeiter-Vereine.* In: *Schweizerische National-Zeitung*, Nr. 5, 7. Januar 1851.—265

Doherty, H. *La question religieuse.* In: *La Phalange.* T. IV, Paris, 1846.—55

Dronke, E. *Aus dem Volk.* Frankfurt am Main, 1846.—164
— *Berlin.* Bd. 1, 2. Frankfurt am Main, 1846.—164
— *Polizei-Geschichten.* Leipzig, 1846.—164

[Dronke, E.] *Allianz der europäischen Polizei.* In: *Neue Rheinische Zeitung*, Nr. 192, 11. Januar 1849.—191

Dureau de la Malle, A. J. *Économie politique des Romains.* T. I-II, Paris, 1840.—425, 433

Eccarius, J. G. *The Last Stage of Bourgeois Society.* In: *The Friend of the People*, Nos. 4, 5, 6, 7; 4, 11, 18 and 25 January 1851.—285
— *Die Schneiderei in London oder der Kampf des großen und des kleinen Capitals.* In: *Neue Rheinische Zeitung. Politisch-ökonomische Revue*, Nr. 5-6, Mai-Oktober 1850.—250

Ewerbeck, H. *L'Allemagne et les Allemands.* Paris, 1851.—475, 478

[Ewerbeck, H.] *Hier Baiern!—Hier Andalusia!* In: *Pariser Horen*, Jg. 1. Paris, April 1847.—112

[Faider, Victor.] *Encore et toujours l'expulsion de M. Marx.* In: *Le Débat Social*, 19 mars 1848.—162, 164

Feuerbach, L. *Das Wesen des Christenthums.* Leipzig, 1841.—12
— *Das Wesen des Glaubens im Sinne Luther's. Ein Beitrag zum Wesen des Christenthums.* Leipzig, 1844.—8
— *Das Wesen der Religion.* In: *Die Epigonen*, Bd. 1, Leipzig, 1846.—54, 68, 75-78

24*

[Fix, Th.] *Bankwesen.—Question des banques.—Un nouveau fantôme en Allemagne,* par Gustave Julius. In-8°. Leipsig, 1846 [review]. In: *Journal des Économistes.* Paris, T. 15, No. 58, septembre 1846.—67
— *Unsre Gegenwart und Zukunft (Notre Présent et notre Avenir),* par Charles Biedermann. 2 vol. in-8°. Leipsig, 1846 [review]. In: *Journal des Économistes.* Paris. T. 15, No. 57, août 1846.—66

Fourier, Ch. *Section ébauchée des trois unités externes.* In: *La Phalange.* T. I, Paris, 1845.—25
— *Théorie des quatre mouvements et des destinées générales.* In: Ch. Fourier. *Oeuvres complètes.* 2 éd. T. I, Paris, 1841.—57

Freiligrath, F. *Abschiedswort der 'Neuen Rheinischen Zeitung'.* In: *Neue Rheinische Zeitung,* Nr. 301, 19. Mai 1849.—198
— *Der Mohrenfürst.*—354, 520
— *Reveille.*—559
— *Trotz alledem!*—377, 398, 527, 531, 558

Godwin, W. *An Enquiry concerning political justice, and its influence on general virtue and happiness.* In two volumes. London, 1793.—27

Goethe, J. W. von. *Faust.* Der Tragödie. Erster Teil.—18
— *Der Fischer.*—266, 474
— *Die Spinnerin.*—500
— *Torquato Tasso.*—264
— *Totalität.*—68

Grün, K. *Die soziale Bewegung in Frankreich und Belgien. Briefe und Studien.* Darmstadt, 1845.—40, 53
— *Über Goethe vom menschlichen Standpunkte.* Darmstadt, 1846.—110

[Grün, K.] *Die preussischen Landtags-Abschiede. Ein Wort zur Zeit.* Birwinken, 1846.—53, 59, 62
— *Über die Ausweisung von Eisermann und Anderen.* In: *Kölnische Zeitung,* Nr. 60, 1. März 1847.—115

Gutzkow, K. *Vorrede zu Börne's Leben.* In: L. Börne, *Urtheil über H. Heine.* Frankfurt a. M., 1840.—38

[Harney, G. J.] [Introduction to the *Manifesto of the German Communist Party.*] In: *The Red Republican,* No. 21, 9 November 1850.—481

Hegel, G. W. F. *Phänomenologie des Geistes.* In: G. W. F. Hegel. *Werke.* 2-te Auflage, Bd. 2, Berlin, 1841.—494

Heine, H. *Atta Troll. Ein Sommernachtstraum.*—265, 418, 430
— *Deutschland. Ein Wintermärchen.*—31, 211
— *Heinrich Heine über Ludwig Börne.* Hamburg, 1840.—38
— *Ein Jüngling liebt ein Mädchen...* In: *Lyrisches Intermezzo.*—64
— *Unsere Marine.* Nautisches Gedicht.—31
— *Zwei Ritter* (Romanzero).—508, 513, 516

Heinzen, K. *An die Herren Hoff und Kapp.* In: *Deutsche Schnellpost,* 13. August 1851.—446-47
— *Die Helden des teutschen Kommunismus. Dem Herrn Karl Marx gewidmet.* Bern 1848.—181

— *Lehren der Revolution.* In: *Deutsche Londoner Zeitung,* Nr. 241, 242; 9., 16. November 1849.—220

— *Meine Religion. Briefe an einen 'frommen' Mann.* In: *Deutsche schnellpost,* 23. Juli 1851.—417

— [Polemik. Karl Heinzen und die Kommunisten.] In: *Deutsche-Brüsseler-Zeitung,* Nr. 77, 26. September 1847.—418

— *Ein 'Repräsentant' der Kommunisten.* In: *Deutsche-Brüsseler-Zeitung,* Nr. 84, 21. Oktober 1847.—139

Hess, M. *Dottore Graziano's Werke. Zwei Jahre in Paris. Studien und Erinnerungen von A. Ruge* [Review]. In: *Deutsche-Brüsseler-Zeitung,* Nr. 62, 63, 5., 8. August 1847.—48

— *Erklärung.* In: *Kölnische Zeitung,* Nr. 209. Beilage; 28. Juli 1846.—48

— *Die Folgen einer Revolution des Proletariats.* In: *Deutsche-Brüsseler-Zeitung,* Nr. 82, 87, 89, 90; 14., 31. Oktober; 7., 11. November 1847.—140

— *Die letzten Philosophen.* Darmstadt, 1845.—16

Historischer und geographischer Atlas von Europa. Bd. 2, Berlin, 1836.—263, 278, 301

Hoff, H. and Kapp, F. *Herrn Karl Heinzen hier.* In: *Deutsche Schnellpost,* 13. August 1851.—446-47

Homer, *Iliad.*—444

Horace (Quintus Horatius Flaccus). *Ars Poetica.*—78

— *Carmina,* Liber III.—357

Imbert, [J.] [Speech at a democratic banquet in Brussels on 27 September 1847.] In: *Deutsche-Brüsseler-Zeitung,* No. 80, 7. Oktober 1847.—124

Jerrold, D. W. *Mrs Caudle's Curtain Lectures.*—533

Johnston, A. K. *The Physical Atlas of Natural Phenomena: a Series of Maps and Illustrations of Geographical Distribution of Natural Phenomena.* Edinburgh and London, 1848.—476

Johnston, I. F. W. *Notes on North America Agricultural, Economical, and Social.* Vol. I-II, Edinburgh and London, 1851.—476

Jones, E. *What is Kossuth? At last he has made his choice.* In: *Notes to the People,* Vol. II, No. 31, 1851.—498

Julius, G. *Bankwesen. Ein neues Gespenst in Deutschland.* Leipzig, 1846.—67

Juvenalis. *Satirae.*—285, 440

Kinkel, G. *Der Brief an die Bürger von St. Louis.* In: *Bremer Tages-Chronik,* Nr. 507, 25. Februar 1851.—430

Kriege, H. *Die kommunistischen Literaten in Brüssel und die kommunistische Politik.* In: *Der Volks-Tribun,* Nr. 25, 26; 20., 27. Juni 1846.—79, 84

La Sagra, Ramon de. *Organisation du travail. Questions préliminaires à l'examen de ce problème.* Paris, 1848.—156

Las Cases. *Mémorial de Sainte-Hélène, ou journal où se trouve consigné, jour par jour, ce qu'a dit et fait Napoléon durant dix-huit mois.* Paris, 1823-1824.—464, 542

Leroux, P. *Lettres sur le fouriérisme. III* e *Lettre. Saint-Simon et Fourier.* In: *Revue Sociale, ou solution pacifique du problème du prolétariat.* No. 11, août 1846.—57

Livius, Titus. *Ab urbe condita libri.* 240

Lubliner, L. [Note on Marx's Expulsion from Belgium.] In: *L'Emancipation,* No. 67, 7 mars 1848.—159

Lüning, O. *Der Volkstribun, redigirt von Hermann Kriege in New York* [Introduction and comments on Marx and Engels' 'Circular Against Kriege']. In: *Das Westphälische Dampfboot,* Juli 1846.—68
— *Neue Rheinische Zeitung, politisch-ökonomische Revue von Karl Marx* [review]. In: *Neue Deutsche Zeitung.* Frankfurt am Main, Nr. 148-151; 22., 23., 25., 26. Juni 1850.—238, 559

MacCulloch, J. R. *A Dictionary Practical, Theoretical, and Historical, of Commerce and Commercial Navigation.* London, 1832.—480

MacGregor, J. *Commercial Tariffs and Regulations, Resources, and Trade of the Several States of Europe and America.* London, 1841-1850.—480
— *The Resources and Statistics of Nations.* London, 1835.—480

Marseillaise (French revolutionary song).—24, 155, 169

Mayer, P. [Comments on Barthélemy's letter.] In: *La Patrie,* No. 71, 12 mars 1851.—318

Mazzini, J. *Au Rédacteur.* In: *Journal des Débats politiques et littéraires,* 18 mai 1851.—361
— *Le Pape au dix-neuvième siècle.* Bruxelles, 1850.—250
— *Republic and Royalty in Italy.* In: *The Red Republican,* Nos. 2, 3, 4, 5, 6, 7, 8, 10, 11, 13, 15, 17, 19, 20, 21; 29 June, 6, 13, 20, 27 July, 3, 10, 24, 31 August, 14, 28 September, 12, 26 October, 2, 9, November 1850.—250, 255

Michelet, J. *Histoire de la révolution française.* T. 2, Paris, 1847.—154

Mieroslawski, L. *Rapports du général Mieroslawski sur la campagne de Bade.* Berne, 1849.—222

Molinari, G. *Un nouveau manifeste rouge.* In: *La Patrie,* 28 novembre 1850.—249

Montecuccoli, R. *Memorie della guerra ed istruzione d'un generale.* [Venezia, 1703.]—371

Moras [C.] [Speech at a democratic banquet in Brussels on 27 September 1847.] In: *Deutsche-Brüsseler-Zeitung,* Nr. 80, 7. Oktober 1847.—124

Moreau de Jonnès, A.—see *Statistique générale de la France*

Mozart, W. *Die Zauberflöte.* Oper in zwei Aufzügen. Libretto E. Schikaneder.—109

Napier, W. F. P. *History of the War in the Peninsula and in the South of France, from the Year 1807 to the Year 1814.* Volumes I-VI, London, 1828-1840.—316, 333, 372

O'Connor, F. *To the Editors of the 'Nottingham Mercury', the 'Nonconformist', the 'Dispatch', the 'Globe', the 'Manchester Examiner' and 'Lloyds' Trash'.* In: *The Northern Star,* No. 522, 23 October 1847.—139

Die Opposition. [Published by K. Heinzen.] Mannheim, 1846.—48

Physiocrates, Quesnay, Dupont de Nemours, Mercier de la Rivière, L'Abbé Baudeau, Le Trosne, avec une introduction sur la doctrine des phisiocrates, des commentaires et des notices historiques, par M. Eugène Daire. P. 1. 2. Paris, 1846.—51

[Pinto, I.] *Traité de la circulation et du crédit.* Amsterdam, 1771.—376

Porter, G. R. *The Progress of the Nation, in Its Various Social and Economical Relations, from the Beginning of the Nineteenth Century.* A new edition. London, 1851.—480

Price, R. *An Appeal to the Public on the Subject of the National Debt.* London, 1771.—423
— *Observations on Reversionary Payments; on Schemes for Providing Annuities for Widows, and for Persons in Old Age; on the Method of Calculating the Values of Assurances on Lives; and on the National Debt.* London, 1771.—423

Proudhon, P.-J. *Gratuité du crédit. Discussion entre M. Fr. Bastiat et M. Proudhon.* Paris, 1850.—492
— *Idée générale de la Révolution au XIXe siècle.* Paris, 1851.—399, 401, 409-16, 419-25, 433, 444, 475, 486, 511
— *Philosophie der Staatsökonomie oder Nothwendigkeit des Elends.* Deutsch bearbeitet von Karl Grün. Bd. 1-2. Darmstadt, 1847.—62, 87
— *Système des contradictions économiques, ou Philosophie de la misère.* T. I-II, Paris, [1846].—62, 63, 70-71, 84, 94, 95-96, 255

Reden, F. von. *Vergleichende Kultur-Statistik der Gebiets- und Bevölkerungsverhältnisse der Gross-Staaten Europa's.* Berlin, 1848.—481

Rodbertus [-Jagetzow, J. K.] *Sociale Briefe an von Kirchmann. Dritter Brief: Widerlegung der Ricardo'schen Lehre von der Grundrente und Begründung einer neuen Rententheorie.* Berlin, 1851.—357

Rotteck, C. von. *Allgemeine Weltgeschichte für alle Stände, von den frühesten Zeiten bis zum Jahre 1831.* Bd. I-IV, Stuttgart, 1832-1833.—322

Rotteck, C. von, und Welcker, C. *Das Staats-Lexikon. Encyklopaedie der sämmtlichen Staatswissenschaften für alle Stände.* Bd. 1-12, Altona, 1845-1848.—322

Ruge, A. *Adresse an die Opposition des Vereinigten Landtages in Berlin.* In: Ruge, A. *Polemische Briefe.* Mannheim, 1847.—135
— *An einen Patrioten.* In: *Telegraph für Deutschland,* Nr. 203, 204; Dezember 1844.—18
— ['London, 13 January'.] In: *Bremer Tages-Chronik,* Nr. 474, 17. Januar 1851.—265, 267
— *Der Rabbi Moses und Moritz Hess.* In: *Die Opposition.* Mannheim 1846.—48, 532
— *Der teutsche Kommunismus. Rheinische Jahrbücher zur gesellschaftlichen Reform, herausgegeben unter Mitwirkung Mehrerer von Hermann Püttmann.* Bd. 1. Darmstadt. In: *Die Opposition.* Mannheim, 1846.—48

Saint-Simon [Cl.-H. de]. *Catéchisme politique des industriels.* In: *Oeuvres de Saint-Simon,* Paris, 1841.—358
— *Lettres d'un Habitant de Genève à ses Contemporains.* In: *Oeuvres de Saint-Simon,* Paris, 1841.—57

Sarrans, B., jeune. *Lafayette et la révolution de 1830, histoire des choses et des hommes de juillet.* T. I-II. Paris, 1832.—279

[Savary, A.-J.-M.-R., duc de.] *Mémoires du duc de Rovigo, pour servir à l'histoire de l'empereur Napoléon.* T. I-VIII, Paris, 1828.—336

Schiller, F. *Die Räuber. Ein Schauspiel.*—66
— *Die Sonntagskinder.*—475

Schmidt, M. *Die Mysterien von Paris. Von Eugène Sue* [review]. In: *Berliner Monatsschrift.* Erstes und einziges Heft. Mannheim, 1844.—11

Schramm, C. *To the Editor of 'The Friend of the People'.* In: *The Friend of the People,* No. 14, 15 March 1851.—313, 315

Shakespeare, W. *Hamlet, Prince of Denmark.*—189, 283
— *King Henry IV.*—507
— *Richard III.*—431

Southey, R. *History of the Peninsular War.* Vol. 1-3, London, 1823-1832.—302

Statistique générale de la France [published from 1835 under the direction of Moreau de Jonnès, A.].—481

Stechan, G. L. ['Hannover, 28. September'.] In: *Zeitung für Norddeutschland,* Nr. 544, 29. September 1851.—474

Stieler's Handatlas über alle Theile der Erde nach dem neuesten Zustand und über das Weltgebäude. Gotha, 1817-1822.—372, 406

Stirner, M. *Der Einzige und sein Eigenthum.* Leipzig, 1845.—11, 13, 16, 393, 397

Struve, G. von. *Grundzüge der Staatswissenschaft.* Bd. 1-4, Mannheim, 1847—Frankfurt a. M., 1847-1848.—322
— *Weltgeschichte in 9 Büchern.* New-York, 1853-1860.—322

Sue, E. *Les Mystères de Paris.* T. I-XIV, Bruxelles, 1843.—7, 11, 28

Techow, G. *Umrisse des kommenden Krieges.* In: *New-Yorker Staatszeitung,* 6. September 1851.—463-71

Tellering, E. *Westdeutscher Zeitungsjammer.* Düsseldorf, 1850.—230

Thiers, A. *Histoire du Consulat et de l'Empire.* T. I-XI, Paris, 1845-1851.—301, 337, 372

Tooke, Th. *A History of Prices, and of the State of the Circulation, from 1793 to 1837; Preceded by a Brief Sketch of the State of the Corn Trade in the Last Two Centuries.* Vols. I-II, London, 1838.—480
— *A History of Prices, and of the State of the Circulation, in 1838 and 1839, with remarks on the Corn Laws, and on some of the alternations proposed in our banking system,* London, 1840.—275, 480
— *A History of Prices, and the State of the Circulation, from 1839 to 1847 inclusive,* London, 1848.—480

Vaulabelle, A. *Chute de l'empire. Histoire des deux restaurations jusqu'a la chute de Charles X., en 1830.* T. 1-7, Paris, 1844-1857.—116

Vidil, J. [Letter to the editors of *La Patrie*.] In. *La Patrie*, No. 69, 10 mars 1851.—318, 381

Virgil, *Aeneid.*—197, 213, 219

Weerth, G. [Speech at the Economic Congress in Brussels on 18 September 1847.] In: *L'Atelier Démocratique*, 29 septembre 1847.—125

Weitling, W. *Aus einem Privatbriefe.* In: *Der Volks-Tribun,* Nr. 26, 27. Juni 1846.—79

[Weitling, W.] *Die Menschheit, wie sie ist und wie sie sein sollte.* [Paris,] 1839.—59, 530
— *Garantien der Harmonie und Freiheit.* Vivis, 1842.—59

Wigand, O. *An Arnold Ruge.* In: *Die Epigonen.* Bd. I, Leipzig, 1846.—58

Wolff, W. *Nachträgliches 'aus dem Reich'.* In: *Neue Rheinische Zeitung. Politisch-ökonomische Revue,* Nr. 4, April 1850.—222
— *Die Schlesische Milliarde.* In: *Neue Rheinische Zeitung,* Nr. 252, 255, 256, 258, 264, 270, 271, 272, 281; 22., 25., 27., 29. März, 5., 12., 13., 14., 25. April 1849.—489

DOCUMENTS

Accounts of the Committee of Support for German Refugees in London (present edition, Vol. 10)
— Rechnungsablage des Anschusses zur Unterstützung deutscher Flüchtlinge in London. In: *Westdeutsche Zeitung,* Nr. 173, 12. Dezember 1849.—234

Accounts of the Social-Democratic Refugee Committee in London (present edition, Vol. 10)
— Rechnungsablage des Sozial-demokratischen Flüchtlingskomitees in London. In: *Westdeutsche Zeitung,* Nr. 68, 21. März 1850.—234

Accounts of the Social-Democratic Refugee Committee in London (present edition, Vol. 10)
— Rechnungsablage des Sozial-demokratischen Flüchtlingskomitees in London. In: *Deutsche Londoner Zeitung,* Nr. 265, 26. April 1850.—233, 234

Address of the French Exiles to Their Countrymen, by Bernard le Clubiste, Louis Blanc and others. In: *The Daily News,* 5 December 1851.—507, 511

Adresse der deutschen Socialreformer zu Philadelphia an Hermann Kriege und die Socialreformer in New York. In: *Der Volks-Tribun,* Nr. 29, 18. Juli 1846.—79

Adresse des Bildungsvereins in London an die deutschen Proletarier. London, 1846. In: *Deutsche Londoner Zeitung,* Nr. 77, 18. September 1846.—69, 91

An den Apostel Ronge [*Address of the London German Workers' Educational Society*]. In: *Telegraph für Deutschland,* Nr. 56, April 1845.—91

An die Deutschen. In: *Bremer Tages-Chronik,* Nr. 534, 28. März 1851.—355, 427

Appeal for the Support for German Political Refugees (present edition, Vol. 10)
— Aufruf zur Unterstützung deutscher Flüchtlinge. In: *Neue Deutsche Zeitung,* Nr. 228, 26. September 1849.—233

Aux Peuples! Organisation de la démocratie. Londres, 22 juillet 1850. In: *Le Proscrit,* No. 2, 6 août 1850.—267

Banquet of the Equals by Landolphe, Barthélemy (Emmanuel), Horace Teggia, Sawaszkiewicz L. L., Vidil (Jules), Willich, Mihaloczy, Schapper, Ronchi, Louis Blanc, Waszkowski (C.), Simonyi. In: *The Friend of the People,* No. 14, 15 March 1851.—282, 292, 293

Bescheidene Erwiederung auf die Beschlüsse der literarischen Repräsentanten des deutschen Kommunismus in Brüssel gegen den Volkstribun, Organ des jungen Amerika. In: *Der Volks-Tribun,* Nr. 26, 27. Juni 1846.—79

Die Centralbehörde an den Bund [1. Dezember 1850]. In: *Dresdner Journal und Anzeiger,* Nr. 171, 22. Juli 1851.—390, 560

Code pénal, ou code des délits et des peines. Cologne, 1810.—181, 183

Le Comité central démocratique européen, aux Allemands [13 novembre 1850]. In: *La Voix du Proscrit,* No. 4, 17 novembre 1850.—249

Correspondence relative to the affairs of Hungary 1847-1849. Presented to both Houses of Parliament by command of Her Majesty, August 15, 1850. London.—325

[*La déclaration de la commission du Banquet des Egaux du 1 mars 1851.*] In: *La Patrie,* No. 66, 7 mars 1851.—313, 381

Instruction du Gouvernement provisoire pour l'exécution du décret du 5 mars 1848, relatif aux élections générales. In: *Le Moniteur universel,* No. 70, 10 mars 1848.—165

Instructions pour la ligue, avant, pendant et près la révolution [translated from the German]. In: *La Patrie,* 17 septembre 1851.—485, 463

[Manifesto of the European Committee of the Democratic Émigrés, 10 November 1850]. In: *Le Constitutionnel,* 18 novembre 1850.—246-47

Manifesto of the Fraternal Democrats. To the Democracy of Europe. In: *The Northern Star,* No. 519, 2 October 1847.—145

Maßregeln vor, während und nach der Revolution. In: *Kölnische Zeitung,* Nr. 225, 19. September 1851.—459, 463, 468

* *Meeting of the Central Authority.* 15 September 1850 (present edition, Vol. 10).—553

Rules of the Communist League (December 1847) (present edition, Vol. 6)
— *Statuten des Bundes der Kommunisten.*—550

Statuten des Communistischen Bundes. In: *Dresdner Journal und Anzeiger,* Nr. 171, 22. Juni 1851.—374, 560

ANONYMOUS ARTICLES AND REPORTS
PUBLISHED IN PERIODIC EDITIONS

Allgemeine Zeitung (Augsburg), Nr. 202, 21. Juli 1846: *Die russische Allianz und die russische Gesandtschaft.*—64
— Nr. 137, 17. Mai 1851: *Paris, 13. Mai.*—358
— Nr. 186, Beilage, 5. Juli 1851: *Der Communistenbund.*—384, 390
— Nr. 189, 8. Juli 1851: *Noch umfassendere Haussuchungen in Aussicht. Umfassende Geständnisse des Schneiders Nothjung.*—389

— Nr. 264, 21. September 1851: *Das revolutionäre Actenstück des Völkerbundes.*— 463
— Nr. 273, Beilage, 30. September 1851: *Neueste Posten, Köln, 26. Sept.*—473

L'Atelier, No. 11, août 1846: *Du manifeste de la presse liberale.*—58
— No. 11, août 1846: *Un Banquet interrompu.*—58
— No. 1, octobre 1847: *Les maîtres et les ouvriers en Angleterre.*—137

Berner-Zeitung, Nr. 361, 27. Dezember 1849: *Anzeige über das Erscheinen der 'Neuen Rheinische Zeitung. Politisch-ökonomische Revue'.*—221

Le Corsaire-Satan, No. 11093, 16, 17 août 1846: *On parlait denièrement dans le salon de M. Ful...*—54

The Daily News, 14 March 1851: *Anniversary of the German Revolution.*—319
— 8 May 1851: *The Debate in the First Chamber...; Germany. Prussia. Berlin, 4 May.*—349
— 1 September 1851: *Remarkable Case of Fraud by an Austrian Spy.*—*Sudden Death of the Impostor.*—450

Le Débat Social, 19 mars 1848: *Encore et toujours l'expulsion de M. Mars.*—164

Deutsche Zeitung, Nr. 262, Beilage, 27. September 1848: *Eine demokratische Volksversammlung.*—543

The Economist, Vol. III, Nos. 17 and 18, 26 April and 3 May 1845: *Remarkable Discovery—Electricity and Agriculture.*—344-45, 350-51, 354
— No. 417, 23 August 1851: *Indigo.*—450

Frankfurter Journal, Nr. 111, zweite Beilage, 9. Mai 1851: *Köln, 8. Mai.*—358
— Nr. 123, 23. Mai 1851: *Köln, 20. Mai.*—365

La Fraternité de 1845, No. 8, août 1845: *La civilisation est l'acheminement de l'esprit humain vers la communauté.*—66
— No. 11, novembre 1845: *La civilisation est le résultat de l'acheminement des sociétés vers la communauté.*—66
— No. 12, decembre 1845: *La civilisation n'est que le résultat de l'acheminement de l'esprit humain vers la communauté.*—66
— Nos. 16, 18, avril, juin 1846: *La civilisation est le résultat de l'acheminement des sociétés vers la communauté.*—66
— No. 20, août 1846: *La civilisation est le résultat de l'acheminement de l'esprit humain vers la communauté.*—66

The Friend of the People, No. 9, 8 February 1851: *Honour to General Bem, the Patriot and Hero.*—289

Illustrierte Zeitung, Nr. 410, 10. Mai 1851: *Rodbertus hat soeben...*—357

L'Indépendance belge, No. 323, 19 novembre 1850: *Nouvelles de France. Notre correspondance nous parle...*—249

Journal des Débats politiques et littéraires, 15 mai 1851: *Message de Mazzini au Comité central de Londres.*—357, 361
— 16 mai 1851: *France. Paris, 15 mai.*—357

Journal des Économistes, T. 14, No. 56, juillet 1846: *Die Lage der arbeitenden Klasse in England—Situation des classes ouvrières en Angleterre, par Frédéric Engels: un volume, Leipsick, 1845* [review].—67

INDEX OF PERIODICALS

Illinois Staats-Zeitung—a German-language daily published in Illinois (USA) from 1851 to 1922.—339

The Illustrated London News—a weekly published from 1842.—355, 358

Illustrierte Zeitung—a German weekly published in Leipzig from 1843 to 1944; in the middle of the nineteenth century was of a moderate liberal orientation.—357

L'Indépendance belge.—Journal mondial d'informations politiques et littéraires—a daily of the liberals founded in Brussels in 1831.—245, 249

Jahrbücher—see *Deutsch-Französische Jahrbücher*

Journal des Débats politiques et littéraires—a daily founded in Paris in 1789; organ of the Government during the July monarchy; took a monarchist stand during the 1848 revolution.—114, 280, 318, 357-58, 361, 363, 458, 484

Journal des Économistes. Revue mensuelle de l'économie politique et des questions agricoles, manufacturières et commerciales—a monthly published in Paris from December 1841 to 1943.—66, 67

Journal des Österreichischen Lloyd—a semi-official daily published in Vienna in 1836-54.—456

Karlsruher Zeitung—a daily newspaper published from 1757, official gazette of the Grand Duchy of Baden, organ of the Brentano Government in 1849.—200

Kölnerin, Kölner Zeitung—see *Kölnische Zeitung*

Kölnische Zeitung—a German daily published under this title in Cologne from 1802 to 1945; organ of the liberal bourgeoisie; in 1848 and 1849 advocated anti-revolutionary tendencies.—48, 83, 94, 114-15, 173, 186, 199, 219, 347, 355, 356, 374, 379, 389, 390, 392, 399, 427-29, 459, 463, 472, 541

Der Kosmos—a weekly of German refugees in England; it was published by Ernst Haug in London in 1851 (only six numbers appeared). Gottfried Kinkel and other leaders of petty-bourgeois democracy contributed to it.—345, 351, 359, 360, 367, 377, 429, 430

Közlöny, hivatalos lap—a Hungarian daily of the Kossuth revolutionary government published in 1848 and 1849 in Pest, Debreczin and Szegedin.—328

Kreuz-Zeitung—see *Neue Preußische Zeitung*

Literatur-Zeitung—see *Allgemeine Literatur-Zeitung*

Lithographische Correspondenz—see *Preußische Lithographische Correspondenz*

Der Lloyd—see *Journal des Österreichischen Lloyd*

The London Telegraph—a daily published in 1848.—175, 176

Mannheimer Abendzeitung—a German radical daily founded in 1842 by Karl Grün, ceased publication in 1849.—200

Le Moniteur Belge. Journal officiel—a Belgian daily founded in Brussels in 1831, official organ of the Government.—163, 164

Weydemeyer. On 6 and 13 January two weekly issues appeared; in May and June two 'non-periodic' issues appeared; Marx and Engels were among the main contributors.—519

Revue—see *Neue Rheinische Zeitung. Politisch-ökonomische Revue*

La Revue indépendante—a monthly propagating the ideas of utopian socialism, it was published in Paris from 1841 to 1848 under the editorship of Pierre Leroux, George Sand and Louis Viardot.—135

Revue Sociale, ou Solution pacifique du problème du prolétariat—a Christian socialists' monthly published by Pierre Leroux in Boussac and Paris in 1845-48 and by the latter's supporters in Paris in 1850.—57

Reynolds's Newspaper. A weekly journal of politics, history, literature and general intelligence—a radical newspaper published in London from 1850; at the beginning of the 1850s supported the Chartists.—497

Rheinische Beobachter—a conservative daily published in Cologne from 1844 to the beginning of 1848.—70; 92

Rheinische Jahrbücher zur gesellschaftlichen Reform—a German magazine, organ of the 'true socialists', published by Hermann Püttmann; altogether two issues appeared: the first in Darmstadt in August 1845, and the second in Bellevue, a place on the German-Swiss border, at the end of 1846; the magazine carried Engels' 'Elberfeld Speeches' and 'The Festival of Nations in London'.—16, 21, 23, 28, 34, 69

Rheinische Zeitung für Politik, Handel und Gewerbe—a German daily founded on 1 January 1842 as an organ of the Rhenish bourgeois opposition, and published in Cologne till 31 March 1843. When edited by Marx (from 15 October 1842 to 17 March 1843), the paper became a mouthpiece of revolutionary-democratic ideas which led to its suppression. Engels was one of its contributors.—17

Schnellpost—see *Deutsche Schnellpost für Europäische Zustände, öffentliches und sociales Leben Deutschlands*

Schweizerische National-Zeitung—a liberal daily, published in Basle from 1842.—186, 222, 438

Le Siècle—a daily published in Paris from 1836 to 1939. In the 1840s it was an oppositional organ which demanded electoral and other reforms.—484

Spiegel—see *Gesellschaftsspiegel*

Staatszeitung—see *New-Yorker Staatszeitung*

Star—see *The Northern Star*

The Sun—a liberal daily published in London from 1798 to 1876.—357, 497

Tages-Chronik—a democratic paper published in Bremen from 1849 to 1851. From January 1851 it appeared under the title *Bremer Tages-Chronik. Organ der Demokratie*. Arnold Ruge contributed to it in 1851.—265, 267, 268, 345, 426

The Telegraph—see *The London Telegraph*

Telegraph für Deutschland—a literary magazine founded by Karl Gutzkow; in 1837 it appeared in Frankfurt am Main, and from 1838 to 1848 in Hamburg. In the

SUBJECT INDEX